ANTARCTIC SECTOR OF THE PACIFIC

FURTHER TITLES IN THIS SERIES

Elsevier Oceanography Series, 51

ANTARCTIC SECTOR OF THE PACIFIC

Edited by

G.P. GLASBY

New Zealand Oceanographic Institute, Division of Water Sciences, Department of Scientific and Industrial Research, Wellington, New Zealand

ELSEVIER

Amsterdam — Oxford — New York — Tokyo   1990

ELSEVIER SCIENCE PUBLISHERS B.V.
Sara Burgerhartstraat 25
P.O. Box 211, 1000 AE Amsterdam, The Netherlands

Distributors for the United States and Canada:

ELSEVIER SCIENCE PUBLISHING COMPANY INC.
655, Avenue of the Americas
New York, NY 10010, U.S.A.

Library of Congress Cataloging-in-Publication Data

Antarctic sector of the Pacific / edited by G.P. Glasby.
      p.   cm. -- (Elsevier oceanography series ; 51)
   Includes bibliographical references.
   ISBN 0-444-88510-2 (alk. paper) : fl 180.00 (est.)
   1. Antarctic Ocean.   I. Glasby, G. P. II. Series.
GC461.A59 1990
   551.46'9--dc20   89-23840
                                                          CIP

ISBN 0-444-88510-2 (Vol. 51)

© Elsevier Science Publishers B.V., 1990

This book is printed on acid-free paper.

Printed in The Netherlands

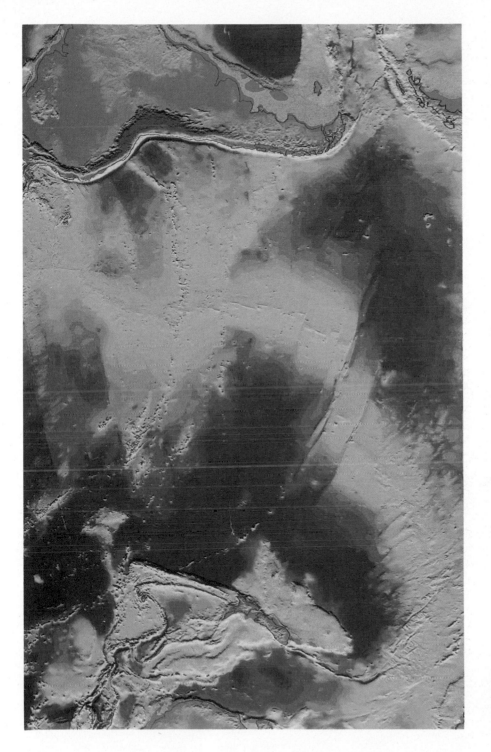

Relief map of the South Pacific showing the main structural features (after Heirtzler, 1985).

LIST OF CONTRIBUTORS

Anderson, J.B.
Department of Geology, Rice University
P.O. Box 1892, Houston, Texas 77251, U.S.A.

Baker, A.N.
National Museum of New Zealand
Private Bag, Wellington, New Zealand

Cook, R.A.
N.Z. Geological Survey, DSIR
P.O. Box 30–368, Lower Hutt, New Zealand

Davey, F.J.
Geophysics Division, DSIR
P.O. Box 1320, Wellington, New Zealand

El-Sayed, S.Z.
Department of Oceanography, Texas A&M University, College Station
Texas 77843–3146, U.S.A.

Glasby, G.P.
N.Z. Oceanographic Institute, Division of Water Sciences, DSIR
Private Bag, Kilbirnie, Wellington, New Zealand

Gregory, M.R.
Department of Geology, University of Auckland
Private Bag, Auckland, New Zealand

Harper, P.C.
Department of Continuing Education, University of Canterbury
Private Bag, Christchurch, New Zealand

Hickman, J.S.
N.Z. Meteorological Service, Ministry of Transport
P.O. Box 722, Wellington, New Zealand

Holdgate, M.W.
International Union for Conservation of Nature and Natural Resources
Avenue du Mont-Blanc, CH–1196 Gland, Switzerland

Keys, J.R.
Department of Conservation
P.O. Box 10–420, Wellington, New Zealand

Mullan, A.B.
N.Z. Meteorological Service, Ministry of Transport
P.O. Box 722, Wellington, New Zealand

Patterson, S.L.
National Oceanographic Data Center
1825 Connecticut Avenue, N.W., Washington, D.C. 20235, U.S.A.

Spurr, E.B.
Forest Research Institute
Private Bag, Christchurch, New Zealand

Taylor, R.H.
Ecology Division, DSIR
Private Bag, Nelson, New Zealand

Whitworth, T.
Department of Oceanography, Texas A&M University, College Station
Texas 77843–3146, U.S.A.

CONTENTS

ACKNOWLEDGEMENTS

As editor, I would like to express my sincere thanks to all the contributors to this book for their tremendous effort in producing manuscripts, to Drs P.J. Barrett and T. Hatherton who kindly reviewed the entire book and D.G. Ainley, W.F. Budd, M.W. Cawthorn, A.E. Gilmour, C.H. Hay, J.R. Keys, K.B. Lewis, R.C. Murdoch, A.D. Pritchard, M.R. Sinclair and B.R. Stanton who reviewed individual chapters, to B. Grant for permission to reproduce the frontispiece, to Ms J.A. McDonald and Mr C.T. Pham who stoically interloaned the many books required in editing this volume, to Mr M. Podstolski who prepared the index, to Mr K.W. Majorhazi who drew a number of diagrams and, most importantly of all, to Mrs R.-M. Thompson who undertook the onerous task of preparing the whole volume to camera-ready copy.

Authors would llke to thank various individuals for their help in producing their chapters. These are listed by chapter.

Chapter 3
Partial support for the preparation of this chapter was provided by grants ATM 8316640 and OCE 8414886 from the National Science Foundation and contract N00014–80–C–0013 from the Office of Naval Research. The following colleagues are thanked for helpful comments: J.D. Cochrane, S.S. Jacobs, W.D. Nowlin, R.G. Peterson, R.D. Pillsbury, J.L. Reid and B.A. Warren.

Chapter 4
This chapter was written under the auspices of the Commission for the Environment and the Department of Conservation, New Zealand. Karen Williams and Dennis Fowler are thanked for their assistance, Margaret Highland for typing and Leigh Hudson for drafting.

Chapter 7
This research is funded by the National Science Foundation Division of Polar Programs (Grant DPP–85–16908). D. Cassidy provided copies of several papers used in the preparation of this paper.

Chapter 10
Dr R. Gambell of the International Whaling Commission is thanked for supplying data on Southern Ocean whaling statistics.

Chapter 11
The Southern Ocean, Subantarctic Islands and Ross Dependency research has been funded by the Research Committee of the University of Auckland and University Grants Committee. Logistic support has come from Antarctic Division, D.S.I.R., Royal New Zealand Navy and United States Coast Guard.

Advice, comment, field assistance and companionship has come from many individuals but I am particularly indebted to P.J. Barrett, R.M. Kirk, M.C.G. Mabin, C. Montieth, I.F. Owen and R.B. Thompson. Skilled technical assistance was provided by L. Cotterall and R. Harris. The manuscript was typed by R. Bunker.

FOREWORD

M.W. HOLDGATE

There is a contradiction in the title of this book. For most volumes about the Southern Ocean stress its circumpolar continuity. The West Wind Drift sweeps around the earth, south of the inhabited southern continents. The main hydrological features of the Pacific Ocean : the East Wind Drift at its southern margin, spilling into the Ross Gyre; the westerly current further north; the northward movement of cold, dense bottom water and of the less saline surface waters with their burden of floating ice; and the counter-balancing southward drift of intermediate water that wells up in the far south and enriches the upper layers with nutrients, are all equally characteristic of the Atlantic or Indian Oceans. The ice phenomena and biology of the Pacific Sector of the Southern Ocean likewise differ in detail rather than fundamentals from those in the other regions of the circumpolar oceanic continuum.

But the point of this book is to bring home to students of the Pacific how that great ocean is transformed in its southernmost part, south of the subtropical convergence and especially south of the Antarctic Convergence or frontal system which lies between 55°S and 60°S. The first chapters, on climate, hydrology and ice bring this out well and also make another important point : that the influence of the cold hub of the Southern Hemisphere, acting through the airs and waters it chills, extends to the climate and oceanic processes far to the north. The Antarctic is an important engine driving world climate. We are still ignorant of many of the inter-linkages between it and other regions — but it is pointless to study Antarctic climate as if it was a separate entity.

The Antarctic Sector of the Pacific is a model demonstrating Southern Ocean features more generally, and pointing up issues that now confront scientists and Governments alike. Much is known about the general patterns of marine circulation and the origins and drift of pack ice and ice bergs — in which the Pacific Sector is rich because so many have their source in the Ross Ice Shelf. But we remain ignorant of many crucial details. We likewise have a broad understanding of the make-up of the oceanic ecosystem — but the factors that determine the productivity of plant plankton in different parts of the region and in turn determine the production of krill and other components of the zooplankton remain only partly established. And while it is a fair generalization that almost anything can eat krill — baleen whales, seals, seabirds, and a number of fish — the trophic interactions between these organisms and others like squid, known to be abundant in the Southern Ocean, have still to be determined precisely. The Ross Sea was the subject of one of the first attempts at mathematical modelling of a part of the Antarctic Marine Ecosystem (Green Hammond, 1981) but the defects in this courageous effort only serve to underline the need for stronger biological research. This need has met with response through the BIOMASS (Biological Investigation of Marine Antarctic Species and Stocks) project, by SCOR and

SCAR, but there is much more to do. And we remain extremely ignorant of the life of the seabed over much of the Antarctic Sector of the Pacific.

The need for research is great because human impact on the Southern Ocean is now increasing again. A century and a half ago, the fur seals (and to a lesser extent the elephant seals) bore the brunt of human exploitation, following the discovery by Cook and others of their vast breeding populations on the Subantarctic Islands, including Macquarie and the New Zealand shelf islands. Because the seal stocks were an "open access" resource, unprotected by sovereign Governments, the sealing industry became a competitive free for all that took millions of skins from the circum-Antarctic zone in 1795–1830 and then collapsed because the resource had been virtually destroyed. Only now are fur seals again becoming numerous in their original haunts (and we cannot be certain that the pattern of species distribution has not been permanently changed). Likewise, shore-based and pelagic whaling gravely reduced the Antarctic stocks of great whales between 1900 and 1970, reducing the population of blue whales to under 5% of its initial size and cutting the sei and fin whales almost as drastically. Whales, too, were (and are) an open-access resource. Although the International Whaling Commission has done much to lead the industry towards responsible self-regulation, there is no certainty that its proposals will be respected by all nations. Meanwhile, the reduction in these whales has almost certainly allowed some other species to increase — including the small minke whale, the crabeater seal and the chinstrap penguin. It may also have left a "surplus" of krill for man to harvest, and a fishery has already been established and is now taking some 200,000 tonnes a year. The fin-fish resources of the Southern Ocean are also being exploited by fleets from far away — many from the Northern Hemisphere — and some have already been reduced by over-fishing.

It is clearly essential that these new fisheries are regulated so that they do not destroy the resources on which they depend, as the sealing and whaling industries did. But such regulation demands science. We need to know whether there really is a surplus of krill, and if so, how much. We need to know whether its harvest by fishing fleets will hamper the recovery of the whales, or endanger other components of the ecosystem. The risk is obvious because krill plays a central part in that ecosystem and makes up 50% of the animal plankton biomass. There is now a Convention on the Conservation of Antarctic Marine Living Resources (CCAMLR) to which all the nations engaged in Antarctic fishery belong, and this is unique in stressing the need to control exploitation so as to safeguard the ecosystem as a whole. But unless we understand that ecosystem, we shall continue to regulate by guess work.

This book highlights another area where our scientific knowledge is insufficient to allow definitive statements about human use of Antarctic resources. There are grounds for believing that there may be hydrocarbon minerals in the Ross Sea, and perhaps elsewhere in the region. The exploitation of such deposits would clearly be extremely difficult and expensive. With the world facing excess rather than shortage of oil, development is clearly highly improbable in the foreseeable future. But we cannot evaluate the probabilities without better geophysical knowledge. Nor can we predict the environmental impact of such developments with certainty unless we know far more about existing pollution levels, about those likely to arise from mineral development, or about the sensitivity of Antarctic marine organisms to the kinds of hydrocarbon likely to be released. The best guess may well be that the Southern Ocean is so vast that even a major oil spillage would have only a localized and transient effect — but we need to know more about the cumulative effects of low levels of pollutant over long periods. The new international agreement on the control of mineral exploration and exploitation demands environmental impact assessments, and it is by no means certain that scientists will be able to carry those out with the requisite certainty.

In the Antarctic, there is a long and good tradition of dialogue between scientists and Governments. The scientists of all the nations working in the region co-operate internationally through the Scientific Committee on Antarctic Research (SCAR) and the parallel Committee on Oceanic Research, SCOR. The Governments are concerned to develop the Antarctic Treaty System not only as a framework for peaceful co-operation in the land areas south of 60°S to which the Treaty applies, but as a series of measures to protect the environment of the wider Antarctic regions from damaging human impact. The CCAMLR Convention covers a broader geographical area than the Treaty and is a pioneering measure in the way in which it applies ecological concepts of resource management in advance of threat and with the aim of preventing damage. It is now being exposed to the test of practicality : is it a strong enough measure to control growing and competing fisheries on the high seas? Equally severe tests of practicality await the measures recently adopted to regulate mineral exploration and exploitation. It is one thing to agree on these well ahead of the commencement of mining activities so that an industry can plan in awareness of the standards it will have to meet and so prevent pollution from the outset. It is another to make them work rigorously in the exacting, and at times hazardous, conditions of the Antarctic. But it is right to try. It is also essential to recognize that these measures could founder unless they are underpinned by good science. This book shows that we know a good deal about the Antarctic Sector of the Pacific Ocean — but we will need to know more if we are to design our policies aright.

CHAPTER 1

INTRODUCTION

G.P. GLASBY

For the English schoolboy brought up in the 1950s, Antarctica was synonymous with Scott's last expedition and Sir Clements Markham's (President of the Royal Geographical Society 1893–1905) romanticized version of the British bluejacket manhauling his sledge to the Pole. Yet the paradox of this view is readily apparent on re-reading the accounts of this expedition and observing that Scott's ship, *Terra Nova*, almost capsized in 1910 in a storm two days out from Port Chalmers, New Zealand. The sea is the gateway to Antarctica and this sea is amongst the most remote, hostile and least studied of the world's oceans.

The region under study here, the Antarctic Sector of the Pacific (lying between Australia and South America and south of latitude 45°S), comprises about 6% of the earth's surface. To the south, the region is bounded by the western coast of the Antarctic Peninsula, Ellsworth Land (Bellingshausen Sea), Marie Byrd Land (Amundsen Sea), King Edward VII Land and Victoria Land (Ross Sea, including the Ross Ice Shelf). Scientific stations in this sector of Antarctica are Russkaya (U.S.S.R.) (Marie Byrd Land), McMurdo (U.S.A.) (Victoria Land) and Scott (N.Z.) (Victoria Land). There are few islands within this sector of the Southern Ocean. Balleny Island, Scott Island, Peter I Island and the islands off the western Antarctic Peninsula lie south of the Antarctic Convergence (or Polar Frontal Zone) but Macquarie Island and the New Zealand Subantarctic islands lie north of the Convergence. Hydrologically, the Antarctic region proper lies to the south of the Antarctic Convergence; the Subantarctic lies between the Subtropical Convergence and the Antarctic Convergence (Tchernia, 1980) (cf. Knox, 1987). Figure 1.1 shows the area under consideration.

The scientific importance of this region is derived from its central role in a number of areas; the reconstruction of Gondwanaland, the influence on Pacific climate and palaeoclimate and the formation of Antarctic Bottom Water, the high biological productivity and the proximity of the magnetic pole (cf. Laws, 1987; Parsons, 1987; Weller et al., 1987). As an example, the Western Boundary Current east of New Zealand transports roughly 20×10^6 m^3 s^{-1} of water northwards (i.e., about 16 times the total continental run-off, Baumgartner and Reichel, 1975) consistent with it being the principal supplier of deep water in the Pacific (Warren, 1981). Indeed, water from the Antarctic is thought to comprise 71% of the Pacific Ocean (Warren, 1971). For comparison, the average transport of the Antarctic Circumpolar Current is about 130×10^6 m^3 s^{-1} (Gordon, 1987; Whitworth, 1988). It has also been argued that the breakup of Pangea resulted in a sequence of climatic, erosional effects that have dominated the history of the earth's surface over the last 250 Ma (Hay, 1981, 1984; Hay et al., 1981). For example, climatic changes in Antarctica have played a key role in determining the palaeoceanography of the world's oceans (Kennett, 1977, 1980, 1983; Loutit et al., 1983; Mercer, 1983; Ken-

2

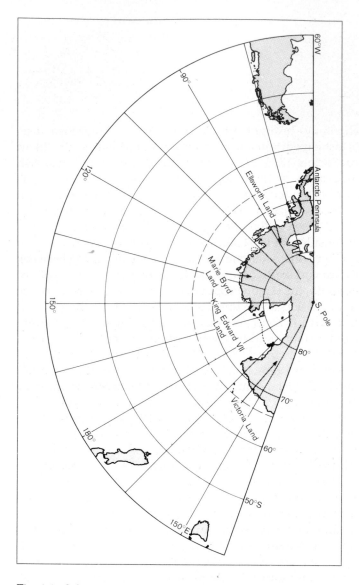

Fig. 1.1. Schematic map showing the Antarctic Sector of the Pacific.

nett and von der Borch, 1986). In addition, it is now believed that the CO_2 content of the atmosphere is transferred to the deep sea through the nutrient content of high latitude surface water. The marked lowering of the CO_2 content of the atmosphere during the last glaciation was therefore markedly dependent on the chemistry of Southern Ocean waters (Toggweiler and Sarmiento, 1985; Wenk and Siegenthaler, 1985; cf. Sarnthein et al., 1988).

Yet, it has only been in the last 30 years (since the International Geophysical Year, IGY, 1957–58) that serious attempts have been made to study this region scientifically and these have been spasmodic. Knowledge of this sector of the

Southern Ocean still lags behind that of the Antarctic continent. It has been said that the broad-scale geographical description of the world's oceans is more or l complete, apart from the polar waters and those of the South Pacific (Hem̨ 1986). Eittreim, Cooper, and Scientific Staff (1984) considered the Antarctic coɪ nental margin to be geologically the least known continental margin. Similaɪ Weller (1986) concluded that the Southern Ocean is the most poorly obser̠ region on earth meteorologically with only a few buoys periodically deployed the open ocean and in the pack ice; this situation is being improved by the use satellites. In many ways, this lack of knowledge is understandable. The extreɪ remoteness of the region is emphasized by the fact that there is only one shippɪ route there (from Christchurch, New Zealand, to Scott Base, McMurdo Sound, a distance of 4,000 km). Its inhospitable nature is emphasized by the strong seas (particularly between 45°S and 50°S) and ice conditions further south (French, 1974; U.S. Navy, 1979).

The disappearance of Captain Robert Johnson (an American sealer) south of New Zealand in 1826 whilst seeking land between 60°S and 65°S, the collision of *Erebus* and *Terror* in front of an iceberg in 1842, the freezing in of Scott's ship *Discovery* in 1902–04 which necessitated a relief expedition being sent from England, the failure of Scott's ship *Terra Nova* to relieve the northern party in 1912, the involuntary drift of Shackleton's ship *Aurora* in the Ross Sea in 1915–16, the double capsize of David Lewis's yacht *Ice Bird* in 1972, the crushing and sinking of the German research vessel *Gotland II* off northern Victoria Land in 1981, the trapping of the Soviet research vessel *Mikhail Somov* in the ice in the Amundsen Sea in 1985, the sinking of the British vessel *Southern Quest* in the Ross Sea in 1986, the grounding and subsequent sinking of the Australian resupply ship *Nella Dan* at Macquarie Island in 1987, the sinking of the Argentinian supply ship *Bahia Paraiso* near Palmer Station on Anvers Island off the western Antarctic Peninsula in 1989 and the grounding of the Peruvian research ship *Humboldt* on King George Island off the western Antarctic Peninsula in 1989 all attest to the dangers of navigation in this region.

HISTORY OF EXPLORATION

For any understanding of this region of the Southern Ocean, some historical perspective is necessary. Perhaps the most comprehensive summary of Antarctic exploration prior to the Heroic Age is that of Mill (1905). Other works consulted include Murray (1886, 1894), Greely (1929), Fleming (1952), Priestley (1956), Kirwan (1959), Brodie (1965), Quartermain (1967), M. Deacon (1971), G.E.R. Deacon (1975a, 1977a, 1984), Lovering and Prescott (1979), Shapley (1985), Walton and Bonner (1985), Hatherton (1986), Mickleburgh (1987) and Walton (1987). A brief summary of exploratory expeditions until the IGY, including cruise tracks, is given by Dater (1975).

The term Antarctica is Greek (Antarktos — opposite the bear) and the idea of a southern landmass Greek. It was Aristotle who first proposed that the earth is a sphere and Eratosthenes (who incidentally has a seamount and abyssal plain off the Nile Delta named after him, Ross et al., 1978) who estimated the size of this sphere. The idea of a southern landmass was based on considerations of symmetry of landmasses with the earth divided into five zones, a northern frigid and a northern temperate zone separated from their southern counterparts by a torrid zone (an impassable gulf of unendurable heat). Although Phoenician sailors traded far into the tropics and had possibly circumnavigated Africa at this time, the belief persisted that the Southern Hemisphere of the globe contained habitable land which could never be reached.

From this time follows 1,500 years in which Greek learning passed to the Arab world and such ideas became the subject of abstruse theological debate in Christendom. It was not until the 15th century that the renaissance, with its revival of classical ideas and its great voyages of exploration, began in Europe. Of these voyages, the circumnavigation of the globe by Magellan (1519–22) in which he passed through the Magellan Straits and saw continuous land of continental appearance to the south is the most significant here. By the early 16th century, cartographers such as Leonardo da Vinci (1515) and Schöner (1515) were producing maps of the world based on these voyages of exploration. The map of Orontius (1531) combined the results of the previous two charts with Magellan's discovery and showed the huge southern continent of Terra Australis (Fig. 1.2). As Mill (1905) stated, "the vast Terra Australis was built entirely of conjecture, save for the Tierra del Fuegian scrap of fact, but was a continent indeed, although not yet fully known, the finding of which would repay any explorer, and place the happy discoverer on a pedestal beside Columbus and Vasco de Gama, perhaps even as high as Magellan himself."

In the middle of the 18th century, the southern continent figured upon all maps as the seat of a great continent awaiting discovery. The last of the firm believers in this idea was Alexander Dalrymple. Dalrymple has been described as an obdurate, cantankerous Scott, of some ability, much self-conceit and no sense of proportion. In his volume of 1770–71 "An historical collection of the several voyages and discoveries in the South Pacific Ocean", he suggested that the Southern Continent was larger "than the whole civilized part of Asia from Turkey to the eastern extremity of China" and that "the scraps from this table would be sufficient to maintain the power, dominion and sovereignty of Britain". However, Dalrymple's map of exploration of the Pacific shows that all voyages to that date had crossed the Pacific north of 30°S so that the area south of this latitude was entirely unknown to Europeans. Dalrymple was first nominated for the leadership of the astronomical expedition to study the transit of Venus in Tahiti in 1769 but quarrels over the overall command of the expedition led him to decline and the appointment was given instead to the man who was to become one of the greatest maritime explorers, James Cook.

It is not necessary here to describe Cook's first voyage of circumnavigation of 1768–71 in the *Endeavour*, from Cape Horn to Tahiti, the circumnavigation and charting of New Zealand, the journey up the coast of Australia and return via New Guinea and Java. Nonetheless, this voyage led Cook to the view that "to make new discoveries the Navigator must traverse or circumnavigate the globe in a higher parallel than has hitherto been done" so that the whole matter of a southern continent could then "be wholy clear'd up".

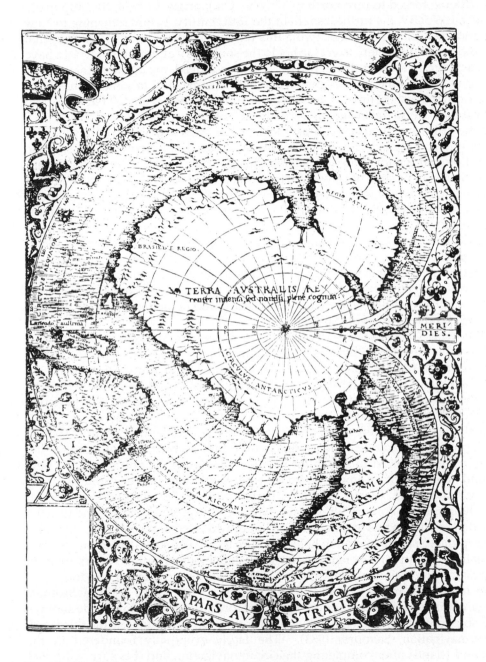

Fig. 1.2. The 1531 Orontius Finaeus map of the Southern Hemisphere.

Cook's second voyage of 1772–75 resulted in the first crossing of the Pacific at high latitude. The *Resolution* left New Zealand on November 26 1773 (the *Adventure* having returned to England) and made 67°31'S at 135°W on December 22 before being forced to turn north to 47°50'S. On January 30 1774, the ship made 71°10'S, 106°54'W, the furthest south of the 18th century, before returning to New Zealand via Easter Island. Following this voyage, Cook wrote "I will not say that it is impossible anywhere to get farther to the south; but attempting it would have been a dangerous and rash enterprise …. It was, indeed, my opinion, that this ice extended quite to the pole, or perhaps joined to some land to which it has been fixed from the earliest time". On November 10 1774, Cook again left New Zealand and reached Tierra del Fuego on December 17 on a course between 57°S and 53°S meeting little ice and no land. Cook's achievement was to dispose of the theory of the southern continent and, on his return, he wrote "should anyone possess the resolution and the fortitude to elucidate this point by pushing yet further south than I have done, I shall not envy him the fame of his discovery, but I make bold to declare that the world will derive no benefit from it". Cook's scientific programme has beem summarized by Rubin (1982a) and his observations of sea ice by Herdman (1969).

On January 14 1775, Cook sighted South Georgia in the South Atlantic. Arriving in the height of summer in the middle of the breeding season, Cook and the naturalists aboard the *Resolution* marvelled at the huge concentrations of wildlife (whales, seals, penguins and seabirds) in the seas around the island (Mickleburgh, 1987). Such a wealth of wildlife was unexpected and helped to foster the myth of the high productivity of the South Ocean.

Following Cook's voyage, there was a long gap in Antarctic exploration as such but his description of the vast abundance of seals in South Georgia fell on attentive ears. In 1778, English sealers brought back from South Georgia and the Magellan Straits 40,000 seal skins and 2,800 tonnes of elephant seal oil. In 1801, the amount of oil imported from these regions reached 6,000 tonnes. The period of destruction of the Southern Ocean marine mammal stock had begun.

Although initial interest of the U.S. and British sealers centred on areas such as the South Shetlands and South Georgia in the South Atlantic, the nature of sealing led to a constant need to search for new grounds since the first to reach a new ground was sure of an immense booty whereas the late comer could go away empty handed (cf. Clark, 1884–87; Turbott, 1952; Bonner and Laws, 1964; Stonehouse, 1972; Bonner, 1982; Laws, 1984). By 1813, New Zealand and the sub-Antarctic islands in this region had been largely divested of their seal populations. The exploitive nature of sealing helped ensure its secrecy so that adequate records of sealing activity are in many cases lost. Nonetheless, some sealers took an interest in exploration and this applied to the Enderby Brothers of London.

In 1830–33, John Biscoe was sent on a sealing voyage by the Enderby Brothers and circumnavigated the Antarctic continent for 160 degrees of longitude south of 60°S aboard the brig *Tula* (150 tonnes) and cutter *Lively* (82 tonnes) (the third such circumnavigation, Savours, 1983). The *Lively* eventually foundered in the Falkland Islands after completing the circumnavigation and it is surprising that such a small vessel could make such a navigation even though conditions onboard must have been wretched (Mill, 1905). In late 1831, Biscoe spent three-months sealing off New Zealand, the Chatham Islands and the Bounty Islands and in 1832 made his first landing in Antarctic territory, probably on Anvers Island off the central stretch of the coast that he named Graham Land. After his return to England, Biscoe made several attempts to push exploration south of New Zealand but was always stopped by ice at about 63°S. In 1838, the Enderbys fitted out the 154 tonne schooner *Eliza Scott* with the 54 tonne cutter *Sabrina* under John Balleny. In February 1832, Balleny reached 69°S, 172°E in the Ross Sea before being stopped by ice and then landed on the Balleny Islands. This was the first time land had been seen in the Antarctic Circle south of New Zealand. Balleny returned to London in time to pass on his results to James Clark Ross. In 1847, the Enderbys obtained a concession from the British Government for a whaling station on the Auckland Islands. This is not the place for a full account of sealing and whaling activities in this region of the South Pacific which is dealt with more fully by Baker (this volume) but it does show that, for a time, these seamen played a leading role in the geographical exploration of these waters.

The next great voyage to concern us is Bellingshausen's circumnavigation of 1819–21. Bellingshausen left Sydney on November 11 1820 and arrived at Rio de Janiero on March 9 1821 via Macquarie Island where they experienced a submarine earthquake and met elephant seal hunters. Bellinghausen's track was immediately north of the ice and it is instructive to note that for the whole cruise Bellingshausen sailed over 242 degrees of longitude south of 60°S of which 41 degrees were within the Antarctic Circle, whereas Cook sailed only 125 degrees of longitude south of 60°S of which 24 degrees were within the Antarctic Circle. Bellingshausen also took care to cross all the great gaps left by Cook thus confirming the existence of a continuous open sea south of 60°S. He also discovered two islands which he named Peter I Island and Alexander Island off the west coast of the Antarctic Peninsula. Unfortunately, whilst Bellingshausen wrote a full account of his voyage, it was in Russian so that details of this expedition were not made available to subsequent expeditions until 1902. Bellingshausen's scientific programme has been summarized by Rubin (1982b).

We now come to the period 1838–43 when four expeditions, of D'Urville (France), Wilkes (U.S.A.), Balleny (Britain) and Ross (Britain), were engaged in Antarctic exploration. Of these, only the expedition of Ross (1839–43) need concern us here, although Walker in *Flying Fish* reached 70°S, 105°W and Ringgold in *Porpoise* 68°S, 95°44'W during the Wilkes expedition (Greely, 1929). The expedition of Ross was described by Murray (1894) as the greatest, most successful and most important expedition to the Antarctic to that date.

In the early 19th century, the study of magnetism had become a pressing problem with the beginning of a new era of maritime activity and Gauss had already predicted that the South Magnetic Pole would be located in the Antarctic at about 60°S, 146°E. The discovery of the South Magnetic Pole became the principal object of the British Antarctic expedition and in 1838 a meeting of the British Association in Newcastle urged the dispatch of an Antarctic expedition for magnetic measurements between Australia and Cape Horn. The man chosen as leader was Captain James Clark Ross, the discoverer of the North Magnetic Pole, who had very substantial experience in the Arctic (Ross, 1982).

The expedition was entirely naval and consisted of two ships H.M.S. *Erebus* (370 tonnes) and H.M.S. *Terror* (340 tonnes) which were specially strengthened for Antarctic work (Richardson and Gray, 1844–75). The first summer's voyage, leaving Campbell Island on December 17 1840, was easily the most successful. Because of their strengthening, the ships were able to penetrate the pack ice where every previous explorer would have had to turn back and on February 1 1841 reached 78°4'S, 173°20'W. Ross was able to land on Possession and Franklin Islands, only the second landings south of the Antarctic Circle (after D'Urville). He discovered and named the mountain chain of Victoria Land, the great volcanoes of Mounts Erebus and Terror and McMurdo Bay, and sailed over 500 km eastwards along the front of the great ice barrier, rising 45–60 m above sea level, that now bears his name (the Ross Ice Shelf). He was able to carry out soundings and dredging (recovering a rich haul of rock fragments dropped by icebergs and a profusion of animal life), take magnetic and meteorological observations, observe the marine life and approach within about 300 km of the South Magnetic Pole. Whales of great size were observed and Ross believed them to be a valuable species, although it was to be 50 years before whaling fleets visited the region. Within 2 km of the ice barrier, he obtained a depth of 480 m with a fine soft mud on the bottom. He also noted the low atmospheric pressure in the Southern Ocean. The success of this first season was rewarded by the award of the next Founder's Medal of the Royal Geographical Society.

In the second season, Ross made his southward approach 2,500 km to the east. On the way, much time was spent measuring the sea temperatures at great depths (but the results were invalid because the thermometers were not protected). In spite of making a latitude of 78°9'S at 161°27'W within 2.5 km of the barrier (the most southerly latitude of the 19th century), conditions were much more difficult than in the first season and the results more disappointing.

In the third season, attention was turned to the Weddell Sea and a latitude of 71°30'S was made in conditions much more difficult than encountered in the Ross Sea. The chief result of this was that, when the assault was finally made on the Pole, it was made from the Ross, and not the Weddell, Sea.

After this burst of activity, there follows a long gap in Antarctic exploration. In Britain, this was due to the search for Sir John Franklin who was lost (aboard *Erebus* and *Terror*) during the search for the North-West Passage in 1845, in the U.S.A. due to the intervention of the civil war (although Wilke's voyage had never been properly supported), and in Germany due to the Franco-Prussian war and the untimely death of Admiral Teggetthoff. The most important development of this period was the H.M.S. *Challenger* expedition of 1872–76 which resulted in the circumnavigation of the globe and observations south of 60°S between Kerguelen Island and Australia. The *Challenger* was powered by sail and steam but not ice strengthened. One of the principal scientists onboard was John (later Sir John) Murray. In this region, the ship carried out soundings and dredgings (Murray, 1894). The hauls contained a more abundant fauna than any others on the whole voyage and recovered glaciated rock fragments including granites, mica schists, grained quartzites, sandstones, limestones and shales which showed the continental nature of Antarctica. A permanent high-pressure zone over the Antarctic continent was also demonstrated. However, the deep-sea thermometers used were found to be inadequate at these latitudes.

During this period there were a number of leading spokesmen for Antarctic research. These included M.F. Maury, Superintendent of the United States Hydrographic Office, who introduced the idea of the great circle route for sailing ships which necessitated sailing from Australia to Cape Horn at high latitudes across the Pacific (Maury, 1963; Williams, 1963), Georg von Neumeyer, Director of the Deutsche Seewarte at Hamburg, whose interests were in magnetism, oceanography and meteorology, Sir John Murray of the *Challenger* expedition, and Sir Clements Markham, later President of the Royal Geographical Society. In this regard, particular mention must be made of Murray's two papers (1886, 1894) which brilliantly summarized the accumulated knowledge gained to that date. Murray (1894) was bold enough to deduce the nature of the Antarctic continent based on existing marine observations and to outline the requirements for a modern Antarctic expedition which would be "of capital importance to British science", although of dubious commercial prospects. He specifically did not advocate "a dash at the South Pole", although, in this, he was to be out-manoeuvred by Markham. In the discussion to Murray's (1894) paper, it was suggested that such an expedition could be justified as knowledge for its own sake and Sir William Flower (described as the greatest authority on marine mammals) noted that commercial exploitation of whales and seals in the region "must end in extermination in a very few years if they are to be killed in the way in which seals have been killed throughout the whole of the southern parts of the world."

The culmination of Victorian debate was the Sixth International Geographical Congress held in London in 1895 in which the resolution was passed "that the Congress record its opinion that the exploration of the Antarctic Regions is the greatest piece of geographical exploration still to be undertaken. That, in the view of the additions to knowledge in almost every branch of science which would result from such a scientific exploration, the Congress recommends that the scientific societies throughout the world should urge, in whatever way seems to them most effective, that this work should be undertaken before the close of the century".

The 19th century ended with the voyage of the *Antarctic* under Captain Kristensen to the Ross Sea in 1894–95 with C.E. Borchgrevink aboard; thus resulting in the first landing on the Antarctic continent at Cape Adare. In 1897–99, the *Belgica* under Gerlache carried out work off the west coast of the Antarctic Peninsula. It was beset for 12 months from March 1898 and drifted between 80°30'W and 102°W to a latitude of 71°32'S resulting in the first wintering over in Antarctica (Owen, 1941). In 1898–1900, Borchgrevink led an expedition on the *Southern Cross* in which a party of 10 wintered over at Cape Adare (the first party to do so voluntarily). A summary of this expedition (including the scientific results) is given by Borchgrevink (1900). By this time, seven non-existent islands had been charted in this region of the South Pacific and it took a number of years before all were expunged from navigational charts (Stommel, 1984).

The 20th century began with the assault on the Pole from the Ross Sea during the expeditions of Scott (1901–04, 1910–13), Shackleton (1907–09, 1914–17), Amundsen (1910–12) and Shirase (1911–12) (although Shirase abandoned his attempt from the Bay of Whales when he heard of the early start of Amundsen and Scott, Lovering and Prescott, 1979). This phase of Antarctic activity became known as the Heroic Age and is too well known to warrant discussion. Nonetheless, the scientific reports of the National Antarctic Expedition 1901–1904 and the British (*Terra Nova*) Antarctic Expedition 1910–1913 added greatly to the scientific knowledge of the Ross Sea region. Scott's first expedition also had a manual written for it summarizing Antarctic scientific methods and results (Murray, 1901). A précis of the oceanographic observations obtained during Scott's last expedition is given by Deacon (1975b) and of foraminiferal distributions by Earland (1935). A substantial account of the Ross Ice Shelf is given by Debenham (1948). Scott's expeditions were, of course, naval expeditions modelled on the search for Sir John Franklin's 1845–48 missing North-West Passage Expedition and the Arctic expedition of 1875–76 (Markham, 1986). This induced a conservatism in equipment and technique and these expeditions have been described as cumbersome, over-manned and inefficient (Markham, 1986). Nonetheless, in spite of Huntford's (1979) scathing account of Scott and his methods, it is evident that Scott's expeditions left by far the greatest scientific legacy of this period.

In 1903–05, Jean Charcot in the *Français* explored the west coast of the Antarctic Peninsula in the vicinity of the Biscoe Islands, and in 1908–10 explored the region again in the *Pourquoi Pas?*, the most modern comfortable polar vessel of its time, and wintered at Petmann Island. Scientific observations were made in the fields of meteorology, glaciology, geology and zoology. During 1915–16, the U.S. vessel *Carnegie* circumnavigated the Antarctic continent between 50°S and 60°S charting the earth's magnetic field (Stommel, 1984; Shapley, 1985). The ship took 118 days to circumnavigate the continent from Lyttelton, New Zealand, to its return. There was precipitation on 100 days and gales on 52, half of which reached hurricane force (Shapley, 1985).

The next phase of exploration had its origin in the First World War (1917) with the realization that the Southern Ocean whaling industry was important to the economy of Britain but that not enough was known about the habits of whales. Ultimately, this led to the *Discovery II* expeditions which can be said to put oceanographic studies in the Southern Ocean on a modern scientific basis. Studies undertaken were wide-ranging and included not only the biology of the whales but also the oceanography of the Southern Ocean and the distribution of the krill upon which the whales feed. The Discovery Reports which run to 37 volumes became a major reference and included such classic hydrological studies as Deacon (1937) and Mackintosh (1946). The concept of the Antarctic Convergence and Subtropical Convergence was first introduced and a chart showing their distribution around Antarctica compiled as a result of these voyages (Deacon, 1977a). Detailed studies of the Pacific Sector were undertaken during the Second Commission (1931–33) which included the fourth circumnavigation of Antarctica and the first in winter, the Third Commission (1933–35) which involved several long voyages through the Pacific, the Fourth Commission (1935–37) in which a circumpolar cruise was planned for the summer months but the ship had to be diverted to the Bay of Whales, Ross Sea, to rescue Lincoln Ellsworth, the Fifth Commission (1937–39) which involved circumnavigation in summer, and the Sixth Commission (1950–51) which involved oceanographic studies around New Zealand as well as a circum-Pacific crossing. Summaries of this work have been given by Herdman (1952), Coleman-Cooke (1963) and Hardy (1967). Some limited sediment sampling was carried out on the west coast of the Antarctic Peninsula during these voyages (Neaverson, 1934).

Whaling was indeed a major factor in the Southern Oceans in the inter-war years (Dawbin, 1952; Priestley, 1956; Quartermain, 1967; Laws, 1977; Stonehouse, 1972; Allen, 1980; Sugden, 1982; Tønnessen and Johnsen, 1982; Brown and Lockyer, 1984; Baker, this volume) and a summary of political regulations governing whaling are listed in Coleman-Cooke (1963, Appendix E). Between 1923 and 1930, 6,111 whales yielding 526,238 barrels of oil were caught in the Ross Sea (Tønnessen and Johnsen, 1982, Table 25). Between 1925 and 1929, pelagic whaling (i.e., based on factory ships rather than shore stations) resulted in a catch of 29,671 whales yielding 2,282,327 barrels of oil in the Antarctic region (Tønnessen and Johnsen, 1982, Table 24). Whaling continued after the war. The total catch of whales in the Antarctic in the period 1904–78 was 1,393,254 whales yielding 83,360,382 barrels (13.9 million tonnes) of oil (Tønnessen and Johnsen, 1982, Table 67). Tønnessen and Johnsen (1982) give no figures for the Pacific sector alone but a chart published by Sugden (1982) shows that 163,000 whales were caught in the area between 130°E and 50°W (the Pacific Ocean sector) during the period 1931–76 whereas 679,200 whales were caught between 50°W and 130°E (the Atlantic and Indian Ocean sectors).

The inter-war phase of whaling activity was also significant in as much as it was the application by the Norwegian, C.A. Larsen, for a whaling concession in the Ross Sea that led to the setting up of the Ross Dependency in 1923 (Tønnessen and Johnsen, 1982; Watt, 1989). Whilst British claims in this region stretched back to Ross's landing on Possession Island in 1841, Britain persuaded a reluctant New Zealand Government to take over administration of the Ross Dependency (stretching between 160°E and 150°W south of 60°S). It was not, however, until 1956 that New Zealand began its permanent scientific programme in the Ross Dependency (Quartermain, 1967). In the Antarctic Peninsula region, the competing claims of Chile (90°–53°W), Argentina (74°–25°W) and Britain (80°–20°W) (all south of 60°S) date from the Second World War period (cf. Lovering and Prescott, 1979).

The inter-war years also saw the use of aircraft and tractors in Antarctica by men such as Byrd and Ellsworth but this is beyond the scope of this chapter (cf. Shapley, 1985). Byrd's work was based on the Little America station in the Bay of Whales. Twelve sediment cores were collected in the Ross Sea (Stetson and Upson, 1937) and echo soundings taken (Roos, 1937) during the Byrd expedition. The U.S. Antarctic Service expedition of 1939–41 also established a permanent base, Little America III, in the Bay of Whales (Shapley, 1985). A key development of this period was the publication of Du Toit's classic book "Our Wandering Continents" (Du Toit, 1937) which recognized the vital role of Antarctica in the reconstruction of Gondwanaland (cf. Sutton, 1977; Craddock, 1978, 1982), a concept first proposed by J.D. Hooker in 1851 (Walton, 1987) and by E. Suess in 1885 (Teichert, 1952). The Norwegians circumnavigated the Antarctic continent in 1930–31 with the *Norvegia* and in 1933–34 with the *Thorshavn*, in both cases carrying out a scientific programme (Holtedahl, 1935).

Following the Second World War, the U.S. Navy mounted a military exercise, *Operation High Jump*, in 1945–47 (Editorial Committee, 1952; Shapley, 1985) which resulted in five bathythermograph sections across the Antarctic Convergence (Pritchard and LaFond, 1952) and the preparation of a sediment chart of the region (Hough, 1956; Thomas, 1959). The great depth of the Antarctic shelf break (420–510 m) was also established during this expedition (Dietz, 1952). In 1954–55, the U.S.S. *Atika* undertook a cruise to the Ross Sea as a reconnaissance for the International Geophysical Year (U.S. Navy Hydrographic Office Tech. Rep. 48) and this was followed by the very extensive U.S. Navy and later Coastguard Programme, *Operation Deep Freeze*, lasting from 1956 to the present, which resulted in wide-ranging hydrological and geophysical studies in the region (cf. U.S. Navy Hydrographic Office Tech. Rep. 190; U.S. Navy Task Force 43, 1969) (cf. Thomas, 1960). The earlier data (up to *Operation Deep Freeze II*) were compiled into an oceanographic atlas of the Southern Ocean (Anonymous, 1957; Lyman, 1958). The Norwegians also carried out numerous hydrological and biological stations in the region during the *Brategg* expedition of 1947–48 (Mosby, 1956) and a summary of oceanographic measurements taken from the Japanese whaling fleet from 1946–52 was presented by Hazawa and Tsuchida (1954). Substantial studies of bottom sediments and geomorphology were also carried out during the cruise of the *Ob* from 1955–58 (Kort, 1962; Lisitzin, 1962, 1970; Zhivago, 1962; Maksimov, 1964). Whilst much information was available on the Pacific Sector of the Southern Ocean by the time of the IGY (particularly in physical oceanography and marine biology), much remained to be learned (Fleming, 1952; Ewing and Heezen, 1956; Deacon, 1963; Brodie, 1965; Angino and Lepley, 1966). This is well illustrated by Ewing and Heezen's review which emphasized the limited geological knowledge in the region (cf. Frakes, 1983). The Pacific–Antarctic Ridge, for instance, was poorly known and the Macquarie Ridge was subsequently shown to be an island arc (Cullen, 1967; Summerhayes, 1967), not a mid-ocean ridge as proposed by Ewing and Heezen.

The IGY of 1957–58 marks the beginning of the most recent phase of Antarctic activity in which scientific research has been pre-eminent. Many nations such as New Zealand mark their permanent occupation of the continent from that date.

Following the IGY, the Antarctic Treaty was ratified in 1961 by the 12 nations that participated in the IGY. There are now 22 nations with consultative status (i.e., have continuing scientific programmes in the region). The provisions of the Antarctic Treaty apply to the area south of 60°S latitude including all ice shelves, although the rights of passage on the high seas are maintained under international law. The principal result of the Antarctic Treaty is that the Antarctic continent has been a region of peaceful international scientific co-operation. Lovering and Prescott (1979) describe the treaty as one of the most successful treaties negotiated for international co-operation (cf. Laws, 1985a). An overview of advances in Antarctic geophysical sciences since the IGY is given in *Antarctic Journal of the*

United States 1986, 21(2). A brief description of Antarctic activities until 1974–75 is given by Dater (1975).

In New Zealand, scientific studies in the southern sector of the Pacific were carried out from U.S. vessels as part of *Operation Deep Freeze* in 1958 (Garner, 1958) and from U.S.C.G.C. *Glacier* in 1964–65 (Hatherton et al., 1965; Forbes, 1966) as well as from H.M.N.Z.S. *Pukaki* and *Hawea* in 1956–57 (Burling, 1961) and H.M.N.Z.S. *Endeavour* in 1957 (forming part of the Trans-Antarctic Expedition) (Cassie, 1963), in 1958–60 (Adams and Christoffel, 1962; Bullivant, 1967) and 1963–65 (Ross, 1967; Summerhayes, 1969; Christoffel and Falconer, 1972) (cf. Burling, 1960; Meade, 1978). Since that time, New Zealand's oceanographic programme in southern waters has been largely in abeyance except as part of international co-operative programmes (Gordon, 1977; Neal and Nowlin, 1979; Bryden and Heath, 1985), on ships of opportunity (Glasby et al., 1975; Davey et al., 1982) or through the ice (Gilmour, 1979; Carter et al., 1981). More recently, New Zealand has been involved in the MSSTS (McMurdo Sound Sediment and Tectonic Studies) (Barrett, 1986) and CIROS (Cenozoic Investigations in the Western Ross Sea) (Barrett and Scientific Staff, 1985; Barrett, 1987, 1989) projects which involved drilling into the seafloor through sea ice. A bathymetric chart of McMurdo Sound is a by-product of this work (Pyne et al., 1985). Sedimentological studies have also been carried out in McMurdo Sound by sampling through the sea ice and from U.S.C.G.C. *Glacier* (Macpherson, 1987; Ward et al., 1987). Korsch and Wellman (1988) have reviewed the tectonic evolution of the region. Fraser (1986) has presented an excellent photographic survey of New Zealand's sub-antarctic islands (cf. Clark and Dingwall, 1985). Vincent (1988) has reviewed microbial ecosystems in the marginal-ice zone and open ocean around Antarctica. Summaries of New Zealand work in the Ross Sea have been given by Knox (1986) and Hatherton (in press).

In the U.S.A., the 1961 *Monsoon* expedition traversed the Pacific–Antarctic Ridge at 64°30'S, 173°E, analyzed rare gases in the South Pacific seawater (Craig et al., 1967; Craig, 1970) and collected manganese nodules from the Southern Ocean (Mero, 1965). Cruises 1–55 of the U.S.N.S. *Eltanin* (1962–72) studied the entire circumpolar region and represent perhaps the most significant advance in the study of all aspects of the Antarctic Sector of the Pacific (cf. *Antarctic Research Series*, vol. 15, 1971; vol. 19, 1972; Hayes and Pitman, 1972). Some of the earlier *Eltanin* data are excellently summarized in the maps of the *Antarctic Map Folio Series*. DSDP legs 28 (1972–73), 29 (1973), 35 (1974) and 90 (1983) were also a key development which played a major role in increasing our knowledge of the palaeoclimatology and palaeoceanography of the region (cf. Johnson et al., 1982). Since the early 1970s, the United States has relied mainly on work from ice-breakers on transit from New Zealand to McMurdo Sound or within the Ross Sea (cf. Jacobs et al., 1981; Anderson et al., 1983, 1984b; Nelson and Smith, 1986; Wilson et al., 1986) or from specific cruises such as those of R.V. *Knorr* (1978–79) (Suess and Ungerer, 1981; Nelson and Gordon, 1982) or S.P. *Lee* (1984) (Eittreim, Cooper, and Scientific Staff, 1984; Cooper and Davey, 1987). In 1974, R.V. *Melville* went to almost 70°S southeast of New Zealand as part of the GEOSECS programme to study seawater chemistry (Broecker et al., 1982). In 1982–83,

U.S.C.G.C. *Polar Star* circumnavigated the Antarctic continent (Holm-Hansen and Chapman, 1983; Hanson and Erickson, 1985). The interdisciplinary RISP (Ross Ice Shelf Project) drilling through the Ross Ice Shelf took place in 1976–77 (Clough and Hansen, 1979). This programme followed the earlier RIGGS (Ross Ice Shelf Geophysical and Glaciological Survey) which took place between 1973 and 1978 (Bentley and Jesek, 1981; Bentley 1984). Bentley also summarized earlier work on the Ross Ice Shelf. The Circum-Pacific Council for Energy and Mineral Resources maps of Antarctica represent the most modern bathymetric and geological syntheses of the region. The Southern Ocean atlas also summarizes hydrological data for the region (Gordon et al., 1982) and the Antarctic Bibliography, now published in 13 volumes by the U.S. Library of Congress, is a major source of references. In addition, a listing of all oceanographic stations in the Southern Ocean has been compiled by Anonymous (1984). The *Antarctic Research Series* published by the American Geophysical Union, now running to 47 volumes, contains a substantial amount of information on the region, particularly in marine biology. For instance, Jacobs (1985) has summarized the oceanography of the Antarctic continental shelf; this volume includes a copy of the GEBCO bathymetric map of the shelf area (cf. Vanney et al., 1981; Johnson et al., 1982). An assessment of U.S. research priorities in Antarctica is given in Anonymous (1983a, 1986a, 1987a). A list of funding allocations within U.S. Antarctic research programmes in selected years is given by Shapley (1985).

Of the other interested nations, German efforts have concentrated on the tectonics and stratigraphy of the Ross Sea region starting in 1979 (Kothe et al., 1981; Tessensohn, 1984; Hinz and Kristoffersen, 1987). The Germans carried out seismic work in the Ross Sea in 1980 using the *Explora*, the French in 1981–82 also using the *Explora*, and the Japanese in 1982–83 using the *Hakurei Maru* (Anonymous, 1982; Behrendt, 1983a). A summary map showing the tracks of the multi-channel seismic surveys in the Ross Sea is given in Eittreim, Cooper, and Scientific Staff (1984). The Italians also carried out seismic work from the *Explora* in the seasons 1986–87, 1987–88 and 1988–89 (Anonymous, 1988, 1989). The Soviet vessel *Ob* began working in the Southern Ocean in 1956 (e.g., Zernova, 1970) and Soviet ships have carried out fisheries surveys in the Pacific Sector of the Southern Ocean since 1968 (USSR, 1985). In the mid 1970s, Soviet scientists developed a programme "Polar Experiment-South (POLEX-South)" to make a long-term study of the Antarctic Circumpolar Current. The results of this work, including a discussion of earlier Soviet physical oceanographic studies in the region, are summarized by Sarukhanyan (1985) (cf. Brigham, 1988). Soviet ships circumnavigated Antarctica in 1982–83 with the *Dmitri Mendeleyev* concentrating its scientific effort southwest of the Campbell Plateau (Anonymous, 1983b). Bek-Bulat and Zalishchak (1985) have reported phosphorite on a seamount in the vicinity of the Eltanin Fracture Zone. The Russian Atlas of Antarctica represented a major synthesis of existing data to that date (Anonymous, 1966a). Soviet ships have also started harvesting krill in the region (Worthington, 1986). Significantly, there has been no winter marine research project in the Ross Sea to rival the 1986 winter Weddell Sea Project undertaken by the German research vessel R.V. *Polarstern* (Hempel, 1988).

There are also a number of international programmes interested in this region such as the World Climate Programme (SCOR Working Group 74, 1985) and the World Ocean Circulation Experiment (Anonymous, 1986b). The International Whaling Commission has also carried out a number of minke whale assessment cruises. These generally include 2–3 Japanese and one Russian whale scouting vessels. The cruises which have taken place in the Antarctic Sector of the Pacific are the Third (1980–81) (130°E–170°W), the Fifth (1982–83) (60°W–120°W), the Sixth (1983–84) (120°W–170°W), and the Eighth (1985–86) (130°E–170°W). The Scientific Committee on Antarctic Research (SCAR) has been involved in a number of projects such as production of the BIOMASS Handbook Series and the BIOMASS Report Series. It has also sponsored a series of symposia on Antarctic geology and geophysics (e.g., Oliver et al., 1983) and on Antarctic biology (e.g., Siegfried et al., 1985). The FAO has put out species identification sheets, including species distribution and fishing grounds, for fishery purposes in the CCAMLR (Commission for the Conservation of Antarctic Marine Living Resources) area of the Southern Ocean (FAO, 1985).

Satellite observations are also becoming increasingly important, for instance to study ocean floor bathymetry (Dixon and Parke, 1983), sea ice distribution (Zwally et al., 1979, 1983, 1985; Gudmandsen, 1983; Robin et al., 1983; Comiso and Zwally, 1984), sea conditions (Mognard et al., 1983; Fu and Chelton, 1984) the relationship of ocean currents to bathymetry (Colton and Chase, 1983) or geoid anomalies (Driscoll and Parsons, 1988).

MINERALS

The honour of being the first to suggest possible economic mineral deposits in Antarctica goes to Borchgrevink who found quartz reefs near Duke of York Island "justifying the belief that in time to come exploration will receive much support from commerce" (Borchgrevink, 1900). Shackleton attempted to finance his expedition in part by floating mining shares. In 1908 at the top of the Beardmore Glacier on their march south, Wild discovered seams of coal between 4 ins and 7–8 ft thick (Shackleton, 1909). In 1912, Wilson found coal seams at all heights in the sandstone cliffs and lumps of weathered coal with fossil plants on Mt Buckley in the Beardmore Glacier. Debenham also discovered coal on the geological expedition to Granite Harbour. Prior to the Southern Journey, Scott had discovered quartz-containing veins of copper near Cape Bernacchi (Scott, 1913). In Adelie Land, Mawson noted small quantities of ore minerals in gneiss which gave "the possibility of mineral wealth beneath the continental ice-cap" (Mawson, 1915). In 1912, the only mineral prospecting licence ever granted in Antarctica was given by the British Colonial Office to Messrs Chr. Salvesen to explore for minerals in the Antarctic Peninsula (Thomson and Swithinbank, 1985). In 1919, Leo Amery, Under-Secretary of State at the Colonial Office, was arguing for British Annexation of Antarctica, partly on the grounds of the "immense potential value of its fisheries and its mineral resources" (Beck, 1983). Priestley, writing much after the event, also considered that there must be "great and valuable mineral resources" in a continent of that size (Priestley, 1956).

An early major review of the economic potential of Antarctic minerals was presented by Potter (1969). Potter not only listed some of the environmental problems associated with Antarctica but also gave detailed costings of working in Antarctica. It was recognized that the only minerals worth exploiting would be those present in high concentrations and of high value with relatively good access. Minerals rated commercial elsewhere would in most cases be uneconomic because of the high costs involved. Based on consideration of the data then available, Potter considered it unlikely that any mineral (metallic, hydrocarbon or manganese nodules) would be commercially exploitable. Whilst some substantial estimates of Antarctic offshore hydrocarbon resources were made in the 1970s (listed in Zumberge, 1979; Auburn, 1982; and Zorn, 1984) stimulating interest, the conclusions reached by Potter remain essentially unchanged today (cf. Pontecorvo, 1982).

Of the possible mineral resources of Antarctica, it is generally accepted that offshore hydrocarbon resources are the most prospective in the forseeable future but that only giant (about 70 million tonnes of recoverable oil) or supergiant (about 700 million tonnes) fields would be considered commercially worthwhile (Behrendt, 1983b). Nonetheless, exploitation of such deposits would present formidable technical problems. An assessment of the economic potential of these deposits is given by Cook and Davey (this volume) and of the environmental aspects of possible recovery by Gregory (this volume).

The distribution of metallic minerals in Antarctica can be inferred by anology with the distribution of minerals in other segments of the Gondwana Super-continent (Runnells, 1970). At present, all mineral observations in Antarctica can be classified as mineral occurrences. In spite of much being written, virtually all authors concede that metallic minerals have only limited potential for commercial exploitation in Antarctica (e.g., Wright and Williams, 1974; Holdgate and Tinker, 1979; Lovering and Prescott, 1979; Zumberge, 1979, 1982; Auburn, 1982; Behrendt, 1983b; Gjelsvik, 1983; Quilty, 1984; Shapley, 1985; Budd, 1986a; Roland, 1986; Tessensohn, 1986; Crockett and Clarkson, 1987; Larminie, 1987; Parsons, 1987; Walton, 1988). The reasons for this include the fact that only 2% of Antarctica is ice-free, the harsh climate, the lack of infrastructure, the tremendous transportation problems, the extreme cost of exploration and mining operations and possible environmental problems. An exception to this viewpoint has been presented by de Wit (1985) who argued that platinum mining might be feasible in the Dufek Massif. However, without a full-scale exploration programme, this really is only an assumption based upon geological setting (Larminie, 1987; Parsons, 1987).

Although deep-sea manganese nodules are known to occur in abundance in the Circumpolar siliceous ooze province, the deposits are also considered to have limited economic potential for various reasons (Anderson, this volume).

In drafting the Antarctic Treaty, it was recognized that agreement would have been impossible if mineral resources issues had been considered. This came to be seen as a weakness of the Treaty system and much effort has gone into negotiating a Minerals Regime for the regulation of mineral exploration and exploitation (Auburn, 1982). An agreement was finally reached in Wellington in 1988. Nonetheless, it should be recognized that exploitation of Antarctic mineral resources (including hydrocarbons) is unlikely in the forseeable future. Quite apart from the considerable technological and environmental problems involved, the high cost of exploiting these deposits means that other sources of minerals or energy can be developed more cheaply elsewhere. This is likely to remain the ultimate barrier to the commercial development of minerals in Antarctica.

MARINE LIVING RESOURCES

Whilst the Antarctic terrestrial ecosystem has an extremely low productivity with a total production of plant material measured in the hundreds of tonnes per year, the Southern Ocean south of the Antarctic Convergence has a very much higher productivity with a total plant (phytoplankton) production measured in thousands of millions of tonnes per year. However, the overall productivity of the Southern Ocean is not as high as previously believed (El-Sayed and Turner, 1977; Holm-Hansen et al., 1977; Knox, 1983; Clarke, 1985; Hempel, 1985; Laws, 1985b; Nelson and Smith, 1986; Wilson et al., 1986) which has implications to the exploitation of living resources from the region (El-Sayed, 1978). It is thought that the large seasonal variations in light and sea-ice cover, and especially the near-freezing temperatures of the surface waters, may be more significant in control-ling the productivity of the Southern Ocean waters than upwelling and the regeneration of nutrients (Knox, 1983). Nonetheless, Knox (1983) has pointed out that, although the Southern Ocean constitutes only 10% of the world's oceans, it has potential resources, principally krill, that could rival the production of the other 90% (cf. Walton, 1987). This makes krill potentially the world's largest fishery stock (Auburn, 1982).

The principal characteristic of the Southern Ocean is the shortness of the food web. The principal herbivore is krill (*Euphausia superba*) which has a biomass of the order of 10^9 tonnes. The consumers of krill include squid, fish, seabirds, crabeater seals and baleen whales. At the top of the food web are the higher predatory species including toothed whales, fish, penguins and Weddell and leopard seals. The shortness of the food web enables a greater proportion of the overall productivity to reach the higher trophic levels and this accounts for the unusually dense populations of birds and mammals. Fish are not as important as elsewhere, in part because the continental shelves are much deeper and narrower (Laws, 1983). Attempts to calculate the consumption of the major food compo-nents by whales, seals and birds have been made by Everson (1977) (cf. Laws, 1985b). However, simple food webs such as found in the Southern Ocean are thought to be ecologically unstable. They exhibit large population oscillations and are vulnerable to significant perturbations.

Because of exploitation, the biomass of whales in the Southern Ocean has declined from about 43 million tonnes originally to about 7 million tonnes today (i.e., a 6-fold decrease). The original whale stocks are estimated to have consumed about 190 million tonnes of krill annually compared to about 43 million tonnes annually today. About 150 million tonnes of krill are therefore thought to be available to other producers (Everson, 1977; Laws, 1977, 1983, 1985a, b; Lovering and Prescott, 1979; Knox, 1983, 1984; Nagata, 1983; Chittleborough, 1984; Walton, 1987). However, the dynamics of the system are still not well understood and it is not possible to say what effect harvesting the "krill surplus" would have, although populations of seals, seabirds, squid, and those populations of baleen whales that have not been exploited may have increased as a result (Knox, 1984).

The early years of Antarctic exploration were characterized by uncontrolled exploitation of marine life, particularly seals and whales. The Antarctic Treaty nations have adopted a number of conservation measures. The Agreed Measures for the Conservation of Antarctic Flora and Fauna (1964) restrict human activities near bird and seal colonies and set aside "sites of special scientific interest". The Convention for the Conservation of Antarctic Seals (1978) established regulations in advance of renewed exploitation. It applies south of 60°S. Ross, elephant, and fur seals are totally protected whilst quotas are set for crabeater, leopard and Weddell seals. At present, there is no commercial exploitation of seals in the Southern Ocean. Whaling is regulated by the International Whaling Commission (1946). The Commission has tended to set catch limits well above natural replacement levels. As the larger whales were hunted to the point of extinction, attention turned to the smaller whales. At present, the U.S.S.R. and Japan are the only IWC countries still hunting whales in the Southern Ocean and the minke whale is the only species abundant enough to catch.

To give some idea of the extent of exploitation of biological resources from the Antarctic Sector of the Pacific, for the statistical area south of 60°S the total krill catch for the 10-year period (1977–86) was 38,707 tonnes of which 49% was taken by the U.S.S.R. and 51% by Japan. This total represents only 1.3% of the total catch from the entire Southern Ocean, a reflection of the lower commercial krill catch rates in this region compared to those in the South Atlantic (Everson, 1977). Total fish catch for this period was reported to be 2,357 tonnes of which the U.S.S.R. took over 99%. This represents a negligible proportion of the total fish catch for the Southern Ocean, reflecting in part the absence of any shallow areas in the region comparable to the Kerguelen Plateau or around South Georgia. These data are taken from SC-CAMLR-V (1985) (cf. Everson, 1977, 1984a; Brewster, 1982; Knox, 1983; Kaczynski, 1984; Clarke, 1985; Kock, 1985, 1987; Anonymous, 1986c; Bardach, 1986; Walton, 1987). The fish catch data do not, of course, include catches from the New Zealand Plateau where southern blue whiting is caught (Brewster, 1982). From 1891 to 1919, approximately 150,000 king and royal penguins were boiled down annually for oil on Macquarie Island (Falla, 1962; Brewster, 1982; Sage, 1985). Seal and whale catch data are given by Baker (this volume).

Much attention has focused on krill as a source of protein in recent years (Mitchell and Sandbrook, 1980; Kaylor and Learson, 1983). Since krill is the basis for marine life in the Southern Ocean (Everson, 1977; Clarke, 1985; Laws, 1985a, b), harvesting krill has enormous implications for all other species.

The Convention for the Conservation of Antarctic Marine Living Resources (CCAMLR) (1982) applied to the area south of the Antarctic Convergence and adopts the "ecosystem approach" in which harvesting of target species is related to the impact on other species (Edwards and Heap, 1981; Nagata, 1983; Powell, 1983; Knox, 1984; Gulland, 1986). The Convention is particularly concerned with the conservation of fish and krill. Nonetheless, to manage living resources by the "ecosystem approach" requires knowledge of the resources, their distribution and behaviour in space and time, their role in the total ecosystem, and their response to fishery and proposed management options.

The BIOMASS (Biological Investigations of Marine Antarctic Systems and Stocks) programme has as its objective the deeper understanding of the structure and dynamic functioning of the Antarctic marine ecosystem as a basis for the management of actual and potential living resources (Knox, 1984; Hempel, 1987; Sahrhage, 1988).   The original intention was that the BIOMASS programme would be a 10-year programme commencing in 1977 in which two major data gathering exercises (FIBEX, 1980–81, and SIBEX, 1983–84 and 1984–85) were undertaken;   these represent one of the largest international programmes in marine biology. The BIOMASS programme involves building an information base which includes (Knox, 1984) :

1. the numerical and functional relationships among key species, particularly the relationships between krill and its predators and competitors;

2. the nature, dynamics and functioning of krill swarms and how they might be affected by harvesting and related activities;

3. the number and distribution limits of independent populations comprising the key species, especially krill;

4. the area and habitats critical for the spawning, survival and productivity of krill and other species; and

5. the major physical/chemical features (e.g., currents, fronts, gyres, upwell-ings, nutrients) that directly or indirectly determine the distribution, movements, abundance, life history, and productivity of the key species and populations, especially krill.

In spite of its ambitious nature, environmentalists have criticized CCAMLR on the grounds that progress in attaining the objectives of the Convention has been extremely slow and that almost all the major fish stocks have been seriously depleted during the last few years. Barnes (1982) considered that the Convention contains serious flaws from the standpoint of sound decision making. In particu-lar, CCAMLR is thought to be hampered by :

1. the refusal of some fishing nations, particularly the Soviet Union, to pro-vide adequate catch and effort statistics;

2. the objective of using the ecosystem approach to the management of krill and fish has enormous data requirements that are impossible to meet given the current level of funding; and

3. the requirement that decisions of the Commission on matters of substance are taken by consensus.

These circumstances have led to the situation where fishing is not regulated unless there is irrefutable evidence that the fish stocks are being depleted.

ENVIRONMENTAL CONSIDERATIONS

For the Southern Ocean, the main environmental hazards are likely to arise from the exploitation of marine living and mineral resources and from climatic changes due to man's activities. These aspects have been discussed in considerable detail (e.g., Holdgate and Tinker, 1979; Brewster, 1982; Zumberge, 1982; Holdgate, 1983, 1987; Bonner, 1984; Keys, 1984; Anonymous, 1985a; Benninghoff and Bonner, 1985; Bolin et al., 1986; Angel, 1987; Bonner and Angel, 1987; May, 1988; Gregory, this volume) and it is not the intention to repeat these arguments here.

Nonetheless, it is worth quoting Zumberge (1982) that knowledge of the Antarctic continent and Southern Ocean remains incomplete. Hundreds of man-years of scientific studies are required before the components of the Antarctic environment and their interdependent relationships are sufficiently understood to permit a reasonably confident assessment of the impact of man's activities on the marine and terrestrial environments in Antarctica. The paucity of basic information in particular, and the lack of knowledge of environmental dynamics in general, makes any attempt to predict the consequences of man's activities on the environment a very tenuous activity. Similarly, Holdgate (1983) has argued that understanding the dynamic and interacting nature of polar environmental conditions is essential if development projects are to be soundly designed. Among the key interactions in the Antarctic about which information is inadequate are those between sea ice and the marine ecosystem, those between marine ecosystems and terrestrial ecology and the extent to which components of the marine system may be vulnerable to pollution. Holdgate also noted that the Antarctic must not be regarded as a pristine environment unmodified by man. Rather, its ecosystems have been widely influenced by past human impacts. Angel (1987) considered three of the main Antarctic habits (terrestrial, inland waters and islands) likely to be fragile whereas the oceanic ecosystem contains few fragile elements. However, the highly dynamic nature of the oceanic environment requires that the whole Antarctic marine environment be thought of as a simple entity and managed as such.

CONCLUDING REMARKS

From the preceding discussion, it can be seen that there has been a very substantial increase in our knowledge of the Antarctic Sector of the Pacific in many scientific disciplines, particularly since the IGY. Nonetheless, much of this remains in specialist journals and is not readily available. Further, the question of the possible exploitation of Antarctic resources has brought Antarctica and its surrounding oceans into increasing prominence over the last few years. It is also seen that the scientific base on which to assess possible environmental impacts as a result of man's activities is inadequate. The aim of this volume is to bring together some of the diverse information from this increasingly important region of the world's ocean in an attempt to show the scientific achievements as well as some of the problems that remain. It is hoped that collating this material will stimulate long-overdue scientific endeavours in this region.

CHAPTER 2

METEOROLOGY

A.B. MULLAN and J.S. HICKMAN

INTRODUCTION

Weather Conditions in the South Pacific

"This 26–27 November [1972] gale was barely over before, on the night of the 27th, the barometer starting dropping again. These repeated gales were seriously beginning to get me down .... I could hardly remember when my storm clothes had last been removed .... On the 28th the bottom fell out of the glass .... The pointer moved right off the scale and continued downwards to about 950 mb during the night ... something altogether new had burst upon us – a storm of hurricane intensity .... The waves increased in height with unbelievable rapidity. Nothing in my previous experience [including North Atlantic autumn gales, a Coral Sea cyclone, gales off Iceland, Cape of Good Hope, and in Magellan Straits] had prepared me for this .... By evening the estimated wind speed was over 60 knots; the seas were conservatively forty feet high and growing taller .... Came a roar, as of an approaching express train .... The tottering breaker exploded right over us ...".

This description of stormy weather (near 60°S, 140°W) is one of many in solo yachtsman David Lewis' book "Ice Bird", describing his journey across the Southern Ocean (Lewis, 1975).

The "second voyage" of James Cook (1772–75) encountered similar weather events. In addition, Cook's experience graphically illustrates the extent of high latitude cloudiness over the oceans. In 1773–74, in the high latitude portion of the New Zealand–Pacific Sector (the same general area covered by Lewis' description), only 1% of weather observations indicate fine, clear weather. Cook also concluded (correctly) that ice in the Southern Ocean is further north in the Atlantic and Indian Ocean sectors than in the Pacific Sector.

Although adverse weather conditions are not encountered all the time in the Southern Ocean, it is as well for travellers through the region to be prepared. Typically, as one travels south from 40°S, conditions progressively deteriorate and the frequency of severe weather increases. South of 50°S in the South Pacific one finds, according to the U.S. Navy Marine Climatic Atlas (1979), low cloud covering more than half the sky at least 70% of the time; precipitation is mentioned in weather observations about 25% of the time; winds are stronger, with speeds above 34 knots (gale force) 10–20% of the time; and wave heights exceed 6 metres (20 feet) 10–15% of the time. Winter conditions are generally worse than in summer, with the additional factor of sea ice to be considered. Greatest storminess occurs in the central Southern Pacific, far from New Zealand and South America. For example, on David Lewis' circumnavigation of Antarctica, the boat capsized twice within a space of two weeks near 60°S between longitudes 140°W and 120°W.

In the latter part of the 19th century, there were sporadic attempts by meteorologists to draw charts showing daily weather conditions over limited geographic regions of the high latitude Southern Hemisphere. At the time, there was little sea level information available apart from very isolated land stations, whaling ships, and other ships of opportunity. This limited flow of information actually declined further with the opening of the Suez Canal in 1869 and the Panama Canal in 1914, which diverted much of the ship traffic from the Southern Ocean. Information on atmospheric conditions above the surface (pressure, temperature, humidity, wind) was not available at all until the development of the balloon radiosonde and radar after World War II. Convincing weather analysis of the Southern Ocean has only been possible since the International Geophysical Year (IGY) in 1957–58, and subsequently with the development of automatic weather stations, buoys and satellites, coupled with the long-term maintenance of a modest network of ground level and upper air weather observing stations in sub-Antarctic and Antarctic latitudes.

Weather Observations in the Southern Hemisphere since 1957

The 18-month period July 1957 to December 1958, known as the International Geophysical Year, was a time of intensive meteorological observations around the world. For Southern Hemisphere meteorologists, the high latitude oceanic areas and continental Antarctica had long been regions where data coverage was very sparse in space and time, and one of the aims of the IGY programme was to improve this situation. A special effort was made to co-ordinate all reports from land stations and ships to produce daily sea level and upper air charts for the entire globe. Nevertheless, coverage of the South Pacific remained poor. Few ships crossed this area and there were no island stations south of 40°S, except for those close to New Zealand (Campbell Island at about 52°S and Macquarie Island at 55°S) and the Antarctic Peninsula.

Thirty-nine stations operated in Antarctica during the IGY (Taljaard, 1972), but their distribution was uneven, with 15 of these clustered close to the Antarctic Peninsula. In spite of these deficiencies, the resulting map series was the best available up to that time and, as the results were analyzed and published during the ensuing decade, much was learned about the general circulation of the Antarctic region, and possible influences of Antarctica on the atmospheric circulation at lower latitudes.

The launching of the first meteorological satellite (TIROS–1) on 1 April 1960 ushered in an exciting new era in which it became possible to receive daily cloud photographs of vast areas of the Southern Ocean. This was also a time of rapid advances in computer technology and in the development of numerical modelling of atmospheric behaviour. The first authoritative treatments of the large-scale circulation in southern latitudes began to appear (e.g., van Loon, 1967; Taljaard, 1972), but most analyses continued to be based on case studies for limited areas and short periods. Then, in May 1972, the Australian Bureau of Meteorology, which assumed the responsibility of World Meteorological Centre for the Southern Hemisphere, began to produce daily numerical analyses of the broadscale features of the hemispheric flow. In the absence of land-based and ship observations in much of the South Pacific and South Indian Oceans, these analyses relied heavily on the interpretation of satellite cloud photographs as pioneered by Australian meteorologists (e.g., Guymer, 1978).

In the last ten years, there have been considerable improvements in the way observational data are assimilated into the computer models, as well as increases in the number of types of data available. Satellite products now include cloud movement vectors and temperature profiles through the atmosphere, in addition to global cloud photographs several times daily. Another special meteorological observation programme, which began in December 1978, was known as the First GARP Global Experiment (GARP = Global Atmospheric Research Programme), or FGGE for short. A particular feature of this 12-month programme was the use of drifting ocean buoys to measure surface air pressure, a parameter not available from satellite observations. These ocean buoys were of great value in defining the intensity of synoptic* weather systems in the Southern Ocean, and generally resulted in observations of lower mean pressures and greater daily variability in the low pressure belt encircling Antarctica than had previously been thought to occur (Guymer and Le Marshall, 1980). Reduced numbers of buoys have continued to be used since the end of the FGGE period. Southern Hemisphere meteorologists working on aspects of the general circulation have therefore had a reasonably uniform and complete set of hemispheric analyses since 1972, although surface pressures in very high latitudes are probably more realistic from 1979 onwards. Satellite measurements of the extent of Antarctic sea ice are also fairly complete from about 1972 and form a second valuable time series.

The temperature of the ocean surface layer is another quantity of value to meteorologists but unfortunately a long homogeneous time series for the Southern Ocean is not yet available. Although satellites are ideal instruments for determining the spatial pattern of sea-surface temperature, obtaining absolute values is not as easy. Water vapour in the atmosphere absorbs radiation of the same wavelengths that satellites use to detect the surface emissions so that a correction factor must be applied to the calculated temperature; liquid water in the form of clouds or rain is a further complicating factor in deducing the temperature from the radiation measurements.

Figure 2.1 shows a typical hemispheric surface pressure analysis and accompanying meteorological satellite cloud mosaic. The satellite images are photographed in the infrared part of the spectrum, which allows changes in cloud features to be followed during hours of darkness. (For daylight satellite passes, photographs are taken in the visible part of the spectrum.) Low pressure centres circulating around the Antarctic continent (Fig. 2.1b) can, in most cases, be identified with distinctive cloud features (Fig. 2.1a); the correspondence may not

---

* In meteorology, the term "synoptic" refers to the use of data obtained simultaneously over a wide area so as to give a nearly instantaneous picture of the atmospheric conditions.

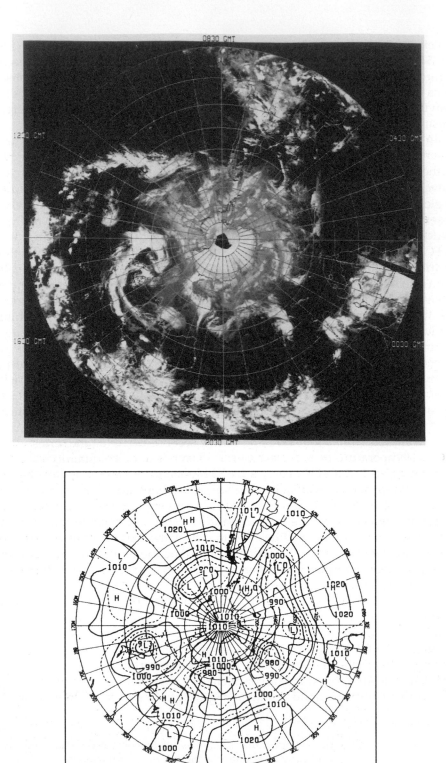

always be exact because the satellite mosaic is a composite of a number of passes over a 24-hour period, whilst the surface pressure analysis is an instantaneous "synoptic" view.

Chapter Outline

Although there are still many gaps in our knowledge of physical processes occurring in the atmosphere at high southern latitudes, the existing data base is sufficient to provide a broad view of the climatology of the region. In the following sections, we describe the main features of the atmospheric circulation over the Pacific south of 40°S. Readers are referred to the World Survey of Climatology series for further discussion of the climate of the South Pacific Ocean (Streten and Zillman, 1984) and the Antarctic (Schwerdtfeger, 1970). Both these volumes contain many useful maps of climatic elements, such as surface pressure, directional frequencies of wind, sea temperature etc. (see also the U.S. Navy Marine Climatic Atlas of the Antarctic, 1965, and of the South Pacific Ocean, 1979).

We are concerned here with the meteorology of the South Pacific over the longitude range from Tasmania eastwards to the Antarctic Peninsula. However, many statements about the Pacific circulation can apply equally well to any longitude of the Southern Ocean. This is hardly surprising considering the relative uniformity of the underlying surface. The sharp contrasts between land and sea that drive the seasonally varying regional circulations of the Northern Hemisphere are absent in the south. The constriction at Drake Passage, which has important consequences for ocean currents, is much less significant for the atmosphere.

The approach taken is therefore to describe the atmospheric circulation over the Southern Ocean from a hemispheric point of view, and to highlight results peculiar to the Pacific Sector wherever possible. The following sections of this chapter describe the meteorology at increasingly higher latitude bands. Firstly, weather systems over the oceanic latitudes are examined. Secondly, we consider the complications of sea ice and thirdly the effect of the Antarctic continent itself. A complete separation of these interacting factors is, of course, not possible, as will quickly become obvious to the reader. Indeed, a synthesis of the various feedbacks between the polar energy balance, seasonally varying sea ice and north-south heat transport by atmosphere and ocean is the ultimate aim of much high latitude climate research. Current research efforts are reviewed briefly in the concluding section of this chapter.

Fig. 2.1. (a) Hemispheric cloud mosaic from NOAA–9 satellite over period 22–23 January 1987, and covering entire Southern Hemisphere from Equator to South Pole. The photographs are taken at infrared wavelengths, and whiter features on the image indicate lower temperatures (usually associated with higher-topped cloud); (b) Mean sea-level pressure analysis at 1200 GMT (or midnight New Zealand Standard Time) on 22 January 1987 drawn to same scale and orientation as (a), but only covering the area from 20°S to South Pole. Isobars drawn every 5 hectoPascals (hPa) and high/low pressure centres denoted by H/L.

ATMOSPHERIC CIRCULATION OVER THE SOUTHERN OCEAN

Mean Circulation

The main feature of the middle and high latitude atmospheric circulation over the Southern Ocean is a wide belt of persistent westerly winds. On the northern side of this belt, at about 30°S, the westerlies give way to a more variable wind pattern coinciding with relatively high atmospheric pressures. Far to the south of the main westerly belt, at about 65°S, winds again become variable, coinciding in this case with the frequent passage of the centres of low pressure that circle Antarctica from west to east (often with a southward component as well).

The 10-year mean surface pressure pattern is shown in Fig. 2.2 for January and July. The middle latitude westerlies are bounded to the north by the subtropical high pressure belt, and to the south by the low pressure region known as the Antarctic Circumpolar Trough or Subantarctic Trough. The location of the circumpolar pressure minimum oscillates with a half-yearly cycle, being furthest north in June and December. Within the trough, there is a tendency for distinct pressure minima to persist in three or four geographic areas, which include the Ross and Weddell Seas. Poleward of the Antarctic Circumpolar Trough is a narrow ring of easterlies around coastal Antarctica, which originates primarily as an outflow of air from the high central plateau, but is reinforced by easterly winds on the southern side of the travelling low pressure systems in the Circumpolar Trough. The high pressure centre depicted over the Pole is unreal, and results from an attempt to estimate the sea level pressure from observations made on the ice surface more than 3 km above mean sea level. Note how much more zonally symmetric the long-term mean flow field is (Fig. 2.2) compared to a daily one (Fig. 2.1. (b)).

The higher altitude airflow is very different from that at sea level. At a pressure altitude of 500 hectoPascals* (approximately 5 km above the surface), where the pressure has reduced to about half that at sea level, the circulation is dominated by a circumpolar westerly flow throughout the year. This westerly flow is not perfectly symmetrical about the Pole but contains large-scale standing-wave perturbations known as "long waves", which are more prominent in winter than in summer. However, even in winter the long waves are of much smaller amplitude than those found in comparable latitudes in the Northern Hemisphere.

An average north-south cross-section of the flow over the sector 130°E–140°W during the austral winter (June–August) 1979 is shown in Fig. 2.3. At very high altitudes (above 100 hPa, or about 16 km) at 60°S, a marked westerly maximum occurs, known as the polar-night jet stream. It is reflected through all levels down to sea level. A second and stronger westerly wind maximum, the subtropical jet

---

* A "hectopascal" (abbreviated "hPa", and equal to 10^{-2} Pa) is the same as the older unit "millibar". The name commemorates Blaise Pascal (1623–62), a French mathematician, who made significant contributions to the theory of hydrostatics and the development of the barometer.

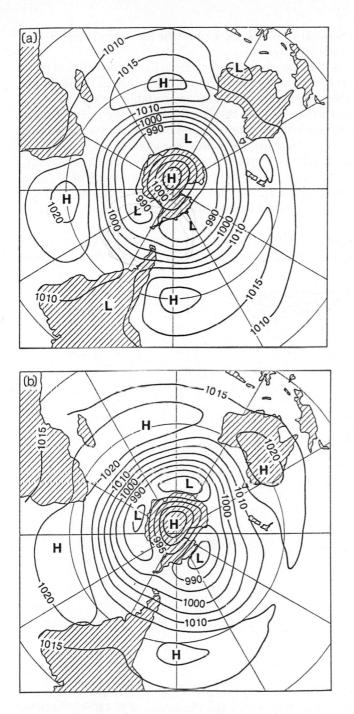

Fig. 2.2. Monthly mean sea-level pressure for (a) January, and (b) July, based on ten years of daily numerical analyses from September 1972 to August 1982. Contour interval 5 hPa (from Le Marshall et al., 1985).

28

stream, occurs at about 28°S at 200 hPa (12 km). Unlike the maximum at 60°S, that near 28°S is not reflected in sea level winds.

This mean jet stream pattern in the central and western Pacific is different from that further westwards over the Indian Ocean sector of the Southern Hemisphere (Mullan et al., 1986). In winter, the subtropical jet is appreciably stronger and the polar-night jet considerably further south in the Pacific than in the Indian Ocean sector. A further difference occurs in the temperature field. In the Pacific, a zone of enhanced north-south temperature gradient lies immediately polewards of both the subtropical and polar-night jet stream axes. In the Indian Ocean sector, there is only one zone of enhanced north-south temperature gradient. These zones produce conditions favourable for the development of cyclones, and we will see later that the patterns of cyclone development in the Indian and Pacific Oceans are quite different

It is worth emphasizing here that the double jet structure that we see in Fig. 2.3 is unique to the Southern Hemisphere winter season. In summer, the jets merge

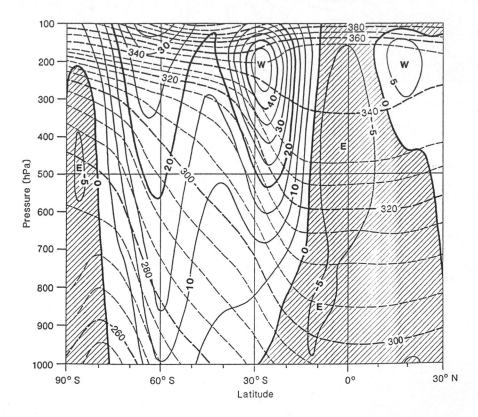

Fig. 2.3. Height-latitude cross-section showing zonal wind and potential temperature fields, averaged over the period June–August 1979 and the sector 130°E–140°W. Isotachs are shown as solid lines, with contours every 5 m.s⁻¹ (and hatched regions indicating easterlies). Potential temperature shown as dotted lines, with contours every 5°K. Vertical scale indicates pressure in units of hPa (from Mullan et al., 1986).

into one. In the Northern Hemisphere, there is only a single westerly wind maximum at all times of the year. The main difference between the westerly wind regime in the two hemispheres is therefore one of pattern in winter (with a double jet in the Southern Hemisphere) and one of intensity in summer (with the stronger westerly jet in the Southern Hemisphere).

Half-yearly Oscillation

Time series of many variables in middle and high southern latitudes show a marked semi-annual oscillation. An example is given in Fig. 2.4, showing the seasonal variation of the mean atmospheric sea-level pressure difference between latitudes 40°S and 60°S. Since the pressure difference is directly related to wind speed, Fig. 2.4 implies that the high latitude westerlies also undergo a semi-annual oscillation in strength, being strongest in autumn and spring. The north-south temperature gradient and the position of the Antarctic Circumpolar Trough exhibit 6-monthly oscillations too. These variations have been recognized for many years, and the explanation put forward by van Loon (1967) is still generally accepted.

Van Loon (1967) noted that at a pressure level of 500 hPa the temperature contrast between middle and high latitudes had a semi-annual oscillation, with maximum latitudinal gradients occurring in March and September. The seasonal temperature cycle at both middle and higher latitudes, however, displays a single

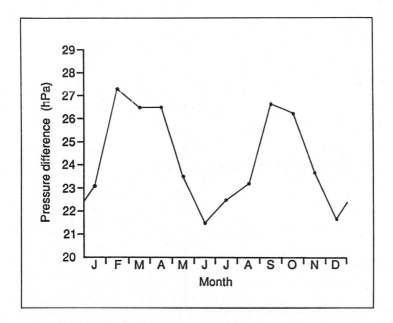

Fig. 2.4. Monthly mean zonally-averaged pressure difference (in hPa) between 40°S and 60°S. Based on daily numerical analyses by the Australian Bureau of Meteorology over the 5-year period 1972–77 (after Streten, 1980).

maximum and minimum (Fig. 2.5). It is the change in the solar insolation regime and nature of the underlying surface between the two latitude bands that produces a semi-annual cycle in the temperature *difference*. At oceanic middle latitudes between 40°S and 50°S, the large thermal inertia of the oceans causes the atmospheric temperature cycle to lag the annual cycle in solar insolation, so that air temperatures do not start dropping until March. The higher latitude region near 65°S, being closer to Antarctica and its surrounding sea ice, displays a more "continental" climate, and air temperatures respond more quickly when solar radiation decreases after the solstitial maximum in December. The 50°–60°S temperature gradient therefore has a maximum in autumn (March).

The second maximum in the spring occurs largely by default, because the lowest temperatures of the year at 65°S are delayed until the very end of winter. To some extent this occurs because there is no clearly defined minimum of insolation during the polar night nearer the Pole, with the sun remaining below or just above the horizon for a long period. Another factor is the large amount of latent heat involved in the formation of sea ice, which acts to buffer the seasonal decline in air temperature (note that autumn is also the season of maximum ice

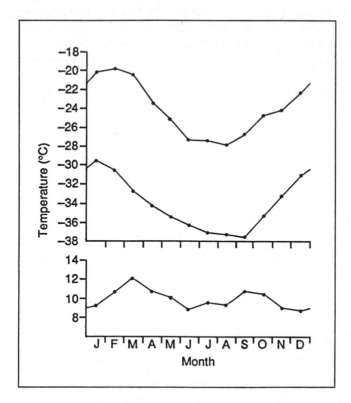

Fig. 2.5. Seasonal cycle of temperature at 50°S and 65°S (upper curves), and meridional temperature gradient 50°–65°S (lower curve), at the 500 hPa level. Based on station data over a 5–8-year period (after van Loon, 1967).

advance; see for example Fig. 2.11). Air temperatures at 65°S and poleward therefore decrease only slowly throughout the winter season, and there is a weaker temperature contrast between middle and high latitudes in winter than in the subsequent spring season.

The steeper temperature gradient in mid-troposphere between 50°S and Antarctica around equinoctial months (March and September) produces an increase in cyclone activity during these two periods. Van Loon (1967) argued that this modulation of cyclonicity over the high latitude oceans shows up in the semi-annual oscillation in the position of the Circumpolar Trough, which is closer to the Pole and somewhat stronger in the autumn and spring seasons. Travelling cyclonic disturbances are indeed a major mechanism for transporting heat into higher latitudes to balance the nett radiation deficit here.

The increased cyclone activity over the Southern Ocean in autumn, with its associated increase in advection of warm air southwards, is also held responsible for a peculiar phenomenon that shows up in Antarctic temperature records. Antarctic temperatures do not decrease regularly to reach a minimum just before the return of the sun. Instead, a slight rise in temperature often occurs about June before further cooling to the minimum in August (Fig. 2.6). Van Loon (1967) found this "coreless" winter pattern could occur in any winter month anywhere

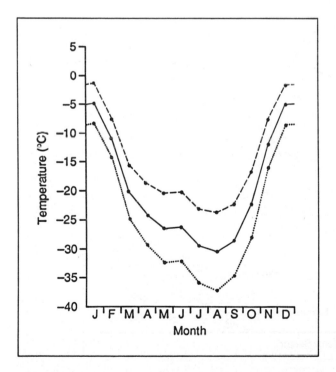

Fig. 2.6. Seasonal cycle of maximum (dashed line), minimum (dotted line), and mean (solid line) temperatures at Scott Base, Antarctica. Based on daily data over the 30-year period 1957–86.

over Antarctica, although the event was strongest and most frequent in the Ross Sea sector.

Cyclones

The dominant feature on mid-latitude weather maps is the series of migratory high and low pressure centres, the anticyclones and cyclones. In the 1920s, a group of Norwegian meteorologists developed a simple model of the structure of a cyclone that is still often used today. This classical structure, redrawn for the Southern Hemisphere, is shown in Fig. 2.7. The model delineates the boundaries between air masses of different characteristics by cold and warm "fronts". At the warm front, there is an upsliding of warm moist air over a wedge of colder air, producing a cloud sheet ranging from high-level cirrus down through gradually thickening middle-level cloud to precipitating nimbostratus near where the front reaches the earth's surface. The cold front is a much steeper wedge of cold air undercutting the warmer moist air to produce a band of deep convective cloud.

Winds circulate around the cyclone centre in a clockwise sense in the Southern Hemisphere, and the associated frontal cloud bands often take on a vortex-like

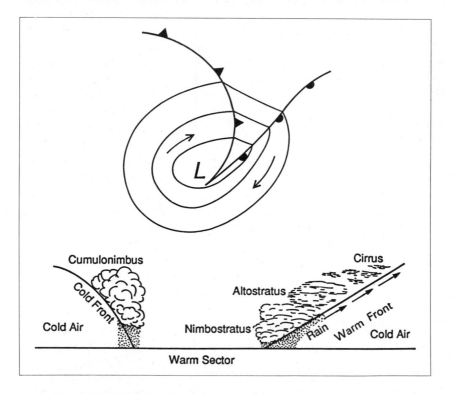

Fig. 2.7. The Norwegian cyclone model adapted to a Southern Hemisphere perspective, showing schematic plan view (above) and indication of associated cloud types and weather (below) (from Hill, 1980).

appearance when viewed from above. Cyclones generally have a well-defined life cycle, going from birth (cyclogenesis) through maturity to decay, during which the three-dimensional atmospheric temperature and pressure fields also undergo systematic changes. The difficulty in the data-sparse Southern Hemisphere is that these changes often cannot be monitored by the conventional meteorological observations of pressure, wind, temperature and moisture at various levels in the vertical (such as might be measured from ships or radiosonde balloon flights). This is where satellites have come to be an invaluable tool, along with models of cyclone structure. Streten and Troup (1973) developed a classification scheme for Southern Hemisphere cyclones using the appearance of cloud vortices in satellite photographs. The structure of the surface pressure field and upper-level temperature and pressure fields, typical of each vortex type, was determined from co-incident conventional observations where these were available. These results could then be applied to regions where ground-truth measurements were absent. Such an approach has proved extremely useful over the Southern Ocean.

The original cyclone climatology as developed by Streten and Troup (1973) was based on data from the ESSA satellite series over the 3-year period 1966–69, but did not include "winter" (defined in this section as June to September inclusive) because of poor illumination in high latitudes at that time of year. Carleton (1979, 1981a) complemented the earlier work by developing a descriptive climatology of cyclone activity for the winter season from five years (1973–77) of satellite infrared imagery. This section briefly reviews the results of these studies. The reader could also consult Trenberth (1981) for further discussion.

The most common cloud vortex types of Streten and Troup's (1973) classification are shown in Fig. 2.8 and Table 2.1. The main sequence is one of development (vortex types W, A or B) through maturity (C) and ultimately decay (D). Cyclogenesis can occur either as a development on a pre-existing cloud band (all type W events are of this type), or in the absence of such a band. Streten and Troup estimated that some 55–60% of "comma cloud" development (types A and B) occurred in the absence of a major cloud band, indicating that such evolutions are more common in the Southern Hemisphere than in the Northern Hemisphere. The distinction between types A and B is mainly a matter of when the satellite passed overhead in the life cycle of the cyclone. Those cyclones that reach and reinforce the Circumpolar Trough (mainly types C and D) are likely to bring severe weather to coastal Antarctica, and may even penetrate far inland.

The frequency distribution of cloud vortex types as a function of latitude for five winter (June–September) seasons is shown in Fig. 2.9. There is a southward trend in the latitude of maximum frequency as we progress from type W through type D. This progression is a little less obvious in summer (not shown), where the wave development (type W) vortices exhibit an approximately constant frequency north of 55°S (Streten and Troup, 1973). The summer peak frequency of type A comma development is also concentrated a little further north at 44°–55°S than evident in the winter figures. The high frequency of lower-latitude cyclone types F and G (also known as "cut-off" lows because they are displaced northwards of the basic westerly current, and are therefore slow-moving) observed by Carleton (1979) seems to be a feature specific to the winter season, when these developments occur preferentially in Australian–New Zealand longitudes.

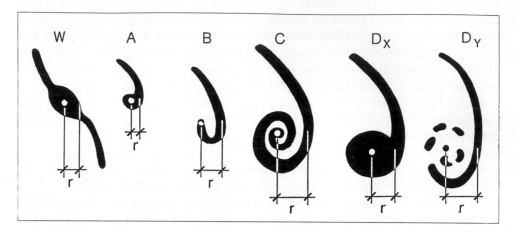

Fig. 2.8. Classification scheme for frontal cloud vortices appearing on Southern Hemisphere satellite imagery (see also Table 2.1). The cross indicates the vortex centre, and r its assumed "radius" (from Streten and Troup, 1973).

TABLE 2.1

Streten cloud vortex classification.

Type	Description
W	Wave development – localized thickening of a cloud band.
A	Early vortex development – "comma cloud" merged with a major cloud band or in isolation.
B	Late vortex development – a hook-shaped cloud with a marked slot of clear air.
C	Vortex at full maturity – spiral of clear air around a well-defined centre.
D	Dissipating vortex – either Dx with considerable cloud near centre, or Dy with fragmentary cloud near centre.
F/G	Frontless vortices (or "cut-off" lows) – corresponding respectively to Dx and Dy types but not associated with a cloud band. (Not shown in Fig. 2.7)

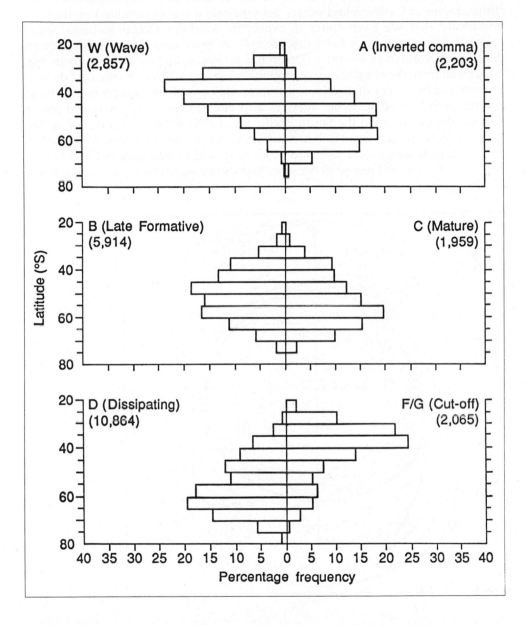

Fig. 2.9. Mean distribution of Streten vortex types as a function of latitude, based on satellite photographs over 5 winters 1973–77. Frequencies in each 5-degree latitude band are presented as the percentage of the total for that type over all latitudes. Values in brackets give the total numbers of cyclones for the five years studied (from Carleton, 1979).

The overall picture then is one of extra-tropical cyclones originating in the middle latitude westerlies and moving gradually southward as they track around the hemisphere, eventually to decay in higher latitudes. Although the cloud climatologies of Carleton and others demonstrate the considerable longitudinal uniformity that we have come to expect in Southern Ocean features, some regional differences have been discovered. A plan view of the frequency of developing vortices in summer (December to March inclusive) is given in Fig. 2.10, taken from the climatology of Streten and Troup (1973). We see that there is a maximum frequency of developing or intensifying cyclones in a concentric band about the Pole near 50°S, but there is also clear evidence of enhanced lower latitude development in the South Pacific and South Atlantic. However, in the Atlantic, the cyclogenetic region is continuous over a broad latitude range, while in the Pacific cyclogenesis seems to occur only within two well-defined bands, with a wedge-shaped region in between that shows significantly weaker activity.

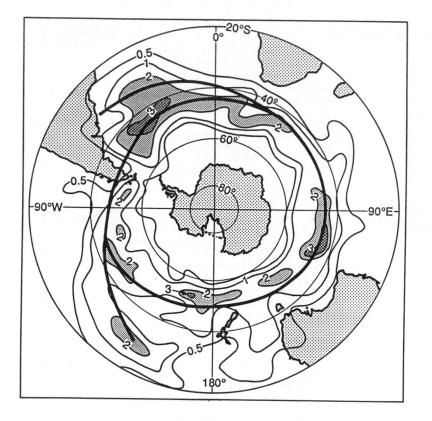

Fig. 2.10. Areal frequency of developing vortices (types W, A and B) in Southern Hemisphere summer, as observed by satellite over the period 1972–77. Full line is the position of the atmospheric polar front in summer (after Taljaard, 1968). Highest frequency regions are shaded (from Streten and Troup, 1973).

Carleton's (1981a) analysis for the winter season shows the same pattern so that the double-band structure is evidently a semi-permanent feature of the South Pacific circulation throughout the year.

The symmetric 50°S band of maximum cyclone frequency is closely related to, and occurs on the equatorward side of, the position of the oceanic Polar Front. This oceanic feature is a zone of steep latitudinal gradient in sea surface temperature, marking the axis of the Antarctic Circumpolar Current (see Patterson and Whitworth, this volume). The lower latitude extension of maximum cyclone frequency in the Pacific occurs in a region where there is a secondary maximum in the north-south atmospheric temperature gradient (Fig. 2.3), and is associated with a feature known as the South Pacific Convergence Zone (see below).

Seasonal variation in cyclone activity has been noted in a number of studies, and some attempts have been made to relate these variations to changes in north-south temperature gradient, location of the Antarctic Circumpolar Trough, and position of the sea-ice boundary. Carleton (1981a) showed in his study of the 1973–77 period that cyclonic vortices of all types were about two and a half times more frequent in the winter months than in summer. August was the month with the highest total frequency of cyclonic vortices, but a latitudinal shift in the occurrence frequencies over the winter months was also apparent. Dividing the hemisphere up into latitude zones (30–39, 40–49, 50–59, and 60–75°S), Carleton found that in July cyclonic activity was highest in the 40–49°S zone and decreased southwards whereas in September the maximum activity was observed in the southernmost zone of 60–75°S.

We have taken Carleton's (1981a) figures for vortex frequencies in various latitude bands, and calculated the latitude of peak frequency, which is plotted in Fig. 2.11. Also shown is the monthly location of the latitude of the Circumpolar Trough and the northern boundary of the Antarctic sea ice, as determined by Streten and Pike (1980) from data over the 5-year period 1972–77. Carleton claimed that the northward shift of maximum cyclonic activity in July and the southward return in September was evidence of the controlling influence of the Circumpolar Trough and, taken in isolation, this result certainly looks reasonable. Also plotted in the figure, however, are the latitudes of peak frequencies of cyclonic vortices calculated from the results of Schwerdtfeger and Kachelhoffer (1973) for the period 1967–70. These authors counted the total number of vortices over two September and three October months (constituting spring), and over three February and March months (autumn). Schwerdtfeger and Kachelhoffer concluded from their limited study that there was a highly significant relationship between the pack-ice border and the latitudinal band of maximum frequency of cyclone occurrence which, of course, is completely at variance with Carleton's (1981a) result. If nothing else, Fig. 2.11 illustrates the difficulty of drawing conclusions about feedbacks between the different aspects of Southern Ocean climate from a limited data base.

38

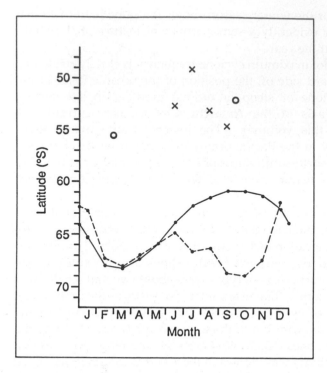

Fig. 2.11. Seasonal cycle of zonally-averaged latitude of Antarctic sea ice margin (solid line) and latitude of axis of the Circumpolar Trough (dotted line) (after Streten and Pike, 1980). Latitudes of maximum cyclonic activity at various times of the year are indicated by crosses (determined from Table 1 in Carleton, 1981a) and open circles (determined from table in Schwerdtfeger and Kachelhoffer, 1973).

Influence of Long Waves on Patterns of Cyclogenesis

We saw in Fig. 2.10 that the South Pacific was unusual in that it had two distinct regions where cyclone activity was high: a zonal belt at approximately 50°S and a second band oriented northwest-southwest in the central South Pacific. This lower-middle latitude zone of frequent cyclogenesis and cloudiness is known as the South Pacific Convergence Zone (SPCZ), and is a semi-permanent feature of the region, although its exact position may vary from month to month. A satellite composite cloud picture over the Southern Hemisphere (Fig. 2.12) shows a well-developed cloud band to the north-east of New Zealand, highlighting the location of the SPCZ at that time. (The reader may also recognize some other cloud vortex patterns with reference to Fig. 2.8.)

A useful start to understanding variations in the behaviour of weather systems at different longitudes is gained by studying the pattern of very long wavelength stationary waves* in the atmosphere. Because of vertical motions associated with these "long waves", weather systems within and eastwards of a long-wave trough

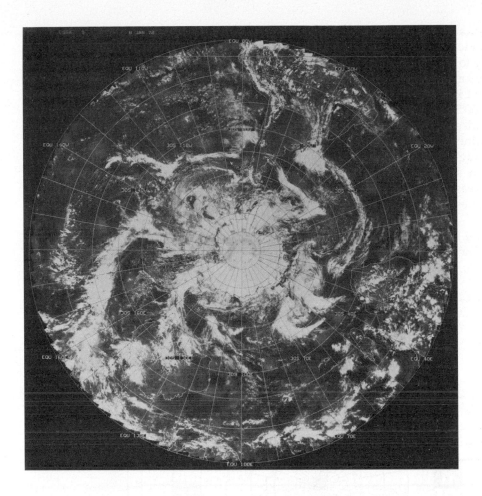

Fig. 2.12. Hemispheric cloud mosaic (visible) for 8 January 1972, photographed by ESSA–9 satellite (from NOAA catalogue, 1974).

---

*   These waves are identified by a wave number (1, 2, 3, etc.) that describes how many complete wavelengths fit around the hemisphere. For example, wave 1 has one trough and one ridge around a latitude circle; wave 3 has three troughs and ridges so that consecutive troughs are separated by 120° of longitude; etc.

are in a more favourable environment for development of cloud systems and cyclonic vortices. Conversely, a cyclone moving into a long-wave ridge position is likely to weaken. The mean locations of the trough and ridge axes of the longest waves at 500 hPa are shown schematically in Fig. 2.13. In terms of amplitude, wave 1 is the dominant wave north of about 40°S, wave 3 is strongest between 40° and 50°S, and waves 1 and 2 are of approximately equal strength in higher latitudes. Trenberth (1980) discussed these details at length, but our interest here is mainly in the overall pattern produced. We see from Fig. 2.13 that a clustering of trough axes occurs in the eastern Indian Ocean, whereas the Tasman Sea and region southeast of New Zealand shows persistent ridging. The northwest-southeast band of trough activity in the central Pacific also extends into lower latitudes, and is associated with the aforementioned South Pacific Convergence Zone.

The long-wave trough-ridge pattern between the Indian and Pacific Oceans influences the movement of cyclones travelling through this region of the hemisphere. Depressions coming out of the Indian Ocean frequently move quickly

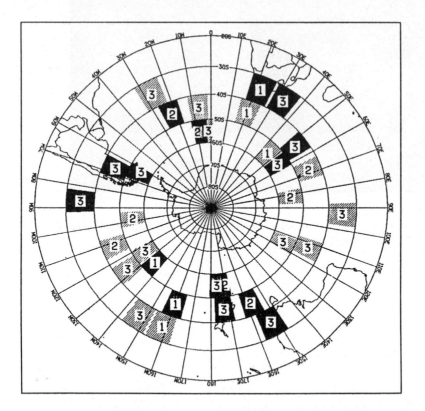

Fig. 2.13. Positions of mean long-wave trough and ridge axes at 35°, 45° and 55°S, at the 500 hPa level. Ridges are shaded and troughs hatched, with central value indicating the wave number. Based on 7 years of daily 500 hPa height data 1976–83. Over this period, wave 2 at 35°S showed no preferred geographic location (adapted from Mullan, 1985).

into higher latitudes as they pass south of Australia and New Zealand (this may be a partial explanation for the persistent pressure minimum in the Ross Sea Sector of the Circumpolar Trough). To the east of New Zealand, stationary long-wave troughs at 35°S coincide with ridges further south at the same longitude. This trough-ridge juxtaposition weakens the north-south pressure gradient and hence the westerlies in the southwestern Pacific. The weaker westerlies mean that the cyclones travel eastward more slowly in this part of the hemisphere, as is shown in Fig. 2.14 from Mullan (1985). In this study, daily 500 hPa height data from 1976–83 were subjected to Fourier analysis and separated into wave components, and the contributions from wave numbers 4 to 9 then recombined to produce what was termed the "medium-wave" field (the medium-wave troughs and ridges can be identified with the travelling cyclones). By tracking the movement of the medium-wave troughs from day to day, the mean speed as a function of longitude at 45°S was calculated. Fig. 2.14 also shows the trough amplitude, and it is apparent that cyclones not only tend to travel faster in the Indian Ocean than in the South Pacific but also are more intense in the Indian Ocean.

The existence of stationary long-wave ridges south of New Zealand, and the reduced speed of weather systems through this region, are key factors in the high incidence of "blocking" in these longitudes. Blocking is associated with a slow-moving long-lived surface anticyclone in high latitudes, commonly with a cut-off low on its equatorward side, that together "block" the progress of the westerlies.

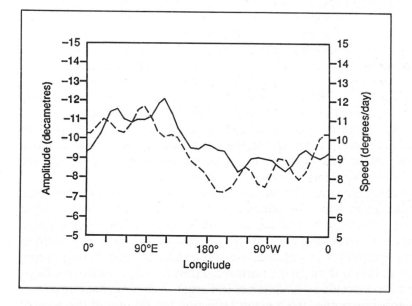

Fig. 2.14. Amplitude (in geopotential metres) and daily movement (in m.s⁻¹) of 500 hPa medium wave trough axes at 45°S. Medium waves defined as the composite over wave numbers 4 to 9 (adapted from Mullan, 1985).

Persistent anomalies created by blocking patterns are of major importance to extended-range forecasting. Although occasional blocks occur southeast of South America and South Africa, the Australia–New Zealand region shows the primary maximum, with more frequent and longer-lasting eposides (Lejenas, 1984; Trenberth and Mo, 1985).

INTERACTION BETWEEN SEA ICE AND ATMOSPHERIC CIRCULATION IN THE SOUTHERN OCEAN

Climatic Considerations

The annual and interannual variability in the amount of sea ice is one of the most significant factors in the energy balance of the Southern Hemisphere atmosphere and ocean. Continental Antarctica, covering an area of approximately $14 \times 10^6 \, km^2$, is cold and dry with a high albedo that is virtually unchanging from year to year. The areal extent of sea ice, on the other hand, undergoes average seasonal changes from approximately $3 \times 10^6 \, km^2$ in February to $20 \times 10^6 \, km^2$ in September, covering at its maximum over 8% of the surface area of the hemisphere. This seasonal variation by more than the land area of Antarctica affects the high-latitude energy balance not only because of the large albedo difference between ice and open ocean, but also because the ice cover is a barrier to energy exchange between the atmosphere and ocean. Latent and sensible heat fluxes over open water can be up to two orders of magnitude greater than over multiyear ice (Weller, 1980) so that it is important to know the fractional coverage by polynyas and open leads within the area enclosed by the maximum extent ice-line. Recent analysis has shown that Southern Hemisphere sea ice is considerably more open than previously thought (Zwally et al., 1979) so that the ocean heat loss is correspondingly higher (by as much as a factor of 6 according to Weller, 1982).

The amount of sea ice present in a particular season can also vary considerably from one year to another. These interannual fluctuations produce large changes in the polar energy balance, which can feed back into sea ice amounts. For example, a delay in the onset of the spring thaw can mean more ice than usual is present in summer at the time of maximum solar radiation and this reduces the amount of oceanic heating which can occur in that season.

There are two other physical processes (in addition to surface-atmosphere heat exchange and the albedo effect) by which sea ice can affect the climate system directly. The first is through thermal inertia of the ice pack, whereby changes in the temperature of the overlying atmosphere are delayed due to the release of latent heat as the ice freezes in autumn and the uptake of heat during spring melting. The other effect is through the northward movement of sea ice (see Keys, this volume, for a more detailed discussion of icebergs). This movement produces a nett equatorward transport of fresh water (affecting the salinity of the oceans) and a nett poleward transport of heat.

The presence of sea ice also affects the poleward heat flux indirectly through modifying the local atmospheric stability and the large-scale north-south temperature gradient; these factors influence the generation of high latitude depressions and their subsequent motion. A complicating factor in understanding the sea ice-atmosphere interactions is that wind stresses generated over the ice pack by travelling storms can affect the position of the maximum ice extent line. Observational studies have so far not resolved this cause and effect problem satisfactorily. We will consider these research efforts further in a later section, and turn our attention first to the seasonal growth and decay of the Antarctic sea ice zone.

Sea Ice Climatology

Present evidence from relatively limited satellite data suggests that at any given longitude there can be large variations in sea ice amount from year to year. However, decreases at one longitude are frequently compensated by increases at another (Zwally et al., 1979) so that interannual variations in total maximum ice extent may not be very great. The seasonal variation in the zonally averaged position of the boundary between Antarctic pack-ice and the open ocean, as shown previously in Fig. 2.11, is therefore fairly well established. Minimum ice extent occurs in February and March, and maximum extent in September and October. The growth and northward advance of the sea ice occurs rather more slowly than the subsequent decay.

Monthly changes in sea ice extent show considerable regional variability in any given year, as well as large differences between years. This variability is greatest in the longitudes of the Antarctic coastal embayments. The regional pattern of ice coverage for three particular dates during 1974 is illustrated in Fig. 2.15. Rapid ice growth has occurred preferentially in the Ross and Weddell Seas between February and June. From June to September, however, there was little further expansion of the ice-ocean boundary at these longitudes: ice tended to be advected downstream by the Antarctic Circumpolar Current, resulting in a more symmetrical distribution about the Pole. Cavalieri and Parkinson (1981) highlighted these pattern changes by Fourier analysis of the latitude of the ice edge. The early-season pattern of February is primarily wave 2, and reflects the shape of the Antarctic continent; the rapid ice-growth phase in the major embayments shows up as a large wave 3 component, and the maximum ice-extent phase when there is greatest symmetry about the Pole shows wave number 1 to be dominant at that time. Such seasonal changes in the high latitude forcing may have important consequences for the standing long-wave patterns in the atmosphere, and hence seasonal forecasting.

Relationships Between Sea Ice and Circulation Features

There is a problem of causality in deciphering relationships between amounts of sea ice and atmospheric circulation features: the ice edge, the position of sea surface temperature gradients, tracks of developing vortices and atmospheric pressure patterns all seem to be correlated but it is not clear whether the physical chain should begin with the atmosphere or the ocean. At the sea-ice boundary,

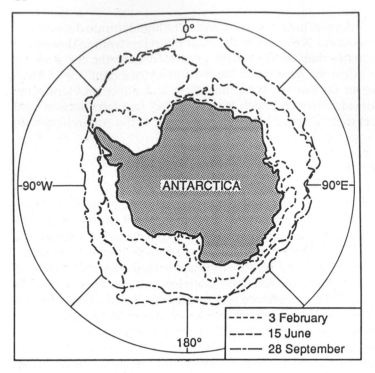

Fig. 2.15. Antarctic sea ice extent for three selected times during 1974, showing examples of dominant wave patterns: 3 February (wave 2 dominant), 15 June (wave 3), and 28 September (wave 1) (from Cavalieri and Parkinson, 1981).

latitudinal temperature gradients are intensified, which may therefore be expected to augment cyclone development downstream (and also equatorward). However, a high frequency of depression centres in a particular location near the ice edge can produce an ice advance to the west of the low centre (and likewise ice to the east may be advected southwards, or at least restrained from advancing). Strong winds around cyclone centres also serve to break up thin ice.

Streten and Pike (1980) examined various characteristics of sea ice extent and the associated atmospheric circulation over the period 1972–77. These authors looked for temporal relationships between ice extent and the strength of the westerlies to the north. Averaged over the whole period, the zonally-averaged westerlies exhibit semi-annual oscillations in strength (Fig. 2.4), and thus display no relation to sea ice extent (Fig. 2.11) over the normal seasonal cycle. There is also no clear correlation between zonally-averaged ice extent and the strength of the westerlies in the preceding or succeeding months. However, on examining interannual variability of the westerlies, they found a greater variability during the time of maximum ice extent: i.e., the westerlies were most variable in October–November, and most consistent year-to-year in February.

Streten and Pike (1980) also showed that the shape of the ice boundary seemed to be related to the location of persistent pressure minima in the Circumpolar

Trough. The mean ice edge in October (near maximum extent) followed the basic continental shape, but was perturbed so that it was located at lower latitudes close to, or just westward of, those longitudes having a high frequency of low pressure centres. However, this association broke down in Weddell Sea longitudes, which led Streten and Pike to argue that regional (i.e., restricted area) rather than hemispheric studies were needed when relating anomalies of ice extent to atmospheric circulation features. Regional relationships are particularly appropriate when looking at interannual fluctuations because of the previously mentioned tendency for an ice anomaly at one longitude to be compensated by one of opposite sign downstream.

In one such regional study by Streten and Pike (1980), interannual variations in the strength of the winter westerlies north of the Ross Sea (160°E–150°W) were found to correlate positively with the amount of sea ice in the following spring. Stronger westerlies in the winter of 1975 were followed by more ice in spring; weaker westerlies in 1977 were followed by less ice. The authors' explanation of this correlation was that weak winds were indicative of a weaker cyclonic gyre in the Ross embayment, and therefore less northward transport of ice. Once again, however, we must emphasize that studies which postulate causative relationships between aspects of polar climate based on short-period correlations must be treated with caution.

Many studies have attempted to relate variations in high latitude cyclogenesis to fluctuations in sea ice extent (Schwerdtfeger and Kachelhoffer, 1973; Streten and Pike, 1980; Carleton, 1981a, b; Cavalieri and Parkinson, 1981). There is no clear relation between the seasonal cycles of mean sea ice extent and cyclonic activity, because of the complicating influence of the semi-annual oscillation (Fig. 2.11) and strong ocean-atmosphere coupling at the oceanic Polar Front (Fig. 2.10). Greater success has been achieved in looking at fluctuations on very short (a few days) or very long (interannual) timescales, where again it is necessary to consider longitudinal variations.

Examining 3-day averages during the time of maximum ice growth in the Ross and Weddell Seas, Cavalieri and Parkinson (1981) found areas of rapid ice growth lying to the west of intense cyclone centres. They attributed this to both equatorward ice transport and *in situ* freezing as a result of advection of cold air from more southerly latitudes. During the months of maximum ice decay, the association between low centres and the regions of ice retreat was not as marked.

Carleton (1981b) compared circulation differences in 1974 and 1976, the two most highly contrasting years in the 1973–77 period in terms of cyclone activity. The greatest total cyclone activity (except in very high latitudes) occurred in 1974, which was also the year with the greatest ice extent. However, the lowest cyclone activity occurred in 1976, an intermediate year as far as ice extent was concerned. Carleton also presented evidence that longitudinal variations in ice extent were due to variations in high latitude cyclone activity, arguing on the same lines as Cavalieri and Parkinson (1981) and Streten and Pike (1980) above. However, a re-analysis of Carleton's data (Fig. 2.16) can be used to argue the reverse relationship: namely, that differences in ice extent between 1974 and 1976 were responsible for the observed longitudinal differences in cyclone frequency.

The upper curve of Fig. 2.16 shows the latitude difference in the sea ice margin between 1976 and 1974. Negative values indicate those longitudes where there was less sea ice in 1976. The lower curve shows the difference in vortex frequencies between 1976 and 1974, negative values indicating those longitudes where the local vortex frequency in 1976 (expressed as a percentage of the 1976 hemispheric mean) was less than the 1974 local vortex frequency. The two curves of Fig. 2.16 look very similar, apart from a phase shift. The maximum correlation (r = +0.70) occurs for a 50 degree eastward displacement of the ice extent curve. Again, there is the question of which is cause and effect but, in this case, it seems rather unlikely that a cyclone (see Fig. 2.16 for typical scale) could affect ice growth 50 degrees westward of the low centre. It is much more probable that an expanded ice line increases the latitudinal sea-surface temperature gradient locally, thus generating more incipient disturbances that reach their maximum intensity some distance downstream.

Budd (1982) and Carleton (1981b) have also found that, on an interannual timescale, the *latitude* of maximum cyclone frequency shifts north or south according to the position of the sea ice margin. Comparing 1975 and 1977, for example, the sea ice was up to 5 degrees further south in 1977 in the region south of eastern Australia, when there was a corresponding southward shift in the distribution of cyclone tracks (Budd, 1982).

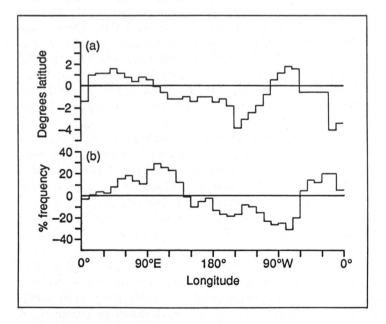

Fig. 2.16. Longitudinal variation of (a) 1976–74 difference in latitude of sea ice margin, and (b) 1976–74 difference in cyclone percentage frequency, over winter June–September period (adapted from Figs 2 and 5 of Carleton, 1981b). The cyclone frequency data have been smoothed before plotting.

EFFECT OF THE ANTARCTIC CONTINENT ON ATMOSPHERIC CIRCULATION IN THE SOUTHERN OCEAN

Katabatic Winds

The term "katabatic" (after Greek for "go down") refers to a wind caused by the local descent of cold air down a slope. In the Antarctic, katabatic winds are a large-scale phenomenon, similar to trade winds in the magnitude of energy transfer (Weller, 1982). A high ice plateau, coupled with low cloud cover, permits intense radiational cooling near the ground, and this sets up strong surface "inversions" (i.e., air temperatures increase with height, which is the reverse of the normal situation in the lower atmosphere). Having the coldest air closest to the ground means an atmospheric column is very stable to vertical motions, and so convection is severely limited. However, the cold air can drain off the plateau down to the coastal regions, with the Coriolis force generating a westward component of motion. With topography playing such a large role in the surface wind regime, the directionality of the flow is often remarkably constant. Some locations are more prone than others to katabatic winds. Cape Denison, site of Sir Douglas Mawson's 1911–14 Australasian Antarctic Expedition, is probably the windiest place on Earth and inspired "The Home of the Blizzard" (Mawson, 1915). According to Mawson, winds of 100 miles per hour (about 45 $m.s^{-1}$) were frequent and, on one occasion, wind speeds of over 200 miles per hour were reported.

In terms of atmospheric dynamics, it is necessary to distinguish between the persistent surface winds (often called "inversion winds") over the gently sloping Antarctic interior, and the unusually strong katabatic winds near the steep coastal escarpment (Schwerdtfeger, 1970; Parish, 1982). The continental inversion winds (of about 2–10 $m.s^{-1}$) can be viewed as an equilibrium flow balancing the sloped-inversion pressure gradient force (determined by topography) and Coriolis and frictional forces. The strong coastal phenomena, where wind speeds can jump almost instantaneously from calm to 15–20 $m.s^{-1}$, are topographically forced patterns of cold air convergence. Katabatic wind flows in other parts of the world are characterized by short lifetimes, as the upstream reservoir of cold air is rapidly depleted. In Antarctica, however, the convergence in the continental interior supplies some coastal sites, such as the Cape Denison region in Adelie Land, with a virtually inexhaustible supply of cold air.

Air draining off the Antarctic continent is turned westward by the Coriolis force to produce the persistent easterlies on the poleward side of the Circumpolar Trough. Other effects of coastal katabatic flows, such as the extreme gustiness and blowing snow of a "katabatic storm", do not extend more than a few kilometres offshore. The persistent winds can also agitate surface waters and prevent ice formation, as has been observed at Terra Nova Bay 300 km north of the Ross Ice Shelf (Bromwich and Kurtz, 1982).

48

Numerical Simulations

Antarctica has a marked topographic and thermal effect on the large-scale atmospheric circulation over the Southern Ocean. Standing-wave patterns in the atmosphere are greatly influenced by mountain barriers and by heat sources and sinks. The continent acts as an elevated heat sink, and the asymmetry of Antarctica about the Pole produces a corresponding asymmetry in the sea surface temperature distribution in high latitudes. At 55°S, for example, surface water temperatures in the South Atlantic and South Indian Oceans are typically about 5°C colder than in the South Pacific Ocean. There are also significant differences between the middle and high latitude circulations of the Northern and Southern Hemispheres, which are in part due to the different land-sea configuration near the poles. In the Southern Hemisphere, the westerlies are stronger and the polar trough much more intense and persistent. It has been suggested (e.g., Mechoso, 1981) that the persistence of the Antarctic Circumpolar Trough results from the Antarctic plateau presenting a physical barrier to the southward movement of cyclones, causing them to cluster along the ice edge. If this were the case, one might expect a rather different sea level pressure pattern if Antarctica were removed. This supposition can readily be tested by experiments with numerical models of the global atmosphere.

Such "general circulation" or "climate" models solve a set of equations describing basic physical laws (such as the second law of thermodynamics, and conservation laws for momentum and water vapour). A detailed treatment is made of the fluxes of solar and infrared radiation through the atmosphere, and the various interactions which can occur at the atmosphere-surface boundary. Because of the complexity of the overall system, it is common for some simplifying assumptions to be made. Usually, at least one of the parameters defining cloudiness, sea-surface temperature or sea ice amount is specified at observed values (rather than allow the model to calculate its own values). Modelling of the oceanic circulation has not yet reached the stage where a coupled atmosphere-ocean climate model can predict ocean heat transports with any confidence. A standard approach is therefore to couple the atmosphere model to a much simpler model of the ocean in which seasonal heat storage (i.e., varying sea-surface temperature) is allowed but no horizontal transport of heat occurs. Unfortunately, neglecting oceanic heat transport in this way tends to produce lower temperatures and more sea ice in high latitudes than observed.

Model calculations of the global atmospheric circulation thus have a number of shortcomings, and the errors tend to be particularly large in polar latitudes. Most climate models underestimate both the strength of the westerlies in the Southern Hemisphere and the intensity of the Antarctic Circumpolar Trough. Herman and Johnson (1980) reported on a "grid-point" climate model which was unable to reproduce the stationary low pressure centres around Antarctica, with the predicted pressures in the Circumpolar Trough being typically 20 hPa too high. "Spectral" models, which did not come into general use until the late 1970s, adopt a different mathematical technique to solve the governing equations, and tend to give a more realistic high latitude simulation than grid-point models. In spectral models, the dynamic variables (e.g., pressure, temperature, wind) are represented by a sum of spherical harmonics, in contrast to the grid-point approach where the variables take values on a network of discrete points. The geometrical formulation of the spectral approach is ideally suited to solving equations on a sphere, and means that spatial derivatives can be evaluated exactly. This is a particularly important advantage in simulating high southern latitude circulation since sharp gradients in many variables occur around the Antarctic escarpment. Manabe et al. (1978) showed that the latitudinal distribution of sea-level pressure, distinctly different in the two polar regions, was reproduced quite well by their spectral model (Fig. 2.17). Increasing the model resolution (i.e., including higher harmonics) strengthened the mid-latitude westerlies in the winter hemisphere, which generally improves the simulation for the Southern Hemisphere but not for the Northern Hemisphere. The January simulation (not shown) had the Antarctic

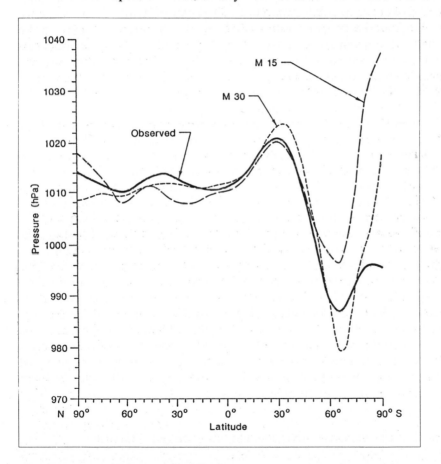

Fig. 2.17. Latitudinal variation of the July zonal mean sea level pressure (in hPa) as observed (solid line), and as simulated by the Geophysics Fluid Dynamics Laboratory spectral model. Two simulations are shown, one at low resolution (M15) and another at high resolution (M30) (from Manabe et al., 1978).

Circumpolar Trough too weak by about 8 hPa at all resolutions and the Northern Hemisphere polar trough much too intense.

Bearing in mind the above comments about the systematic errors in the models, we now consider two experiments which attempt to highlight possible effects of Antarctica on high latitude circulation. Mechoso (1981) examined topographic influences on the Southern Hemisphere general circulation by comparing a "control" circulation with an "anomaly" circulation where all topography in the Southern Hemisphere was reduced to zero. The simulation was for the month of July and used the spectral model of Manabe et al. (1978) referred to above, whose control simulation was known to be fairly realistic. In the absence of all mountains (the "anomaly" run), the high latitude surface westerlies were weaker and extended further poleward. The areal extent of the surface easterlies was much reduced, with the axis of the Circumpolar Trough being near 80°S over continental "Antarctica". Depressions which formed in mid-latitudes still followed a general south-easterly track, but no longer showed the clustering around the Antarctic coast. Very little high latitude cyclogenesis occurred in the no-mountain case as compared to the control run. In the absence of Antarctica, the atmospheric standing waves in high latitudes were also much weaker, with their phases unrelated to observations, in spite of the model prescribing the observed sea-surface temperature pattern.

Simmonds and Lin (1983) used the Australian Numerical Meteorology Research Centre spectral model, and compared a January control simulation with the circulation in three anomaly experiments: no mountains anywhere in the Southern Hemisphere, the removal of just Antarctica (replacing it by sea at −1°C), and the imposition of a longitudinally uniform sea-surface temperature. The control simulation had the common failing of a Circumpolar Trough substantially weaker than observed. Rather surprisingly, the topographic anomaly experiments showed little significant change in the surface pressure field — the subtropical highs and Circumpolar Trough were present in all runs, in much the same location. Larger changes were noted at upper levels, where the intensity of the standing-wave pattern was much reduced. The removal of Antarctica affected the 500 hPa height field as far north as 45°S. The zonally uniform sea-surface temperature run produced little effect in high latitudes, but thermal forcing was shown to be the dominating influence in locating the subtropical oceanic highs on the eastern sides of the ocean basins. Although Mechoso (1981) and Simmonds and Lin (1983) reached somewhat different conclusions, they both showed that the presence of Antarctica can have effects on the circulation of the Southern Hemisphere far away from the continent itself.

PRESENT RESEARCH EFFORTS AND PROBLEMS FOR THE FUTURE

A comprehensive review of polar processes and their role in the global climate system has recently been given by the Polar Group (1980). They acknowledge that the most pressing problem at the present time is the lack of ground-truth observations (particularly in winter) needed to adjust the numerical models to improve their portrayal of physical processes. To increase the data base in the polar regions, it is important to continue employing drifting buoys and automatic weather stations in the Southern Ocean and in the southern pack-ice zone. Modelling studies also need to be conducted in parallel with the observational programme, with particular attention focused on the interrelations between sea ice extent and climate. Current general circulation models are unable to simulate realistically the seasonal variation of sea ice and polar cloud cover, probably because the representation of boundary layer fluxes in the models is inadequate.

An understanding of the circulation of polar regions, and how this is related to lower latitude climate, is today more crucial than ever because of growing concern about the fragile environment of Antarctica and the prospect of ever larger numbers of people living and working on the ice. Climate studies have shown the sensitivity of high latitudes to global climate changes. For a doubling in the carbon dioxide content of the atmosphere, Washington and Meehl (1984) predicted an increase in the globally-averaged surface air temperature of approximately 2–3°C (the so-called "greenhouse effect"). At high latitudes, however, the temperature changes were much larger, with increases in excess of 10°C in winter and 5°C in summer predicted around the Antarctic coast. Such a large temperature change and the associated presumed increase in precipitation would have a significant effect on coastal ice, the coastline and ice-free areas.

The atmospheric ozone layer, which presently absorbs much of the damaging ultraviolet radiation from the sun before it can reach the surface of the Earth, also seems to be especially sensitive in polar latitudes. The chlorofluorocarbons (man-made chemicals used as aerosol propellants, refrigerants and for other industrial purposes) destroy ozone on reaching the stratosphere, and could be partly responsible for recently observed declines in global ozone concentration. There is now little doubt that these trace gases are implicated in the "ozone hole" phenomenon, which is a drastic reduction in ozone levels that occurs in the Antarctic each spring (Lindley, 1987; Bell, 1988). The ozone depletion apparently began in the late 1970s and the situation has deteriorated such that by 1987 ozone levels over the continent in October were only about 50% of the historic levels of the 1960s. Short durations of almost 100% ozone loss have been observed in narrow layers within the 12–20 km height range (Farman and Gardiner, 1987). Changing ozone levels affect the atmospheric temperature structure and consequently the wind field.

The problem of climate change in Antarctic regions is two-sided. We have mentioned how modifications of the global atmosphere (driven primarily from the industrialized countries of the Northern Hemisphere) could influence Antarctic circulation. The other side of the coin is that changes specific to the Antarctic could feed back into the ocean-atmosphere system at lower latitudes. Antarctica represents a major global heat sink which sets up the temperature gradient that drives the Southern Hemisphere atmospheric circulation. High latitude changes could therefore have far-reaching consequences on, for example, cyclone tracks over the Southern Ocean and thus the climates of Australia, New Zealand and South America. It is also possible that the polar energy balance could be affected by commercial activities that introduce oil spills or low-level air pollution.

The feedback effects from ozone losses and greenhouse warming could potentially have even more serious long-term consequences. The ozone hole itself is restricted to Antarctic (and possibly Arctic) latitudes because of the unique meteorological conditions there, but its recurrence every spring could accelerate the overall global depletion. It is estimated that a 1% decline in global ozone levels could result in a 4–6% rise in the incidence of some skin cancers. The danger from the greenhouse warming lies in accelerating the rise in world sea level. The West Antarctic Ice Sheet is largely grounded below sea level, but is surrounded by floating ice shelves that retard the seaward progress of the outflowing ice streams. If these floating ice shelves around the continental margin were to disappear, the stability of the West Antarctic Ice Sheet would be threatened. People have speculated that the ice sheet could eventually melt and result in sea level rises of 5–6 metres or more over a period of several hundred years (e.g., Mercer, 1978).

SUMMARY

The first recorded voyage south of the Antarctic Circle, by Captain James Cook, provided the first broad description of high southern latitude weather sequences in the region. Some of the general conclusions reached by Cook are still valid: for example, ice in the Southern Ocean is further north in the Atlantic and Indian Ocean Sectors than in the Pacific Ocean Sector. Other mariners provided further initial information, and those who named the "roaring forties" also identified, with more alliteration, the "furious fifties" and "screaming sixties".

The middle and high latitude atmospheric circulation is indeed dominated by the westerly winds, that start south of 30°S and increase in intensity as latitude increases until the Antarctic Circumpolar Trough is reached near 65°S. A narrow zone of easterlies exists between coastal Antarctica and the Circumpolar Trough. The westerlies are marked by a half-yearly oscillation so that they are strongest in spring and autumn.

The oscillation in intensity of the westerlies is due in part to the large thermal inertia of the oceans that causes atmospheric temperature cycles to lag the annual cycle of solar insolation. This means that air temperatures over the oceans do not drop as rapidly in early autumn as temperatures over the continents. Latent heat released as sea ice forms in autumn also slows the high latitude temperature decrease as autumn and winter advance.

Again, increased storm activity in autumn drives warmer air from lower latitudes towards and over Antarctica. This is held responsible for a slight rise in temperature sometimes seen over the continent about June, before further cooling to a minimum in August. The absence of a single clearly defined minimum in winter temperatures, known as a "coreless" winter pattern, is a characteristic found in many parts of Antarctica. The pattern is strongest and occurs most frequently in the Ross Sea Sector.

The rotating storms, or cyclones, that develop in the middle latitude westerlies move gradually across higher latitudes towards Antarctica as they travel around the globe. The maximum frequency of cyclones is found in a concentric band centred about 50° S. A second region of high cyclone occurrence is found along a north-west to south-east band in the South Pacific.

Looking at the longitudinal variation of atmospheric pressures on a hemispheric scale, a long-wave trough (or region of relatively lower pressures) is dominant in the eastern Indian Ocean, whereas the Tasman Sea and the region southeast of New Zealand show persistent ridging (or relatively higher pressures). This pattern influences the movement of cyclones leaving the Indian Ocean, as they travel south of Australia and New Zealand and into the Pacific.

At higher latitudes, there is no clear relationship between seasonal cycles of mean sea-ice extent and cyclone activity. However, some relationships between fluctuations in sea ice and cyclone activity on very short (a few days) and very long (interannual) timescales have been found. For example, 3-day averages of sea ice position have shown that rapid growth of ice occurs to the west of cyclone centres. Annual latitudinal differences in sea-ice extent in the region south of eastern Australia have been shown to correspond with similar latitudinal shifts in the distribution of cyclone tracks.

There is a constant draining of cold air from the interior of Antarctica, outwards to the coast. This flow turns towards the west near the coast, producing the narrow ring of easterlies winds about the continent. Sometimes, persistent severe gales occur at coastal sites as a result of the forced cold air convergence and drainage off the plateau. These blizzards seldom extend more than a few kilometres offshore. The constancy in direction of winds at the coast was remarked on by early explorers such as Sir Douglas Mawson. The often violent coastal phenomena contrast with winds on the inland plateau, which are also remarkably constant in direction, but are usually relatively gentle.

Antarctica has a marked effect on the large-scale atmospheric circulation over the Southern Ocean. Heat sources and sinks, and mountain barriers, have a strong influence on the "standing wave patterns" in the atmosphere that set up the background environment under which smaller scale weather systems develop and move. Antarctica not only affects the atmosphere directly in this way, but its asymmetry about the Pole produces a corresponding asymmetry in ocean temperatures at high latitudes. At 55°S, surface water temperatures in the South Atlantic and South Indian Oceans are about 5°C colder than in South Pacific longitudes.

Numerical simulations of atmospheric flow still have a number of shortcomings, and the errors tend to be largest in polar latitudes. The relative contributions of the heat sink and land mass effect of Antarctica remain to be more precisely defined, but models are sufficiently meaningful to demonstrate that the presence of Antarctica has widespread effects on the Southern Hemisphere circulation.

Present research efforts, directed towards a better understanding of the role of Antarctica in the global climate system, are both observational and theoretical in nature, supported by numerical modelling. Antarctica represents a major global heat sink which sets up the temperature gradient that drives the atmospheric circulation of the Southern Hemisphere. Any high latitude changes can therefore have far-reaching consequences on, for example, cyclone tracks over the Southern

Ocean and thus on the regional climates of middle latitude land masses. Climate studies have also shown the sensitivity of high latitudes to global climate changes. The possible break-up of the West Antarctic Ice Sheet under the predicted "greenhouse" warming, and the appearance each spring since about 1980 of a "hole" in the ozone layer, are two examples of how global climatic variations can be amplified by the unique conditions of the Antarctic atmosphere and oceans.

CHAPTER 3

PHYSICAL OCEANOGRAPHY

S.L. PATTERSON and T. WHITWORTH

INTRODUCTION

The ocean circulation in the Antarctic Sector of the Pacific is dominated by the continuous eastward-flowing Antarctic Circumpolar Current (ACC), a deep-reaching current driven by strong, prevailing westerly winds. Waters with diverse properties are entrained into the ACC all along its path and are subsequently blended into a more or less zonally uniform flow. The southern-most waters in the Pacific Ocean are therefore more similar to their counterparts in the Atlantic and Indian Oceans than they are to the waters further north in the Pacific. Because of their distinct and relatively homogeneous properties, the waters within and to the south of the ACC are collectively referred to as the Southern Ocean.

Besides being important as the primary connecting link between the three major ocean basins, the Southern Ocean is also the region of the major oceanic heat loss that drives the meridional circulation of the world ocean thermally. Heat advected poleward within the deep water is lost by radiation and either direct or indirect interaction with the cold Antarctic atmosphere and ice. The newly-formed cold water masses then spread northward at intermediate (~ 1,000 m) and abyssal (> 4,000 m) depths.

In this chapter, we present a general review of the descriptive physical oceanography of the Antarctic Sector of the Pacific Ocean, whose geographic limits and major bathymetric features are shown in Fig. 3.1. The Pacific constitutes by far the largest sector of the Southern Ocean, but its influence on the water mass properties of the ACC and the adjacent oceans is relatively weak in contrast to that of the Atlantic, which contains major sources of both deep and bottom waters. The chief influence of the Pacific is its contribution of a dissolved oxygen minimum and nutrient maximum to the Upper Circumpolar Deep Water. There are also identifiable sources of Antarctic Bottom Water (AABW) within the Ross Sea and along the Adelie Coast (130°E to 150°E), but their influence seems to be confined to the vicinity of the sources.

Ocean circulation within the Pacific Sector is driven by both wind and thermo-haline forcing. Both modes of circulation are influenced by bottom topography and the earth's rotation. The review begins with a description of the mean wind-driven circulation in the Pacific Sector. This is followed by a discussion of the velocity structure of the ACC, its interaction with bottom topography, and its estimated volume transport. The tendency for water properties to vary from north to south (meridionally) but to be uniform from east to west (zonally) has led to a characterization of the ACC as consisting of broad, distinct and continuous zones separated by narrow fronts. This "zonation" of the ACC is described in some

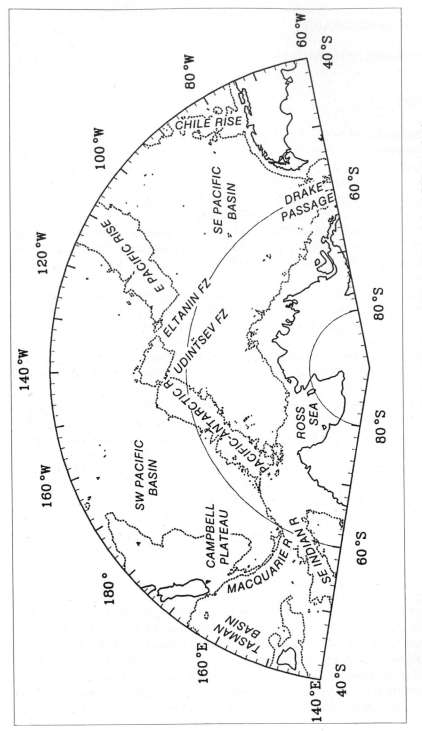

Fig. 3.1. Major bathymetric features of the Pacific Sector of the Southern Ocean. Dashed line is the 3,500 m isobath.

detail and is followed by a brief discussion of mesoscale variability within the ACC. The next section presents a discussion of the large-scale thermohaline circulation and includes a description of sources, formation mechanisms, identifying properties, and circulation of the major water masses present in the Pacific Sector. The final section presents a summary and identifies some of the major gaps in our knowledge of this vast and remote area.

MEAN WIND FORCING AND LARGE-SCALE OCEANIC RESPONSE

Although detailed knowledge of the wind fields over the southern hemisphere at any particular time is limited by a chronic shortage of observations over large, remote areas of the ocean, the major climatological features of these fields have been fairly well documented (e.g., Taljaard et al., 1969; Jenne et al. ,1971; Han and Lee, 1981). The climatological sea-level pressure distribution is dominated by subtropical highs centred over the oceans at approximately 30°S, low pressure cells around the edges of the Antarctic continent at 65°S to 70°S, and a permanent high over the South Pole. The high gradient region between 40°S and 65°S maintains a strong and prevailing westerly wind. Nearer the Antarctic continent, on the southern flank of the low pressure cells, the mean wind direction (usually between southerly and easterly) is influenced by both the horizontal pressure gradient and the katabatic effects of the massive continental ice shield (*see* Mullan and Hickman, this volume).

An extensive effort to collect atmospheric data was carried out between December 1978 and December 1979 as part of the First GARP (Global Atmospheric Research Program) Global Experiment (FGGE). The quantity of data obtained and the spatial coverage realized by this effort, especially in the southern hemisphere, are unpredecented. The mean wind stress field over the Pacific Sector of the Southern Ocean as derived from the FGGE data set (Ploshay et al., 1983) is presented in Fig. 3.2. Although these stresses were obtained during only a single year, the distribution is generally consistent with the historical climatology of wind stress presented by Han and Lee (1981).

North of 70°S, the mean wind stress drives the surface waters eastward with some deflection to the left of the wind stress direction due to the influence of the earth's rotation (Ekman, 1905). The northward Ekman transport of surface water sets up a north-south pressure gradient within the Southern Ocean that in turn supports the eastward geostrophic flow. This eastward wind-driven flow has been referred to as the West Wind Drift (Deacon, 1937). As the flow approaches the western coast of the South American continent, it splits into a northward and southward branch at approximately 43°S (Reid and Arthur, 1975). The northern branch, called the Peru or Humboldt Current, forms the eastern limb of the South Pacific subtropical gyre, and the southern branch flows through Drake Passage as the ACC. Most of the eastward-flowing waters south of 40°S in the Pacific are within the ACC. Fig. 3.2 reveals a zonal band of high mean wind stress (greater than 0.15 Nm^{-2}) between 45°S and 65°S. Within this band the stress is highest (greater than 0.25 Nm^{-2}) south of New Zealand between 160°E and 160°W. That

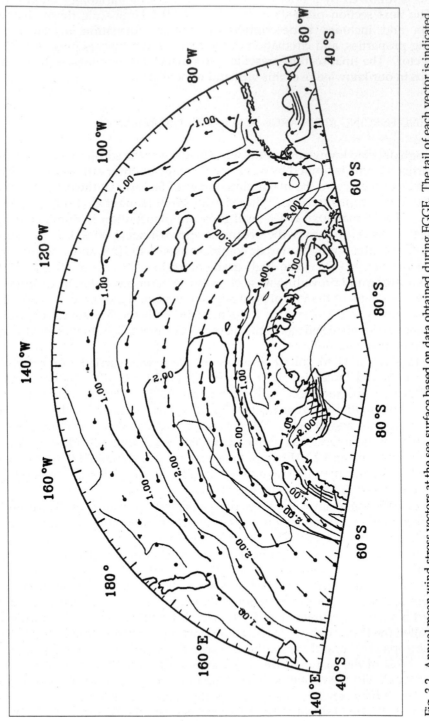

Fig. 3.2. Annual mean wind stress vectors at the sea surface based on data obtained during FGGE. The tail of each vector is indicated by a large dot. Spatial variations in stress magnitude are emphasized with contours. Units are 10^{-1} Nm^{-2}.

this band coincides with the region of highest mean ocean current velocities has been confirmed by both indirect (Gordon et al., 1978) and direct (Hofmann, 1985; Patterson, 1985) methods. Within this band, vector-averaged surface velocities inferred from satellite-tracked drifting buoys are typically greater than 20 cm sec.$^{-1}$. In some locations, such as south of New Zealand and South America, they exceed 40 cm sec.$^{-1}$ (Patterson, 1985).

Although the wind variability increases toward the south, the mean wind stress near the Antarctic continent is relatively large (Fig. 3.2) and induces a net flow toward the west. Deacon (1937) referred to this flow as the East Wind Drift and claimed that it was nearly circumpolar, being interrupted only at Drake Passage. More recent evidence (Treshnikov, 1964) indicates that easterly winds help maintain several distinct clockwise gyres south of the ACC, including the Ross Sea Gyre in the Pacific and the Weddell Gyre in the Atlantic. The continuity of the East Wind Drift is therefore probably interrupted in several locations around Antarctica.

MEAN CURRENT STRUCTURE AND
INTERACTION WITH BOTTOM TOPOGRAPHY

While the large-scale features of the mean surface circulation generally conform to the pattern imparted by wind forcing, this basic pattern is modified or perturbed by interaction of the flow with bottom topography. Sverdrup et al. (1942) pointed out that the configuration of the ACC is strongly influenced by major bathymetric features.

With the exception of the large array of drifting buoys deployed during FGGE (Garrett, 1980), direct current observations in the Pacific Sector of the Southern Ocean are sparse. The configuration of the flow field has therefore been largely inferred through indirect methods based on the distribution of tracers and the internal density structure (e.g., Reid and Arthur, 1975). In a comprehensive monograph on the South Pacific, Reid (1986) adjusted the flow inferred from tracer patterns with estimated values of bottom currents necessary to satisfy continuity of mass. Only the flow calculated by Reid near western boundaries or in very deep water differs significantly from the patterns that are revealed by tracers alone. We will note such differences later.

A good description of the mean surface circulation of the entire Southern Ocean inferred from the internal density structure was presented by Gordon et al. (1978). Fig. 3.3 is an adaptation of their map (incorporating data from Gordon and Molinelli, 1982) showing the dynamic height of the sea surface relative to 1,000 decibars within the Pacific Sector. The magnitude of the relative geostrophic flow at the sea surface is proportional to the closeness of the contours and is directed parallel to the contours such that higher values are to the left (in the southern hemisphere) of the flow. In this figure, the strong influence of major bathymetric features on the flow is evident. In the following discussion, observational evidence of such interactions throughout the Pacific Sector is reviewed.

South of Australia, the Southeast Indian Ridge is zonal in orientation and the

60

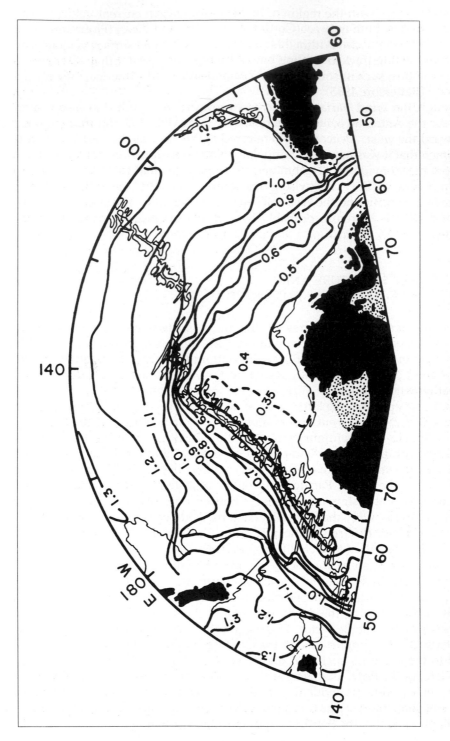

Fig. 3.3 Dynamic height of the sea surface relative to the 1,000 decibar level. Units are dynamic metres. Thin line is the 3,000 m isobath. Adapted from Gordon and Molinelli (1982).

most intense flow is along the northern flank of this ridge. Analyses of synoptic sections across the ACC usually reveal that the flow is streaky; that is, concentrated into multiple high velocity cores. These cores are frequently aligned along the flanks of major bathymetric features. Callahan's (1971) analysis of meridional sections along 115°E, 132°E, and 140°E across the ACC reveals an intense jet of eastward flow along the northern flank of the Southeast Indian Ridge and a broader, less-intense, eastward flow south of the ridge. These two eastward cores are separated by a zone of relatively weak flow (eastward or westward) over the ridge crest.

South of Tasmania at 145°E, the Southeast Indian Ridge turns abruptly toward the southeast until it merges with the Antarctic continental rise at approximately 160°E. The intense flow on the north flank of the ridge also turns to the southeast. Downstream of this turn, the trajectories of satellite-tracked drifting buoys (Fig. 3.4) exhibit a persistent wave-like pattern suggestive of a stationary Rossby wave. Such waves are to be expected in eastward flow downstream of large topographic obstructions due to the conservation of potential vorticity (McCartney, 1976).

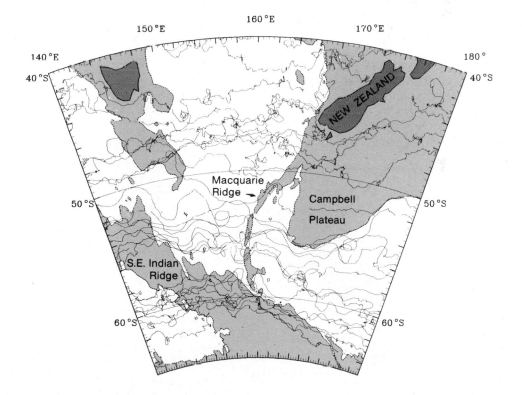

Fig. 3.4. Trajectories of FGGE drifting buoys south of Tasmania and New Zealand. Shaded area is shallower than 3,500 m.

Gordon (1972a) reported that the ACC appears to split into three velocity cores as it flows over the Macquarie Ridge at 158°E (Fig. 3.4). Most of the ACC flows through the passage (58°–60°S) south of the southern tip of the Macquarie Ridge, but two other velocity cores coincide with deep gaps in the ridge at 53.5°S and 56°S. Numerous researchers have described the downstream circulation south of New Zealand (e.g., Burling, 1961; Houtman, 1967; Gordon and Bye, 1972; Gordon, 1975; Heath, 1981). The two northern velocity cores appear to merge into a single jet south of the Campbell Plateau. This jet then follows the southeastern flank of the plateau northward to about 50°S where it turns eastward (Fig. 3.3). The southern branch flows northeastward along the northern flank of the Pacific–Antarctic Ridge until it reaches the two major fracture zones (Udintsev and Eltanin) between 150°W and 120°W (Fig. 3.1). Here, the two branches of the ACC converge before crossing the ridge system over the fracture zones.

Corroborating evidence of this inferred flow pattern near the fracture zone is provided by buoy trajectories (Fig. 3.5). Flow approaching from the west is deflected northeastward by the Pacific–Antarctic Ridge. Although some buoys managed to cross the ridge further south, the remaining buoys turned to the southeast near the fracture zones. Two buoys that did not successfully negotiate the Eltanin Fracture Zone were deflected northeastward along the northwest flank of the East Pacific Rise.

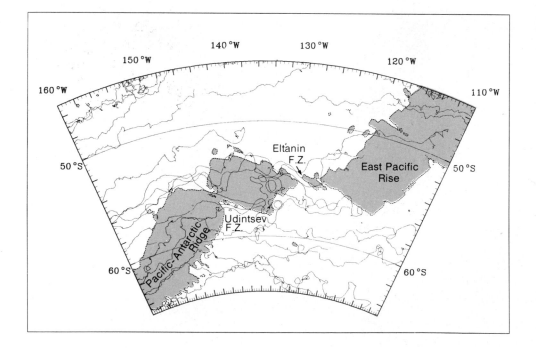

Fig. 3.5. Trajectories of FGGE drifting buoys near the Udintsev and Eltanin Fracture Zones. Shaded area is shallower than 3,500 m.

On the southern flank of the Pacific–Antarctic Ridge, there is a trough in the dynamic topography (Fig. 3.3). The inferred circulation around the trough is clockwise. It is not clear whether the surface flow in this region forms a closed gyre as is known to exist in the Weddell Sea, but topographic constraints would suggest that such a gyre is likely in the deep circulation. By analogy with the Weddell Sea therefore, the flow in this region is referred to as the Ross Sea Gyre. Although the dynamic topography (Fig. 3.3) and iceberg drift trajectories (Tchernia and Jeannin, 1983) suggest that the Ross Sea Gyre is confined to the southwestern sector of the Southeastern Pacific Basin, they may portray only the most intense portion of the flow. Some property distributions (discussed later) suggest that the gyre may extend eastward almost to Drake Passage.

Across the Southeastern Pacific Basin, the dynamic topography (Fig. 3.3) exhibits no persistent sharp gradients, which suggests that the ACC here is characterized by a broad and more-or-less uniform eastward flow until it reaches Drake Passage. This apparent lack of velocity cores may be an artifact of the sparseness of data, or may be related to the rather featureless bathymetry in this region. In any event, conditions appear to be quite different from those within Drake Passage.

Prior to 1975, numerous researchers (e.g., Ostapoff, 1961; Gordon, 1967a; Reid and Nowlin, 1971) presented vertical sections of geostrophic velocity for Drake Passage that exhibited multiple velocity cores. However, the station spacing in these early sections was too wide to resolve the velocity structure adequately. Between 1975 and 1980, this area was intensively examined during field experiments conducted as part of the International Southern Ocean Studies (ISOS) program. One of the major findings of ISOS was that the flow through Drake Passage is almost always organized into three narrow eastward jets separating four wider zones of weaker eastward flow (Nowlin et al., 1977; Whitworth, 1980; Nowlin and Clifford, 1982). These jets are seen to extend to the bottom in meridional setions of potential density, which exhibit three vertically-coherent bands in which isopycnal slope is somewhat steeper than the general downward slope of isopycnals toward the north.

TRANSPORT

Until recently, the best available estimates of the transport of the ACC were based on the density field alone. Such relative transport estimates assume that the current speed approaches zero at great depth. The most consistent transport figures come from regions where the ACC is geographically constrained: between Australia–New Zealand and Antarctica and in Drake Passage. The relative transport through Drake Passage is about 115 Sv (1 Sverdrup = 10^6 m^3 sec.$^{-1}$) according to Reid and Nowlin (1971) and that south of Australia and New Zealand is about 145 Sv (Gordon, 1975). The lesser value at Drake Passage is largely attributable to the shallower bottom depth there.

The introduction of reliable internally-recording current meters made it possible to measure deep currents rather than assume that they vanished. This technology is especially important in the ACC, which is known to be deep-reaching and have non-negligible bottom speeds. Speed estimates from current meters provide a reference with which to adjust the relative speeds obtained from the density field and permit estimates of the net transport. Using this technique, Reid and Nowlin (1971) measured a transport of 237 Sv at Drake Passage, and Callahan (1971) estimated the transport south of Australia at 233 Sv. It is now believed that both of these estimates are too high since both relied on a few widely-spaced current measurements of only a few days duration. Because of the banded nature of the flow in the ACC, many direct measurements are needed to characterize the deep flow accurately, and the agreement of these two estimates is doubtless fortuitous.

During ISOS, transport calculations were made by adjusting density measurements to more extensive current meter and pressure gauge data. In 1979, the net transport through Drake Passage averaged 130 Sv (Whitworth et al., 1982). Over a three-year period, the net transport ranged between 95 and 158 Sv (Whitworth and Peterson, 1985). Excluding Drake Passage, transport out of the Pacific is limited to the Bering Strait and the East Indian Archipelago. The out-flow through the Bering Strait has been estimated at 0.8 Sv by Coachman and Aagaard (1981) and 0.6 Sv by Aagaard et al. (1985). Various estimates of the transfer of Pacific waters to the Indian Ocean through the Indonesian Sea have been summarized by Gordon (1986). The estimates range from 1.7 to 14 Sv, and the average transport from all estimates is 9.2 Sv. The mean transport of the ACC as it enters the South Pacific is therefore about 140 Sv (130 + 0.7 + 9.2 Sv). In the open ocean, it is more difficult to establish northern and southern bounds of the ACC, and there are therefore no reliable transport estimates in the central part of the Pacific Sector.

ZONATION

The continuous eastward flow of the ACC causes the horizontal distribution of water properties in the Southern Ocean to be relatively uniform in the zonal direction while varying meridionally. In most longitudes, the meridional gradients in water properties are not uniform, but occur in steps. That is, relatively broad zonal bands (zones) characterized by weak horizontal gradients are separated by narrow fronts with sharp gradients (e.g., Gordon and Goldberg, 1970; Gordon and Molinelli, 1982). A schematic representation of the zonation is given in El-Sayed (this volume, Fig. 9.1). The gross features of this zonation in water properties have long been recognized (e.g., Deacon, 1937; Mackintosh, 1946) but only in recent years with the advent of instruments capable of recording continuous vertical profiles of temperature and salinity has this phenomenon been described in some detail south of Australia and New Zealand (Gordon, 1973, 1975; Gordon et al., 1977b), in Drake Passage (Nowlin et al., 1977; Whitworth, 1980; Nowlin and Clifford, 1982), and in the western Scotia Sea (Gordon et al., 1977a). The studies have revealed that the various zones can be characterized on the basis of distinctive vertical stratification or temperature-salinity relationships of the surface and intermediate waters. Characteristics of the deep and bottom waters undergo more subtle transitions across the ACC. The zonation within these deep layers is most evident as an abrupt change in depth of common water properties from one zone to the next.

In each of the regions studied, the zonation is remarkably similar. The zones are, from north to south, the Subantarctic Zone, the Polar Frontal Zone, the Antarctic Zone, and the Continental Zone. As noted earlier, the narrow boundaries or fronts separating the zones in Drake Passage and the western Scotia Sea coincide with jets of eastward flow. The front separating the Subantarctic Zone from the Polar Frontal Zone is called the Subantarctic Front, that separating the Polar Frontal Zone from the Antarctic Zone is called the Polar Front, and that separating the Antarctic Zone from the Continental Zone is called the Continental Water Boundary. A similar configuration is observed south of Australia and New Zealand (cf. Callahan, 1971; Gordon et al., 1977b). One difference observed in this latter region is the presence of an additional zone, the Subtropical Zone, to the north of the Subantarctic Zone. The front separating the Subtropical waters from the Subantarctic waters is called the Subtropical Front or Subtropical Convergence.

The similarity of zonation and velocity structure among the regions which have been studied so far has led to the conjecture that the ACC may everywhere be characterized by two separate and distinct fronts, the Subantarctic Front and the Polar Front, and their associated eastward jets. As will be discussed later, the circumpolar continuity of this structure has not yet been convincingly demonstrated. However, this conceptual model of the ACC provides a useful framework for the following discussion of zonation in the South Pacific.

Figs 3.6a–e present distributions of potential temperature, salinity, oxygen, silicate, and potential density on a meridional section through the central part of the Pacific Sector. The locations of the stations used to construct the section are shown in Fig. 3.7. Since the section combines data from different seasons and different cruises, it is not synoptic. Nonetheless, the major features revealed in the distributions are representative of conditions in the area. Although it would have been desirable to present distributions of phosphate and nitrate along this section, high quality nutrient data were not available.

Subtropical Front

The Subtropical Front separates the relatively warm, salty subtropical waters from the cooler, fresher waters of the Subantarctic Zone. Although this front passes south of New Zealand (Heath, 1981), it lies to the north of 40°S throughout most of the South Pacific east of 150°W (Deacon, 1982). Since this front is not observed in Drake Passage, it is not circumpolar in extent.

Subantarctic Zone

The northernmost zone in the ACC is the Subantarctic Zone. This zone has two distinguishing characteristics. First, vertical sections across the ACC show that

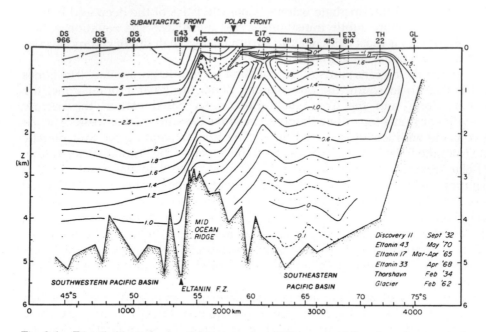

Fig. 3.6a. Distribution of potential temperature (°C) on a meridional section approximately along 135°W. Dotted line indicates the core of the subsurface temperature minimum. Station positions are shown in Fig. 3.7.

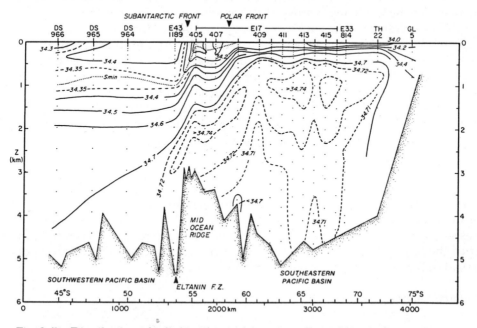

Fig. 3.6b. Distribution of salinity (‰) on the section. Dotted line indicates the core of the subsurface salinity minimum.

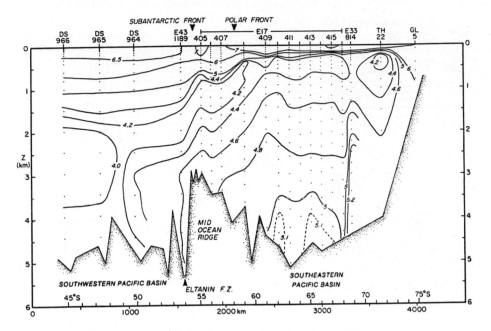

Fig. 3.6c. Distribution of dissolved oxygen (ml/l) on the section.

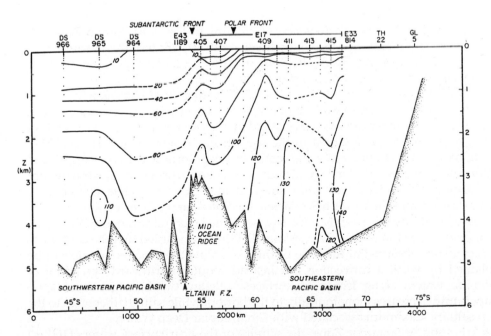

Fig. 3.6d. Distribution of silicate (μg-atoms/l) on the section.

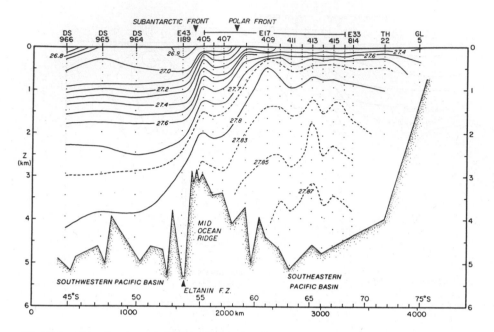

Fig.3. 6e. Distribution of the density parameter σ [σ = (ρ − 1) x 1,000) where ρ is potential density] on the section. Units are mg/cm³.

the temperature-salinity relationships of stations in the Subantarctic Zone fall within a very tight envelope (e.g., Nowlin et al., 1977). Second, the southern part of the zone, just to the north of the Subantarctic Front, contains a thick, nearly homogeneous layer extending from near the sea surface to depths of 400 m or more (e.g., stations 964 and 1189 in Fig. 3.6). The degree of homogeneity varies with geographical location and season. The deepest and most homogeneous layers seem to be those in the southeast Indian Ocean, while the coldest, freshest and densest layers are observed in the southeastern Pacific (McCartney, 1977). The homogeneity is apparently the result of deep vertical convection induced within the Subantarctic Zone by air–sea interaction during the austral winter (McCartney, 1977). However, some stratification within this layer is noted. In Drake Passage and the western Scotia Sea, the Subantarctic Zone exhibits a slight decrease in salinity with depth (a "nearly isohaline layer") associated with a weak thermocline (Gordon et al., 1977a). Molinelli (1978) concluded that the cold, fresh characteristics observed at the base of this "isohaline thermocline" could not be explained by vertical convection but instead require northward spreading of Antarctic waters along isopycnal surfaces. Below the homogeneous layer, temperature decreases monotonically to the bottom while salinity increases to the deep salinity maximum associated with Circumpolar Deep Water.

Within the Subantarctic Zone, the salinity of the near-surface waters (100 m) decreases from west to east across the South Pacific (Fig. 3.8). South of Australia

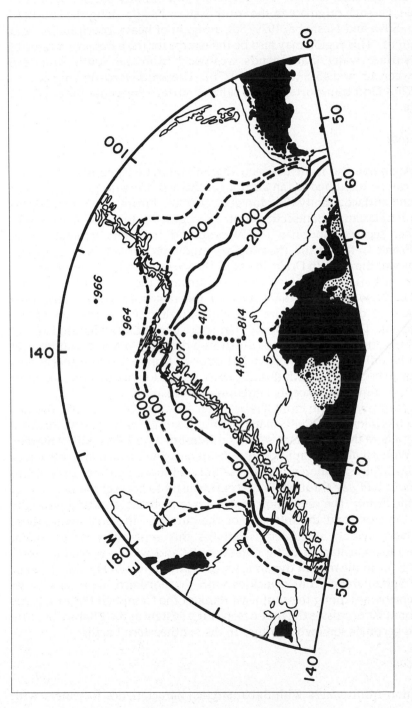

Fig. 3.7. The locations of the Subantarctic and Polar Fronts as determined by the diving of the salinity and temperature minima, respectively. The dashed lines show the 400 m and 600 m isobaths of the salinity minimum layer. The heavy solid lines show the 200 m and 400 m isobaths of the temperature minimum layer. The contours are from Gordon and Molinelli (1982). The light solid line is the 3,000 m isobath. Dots indicate the positions of stations used to construct the vertical sections shown in Fig. 3.6.

these waters have salinities greater than 34.5‰ while in northern Drake Passage the salinities are less than 34.1‰. The relatively low salinity surface waters in northern Drake Passage originate in the southeastern Pacific along the southern coast of Chile (Silva and Neshyba, 1979/80), a region of heavy precipitation and continental runoff. This region may also be the source for the extensive tongue of low salinity surface water that extends westward from the South American continent between 40° and 45°S (Deacon, 1977b). The southward-flowing branch of the West Wind Drift transports the low salinity surface layer into the northern Drake Passage.

Subantarctic Front

South of Australia, the front between the Subantarctic Zone and the Polar Frontal Zone can be identified by an abrupt southward decrease in both surface temperature and surface salinity (Gordon et al., 1977b). Burling (1961) called this feature the Australasian Subantarctic Front. Recognizing that this front might extend to other sectors, Houtman (1967) proposed the more general name, Subantarctic Front. In the Pacific, the property gradients across this front appear to diminish toward the east. In Drake Passage, the surface gradients are relatively weak, and, in fact, surface salinity increases toward the south (Sievers and Nowlin, 1984). Nowlin et al. (1977) selected the relatively sharp meridional density gradient at depth as a more reliable indicator of the position of the Subantarctic Front. The different salinity characteristics of the Subantarctic Front south of Australia and at Drake Passage illustrate a difficulty often encountered in attempting to identify a single objective indicator of frontal position that works equally well in all sectors. Indeed, this difficulty serves to illustrate one inherent difficulty in confirming the concept of circumpolar zonation.

In Fig. 3.6, the Subantarctic Front lies between stations 1189 and 405. Besides the intensified meridional gradients in temperature, salinity and density, the front is also the site where the subsurface salinity minimum associated with Antarctic Intermediate Water makes its rapid descent from near the surface to depths near 1,000 m. In Fig. 3.7, the location where the salinity minimum layer crosses 400 m and 600 m (about halfway through its descent) is used to bracket the position of the Subantarctic Front. The separation of these two isobaths is indicative of the sharpness of the front and the intensity of the current. In some areas, these isobaths are very widely separated. Perhaps this separation is somewhat misleading and is an artifact of using non-synoptic and widely-spaced stations. Comparing Fig. 3.7 to the map of dynamic topography shown in Fig. 3.3, it can be seen that the Subantarctic Front coincides with the northern high velocity jet which flows northward along the southeast flank of the Campbell Plateau, turns eastward at about 50°S, crosses the mid-ocean ridge system at the Eltanin Fracture Zone and then becomes somewhat diffuse in the southeastern Pacific.

Polar Frontal Zone

The transition from waters with Subantarctic characteristics to waters with

Antarctic characteristics occurs within the Polar Frontal Zone. In their description of zonation south of Australia and New Zealand, Gordon et al. (1977b) aptly referred to this as the Complex Zone. Vertical profiles of temperature within the Polar Frontal Zone exhibit multiple inversions which are accompanied by density-compensating salinity fluctuations. This interleaving of warm, salty waters from the north with cold, fresh waters from the south exhibits vertical scales between 10 m and 200 m. Inversions are most prevalent within the upper 500 m of the water column where lateral gradients of temperature and salinity along density surfaces are greatest. Apart from this interleaving, salinity generally increases monotonically with depth until the salinity maximum of Circumpolar Deep Water is reached. Weak subsurface minima in temperature between 200 m and 500 m depth can often be traced continuously southward to the intense minimum at depths of about 100 m south of the Polar Front.

Polar Front

In the early literature, the Polar Front, or Antarctic Convergence, was considered to be the boundary separating Subantarctic and Antarctic waters (Deacon, 1937; Sverdrup et al., 1942; Mackintosh, 1946). Many different surface and subsurface criteria were used to determine the position of this boundary (cf. Gordon, 1971). As more and better quality data became available, the zonation concept emerged, and it is currently popular to refer to the boundary between the Polar Frontal Zone and the Antarctic Zone as the Polar Front (Emery, 1977; Whitworth, 1980). So defined, the Polar Front coincides with the northern terminus of the well-defined temperature minimum layer of the Antarctic Zone. Here the temperature minimum layer begins its steep descent from depths of approximately 150 m to depths of approximately 500 m. As it deepens, the temperature minimum layer breaks up into multiple weaker minima characteristic of the Polar Frontal Zone. Consistent with the earliest descriptions of the Polar Front, this boundary is often marked by relatively sharp gradients in surface temperature, salinity and silicate (Patterson and Sievers, 1979/80; Sievers and Nowlin, 1984). In Fig. 3.6, the Polar Front is located between stations 407 and 408. The reversal in the slope of the isolines suggests the presence of a current meander between stations 405 and 408, which probably accounts for the two apparently detached temperature minima observed at station 405. The buoy trajectories shown in Fig. 3.5 confirm that meanders are common over the ridge near 135°E.

The depth of the temperature minimum core layer has been plotted by Gordon and Molinelli (1982). Its location at 200 m and 400 m is shown in Fig. 3.7 to bracket the position of the Polar Front. The break in the 400 m isobath between 140°W and 170°W implies that in this region the temperature minimum erodes away before it attains a depth of 400 m. The Polar Front coincides with the southern high velocity jet revealed in Fig. 3.3. It follows the northern flank of the Pacific–Antarctic Ridge northeastward to the Udintsev Fracture Zone where it crosses into the Southeastern Pacific Basin and then, like the Subantarctic Front, weakens until it reintensifies west of Drake Passage.

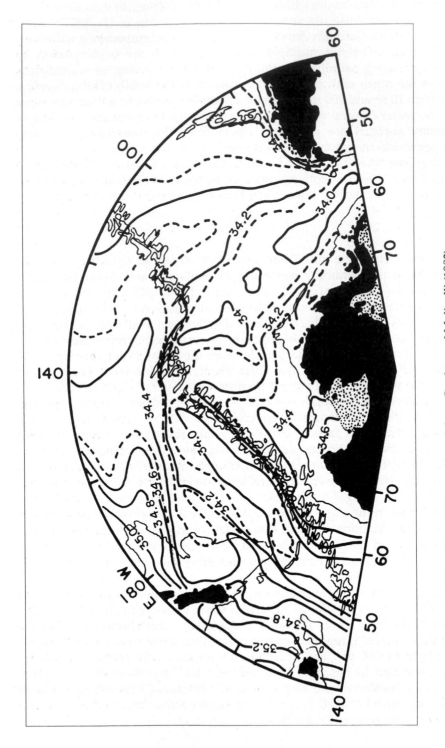

Fig. 3.8. Distribution of salinity (‰) at 100 m. Adapted from Gordon and Molinelli (1982).

Antarctic Zone

The Antarctic zone is south of the Polar Front and is characterized by relatively smooth vertical profiles of temperature and salinity that exhibit a well-defined subsurface temperature minimum embedded within a halocline above 200 m. The temperature minimum marks the base of the winter mixed layer. Surface heating and melting of ice during summer warms and freshens the surface water and leaves as a residual the characteristic subsurface temperature minimum. Below the minimum, temperature and salinity increase monotonically to the maxima associated with Circumpolar Deep Water.

Within the Antarctic Zone, the isolines in the various property distributions shown in Fig. 3.6 continue to rise toward the south as far as station 409. This station is within the eastward-flowing northern limb of the Ross Sea Gyre (Fig. 3.3). South of this point the isolines become more or less horizontal across the Southeastern Pacific Basin, indicative of weak zonal flow (possibly southward flow) in this location. South of station 413 the deep isopycnals slope downward to the south. This configuration is consistent with westward flow (East Wind Drift) in the southern limb of the Ross Sea Gyre.

Continental Water Boundary and the Continental Zone

In the southern part of the Antarctic Zone, the temperature and salinity maxima of the Circumpolar Deep Water attenuate and there is a transition to the more vertically homogeneous water column of the continental shelf and slope. In Drake Passage, the transition is referred to as the Continental Water Boundary (Sievers and Emergy, 1978) and the waters to the south are in the Continental Zone. In Fig. 3.6, the Continental Water Boundary is between stations 22 and 5. The direction of flow at the Continental Water Boundary apparently varies with location. Eastward flow is reported in Drake Passage (Nowlin et al., 1977), at 60°E (Jacobs and Georgi, 1977), and at 132°E (Callahan, 1971). In the Weddell and Ross Seas, however, this transition occurs within the westward flow of the southern limbs of the subpolar gyres.

Flow within the Continental Zone south of the Continental Water Boundary is poorly resolved. In southern Drake Passage, direct current measurements have shown persistent subsurface flow to the west along the continental shelf and slope (Whitworth et al., 1982). This current has been studied by Nowlin and Zenk (1987) who identified the source waters as coming from the Weddell Sea. They noted that the current cannot be part of the wind-driven circulation because the mean winds throughout Drake Passage are from the west. Rather, the flow is probably a thermohaline feature: a westward extension of the Polar Slope Current of the Weddell Sea. All around the Antarctic continent, shelf waters are colder and denser than the waters offshore. While much of this shelf water is not dense enough to form Antarctic Bottom Water, Killworth (1983) has noted that it may sink to some shallower depth, turning to the west because of the earth's rotation as it sinks. Since dense shelf waters are a circumpolar feature, the implication is that a thermohaline-driven westward flow may exist in most regions within the

Continental Zone. In regions with subpolar gyres (e.g., the Weddell Gyre and the Ross Sea Gyre) such thermohaline currents may supplement the westward wind-driven flow.

Continuity of Fronts and Jets

As noted earlier, the similarity of zonation observed in the various sectors has led to the idea that the Subantarctic and Polar Fronts and their associated high-velocity jets exhibit circumpolar continuity. Emery (1977), in his analysis of historical expendable bathythermograph (XBT) and hydrographic station data, attempted to assess the extent of continuity across the Pacific Sector of the Southern Ocean. He concluded that the distinctive interleaving and temperature-salinity relationships which characterize the Polar Frontal Zone can be traced continuously across the Pacific, but that the bordering fronts and their associated jets seem to become diffuse and ill-defined in the southeastern Pacific. The same interpretation of flow structure in this region is suggested by dynamic topography (Fig. 3.3) and the zonally varying width of the fronts as revealed by Fig. 3.7. As noted earlier, the failure to detect high-velocity jets in this region may be an artifact of inadequate sampling, but Emery speculated that, in response to the lack of any topographic constraints in the Southeastern Pacific Basin, the jets may spread out into a broader and weaker flow.

In her analysis of the FGGE drifting buoys, Hofmann (1985) noted that in some sectors, especially south of Australia and New Zealand, the buoys drifted along preferred paths which coincide with frontal positions. These paths are evident in Fig. 3.4. The northernmost path lies between 46°S and 50°S and coincides with the Subtropical Front. Farther south the next path, which corresponds to the Sub-antarctic Front, crosses 140°E between 52°S and 54°S, then turns southeastward and passes around the southern flank of Campbell Plateau (cf. Fig. 3.7). The southernmost path preferred by the buoys, which corresponds to the Polar Front, crosses 140°E between 58°S and 60°S, then crosses the Southeast Indian Ridge at about 59°S, 150°E and continues eastward along the northern flank of the ridge system. Using the frontal positions defined by Clifford (1983) and surface velocities derived from the buoy trajectories, Hofmann concluded that the jets associated with the Subantarctic and Polar Fronts are continuous over large sectors of the Southern Ocean, especially in regions influenced by major bathymetric features. In the southeastern Pacific, however, this continuity could not be demonstrated.

If the jets are continuous, a dynamical explanation is lacking. It has been noted that there is consistency between the mean positions of Southern Ocean fronts and specific features of the wind-induced Ekman flow and the seasonal sea-ice distribution (Taylor et al., 1978; Deacon, 1982; Clifford, 1983). However, it is not clear how these surface forces acting alone can develop and maintain the jets which extend to the bottom. Other investigators (Thompson, 1971; Gordon, 1972a; McCartney, 1976) have related the jets in specific locations to bottom topography, but it is not clear how a zonally variable bottom configuration can produce zonally continuous jets.

MESOSCALE VARIABILITY

Although the preceding discussion has attempted to describe the configuration of the mean flow within the Pacific Sector, the currents actually exhibit substantial spatial and temporal variability. In his description of the Polar Front, Mackintosh (1946) noted that "it forms twists and loops that may extend as much as 100 miles north or south, and it possibly even forms isolated rings." Since the jets within the ACC extend to great depths, interactions with bottom topography influence the nature and intensity of current variability. For example, Gordon (1967b) noted the unusual complexity of the Polar Front downstream of the Udintsev and Eltanin Fracture Zones which he characterized as a "double" polar front. He later described similar complexity downstream of the Macquarie Ridge (Gordon, 1972a) and speculated that it might be due to rings shedding from the ACC at the ridge and advecting downstream. His speculation was supported by the results of a numerical model (Boyer and Guala, 1972).

The belief that current jets within the ACC tend to meander and occasionally form detached rings has subsequently been confirmed by ship surveys (Joyce and Patterson, 1977; Savchenko et al., 1978; Patterson and Sievers, 1979/80; Joyce et al., 1981; Peterson et al., 1982), moored current meter arrays (Sciremammano, 1979; Hofmann and Whitworth, 1985) and satellite imagery (Legeckis, 1977; Peterson, 1985).

Extensive meandering of the fronts within the ACC has been observed within Drake Passage and south of New Zealand. Within the restricted confines of Drake Passage, meanders can shift the location of the Subantarctic Front by more than 100 km in a few weeks (Hofmann and Whitworth, 1985). In the open ocean, such shifts in frontal position might be several times larger. In the seven months between two surveys of a region southeast of New Zealand, Bryden and Heath (1985) found that the flow just north of the Subantarctic Front had changed direction by 180°. That current meanders extend to the bottom was confirmed by Sciremammano (1979), who detected such a feature in the Polar Front from current meter data at 2,700 m, and found the signal to be coherent with the surface expression as revealed by satellite images (Legeckis, 1977).

Bryden (1983) reviewed eddy observations in the Southern Ocean and noted that a typical eddy south of New Zealand or in Drake Passage has a radius of 30–50 km and surface speeds of 30–40 cm sec.$^{-1}$. The frequency of formation of detached rings is not known, but using eight-month current records from central Drake Passage, Pillsbury and Bottero (1984) inferred the presence of five cold-core rings and one warm-core ring. Also, during a one-year study in Drake Passage, one warm-core and three cold-core rings were detected passing through an extensive array of current, temperature and pressure sensors (Hofmann and Whitworth, 1985).

In the open South Pacific, there are fewer direct observations of mesoscale variability. However, distributions of buoy-derived eddy kinetic energy (Patterson, 1985), the variance in geopotential anomaly (Lutjeharms and Baker, 1980), and the variance in altimeter-derived sea surface height (Cheney et al., 1983) all exhibit large values near the Macquarie Ridge and the Udintsev and Eltanin Fracture

Zones (e.g., Fig. 3.9). Current meter data in northern Drake Passage and southeast of New Zealand reveal eddy kinetic energies at depth comparable to those found within the Gulf Stream and Kuroshio (Nowlin et al., 1981; Bryden and Heath, 1985).

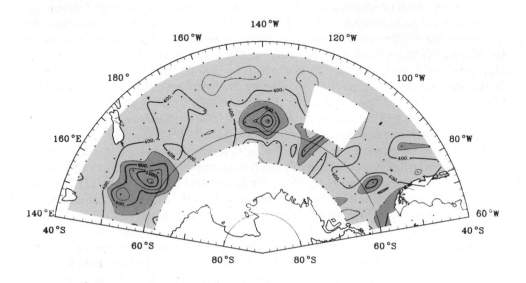

Fig. 3.9. Distribution of eddy kinetic energy per unit mass (cm² sec.⁻²) of the surface flow based on 5° square analysis of FGGE drifting buoys (Patterson, 1985).

WATER MASSES AND THERMOHALINE CIRCULATION

The water column in the deep ocean is stably stratified into several layers which are traditionally identified by extrema (cores) in vertical profiles of temperature, salinity, oxygen or nutrients. The distinguishing characteristics of each core layer reflect the unique properties input at the source region and the subsequent modifications of the water mass within that layer. The conservative properties, such as potential temperature and salinity, are modified only by diffusion and mixing as they sink and spread. Non-conservative properties, such as oxygen and nutrients, have their source values altered by biological or chemical processes. Nonetheless, extrema in the non-conservative properties persist over great distances and are very useful as water mass tracers. A subsurface oxygen maximum, for example, usually indicates that water within the layer occupied by that maximum was more recently exposed to the atmosphere than the waters immediately above and below. Maxima in oxygen are usually accompanied by minima in phosphate and nitrate. Some extrema are not true cores that can be identified with a particular source region, but instead are "induced" by underlying or overlying true cores (Gordon, 1967b). When highly oxygenated surface water sinks to intermediate depths (e.g., Subantarctic Mode Water), an induced oxygen minimum core layer is formed between the maximum at the surface and that at intermediate depth.

Since water parcels tend to flow along surfaces of constant potential density, the individual core layers tend to conform to these surfaces which ascend toward the sea surface in polar latitudes. Here, the waters are subjected to the modifying influence of interactions with cold Antarctic air and ice. The classical picture of the meridional circulation driven by thermohaline exchanges in the Antarctic was given by Deacon (1937, fig. 1). Relatively warm and salty deep waters flow with a southward component of motion toward Antarctica. South of the Polar Front, this water mass, which is here referred to as Circumpolar Deep Water, rises to shallow depths and is cooled, freshened, and oxygenated to form both Antarctic Surface Water and Antarctic Bottom Water. Subsequently, these water masses spread northward within the surface and bottom layers, respectively. Within the Polar Frontal Zone, the layer containing Antarctic Surface Water descends below the warmer and less dense Subantarctic Surface Water. North of the Polar Frontal Zone, this layer is identified by a relative minimum in salinity and is referred to as Antarctic Intermediate Water. The thermohaline circulation is believed to play an important role in the redistribution of heat from the equator to the pole and in the ventilation of the deep and abyssal waters.

Recent studies (e.g., Reid et al., 1977; Schlemmer, 1978; Sievers and Nowlin, 1984) have demonstrated that core layers coincide with local minima in vertical profiles of stability, while the boundaries between layers coincide with stability maxima. This technique for tracing water masses can also be implemented in terms of the distribution of potential vorticity (e.g., Keffer, 1985). These studies have revealed that the major water masses mentioned above consist of numerous sublayers that are distinct in more subtle ways.

The following discussion of the various water masses in the Pacific Sector will be arranged more or less in order of decreasing density. That is, it begins with a description of the very cold, dense waters observed over the continental shelf, continues with a discussion of Antarctic Bottom Water, and proceeds generally upward and northward through the various water mass layers. Table 3.1 enumerates the water masses of the Pacific Sector of the Southern Ocean and summarizes their characteristics. Where no geographical limits are noted, the water mass can be found throughout the Pacific Sector.

Waters over the Antarctic Continental Shelf

During summer, when the coastal region is accessible for sampling, all of the waters over the Antarctic continental shelf exhibit temperatures within a few degrees of the *in situ* freezing point, but the salinities vary considerably. The variations in salinity are probably due to geographic differences in exchanges across the air-sea interface. Highest salinities seem to occur in regions of persistent wintertime leads and polynyas which prolong the exposure of the sea to the cold Antarctic atmosphere. During summer, the cold shelf waters are overlain by a layer of relatively warm surface water that is diluted by melting ice. According to

TABLE 3.1

Summary of water mass characteristics in the Antarctic Sector of the Pacific Ocean.

Water Mass	Location (Depth)	Characteristics	Source of Characteristics
1. Waters over the Antarctic Continental Shelf			
Surface Water	Upper 50 m	$\theta > -1.6°C$, $S < 34.50‰$	air/sea ice/AASW
Modified Circumpolar Deep Water	200–300 m	$\theta > -1.6°C$, $S > 34.50‰$	CDW/AASW/shelf waters
High Salinity Shelf Water (HSSW)	S.W. Ross Sea Shelf	$\theta \sim -1.9°C$, $S > 34.75‰$	air/sea ice/AASW
Low Salinity Shelf Water (LSSW)	Most of continental shelf	$\theta > -1.9°C$, $S < 34.60‰$	air/sea ice/AASW
Deep Ice Shelf Water (DISW)	300–600 m, S.W. Ross Sea shelf	$\theta < -1.9°C$, $S > 34.60‰$	HSSW/ice shelf
Shallow Ice Shelf Water (SISW)	50–250 m, Ross Sea shelf	$\theta < -1.9°C$, $S < 34.60‰$	CDW/ice shelf
2. Antarctic Bottom Water (AABW) "new" bottom water			
Low salinity bottom water	Bottom, near sources	θ min, S min, O_2 max. PO_4 min, NO_3 min, SiO_3 min	Weddell Sea, Adelie Coast, eastern Ross Sea, etc.
High salinity bottom water	S.E. Australia–Antarctic Basin and S.W. Southeastern Pacific Basin	θ min, S max, O_2 max, PO_4 min, NO_3 min, SiO_3 min	N.W. Ross Sea (HSSW/CDW)
"old" bottom water	Bottom, away from sources; above "new" bottom water near sources	PO_4 max, NO_3 max, SiO_3 max	sediments; off-bottom core induced by "new" bottom water
3. Circumpolar Deep Water (CDW)			
Lower Circumpolar Deep Water (LCDW)	1,000 m in Antarctic Zone to 3,000 m in Subantarctic Zone	S max, PO_4 min, NO_3 min	North Atlantic Deep Water
Upper Circumpolar Deep Water (UCDW)	400 m in Antarctic Zone to 1,800 m in Subantarctic Zone	O_2 min, PO_4 max, NO_3 max (θ max in Antarctic Zone)	Subtropical waters of Pacific and Indian Oceans

TABLE 3.1 (*continued*)

Water Mass	Location (Depth)	Characteristics	Source of Characteristics
4. Antarctic Surface Water (AASW)	Antarctic Zone above 200 m	Cold and low salinity surface layer	air/sea ice/CDW
5. Antarctic Intermediate Water (AAIW)	Surface in Polar Frontal Zone to 1,000 m in Subantarctic Zone	S min north of Polar Front	AASW/SAMW
6. Subantarctic Mode Water (SAMW)	Surface (winter) to 700 m in Subantarctic Zone	O_2 max, pycnostad	air/SASW
7. Shallow Oxygen Minimum Layer	200–400 m in Subantarctic Zone	S max, O_2 min	Induced by SAMW (below) and SASW (above)
8. Subantarctic Surface Water (SASW)	Surface in Subantarctic Zone	Surface θ max, O_2 max, PO_4 min, NO_3 min, SiO_3 min; S varies regionally	air/sea interaction (above) and shallow oxygen minimum layer (below)

Carmack (1977), the summertime mean temperature of shelf water in the Pacific Sector of the Southern Ocean (– 1.03°C) is somewhat warmer than that in the other two sectors; the mean salinity is 34.46‰. Fig. 3.10, adapted from Ainley and Jacobs (1981), shows vertical sections of temperature and salinity across the Ross Sea Shelf near 170°W, and illustrates several of the water masses described below.

The densest water mass in the Southern Ocean is High Salinity Shelf Water observed over the broad continental shelf in the southwestern Ross Sea. Its salinity increases with depth from 34.75‰ to 35.00‰ or greater (Jacobs et al., 1970). Since this water mass is nearly isothermal at the surface freezing point (approximately –1.9°C), it is probably formed during winter by freezing and evaporation in the leads and polynyas in the western Ross Sea along the Victoria Land Coast (Jacobs et al., 1985). High Salinity Shelf Water appears with salinities greater than 34.80‰ in Fig. 3.10. It is presumed that most of this dense water is dynamically constrained to circulate in a clockwise gyre over the shelf (Jacobs et al., 1970). That portion which escapes from the shelf contributes to the formation of the high salinity variety of bottom water.

Shelf waters with somewhat lower salinities (34.60‰–34.75‰) are still dense enough to contribute to the formation of bottom water. Such shelf waters are

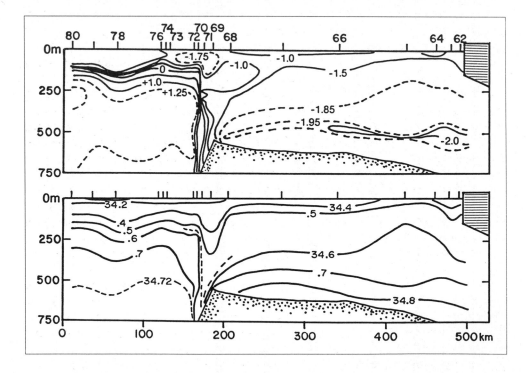

Fig. 3.10. Distribution of temperature (top panel) and salinity (bottom panel) constructed from stations occupied along approximately 170°W across the Ross Sea continental shelf in austral summer. The barrier of the Ross Ice Shelf is indicated at upper right in each panel. Adapted from Ainley and Jacobs (1981).

present within the eastern Ross Sea (Jacobs et al., 1979) and along the Adelie Coast near 140°E (Gordon and Tchernia, 1972).

Most of the continental shelf in the Pacific Sector is occupied by water with salinity lower than 34.60‰ (Carmack, 1977) which is referred to as Low Salinity Shelf Water. While mixtures containing this water are not dense enough to sink to abyssal depths, they may sink along the continental slope and spread at intermediate depths (Carmack and Killworth, 1978; Killworth, 1983) thereby ventilating the water column.

About half of the continental shelf in the Ross Sea is covered by the thick permanent floating glacial ice of the Ross Ice Shelf. Some of the subsurface water observed over the continental shelf is colder than the sea surface freezing point and therefore could not have formed at the sea surface. Since the freezing point of seawater decreases with increasing pressure, this very cold water must be cooled at depth by interaction with the ice shelf. This water is therefore called Ice Shelf Water.

Two distinct layers of Ice Shelf Water have been observed in the Ross Sea (Jacobs et al., 1979). Shallow Ice Shelf Water with salinity less than 34.60‰ is seen emerging from the edge of the ice barrier at depths between 50 m and 250 m. Relatively warm water originating from Circumpolar Deep Water penetrates over the continental shelf and beneath the Ross Ice Shelf at approximately 175°W (Jacobs et al., 1979; Pillsbury and Jacobs, 1985). Fig. 3.10 shows a tongue of modified Circumpolar Deep Water with temperatures greater than −1.0°C penetrating the shelf above 250 m. Shallow Ice Shelf Water presumably forms as a result of interaction of this warm water with the ice shelf (Jacobs et al., 1985).

Deep Ice Shelf Water is observed at depths between 300 m and 600 m offshore of the ice shelf. Its salinity is greater than 34.60‰ and in Fig. 3.10 appears as a tongue of water colder than −2.0°C near 500 m. MacAyeal (1984) has described the likely formation mechanism of Deep Ice Shelf Water. From its source region in the northwestern Ross Sea, High Salinity Shelf Water flows to the southwest along the western margin in a deep depression under the ice shelf. In the southwestern Ross Sea, the ice shelf is thick and the water column below is relatively thin. Tidal currents are strongest in such regions and capable of supplying the mechanical energy necessary to allow the High Salinity Shelf Water to penetrate the thin layer of melt water which separates it from the base of the ice shelf. Subsequent basal melting reduces the salinity and results in the Deep Ice Shelf Water observed further north.

The circulation on the Ross Sea Shelf has been inferred from density distributions supplemented by some bottom photographic evidence and a few direct current measurements (e.g., Pillsbury and Jacobs, 1985). It is thought that the circulation on the shelf is clockwise with westerly flow along the edge of the ice shelf and eastward flow along the shelf break (Jacobs et al., 1970; Ainley and Jacobs, 1981). The salinity field (which is generally parallel to the density field) supports this view if it is assumed that currents at the shelf floor are negligible (Fig. 3.10).

Waters of the continental shelf regime are separated from those of the oceanic regime by a wedge of relatively fresh water at the shelf break (Fig. 3.10). Ainley and Jacobs (1981) referred to this feature as the Slope Front. This separates the eastward-flowing northern limb of the Ross Sea Shelf circulation from the west-ward flow of the Circumpolar Deep Water. Gill (1973) noted a similar V-shaped salinity distribution in the southern Weddell Sea, but interpreted the flow field differently: he assumed that there is a substantial westward bottom flow at the edge of the shelf and concluded that both shelf and slope waters are flowing westward. Direct current measurements are needed to resolve the flow in these two regions.

Antarctic Bottom Water

Although some investigators (Gordon, 1978; Killworth, 1983) have noted the potential importance of open ocean convection in bottom water formation, most Antarctic Bottom Water is believed to form near the Antarctic continental margins. There, very cold, dense waters ($\theta < -1.8°C$, $S > 34.60‰$) of the continental shelf mix with components of Circumpolar Deep Water available near the shelf break and over the continental slope. Due to its high density, this mixture tends to sink to the ocean floor along the continental slope but, because of the influence of the earth's rotation, it is deflected to the left and flows approximately parallel to the isobaths as a contour current. When the dense water finally reaches the ocean floor, it spreads laterally along the bottom of the basins adjacent to Antarctica. Exchange between basins is restricted to deep gaps and fracture zones in the submarine ridge system.

Because of its components from the waters over the continental shelf, newly formed Antarctic Bottom Water is characterized by a maximum in dissolved oxygen and minima in potential temperature, silicate, phosphate, and nitrate. The salinity of bottom water varies but, with the exception of that formed in the northwestern Ross Sea, is characterized by a bottom minimum in salinity. Cir-cumpolar Deep Water, which overlies the bottom water, is also identified by minima in phosphate and nitrate, so there must be an induced nutrient maximum between newly formed Antarctic Bottom Water and Circumpolar Deep Water. We will refer to the layer of maximum phosphate, nitrate, and silicate as "old" bottom water. Away from source regions, the newly-formed bottom water is absent and the layer of old bottom water intersects the bottom. Even further away, the old bottom water is absent and Circumpolar Deep Water intersects the bottom.

The contrast between new and old bottom water is strongest near source regions and is particularly evident in vertical profiles of silicate presented by Edmond et al. (1979) from various sites in the Southern Ocean and in the vertical sections of phosphate and silicate presented by Reid et al. (1977, fig. 6) for the Atlantic Sector. Similar stratification is observed south of New Zealand near the Ross Sea source of bottom water in vertical sections of silicate and nitrate (Craig et al., 1981, plates 83 and 85). Fig. 3.11 shows profiles of properties in the Ross Sea Gyre from a station at 73°S, 159°W. Although the phosphate and nitrate profiles are plotted on an expanded scale that reveals the precision of the measurements, the overall trend is clear: the near-bottom minima in potential temperature and

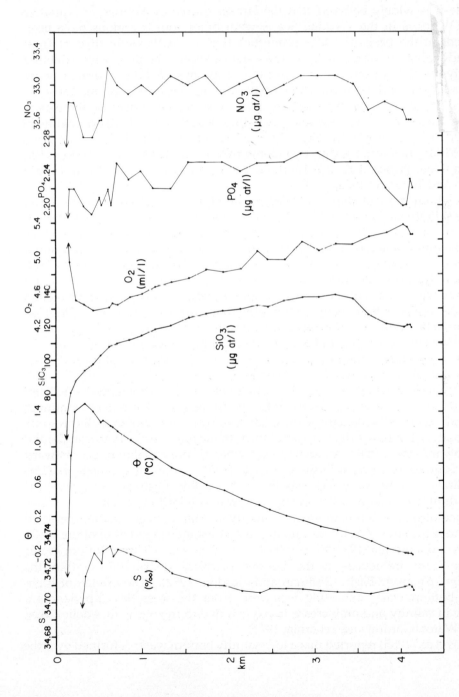
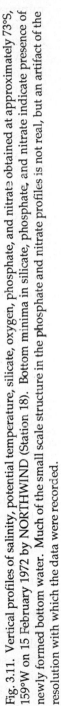

Fig. 3.11. Vertical profiles of salinity, potential temperature, silicate, oxygen, phosphate, and nitrate obtained at approximately 73°S, 159°W on 15 February 1972 by NORTHWIND (Station 18). Bottom minima in silicate, phosphate and nitrate indicate presence of newly formed bottom water. Much of the small scale structure in the phosphate and nitrate profiles is not real, but an artifact of the resolution with which the data were recorded.

and nutrients and the maxima in oxygen and salinity show newly formed high-salinity bottom water. The overlying nutrient maxima and relative salinity minima are probably a mixture of old bottom waters from various sources. Further east, new bottom water appears as a bottom minimum in silicate at stations 414 and 415 in Fig. 3.6d.

While it is widely believed that the largest source by volume of Antarctic Bottom Water is in the Weddell Sea, several other source regions have been identified on the basis of water properties that are sufficiently distinct from surrounding bottom waters to indicate local formation. The properties exhibited by newly-formed bottom water reflect the properties of the constituent water masses available at the source. There is speculation that the importance of some sources of Antarctic Bottom Water are not fully appreciated because the waters formed at these sources are essentially indistinguishable from those originating in the Weddell Sea (e.g., Mosby, 1968; Carmack and Killworth, 1978; Jacobs et al., 1985). Within the Pacific Sector, two identifiable source regions are the Ross Sea (Gordon, 1966; Jacobs et al., 1970) and the Adelie Coast between 130°E and 150°E (Gordon and Tchernia, 1972).

Throughout most of the Pacific Sector, salinity values decrease with depth from the salinity maximum (> 34.73‰) of the Lower Circumpolar Deep Water to a minimum (34.69–34.72‰) at the bottom. The northwestern Ross Sea is anomalous due to the introduction of a high-salinity (> 34.72‰) bottom water formed along the continental slope in the western Ross Sea from a mixture of High Salinity Shelf Water and Circumpolar Deep Water (Jacobs et al., 1970). Between the salinity maximum associated with Lower Circumpolar Deep Water and that associated with high-salinity bottom water is an intermediate salinity minimum (< 34.71‰) which probably represents the upper limit of influence of the high-salinity bottom water. However, Carmack and Killworth (1978) presented evidence to suggest that this deep salinity minimum may be locally reinforced by plumes of low-salinity water flowing down the continental slope.

The high-salinity bottom water initially flows westward towards the Balleny Islands (67°S, 160°E) where it splits into two branches. One branch continues westward, south of the Balleny Islands, into the Australian–Antarctic Basin south of the Southeast Indian Ridge; the other turns to the north, east of the islands, and heads towards the Pacific–Antarctic Ridge where it presumably turns eastward into the Southeastern Pacific Basin (Carmack, 1977). The small areal extent of this high-salinity bottom water suggests that it has a low formation rate and it is quickly diluted by mixing with surrounding waters (Gordon, 1972b).

Anomalously low temperature and salinity and high oxygen values observed off the Adelie Coast (67°S, 140°E) identify this as a source region for bottom water (Gordon and Tchernia, 1972; Carmack, 1977). This Adelie Coast Bottom Water has significant influence on the bottom property distribution within the Australian–Antarctic Basin (Rodman and Gordon, 1982). The branch of high-salinity bottom water advecting westward from the Ross Sea experiences a decrease in salinity and an increase in oxygen due to mixing with Adelie Coast Bottom Water (Gordon and Tchernia, 1972).

Jacobs et al. (1985) reported that a low-salinity bottom water is formed over the continental slope in the eastern Ross Sea from a mixture of Circumpolar Deep Water and the local shelf water (containing some Ice Shelf Water), which is less saline than that in the western Ross Sea. This bottom water presumably contributes to the rapid dilution of the high-salinity variety. On the other hand, Carmack (1977) speculated that it is low-salinity bottom water, primarily of Weddell Sea origin, flowing from the west into the Southeastern Pacific Basin that dilutes the high-salinity Ross Sea bottom water.

As noted earlier, water parcels tend to flow along surfaces of constant potential density, and these surfaces slope down toward the north. Except for a few deep fracture zones, the Southeast Indian Ridge, Pacific–Antarctic Ridge and East Pacific Rise are continuous at depths greater than about 4,000 m. Density values associated with Antarctic Bottom Water do not occur north of this ridge system, so Antarctic Bottom Water is confined to the Australian–Antarctic and Southeastern Pacific Basins. North of this ridge line, the bottom waters are a mixture of Antarctic Bottom Water and Lower Circumpolar Deep Water (Schlemmer, 1978). The volume of Antarctic Bottom Water in the Pacific is about five times less than in the Atlantic or Indian Ocean Basins (Carmack, 1977).

The mixture of Antarctic Bottom Water and Lower Circumpolar Deep Water that comprises the abyssal waters of the southern Tasman Basin come from the Australian–Antarctic Basin through the Balleny Fracture Zone near 155°E. It appears to flow in a clockwise loop through the Tasman Basin and then eastward through gaps in the Macquarie Ridge and into the Southwestern Pacific Basin (Rodman and Gordon, 1982).

From theoretical considerations, Stommel (1957) predicted equatorward flowing bottom boundary currents along the western sides of ocean basins. The SCORPIO section along 43°S (Warren, 1973) shows the western intensification of the bottom flow against the Chatham Rise, and the influence of Lower Circumpolar Deep Water is clear from the salinity maximum between 3,000 and 4,000 m. Northward abyssal flow extends some 1,000 km east of the intense western boundary jet, and transport within the northward flow is estimated to be about 20 Sv (Warren, 1973, 1976). Similar deep western boundary currents have been observed to exhibit variable, and occasionally quite high, velocities that are capable of significant sediment transport (Londsdale and Smith, 1980; Glasby, 1983; Hollister et al., 1984; Carter and Mitchell, 1987).

The northward-flowing bottom boundary current follows the western margin of the Southwestern Pacific Basin along the Tonga–Kermadec Ridge to about 30°S, where it splits into two parts (Reid, 1986). The northern branch extends to the northern end of the basin near 10°S. Here, the salinity and silicate maxima of Lower Circumpolar Deep Water intersect the bottom, and there is no remaining trace of Antarctic Bottom Water (Mantyla and Reid, 1983). An eastward branch of the abyssal flow extends to the East Pacific Rise before turning to the north (Reid, 1986). The inferred flow pattern in the northern part of the Southwestern Pacific Basin is counter-clockwise, similar to the overlying Subtropical Gyre.

Bottom property distributions suggest a clockwise circulation in both the Australian–Antarctic Basin and the Southeastern Pacific Basin (Gordon, 1972b; Rodman and Gordon, 1982; Mantyla and Reid, 1983; Reid, 1986). The relatively high bottom silicate and low oxygen content of waters in the northern and eastern portions of the Southeastern Pacific Basin suggest long residence times and therefore sluggish flow. Newly-formed Ross Sea bottom waters seem to be confined to the southwestern portion of the basin. Vertical sections across Drake Passage (Sievers and Nowlin, 1984) show that the densest waters flowing from the Pacific to the Atlantic are the older, high silicate bottom waters of the Southeastern Pacific Basin.

Circumpolar Deep Water

By far the most voluminous water mass in the Pacific Sector of the Southern Ocean is Circumpolar Deep Water (Carmack, 1977). It is this water mass which occupies the deep and bottom layers throughout most of the Pacific Ocean. Since Circumpolar Deep Water is continuously flowing around the Antarctic Continent, its properties are relatively homogeneous, but it can be divided into two layers (Gordon, 1967b) that derive their distinguishing properties from two different northern sources.

Lower Circumpolar Deep Water is characterized by a deep maximum in salinity and minima in phosphate and nitrate. These properties are derived from North Atlantic Deep Water that is entrained into the eastward-flowing ACC in the southwestern Atlantic (Reid et al., 1977). Although the extrema that mark the core of Lower Circumpolar Deep Water erode slowly downstream because of both lateral and vertical mixing (Reid and Lynn, 1971), the core is still clearly observed in the flow from the Pacific through Drake Passage (Sievers and Nowlin, 1984). The core of Lower Circumpolar Deep Water rises from depths greater than 3,000 m north of the Subantarctic Front to depths less than 1,000 m south of the Polar Front (Fig. 3.6b). Within the Pacific Sector, salinity values at the core decrease from 34.76‰ near the Macquarie Ridge south of New Zealand to 34.73‰ in Drake Passage (Fig.3.12). Corresponding phosphate values increase from 2.0 to 2.2 μg-atoms/l and nitrate values increase from 31 to 32 μg-atoms/l (Bainbridge, 1981; Craig et al., 1981). The remarkable persistence of these extrema suggests that the distributions of properties deep within the ACC are determined largely by advection rather than diffusion. The highest salinity within the salinity maximum core layer in the Pacific is found close to the position of the Polar Front (cf. Figs 3.7 and 3.12), and has been used by Gordon (1972a) to mark both the axis of spreading of Lower Circumpolar Deep Water and the axis of flow of the ACC. The patchiness in the distribution of salinity within this core layer (e.g., Fig. 3.12) is a commonly reported phenomenon (e.g., Gordon, 1975; Jacobs and Georgi, 1977). Although most of this patchiness is probably an artifact of inadequate sampling, the known mesoscale variability in the ACC suggests that some of the patchiness is real.

Besides the general eastward flow of the ACC, other features of the deep circulation can be inferred from the distribution shown in Fig. 3.12. The northward protrusion of high salinities east of New Zealand is indicative of northward flow of Lower Circumpolar Deep Water in this region. The lower salinity tongue (< 34.74‰) extending northeastward along the southern flank of the Pacific–

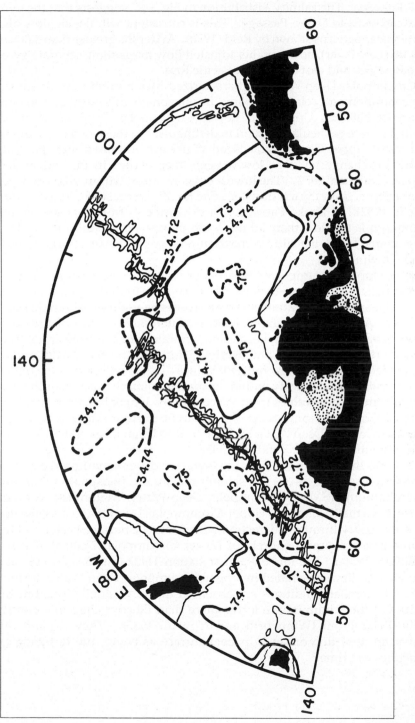

Fig. 3.12. Distribution of salinity (‰) on the surface defined by the deep salinity maximum. Adapted from Gordon and Molinelli (1982).

Antarctic Ridge is also consistent with a topographically steered clockwise gyre north of the Ross Sea. The salinity distribution in Fig. 3.12 suggests that the gyre may extend eastward to Drake Passage. This is consistent wih the shallow and intermediate tracer patterns shown by Reid (1986). At depths greater than 3,000 m (e.g., below this core layer), however, his adjusted flow maps show separate gyres north of the Ross Sea and east of the East Pacific Rise.

Upper Circumpolar Deep Water is characterized by a minimum in dissolved oxygen concentration and relative maxima in phosphate and nitrate. The contrasting extrema between Upper and Lower Circumpolar Deep Water make phosphate and nitrate particularly useful in distinguishing these two deep layers. The properties of Upper Circumpolar Deep Water are entrained into the ACC through lateral exchange with the low-oxygen deep waters in the Indian and Pacific Oceans (Callahan, 1972). The lowest oxygen values within this core layer (< 3 ml/l) are observed in the southeastern Pacific off the coast of Chile (Gordon and Molinelli, 1982). In Drake Passage, just downstream from this source, the oxygen minimum is still less than 4.0 ml/l, the phosphate maximum is greater than 2.4 µg-atoms/l and the nitrate maximum is greater than 35 µg-atoms/l (Sievers and Nowlin, 1984).

The core of Upper Circumpolar Deep Water rises from depths greater than 1,800 m in the Subantarctic Zone to depths less than 400 m in the Antarctic Zone (Fig. 3.6c). In the Subantarctic Zone, this core layer is overlain by Antarctic Intermediate Water. As Upper Circumpolar Deep Water shoals south of the Polar Front, its low oxygen, high phosphate, and high nitrate core begins to erode from above due to vertical mixing with the overlying Antarctic Surface Water, which has relatively high oxygen and low nutrient values. This is reflected in the higher oxygen concentrations and density within the oxygen minimum layer south of the Polar Front as compared to values from the core of the Upper Circumpolar Deep Water north of the Polar Front. Since the Antarctic Surface Water is relatively cold, Upper Circumpolar Deep Water is characterized by an induced temperature maximum within the Antarctic Zone (Fig. 3.6a).

Fig. 3.11 shows that, within the Ross Sea Gyre, the oxygen minimum occurs at approximately the same depth as the salinity maximum, phosphate minimum, and nitrate minimum of Lower Circumpolar Deep Water. Within the Ross Sea Gyre, therefore, virtually all of the Upper Circumpolar Deep Water has shoaled and been eroded away through interaction with Antarctic Surface Water and the water column consists almost entirely of Lower Circumpolar Deep Water and Antarctic Bottom Water. The low oxygen at station TH22 (Fig. 3.6c) occurs at a density too great to have originated in Upper Circumpolar Deep Water north of the Polar Front. Similar conditions are observed in the Weddell Gyre, but the oxygen values at the minimum are lower there than those at the same density north of the Polar Front (Whitworth and Nowlin, 1987). They explain this apparent oxygen depletion on an isopycnal surface as being due to biological processes acting over time.

Antarctic Surface Water

The most distinctive feature of the Antarctic Zone is the relatively cold, low-salinity surface layer referred to as Antarctic Surface Water. As noted earlier, the relatively warm, salty Circumpolar Deep Water rises to shallow depths south of the Polar Front and Antarctic Surface Water is formed by modifying this basic water mass. Heat is lost by interaction with the cold atmosphere and ice, and fresh water is added in the form of precipitation and runoff of ice from the continent. Superimposed on this mean flux of heat and salt through the Antarctic Surface Water layer is a pronounced annual oscillation. Winter cooling and sea ice formation induce vertical convection to produce a winter mixed layer down to the permanent pycnocline. During summer, warming and ice melt create a thin, low density surface layer overlying the residual "winter water" identified by a pronounced subsurface temperature minimum (Fig. 3.6a). The depth of this minimum ranges from approximately 50 m near the Antarctic continent and in the centre of the Ross Sea Gyre to approximately 200 m at the Polar Front.

Distributions of temperature and salinity on the temperature minimum surface are presented by Gordon and Molinelli (1982). Temperature increases from near freezing (approximately –1.9°C) adjacent to the Antarctic continent to approximately 2°C at the Polar Front. The salinity distribution is more complex. There is a patchy band of relatively low salinity (< 34.00‰) to the south of the northern limit of the temperature minimum core layer. Salinity increases from this band toward both the north and south with highest salinities (> 34.30‰) being observed in the Ross Sea Gyre. The increase toward the north is due to mixing with more saline Subantarctic Zone waters. The southward increase in the salinity of the temperature minimum layer may reflect mixing with upwelled Circumpolar Deep Water in these areas. Another contributing factor may be the meridional difference in the effects of sea ice formation and melting. During autumn, surface freezing begins to dominate melting near the continent and sea ice begins to accumulate. As sea ice forms, brine is ejected raising the salinity of the underlying layer of Antarctic Surface Water. Once formed, some of the ice drifts northward away from the continent and toward warmer waters. As the dominance of freezing over melting advances northward, so does the northern edge of the ice pack. The maximum northward extent of the pack remains south of the Polar Front (Deacon, 1982). During spring, melting begins to dominate freezing and the ice edge retreats toward the south. The net effect of this annual freezing cycle is to fractionate fresh water from the southern portions of the Antarctic Surface Water layer and transport it northward.

Antarctic Intermediate Water

Besides Antarctic Bottom Water, the second major water mass spreading northward from sources in the Southern Ocean is Antarctic Intermediate Water. Unlike Antarctic Bottom Water, whose northward flow is concentrated in deep western boundary currents, Antarctic Intermediate Water diffuses northward in all longitudes with a northward component that may vary, but is significantly slower than the eastward component of the ACC. This water mass is apparently formed within the Polar Frontal Zone where the layer of relatively cold and fresh Antarctic Surface Water flows beneath, and is mixed with, warmer, saltier, and less dense Subantarctic waters. Although the subsurface temperature minimum of Antarctic Surface Water is eroded away by vertical mixing within the Polar Frontal Zone, the low salinity waters above the temperature minimum provide Antarctic Intermediate Water with its identifying characteristic, a salinity minimum (Fig. 3.6b). The properties of Antarctic Intermediate Water vary somewhat within and between the major oceans of the southern hemisphere. This is due in part to regional differences in the properties of the Subantarctic contributions to the water mass. The Antarctic Intermediate Water near its formation region in the Pacific is the warmest ($> 5°C$) and least dense ($\sigma \sim 27.1$ mg/cm^3) variety (Piola and Georgi, 1982).

In the South Pacific, the salinity minimum core layer is near the sea surface in the vicinity of the Polar Frontal Zone (Fig. 3.6b). In some sections, the minimum can be traced southward across the Polar Frontal Zone to the Polar Front (Sievers and Nowlin, 1984). The core layer deepens rapidly toward the north at the Subantarctic Front, reaches depths of approximately 1,000 m within the subtropical anticyclonic (counter-clockwise) gyre, and can be traced northward to at least 10°S (Craig et al., 1981). The low-salinity surface waters in the south-eastern Pacific off the coast of Chile (Fig. 3.8) provide little contrast with the underlying salinity minimum layer. The core of Antarctic Intermediate Water is therefore rather poorly defined in this region.

Spreading of Antarctic Intermediate Water is strongly influenced by the wind-driven surface circulation. Most of the flow in the Pacific Sector is eastward with the ACC. However, there is a westward-intensified, subtropical anticyclonic gyre over the Southwestern Pacific Basin east of the North Island of New Zealand (Reid, 1965; Piola and Georgi, 1982). At approximately 1,000 m, the gyre is centred along 40°S. Core layer properties attenuate along the flow path because of vertical and lateral mixing. Near the source, the core layer is characterized by salinities less than 34.20‰, temperatures less than 4°C, and dissolved oxygen values greater than 6 ml/l. These values attenuate northward along the eastern limb of the subtropical gyre and westward along the northern limb. Within the centre of the gyre and throughout the Tasman Basin, salinities are greater than 34.40‰, temperatures are greater than 5.5°C, and dissolved oxygen is less than 4.5 ml/l (Gordon and Molinelli, 1982). The properties of Antarctic Intermediate Water in the southwestern Pacific reflect the entrainment of warm, salty, and low oxygen waters from the Coral Sea (Reid, 1965).

Subantarctic Mode Water

One of the distinguishing characteristics of the Subantarctic Zone is a thick, nearly homogeneous layer (referred to as a pycnostad) near the sea surface just to the north of the Subantarctic Front (McCartney, 1977, 1982). The large volume of water contained in this pycnostad emerges as an isolated peak or "mode" in regional volumetric censuses (e.g., Cochrane, 1958; Montgomery, 1958; Worthington, 1981; Piola and Georgi, 1982). Consequently, this water has been named Subantarctic Mode Water (McCartney, 1977). The homogeneity of this layer is apparently the result of deep vertical convection driven by winter cooling at the sea surface. The convective overturning also serves to ventilate this water as evidenced by its high dissolved oxygen content (> 6 ml/l). As noted earlier, properties within the Subantarctic Zone vary from west to east across the Pacific and this variation is reflected in the properties of Subantarctic Mode Water observed in the SCORPIO section along 43°S (Reid, 1973; McCartney, 1982; Piola and Georgi, 1982). The potential density (in σ units) of this water increases from 26.9 mg cm^{-3} in the Tasman Basin to 27.1 mg cm^{-3} in the Southeastern Pacific Basin and is accompanied by a decrease in temperature from 8.5°C to 5.5°C and a decrease in salinity from 34.62 to 34.25‰.

As Subantarctic Mode Water is advected northward by the subtropical anti-cyclonic gyre, it occupies a layer above the salinity minimum of Antarctic Intermediate Water (Piola and Georgi, 1982) and it retains its identifying characteristics of a pycnostad and an oxygen maximum. Although these features attenuate along the flow path, they can be traced to the northern limb of the subtropical anticyclonic gyre along 15°S (Reid, 1973; McCartney, 1977; Craig et al., 1981). The warmer, saltier, and lighter variety of Subantarctic Mode Water observed in the southwestern Pacific is apparently confined to this part of the ocean (McCartney, 1982). The oxygen maximum core layer descends to a maximum depth of approximately 700 m at about 28°S and then rises to approximately 500 m at 15°S where oxygen values at the core have decreased to less than 4 ml/l (Craig et al., 1981). In the SCORPIO section along 43°S, there is only a weak and poorly-defined oxygen minimum separating the Subantarctic Mode Water from the high oxygen surface layer. However, at 28°S, the separation is distinct (Reid, 1973). This may explain why the subsurface oxygen maximum of Subantarctic Mode Water is not detected in the vertical section shown in Fig. 3.6c, which extends northward only to 45°S.

Shallow Oxygen Minimum Layer and the Peru–Chile Undercurrent

Throughout much of the South Pacific, the weak oxygen minimum layer overlying the maximum in the Subantarctic Mode Water appears as a relative minimum because of the presence of higher dissolved oxygen concentrations in the surface layer (Reid, 1965, 1973). East of about 160°W, this shallow oxygen minimum layer is also characterized by a salinity maximum induced by the overlying low-salinity surface layer of the southeastern Pacific (Fig. 3.8). However, along the eastern boundary of the South Pacific, the extrema in this layer are not merely induced features. Instead, waters with very low dissolved oxygen values (< 2 ml/l) and relatively high salinities (> 34.40‰) are advected into this layer from the tropical Pacific by the southward-flowing Peru–Chile Undercurrent. The water in this current is clearly distinguished from that further west in this same layer by its high phosphate, nitrate and silicate concentration (Reid, 1973). The nutrient concentrations within the core of this undercurrent are high enough to cause the underlying Subantarctic Mode Water to be locally characterized by an induced minimum in nutrients.

The properties marking the core of the Peru–Chile Undercurrent become shallower and attenuate toward the south, but are still clearly evident in the SCORPIO section at 43°S (Reid, 1973), and can be traced southward to approximately 50°S (Silva and Neshyba, 1979/80). At 43°S, the core is at a depth of approximately 250 m with salinity greater than 34.40‰, oxygen less than 3 ml/l, phosphate greater than 2.6 µg-atoms/l, nitrate greater than 30 µg-atoms/l, and silicate greater than 20 µg-atoms/l. At 50°S, the core has shoaled to a depth of approximately 200 m with salinity less than 34.20‰, oxygen greater than 4 ml/l, phosphate less than 2.0 µg-atoms/l, nitrate less than 30 µg-atoms/l, and silicate less than 15 µg-atoms/l. South of this latitude, the undercurrent loses its identifying characteristics.

Subantarctic Surface Water

Although the properties of the surface waters within the Subantarctic Zone are subject to much spatial and temporal variability due to exposure to the atmosphere, these waters are normally characterized by a surface maximum in temperature and dissolved oxygen and a corresponding minimum in nutrients. There is also a general southward decrease in temperature and an increase in oxygen and nutrients. Salinity in the southeastern Pacific has a somewhat more complex distribution because of the extensive tongue of low-salinity surface water (Deacon, 1977b) that extends westward from the South American coast (Fig. 3.8). In the region covered by this tongue, the surface waters are characterized by a salinity minimum; elsewhere the surface waters are characterized by a salinity maximum (Reid, 1973). The apparent source of this feature is the fresh water input along the southern coast of Chile by heavy precipitation and continental runoff (Silva and Neshyba, 1979/80), but the mechanism for distributing this low-salinity water westward remains unresolved. Throughout this region, the large-scale mean flow, in both the atmosphere and ocean, is toward the east. The area occupied by the tongue coincides with the area in which the West Wind Drift splits into northward and southward flowing branches. However, since salinity in this region increases with depth in the upper layer, the low-salinity tongue cannot be maintained by divergence and upwelling. The hypothesis of westward surface flow to maintain this distribution has been advanced (Deacon, 1977b; Neshyba and Fonseca, 1980), but confirmation by direct measurements is lacking.

SUMMARY AND CONCLUSIONS

In this chapter, we have presented a general qualitative description of the major water masses and the large-scale features of the mean circulation in the Pacific Sector of the Southern Ocean. The circulation is dominated by the wind-driven eastward flow of the Antarctic Circumpolar Current. In the Southwestern Pacific Basin, this current consists of at least two relatively narrow jets of intense flow associated with sharp horizontal gradients (fronts) in the property field.

These jets appear to be steered and perhaps maintained by the bathymetry. The Subantarctic Front, which meanders northward east of the Campbell Plateau, and the Polar Front, which follows the northern flank of the Pacific–Antarctic Ridge, move close together to cross the ridge system above the Udintsev and Eltanin Fracture Zones. In the Southeastern Pacific Basin, the jets appear to weaken and become more diffuse, and their continuity west of Drake Passage cannot be demonstrated with available data.

South of the Antarctic Circumpolar Current, the data are sparser in part due to the presence of ice. Here, a generally acknowledged feature of the large-scale mean flow, the Ross Sea Gyre, is only poorly resolved by the existing data. The strength, persistence and areal extent of this feature remains to be determined. The structure and persistence of circulation near the Antarctic continental slope throughout the Pacific Sector is also largely unresolved. Further north, the mechanism responsible for maintaining the tongue of low-salinity surface water extending westward from the southern coast of Chile remains a mystery.

The major influences on the water masses of the Southern Ocean are derived from the North Atlantic and the Weddell Sea. Far downstream in the South Pacific, the relatively minor changes experienced by these water masses can be attributed to diffusion and mixing. The most distinguishing contribution of the Pacific Sector to the properties of the Southern Ocean is the oxygen minimum and nutrient maximum of the Upper Circumpolar Deep water. Most of the dense water formed over the continental shelf in the Ross Sea appears to be dynamically constrained to circulate over the shelf. The small amount of high-salinity shelf water that flows off the shelf and down the continental slope contributes to the formation of high-salinity bottom water. However, the influence of this water appears to be confined to a limited region near the source and is therefore minor compared to the influence of Weddell Sea Bottom Water. Because of its similarity to Weddell Sea Bottom Water, the extent of influence of low salinity bottom water formed near the Adelie Coast and in the eastern Ross Sea has not yet been clearly established.

In conclusion, we have been only marginally successful at describing even the large-scale mean picture. Clearly, more strategically-placed modern hydrographic stations are needed to help bring this mean picture into sharper focus. The extrema in phosphate and nitrate profiles are particularly useful in identifying all of the major water mass layers within the deep and bottom waters of the Southern Ocean. The increasing availability of high-quality nutrient and transient tracer data provided by modern hydrographic stations should be very helpful in the investigation of water mass formation and spreading. However, the most critical data deficiency in the Pacific Sector of the Southern Ocean is the lack of direct current measurements throughout the water column to quantify better water mass spreading, heat flux and associated phenomena. In this remote region, such data are exceedingly sparse. Future efforts to fill this void are essential.

CHAPTER 4

ICE

J.R. KEYS

INTRODUCTION

Ice visually dominates most of the surface of the globe south of the Antarctic Circle for all or part of the year. This ice is either *glacial ice* formed by accumulated and compacted snow or *sea ice* formed from the freezing of sea water.

Ice covers 97.6% of the continental land mass, mainly in the form of an immense *ice sheet* up to 4,500 km wide, and with an area of about 12 million km². This ice mass extends north of 66°S latitude in Wilkes Land, Enderby Land and the Antarctic Peninsula. The ice sheet is fringed by glacial ice in the form of floating ice shelves and other glaciers over half of its perimeter. This adds another 1.6 million km² of ice. *Icebergs* break off these glaciers to drift around the continent and north into the Southern Ocean as far as 30°S (Burrows, 1976).

During winter, the area of ice doubles with the formation of sea ice. At its maximum in late winter, sea ice forms a belt 400 to 2,000 km wide from the coast of Antarctica to as far north as 53°S (Jacka, 1983). The maximum extent of this ice, including areas of open water within it varies from 17.3 to 20.2 million km² or 18.5 million km² on average (U.S. Navy, 1985). During spring and summer, this ice recedes south to the coast in several places. The sea ice extent reaches a minimum in February and varies depending on the summer, between 2.4 and 5.1 million km² or 3.6 million km² on average. The area of ocean actually covered by sea ice at the February minimum averages only 2.8 million km².

In contrast, the snow coverage of the Antarctic continent changes little with the snow line being at, or close to, sea level year-round. Summer melting is confined to narrow coastal zones, the snouts of glaciers which end on ice-free terrain and the margins of some ice-free areas. Probably less than 4% of Antarctica's surface is either ice-free land or snow-free ice (Drewry, 1983; Robin, 1986); some of this area may be covered by snow at any time of the year, although such snow-falls do not normally last for more than a few days or weeks. Beneath the surficial snow, the seaward margins of the floating glaciers change on time scales of years to decades while the ice sheet margins take hundreds or thousands of years to alter.

This chapter examines Antarctic ice, concentrating on that in the Antarctic Sector of the Pacific Ocean. The significance and characteristics of this ice are discussed with emphasis placed on ice shelves, icebergs and sea ice as these are the main features in the marine environment.

THE ANTARCTIC ICE SHEET

The Antarctic ice sheet has the form of two coalesced ice sheets and is basically

dome shaped (Fig. 4.1). The larger thicker East Antarctic Ice Sheet is classed as terrestrial because its base is resting on land which is mostly above sea level. (The mean elevation of bedrock in East Antarctica is 15 m, Drewry et al. 1982). The smaller, lower elevation West Antarctic Ice Sheet is a marine ice sheet because it is grounded mostly well below sea level (Fig. 4.1 inset). The mean elevation of bedrock here is 440 m below sea level (Drewry et al., 1982). The ice reaches 4,000

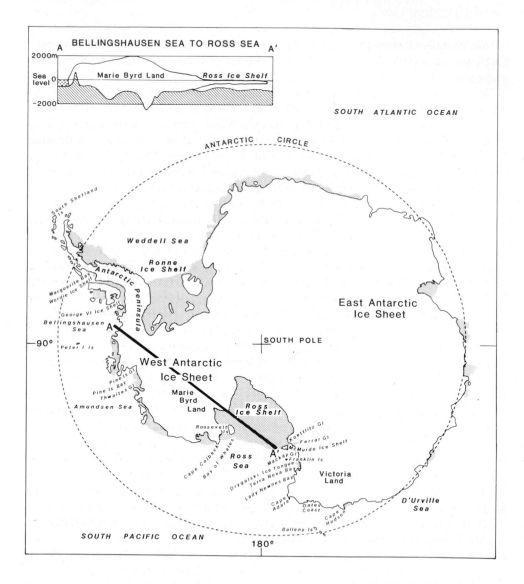

Fig. 4.1. Antarctica showing the extent of glacial ice in West and East Antarctica and ice shelves (shaded). The inset is a cross-section through the West Antarctic Ice Sheet which is grounded well below sea level in most places.

metres above sea level near the centre of East Antarctica, and 2,538 m below sea level in West Antarctica. Maximum measured thickness is up to 4,776 m (Drewry, 1983).

The Antarctic Ice Sheet is by far the largest body of ice on earth. It contains 29 million km³ of ice which is about 90% of the world's supply of ice and about 70% of all fresh water. Wind blown and fallen snow accumulates on the surface at a mean rate of about 150 kg m^{-2} yr^{-1} and is compacted with increasing depth of burial. True glacial ice is formed at depths between 40 m near the coast and 160 m inland. This ice moves under gravity generally downwards and outwards from the interior of Antarctica towards the coast, increasing from close to zero as ice divides to about 4 km yr^{-1} in the fastest outlet glaciers. Movement is concentrated in ice streams (Bentley, 1987) which flow at speeds typically about 1,000 m yr^{-1} into valley or outlet glaciers onshore, or ice shelves or tongues of glacial ice protruding offshore. Further details of the ice sheet are given in many publications including Gow (1965), Drewry (1983, 1986), Robin and Swithinbank (1987) and Robin (1988).

Because of its size, composition and geographic position, the ice sheet is an important feature of the earth. It affects global climate and sea level, as well as patterns of weather and ocean currents in the Southern Hemisphere. It is believed to respond slowly to change and may be a stabilizing component of the dynamic atmosphere–ocean–cryosphere system which dominates the global environment. At depth, it contains a detailed and probably unparalleled record of past climate, snowfall, air temperature, atmospheric gases and solids such as dust and volcanic products deposited over the last 200,000 years or so. It has been shown, for example, that present concentrations of CO_2 in the atmosphere are greater than they have been over the last 160,000 years, including the last interglacial period (Barnola et al., 1987). Measurement of impurities in the snow and ice including methane, lead and radioactive elements provides a guide and baseline to global pollution. Ice plays and has played an important role on our planet and Antarctica contains the only marine and terrestrial ice sheets of continental size enabling the study, dating, modelling and even prediction of a wide range of processes that occurred before, during and after world glaciations. Antarctica is also the largest collector and preserver of extraterrestrial matter (e.g., meteorites and dust) on earth. A proposal to bury high-level radioactive waste in the ice sheet (Zeller et al., 1974) was dropped when it was discovered that the base of the ice sheet is melting in places (Robin and Swithinbank, 1987).

The mechanisms by which the Antarctic ice sheet interacts with the rest of the globe, global processes and the biosphere are known in a general way but not always in detail (e.g., Deacon, 1984; Oerlemans and van der Veen, 1984). Ice sheets exist as a consequence of climate, geographic position and topography. Antarctica itself strongly influences climate through powerful feedback processes. The growth and decay of Antarctic ice perturb and are perturbed by the global energy and water budgets. The high albedo (a ratio of reflected and incident radiation) of snow and ice interact with various climate-determining factors to influence the response of the climate system. The accumulation of ice has completely changed the colour and relief of Antarctica burying whole mountain ranges. Being white and covered with snow, the ice sheet reflects back most incoming solar radiation and radiates long-wave radiation as well. A vast, powerful heat sink has therefore been created which helps drive both the poleward transport of energy and mass from the solar-heated equatorial regions and the circulation of atmosphere and oceans. Cyclonic storms and frontal waves are continually being formed in the circumpolar interface between cold Antarctic and warm, moist subtropical air masses. These storms orbit Antarctica from west to east and with the predominantly westerly wind they create north of 60°S, help drive the Antarctic Circumpolar Current which flows eastward around the continent (Deacon, 1984). Weather patterns and ocean currents far to the north are also affected. Seasonal changes driven by earth–sun relationships impact on these processes and directly influence biota, for example through animal and bird migrations.

Global sea levels are possibly the most spectacular linkage between Antarctica, the atmosphere and the oceans. The Antarctic Ice Sheet contains sufficient ice that, if melted, would raise sea level by about 73 m (Robin, 1986). A rapid or imminent rise of this order is most unlikely because of the slow response time of most of the ice sheet to atmospheric or climatic changes and the large amount of warming (up to 15°C; Robin, 1986) required. However, recent evidence suggests that growth and collapse of substantial parts of the ice sheet occur on time scales of a million years rather than ten million years as previously thought (Webb et al., 1984). On the other hand, the West Antarctic Ice Sheet is in close contact with the ocean via large ice shelves and could be susceptible to changes in it as well as climatic changes. The ice sheet has fluctuated in thickness and diameter on time scales of thousands to tens of thousands of years, especially between glacial and interglacial periods, but there is disagreement about the precise nature and scale of changes to it (Stuiver et al., 1981; Robin, 1986). Possible fluctuations over time periods of hundreds of years could produce catastrophic change in sea level of up to 6 m. This ice sheet is situated mainly in the Pacific Sector of the Antarctic region.

Such a catastrophic change in sea level could come about due to future climatic warming, particularly oceanic warming, induced by an increased concentration of gases in the atmosphere due to the 'greenhouse effect' (Anonymous, 1985a). Climatic warming is likely to initiate a small rise in sea level due to thermal expansion of the oceans and increased melting of glaciers outside the Antarctic (Robin, 1986). This could be of the order of 20–140 cm (Bolin et al., 1986). In theory, the higher sea level would tend to cause Antarctic glacial ice to be afloat slightly further south than it is now. In addition and possibly more important, higher sea temperatures may accelerate bottom melting and frontal decay of ice shelves, reducing the size of the shelves (Mercer, 1978; Anonymous, 1985a). While decay of floating ice does not alter sea level, it would reduce the friction between ice shelf and coast, lessening the back pressure which ice shelves exert "upstream" on the inland ice and increasing the flow of ice off the land (Thomas, 1979a). The ice sheet which most scientists believe at present is either in mass balance (that is, total accumulation equals total wastage) or slowly thickening may therefore begin to discharge faster and retreat in areas where it is presently resting on land far below sea level (Anonymous, 1985a). In theory, such a retreat could also start naturally due to a natural increase or decrease of continental ice or other glacial instabilities. Wilson (1964), Hughes (1973), Weertman (1974) and others have suggested or modelled ways in which the Antarctic ice sheet, particularly the West Antarctic Ice Sheet, may become unstable naturally. Such a retreat would represent a negative mass balance of (or a loss of mass from) the ice sheet.

A negative mass balance or retreat of a grounded ice sheet adds mass (water) to the ocean and atmosphere, causing sea level to rise. The ice in West Antarctica is grounded 500–1,200 m below sea level and the land beneath slopes down towards the ice sheet interior in many places (Fig. 4.1). These key factors may mean that a retreat of this nature once started may become irreversible leading to a disintegration of the West Antarctic Ice Sheet and a rise in sea level of a few metres.

There is no conclusive evidence that such a disintegration has ever occurred before (Robin, 1986; Robin and Swithinbank, 1987). Moreover, the likelihood, sequence or time scale of such events or counteracting processes (e.g., increased snowfall) are not certain (Robin, 1979; Anonymous, 1985a). Differences in snow accumulation rates over the Antarctic ice sheet during glacial and interglacial times may be more important to sea level because of the sheer size of the ice sheet and the amount of ice it contains. Corresponding differences in the elevation of the ice sheet surface may, therefore, account for much of the 7 m rise in sea level that is believed to have occurred during the last interglacial (Robin, 1986). In addition, it is believed that greenhouse-induced changes of melting and accumulation in the ice sheets of Greenland and Antarctica will tend to counterbalance each other. The topography and dynamics of ice sheet outlets may also stabilize discharge of the ice sheet (McIntyre, 1985). Further study is needed of the processes of ice dynamics involved in the Pacific Sector of the Antarctic. Ice streams draining the West Antarctic Ice Sheet and flowing into the Ross Ice Shelf are being studied for the part they may play in these processes (Anonymous, 1985a; Bentley et al., 1987).

The ice sheet–atmosphere–ocean interaction has other significant aspects. It drives the annual cycle of Antarctic sea ice which is important biologically, logistically and climatically. Formation and decay of this sea ice, melting at the base of ice shelves and iceberg decay affect salinity and hence the density and vertical circulation of Antarctic sea water, and especially the production of Antarctic Bottom Water. Higher Antarctic temperatures, melting and increased production of icebergs would tend to lessen surface seawater density and therefore alter the density structure of the world's oceans and deep circulation. A decrease in sea ice extent and increases in snowfall and the albedo of sea ice, all possible consequences of higher temperatures, would also alter the energy and moisture exchange between the ocean and atmosphere as well as between the subtropical and Antarctic regions.

It is still not clear whether the Antarctic ice sheet is growing or shrinking. The vast size of Antarctica plus a scarcity of data on snow accumulation, glacier flow and ice-shelf wastage have made it difficult to make an accurate assessment of the mass balance of the ice sheet. Climate change is underscoring the need to make a reliable assessment as a 1% change in the volume of the ice sheet is equivalent to a 70 cm rise or fall in sea level. Comparison of ice dynamic model predictions with layering observed in the West Antarctic Ice Sheet suggests that a large part of it has been stable with no signficant changes in mass balance, ice velocity or shape during the past 20,000–40,000 years (Whillans, 1976). Recent calculations for the whole Antarctic ice sheet suggest that total accumulation of snow and ice of about 2×10^3 km^3 yr^{-1} (2×10^{15} kg yr^{-1}) (Giovinetto and Bentley, 1985) is probably nearly balanced by the outflow and wastage. A discrepancy of between zero and plus 20% possibly implies a growing ice sheet (Budd and Smith, 1985). Proxy information from deep bore-holes in the ice sheet leads to similar conclusions (Robin and Swithinbank, 1987). However, the rate of iceberg formation may have been grossly underestimated and, if so, Antarctica may be losing, not gaining, mass (Orheim, 1985).

Research including the development of various computer models on Antarctic ice mass balance, dynamic behaviour, and decay as well as past climate and physical conditions in surrounding seas are continuing. By the year 2100, a global warming may have produced a sea level rise of an appreciable fraction of a metre (Anonymous, 1985a; Bolin et al., 1986) and probably a significant increase in Antarctic snowfall. Increased discharge of glacial ice from the West Antarctic Ice Sheet into the sea is therefore a possibility. Some workers believe that this may have already started on the coast of the Amundsen Sea (Stuiver et al., 1981; Hughes, 1983), although others indicate that nothing unusual is happening there (Crabtree and Doake, 1982; Robin, 1986).

ICE SHELVES AND OTHER MARINE GLACIERS

Glaciers in contact with the sea can be given a general name of marine glaciers. Such glaciers are significant because their ice discharge is sufficient to bring them into contact with the sea and its powerful eroding forces. Most Antarctic glaciers reach the sea and some extend many hundreds of kilometres offshore. The Pacific Sector of the Antarctic contains a representative selection of different types of marine glaciers, from ice shelves to fjord glaciers to those that terminate on beaches below the high tide mark. Examples and explanations of these are given below.

Ice shelves appear as quite flat bodies of generally snow-covered glacier ice floating over most of their area but grounded along coastlines and over other shallow parts of the seafloor. They are formed from glaciers, particularly ice streams flowing off grounded ice sheets to merge offshore, and by thickening of old sea ice in bays near such glaciers, particularly where this sea ice is anchored by islands or grounded icebergs. Ice shelves spread outwards over the sea driven by the flow of the feeder glaciers and by thinning under their own weight. Thicknesses range from as much as 1,300 m at their inland margins to less than 10 m at free floating seaward fronts. Where the ice runs aground or ice streams merge, the ice tends to thicken and may buckle as it deforms to produce pressure rollers (ridges) with wavelengths of a few hundred metres or less and amplitudes up to 15 m. Other undulations or depressions with wavelengths of 1–10 km and amplitudes up to 5 m are widespread due to complex but incompletely understood dynamics (Swithinbank and Zumberge, 1965; Thomas, 1979b; Collins and McCrae, 1985). In general, however, an ice shelf appears quite flat and covered with snow. Ross Ice Shelf, for instance, has a slope mostly between 1 in 10^3 and 1 in 10^4. Snow-free surfaces and exposures of sediment are rare. The western portion of the McMurdo Ice Shelf which is covered with seafloor debris through freeze on below and ablation above (Swithinbank, 1970), and the Nansen Ice Shelf in Terra Nova Bay, seem quite exceptional in this respect.

Ice shelves are nourished mainly by influx of glacier ice and by accumulation of snow and rime on their top surface. Seasonal stratification in the consolidating snow pack is normally conspicuous along ice fronts and crevasse walls. In circumstances where thermal conduction (e.g., western McMurdo Ice Shelf) or cold-water circulation allows it, water freezes on their underside.

Wastage is mainly by calving from seaward edges at rates averaging probably some hundreds of metres per year to produce icebergs. Bottom melting is also significant, especially near the ice front, with rates estimated to be up to 10 m yr^{-1} (Robin, 1979). Loss by surface ablation, particularly wind erosion, is relatively small but looks spectacular when blowing snow pours over the ice front.

Glacier (or ice) tongues are narrower protrusions of floating glacier ice usually formed by single or converging ice streams or glaciers laterally confined at the coast and discharging into the sea. These tongues extend seaward because discharge of ice across their landward grounding line (the junction between the grounded feeder glacier and the floating ice) is normally faster than the rate at which icebergs break off. Thinning proceeds seaward of the grounding line and towards the sides of the tongue. Serrations or "teeth", with horizontal amplitudes and wavelengths of some hundred metres, are common along the sides of many tongues (e.g., Erebus Glacier Tongue, Ross Island); their formation may be due to lateral deformation and expansion (due to relaxation of pressure) of the glacier as it moves out of the constraining valley causing periodic variations in ice discharge. Wastage is again mainly by calving and bottom melting but melting and sublimation from the surface of glacier tongues is probably much more widepread than on ice shelves as shown by the relative extents of snow-free firn (old snow that has been transformed into a denser form), ice and meltwater features. Some glacier tongues are actually partly grounded on the seafloor, often becoming quite crevassed and even breaking up to form an iceberg tongue (e.g., Thwaites Iceberg Tongue, Marie Byrd Land).

Other glaciers that reach the sea do not extend out past their valley sides or, in extreme cases, past the high-tide level because their rate of ablation in contact with the sea is relatively high compared to ice discharge. The combined rates of wave erosion, minor calving of ice, iceberg production, submarine melting and surface ablation equal the forward motion of the ice much closer to the grounding line than in ice shelves or glacier tongues. Marine glaciers flowing down valleys may terminate at the valley mouth (e.g., Pine Island Glacier, Marie Byrd Land) or part way up a fjord (e.g., Ferrar Glacier, South Victoria Land). Unconfined glacial ice (such as slow moving parts of a grounded ice sheet, glaciers which mantle low-lying coastal terrain, or lobe-shaped glaciers ending in the sea below coastal mountains) ends just seaward of the grounding line, or closer inshore.

Grounded ice cliffs are termed ice walls and rest on beaches or on the seafloor in water up to at least 400 m deep (Robin, 1979). Ice walls terminating on pebbly beaches exposed at low tide are typical of the western coast of the Antarctic Peninsula, from its northern tip to 69°S at the northern edge of the Wordie Ice Shelf.

The state of equilibrium, mass balance and seaward extent of floating glaciers are influenced by a variety of glacial and non-glacial processes acting over periods of a few hours (e.g., storm surges and tides) to many tens of thousands of years. Changes in the position and geometry of the grounding line, in ice thickness and in the position of the seaward margin, all reflect a complex inter-related set of processes. For instance, an ice shelf that is growing thicker may be due to : an increase in drainage from the ice sheet because of accelerated thinning or increased snowfall; a reduction in creep-rates and/or velocities in the ice shelf (caused by cooling temperatures or development of grounding areas offshore as sea level falls or the seabed rises); an increase in snowfall or a decreased rate of bottom melting on the ice shelf; and a decrease in the rate of iceberg production leading to growth in the ice shelf area and a greater mass for the ice shelf to push past its margins (Thomas, 1979b). Similar factors apply to glacier tongues.

Islands, headlands or shoal areas seem particularly important for pinning or protecting the seaward margins of some ice shelves and fjord glaciers and hence influencing their seaward extent (Fig. 4.1). Lateral stretching and thinning of the ice beyond these anchoring points leads to ice failure. A calving front is established near the pinning points along a relatively narrow zone across which outward ice flow is in approximate equilibrium with the rates of iceberg production and bottom melting. However, iceberg production is not regular in space or time and therefore the position of the calving front (or seaward end of an ice tongue) may vary (e.g., Fig. 4.2) over a cycle of several years or even decades, irrespective of more fundamental trends (if any) in mass balance. The length of ice tongues may vary even more noticeably due to their smaller size and perhaps a greater vulnerability to iceberg formation, for instance (Swithinbank et al., 1977) by impact of colliding icebergs.

A sustained retreat of an ice shelf is signficant because it produces an increased number of icebergs and possibly speeds up the drainage of the inland ice. Recent extreme retreats of possibly three ice shelves in the Pacific Sector illustrate that ice shelves are not perennial features. George VI Ice Shelf in the Antarctic Peninsula may have disappeared about seven thousand years ago (Clapperton and Sugden, 1982). Microfossils in seafloor sediments in Pine Island Bay, Marie Byrd Land, suggest that an expanded ice shelf was present a few hundred years ago (Kellogg and Kellogg, 1986) where only ice tongues and small ice shelves exist today. An ice shelf in Lady Newnes Bay, North Victoria Land, may have broken up and disappeared between 1912 and 1960 (Anonymous, 1966b) leaving a series of glacier tongues. The last Ice Age saw major advances and thickening of Antarctic ice shelves (Drewry, 1979; Stuiver et al., 1981).

Ice shelves are especially significant in the Pacific Sector of the Antarctic.

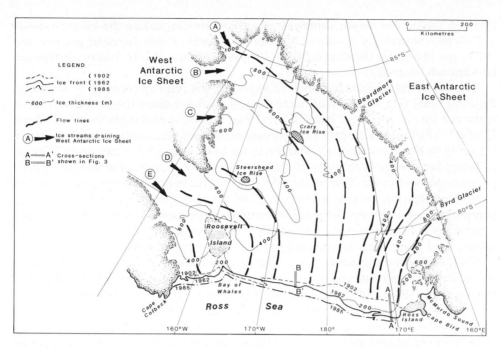

Fig. 4.2. The Ross Ice Shelf showing the position of the ice front in 1902, 1962 and 1985, as well as ice thickness contours and glacial flow-lines (adapted from Bentley et al., 1979; Neal, 1979; Jacobs et al., 1986).

Between Cape Adare in North Victoria Land and Marguerite Bay in the Antarctic Peninsula about 40% of the coastline is occupied by ice shelves. Ice shelves are barriers to southern movement of ships and are the major sources of Antarctic icebergs. The 750 km wide Ross Ice Shelf and the 70 km long Drygalski Ice Tongue (western Ross Sea) affect sea currents and sea ice distribution in parts of the Ross Sea.

Ice shelves, particularly large ones, are important because of their role in restricting the discharge of the Antarctic ice sheet. The Ross Ice Shelf is especially so because it buttresses the West Antarctic Ice Sheet.

Knowledge of ice shelves, including modelling of their flow and dynamics, has been reviewed by Swithinbank and Zumberge (1965), Thomas (1979b) and Barkov (1985). The next three sections look at the Ross Ice Shelf and some other marine glaciers in the Pacific Sector emphasizing their seaward margins and recent behaviour as these relate closely to the coastline of the Pacific Sector.

ROSS ICE SHELF

The Ross Ice Shelf is the largest ice shelf on earth having an area of 536,000 km^2 (twice the area of New Zealand) and a volume of 23,000 km^3 (Stuiver et al., 1981;

Drewry, 1983). The ice shelf drains 2.86 million km² (including the ice shelf itself) or 21% of Antarctica (Giovinetto and Bentley, 1985). Extensive field work in the 1970s, mainly under the Ross Ice Shelf Project (Thomas, 1979b), has made this the best known ice shelf.

The thickness of Ross Ice Shelf is anything but regular (Bentley et al., 1979; Bentley, 1985) (Fig. 4.2). Broad intrusions of thick ice enter the shelf from West Antarctic ice streams (e.g., B and C) and East Antarctic outlet glaciers (e.g., Byrd Glacier). Thicknesses are greater upstream of ice rises because these present major obstacles to flow. Roosevelt Island forces ice to flow around it, causing a thinner convergence zone downstream in which (and mainly because of which) the quasi-permanent indentation(s) known as the Bay of Whales is formed (Fig. 4.2). In this zone, compression, rifting and differential thinning cause probably the most complex topography on the shelf. Complex topography is also created where large glaciers float free of their bed as they flow into the ice shelf, forming poorly understood transverse crevasse patterns (Lucchita and Ferguson, 1986).

The shelf is thinnest along the ice front but here also thickness is quite variable. At present the ice front is consistently less than 100 m thick west of 173°E (Fig. 4.3) (Jacobs et al., 1986) and thicknesses of 70 to 133 m were quoted for Bay of Whales by Markov et al. (1970). The ice front is thickest in the central portion between 178°E and 167°W (Bentley et al., 1979) — but even here it may not be much thicker than 100 m after periods of prolonged basal melting in places (Fig. 4.3). The ice

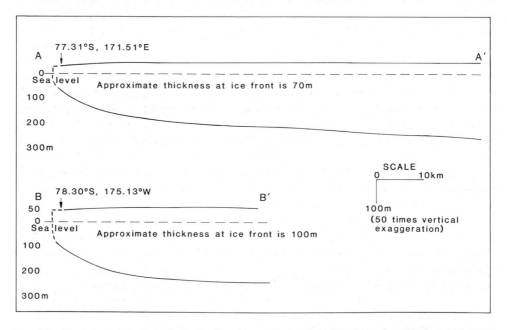

Fig. 4.3. Two cross-sections through the seaward margin of the Ross Ice Shelf showing the pronounced thinning which occurs towards the ice front (drawn from radio echo sounding data obtained in 1974 by the Scott Polar Research Institute, courtesy of P. Cooper). The positions of sections are shown on Fig. 4.2.

shelf generally slopes down towards the ice front (Fig. 4.3) because of loss of ice at depth.

The height of the ice front above sea level varies from a few metres to about 50 metres (Wright and Priestley, 1922) reflecting ice front thickness and vertical profile, ice shelf density and hydrostatic forces. Shabtaie and Bentley (1982) derived buoyancy relationships between height and thickness for the ice shelf and icebergs from it. Such relationships may be least accurate for thin ice fronts (and icebergs) where basal melting has removed the densest basal ice accentuating the effect of density variations in the snow and firn above.

The dynamics and mass balance of Ross Ice Shelf have been major themes of study. Glacier flow lines (Fig. 4.2) and velocity vectors have been mapped (Bentley et al., 1979; Neal, 1979) and show that velocity increases to a maximum of 1.1 km yr^{-1} in the centre of the shelf at the ice front. Surface accumulation has been determined by Clausen et al. (1979) and varies from 0.1 m yr^{-1} (water equivalent) in the interior to a maximum of 0.2 to 0.3 m yr^{-1} along the ice front. Total ice input has been estimated to be between 224 and 327 km^3 yr^{-1} (Bentley, 1985; Doake, 1985). Bottom mass balance is complex with some evidence for saline bottom ice due to brine infiltration and bottom freezing (Neal, 1979; Zotikov et al., 1980). There is also good evidence for bottom melting especially near the ice front, for instance near Ross and Roosevelt Islands (Bentley et al., 1979; Neal, 1979; MacAyeal and Thomas, 1986). Modelling and mass balance considerations suggest that these melt rates are as large as 2.5 m yr^{-1} at the ice front decreasing to ± 0.1 m yr^{-1} 100 km inland (Thomas and MacAyeal, 1982; Jacobs et al., 1986). Basal melting may total 60 to 155 km^3 yr^{-1} similar to the estimated 150 km^3 yr^{-1} lost on average by calving and minor attrition (Doake, 1985; Jacobs et al., 1986; Bentley et al., 1987). However, these estimates are not yet accurate enough to give a reliable estimate of mass balance.

Ice thickness patterns and basal mass balance vary so much across the shelf that it is not likely to be in equilibrium everywhere (Bentley, 1985). Dynamic changes may occur on a time scale of a century or so. However, the shelf is believed to be in, or close to, steady state (i.e., accumulation rate, thickness, velocity, temperature do not change with time) and has been so for perhaps 200 years in the east and 1,500 to 2,500 years elsewhere (Thomas and MacAyeal, 1982; Jezek and Bentley, 1984; Bentley, 1985).

Nevertheless, the position of the ice front has moved north over recent years, although the general trend of its coastline has been maintained (Jacobs et al., 1986) (Fig. 4.2). The ice front has reached its most northern point (77°10'S) in recorded history (i.e., since 1841) at longitude 170°30'E. The Bay of Whales has persisted for most, if not all, of this period.

Between 1962 and 1985, the whole ice front moved an average of 19.3 km north while between 170°E and 178°E the advance was 13.9 km (Jacobs et al., 1986). The average annual rate of advance in this period agrees quite well with measured ice velocities indicating that no major calving has occurred in those 23 years.

Major calving is propably episodic with intervals of several decades, when hundreds of cubic kilometres of ice shelf break off. This happened in late September–early October 1987 when a giant iceberg (B–9) calved from the eastern

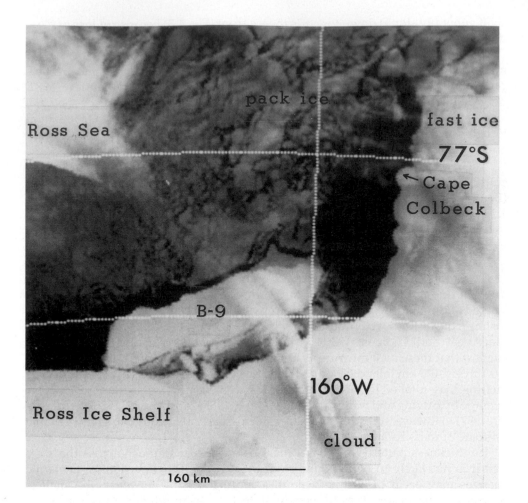

Fig. 4.4. NOAA–9 satellite infrared image of the 154 km long iceberg B–9 on 9 November 1987, four weeks after its separation from the eastern front of the Ross Ice Shelf. Several other bergs up to 20 km long that calved at the same time can be seen between B–9 and the ice shelf. These had drifted as far west as Ross Island (approximately 600 km) by March 1988 whereas B–9 was only 150 km west-north-west of its calving site at that time. By May 1988, B–9 was close to the north-eastern boundary of the Ross Sea at the edge of the continental shelf along which flows a strong north-west setting current. This image, obtained by U.S. Navy scientists at McMurdo Station, was supplied by the Antarctic Research Center at Scripps Institution of Oceanography.

front of the ice shelf (Anonymous, 1987b) (Fig. 4.4). The iceberg contained about 1,100 km³ of ice which is many times the average annual production of the Ross Ice Shelf. The former Bay of Whales feature was destroyed during the calving but a new indentation was formed some 40 km further east and a similar distance south of the old ice front. It is possible that such a large and sudden mass loss could affect the dynamics of the ice shelf upstream of the calving site.

Minor calving occurs more frequently, probably many times each year. Jacobs et al. (1986) considered that such calving has been most prevalent west of 178°E. About 0.3–0.4 km yr[-1] appears to calve off this 200 km length of the ice front (including minor attrition) which represents probably less than 10 km³ yr[-1] (from Fig. 4.3). Averaged over the whole ice front, recent calving before September 1987 appears to have totalled much less than the estimated 150 km³ yr[-1] required to maintain a stationary ice front assuming realistic melt rates (Doake, 1985; Jacobs et al., 1986). Clearly, the ice front does not maintain a precise equilibrium position.

OTHER MARINE GLACIERS

The ice front of three other ice shelves in the Pacific Sector have retreated in recent years. The fronts of the Wordie and George VI Ice Shelves on the west coast of the Antarctic Peninsula have retreated by several kilometres over the last 10 to 30 years (Doake, 1982). About one-third of the Wordie Ice Shelf has disappeared. This behaviour may be due to a warmer climate and decreasing snowfall in recent years, although glaciers in parts of the Peninsula are still thickening apparently in response to a high accumulation rate experienced several hundred years ago. It is, therefore, not possible to attribute the retreat unambiguously to disintegration of the ice sheet in the Antarctic Peninsula (Doake, 1985). Similarly, the retreat of the northern margin of the McMurdo Ice Shelf in the south-west Ross Sea, shown in maps by, for example, Prebble (1968) and Pyne et al. (1985), may be due simply to short-term disequilibrium between ice input, bottom melting, and the rates of calving. The Nansen Ice Shelf in western Terra Nova Bay is presently advancing after a calving event between 1957 and 1973 removed about 15% of the ice shelf area, as indicated by comparing photographically derived maps and Landsat imagery. These four ice shelves exist near the limits for their climatic and oceanographic environments and should be monitored for possible response to climate change (Mercer, 1978; Doake, 1982).

The dynamic behaviour of these ice shelves is different from that of Ross Ice Shelf. Descriptions in Swithinbank (1970) and Doake (1982, 1985) suggest that brine percolation, surface and bottom melting, and calving are more significant relative to the size of the ice shelf than in the case of the large ice shelf. Ice velocities are also less than on the Ross Ice Shelf (Heine, 1967; Swithinbank, 1970; Doake, 1985; J.R. Keys, unpubl. data).

The Erebus Glacier Tongue is the most studied ice tongue in the Pacific Sector. Holdsworth (1978, 1982) has described its morphology, dynamics and possible modes of calving. The tongue, currently 14 km long (1988), thins from 300 m thick and 2.8 km wide at the grounding line on Ross Island to 60 m thick and 1 km wide at its snout. Surface densities vary from that of snow to ice (at 0.87 ± 0.02 g cm[-3]) while surface mass balance is calculated to be ± 0.1 m yr[-1] along the tongue. Bottom melting appears to predominate and derived rates are up to 4 myr[-1] on the base and 10 m yr[-1] on the sides. Ice velocity near the centre-line increases from

90 m yr[-1] near the hinge-line where the ice flows off Ross Island, to 150 m yr[-1] at the snout. The tongue underwent its most recent major calving in the early 1940s and has been advancing at an accelerating rate since then, with speeds similar to the ice velocity at the snout (from Holdsworth, 1985).

Various maps and recent observations of the snow-covered Drygalski Ice Tongue in the western Ross Sea suggest that this 70 km long, 20 km wide tongue has advanced in recent years at a rate similar to the speed of its ice (730 m yr[-1]) about 50 km from the snout) (Holdsworth, 1985). Up-warping of floating "capes" is prominent along the northern margin of the tongue, indicative of strong wave action or surface currents causing ablation near sea level to exceed melting at depth.

The tongue of the Thwaites Glacier in the Amundsen Sea has undergone complex behaviour in recent times. Visual imagery from Kosmos–226 satellite suggests that the glacier tongue apparently doubled in length between 1961 and 1969 to about 200 km, but also broke off and buckled laterally towards the west in this period (Savatyugin, 1970; Holdsworth, 1985). A glacier tongue 70 km long was present in 1972 with an iceberg tongue 130 km long immediately to the north. This iceberg tongue appears to be rotating anticlockwise about a probable pinning point roughly 200 km from the glacier's grounding line (Hughes, 1983). Glacier flow and the west-setting Antarctic coastal current (East Wind Drift) may be causing this rotation. The glacier tongue has advanced since 1972 apparently at a rate similar to the surge-like speed of its ice near the ice front (3.7 km yr[-1]) (Lindstrom and Tyler, 1984).

Complex, dynamic behaviour of the Thwaites Glacier and its neighbour, the Pine Island Glacier, in the Amundsen Sea is not inconsistent with the theories of Hughes (1973, 1983) linking these glaciers to a drop in the level of their drainage basins and collapse of the West Antarctic Ice Sheet. These fast-moving glaciers also seem to have high basal melt rates which might accelerate decay of ice shelves formed in the embayment there or prevent them forming at all. However, radio echo sounding shows that the grounding line of the Pine Island Glacier is held at the foot of a rock bar 200 m high which, together with simple modelling, suggests that the glacier is stable and not undergoing any unusual behaviour (Crabtree and Doake, 1982; Doake, 1985). This also applies to the Thwaites Glacier (McIntyre, 1985).

Nevertheless, neither glacier is necessarily in equilibrium. If either of their grounding lines began a rapid retreat, they could accelerate their drainage and possibly destabilize the West Antarctic Ice Sheet. Modelling has suggested that it could take a few hundred to a few thousand years for the Ice Sheet to collapse in this way (Anonymous, 1985a), but estimates are tentative because of the lack of knowledge of the dynamics of fast-moving ice streams (Robin, 1986).

ICEBERGS

Icebergs are masses of ice that have broken away from marine glaciers. They have a wide variety of shapes and sizes, depending on source and decay process and they may be floating or grounded on the seafloor. By definition, icebergs show more than 5 m of ice above sea level and are 100 m² or more in area. The longest iceberg ever recorded was about 180 km long (Wordie and Kempe, 1933). Its mass would have been about 10^{12} tonnes. The median width of all Antarctic icebergs is probably less than 200 m, although tabular bergs are larger (Budd et al., 1980; Neshyba, 1980; Keys, 1984; Pyne, 1986).

Icebergs are the largest objects to have floated in the sea and can be a serious hazard to shipping. Three ships are thought to have sunk or been written off after striking Antarctic icebergs in the last 100 years (Table 4.1) and many others have been similarly threatened. Production of icebergs is the main way the Antarctic ice sheet loses mass, so it is important to understand and quantify iceberg sources, production, total mass, distribution and decay. Icebergs cause local mixing of the water through which they drift and in pack ice can create open water in their wake. Speculation persists about their possible future use as sources of fresh water (e.g., Weeks and Campbell, 1973; Lovering and Prescott, 1979; Hantke, 1986). Various aspects of Antarctic icebergs have been reviewed by Weeks and Mellor (1978), Schwerdtfeger (1979) and Kristensen (1983). This section examines the life history and some other characteristics of bergs in the Pacific Sector.

The mean annual production of Antarctic icebergs has been estimated to be 0.6–2.3 x 10^{15} kg or 750–3,000 km³ (Orheim, 1985). This estimate is made complicated by the large size of the Antarctic, complex iceberg distribution and uncertainties in decay rates, but is equivalent to some hundreds of thousands of bergs. Production in the Pacific Sector is probably almost half of this Antarctic total. Most icebergs (perhaps 60–80% by volume) separate from the flat-topped ice shelves. Tabular icebergs are, therefore, common (e.g., Wright and Priestley, 1922). In addition, a significant proportion of bergs come from ice streams and active outlet glaciers.

Icebergs are produced (berged or calved) by different mechanisms. These are still not completely understood but are believed to be affected by : weaknesses in ice shelves or glacier tongues including surface and bottom crevasses and hinge-lines; lateral and vertical stresses developed during glacial thinning, flotation, vertical vibration, horizontal bending and impact of colliding icebergs; ocean swells, storm surges, tsunamis and tides; seafloor or shore topography (e.g., Wright and Priestley, 1922; Swithinbank et al., 1977: Holdsworth, 1978, 1985; Robin, 1979; Shabtaie and Bentley, 1982; Keys, 1984). Different mechanisms and different marine glaciers may produce icebergs at different rates and sizes.

Icebergs are most numerous near the coast but there is considerable spatial and temporal variation in their concentration. In the Pacific Sector, the highest concentrations of drifting bergs occur in the Amundsen and Bellingshausen Seas (Romanov, 1984) (Fig. 4.5). Average coastal concentrations vary spatially between about 5 and 9 bergs detected by radar per 1,000 km². Maximum concentrations of drifting bergs in the western Ross Sea are at least as high as 25 bergs per 1,000 km². However, well over 200 bergs might be visible by eye in the most concentrated areas (Deacon, 1984) near active iceberg-producing glaciers and because of icebergs drifting in clusters or collecting (grounded) on shallows (Keys, 1983, 1985). Very high concentrations, up to four bergs per square kilometre have been

TABLE 4.1

Ships sunk or wrecked by ice in the Antarctic (from Ingram and Wheatley, 1961; Anonymous, 1979; and the Alexander Turnbull Library, Wellington, N.Z.).

Vessel	Route and general location	Cargo	Incident
H.M.S. Guardian	U.K. to Botany Bay, Australia	?	Seriously damaged and abandoned after colliding with iceberg in dark fog, 24 Dec. 1789.
Matoaka (1,110 t gross)	Lyttelton, N.Z. to London	Wool, gold, 45 passengers	Lost at sea in 1869 [1]. May have struck ice.
Marlborough (1,210 t)	Lyttelton, N.Z. to London	Frozen meat and wool	Presumed to have struck an iceberg and sunk near Cape Horn, 1890.
Antarctic	Antarctic Sound to Snow Hill Island, Antarctic Peninsula	Expedition	Crushed by pack ice and sunk on 12 Feb. 1903 after being beset for 5 weeks in the north-west Weddell Sea.
Havfruen (1,321 t)	South Georgia to Sandwich Islands (on tow)	?	Sunk by ice in the south-west Atlantic Ocean, 3 Dec. 1911.
Endurance (354 t)	South Georgia to Weddell sea	Expedition	Crushed by pack ice and sunk on 21 Nov. 1915 after being beset for 44 weeks in the Weddell Sea [2].
Garthforce (1,972 t)	Liverpool to Newcastle, Australia	?	Severely damaged after striking iceberg near Marion Island. Sold as a hulk 28 Jan. 1922.
Professor Gruvel (3,363 t)	Sandefjord to South Shetland	General	Struck by ice and foundered off South Shetlands, 12 Oct. 1927.
Southern Queen (5,739 t)	?	Whale oil	Wrecked by ice off the South Orkneys, 24 Feb. 1928.
Gotland II (1,500 t)	Wellington to Yule Bay	Expedition	Crushed and sunk between pack and fast ice in Yule Bay, Oates Coast, 17 Dec. 1981.
Southern Quest (328 t)	Hobart to McMurdo Sound	Expedition	Caught and sunk by pack ice near Beaufort Island, south-west Ross Sea, 11 Jan. 1986.
Bahia Paraiso (9,600 t)	Marguerite Bay to Esperanza	Expedition, 82 tourists	Ran aground and sank off Anvers Island, off Antarctic Peninsula, 31 Jan. 1989

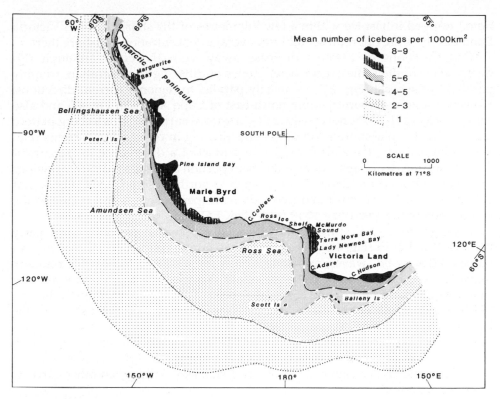

Fig. 4.5. Distribution and mean concentration of icebergs in the Pacific Sector (after Romanov, 1984). Various zones delineate areas where a given number of icebergs per 1,000 km² of ocean can be expected.

1　Other vessels lost at sea from unexplained causes plying this or similar routes were the *Glenmark*, 968 tonnes (1872), *Loch Dee*, 738 tonnes (1883), *Kilmery*, 813 tonnes (1882), *Loch Fyne*, 1,290 tonnes (1883), *Dunedin*,1,341 tonnes, (1890). Other vessels not involved in the New Zealand trade would have been lost on other shipping routes in the Southern Hemisphere. Ice could have been involved.

2　Numerous ships have been beset by pack ice and some were damaged or severely threatened before escaping.

In the Pacific Sector, the *Belgica* (trapped for one year in the Bellingshausen Sea from March 1898), *Aurora* (10 months in the Ross Sea and south-west Pacific Ocean from May 1915), *Ob* (3 months off Oates Land from April 1973), and *Mikhail Somov* (8 weeks off Oates Land in 1977, and 19 weeks east of the Ross Sea from March 1985) gave useful information on ice movement and currents as they drifted with the pack. Other vessels have been stuck for shorter periods where pack ice concentration is high, for instance early in the navigation season (e.g., *Gotland II*, for several days from 23 November 1981 north of the Ross Sea; *John Biscoe* for a few days from 13 November 1985 off the western coast of the Antarctic Peninsula) or in areas of persistent pack ice (e.g., *Polar Sea* once or twice in late February 1984 in the Amundsen Sea).

noted trapped in fast ice within a few kilometres of the shore of South Victoria Land but these are not representative of average concentrations offshore there.

Concentrations of icebergs decrease away from the coast although this decrease is not the same everywhere. Zones of differing concentration, roughly parallel to the coast (Fig. 4.5) are mostly parallel to regional current directions. However, a zone shown trending north-east of Cape Adare in Fig. 4.5 and also shown by Keys (1983) is not consistent with known currents. This iceberg pattern may be due to an accumulation of icebergs drifting in converging currents (Fig. 4.6). Alternatively, the zone could be an artifact of a divergence in the coastal current north-east of Cape Adare as the main portion of the coastal current swings to the west around the Cape. A zone north to north-west of Cape Colbeck, not shown on Fig. 4.5, is illustrated by O. Orheim (pers. comm.) and is due to the subdivision of the East Wind Drift there (Fig. 4.6) .

Icebergs move around the continent initially in coastal currents, particularly the East Wind Drift (Fig. 4.6). They drift in an erratic fashion because of current eddies, tides, wind, waves, and the Coriolis force due to the earth's rotation. However, the nett drifts of icebergs follow the west-setting currents at rates thought to be between 50% and 75% of the speed of the surface currents (Tchernia, 1977; Swithinbank et al., 1977; Tchernia and Jeannin, 1983). Offshore in the Pacific Sector, measured speeds average 3–12 km day^{-1} (0.03–0.14 m sec.$^{-1}$). Various studies have shown that ocean currents are more important than winds (even strong ones) in determining directions of movement (e.g., Tchernia and Jeannin, 1983) but wind can be significant (Veskin, 1982), especially when other currents are slow or absent.

Near shore, average speeds are much slower and the bergs frequently run aground. The giant berg B-9 averaged a little over 1 km day^{-1} during the first three months of its drift in which time it collided with the ice shelf (Keys, 1988, 1989) (Fig. 4.4). The furthest distance a positively-identified berg has travelled in one open-water season northwards up the coast of South Victoria Land is only about 100 km, which gives a minimum estimate of iceberg drift rate, including any time spent aground, of 1–2 km day^{-1} (Keys and Fowler, 1989). This is about half the mean current speed inferred by Lewis and Perkins (1985) for the north-setting current there. These speeds are much slower than the drift of some icebergs that kept apace with the *Aurora* while it was beset in pack ice in western Ross Sea in 1915 (8 km day^{-1}, from Wordie, 1921). Wright and Priestley (1922) reported that some icebergs moved as fast as 2 m sec.$^{-1}$ for short periods in coastal areas.

There are a number of places around the continent where drifting icebergs turn north from the coastal zone (Tchernia and Jeannin, 1983). In the Pacific Sector, the best defined of these appears to be north of Cape Colbeck east of Ross Sea (Fig. 4.6) where the continental shelf break starts trending north-west and so subdivides the East Wind Drift. Consequently, relatively few bergs seem to enter Ross Sea from the east, most instead being carried northwards. Thereafter, they are carried into the great Antarctic Circumpolar Current (West Wind Drift) with sinuous but generally eastward drifts. A similar north-turning zone is located north of Cape Hudson (Fig. 4.6) west of Cape Adare on the Oates Coast (Tchernia and Jeannin,

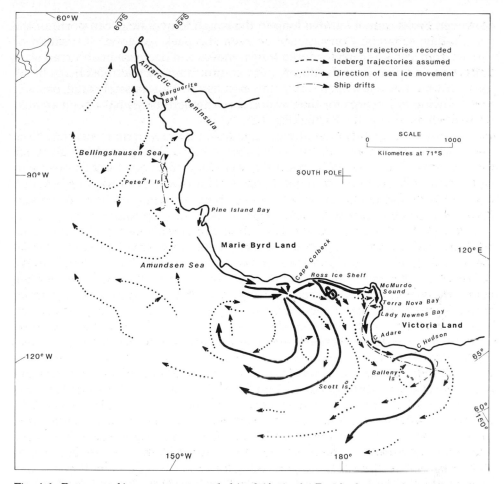

Fig. 4.6. Patterns of ice movement and ship drifts in the Pacific Sector, adapted from Elliot (1977), Swithinbank et al. (1977), Tchernia and Jeannin (1983), Romanov (1984), Sturman and Anderson (1986), Keys and Fowler (1989), R. Moritz, D. Harrowfield and B. McIntosh (pers. comm.) and miscellaneous ice charts from the U.S. Joint Ice Center.

1983). Icebergs may also turn north from the coast in the Bellingshausen Sea in a possible current gyre revealed by the year-long drift of the barque *Belgica* beset in the ice pack from March 1898. Cape Colbeck, Cape Hudson and Thurston Island may all mark places where iceberg populations are subdivided by regional current patterns and only those icebergs driven by local and tidal currents mix across them.

The extreme northern limit reached by icebergs in European history (c. 200 years) is approximately 40°S in the Pacific Ocean near the Subtropical Convergence (Brodie and Dawson, 1971; Burrows, 1976). Furrows gouged on the Chatham Rise by grounding icebergs imply that bergs were common in New Zealand waters during the Pleistocene Glaciation (Kudrass and von Rad, 1984).

However, bergs cannot survive long in the rough temperate ocean north of the present-day Antarctic Convergence or even the pack ice zone. Cessation of signals from icebergs carrying radio transponders and decrease in observed sizes of icebergs in open water (I. Allison, pers. comm.) suggest that most bergs break up soon after they reach open water; this creates a serious, possibly fatal, obstacle to the towing of icebergs for their water. Few modern bergs have been sighted north of about 55°S in the Pacific (Fig. 4.5).

Icebergs decay mainly by splitting, wave action at the waterline, melting below the waterline and calving off the sides above the waterline (Budd et al., 1980; Orheim, 1980; Keys and Williams, 1984; Hamley and Budd, 1986), probably in that order. Observations near the coast of south-west Ross Sea suggest that splitting is caused mainly by stresses developed during grounding on the sea-floor, collisions by other bergs and upwards buoyancy on underwater portions (J.R. Keys, unpubl.). Offshore, stresses induced by ocean waves (Wadhams et al., 1983) are probably more important. Calving occurs when waves erode notches at the waterline, undercutting the ice at about 100 m yr^{-1} (Keys and Williams, 1984). This often leads to caves, arches and wave-cut platforms at the waterline. Melting below the waterline is enhanced by roll-over and wallowing of bergs, strong currents and higher sea temperatures. Iceberg melt rates, which have been estimated from measurements of side melting to be about 20 m yr^{-1} at −1°C (Keys and Williams, 1984), are therefore much faster than basal melt rates of ice shelves in water of the same temperature.

The life expectancy and residence time of icebergs depend on the mechanisms and rates of decay, drift speeds and on their initial size. Various tabular bergs drifing in the Pacific Sector were tracked by Tchernia and Jeannin (1983) and the U.S. Joint Ice Center (R. Godin, pers. comm.) for up to two years but their average lifetime is thought to be longer than this (Hult and Ostrander, 1973) (some icebergs elsewhere in the Antarctic have been tracked for several years, Swithinbank et al., 1977). The sparse data given above suggest that it might take one to two years for bergs to drift up the 800 km long Victoria Land coast of Ross Sea. In general, the half-life of bergs near the coast is possibly two to five years but only a year for bergs that have drifted north from the coast (Orheim, 1985). For example, the average half-life before breakage or roll-over of bergs less than 1,000 m wide in water of about + 1°C (north of the coastal zone) is estimated to be about 0.2 years (Hamley and Budd, 1986). However, bergs grounded near the coast have been known to survive for many years, perhaps decades, in the cold water there, especially when they are locked in fast sea ice for most of the year and protected from the effects of waves.

In coastal waters in the Ross Sea Sector, icebergs commonly ground in water depths less than 200 m, although a few ground in up to 300 m. About 75% of 285 bergs trapped in fast ice near the coast in the south-west Ross Sea were aground (Keys, 1985). Soundings, using a weighted wire line deployed through holes drilled in fast ice beside grounded bergs there, revealed water depths from 10 to 273 m. Icebergs in seaward extensions of fast ice off Cape Colbeck and Grant Island further east (Hult and Ostrander, 1973) were in about 200 m of water and were also probably aground. Stationary icebergs observed in open water off Cape

Adare Peninsula and Franklin Island were also in less than 200 m (Keys, 1983). No bergs have been observed grounded in water deeper than 300 m in this area. The draft of most modern bergs in Ross Sea is therefore probably less than 300 m.

Icebergs having drafts of more than 300 m may occur in the Ross Sea, for example some derived from the thick Mackay Glacier Tongue (Keys, 1983). Measured thicknesses (Bentley et al., 1979; Jacobs et al., 1986) and post-measurement deformation of the source area in Ross Ice Shelf of the giant berg B–9 suggest that its maximum draft may be about 300 m. Fragmentation and tilting of B–9 could produce bergs with drafts deeper than this. Its slow and seemingly erratic behaviour while over a deep submarine bank at 77°40'S, 166°50'W suggests that it was temporarily grounded there (Navy Polar Oceanographic Center, written communication, February 1988). Water depths between 400 and 500 m have been measured in the area (Davey and Cooper, 1987) so an alternative reason for its erratic behaviour may be a lack of strong currents over the bank.

About one-third of the bergs near the coast of south-west Ross Sea are tabular (Keys, 1985). Irregular shaped and rounded bergs are present in similar proportions. Close inspection indicates that about one-third of all bergs contain some dirt in the full range of environments for glacial sediments. About half of the tabular bergs are quite featureless in that they have no distinguishing upper surface that could be used to trace their source.

About 40% of the tabular bergs are less than 100 m thick and probably come from Ross Ice Shelf. The water depth beside grounded icebergs, together with their height (freeboard) give an indication of their thickness. Table 4.2 lists 10 tabular bergs representative of those in south-west Ross Sea which have a stratified snow pack and a planar upper (top) surface. The composition and density of these bergs are similar to that of Ross Ice Shelf (Keys, 1985) whose thickness at the ice front is thinner than 100 m west of 173°E (e.g., Fig. 4.3) and in Bay of Whales (see above). Calving of the ice shelf in recent years has probably been most prevalent west of 178°E (Jacobs et al., 1986 — see above). Most bergs calved from the Ross Ice Shelf probably drift westwards, parallel to and within about 100 km of the ice front (Keys and Fowler, in press). It is therefore highly likely that most of the bergs listed in Table 4.2 came from Ross Ice Shelf west of 178°E.

It is unlikely many tabular bergs of similar thickness come from sources east of Cape Colbeck as the subdivision of the East Wind Drift north of this cape (Fig. 4.6) would tend to prevent this. However, the Sulzberger Ice Shelf immediately to the east of Ross Sea is probably up to about 40 to 70 m thick near the ice front (Anderson, this volume) and may have produced some of the bergs present.

These "Ross Ice Shelf" tabular bergs are in a minority near the South Victoria Land coast. Only about 10% of the bergs trapped in fast sea ice near this coast in November 1984 were tabular bergs which appeared to have been little decayed and therefore must have been derived relatively recently from the Ross Ice Shelf west of 178°E. The composition and shapes of a further 30% of bergs suggest that they too had been derived from the ice shelf. Their combined volume was estimated to be in the order of 0.1 km^3, only 1% of the 10 km^3 that may be calved annually on average from this part of the ice shelf (see Ross Ice Shelf, above). It is

TABLE 4.2

Estimated thicknesses of some grounded tabular icebergs containing stratified snow pack and having planar upper surfaces. These icebergs are thought to have been calved from the western front of the Ross Ice Shelf.

Iceberg Number (1984/85 season)	Maximum Height (m)	Mean Height (m)	Approx. Water Depth (m)	Estimated Maximum Thickness (m)
CI–9	36	20–25	65	100
CR–6	15	15	40	55
CR–8	30	26	50	80
CR–32	30	10–15	60	90
CR–33	24	20	50	70
BS–11	24	15	30	50
BS–85	22	20	30	50
BS–93	30	25	45	75
BS–94	35	25	45	80
BS–97	25	10–15	30	55

therefore likely that only a very small proportion of bergs calved from the ice shelf are grounded near shore.

Other tabular bergs in western Ross Sea have uneven upper surfaces and many of these are composed of stratified firn and ice without snow. Most of these bergs calved from glacier tongues, piedmont and other marine glaciers along the Victoria Land coast (Keys, 1985).

Iceberg populations are therefore complex. They are composed of bergs derived from sources both near and far and vary in concentration depending on sources, production rates, drift patterns, grounding and decay.

SEA ICE

Sea ice is frozen sea water and in the Antarctic is mostly mobile pack ice less than one year old. When the sea surface begins to freeze, from about mid February on, small needles or platelets of ice appear, growing and agglomerating to form a slush known as *grease ice*. As it thickens, this slush coagulates and breaks up under the influence of waves and wind into intermediate soft and hard plates which collide with each other and may form *pancake ice*. Still thickening, these alternately freeze together and break up forming even larger, still thickening slabs of ice called *floes*. Colliding floes may raft over one another when still thin or form *pressure ridges* of ice rubble along the colliding margin, particularly in shear zones near the coast. The whole accumulation of broken sea ice is termed pack ice and collectively referred to as the *ice pack* (or simply *pack*).

In most places, Antarctic pack is not constrained by land and so divergent motion is common. Floes move under the influence of wind, storms and currents. Cracks and linear openings (*leads*) formed between (or through) floes, and non-linear openings (*polynyas*) are sites of rapid formation of new ice during autumn, winter and spring. The areal ratio of ice to water is greatest during winter (when ice concentration is mostly nine-tenths or more) and least in late summer. Other characteristics of Antarctic pack ice include an extensive snow cover, a high pro-portion of fine-grained spicule and plate crystals, a frequent underlayer of uncon-solidated ice platelets, algae growth within the ice and a general lack of surface melt features (Lewis and Weeks, 1970; Gow et al., 1982; Jacka et al., 1987). These characteristics are in large part due to the dynamic and climatic regimes pro-ducing divergent ice motion, lead formation, ice formation and snowfall.

In the Pacific Sector (160°E to 60°W), the pack ice reaches a maximum extent averaging 6.3 million km² by late September (U.S. Navy, 1985), one-third of the total Antarctic ice pack extent. By the end of the growth season, undeformed sea ice has thickened to about 3 m at 77°S (Budd, 1981). Floe size and thickness probably vary greatly at all locations but generally increase from north to south (Gilbert and Erickson, 1977; Jacka et al., 1987). Thickness averaged over time and space perhaps 0.5 to 1.5 m (Budd, 1986b) because of continual formation of leads, new ice and northwards advection of ice. From October to February, the pack decays by breakage, dispersal and melting to a minimum extent of about 1.5 million km² in the Pacific Sector. Most of the ice is therefore less than one year old (*first-year* ice).

Other forms of sea ice also occur in the Pacific Sector. *Fast ice* (ice in a sheet attached to the shore) develops along most of the coastline during winter, especially in coastal indentations sheltered from the wind and waves. The fast ice belt extends up to 150 km offshore near Russkaya Station (74°50'S, 137°E) (Romanov, 1984). Most of this fast ice has broken up and dispersed by February, except in some coastal indentations some years. *Second-year* (or multi-year) pack ice is found in areas of pack which survive the summer melting (Fig. 4.7). It there-fore tends to be thicker than first-year ice and takes longer to melt. An *ice-foot* consisting of frozen sea water with blocks of sea ice and glacial ice, or *ice-push* ridges of heaped up sea ice, develop along rocky shores throughout the year but most invariably melt in summer.

Antarctic sea ice has a significant effect on the climate, weather, seas, and ecosystems of the region and human activities there. The seasonal sea ice cover varying so much between light coloured ice and dark ocean or thin ice modifies the surface albedo and energy exchange affecting the earth's heat balance in the Antarctic region. Sea ice acts as an insulator between the cold polar atmosphere and the relatively warm ocean, so moderating the exchange of heat and moisture between them, and hence affecting their characteristics, particularly of the upper layer of the ocean and deep oceanic circulation. Snow-covered pack ice reflects most of the incoming solar radiation, amplifying the cooling effect of the region as well as delaying and limiting the summer warming of the continent and its surrounding seas. The generation and paths of storms in the Southern Ocean are related to the ice pack extent (*see* Mullan and Hickman, this volume). Sea ice formation increases the salinity of the sea water beneath causing vertical mixing in the water column. In particular, polynyas and leads in the pack are thought to contribute to the high salinity Antarctic Bottom Water (Zwally et al., 1985) found throughout the world's oceans. Melting in summer dilutes and can increase the stability of the upper part of the water column increasing phytoplankton activity there (Ainley and Jacobs, 1981; Smith and Nelson, 1985; Smith, 1987). The ice algae that grow in sea ice are believed to be an important source of food for secondary consumers as indicated by increased productivity at the pack ice edge and the ecosystem characterstics (Ainley et al., 1986). Polynyas in the pack are thought to be important biologically as they may contribute to ecosystem productivity and provide winter refuges. Pack ice effectively limits most Antarctic shipping to less than four months of the year from mid November and has recently caused two ships to sink in the Pacific Sector (Table 4.1).

This section outlines the distribution and movement of sea ice in the Pacific Sector. Further information and reviews of Antarctic sea ice are given by Lewis and Weeks (1970), Ackley (1981), Zwally et al. (1983a, b), Romanov (1984), Keys (1984), U.S. Navy (1985), Sturman and Anderson (1986) and Lewis (1987). Most of our knowledge of Antarctic ice pack has been derived using remote sensing techniques especially satellite-borne sensors. These may underestimate the amounts of new or young ice present (Jacka et al., 1987).

Different methods of interpretation and analysis have produced different results. Our knowledge is therefore still incomplete especially since satellite observations of the whole pack have been made only over the last 15 or so years and not all sea ice parameters can be measured in this way. In addition, the distribution of pack ice is complex and variable due to a variety of dynamic, thermal, climatic and oceanographic factors.

The main feature of pack ice distribution in the Pacific Sector, like elsewhere in the Southern Ocean, is the large seasonal change in ice extent (area covered by pack ice) between summer and winter. This change is particularly evident in the Ross Sea. Fig. 4.7 shows the mean extent of the pack in late September and in mid Feburary, the latter time being close to the end of the summer melt season. Four areas of pack normally survive the summer. Although the two relatively small areas in the western Ross Sea have completely dissipated some summers (Fig. 4.7), persistent cores of pack ice survive mainly in the Amundsen and Bellingshausen Seas but also off the Oates Coast (Zwally et al., 1983a; U.S. Navy, 1985). Extensive freezing occurs from the south from late Feburary–March due to rapidly cooling air and sea temperatures. Together with ice advection driven by wind and currents (*see* below), this freezing leads to rapid areal increase in sea ice cover from early April to late July (Ackley, 1981; Zwally et al., 1983a). Thereafter, the pack continues to expand more slowly until September–October (Figs 4.7; 4.8). The rapid decrease in ice cover from mid November to January is thought to be due to upwelling of relatively warm deep water, for example, along the Antarctic Divergence, and to exchange of heat between sea and air (Gordon, 1981).

Two other important and related features of pack ice distribution are the

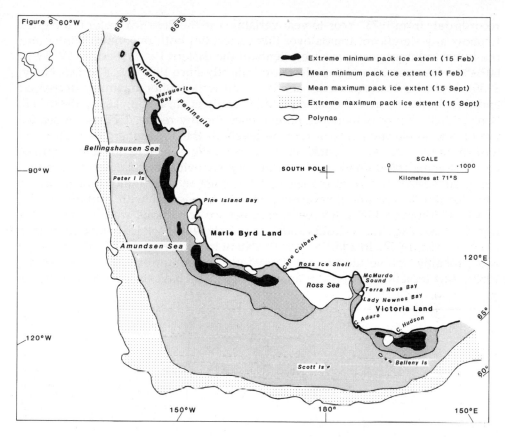

Fig. 4.7. Sea ice in the Pacific Sector adapted from U.S. Navy (1985) showing ice extents in mid September (extreme maximum and mean maximum), and mid February (mean minimum and extreme minimum) averaged over the years 1973 to 1982. Recurring or intermittent polynyas (areas of relatively thin pack ice with a higher incidence of open water) within the ice pack and along the coast are also shown, after Romanov (1984) and Zwally et al. (1985). Other small polynyas probably occur at the edge of the fast ice similar to the polynya in McMurdo Sound.

differences in area from year to year of pack ice extent, and polynyas (areas of open water or reduced ice concentrations within the ice pack). Variability is most pronounced in the summer months (Fig. 4.8) when the area of the ice pack at any given time may vary by up to 50% between years (Zwally et al., 1983a; U.S. Navy, 1985). The Ross Sea pack is especially variable. Some summers are heavy ice seasons when the pack is very slow to dissipate (e.g., 1975–76, 1976–77, 1977–78) and others have extensive and long (e.g., three months) open-water seasons (e.g., 1978–79, 1979–80) (Zwally et al., 1983b; Keys, 1984). Jacka (1983), Romanov (1984) and U.S. Navy (1985) also portray the pack ice distribution and the variability of the present-day ice edge.

The areal extent of sea ice also varies over longer periods but the most reliable records date from 1973. Year-to-year variability in the Ross Sea sector is too great to show any significant trends over this period but both maximum winter and minimum summer yearly sea ice extents in the eastern Pacific Sector (130°W to 60°W) have increased and then decreased slightly since 1973 (Fig. 4.8; U.S. Navy, 1985). However, total Antarctic pack ice extent at the winter maximum decreased and then increased over the same period (Zwally et al., 1983b; Jacka, 1983; U.S. Navy, 1985). There is therefore no evidence for any recent decrease in sea ice extent due to elevated carbon dioxide levels in the atmosphere or higher sea temperatures. Antarctic pack ice may be quite sensitive to such changes (Parkinson and Bindschadler, 1984) but geologic evidence relating to ice-rafted debris suggests that current models which predict an early removal of Antarctic pack ice due to greenhouse warming should be viewed with caution (Robin, 1986). During the 1930s, however, summer ice conditions were heavier than during present summers (Kukla and Gavin, 1981) and pack ice extended further north (Doake, 1985). In addition, sea ice extent in winter–spring 18,000 years ago was probably double the present day winter maximum extent (Burckle et al., 1982). Any local influence that human activity might have on ice extent, duration

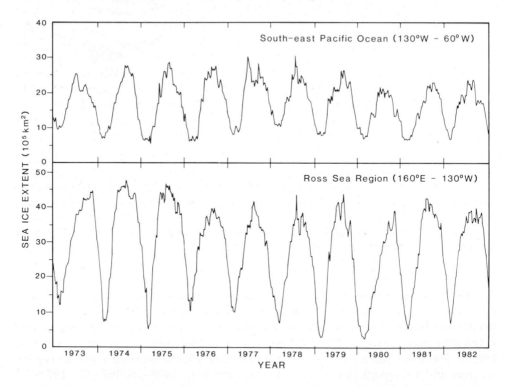

Fig. 4.8. The extent of sea ice, mainly pack ice, in the Pacific Sector as interpreted from visual, thermal, infrared and passive microwave satellite imagery (after U.S. Navy, 1985). These weekly observations show the marked seasonal change in ice extent between late summer and winter and indicate the interannual variability between January 1973 and December 1982.

or albedo is likely to be outweighed by such seasonal and interannual variability of the highly mobile pack.

The development of polynyas strongly influences pack ice distribution and dissipation including the length of the open-water season. At least nine intermittent or recurring polynyas have been recognized in the Pacific Sector (Fig. 4.7). These areas of reduced ice concentration (and thickness) or open water are thought to be caused by a combination of synoptic (as produced in a regional weather event or events) and katabatic winds acting in concert with suitable topography of land, coast and seafloor (Kurtz and Bromwich, 1985; Zwally et al., 1985). Probably some vertical component of water motion is also involved.

The stable, recurring polynya in Terra Nova Bay (Fig. 4.7) is most convenient for study and its existence has been the most fully explained. Strong, persistent westerly katabatic winds blowing offshore and the Drygalski Ice Tongue which blocks northward advecting sea ice from moving into the Bay are the primary cause of the polynya (Kurtz and Bromwich, 1985). Synoptic winds, deep water and water circulation patterns are secondary influences. Sea ice is continually forming in this 1,000 km² polynya for probably 9–10 months of the year to be advected eastwards contributing to the persistent pack ice zone in the north-west Ross Sea (Fig. 4.7). The same polynya, however, also helps disperse the pack there in late summer due probably to the increased ice divergence and upwelling of deeper water.

The large Ross Sea polynya appears to be driven by southerly through easterly winds and probably by some upwelling of warmer or more saline water as well (Jacobs et al., 1970; Keys, 1984; Pillsbury and Jacobs, 1985; Zwally et al., 1985). Ice advection into the southern and central Ross Sea is limited because of the current and wind directions (Fig. 4.6), whereas the winds and upwelling act to drive and melt ice out of this area. The polynya therefore tends to open the Ross Sea from the south due to enhanced advection and melting (especially in summer). The strong but variable synoptic forcing of the polynya is probably the main reason why the development of open water in the area is not the same from year to year (Zwally et al., 1985).

The large seasonal changes in pack ice extent mean that the region, especially the Ross Sea, has an extensive marginal ice zone. This is the zone across which the advancing or retreating edges of pack ice sweep during the year. Studies made of this zone in the Arctic have considerable relevance to the Antarctic. The complex vertical and horizontal air-sea-ice interactions of the zone are, in general terms, likely to be the same in both polar regions. For example, direct observations of Arctic ice edge compaction during on-ice winds and divergence during off-ice winds also apply to the Antarctic. Divergence is also due in part to ice advecting over warmer water and thinning, and to warm water incursions into the pack in eddies. Such processes together with synoptic weather events and local ice and ocean dynamics help explain the pronounced variability in the position of the ice edge (e.g., Jacka, 1983).

The patterns of sea ice movement in the Pacific Sector are known only in general terms. Average directions and speeds of regional ice movement are portrayed by Romanov (1984) and Sturman and Anderson (1986) and shown here in Fig. 4.6. Near the coast, from about Thurston Island west to Cape Colbeck, ice drift is generally westwards apart from localized areas where katabatic winds force the ice offshore. In most of the Ross Sea, drift appears to be more towards the north-west and north especially in the north. However, in the southern Ross Sea, westward drift may also occur turning to the north near Ross Island then north-west again around Cape Adare. North of the Ross Sea, northward movement appears to be most common until the latitudes of the West Wind Drift are reached and where eastward drift predominates (Fig. 4.6). These sea ice drift directions are not always consistent with iceberg trajectories. Elsewhere in the Pacific Sector, sea ice movement tends to be more variable and information less reliable but there is evidence for circular (gyral) motion in the vicinity of the Antarctic Divergence (Romanov, 1984). Southwards drift may be most common at longitudes 130° to 140°W (Fig. 4.6).

The pattern and direction of predominant winds (e.g., Weyant, 1967), surface currents (e.g, Elliot, 1977) and the drifts of ships beset in the pack (Tchernia and Jeannin, 1983) are similar to that of the ice (Fig. 4.6). This implies that ice advection can be attributed qualitatively to both wind and current. However, the direction of ice drift can be highly variable over short periods (De Rycke, 1973). Drift rates are highly variable also with mean speeds normally less than 17 km day^{-1} (0.2 m sec.$^{-1}$; Romanov, 1984; R. Moritz, pers. comm.) but maximum speeds probably exceeding 1.2 m sec.$^{-1}$ when driven by strong winds or tides (Wordie, 1921; De Rycke, 1973; Keys, 1984). Probably sea ice drifts faster than icebergs on average due to the greater influence of wind on the former but it is not uncommon to see icebergs caught in strong currents ploughing through slower moving pack ice.

There is as yet no widely used model to describe the persistent areas of pack ice (Fig. 4.7) in the Pacific Sector. Sturman and Anderson (1986) concluded that higher concentrations in the eastern Ross Sea and north of the Oates Coast were probably due to slower ice movement, convergence and accumulation of ice in these areas throughout the year. Persistent pack in the western Ross Sea was thought to be due to convergence caused by both offshore (katabatic) winds off Victoria Land and southerly (and south-easterly) winds further out to sea and in the south. While this model is very plausible, advection of ice and cold water in regional currents may have been underestimated. Advection appears to be significant off the Oates Coast and the eastern Ross Sea where regional currents have been best defined by iceberg drift (Fig. 4.6).

Nevertheless, convergence remains an underlying factor. It seems a fundamental cause of the two other major areas of persistent pack ice in the Pacific Sector, in the Amundsen and Bellingshausen Seas (Figs 4.6; 4.7). Surface air temperatures in these areas are about –2° to –6°C in January, colder than elsewhere along the coast of the Pacific Sector at this time (Schwerdtfeger, 1970). Sea ice, therefore, probably forms in the vicinity throughout the year and is made to converge in these areas by the pattern of winds and currents. Katabatic winds off the continent could contribute to this convergence for instance north of the coastal polynyas at 110° to 150°W (Fig. 4.7). Elsewhere such coastal polynyas tend to develop sufficiently to break through the most persistent band of pack ice further offshore (Fig. 4.7). Convergence may also be increased locally by coastal topography for example in Lady Newnes Bay where the coastline trends north-east approximately normal to south-easterly winds and the regional current in the western Ross Sea.

A further example of local convergence may be caused by the Drygalski Ice Tongue which is advancing out into south-west Ross Sea. This could tend to increase sea ice convergence south of it (up current and up wind) and would have implications for logistic, scientific and biological activities in McMurdo Sound.

CONCLUSIONS

This survey of ice in the Antarctic Sector of the Pacific has shown that the diverse ice forms there are understood in general terms. Their distribution and other characteristics are complex and very significant in environmental and human terms.

However, important information on physical process is still lacking. More data on the mass balance and flow of the Ross Ice Shelf and the major glaciers in Pine Island Bay are needed so that the ice sheets response to global change, for example the stability of the West Antarctic Ice Sheet, can be determined and properly modelled. The distribution, volume, production and decay of icebergs need to be better known to help refine estimates of the mass balance of the ice sheet, iceberg production rates and to quantify the iceberg hazard. More information on the distribution and properties of sea ice, especially in winter, is needed to produce better models and improve our understanding of this important component of the earth. Obtaining such information is becoming increasingly urgent with the likelihood of significant climate change in the next few decades and its effects on Antarctic ice.

CHAPTER 5

STRUCTURE AND TECTONICS

F.J. DAVEY

INTRODUCTION

The southern Pacific Ocean is bounded by South America, West Antarctica and Australia (Fig. 5.1). The morphology of the deep ocean floor, which lies at depths of about 5,000 m, shows three main basins separated in the east by a major submarine ridge (the Pacific–Antarctic Ridge which continues into the East Pacific Rise) and in the west by the New Zealand continental block. These basins are, from west to east, the Tasman Basin, the Southwestern Pacific Basin and Southeastern Pacific Basin. Complex morphology south of New Zealand defines the smaller Emerald Basin, west of Campbell Plateau, and East Balleny Basin, north of Ross Sea. Major fracture zones (e.g., Eltanin Fracture Zone) offset the major oceanic rises. Oceanic trenches, reaching depths of up to 6,000 m, lie along the Pacific margin of South America and northern Antarctic Peninsula and along part of the Macquarie Ridge south of New Zealand. Continental shelves are narrow, apart from the broad shelves of the Bellingshausen, Amundsen and Ross Seas of Antarctica, with the other main shallow water area being the Campbell Plateau near New Zealand. This morphology of the southern Pacific Ocean and its margins has resulted from the geological development of the region during the past 150 Ma.

The southern Pacific Ocean has evolved primarily as a result of the breakup and dispersal of the super-continent of Gondwana (Fig. 5.2). The similarities in geology of South America, South Africa and India led Suess (1909) to propose the existence in the past of a continuous continent which he termed "Gondwana Land". Wegener at about this time was developing his ideas on continental drift enabling the reconstruction of this super continent by reassembling the positions of Antarctica, Africa, South America, India and Australasia using geological and geomorphological constraints (Wegener, 1924). He considered that the fragmentation of Gondwana commenced in the late Mesozoic (about 100 Ma B.P.). Du Toit (1937) reviewed and developed the evidence and theories associated with continental drift and reconstruction. He noted the position of Antarctica as the 'key piece' of Gondwana, the drift northwards of the surrounding continents and the pre-breakup continuity of the late Palaeozoic Samfrau Geosyncline, or orogenic belt, along the Pacific margin of Gondwana.

The process of breakup and dispersal of Gondwana, with various continental fragments breaking away at different times, can be described in a coherent fashion by means of the theory of plate tectonics. This theory also helps us understand the tectonic development of both the southern Pacific Ocean and the continental margins bordering the Pacific.

The surface of the earth is covered by a brittle crust of two main types : oceanic

126

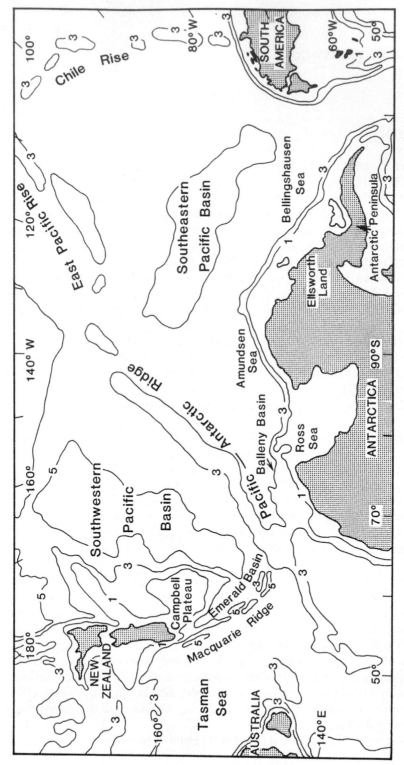

Fig. 5.1. Morphology of the southern Pacific Ocean and its margin. Contours are water depths (km) (Polar Stereographic projection).

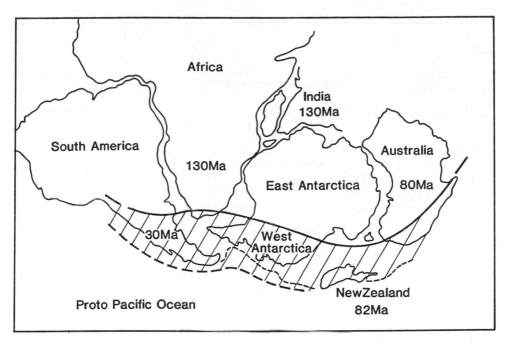

Fig. 5.2. Gondwana showing the age of separation (Ma) of the continents from Antarctica. The Samfrau Geosyncline (Du Toit, 1937) is shaded.

crust, about 5 km thick, and continental crust, about 35 km thick. These are underlain by a more ductile rock layer termed the mantle. The two types of crust correspond, in general terms, with the deep ocean basins and with the continental land areas respectively. In plate tectonics, the surface of the earth is considered to be formed by several thin (5–60 km) rigid plates (Fig. 5.3a). These plates consist of the crust and uppermost mantle (lithosphere) and are moving relative to each other (Fig. 5.3b). Where the plates are moving apart, a spreading centre (or ridge) is formed at a boundary where new hot, mantle-derived, rocks rise to the surface and solidify to form new oceanic crust (e.g., Pacific–Antarctic Rise). Three spreading centres may join to give a 'triple junction' which is a stable spreading configuration. In the regions where plates converge, one plate is usually thrust under the other and descends to depths of up to 600 km. This underthrusting is referred to as subduction. Where this type of plate boundary occurs, a trench is often formed with uplift and volcanic activity occurring in the adjacent overlying plate close to the boundary (e.g., Chile Trench). However, if continental crust occurs at the convergent boundary, the crust tends not to subduct but to crumple up forming mountain ranges (e.g., Southern Alps of New Zealand). If the rate of formation of new crust at a spreading centre is slower than the rate of consumption (subduction) at the adjacent plate boundary, then the spreading centre will migrate to the trench (subduction zone) and the system will ultimately die. Where the relative plate motion at the boundary is parallel to the boundary, a transcurrent boundary is formed.

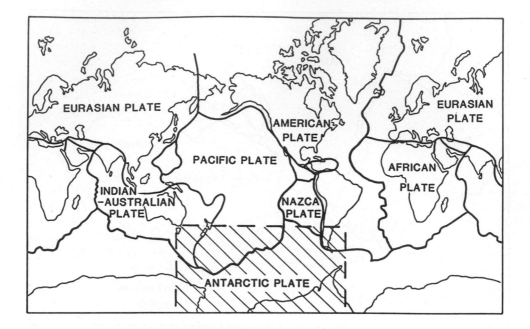

Fig. 5.3a. Major lithospheric plates (Mercator projection). The Antarctic Sector of the Pacific Ocean is outlined by heavy dashed line.

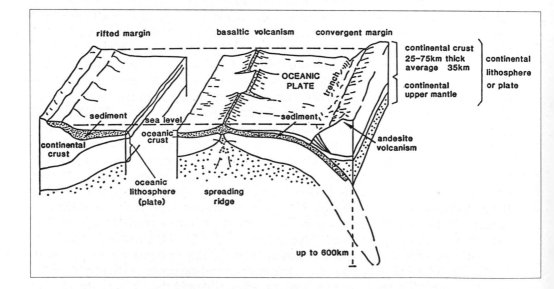

Fig. 5.3b. Schematic diagram showing the mechanism of seafloor spreading.

The rifting processes coinciding with the onset of a new spreading centre typically start with an upwelling of hot mantle rocks under continental lithosphere, the heat leading to uplift and associated erosion. As the process continues, major block faulting occurs along the line of the increased heating giving rise to major continental rift structures, such as the East African Rift, with associated crustal stretching and thinning and downwarp of the land surface. Eventually, the stretching of the continental crust reaches its limit and molten mantle rocks rise to the surface, cool and solidify to form new oceanic crust. The time between the initial heating, uplift and continental rifting and the first intrusion of new oceanic crust may take many million years.

The Pacific margin of Gondwana consisted of the continental blocks now forming South America, west Antarctica (Antarctic Peninsula, Ellsworth Land), and New Zealand (Fig. 5.2). Convergent plate margins occurred along this region prior to the Cretaceous (100 Ma B.P.) with the oceanic Pacific, Phoenix and Farallon plates being underthrust under the Gondwana continent. In Jurassic (150 Ma B.P.) and possibly earlier times, rifting processes started to occur along most of the present Antarctic margin resulting in the breakup of Gondwana and the isolation of Antarctica. Oceanic lithosphere started forming about 130–150 Ma ago between South Africa/India and Antarctica and about 80–85 Ma ago between Australia/New Zealand and Antarctica. The South America/Antarctic Peninsula/Ellsworth Land margin of Gondwana remained a subducting convergent margin during this period with subduction ceasing in Oligocene times (30 Ma B.P.) along Ellsworth Land and at successively younger times for the margin eastwards along the Antarctic Peninsula. The present oceanic lithosphere of the southern Pacific Ocean was therefore produced by seafloor spreading over the last 85 Ma, associated in part with the rifting of New Zealand from Antarctica. In the eastern part of the southern Pacific Ocean, the continental margins coincide with convergent plate margins whereas, in the western southern Pacific Ocean, the continental margins are dominantly passive margins arising from rifting of continental lithosphere during the past 150 Ma.

PLATE TECTONIC DEVELOPMENT OF THE SOUTHERN PACIFIC OCEAN

Seafloor Spreading

The basic pattern of seafloor spreading in the southern Pacific Ocean has been derived from the analysis of seafloor magnetic anomalies. The upper part of the oceanic lithosphere is highly magnetic. It acquires the direction of magnetization of the earth's magnetic field in existence at the time it is formed at seafloor spreading centres by the solidification of igneous rocks injected into and onto the crust at the spreading centre. The earth's magnetic field has undergone reversals in direction at irregular intervals in the past and this gives rise to a distinctive magnetic anomaly pattern across the seafloor from younger to older oceanic crust (Fig. 5.4). New oceanic lithosphere is usually formed at spreading centres at a fairly constant rate for significant periods of time. This enables the identification

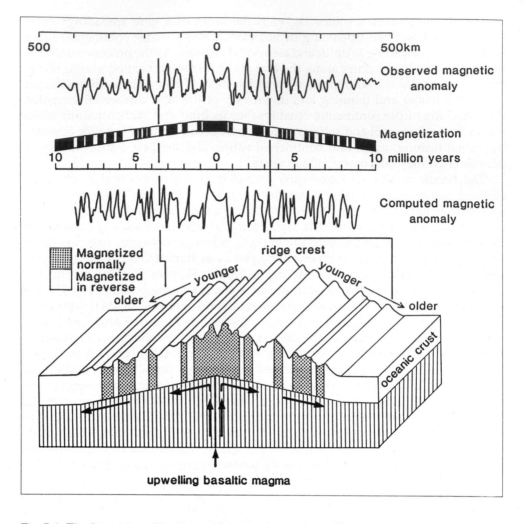

Fig. 5.4. The formation of linear magnetic anomalies at seafloor spreading centres, showing a comparison between the observed magnetic anomaly and a theoretical computed magnetic anomaly based on reversals in magnetization of the oceanic crust.

of distinctive magnetic anomaly sequences from their shape and hence the age of the crust giving rise to them. Marine magnetic surveys, particularly by U.S.N.S. *Eltanin* in the late 1960s and early 1970s, have enabled the ages of a large portion of the oceanic crust of this region to be ascertained. The basic pattern of seafloor spreading in the area south of 45°S between South Australia and South America has been defined and described by many authors including Pitman et al. (1968), Herron and Hayes (1969), Herron (1971, 1972), Christoffel and Falconer (1972), Weissel and Hayes (1972), Hayes and Ringis (1973), Molnar et al. (1975), Handschumacher (1976), Herron and Tucholke (1976), Weissel et al. (1977), Cande et al.

(1982) and Stock and Molnar (1987). However, gaps in data exist, especially on the Antarctic plate north of Ross Sea and Marie Byrd Land.

Mesozoic Spreading

Although the Pacific margin of Gondwana has been a convergent oceanic-continental plate boundary for a large portion of time since the Precambrian (570 Ma B.P.) (Scotese, 1987), the present oceanic lithosphere of the Pacific Basin is largely 150 Ma or younger in age. To define the Early-Middle Cretaceous (90–135 Ma B.P.) development of the southern Pacific Ocean, the Early Cretaceous spreading patterns in the north and western Pacific (Larson and Chase, 1972) must be studied. As no magnetic anomalies of that age occur in the south, these Mesozoic spreading systems must have evolved into the later Cretaceous–Cenozoic system in the southern and eastern Pacific but details of this evolution are not obvious because of the lack of magnetic reversals recording the spreading pattern from 110–85 Ma B.P. (the Cretaceous Magnetic Quiet Zone). This was also a period of very rapid spreading at all ridges. The Mesozoic spreading pattern is interpreted in terms of a four plate system (Fig. 5.5), the Kula, Farallon, Phoenix and Pacific plates with two triple junctions (T, Fig. 5.5), one at the northern and one at the southern end of the Pacific–Farallon spreading centre. These triple junctions migrated north and south rapidly as a result of jumps in ridge (spreading centre) positions. The formation of new oceanic crust caused the southern spreading centres to migrate to the southeast and rotate anticlockwise to align with their Cenozoic counterparts. The southeastern ridge (Farallon/Phoenix) jumped to the west between 100 and 120 Ma B.P. to give the observed offset to the southwest of the Pacific/Farallon plate boundary (T1 to T2, Fig. 5.5). The Phoenix and Farallon plates were being continually subducted under South America and Antarctica with the Phoenix/Farallon spreading centre also being subducted, presumably at the South American margin. The Farallon plate broke up during the late Tertiary and the Nazca plate (Fig. 5.6) is the remaining fragment in the southern Pacific Ocean. The Aluk plate (Fig. 5.6) is another name for the last fragment of the Phoenix plate. As the Pacific–Phoenix spreading centre migrated southwards during the Cretaceous, possibly terminated to the west by the Eltanin Fracture Zone (EFZ, Fig. 5.5), it linked up with the Antarctic–New Zealand spreading centre which commenced spreading in the Late Cretaceous, about 85 Ma ago (Christoffel and Falconer, 1972).

Late Cretaceous–Cenozoic Spreading

Details of the initiation of the Late Cretaceous–Cenozoic (85 Ma to present) spreading episode are uncertain. If the Pacific–Phoenix spreading centre extended to the west of the Eltanin Fracture Zone (Fig. 5.5), subduction of the Phoenix plate would have occurred along the northern margin of the New Zealand block until this western portion of the spreading centre reached the subduction zone, at or just prior to anomaly 34 time (80 Ma), where it presumably aligned with the proto New Zealand–Antarctic rift zone (Larson et al., 1979). At this time,

132

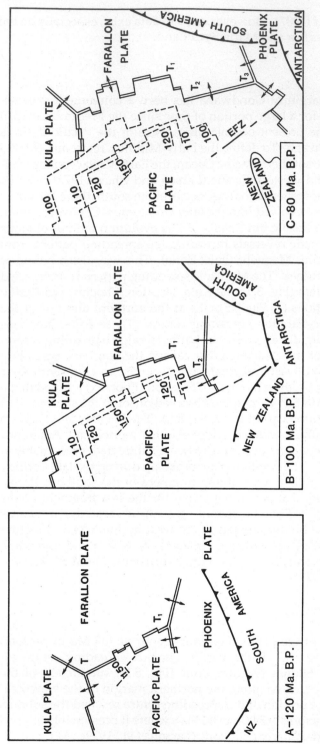

Fig. 5.5. The major plates in the Pacific Ocean and their development during the Cretaceous relative to a fixed Pacific plate (after Larson and Chase, 1972). T marks position of spreading ridge triple junctions. Anomaly ages (Ma) and position (dashed lines) are marked. EFZ = Eltanin Fracture Zone.

spreading ceased on this segment of the Pacific–Phoenix spreading centre which jumped southwards to between the New Zealand block and Antarctica, with the New Zealand block becoming incorporated into the Pacific plate and a major transcurrent boundary (1,000 km total offset (Larson et al., 1979)) lying along the Eltanin Fracture Zone. This boundary subsequently formed the southern boundary of the greater Antarctic Peninsula, with subduction occurring to the east but not the west (Fig. 5.6) (Barker, 1982).

The Late Cretaceous–Cenozoic development of the region is complex. Five spreading centres were operating for all or part of this period; the Pacific–Antarctic Ridge, the Chile (Antarctic–Nazca) Ridge, the Indian–Antarctic Ridge, the Central Tasman spreading centre and the Farallon–Phoenix (Aluk) Ridge (Fig. 5.6). Recent work (Stock and Molnar, 1987) indicates a possible sixth ridge,

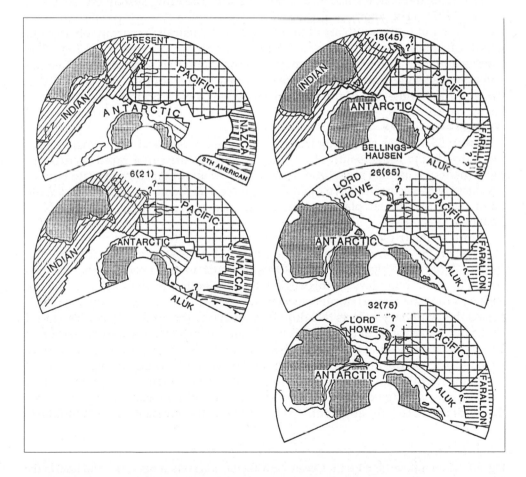

Fig. 5.6. The major plates in the Pacific Ocean and their development during the Cenozoic (after Weissel et al., 1977; Stock and Molnar, 1987). Magnetic anomaly number and ages in brackets shown at top of each diagram. (Polar Stereographic projection).

Bellingshausen–Antarctic Ridge, and an additional minor plate, the Bellingshausen plate, in the vicinity of Bellingshausen Sea (Fig. 5.6). The development of the present oceanic lithosphere on the Pacific Sector of the Antarctic plate commenced about 85 Ma ago with the onset of rifting of New Zealand (Pacific–Lord Howe plate(s)) from Australia and Antarctica (the Antarctic and Bellingshausen plates) along the spreading centres of the central Tasman Sea and the Pacific–Antarctic Ridge. Spreading continued along the existing Pacific–Phoenix and Farallon (Nazca)–Phoenix spreading centres. Very slow spreading was probably occurring between Australia and Antarctica (Cande and Mutter, 1982).

Southwestern Pacific Ocean

The Tasman Basin formed as a simple 2-plate spreading system (Weissel and Hayes, 1977). The anomaly lineations in the Tasman Sea are parallel to Lord Howe Rise but in the north are oblique to the east Australian margin where right lateral offsets in the spreading centre to the north are inferred (Fig. 5.7). The southern margin of the basin is a major fracture zone that separates the Tasman spreading episode from younger oceanic crust to the south. The part of this fracture zone to the east of the Tasman Ridge was a plate boundary between the Pacific plate and a "Lord Howe" plate in the Late Cretaceous to Palaeocene (Weissel et al., 1977).

About 55 Ma ago, spreading in the Tasman Sea ceased and was transferred to the Indo–Pacific Ridge south of Australia. This resulted in a rapid increase in movement of Australia away from Antarctica. At about this time, a plate boundary, largely transcurrent, developed through New Zealand separating the Pacific plate from the Indian plate and resulting in a triple junction south of New Zealand.

South of the triple junction, magnetic anomalies 1–18 (present to 45 Ma B.P.) mapped on the Antarctic plate were generated at the easternmost segment of the Indian–Antarctic Ridge (Fig. 5.7). Oceanic crust to the north of the Pacific–Antarctic plate boundary in this region was generated at the Pacific–Antarctic Ridge in the Late Cretaceous–Palaeocene (85–60 Ma). A change in crustal depth across this boundary reflects this difference in age of the oceanic crust. The trend of the older lineations in the south is NNE and intersects the Antarctic margin at a high angle suggesting that the northwestern Ross Sea margin was produced by strike slip action during the early stages of Antarctic– Australia rifting.

To the north of the triple junction, the Indian–Pacific plate boundary lies along the Macquarie Ridge complex. Here, the ENE-trending Cenozoic lineations on the Indian plate are apparently truncated at the present plate boundary.

Fig. 5.7. The southwestern Pacific Ocean showing the magnetic anomalies (solid line) in the Tasman Sea and the region of the Pacific–Indian–Antarctic triple junction (T). Fracture zones are marked by dotted lines, Fracture zone Z referred to in text. Plate boundaries marked by double line. 2,000 m bathymetry contours marked by dashed line. Anomaly numbers after Heirtzler et al. (1968) (Mercator projection).

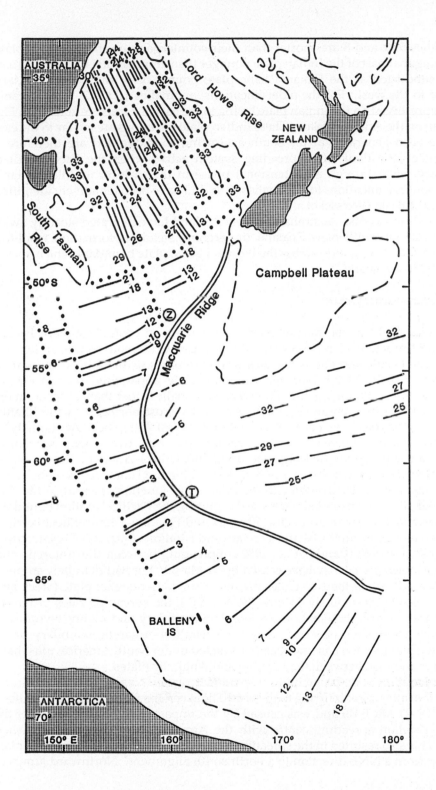

Anomalies 5, 6, and 8 are shorter than their counterparts on the Antarctic plate indicating that part of the Indian plate younger than anomaly 10 is missing. It was either subducted at the Indian–Pacific plate boundary or the plate boundary jumped to the west. For the older lineations, anomalies 10 to 22, more oceanic crust is preserved on the Indian plate laying to the east of a fracture zone (Z in Fig. 5.7) than on the Antarctic plate. These Indian plate lineations are too far to the east to have been generated at the southeastern Indian Ridge and are therefore a remnant of one flank of a spreading system active when the Pacific–Indian boundary went through an extensional phase in the early to middle Tertiary. Corresponding lineations for anomalies 12 and 13 have been tentatively identified in Emerald Basin (Weissel et al., 1977).

Since these events, Australia and New Zealand have migrated steadily away from Antarctica with New Zealand undergoing steady deformation resulting from relative plate motion across the Indian–Pacific plate boundary which passes through New Zealand.

Southeastern Pacific Ocean

A major bight in the magnetic anomaly pattern of central southern Pacific Ocean indicates that a 3-plate system existed in Late Cretaceous time (Cande et al., 1982). The Pacific and Farallon plates were two of these, the third is unknown. Prior to anomaly 29 (65 Ma), the Antarctic plate apparently did not extend northeast of the Eltanin Fracture Zone, as no anomalies older than 29 occur on the Pacific plate in this region (Fig. 5.8). Any older crust northeast of the Eltanin Fracture Zone must have been subducted under West Antarctica. At anomaly 29 time, the Pacific–Phoenix spreading centre split into two slower spreading centres, a Pacific–Antarctic Ridge and a Phoenix (Aluk)–Antarctic Ridge, a split which has propagated eastwards with time reaching the Tula Fracture Zone about 64 Ma B.P. and the Pacific–Phoenix–Farallon triple junction at about 50 Ma B.P. Since then, it has propagated northwards splitting the Pacific–Farallon boundary and replacing the Antarctic–Pacific–Phoenix and Farallon–Pacific–Phoenix triple junctions by the Antarctic–Pacific–Farallon and Farallon–Antarctic–Phoenix triple junctions (Fig. 5.6) (Cande et al., 1982). Spreading between the Antarctic and Bellingshausen plates may have ceased by 51 Ma B.P. but had definitely stopped by 43 Ma B.P. when the two plates became a single (Antarctic) plate (Stock and Molnar, 1987). At anomaly 24 time (56 Ma B.P.), the spreading rates increased significantly across the Farallon–Pacific plate boundary and highly asymmetric spreading must have occurred across the Farallon–Antarctic boundary or an unknown plate, which has since been subducted under South America, must have existed to the east, between the Farallon and Antarctic plates.

The Farallon plate broke into three smaller plates (Nazca, Cocos and Gorda plates, the latter two occurring to the north) between the formation of anomalies 6 and 7 (27–21 Ma B.P.) and was caused by the impact in the north Pacific of the Pacific–Farallon spreading centre with the American plate (Handschumacher, 1976). This also resulted in the spreading centre to the north of the Antarctic plate rotating from a NNE direction to a north-south alignment. Northward jumps of

137

the Pacific–Nazca–Antarctic triple junction have occurred several times during the past 20 Ma.

The northeast trending anomalies off west Antarctic become younger towards the Antarctic coast indicating that the other half of the oceanic crust formed at the

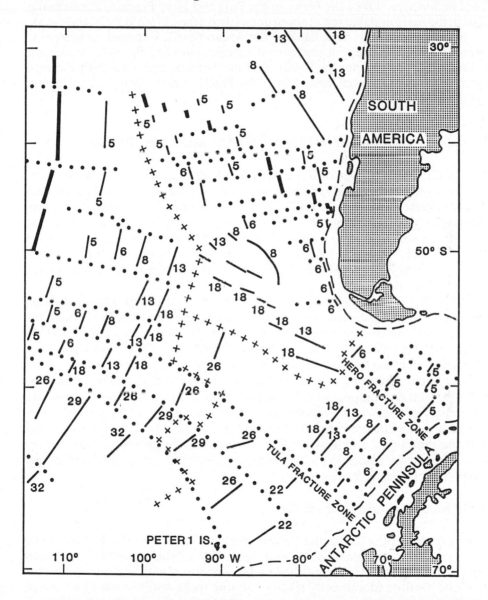

Fig. 5.8. The southeastern Pacific Ocean showing magnetic lineations (after Cande et al., 1982) with anomaly numbers after Heirtzler et al. (1968). Spreading ridges shown by heavy solid lines. Fracture zones are marked by dotted lines. Inactive plate boundaries by cross lines. 2,000 m bathymetry contours marked by dashed line (Mercator projection).

Aluk Ridge has been subducted under West Antarctica (Fig. 5.8). When this spreading centre, between the Tula Fracture Zone and Peter I Island, reached the trench axis, sometime after anomaly 22 time (55 Ma B.P.), the corresponding part of the Aluk (Phoenix) plate had been completely subducted and the plate boundary became inactive. Likewise, between the Tula and Hero Fracture Zones to the northeast, the margin stabilized at about anomaly 6 time (30 Ma B.P.) (Cande et al., 1982). Subduction of the Aluk flank of the Antarctic–Aluk spreading system is continuing along the adajcent continental margin, between the Shackleton and Hero Fracture Zones, under the South Shetland Islands, and a spreading centre was active in Drake Passage, east of the Hero Fracture Zone from early Miocene time until 5 Ma B.P.

TECTONIC HISTORY OF THE MARGINS OF THE SOUTHERN PACIFIC OCEAN

The Pacific Ocean margin of Gondwana (South America, Antarctica and Australasia), as noted earlier, had been an active orogenic zone from the Precambrian to the Late Cretaceous (Scotese, 1987). It formed the boundary zone between the Pacific Ocean and the stable shield area comprising the Precambrian metamorphic rocks which occur in Brazil, Uruguay, northeastern Argentina, Falkland Islands, Falkland Plateau, East Antarctica and Australia. Knowledge of the area is highly variable reflecting the limited information and rock exposure, particularly in parts of Antarctica.

The margin falls into two major regions; one has a more or less continuous history of convergent plate tectonics (South America and Antarctic Peninsula), the other is strongly affected by the extensional rifting tectonics of the past 80–100 Ma B.P. (Southwestern Pacific). The geology of coastal Marie Byrd Land and Ellsworth Land covers the transition between these two geological environments.

The continental margin of the ocean/continent convergent plate boundary has three major tectonic components. These are, from ocean to continent, a fore-arc sedimentary province which includes an accretionary sedimentary pile and fore-arc basin, a magmatic arc consisting mainly of calc-alkaline volcanic rocks and underlying granitoids, and a back-arc sedimentary basin province. Rifted margins, in contrast, are associated with initial uplift and erosion, major faulting and the extrusion of basic volcanics.

South America and Greater Antarctic Peninsula

The development of the Pacific Ocean margin of South America and Antarctic Peninsula falls into two main phases represented by (a) the present Pacific Ocean margin cordillera, initiated in middle-late Jurassic times with widespread extrusion of calc-alkaline (dominantly silicic) volcanic rocks and the site of an active subducting plate boundary between the Pacific Ocean (Farallon) and American plates, and (b) a previously deformed and metamorphosed basement complex separated from the overlying younger rocks by a major unconformity (Dalziel, 1982). This major unconformity represents uplift and erosion of the basement complex in Late Triassic–Jurassic times.

In southern South America, basement comprises a central late Palae-ozoic–early Mesozoic magmatic arc, an eastern back-arc epicratonic sedimentary province, which corresponds to the Samfrau Geosyncline of Du Toit (1937), and a fore-arc province to the west, (Fig. 5.9) (Forsythe, 1982). Dalziel (1982) considered that the basement geology of the Antarctic Peninsula represents a portion of the fore-arc and main magmatic arc of a pre-Middle Jurassic subduction zone (Fig. 5.9). A Palaeozoic–early Mesozoic subduction complex therefore existed along the South American–Antarctic Peninsula margin of Gondwana and extended to New Zealand.

A major unconformity occurs between this basement complex and the overly-ing Late Jurassic–Cretaceous arc sequences. Dalziel (1982) concluded that the uplift and erosion of the basement, following deformation and metamorphism, which resulted in this unconformity was related to the initial phases of the break-up of Gondwana. Overlying the major middle Jurassic unconformity are primar-ily volcanic rocks interlayered with volcaniclastic sandstone and shales indicative of a shallow marine environment. Deposition of these rocks accompanied wide-spread extension in the latest Jurassic–Early Cretaceous, probably associated with Gondwana fragmentation (Dalziel, 1982) when vast quantities of extrusive and intrusive igneous rocks were associated with extensional tectonics in the southern continents. Convergent margin tectonics continued in southern South America, where a marginal (back-arc) basin of Late Jurassic–Cretaceous age formed behind the calc-alkaline volcanic chain that was developing along the South American continental magin (Dalziel, 1981). Central and southwestern Antarctic Peninsula was the site of a narrow, more or less continuous, volcanic arc terrane by Late Jurassic times. A fore-arc basin was developing in the Alexander Island area, while along the eastern Antarctic Peninsula, from James Ross Island to Hope Bay and South Orkney Islands in the north, and along the southeastern Antarctic Pen-insula, sedimentation was occurring in a back-arc basin environment.

The continental margin of South America underwent considerable defor-mation and uplift in the mid-Late Cretaceous (Andean Orogeny). These processes resulted in the initiation of the present southern Andean Cordillera (Bruhn and Dalziel, 1977). This compressional deformation coincided closely in time with the period of fast seafloor spreading in the southeastern Pacific (Larson and Pitman, 1972) and a change in relative plate motion between the South American and African plates (Rabinowitz and LaBreque, 1979). No fore-arc sediments of Late Cretaceous age are known in the Antarctic Peninsula and the uplift and deformation of the late Jurassic–Early Cretaceous Fossil Bluff formation of Alexander Island possibly commenced at this time. Widely scattered volcanic centres erupted chiefly basalts during the late Cenozoic in southern Patagonia and Tierra del Fuego (Dott, 1976). Volcanism continued into the early Cenozoic in South Shetland Islands and Alexander Island but late Cenozoic volcanism is restricted to South Shetland Islands and east of northern Antarctic Peninsula, reflecting the cessation of subduction further to the southwest.

The continental shelf of the Antarctic Peninsula is at depths of 250–300 m in the northeast, deepening to 500 m or greater in the southwest near Thurston Island. The shelf varies in width, reaching a maximum of 500 km in the Bellingshausen

140

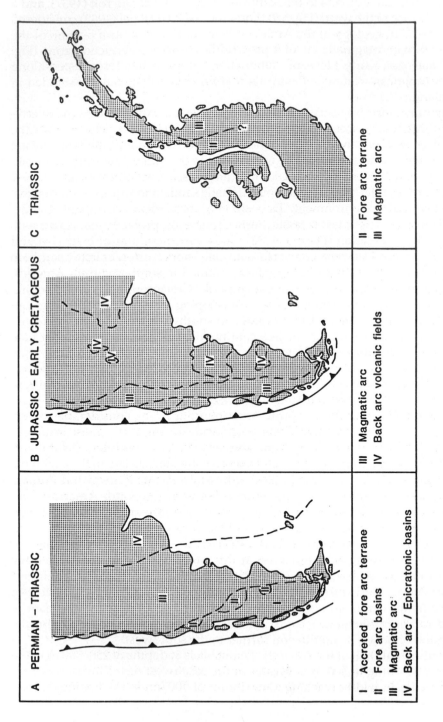

Fig. 5.9. Major pre-Jurassic and Jurassic–Early Cretaceous tectonostratigraphic provinces of South America (A, B) (after Forsythe, 1982) and Antarctica (C) (after Dalziel, 1982).

Sea (Fig. 5.10) and possibly 400 km in Amundsen Sea (Fig. 5.13). Sediments thicken in a southeast direction under the continental rise to reach thicknesses in excess of 3 km under the continental slope and over 5 km on the shelf northwest of the South Shetland Islands (Fig. 5.11) (Ashcroft, 1972; Houtz, 1974; Tucholke and Houtz, 1976; Kimura, 1982). The age of these sediments is not well constrained but they probably are Mesozoic or younger in age.

Off central Antarctic Peninsula, where active subduction ceased after ridge-trench collision, a palaeo island arc sequence has been interpreted in the sediments of the continental margin (Fig. 5.12) (Kimura, 1982). The morphological expression and large negative free air gravity anomaly of the palaeo-trench has deteriorated through isostatic rebound since the trench-arc system was transformed into a passive margin after ridge subduction during the Oligocene. In the north of the Antarctic Peninsula, the present convergent plate boundary gives rise to the South Shetland Trench and to the back-arc basin (Bransfield Strait) which lies to the east of the South Shetland Islands. Thin crust (25 km) occurs in this back-arc basin (Guterch et al., 1985).

The similarity and presumed continuity of the pre-Cretaceous geology of South America, Antarctic Peninsula and the South Georgia and South Orkney continental blocks allow a reconstruction to be made of Gondwana for this region (Dalziel, 1983) (Fig. 5.12) and demonstrate the complex movement that has occurred since breakup.

Western Ellsworth Land and Marie Byrd Land

The older basement geology along the coastal region between Antarctic Peninsula and Ross Sea includes low grade metasedimentary rocks (quartzose flysch deposits) of possibly Precambrian–Palaeozoic age (Swanson Group) in the west (Marie Byrd Land) and possible correlatives (or older), comprising higher grade metamorphic rock sequences and igneous rock (Fosdick Complex), in western Marie Byrd Land and Thurston Island (Fig. 5.13). Sporli and Craddock (1981) suggested that these latter rocks may have correlatives along the Ruppert and Hobbs Coasts of central Marie Byrd Land (Wade and Wilbanks, 1972).

A younger basement complex of widespread granitoids and rhyolitic volcanics of calc-alkaline affinities were emplaced throughout Marie Byrd Land and in the Thurston Island–Eights Coast region of western Ellsworth Land. They are very similar to the suites of Mesozoic volcanic rocks of Antarctic Peninsula (Metcalfe et al., 1978) and may form part of a magmatic arc of Late Palaeozoic–Early Mesozoic age that was continuous with a contemporaneous arc in the Antarctic Peninsula. Since that time, the geological history of the region has differed from that of the Antarctic Peninsula, reflecting the effect of the rifting of the New Zealand region from Antarctica.

During Cretaceous times, mafic dyke swarms intruded the coastal region of Marie Byrd Land. They increase in number towards the coast and trend sub-parallel to the continental margin reflecting the extensional regime which existed prior to the separation of New Zealand from Gondwana.

A widespread erosional surface formed during the Late Cretaceous–Early

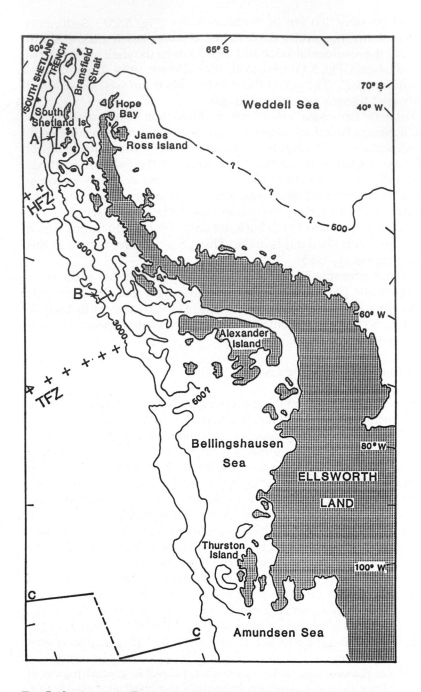

Fig. 5.10. Antarctic Peninsula. Location of geophysical profiles (A, B and C in Fig. 5.11) across the western Antarctic Peninsula–Bellingshausen Sea margin. HFZ - Hero Fracture Zone, TFZ - Tula Fracture Zone. Bathymetry contours at 500 m and 3,000 m delineate continental slope and shelf (Polar Stereographic projection).

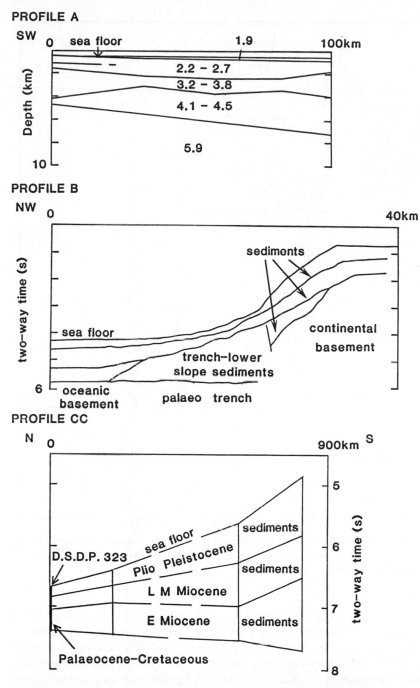

Fig. 5.11. Profiles across the western Antarctic Peninsula–Bellingshausen Sea margin (after Ashcroft, 1972; Kimura, 1982). Profile A shows seismic velocities in km sec.[-1]. The locations of the profiles are shown in Fig. 5.10. On profiles B and C, a 2-way travel time of 1 sec. is equivalent to about 1 km thickness in the sedimentary layers.

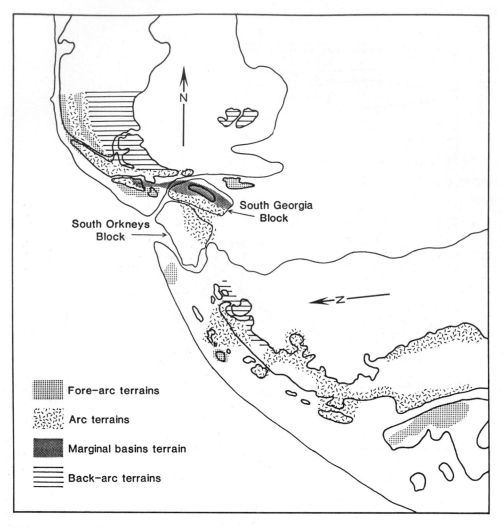

Fore-arc terrains

Arc terrains

Marginal basins terrain

Back-arc terrains

Fig. 5.12. Possible reconstruction of South America to western Antarctica (after Dalziel, 1982). The arrows indicate north directions for the present-day orientation of South America and Western Antarctica.

Cenozoic as a result of subsidence during the early rifting of New Zealand from Antarctica. Tectonism resumed in the Oligocene when extensive eruptions of calc-alkaline volcanic rock (hyaloclastite deposits) of Late Cenozoic age (up to 28 Ma B.P.) occurred (LeMasurier and Rex, 1982). These hyaloclastite deposits are considered to be the product of alkaline volcanic eruption under a continental ice sheet and, along with major normal faulting, suggest an extensional tectonic regime and the existence of a continental ice sheet for the last 28 Ma.

There are few bathymetric or other data across the shelf between Thurston Island and Sulzberger Bay (Vanney and Johnson, 1976), but the limited data

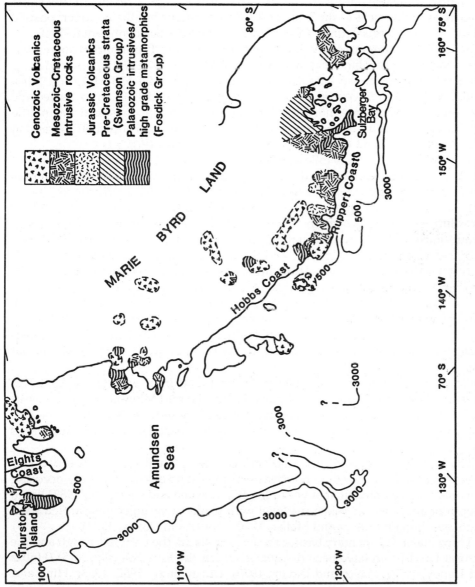

Fig. 5.13. Geology of Marie Byrd Land. Bathymetry contours at 500 m and 3,000 m (where available) delineate continental slope and shelf (Polar Stereographic projection).

indicate the shelf may reach 400 km in width in Amundsen Sea. About 4–5 km of sedimentary cover of Cretaceous or younger age (Fig. 5.12) probably built out as a prograded shelf under the upper continental rise (Kimura, 1982).

The Ross Sea Region

The Ross Sea covers the extensive, deep continental shelf area lying between Marie Byrd Land and the Transantarctic Mountains of East Antarctica. It originally lay on the continental side of the pre-80 Ma B.P. Pacific convergent margin which now forms the Campbell Plateau. The early geological history of the region is recorded in the rocks of the Transantarctic Mountains but the younger, post-80 Ma B.P. history, largely comes from studies of the Ross Sea continental shelf.

In the Transantarctic Mountains, basement comprises Precambrian and Lower Palaeozoic metamorphic rocks which were folded and metamorphosed during the Ross Orogeny in the Late Cambrian–Ordovician (500–530 Ma) (Fig. 5.14). Similar rocks occur in central Ross Sea. Sedimentary rocks of Lower Palaeozoic age were deposited in a northwest-southeast elongate extensional basin (the Bowers Trough) and now occupy a 350 km long fault controlled belt traversing northern Victoria Land from Ross Sea to the Oates Coast (Fig. 5.14).

The Ross Orogeny was followed by extensive erosion in the Ordovician and Silurian. The deposition of the flatlying shallow water alluvial sandstones, shales and coal measures of the Beacon Supergroup (Barrett, 1981) commenced in the Early Devonian in Victoria Land with intrusion of Late Devonian granites (Admiralty Intrusives) in Northern Victoria Land. An extensive Late Carboniferous–Early Permian glaciation removed a large part of the sequence. Sedimentation ceased in the Early Jurassic and the Beacon Group sediments were subsequently widely invaded by tholeiitic intrusives and extrusives of Middle Jurassic age (Ferrar Dolerites and Kirkpatrick Basalts) associated with the fragmentation of Gondwana. These rocks have been uplifted by at least 5 km, largely in the Late Tertiary, with rapid uplift (100 m/Ma) occurring during the last 50 Ma (Gleadow and Fitzgerald, 1987) perhaps associated with changes in plate motion (e.g., major Australia–Antarctic spreading) that occurred in the southwestern Pacific at that time.

No Cretaceous or pre-Oligocene rocks are found in or west of the Ross Sea. Extensive basaltic volcanism has occurred since the mid Miocene along the western Ross Sea margin. Late Tertiary and Quaternary sediments occur in the Dry Valley region of south Victoria Land and along the coastal region of western Ross Sea.

The Ross Sea (Fig. 5.14) has a 500 m deep continental shelf with broad low ridges running north-south to northeast-southwest across it. A widely occuring erosional surface dated at about 4–10 Ma B.P. (Savage and Ciesielski, 1983) lies at a depth of about 500 m below sea level with banks of younger unstratified sediments overlying it (Houtz and Meijer, 1970; Houtz and Davey, 1973).

Three major sedimentary basins, the Eastern Basin, the Central Trough and the Victoria Land Basin have been delineated under the Ross Sea (Fig. 5.15) (Houtz and Davey, 1972; Hayes and Davey, 1975; Davey et al., 1982, 1983; Hinz and

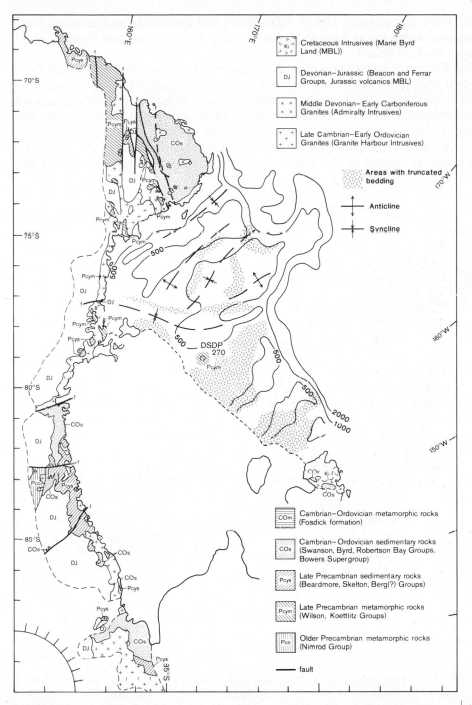

Fig. 5.14. Generalized pre-Cenozoic geology of the Ross Sea region (after Davey, 1987). Simplified bathymetry of the Ross Sea showing near surface geological structures (after Houtz and Davey, 1973) (Polar Stereographic projection).

148

Block, 1983; Cooper and Davey, 1985, 1987) and are considered to result from extensional tectonics in the late Mesozoic–early Tertiary and late Tertiary times (Cooper et al., in press).

The Eastern Basin covers most of the eastern Ross Sea continental shelf from the shelf edge in the north to and under the Ross Ice Shelf to the south, an area of about 100,000 km². The basin is a simple sediment filled basin or trough at least 3.7 km deep (Davey et al., 1982) with gentle folding along its flanks (Houtz and Davey, 1972). A north-south trending trough, up to 2 km deep, of pre-Late Oligocene sediments underlies the western margin (Hinz and Block, 1983) and may either be related to the separation of New Zealand from Gondwana and

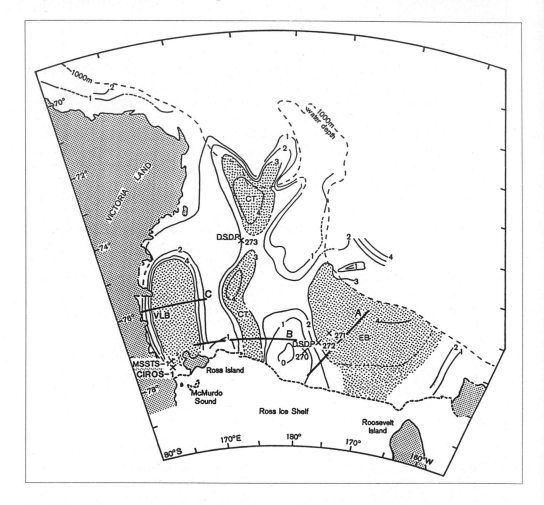

Fig. 5.15. Sedimentary basins of the Ross Sea (modified after Davey et al., 1983 and Cooper et al., 1987). Isopachs of sediment thickness in kilometres, light shaded where basement > 3 km below seafloor. The isopachs represent minimum sediment thicknesses. Profiles marked A to C are illustrated in Fig. 5.16. VLB - Victoria Land Basin, CT - Central Trough, EB - Eastern Basin (Polar Stereographic projection).

hence of Late Cretaceous age or be lowermost Tertiary in age (Fig. 5.16). DSDP sites 270–272 (Hayes et al., 1975a) along the western margin of the Eastern Basin show thin subaerial or shallow-water sediments of Oligocene age overlying metamorphic basement, which in turn are overlain by Late Oligocene and Miocene marine glacial sediments. This upper sedimentary sequence (Hinz and Block, 1983; Sato et al., 1984) is interpreted as a series of mostly fluvial delta lobes, with a thin delta plain facies to the south and a prograding prodelta facies to the north on a subsiding platform. The unconformity between the younger sequence and the older sedimentary sequence corresponds, at DSDP site 270, to the boundary between basal glacial sediments with an inferred age of 25 Ma (Allis et al., 1975) and preglacial greensands with a K/Ar date of 26 Ma (McDougall, 1977) and coincides with the development of an unrestricted Circum Antarctic Current (Kennett, 1980).

The Central Trough is an elongate sedimentary basin over 500 km long and about 100 km wide (Fig. 5.15). It has a north-south trend, extending from the continental shelf edge to under the Ross Ice Shelf and coincides approximately with 175°E longitude (Davey et al., 1983). It contains two sub-basins with the northern sub-basin offset to the east from the southern one by about 50 km at about 75°S (Davey et al., 1983; Hinz and Block, 1983). Thicknesses of about 6 km of sediment are present in the deepest part of the basin (Hinz and Block, 1983) and the oldest sediments may be Late Cretaceous in age. The basin is considered to be a major north-south trending graben extending from the ice shelf to the continental margin and coinciding with a thinned crust (Fig. 5.16) (Hayes and Davey, 1975).

The Victoria Land Basin (Wilson et al., 1981; Davey et al., 1982) contains up to about 5–6 km of sediments, underlain by a stratified, presumably low-grade metasedimentary layer up to 6 km thick with seismic velocities of about 5.5 km sec.$^{-1}$ (Fig. 5.16) (Cooper et al., 1987). Drillhole data (Barrett and McKelvey, 1986; Barrett, 1987) from the western flank of the basin in McMurdo Sound show marine glacial sediments dating back to Early Oligocene for the upper 700 m of sediments. The axis of the basin is a rift depression about 20 km wide extending between the Late Cenozoic volcanic provinces at Ross Island and Mt Melbourne (Cooper and Davey, 1985). The crust thickens from about 22 km under McMurdo Sound (McGinnis et al., 1985; Davey and Cooper, 1987) to over 35 km under the Transantarctic Mountains. Sedimentary sequences along the western flank of the basin are truncated at the seafloor and dip towards the central rift reflecting the uplift of the Transantarctic Mountains (Northey et al., 1975; Wong and Christoffel, 1981; Cooper et al., 1987).

The basin probably formed in two extensional eipsodes. The first, in the Cretaceous, was associated with the fragmentation of Gondwana and formed the lower part of the basin. The second in the Cenozoic (50 Ma and later) was associated with the uplift of the Transantarctic Mountains and the formation of the central rift depression and resulted in the younger sedimentary sequence (Cooper et al., 1987). High heatflow in McMurdo Sound (Risk and Hochstein, 1974; Decker, 1978) and in northern Victoria Land Basin (Blackman et al., 1984) and the presence of numerous Late Cenozoic volcanic centres in western Ross Sea supports the idea of an extensional environment.

PROFILE A

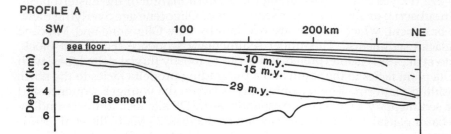

PROFILE B

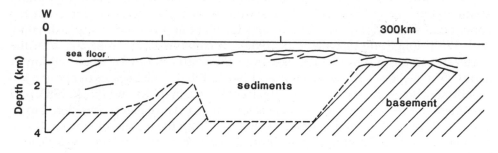

PROFILE C

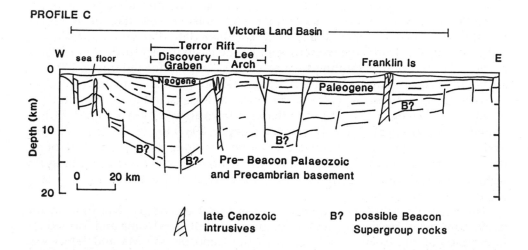

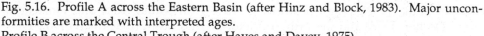

Fig. 5.16. Profile A across the Eastern Basin (after Hinz and Block, 1983). Major unconformities are marked with interpreted ages.
Profile B across the Central Trough (after Hayes and Davey, 1975).
Profile C across the Victoria Land Basin (after Cooper and Davey, 1985).

Iselin Bank, which lies between the eastern and western Ross Sea continental margins, is continental in character (Hayes and Davey, 1975). It forms part of a structural boundary between the east and west Ross Sea (the line of basement highs from the ice shelf ot Iselin Bank) and may also have existed in pre-Tertiary times as it coincides with the junction of the New Zealand and Australian continental blocks in Gondwana reconstructions (e.g., Grindley and Davey, 1982).

The Campbell Plateau

The Campbell Plateau is a continental margin plateau laying to the southeast of New Zealand (Fig. 5.17) at a depth of about 1,000 m. The basement rocks underlying the south and west Campbell Plateau at Campbell Island and in drillholes (Fig. 5.17) comprise schists similar to the Palaeozoic schists and gneisses of the Transantarctic Mountains and Tasmania (Anderton et al , 1982). During the Early to Mid Mesozoic, deep sedimentary deposits developed seaward of these Gondwana coast sequences. The associated volcanics and accreted ophiolites occurring in these thick flysch sequences indicate the existence of a convergent subducting margin during Permian and Jurassic times. Exposures of this partially- to fully-metamophosed belt of geosynclinal fore-arc sediments are known in the Southern Alps of New Zealand, Marie Byrd Land, Ellsworth Land and the Antarctic Peninsula. They constitute basement rocks on the northern Campbell Plateau and on the Chatham Rise.

New Zealand started to rift from Antarctica in the Mid Cretaceous, thinning the crust and giving rise to deep grabens forming a number of large depocentres parallel to the axes of rifting (Fig. 5.17). Bounty Trough was initiated as a rift valley at this time, separating Campbell Plateau from the Chatham Rise, but subsequently failed to spread. Five main basins occur on the Campbell Plateau (Fig. 5.17). The Great South Basin is the largest and most complex with a fault-controlled northwestern margin and with southwestern and southeastern flanks formed by sediments thinning and onlapping on to shelving basement. The central part of the basin contains sediments up to 8 km thick and mainly Mid Cretaceous to Eocene in age.

The Pukaki Trough (the Pukaki Basin and the Pukaki Embayment), an elongate trough of sediments which runs off the southern corner of the Great South Basin, and the Campbell Embayment, which extends eastwards from near Campbell Island, both contain in excess of 3.5 km of sediments (Sandford, 1980). Most of the sediments are older than Palaeocene, and there has been little local subsidence since that time. The arcuate Campbell Basin, at the southwest corner of the Campbell Plateau, contains a maximum sediment thickness in excess of 2 km, mostly of pre-Middle Palaeocene age.

The commencement of drifting and the formation of new oceanic crust that occurred about 85 Ma B.P. is marked by an unconformity in the sedimentary layers and a change from non-marine to marine or restricted marine sedimentation as the land surface sank. By uppermost Cretaceous–Palaeocene, a full marine transgression covered the Campbell Plateau with the far offshore areas starved of sediments.

During the Mid Miocene (15 Ma B.P.), the Kaikoura Orogeny commenced. Oblique convergence at the Indian–Pacific plate boundary through New Zealand led to the uplift of the Southern Alps providing a source for the significant amounts of Mio-Pliocene sediments which accumulated in northern coastal areas. Further offshore, shelf and deep-water carbonates have predominated with minor Mio-Pliocene volcanism in scattered localities.

Fig. 5.17. Campbell Plateau. Bathymetry - light line. Drillholes reaching metamorphic basement - filled circles. Metamorphic basement geology shown for offshore region. Heavy dashed line marks northeastern limit of high temperature –high pressure metamorphic basement. Major sedimentary basins of Campbell Plateau. Sediment thickness in kilometres (modified after Sandford, 1980). Dashed line marks the major strike slip faults along the northeast margin of Great South Basin (Mercator projection).

Sedimentary sequences within the Bounty Trough show mainly pelagic sedimentation during the Early–Mid Cenozoic, when there was a very low relief in the adjacent landmass, followed by more turbiditic sedimentation resulting from uplift of the adjacent South Island since the Mid Miocene (Kaikoura Orogeny), as indicated by results from DSDP site 594 (Kennett et al., 1986).

The South Tasman Rise

The East Tasman Plateau and South Tasman Rise (Fig. 5.18) are probably subsided continental crust that fragmented during the initial separation of Australia from Antarctica. DSDP site 281 (Kennett et al., 1975a) sampled a quartz mica schist basement, possibly a correlative of the Palaeozoic schist found in Tasmania. The plateau and rise are separated from the narrow continental shelf and steep upper continental slope of Tasmania by troughs. The northern portion of the South Tasman Rise shows flanking horst and graben structures with a central platform region and sediments up to 3 km thick but of unknown age on the flanks.

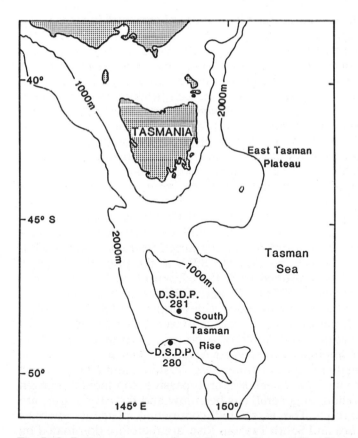

Fig. 5.18. Bathymetry of the South Tasman Rise and East Tasman Plateau. DSDP sites 280 and 281 marked by solid circles (Mercator projection).

Post break-up deposition commenced in the Late Eocene (DSDP site 281) (Kennett et al., 1975a). The East Tasman Plateau has been poorly surveyed but it is probably continental. Oceanic basement abuts its eastern margin with no marginal rift suggesting a transcurrent rather than extensional margin.

Macquarie Island

Macquarie Island is part of the ridge crest of the Macquarie Ridge which forms the Indian–Pacific plate boundary from New Zealand to the triple junction at about 60°S, 160°E (Fig. 5.7). It is elongate parallel to the ridge and extends over an area of about 170 km². It is formed of fault-bounded blocks of basic extrusive rocks and associated sediments characteristic of deposition on the ocean floor at water depths of about 2,000–4,000 m (Varne et al., 1969) and represents a faulted section through oceanic crust (Varne and Rubenach, 1972).

SUMMARY

The southern Pacific Ocean has a complex geological structure incorporating two major temporal and spatial elements. Prior to the Late Jurassic (150 Ma B.P.), the present continental margin elements of the South Pacific formed part of the convergent, or actively subducting, margin of Gondwana. The oceanic crust of the proto-Pacific Ocean was being subducted under Gondwana, but no trace remains of this older crust at present. About the late Jurassic, the Gondwana continent broke up with rifts forming between New Zealand/Australia and Antarctica and between South America and Antarctica. This breakup of Gondwana and the subsequent drift of the other continents from Antarctica led to the development of the southern Pacific Ocean as a feature of Cenozoic age, the continuation of the West Antarctic margin as a convergent plate margin and the development of continental rift (passive) margins between Australasia and Antarctica.

The structure and geological history of the old Gondwana margin (South America, West Antarctica and New Zealand) therefore results from the continued existence of a convergent margin from at least the early Mesozoic (200 Ma B.P.), probably as early as the Precambrian (600 Ma B.P.), to the present. A major unconformity (erosional event) resulted from the breakup tectonics of Jurassic (150 Ma B.P.) – Early Cretaceous (100 Ma B.P.) age. Other perturbations reflected in the geological history of the margin include the development of the active plate boundary through New Zealand during the mid-late Cenozoic and the sequential cessation of convergence at the West Antarctic subducting margin as the Aluk–Phoenix spreading centre impinged on the West Antarctica trench.

In contrast, the conjugate margins of Antarctica, Australia and New Zealand reflect younger (Cretaceous and later) rift and passive continental margin development. Sedimentation, in general, has been low and the rift margins are relatively sediment starved. The associated continental plateaus, such as Campbell Plateau, Ross Sea and South Tasman Rise, are therefore dominated by late Mesozoic–Cenozoic extensional tectonics with rift structures and crustal downwarp.

CHAPTER 6

HYDROCARBON EXPLORATION AND POTENTIAL

R.A. Cook and F.J. Davey

INTRODUCTION

The search for hydrocarbons continues to be a major emphasis of the modern world. Whilst vast reserves are held within the OPEC nations, the strategic value of resources outside of the Middle East continues to bring exploration interests to higher risk and more marginal areas. The sector of the Pacific south of 45°S is no exception, although most parts of it have some of the severest climates which will test the ingenuity of any explorers or developers.

South of 45°S in the Pacific, there is at present no production of hydrocarbons, although the continental margins of the area have several large sedimentary basins. The sedimentary basins on the Antarctic shelf have now undergone quite detailed scientific scrutiny (Behrendt, 1983a,b; Davey, 1985; St. John, 1986; Hinz and Kristoffersen, 1987) and those around the New Zealand coast major oil exploration programmes (Anderton et al., 1982; Katz and Herzer, 1986). The traces and subcommercial finds of hydrocarbons have encouraged speculation about commercial prospects. Adding to this speculation is the presence of two productive basins with significant reserves of oil and gas immediately to the north of the region, namely the Gippsland Basin off the southeastern coast of Victoria, Australia, and the Taranaki Basin on the western margin of New Zealand (Fig. 6.1).

While the Taranaki and Gippsland basins fall outside the region, they were in much closer proximity to the basins of the Ross Sea and Campbell Plateau prior to the breakup of the supercontinent Gondwanaland (Fig. 6.2) (Davey and Houtz, 1977; Grindley and Davey, 1982; Katz, 1982). Their similar origins and early history during the breakup phase about 100 Ma B.P. offer a valuable comparison when evaluating the less explored basins of the region for the major factors required to generate and accumulate commercial hydrocarbons.

In addition to Gippsland and Taranaki, several basins of the region are worthy of exploration (Fig. 6.1). The Bellingshausen continental margin of Antarctica from the Amundsen Sea to the Antarctic Peninsula is distinctly different from that of the rest of Antarctica as it is the only margin of the continent which was not formed by the breakup of Gondwanaland. It has faced a deep ocean basin since the Palaeozoic or earlier (Craddock and Hollister, 1976; Davey, 1985). The shelf varies in width throughout this region reaching a maximum of 500 km in the Bellinghausen Sea where 2–3 km of Mesozoic and Tertiary sediment has built up (Davey, 1985; St. John, 1986). Further east and north, the Pacific margin along the South American coast consists of an active subduction zone backed by the Patagonian and Andean Cordillera which contain no sedimentary basins with potential for hydrocarbon generation. The petroleum producing basins of the

Argentina area are to the east of these cordillera and do not lie within the Pacific margin (Cameron, 1981).

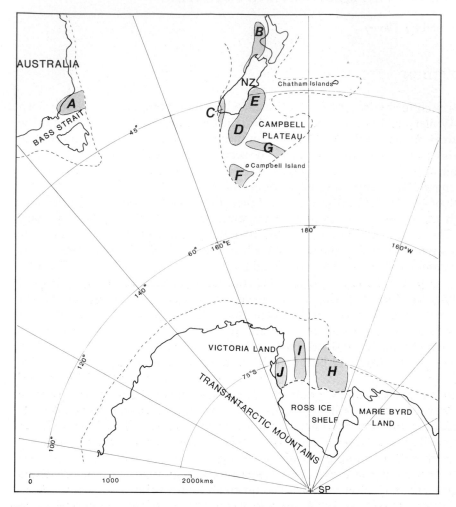

Fig. 6.1. Present-day distribution of the sedimentary basins of the southwest Pacific. A = Gippsland Basin, B = Taranaki Basin, C = Solander and Waiau Basins, D = Great South Basin, E = Canterbury Basin, F = Campbell Basin, G = Pukaki Basin, H = Eastern Ross Basin, I = Central Ross Sea Basin, J = Victoria Land Basin.

EXPLORATION HISTORY

The onshore parts of the Gippsland and Taranaki basins have long histories of exploration. Shallow drilling in Taranaki started in 1866 adjacent to seepages (Katz, 1968) and in Gippsland in 1924 after the indications of oil in water wells (Colman, 1976). Significant production took place onshore in both basins before

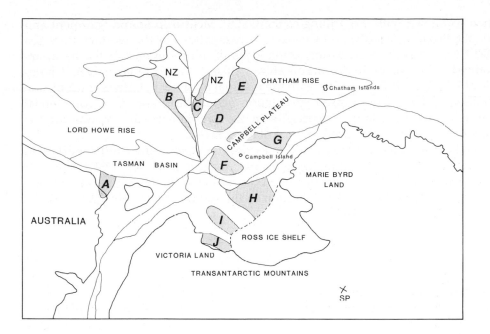

Fig. 6.2. Distribution of the sedimentary basins of the southwestern Pacific during the Upper Cretaceous when the breakup of Gondwana began (after Grindley and Davey, 1982). Basin identification is given in Fig. 6.1.

exploration moved offshore in Gippsland in 1951 and in Taranaki in 1965. Subsequent major oil and gas finds have vastly increased the reserves of both basins and encouraged further exploration. The present levels of knowledge of the geology of these basins and of the hydrocarbon sources and reservoirs are considerable (Threlfall et al., 1976; Shibaoka et al., 1978; Thomas, 1982; Cook, 1988; King and Robinson, 1988). The basins south of 45°S, which are entirely offshore, have much lower levels of exploration.

All the basins of the Campbell Plateau have at least reconnaissance seismic data. The Great South Basin has had 8 wells drilled in it and the Canterbury Basin 4 wells since 1970. Subcommercial finds of gas and traces of oil have been reported from several of these wells (Katz and Herzer, 1986). These have encouraged explorers and helped focus on areas with better potential for further work. The Solander Basin has also been drilled with 2 wells since 1975 but no hydrocarbons were recorded. The other basins of the Campbell Plateau (Campbell Basin and Pukaki Basin) have yet to be drilled, although they have been defined by good reconnaissance seismic and the Deep Sea Drilling Project (DSDP) site 277 (Anderton et al., 1982).

Under the Antarctic Treaty, no commercial exploration has been carried out in the Antarctic or on its adjacent continental shelf, although scientific work carried out in the region has produced enough regional seismic data to define the basins of the Ross Sea (Davey et al., 1982; Davey, 1985; Hinz and Kristoffersen, 1987).

When combined with the drilling of the DSDP, McMurdo Sound Sediment and Tectonic Studies (MSSTS) and Cenozoic Investigations of the western Ross Sea (CIROS) projects in these basins, some ideas of the sediments of the basin are obtained. The minor hydrocarbon shows during the drilling of DSDP holes 271–273 (McIver, 1975) together with the residual oil show in CIROS–1 (Cook and Woolhouse, 1988) have caused speculation about the presence of commercial hydrocarbon accumulations especially in the preliminary discussions for the minerals regime to be attached to the Antarctic Treaty.

The Bellingshausen area has had no exploration and less scientific work than the Ross Sea. No DSDP drilling has taken place on this shelf area. DSDP holes 323 and 445 were drilled in the deeper area beyond the shelf. Only the very limited seismic coverage allows some definition of the sediments present (Davey, 1985; Hinz and Kristoffersen, 1987).

ASSESSMENTS OF HYDROCARBON POTENTIAL

Techniques used in the assessment of the hydrocarbon potential of specific basins vary considerably with the amount of knowledge available for that basin. The simplest is to compare the basin size with other producing basins and to use a worldwide average hydrocarbon yield. The normally used yield is 1900 m^3 (12,000 barrels) of oil or oil equivalent (1070 m^3 gas equivalent to one m^3 oil) per km^3 of sediment (Miller et al., 1975; St. John, 1986). The accuracy of this method can be questioned as the validity of the worldwide analog chosen depends on the presence in the basin of the basic requirements of oil generation. Hence, the preferred evaluation method is to compare the various parameters which control the generation and accumulation of oil or gas with those for nearby producing basins with similar geological settings and histories. Once a basin has been drilled and most of the exploration parameters have been defined, then a basin can be separately evaluated much more accurately. As most of the basins of the southern Pacific have not yet been explored in detail, it is necessary in most instances to use the comparative techniques to evaluate the various controlling conditions for hydrocarbon generation and accumulaton.

There are four principal parameters which control hydrocarbon accumulation.

Source material

Natural oils and gases are a complex mixture of hydrocarbon compounds that range from methane to long chain waxes and aromatic molecules. They are formed from non-skeletal organic debris that has been buried in sedimentary rock. The first major criterion for exploration is to have large enough concentrations of organic material present to form a potential source bed. The type of the organic debris can affect the type of hydrocarbon generated. When coals or shales contain the debris of terrestrial higher plant-life of trees and shrubs, gases and gas condensates or waxy light crude oils are produced (Tissot and Welte, 1978). This is the normal situation in New Zealand and in the Gippsland Basin. When marine shales contain planktonic debris as the primary source of organic matter, heavier to light crude oil with smaller amounts of gas tend to be formed. These are the types of oils found in the North Sea and Middle East. Until well samples become available to assess whether sufficient organic matter is present, the presence and type of source rock are inferred. These inferences are based on the assumption of similar geologic conditions being present in similar basins and knowledge of present-day oceanography (Demaison, 1984).

Maturation

When organic matter is buried for a sufficient period, the temperature and pressure increase and the transformation from organic debris to natural oils and/ or gases takes place. The source rock at this point is said to be "mature". At more extreme conditions beyond the "maturation" level, the more complex hydro-carbon molecules start to break down to simple gases and eventually these will dissociate to carbon and hydrogen. There is therefore an optimum set of con-ditions for the formation of oil and gas known as the "oil window". The definition of the maturation conditions for the potential source rocks is therefore the second criterion for exploration. Normally, this is measured within a well using the effects of chemical change on the reflectance of coaly particles or the colour change in pollens and spores (Héroux et al., 1979; Hood et al., 1975). The zone of maturation for oil is accepted when a reflectance (Ro) of 0.6 for marine and 0.7 for non-marine source rocks has been reached. Even if no wells have been drilled in a basin, it is possible to model the depth at which maturation is reached using the basic knowledge of the burial history of a basin and the heat flow (Tissot and Welte, 1978).

Reservoir

Once hydrocarbons have been formed they are disseminated through the source rock. Before any commercial recovery can be made, the hydrocarbons must be concentrated in a reservoir rock. Commonly, these are well-graded sandstones or porous limestones with 20–30% pore space. Along with the poros-ity, it is necessary to have good permeability that will allow the free flow of oil and gas from the rock under production. As with source rocks, the presence of reservoir rock can only be inferred until the area has been drilled.

Trap

The final criterion for hydrocarbon accumulation is the presence of a trap. Just as oil and gas float on water so they rise in a reservoir rock. In situations where the reservoir rock is sealed by a cap rock and is a raised structure, hydrocarbons can accumulate. Good knowledge of the rock sequences (stratigraphy) allows inter-pretation of whether a cap rock or seal is present. The raised structural positions are formed by folding and/or faulting if they are not a natural feature of the rock such as a buried reef. Detailed seismic surveys are used to find such structural features. These surveys also delineate the extent of the structures. By combining this with the thickness of the reservoir, an estimate of the likely size of any potential reserves can be obtained. The faulting and folding in a basin are the result of the forces acting on the sediments. These are often active well after the sediment has been laid down and are usually unique to each basin. The broad geological situation of a basin, including the timing of major compressional or tensional events, can give some idea of the type of structure to be expected in an unexplored basin.

REGIONAL HYDROCARBON EVALUATION

Exploration provinces limited to Cretaceous–Tertiary basins

The southern Pacific coast of the Gondwana supercontinent consisted of portions of what has become eastern Australia, New Zealand and western Antarctica. The Palaeozoic interior of Gondwana was composed of sedimentary and igneous rocks which have become the schists and gneisses of the Transantarctic Mountains of Antarctica, the Great Dividing Range of Tasmania and Australia and the western province in New Zealand which consists of Nelson, Fiordland and, in the east, the Campbell Plateau.

Seaward of the old Gondwana Coast, deep ocean basins filled with sediment during the early to Mid-Mesozoic. The rocks so formed, together with their associated volcanics and accreted ophiolites, suggest subduction along this ancient coastline during Permian to Jurassic times (St. John, 1986). These rocks now make up a partially to fully metamorphosed belt exposed in the Southern Alps of New Zealand and in Marie Byrd Land, Ellsworth Land and the ranges of the Antarctic Peninsula.

Because all of these rocks have been exposed to the extreme temperatures and pressures of metamorphism, their source and reservoir potentials have been degraded. The hydrocarbons in the rocks have been degraded and any pore space has been filled by minerals. The main hydrocarbon potential is therefore restricted to those basins containing the younger Cretaceous and Tertiary sediments.

Sedimentary infill and reservoir rock similarity

To evaluate the hydrocarbon potential of the basins of the southern Pacific, we compare them with hydrocarbon-producing basins close by, namely the Taranaki and Gippsland Basins. This is necessary because some of the basins have not been drilled and their rock infill sequences are as yet unknown.

With the basins now spread over a latitudinal range of 38°S to 78°S with vastly different present-day climates, it is difficult to see how any analogy of the basins could be valid. We must, however, go back 100 million years to the Late Cretaceous when the continents of the region made up part of the Gondwana supercontinent. The areas that would subsequently contain the prospective basins of

Gippsland, Taranaki, Campbell Plateau and the Ross Sea were then grouped very closely (Fig. 6.2) (Grindley and Davey, 1982).

With the onset of the breakup of Gondwanaland, a series of depressions and failed rifts formed and it was these depressions which began to accumulate the sediments that now form the various basins (Falvey, 1974).

Typically, such basins formed through separation are initially infilled by non-marine river sediments followed progressively, as the sea encroaches, by deltaic coal measures, then beach and marine sands and shales leading eventually to open ocean carbonate muds. It can be expected that similar reservoir rocks (porous and permeable sandstones) will occur in all of these basins.

Source rock similarity

While the similar geological environments will give rise to similar sediments, it is the climate which controls the type and amount of organic matter growing in a region and this in turn controls the hydrocarbon source rock potential.

Given that the basins were all grouped together within a narrow latitude range of 10–20° and had similar non-marine to marginal marine depositional environments during the Upper Cretaceous, it is not unreasonable to suggest that all the basins were receiving very similar organic debris. From the reconstructions of Gondwanaland, we find, however, that these basins lay at latitudes of 70–80°S. This is well south of what could be considered a temperate forest zone today. Yet, the deposition of extensive coals containing dominantly temperate climate podocarps with lesser beeches and ferns in the New Zealand and the Gippsland basins (Mildenhall, 1980) means that the latitudinal climatic zonation during the Late Cretaceous to Eocene was not similar to the present regime. Recent work by Hallam (1984) on the distribution of minerals deposited in environments controlled by specific climates and the distribution of coals worldwide suggests that a much broader temperature versus latitude zonation occurred during the Jurassic and Cretaceous than at the present. During this time, the variation of temperture from pole to equator was possibly 20°C instead of the present 40–50°C. In the southern Pacific, such a zonation probably continued up to the Eocene about 40 million years ago when polar ice sheets began to dominate the Antarctic continent (Barron et al., 1988).

Overall, it is reasonable then to expect that all the basins of the southern Pacific during the Late Cretaceous up to the Eocene had the same marginal marine and lowland temperate forest floral types leading to similar potential source rocks.

This Cretaceous to Palaeocene period is also a period of significant marine organic deposition throughout the world (Fischer, 1982; Dean et al., 1984; Schlanger, 1986; Brooks and Fleet, 1987). These organic-rich marine sediments would provide potential source rocks if similar deposits were present in the basins of the region. As mentioned earlier, these marine sediments would also be most likely to generate oil rather than gas.

By the Late Oligocene, the picture had changed as the opening seaways started to affect the climate and cause botanical isolation (Kennett et al., 1972; Kennett, 1977, 1980). However, as will be shown later, the important source rocks occur in the Eocene and earlier sequences. Valid analogies of source potential between the basins can therefore be made.

Maturity and trap comparisons

Unlike the controls on the source and reservoir, the controls on maturity and trap geometry are not limited to the Late Cretaceous and Early Tertiary. The maturity is controlled by the depth of burial of the source sediments and this is highly variable between the basins. To evaluate it, each basin must therefore be considered independently.

The structural configurations are also unique to each basin as the stresses associated with each basin following the breakup of Gondwanaland have varied widely both in timing and strength.

To evaluate the hydrocarbon potential of the basins of the Antarctic Sector of the Pacific, it is therefore important to look at the various basins in detail and to draw comparisons between them so as to evaluate the various parameters needed for hydrocarbon accumulation. The first stage is to describe the hydrocarbon occurrences in the two adjacent productive basins, the Gippsland and Taranaki Basins.

Gippsland Basin

The Gippsland Basin lies at the eastern end of the Bass Strait, in southeastern Australia (Fig. 6.3) and is one of the world's major coal- and petroleum-bearing basins. The basin is wedge-shaped and approximately 50,000 km² in area of which four-fifths lies offshore. It contains up to 5 km of Cretaceous and Tertiary sediments with an average thickness of 3.5 km.

Exploration since 1964 has resulted in the discovery of several commercial oil fields, three of which are in the giant category (8×10^7 m³, Halbouty et al., 1970). The total recoverable reserves for this basin are now quoted at 3.2×10^8 m³ of oil, 6.4×10^7 m³ of LPG and 2×10^{10} m³ of gas. This equates to a reserve factor of 2300 m³ oil equivalent/km³ of sediment which is close to the figure of 1900 m³/km³ mentioned earlier as a worldwide average.

Most of the hydrocarbons found in the Gippsland Basin are trapped at the top of the Late Cretaceous to Eocene Latrobe Group. Here, erosional and structural highs occur under the unconformably overlying shales. The reservoirs are therefore the alluvial-deltaic sands of the Latrobe Group. Most of the sedimentary rocks below the reservoirs are of non-marine origin, and the coal material within the Latrobe and Early Cretaceous Strzelecki Groups has been suggested as the source of the hydrocarbons (Threlfall et al., 1976; Shibaoka et al., 1978). The main Gippsland oils are high in wax and the distribution of biological markers confirms that terrestrial organic material was the source of oil (Thomas, 1982; Burns et al., 1984). At the western margin of the basin, a number of low to medium gravity naphthenic crudes has been recovered. These show the biological marker characteristics of the other waxy and plant-derived oils. However, they have subsequently been biodegraded due to the invasion by meteoric water (Threlfall et al., 1976; Thomas, 1982).

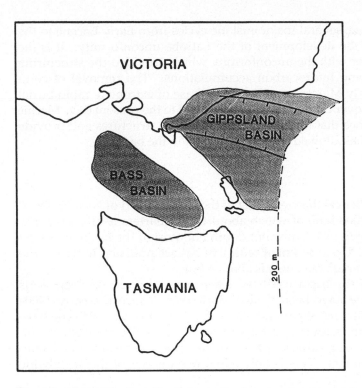

Fig. 6.3. Map of the Bass Strait Australia showing the area of the Gippsland Basin.

The measured maturation levels within the basin show that the main generation zone lies at a depth of about 2.8 km. At the centre of the basin, this lies within the top of the Latrobe Group. However, extrapolation of the maturation/depth trend suggests that the Strzelecki Group is overmature to have generated oil in the recent past (Shibaoka et al., 1978).

The seal over the structures is provided by the calcareous mudstones and marls of the Miocene Lakes Entrance formation and the Gippsland limestone.

The structural development under the erosional unconformity at the top of the Latrobe Group has given rise to the majority of the hydrocarbon traps of the basin. The initial basin formation resulted from a rifting phase between the Jurassic and Early Cretaceous (Smith, 1982). This led to the deposition of the Strzelecki Group, consisting of non-marine sandstones, volcaniclastics and conglomerates on the basin margins with more mudstones and coals accumulating along the central axis of the basin. Towards the end of the Early Cretaceous, subsidence decreased with some uplift in the latter part of the Early Cretaceous (Threlfall et al., 1976). The resultant unconformity was then followed in the Late Cretaceous by a second rifting phase. This led to the deposition of the Late Cretaceous to Eocene coal-bearing deposits of the Latrobe Group. Cessation of ocean formation in the Tasman Sea by the Early Eocene marked the end of the rift-associated subsidence which was replaced by compression and wrench faulting (Smith, 1982). During this compressional phase, several major eustatic cycles from Early Eocene to the Early Oligocene led to the development of the Latrobe unconformity. It is the wrench faulting together with the unconformity which provided the structuring of the reservoirs allowing hydrocarbon accumulations. The removal of compression during the Early Miocene resulted in a phase of extremely rapid burial and shelf development over the basin which has lasted to the present day. Marine sediments deposited since that time form the seal for the structures and provide the overburden which has allowed the oil generation in the basin.

Taranaki Basin

The Taranaki Basin lies off the west coast of the North Island of New Zealand. It covers more than 80,000 km^2, of which about three-quarters is offshore. The offshore parts range down to 500 m water depth but most of the basin lies in the 100–250 m depth range. Up to 11 km of sediment has accumulated in part of the graben, although the average thickness is about 4 km.

Seismic coverage of the basin has been extensive and some 56 deep wells onshore and 30 offshore have been drilled since 1965. Since the early 1960s recoverage reserves of 10^{11} m^3 of gas and 4.3 x 10^7 m^3 of oil and condensate have been located in the Maui, Kapuni and McKee Fields (Cook, 1985) together with several new fields yet to be produced. This equates to a reserve factor of 500 m^3 oil equivalent/km^3 sediment. This is only about one-quarter of the worldwide average of 1900 m^3/km^3.

Most hydrocarbons discovered in the Taranaki Basin are trapped near the top of the Eocene Kapuni Group. The reservoirs are the alluvial and marginal marine sandstones associated with coal measure sequences, although other marine sandstones in the Miocene and Pliocene have also contained hydrocarbons (Robinson and King, 1988). The hydrocarbons have been shown geochemically to be derived from coals, probably from the Late Cretaceous Pakawau and the Kapuni Groups (Cook, 1988). These hydrocarbons are primarily gas/condensates, although a significant amount of high wax oil has also been found. The measured maturation levels from the biomarkers and the well samples suggest that the oils have been generated at depths greater than 5 km (reflectance 0.9%) which confirms that the Pakawau Group coals are the primary source. Kapuni Group members may well also have generated hydrocarbons in the northern parts of the graben (Cook, 1988). The marine equivalents to the Kapuni Group and the overlying Oligocene and Miocene limestones and mudstones provide seals for the various reservoirs throughout the basin.

The Taranaki Basin developed during the Late Cretaceous to Eocene as a result of the rifting phase associated with the opening of the Tasman Sea. However, with the onset of compression during the Upper Oligocene to Miocene, the basin separated into the more stable Western Platform and the Taranaki Graben complex. The northern part of the Graben is an area of continuous subsidence and oblique faulting (Knox, 1982) and contains extensive Miocene and Pliocene volcanics (Pilaar and Wakefield, 1984). This contrasts with the southern Taranaki Graben where predominantly reverse faulting occurred (Knox, 1982). The Late

Eocene to Late Miocene faulting is recognizable along the Cape Egmont Fault Zone which separates the Graben from the Western Platform. This faulting is probably related to the development of the active plate boundary beneath the North Island and the dextral transform faulting along the Alpine Fault 35–10 Ma B.P. (Carter and Norris, 1976; Knox, 1982). From the Late Miocene to Pleistocene, the graben underwent compressional deformation which caused reverse faulting, especially low angle thrust faults. These thrust faults along the eastern margin of the graben are particularly important as they form the structures of the McKee, Tariki, Ahuroa and Waihapa Fields. This complex tectonic history has given rise to the structures associated with the various fields and most have a combination of fault and fold closure. In size, they range from giant, as found in the Maui gas/condensate Field, down. While the obvious large structures of the basin have now been drilled, there remain many more intermediate and commercially viable structures to be drilled. The complex tectonics of the region may also give rise to other types of structure and reservoir combinations which are as yet untested.

SEDIMENTARY BASINS OF SOUTHERN NEW ZEALAND

Solander Trough

The Solander Trough lies at the southern end of the South Island of New Zealand. It forms a submarine depression between the continental Campbell Plateau and the oceanic Macquarie Ridge to the west. At its head are a series of

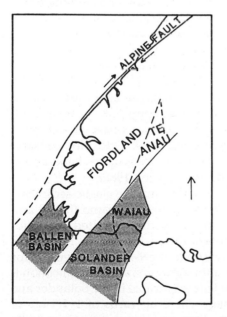

Fig. 6.4. Map of southwestern New Zealand showing the location of the sedimentary basins.

small sub-basins which are considered to have some hydrocarbon potential. They are the Solander, Balleny and the onshore Waiau and Te Anau Basins (Fig. 6.4).

The two offshore basins extending to the 1,000 m isobath cover about 14,000 km^2 whilst the onshore basins cover about 6,000 km^2. Although the offshore basins extend well to the south, possibly tripling the area, water depths there exceed 1,500 m. Little work has been completed in the deepwater region and the full extent of the basin has yet to be defined. The thickest sedimentary section in all the basins is about 6 km, with an average of about 3 km. This would suggest that the basin has a hydrocarbon potential of 1×10^8 m^3 oil equivalent, although none of this has yet been found.

Early exploration interest in the onshore part of the region resulted from the thin oil shale deposits discovered near the coast in the Waiau Basin. However, it has only been in the last decade and a half that there has been interest in the off-shore area. Over this time, the area out to about 1,000 m water depth has received extensive seismic coverage. Since 1975, two wells have been drilled offshore and two onshore but these had disappointing results.

The subsidence in the basins has been controlled by major faults and has a complicated tectonic history resulting from the response to the regional stresses and the proximity of the area to the southern end of the Alpine Fault and hence Pacific plate margin (Norris and Carter, 1980; Grant, 1985).

While any one of the local histories of the basins is complex, especially during the Late Tertiary, all the basins have a similar framework to their stratigraphy and tectonics.

During the Late Cretaceous and Early Tertiary, the initial relief on the stable landscape of mostly Palaeozoic rocks was reduced by erosion and infilling of the block-faulted topography. The Cretaceous to Eocene sediments show relatively steep dips on the regional seismic profiles. They are assumed to be relatively coarse sediments derived from the west of the bounding faults and make up to 3 km of the sequence. The coal measure sequence seen on the eastern margin of the Waiau Basin could well be a major part of these sequences. They occur in a similar situation to those in the Taranaki Basin where the Pakawau coal measures are locally deposited within the middle Cretaceous topography. The mature land-surface during the Late Eocene was abruptly affected by a phase of tectonism which allowed a rapid marine incursion. This resulted in the deposition of coarse breccias, arkosic sandstones and flysch which in the west pass up to chalks and in the east to fine-grained clastic sediments (Norris and Carter, 1980).

The Plio-Pleistocene deposition consisted of further marine clastic sediments in the south but in the north of the Waiau Basin deposits became fluvial and glacial. Throughout the area, these sediments are warped and faulted with Plio-cene fault reactivation and the large-scale uplift of the basins (Grant, 1985). The basins have not been uplifted much by comparison to the 9–15 km suggested for the adjacent Fiordland region (Suggate, 1963), although some surface truncation is suggested in seismic profiles. While the uplift is recognizable in the Solander and Waiau region, it is greater in the Balleny Basin where upwards of 1–1.5 km of section loss is shown (Grant, 1985).

Hydrocarbon potential

The 3 km of Cretaceous and lower Tertiary sediments at the base of the basins holds the key to their hydrocarbon potential. These are the Ohai Group coal measures as seen in the eastern margin of the Waiau Basin and the conglomerates and Eocene sands of the western margin.

While the conglomerates would be of no interest as a source of hydrocarbons or as a potential reservoir, the coals are similar to those found in the Taranaki Basin. Such coal measures are therefore the primary objective for exploration as they would provide both the oil and gas source together with reservoir-quality sands.

Whether such coal sequences are buried deep enough to have generated significant hydrocarbons is questionable (Cook, 1988). Because of the widespread uplift since the Pliocene, large volumes of the more mature section may be closer to the surface than normal. Present burial depths cannot therefore be used to exclude the maturation potential of the basins. This is borne out by the Ohai coal measures being on the present-day surface with a rank of high volatile bituminous equivalent to reflectance of 0.53 (Black, 1980). The Late Tertiary marine sequences would provide surficial seal for any trap.

While detailed structural maps have not been made for the Solander Trough basins, the regional work of Grant (1985) suggests that significant to large folded and faulted structures are present.

BASINS OF THE CAMPBELL PLATEAU

The Campbell Plateau is a large submerged block of continental crust lying to the east and southeast of the South Island of New Zealand. This block was originally part of Gondwanaland and several tensional basins formed within it during its separation from Antarctica (Davey, this volume). Four of these basins have commercial potential for hydrocarbons. They are the Canterbury, Great South, Pukaki and Campbell Basins (Fig. 6.5)

Canterbury Basin

The Canterbury Basin lies to the east of the alpine area of the South Island and continues up to 150 km offshore to water depths of up to 1,500 m. Overall, the basin covers some 48,000 km² with a maximum thickness of over 5 km of sediment and average of 3 km. This would suggest that there is a potential for some 3×10^8 m³ oil equivalent to be found in the basin based on world average figures.

Because of the great water depths of the eastern side of the basin, exploration has been limited to the western onshore and the continental shelf sectors. Extensive exploration seismic profiles have been carried out on the continental shelf but the deeper parts of the basin have only had limited reconnaissance seismic work. However, this is sufficient to delimit the extent of the basin. Seven wells have been drilled in the area with three onshore and four offshore. The onshore wells

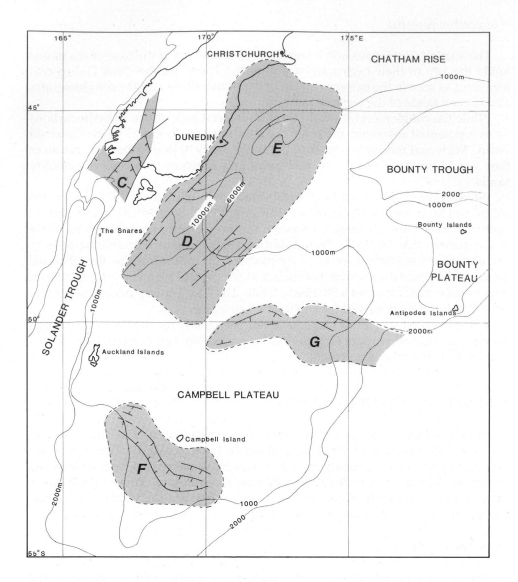

Fig. 6.5. Map of the Campbell Plateau showing the major sedimentary basins and their gross structuring. Basin identification is given in Fig. 6.1.

showed that the potential reservoirs had been flushed with fresh water but two of the offshore wells did have good condensate and gas shows present. Galleon-1 proved sub-commercial reserves of 4×10^8 m^3 gas and 0.2×10^6 m^3 of condensate.

From geochemical studies of the condensate, the source of the oil appears to be terrestrial organic material suggesting that the coal measure sequence has provided the hydrocarbons. Studies also show that the Palaeocene marine shales are rich enough to be potential source rocks for hydrocarbons in the area.

The potential reservoirs for the area lie in the sandstones of the Late Cretaceous coal measures and the Palaeocene to Eocene marine sandstones.

The marine mudstones and non-marine shales associated with the reservoir sands would provide a good sealing cap rock for the structures. From the studies carried out by the oil industry, maturation levels for the generation of hydro-carbons would be reached at around 2,800–3,600 m.

The stratigraphy includes a broadly transgressive sequence of synrift and early post-rift coal measures and conglomerates followed by marine sandstones, mud-stones and finally limestones. A strong regional unconformity within the Oligo-cene limestone separates this lower transgressive sequence from an overlying regressive sequence of marine siltstones and sandstones that filled the western part of the basin during the Neogene orogenic uplift of the Southern Alps. Local episodes of volcanism occurred at intervals throughout the basin's history.

As the lower transgressive sequence onlapped to the west, stratigraphic pinch-out structures are present in combination with the extensional faulting. This faulting is not normally observed above the Palaeocene sequence. However, reverse movement occurred on pre-existing fault zones during the beginning of the Miocene giving rise to anticlinal structures. The third kind of structures found in the basin are those associated with volcanic doming.

Great South Basin

The Great South Basin lying southeast of the South Island is the largest of New Zealand's sedimentary basins. It covers about 85,000 km² with all but a few hundred km² offshore (Fig. 6.5) and extends to water depths of up to 1,500 m. However, two-thirds of the basin lies in the water depths less than 1,000 m. The maximum sediment thickness is 7.5 km with an average of around 4 km. Using world average figures this would suggest that reserves of 6.5×10^8 m³ oil equiva-lent should be present. Commercial exploration of the basin began in the mid 1960s. The information base for the area now includes more than 50,000 km of seismic profiles and eight offshore wells. These wells have confirmed some potential for the basin, with shows of gas and condensate in two wells together with the sub-commercial test of 1.9×10^5 m³/day gas and minor amounts of condensate at Kawau-1A.

Unfortunately, a large percentage of the basin is in water deeper than 500 m and ranges up to 350 km from land (Fig. 6.5). To be commercial, any field will therefore have to be in at least the giant category of reserves.

The Great South Basin is a fault-controlled basin. The majority of the faulting appears to have been active up to the Palaeocene but not since. The basin floor is block faulted in a series of horst and graben structures, typical of tensional tectonics. The tensional nature of the faulting around the whole basin, the trend of the basin parallel to the eastern margin of the Campbell Plateau and its timing all suggest that the basin had its origin as the response to the crustal thinning under the plateau during the separation of the region from Antarctica.

The sedimentary sequence contains over 5 km of mainly Cretaceous and Early Tertiary rocks. These consist of thick basal coal measures and fluvial deposits

overlain by a Late Cretaceous to Eocene marine clastic sequence. By the Oligocene, the source of clastic material was removed from most of the basin and for
most of the Late Tertiary the sequence was dominated by fine-grained calcareous
deposits. During the Pleistocene, a clastic wedge of sediment was deposited over
the western margin of the basin.

In the wells drilled in the Great South Basin, the hydrocarbon indications have
been restricted to the Cretaceous section. Geochemical analyses of the only test
gas and condensate in the Kawau-1A well indicates that these hydrocarbons have
been derived from terrestrial and coaly organic matter.

The rocks of the basal Cretaceous sequence contain abundant humic kerogen
and some thick coals. In addition, the Late Cretaceous and Palaeocene restricted
marine mudstones contain organic material which has the potential to generate oil
(Anderton et al., 1982). The character of the source rocks indicates that the basin
should be considered as a primary gas condensate source with some light waxy oil
potential.

The maturation level of the potential source has been measured in all of the
wells drilled to date. It has been found that only the Cretaceous sediments have
reached maturity with reflectance levels of 0.75% at the 3,600–4,200 m level.
Extrapolation of the maturation level into the thickest parts of the basin, however,
shows that some of the Lower Palaeocene sediments will have reached maturity.

With the assumption that the basin has had a similar geothermal gradient
throughout its geological history (and therefore similar depths of burial have been
required to reach maturity in the past), it can be shown that there has been some
generation of hydrocarbons since the Palaeocene.

The Late Cretaceous to Early Tertiary marginal marine sandstones are the
principal reservoir targets of the Great South Basin, although the fluvial sands
associated with the coal measures of the Late Cretaceous have potential. Where
these have been encountered in wells, they show good reservoir porosities of
17–20% and permeabilities of between 10 and 100 millidarcies.

With very little tectonic deformation in the Great South Basin, the structures
with hydrocarbon potential are derived primarily from sediment drape over
basement highs combined with limited faulting. The sizes of these structures are
of the order of 200 km^2, with up to 300 m of vertical closure. The potential for
finding large quantities of reserves in the Great South Basin is still good if any one
of these structures is found to produce oil.

The mudstones and siltstones deposited during the marine transgression provide good reservoir seals, especially in the southern and eastern areas. However,
these mudstones were only present on the western side of the basin from the
Eocene, so the seal potential of this region is not good.

Campbell Basin

The remoteness of the Campbell Basin from New Zealand together with its
location in the circum-polar rough weather belt (Fig. 6.5) has meant that it has not
been the focus of much exploration activity to date. However, since 1970, this
basin has received good seismic coverage and has been mapped and evaluated

(Anderton et al., 1982). No exploration wells have been drilled within this basin but DSDP hole 277 was drilled on its western margin.

The basin has a total area of about 20,000 km^2 and, like the Great South Basin, is a deep, essentially linear, normal fault-controlled depression. It had its origin during the rifting of the Campbell Plateau from Antarctica when the basement crust thinned. The basin lies in water depths of 200 m in the northeast towards Campbell Island to about 850–1,000 m at its southern edge.

Upwards of 5 km of sediment is present in the large graben located on the southern side of the basin. To the north of this deep graben lies a series of sub-parallel horsts and grabens of lesser relief. The basin may be open to the south (i.e., has been truncated by the Antarctic/Campbell Plateau Rift) but this is unproven.

The fault growth in the basin follows the same pattern as the Great South Basin. Very rapid fault movement occurred during the early stages of development of the basin which was then followed by a general downwarping during the latter part of the basin subsidence with none of the upper beds cut by the initial faulting.

No direct control is available for the stratigraphy of the Campbell Basin but a sequence of Late Cretaceous and Tertiary rocks are present on the adjacent Campbell Island (Beggs, 1978; Cook 1981). Within the basin, seismic mapping has been used to separate three main sedimentary groupings (Anderton et al., 1982).

On Campbell Island, the latest Cretaceous (Maastrichtian) to Palaeocene Garden Cove Formation consists of fluvial channel/point bar deposits at the base grading up through estuarine channel and mud deposits to fully marine mudstones at the top. This transition from non-marine to marine approximates the same transition as in the Great South Basin. Within the Campbell Basin, the seismic response of the Cretaceous sequence has been interpreted as lacustrine shales which have been flanked by fluviatile, lake shore and coal swamp facies where sands and silts predominate (Anderton et al., 1982). Immediately overlying the horizon mapped as the top of the Cretaceous is the marine transgressive sequence; its seismic character indicates good sand horizons. On Campbell Island, the facies equivalent is seen in the middle estuarine channel deposits of the Garden Cove Formation. The slightly later age of the transgression on Campbell Island reflects its marginal location beyond the basin edge. Above the Palaeocene, the sequence within the basin is undoubtedly equivalent to the Tucker Cove Limestone of Campbell Island with fine-grained limestone and chert, as was also seen in cores from DSDP site 277. It is unknown if sedimentation has been continuous in the Campbell Basin throughout the Late Tertiary. There is no immediate evidence of any of the Miocene–Pleistocene volcanics of Auckland and Campbell Islands being present within the basin.

Although no wells have been drilled in the basin, the parameters required for hydrocarbon accumulations can be assessed from the outcrop data on the Campbell Island and by comparison to the Great South Basin.

Samples taken from Campbell Island are consistently less than the 0.5% total organic carbon which is considered the minimum necessary for a source rock (Phillips Petroleum, 1976). This is to be expected in the sedimentary environ ments represented. In the Campbell Basin itself, it is concluded that the total organic carbon content of the lacustrine and any lake-margin coal measures would be much higher than their equivalent fluvial rocks on Campbell Island. As in the Great South Basin, the Cretaceous coals probably contain a similar flora to those of the western side of New Zealand. These coals could therefore be the source of liquid hydrocarbon as well as gas.

Given that the geothermal gradients have been about the same as those in the Great South Basin, we can expect maturation to have started in the Campbell Basin below 3.5 km. In fact, due to the much closer proximity of the Antarctic–Campbell Plateau rift, this assumption of the same geothermal gradient as the Great South Basin is probably on the conservative side. This could mean more of the Campbell Basin sequence would have reached maturity.

Widespread clastic reservoir development probably has not occurred in the Campbell Basin. However, two zones could well act as reservoirs. The marginal beach sands of the lacustrine facies and associated channelling of any coal swamps could be one reservoir sequence while the development of transgressive beach sands overlying the lower sequences may have developed at the time of the Late Cretaceous–Palaeocene transgression. Given the quartz-rich nature of the basement rocks, the presence of well sorted quartzose sands is reasonable in the above environments.

Sediment drape over the irregular basement is the major source of structures in the Campbell Basin. As these decrease rapidly up into the overlying sequence, closure associated with the marginal faults would therefore be more viable for hydrocarbon traps. Sealing for these trap types would come from the shales and chalks which predominate in the upper sequence. Location of reservoir sands would be a greater problem than sealing with fine-grained sediments.

While the Campbell Basin has not yet undergone extensive exploration, it does have a thick sedimentary fill with the potential of some of it being mature for hydrocarbon generation. The similar tectonic setting and seismic reflection character of this basin to the Great South Basin allows consistent geological interpretations to be made incorporating the evidence from both Campbell Island and DSDP site 277. Until it is drilled, the hydrocarbon potential of the basin is speculative. However, the interpretations suggest that it is worth considering on strategic grounds even if it is not viable economically.

Pukaki Basin

On the Campbell Plateau, an elongate basin trends east-west from the continental margin in the east to the southeast corner of the Great South Basin (Fig. 6.5). This relatively small basin (40,000 km²) is not joined to the Great South Basin but has a basement ridge separating the two. Two sedimentary sub-basins, the Pukaki Basin and the Pukaki Embayment, have been recognized. Within this trend, each sub-basin has up to 3.5 km of supposed Cretaceous–Tertiary section.

To date, no drilling has been carried out within the basin but 3,700 km of reconnaissance seismic profiles have been run. While the initial definition of the Pukaki Basin was made at the same time as both the Great South Basin and

Campbell Basin, no seismic mapping or evaluation has been carried out on this basin to date. An overview of the seismic data suggests that, like the Campbell Basin, the Pukaki Basin originated through extensional faulting and is therefore of comparable age. The sedimentary fill is unknown but seismic reflectors similar to those in the Campbell Basin and Great South Basin are present. The same model of sedimentation, source and reservoir are therefore taken for this basin as for the Campbell Basin. The only difference is that the marine transgression may have occurred much earlier as this rifted basin was open to the primary rift zone which eventually separated New Zealand and Antarctica.

Because of the limited thickness of sequence and by comparison with the Great South Basin, any source rock could only just be mature at 3.5 km depth. This, together with its great distance from the South Island, means that it is considered the poorest hydrocarbon prospect of the Campbell Plateau.

BASINS OF THE ROSS SEA

Geophysical research in the Ross Sea shows that thick sedimentary sequences are present over large areas (Houtz and Davey, 1973; Wong and Christoffel, 1981; Davey et al., 1982, 1983; Hinz and Block, 1983; Sato et al. 1984; Cooper et al., 1987). Drillhole data from the Deep Sea Drilling Project (DSDP) Leg 28 (Hayes et al., 1975a, b), McMurdo Sound Sediment and Tectonic Studies (MSSTS-1) drillhole (Harwood, 1986) and Cenozoic Investigations of Ross Sea (CIROS-1) drillhole (Barrett, 1987) show that the sediments which underlie the Ross Sea are up to Oligocene in age with older rocks being found only in McMurdo Sound as erratics (Webb, 1983). The deeper sediments in the Ross Sea basins are probably at least Early Tertiary in age and possibly as old as Late Cretaceous (Houtz and Davey, 1973; Davey et al., 1982; Hinz and Block, 1983). Cooper et al. (1987) interpreted an older sedimentary sequence in the western Ross Sea as being as old as Upper Palaeozoic in age.

Three major basins have been delineated : the Eastern Basin, the Central Trough and the Victoria Land Basin (Fig. 6.6) (Davey, this volume). Multichannel seismic reflection data have defined the extent, sedimentary structure and stratigraphy of the basins in detail (Hinz and Block, 1983; Sato et al., 1984; Cooper et al., 1987; Hinz and Kristoffersen, 1987).

Eastern Basin

The Eastern Basin covers most of the eastern Ross Sea continental shelf, an area of about 100,000 km² (Houtz and Davey, 1973 (Fig. 6.6). It contains up to about 6 km thickness of sedimentary rocks with an average of 3 m, suggesting a potential for about 6×10^8 m³ oil equivalent to be found in the basin, based on worldwide averages. The seafloor lies at an average depth of about 500 m. Reconnaissance multichannel seismic data since 1980 cover the area (Hinz and Block, 1983; Sato et al., 1984; J. Wannesson, pers. comm.) and, with the results of the DSDP drillholes, enable a preliminary stratigraphy to be derived.

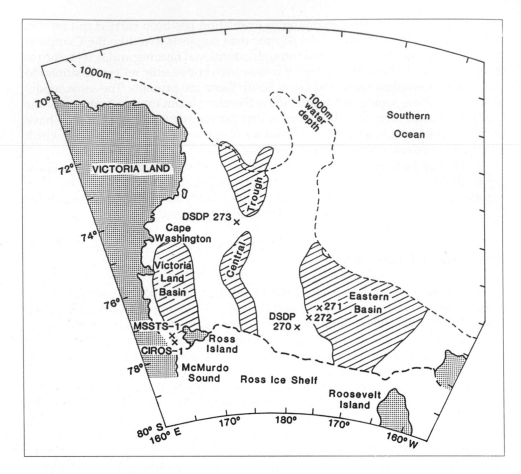

Fig. 6.6. Sedimentary basins of the Ross Sea (after Davey, this volume), lightly shaded where basement > 3 km below seafloor (Polar Stereographic projection).

The basin is a simple open basin or trough, opening towards the shelf edge in the north and extending to, and under, the Ross Ice Shelf in the south (Davey, this volume). Beneath a shallow widespread unconformity, separating Middle Miocene sediments from those of Pleistocene and younger age, the sedimentary layers dip gently towards the centre of the basin and towards the shelf edge where they reach a thickness of 4 km and have the form of prograded beds. Along the margins of the basin, these Late Oligocene and Miocene sediments are folded into north-south trending broad open folds. Seismic data at the continental slope can be interpreted as showing 2 km of pre-Oligocene sediments and this thickness may continue under the main basin. Hinz and Block (1983) detected a north-south trending trough of pre-Late Oligocene sediments, up to 2 km deep, under the western margin of the Eastern trough which may continue under the southern part of the basin. The lower sequence could be either related to the separation of

New Zealand from Gondwana and therefore of Late Cretaceous age (Cooper et al., 1988) or be lowermost Tertiary in age.

The thin Oligocene sequence drilled in DSDP hole 270 suggests that the lower sequence consists of terrestrial to marginal marine sediments. The unconformity overlying the older sedimentary sequence has an age of 25–26 Ma which coincides closely with the development of the Circum-Antarctic Current (about 30 Ma), and a widespread Oligocene regression in the Southern Hemisphere. Above this older sedimentary sequence, Hinz and Block (1983) detected six depositional sequences, the upper five prograding sequences being interpreted as a series of mostly deltaic lobes, with a thin delta plain facies to the south and a prograding prodelta facies to the north on a subsiding platform. The uppermost unconformity corresponds to an age gap of 4–10 Ma (Savage and Ciesielski, 1983) and is widespread over the whole Ross Sea. It truncates the dipping reflections forming the margin of the basin in the south, therefore indicating a lack of subsidence of the basin in this region since 10 Ma ago. A thickness of several hundred metres of sediments has been removed.

Small amounts of methane and ethane were found in the Miocene glacial marine sediments of DSDP sites 271–273 (Hayes et al., 1975a, b). McIver (1975) found that the gas extracted from the sealed cores from these drillsites had a significant fraction of higher homologues than ethane which, together with their consistent nature throughout, suggested that local organic diagenesis could have occurred and that liquid hydrocarbons may have been generated somewhere in the sedimentary section.

Modelling of the thermal maturity of the sediments to see if conditions suitable for hydrocarbon generation have been reached has been carried out by Hinz and Block (1983) and Cook and Davey (1984). Information for the models is sparse. No measurements of heat flow or geothermal gradient have been made in the Eastern Basin and the value assumed was based on the nearest heat flow measurements on Roosevelt Island (Fig. 6.6). A basic assumption for the model is that heat flow has not varied with time. This is conservative for a basin lying close to a rifted continental margin where heat flows are probably significantly higher at breakup and slowly decay with time (Turcotte, 1980). The thermal conductivities assumed were related to the sediments predicted or shown to exist in the basin without allowing for compaction. For example, the Late Oligocene to Holocene glacial marine sequence is predominantly fine-grained shales and mudstones with glacial erratic pebbles floating in the fine-grained matrix (Hayes et al., 1975a). The fine-grained nature of the sediment places a control on its thermal conductivity with a higher value for the deeper, more sandy, marginal marine/terrestrial sequence. The ambient surface temperature from time of deposition to present was taken as 0°C, assuming high latitudes for the terrestrial and marine sequence throughout the Tertiary. The models for the Eastern Basin suggest that hydrocarbons generation is possible but only in the pre-Late Oligocene sediments.

Source rocks in the basin probably occur in the older sequence as the younger sediments comprise marine glacial sequences. Since the lower sequence has not been drilled or sampled, a measurement of the organic carbon content of the sequence has not been made. Comparable terrestrial marginal marine sequences related to breakup (i.e., Gippsland Basin) do, however, contain sufficient carbonaceous material to provide a source for hydrocarbons.

Little information exists on which to base an assessment of reservoir rocks. In the Tertiary, drillhole data through marine glacial sequences (DSDP, MSSTS-1, CIROS-1) indicate adequate porosity for some horizons but permeability is unknown. The older, preglacial rocks of probable Late Cretaceous to Oligocene age may have reservoir rocks in marine or non-marine sandstones, by analogy with coeval basins in western Tasmania and Campbell Plateau.

Many types of stratigraphic or structural traps may exist related to the tectonic history (two-phase rifting) including traps resulting from sediment drape over early rift faulting and stratigraphic traps arising from the numerous unconformities seen in the sedimentary section, particularly associated with the thick prograding sequence of glacial deposits.

Central Trough

The Central Trough (Davey, this volume) is an elongate sedimentary basin trending north-south and extending from the continental shelf edge to under the Ross Ice Shelf. It coincides approximately with 175°E longitude. The Central Trough is over 500 km long and about 100 km wide, with one major dextral offset at 74°S and a possible minor one at 73°S. Thicknesses of about 6 km of sediment are present in the deepest part of the basin and a possible oil reserve of 2.5×10^8 m^3 is indicated based on worldwide averages.

DSDP site 273 (Fig. 6.6) was located over the basin and penetrated to 346 m sub-seafloor. It encountered only one major unconformity, which was at shallow depth, corresponding to the time interval 4–10 Ma.

The axis of the trough coincides with a large gravity high indicating a rift origin with associated crustal thinning and/or intrusions of high density rocks into the crust beneath the basin (Hayes and Davey, 1975). Seismic data indicate steep margins to the trough with the adjacent basement either near seafloor (Houtz and Davey, 1973) or at depths of up to 2 km where the rift contains only the oldest sediments (Davey et al., 1982). Davey (1981) postulated an Early Tertiary age, suggesting that the trough is a graben structure formed as a failed arm of the spreading centre which abutted the continental margin of the western Ross Sea at about 55 Ma (Weissel et al., 1977). Hinz and Block (1983) and Cooper et al. (1988), however, suggested that the oldest sediments may be Late Cretaceous in age.

The stratigraphy for the Central Trough is poorly known. At DSDP site 273 (Fig. 6.6), the oldest sequence penetrated was Early Miocene (Hayes et al., 1975b). This sequence was predominantly a pebbly silty claystone of marine glacial origin. The sediments in the deeper part of the trough are probably as old as Early Tertiary–Late Cretaceous (Davey et al., 1982). A coarse sandstone sequence is suggested by the complex seismic velocity-depth profile for the trough (Davey et al., 1982) and would be consistent with a graben formation and terrestrial sequence for the lower part. Two lithological models were used by Cook and Davey (1984) for maturation assessment because DSDP 273 drilled marine glacial sediments back to Early Miocene. The first model assumed a pre-Oligocene terrestrial sandy sequence overlain by marine glacial sediments. The second assumed a sandy mudstone sequence averaging 20% sand throughout.

The input parameters for maturation modelling are poorly controlled. Assuming a constant sedimentation rate and an Early Tertiary age of formation, the central part of the basin, where a total sedimentary thickness of 4,200 m has been measured, contains 200 m of Plio-Pleistocene, 2,100 m of Oligocene to Miocene and 1,900 m or more of Eocene–Upper Palaeocene sediment (Davey et al., 1982). Hinz and Block (1983) inferred up to about 3,500 m of Late Oligocene or younger sediments in the deepest part of the basin. The heat flow measurements on the south-eastern margin of the trough (Sato et al., 1984) are unusually high for the tectonic regime and may be affected by seasonal bottom water temperature variations. The value assumed for the Eastern Basin was taken to be more realistic. The thermal conductivities used were based on the inferred or observed lithologies.

The maturation models for the Central Trough give unprospective results with maximum maturation values well below the onset of hydrocarbon generation, even if the higher heat flow values are used. On present knowledge therefore, the hydrocarbon potential of the Central Trough is considered to be poor.

Reservoir rocks are not well defined for the Central Trough. However, if the older sedimentary sequences are of early rift terrestrial sandy sediments, then moderate to high porosity and permeability may be expected provided no diagenesis has occurred.

Probable traps are less well defined than for the Eastern Basin as the lack of prograding sequences downgrades the possibility of stratigraphic traps.

Victoria Land Basin

The Victoria Land Basin covers an area of some 80,000 km^2 and contains up to 6 km of young (?Late Cretaceous to Tertiary) sediments (Davey, this volume). Probable oil reserves would total some 4×10^8 m^3, based on worldwide averages.

The Victoria Land Basin is a broad basin some 150 km wide extending along the western margin of Ross Sea from Ross Island to Cape Washington, a distance of over 500 km (Fig. 6.6). The basin contains two main sedimentary sequences (Cooper et al., 1987). The upper sequence has a thickness of about 5–6 km and is underlain by a stratified, presumably low grade, metasedimentary sequence up to 6 km thick with a seismic velocity of about 5.5 km sec.$^{-1}$. The western flank of the basin contains a sedimentary sequence which dips towards the centre of the basin and is truncated at or near the seafloor. Basement underlying this western flank is apparently blockfaulted down to the east reflecting the uplift of the Transantarctic Mountains. A rift depression about 20 km wide lies along the axis of the basin linking the volcanic provinces of Ross Island and Cape Washington. The rift is marked by numerous faults, especially on the eastern flank, which apparently have been recently active. The older sedimentary sequence thins over the eastern flank of the basin, onlapping against basement. Back-tilted blockfaulting and igneous activity also occur over the eastern flank. The crust under the Victoria

Land Basin is thin for continental regions, being about 22 km under the basin and thickening to about 28 km at the coast and in the Ross Sea to the east of the basin (McGinnis et al., 1985; Davey and Cooper, 1987), increasing to probably 35–40 km under the Transantarctic Mountains (Davey and Cooper, 1987).

The two main sedimentary sequences suggest two main episodes of basin formation. The older episode indicates a broad downwarp and sediment deposition in probably post-mid Jurassic (Beacon Supergroup) and pre-Late Cretaceous (New Zealand–Antarctic separation) time. Tectonics associated with continental breakup led to the major unconformity between the two main sedimentary sequences. Subsequent downwarping, presumably since Late Cretaceous times, has led to the deposition of the younger sequence. The tectonic activity increased in the Neogene with the formation of the active rift, which links the active Late Cenozoic volcanic centres of Ross Island and Cape Washington, and is also reflected in the uplift of the Transantarctic Mountains which increased markedly (15 m/Ma to 90 m/Ma) about 50 Ma ago (Gleadow and Fitzgerald, 1987).

The MSSTS-1 drillhole, sited on the western flank of the basin in McMurdo Sound, penetrated a thin sequence (226 m) of Late Oligocene and younger sediments (Harwood, 1986). Correlation of these data with seismic reflection data suggests that about the upper 1–2 km of sediments in the deeper part of the basin are Late Oligocene or younger in age (Davey and Christoffel, 1984; Cooper and Davey, 1985). The remainder and thickest part of the younger section is therefore probably Palaeogene and perhaps Late Cretaceous (Cooper et al., 1987) with deposition following the rifting of New Zealand from Antarctica. The older sequence is considered to have an age range commencing after the end of Beacon sedimentation (mid-Jurassic) and finishing before continental breakup in the Late Cretaceous. Sedimentological studies (Barrett, 1981) indicate that the Ross Sea was an elevated region during Beacon sedimentation. The tectonic activity during continental fragmentation provides a mechanism for the inferred major break in sedimentation and low grade metamorphism of the older sequence.

Source rocks are unlikely to occur in the younger, marine glacial sediments. Marine sediments, possibly interbedded or underlain by non-marine sediments probably occur in the lower part of the sequence as suggested in the recycled marine microfossils of Late Cretaceous and Early Tertiary age. These marginal marine sediments have been suggested as the source of the oil found in the CIROS-1 hole (Cook and Woolhouse, 1989). Coal measures occur in the Beacon Supergroup rocks and, if these are not as heavily metamorphosed by contact with volcanic sills as they are in the Transantarctic Mountains, they could also be potential source rocks.

The maturation levels for the Victoria Land Basin have been modelled by Cook and Davey (1984) and Cooper et al. (1988). Cook and Davey (1984) assumed a sedimentation rate based on the uplift rates for the Transantarctic Mountains in the region (Gleadow and Fitzgerald, 1987) to obtain the age of the sediments. A total sediment thickness for the younger sedimentary section in the Victoria Land Basin was used (Davey et al., 1982; Cooper and Davey, 1985). Cooper et al. (1988), on the other hand, used the stratigraphy for the basin (Cooper et al., 1987) to define the age-depth relationships for the whole of the sedimentary section of younger (post-Late Cretaceous) rocks and older (pre-Late Cretaceous) rocks. The MSSTS-1 and DSDP 270–273 drillholes encountered a regional hiatus which occurred during the Late Miocene and Pliocene (Hayes et al., 1975a) which has been included in the model for the basin.

Heat flow measurements in the basin are highly variable. Most of the measurements were taken in the McMurdo area, adjacent to active volcanism and plutonic granites and are therefore associated with high local heat flows. However, the MSSTS-1 drillhole gave a value of 60 mW/m², assuming marine glacial sediments with thermal conductivity of 1.7 W/m°C (Sissons, 1980), and values of about 100 mW/m² were obtained in Terra Nova Bay at the northern end of the Victoria Land Basin (Blackman et al., 1984). The sedimentary sequence in the MSSTS-1 hole is glaciomarine (Barrett and McKelvey, 1986) and an appropriate thermal conductivity value was used by Cook and Davey (1984) in the modelling. However, Cooper et al. (1988) assumed marine sediments for the pre-38 Ma sediments with possible non-marine sediments in the older part (pre-85 Ma) of the sedimentary section corresponding to pre-breakup sedimentation.

The maturation calculations for the Victoria Land Basin indicate that, even in the low heat flow model of Cook and Davey (1984), the lowermost 1 km or more of the younger sedimentary sequence of the basin have reached maturation values corresponding to the onset of oil generation. The thicker, younger sequence in the deepest part of the Victoria Land Basin would have a thicker mature section and the older sedimentary sequence would also be a potential source having passed through the "oil window". These results are consistent with the drillhole data from the CIROS-1 drillhole in western McMurdo Sound where a 2 m thick sandstone containing traces of residual oil was detected (Barrett, 1987). The sandstone is considered to contain a residue of a hydrocarbon generated at greater depth and migrated through the sandstone. Detailed chemistry of this oil residue indicates that its source was a nearshore marine sediment (Cook and Woolhouse, 1988).

The organic content of the sediments in the MSSTS-1 hole reached a maximum of 0.18% wt (Collen and Froggatt, 1986) which is below the industry-accepted minimum source rock requirement. Similar sediments measured in DSDP holes 271–273 where the sedimentation rate is higher have organic contents of 0.25–0.7% (McIver, 1975). Possible reservoir rocks are again poorly defined but are indicated by high porosity sediments sampled in the drillholes and by analogy with older rocks from coeval basins on Campbell Plateau and Tasmania.

Possible hydrocarbon traps would include stratigraphic and structural forms. Vertical deformation, especially Late Tertiary deformation associated with the Terror Rift system and its associated intrusive structures, may be expected to give rise to many late rift structural and stratigraphic traps associated with numerous unconformities.

The older sedimentary sequence, if deposited during early rift formation prior to continental breakup, may contain synrift sediment of terrestrial or shallow water, alluvial plain origin, similar to those found along the southern Australian margin and therefore include significant source material.

WESTERN ANTARCTIC PENINSULA AND WESTERN ELLSWORTH LAND

Few data exist over the continental margin of Antarctica between the Ross Sea and Thurston Island. Further to the east, geophysical data over the upper continental rise and shelf are confined to detailed studies in the northern Antarctic Peninsula region (e.g., Ashcroft, 1972) and to widely spaced profiles (Houtz, 1974; Tucholke and Houtz, 1976) including multichannel seismic data (Kimura, 1982) across the continental margin between Anvers Island and Thurston Island (Fig. 6.7).

The continental shelf varies in width, reaching a maximum of 500 km in the Bellingshausen Sea and 400 km in the Amundsen Sea (Davey, this volume). Long narrow depressions on the shelf lying sub-parallel to the shelf edge have been interpreted as marking the boundary between old continental rock and more recent sedimentary wedges forming the outer continental shelf, slope and rise for the region west of the Antarctic Peninsula (Vanney and Johnson, 1976). A well-developed continental rise exists along the central and western sector of the margin. Seismic data show sediments under the rise to reach about 3 km thickening under the continental slope. Data coverage is poor for the shelf region apart from in the north where Ashcroft (1972) measured a sedimentary thickness of 5 km (seismic velocity less than 4.2 km sec.$^{-1}$) to the northwest of the South Shetland Islands.

In the Jurassic to Early Cretaceous, the Antarctic Peninsula was the site of a volcanic arc associated with subduction along the Pacific margin (Dalziel and Elliot, 1973). During this time, sediments of the Fossil Bluff Formation in Alexander Island were laid down in a fore-arc basin. Over 5,000 m of sediments of dominantly shallow water origin (mudstone, sandstone, and conglomerate) occur with lavas interbedded in the lower part and plant-bearing sequences, possibly terrestrial, containing local coal measures in the upper part. Marine deposits, similar to the lower part of the section, occur farther north at South Shetland Islands (Thomson, 1982) . Uplift and erosion took place in middle Late Cretaceous followed by the extrusion of mid-Late Cenozoic basic volcanics and pyroclastics in Marie Byrd Land and Late Cenozoic volcanics and conglomerates in northern Antarctic Peninsula. The structural development of the region throughout the Mesozoic and Tertiary has been controlled by the development of the active plate margin which is now active only north of the Hero Fracture Zone (Fig. 6.7, Davey, this volume).

Hydrocarbon maturation models have been produced for the upper continental rise sediments off Thurston Island and for the outer shelf sediments near the South Shetland Islands (Davey, 1985). The age of the sediments for the Thurston Island model was based on the results of DSDP sites 323 and 324. An average heat flow was assumed using a heat flow age relationship for oceanic crust. The sediment conductivity was based on the lithologies sampled at the drill sites and a geothermal temperature gradient derived. The computed maturation value was well below the onset of oil generation. The region, however, lies where a spreading ridge passed through the region such that the sediments experienced higher temperatures. However, based on the assumptions made, the margin does

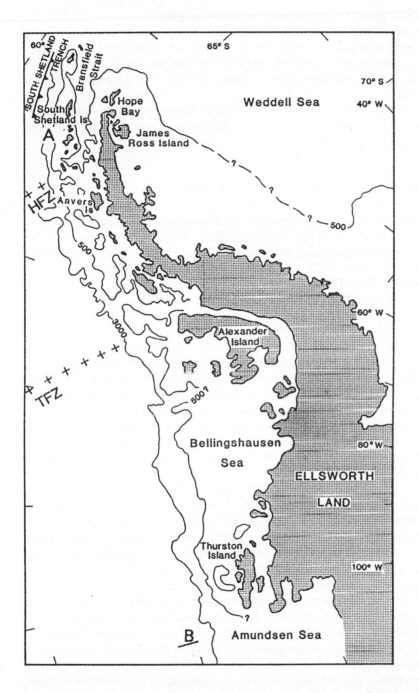

Fig. 6.7. Antarctic Peninsula. The western Antarctic Peninsula–Bellingshausen Sea margin. HFZ = Hero Fracture Zone, TFZ = Tula Fracture Zone. Bathymetry contours at 500 m and 3,000 m delineate continental slope and shelf (Polar Stereographic projection).

not appear to show good hydrocarbon maturation potential.

The age of the sediments, lithology and heat flow for the South Shetland Islands model were very poorly constrained. Although a significant sedimentary section exists, the model served mainly to point out the paucity of useful data in the Antarctic region. On the assumptions made, Davey (1985) derived a very low maturation value.

The geology of the fore-arc basin sediments indicates possible source rocks (coal measures) and possible reservoir rocks (sandstone) in the sequence. The information is, however, too sparse to justify further discussion.

HIGH LATITUDE EXPLORATION AND PRODUCTION

There has been much speculation on the hydrocarbon potential of Antarctica (e.g., Wright and Williams, 1974; Ivanhoe, 1980; Mitchell and Tinker, 1980; Cameron, 1981; Apostolescu and Wanneson, 1982; Auburn, 1982; Behrendt, 1983b, in press; Bergsager, 1983; Guillaume, 1983; Garrett, 1984; Quilty, 1984, 1987; Tessensohn, 1984, 1986; Aleyeva and Kucheruk, 1985; Cortes, 1985; Shapley, 1985; Davey, 1985; Ivanov, 1985; Roland, 1986; St. John, 1986; Anderson, 1987; Crockett and Clarkson, 1987; Larminie, 1987; Parsons, 1987; Elliot, 1988). For instance, St. John (1986) identified 21 sedimentary basins for the Antarctic and immediately adjacent areas. Of these, 10 basins were estimated to contain approximately 16.9 million km^3 of sediment with a potential hydrocarbon yield of 203 billion barrels of oil equivalent. However, Parsons (1987) would speak for most in stating that estimates of the hydrocarbon resources of Antarctica are without scientific foundation and at best can only be categorized as guesses. In his opinion, it is hard to see how Antarctica could come anywhere but last on a global rating of known sedimentary basins in terms of the hydrocarbon potential. Further, unconventional sources of hydrocarbons may well be cost competitive with Antarctic oil (Garrett, 1984).

While hydrocarbons may or may not be present in the basins offshore Antarctica, it is important to recognize that, unlike other regions of the world, the harsh climate and remoteness bring into question the viability of exploring areas with even good geological potential. It is an important part of assessing the overall potential of these Antarctic basins to review the physical and logistical difficulties that would have to be overcome (Holdgate and Tinker, 1979; Mitchell and Tinker, 1980; Sanderson, 1983; Anonymous, 1986c; Parsons, 1987).

Exploration in the Northern Hemisphere high latitudes has shown that explorers can now cope with the cold, ice and snow (cf. Anonymous, 1986b; Curlin et al., 1986). Even the problem of icebergs off the east coast of Canada has been overcome for exploration purposes so that the north can be explored without too many problems apart from seriously raising costs.

While the problems of cold, snow and ice are similar in the Southern Ocean, these factors are compounded in the south by major additional factors. Winter temperatures are more extreme with low temperatures from –80°C on the high ice plateau to –60°C near sea level. The continental size more than doubles during the winter with the ocean freezing out beyond the 200 m isobath (Ivanhoe, 1980). The land and sea distribution of the Antarctic and Arctic are in fact reversed. The Arctic is an ocean surrounded by land whereas the Antarctic consists of a continent surrounded by ocean. Throughout the year, the ice-choked and stormy seas around the Antarctic continent hinder access. Great cyclonic storms circle the Antarctic with no land to break their progress and relentless force. Moist maritime air interacts with the cold polar air which makes the Antarctic Ocean in the vicinity of the Polar Front one of the world's stormiest.

Access

The extreme remoteness of Antarctica contrasts with the Arctic. In the Arctic, materials can be moved north to the Arctic sea coast from ice-free harbours or across land whereas Antarctica is surrounded by vast Southern Ocean where 2–3,000 km of some of the world's roughest waters must be negotiated. In addition, there is a very short period of only 2–4 months a year when the continent can be reached by ship and then only with icebreaker assistance. This means that supply lines would be tenuous.

Drilling

Then come the problems with drilling. Since all of the Cretaceous and Tertiary basins of the Pacific margin of Antarctica are located under major shelf ice or in the offshore areas, conditions relevant to these areas must be considered. The Ross Ice Shelf is not a stable platform but has a horizontal movement of up to 6 m per day. This would cause serious drilling problems necessitating continuous hole widening and moving of the rig. Offshore, in the Ross Sea (the most likely area for initial exploration), the first problem is the depth of water. Water depths are typically 400–600 m and almost never less than 200 m. The sea is subject to violent wind and wave conditions and during much of the year is covered with 1–2.5 m of ice. Extremely large icebergs are common in these Antarctic waters. They are typically 200–400 m thick and 700–1,000 m across but have been known to exceed 150 x 70 km.

To overcome these drilling problems, Sanderson (1983) has suggested that, while there is often only about 10 m of water beneath the Ross Ice Shelf, there are points where the ice grounds on a shoal. The ice then becomes stationary and this would allow year round drilling. However, there are only a few shoals. Only a very limited area for exploration would therefore be available from these locations.

Another solution suggested by Sanderson (1983) would be to form an ice island by grounding a large iceberg at the location of interest by adding ice to its upper surface. This is a much cheaper and environmentally more acceptable than building an artificial island of gravel (which would require up to 5 km³ of gravel at these water depths) since on completion of the work the grounded berg can be left to melt and drift away.

Production

While exploration is used to assess the potential of a region, there is little point in finding oil unless it can be produced economically. To be economic, almost year-round production would be required. Whereas exploration requires suitable conditions over a few months, production requires these conditions over many years. With the water depths involved, the only realistic techniques would again be to ground an iceberg and to keep adding new ice to it to keep it grounded over many years or to produce from a totally subsea system where the units would be buried 25–30 m below the seafloor in water depths of up to 500 m to protect them from ice scour (cf. Keys, 1984; Barnes and Lien, 1988). These units would only be able to be maintained during the summer ice-free period and by submarine.

At present, this is still not technically feasible (Mitchell and Tinker, 1980; Sanderson, 1983; Crockett and Clarkson, 1987; Parsons, 1987). Even when the problems in developing the production facility have been overcome, the oil has still to be transported to markets. Unlike in the Arctic, the oil cannot be piped ashore and then overland to markets.

In the Antarctic, there are still the problems of nine months of sea ice and the vast Southern Ocean over which to transport the oil. Only questions can be raised at this point. Is it viable to store the whole year's product adjacent to the facility and ship it out during the summer? This idea ignores the fact that, as in 1985–86, severe ice can restrict or curtail all shipping even during the normal time period. It also ignores the environmental questions of storing and moving huge quantities of oil through very dangerous and difficult regions. Would a pipeline north to Australia or New Zealand be possible considering it would be 2–3,000 km long with ocean depths in excess of 5 km? Whatever, the cost of production of Antarctic oil it is likely to be extremely high and this is likely to be the main constraint to exploitation (Garrett, 1984).

SUMMARY

Of the basins bordering the Pacific south of 45°S, those of the Campbell Plateau and surrounding southern New Zealand have already undergone limited exploration for hydrocarbons. This exploration has been partially successful with gas condensates and oil shows being recorded in the Canterbury and Great South Basins. The condensates and oil shows indicate that their source is the basal coal measure sequence in the basins.

Two other basins, the Campbell and Pukaki Basins, have yet to be drilled. However, their similar geological settings to the Great South Basin suggest that they too have potential but their locations far from land have meant their potentials have yet to be fully evaluated.

The basins of the Ross Sea have only very limited geophysical coverage but nonetheless their extent and sediment infill have been defined. The stratigraphic drilling by the Deep Sea Drilling Project (DSDP holes 270–273) and the Cenozoic Investigations in the Western Ross Sea (CIROS-1) encountered indications of higher hydrocarbons within these basins. This suggests that there is potential for hydrocabon reservoirs to be found at least in the Eastern Basin and the Victoria Land Basin.

The sediment accumulations of the Western Antarctic Peninsula and Western Ellsworth Land have been little studied. Based on the available data and assumed maturation models for the sediments off Thurston Island and the outer shelf near the South Shetland Islands, the deepest sediments are too immature to have generated hydrocarbons. This suggests that the Pacific margin east of the Ross Sea does not have good hydrocarbon potential unless volcanic arc environments have provided much higher than normal temperature gradients in the sediments than modelled.

While superficially the Antarctic and Arctic may appear to pose similar problems for hydrocarbon exploration and production, the Antarctic is logistically a much more difficult region, even before the sensitive environmental conditions are considered. It is most unlikely that, under the present price regime and known world reserve levels for hydrocarbons, even reconnaissance exploration will be made for more than scientific purposes.

CHAPTER 7

SEDIMENTS

J.B. ANDERSON

INTRODUCTION

This chapter describes sediment types, distribution patterns, and processes which regulate sedimentation on the seafloor of the Antarctic Sector of the Pacific Ocean. It is based largely on sediment cores and samples, bottom photographs, and nephelometer profiles acquired during previous cruises of the United States vessels U.S.N.S. *Eltanin*, R.V. *Conrad* and U.S.C.G.C. *Glacier* (Deep Freeze Expeditions) and, to a lesser extent, on published sediment descriptions and maps of Russian (Lisitzin, 1962, 1970) and French (Dangeard et al., 1977) scientists.

CONTINENTAL MARGIN SEDIMENTATION

The Antarctic Sector of the Pacific is bounded on the south by the Antarctic continent, which is the primary source of terrigenous sediment to this region. For this reason, sedimentation on the Antarctic continental margin is discussed in some detail.

Continental Shelf Sedimentation

The Antarctic continental shelf is unique compared to other continental shelves of the world for the following reasons : (1) glaciers flow directly into the sea so that sediment supply is by ice; surface meltwater runoff is presently minimal; (2) it is covered by sea ice for most of the year and large portions of the shelf are covered by perennial sea ice; and (3) it is deep (average 450 m) and has considerable topographic relief.

Prior to the late 1960s, very few sediment samples had been acquired on the Antarctic continental shelf and slope so that the character of sediments there and the processes responsible for these deposits were poorly understood. Since then, there has been a major marine geological programme on the Antarctic continental shelf, mainly as a result of *Eltanin* and Deep Freeze (U.S.C.G.C. *Glacier*) cruises. Most of this work has concentrated on the Ross Sea region. The following discussion is therefore based mainly on studies of sediments from this area.

The marine setting of the Ross Sea region includes virtually every kind of glacial terminus, including large ice shelves (the Ross Ice Shelf and Sulzberger Ice Shelf), ice tongues, ice cliffs, outlet glaciers, and valley glaciers which flow directly into the sea, as well as those whose terminus is situated well inland of the coast (the Dry Valleys regions, Fig. 7.1). The Ross Sea therefore provides an ideal setting in which to study glacial marine sedimentation.

188

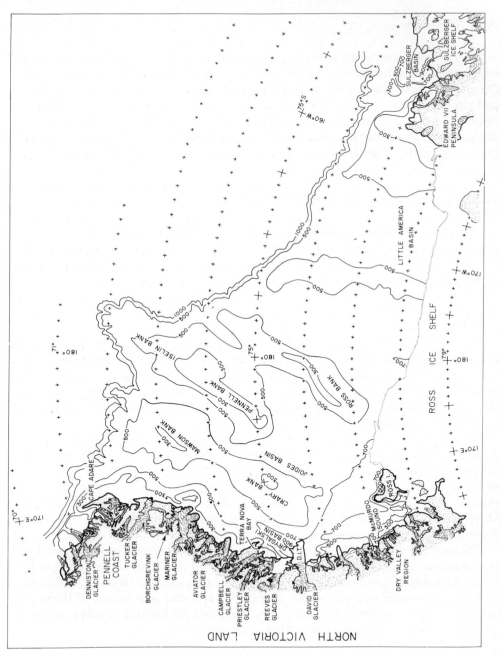

Fig. 7.1. Geography, glaciology and bathymetry of the Ross Sea region. Bathymetry in metres.

The dominant glacial feature in the Ross Sea is the Ross Ice Shelf (Fig. 7.1). It is the glacial terminus of ice draining an area of approximately $2.3 \times 10^6 \, km^2$, and its drainage basin includes both the east and west Antarctic ice sheets (Fig. 7.1).

Ice flowing into the Ross Sea from East Antarctica must make its way either over or through the Transantarctic Mountains, and is channelled into rapidly flowing ice streams. The largest of these is David Glacier, which extends presently some 70 km off the coast as a vast ice tongue, the Drygalski Ice Tongue (Fig. 7.1). David Glacier is the largest glacial outlet in the Ross Sea. For the most part, the ice sheet in the region is ponded behind the Transantarctic Mountains. Drainage into the Ross Sea is mainly from large valley glaciers. The largest of these include Tucker Glacier, Borchgrevink Glacier, Mariner Glacier, Aviator Glacier, Campbell Glacier, Priestley Glacier and Reeves Glacier (Fig. 7.1).

Because of their much smaller drainage basins and channel characteristics, these glaciers flow into the Ross Sea at slower rates than David Glacier. They therefore form smaller ice tongues. Ice tongues such as the Borchgrevink, Mariner and Aviator are protected from wave erosion by perennial sea ice in the north-western Ross Sea.

South of the Dry Valleys, the East Antarctic Ice Sheet flows into and becomes part of the Ross Ice Shelf (Fig. 7.1). The Ross Ice Shelf is the largest ice shelf in the world (total surface area is approximately $5.4 \times 10^5 \, km^2$). Its grounding line is situated some 960 km inland from its calving line. It produces the largest icebergs on average in the Ross Sea region and its steep calving wall occupies approximately 10% of the Antarctic coastline. The largest icebergs that calve from the Ross Ice Shelf are as large as or larger than the ice tongues of the northwestern Ross Sea and have drafts in excess of 200 m, although shallower drafts may be more common. Some thick icebergs calved from ice tongues, however, have drafts of the order of 300 m (Keys, this volume).

East of the King Edward VII Peninsula, large outlet glaciers flowing down from the mountains of Marie Byrd Land converge to form the Sulzberger Ice Shelf (Fig. 7.1). It is much smaller ($1.6 \times 10^4 \, km^2$) than the Ross Ice Shelf and its calving wall stands only 6–10 m high, compared to the 20–50 m high calving wall of the Ross Ice Shelf. Icebergs calved from the Sulzberger Ice Shelf therefore have much shallower drafts, probably on the order of 40 to 60 m.

Surface sediments of the Ross Sea region have been examined in detail by Stetson and Upson (1937), Chriss and Frakes (1972), Glasby et al. (1975), Anderson et al. (1980, 1984b), Barrett et al. (1983), Dunbar et al. (1985, 1989), Kellogg and Kellogg (1988), Leventer and Dunbar (1988), Anderson and Smith (1989), Karl (1989) and Harwood et al. (1989). Piston cores from the Ross Sea continental shelf typically terminate in cohesive sediments believed to be basal tills (products of subglacial sedimentation). This interpretation is based on the fact that these deposits are characterized by high cohesive strength, a lack of sorting, lack of stratification, absence of marine fossils (other than reworked fossils), pebbles that are rounded relative to those found in glacial marine sediments, and textural and mineralogical homogeneity within individual units. Kellogg et al. (1979) and Anderson et al. (1980, 1984b) have given more detailed descriptions of these glacial deposits.

Basal tills extend almost to the continental shelf edge. This indicates that the ice sheet was at one time grounded on most of the shelf. In fact, a detailed analysis of the mineralogies and pebble lithologies of Ross Sea basal tills has revealed that distinct petrographic provinces do occur on the continental shelf and these have been used to reconstruct the late Wisconsinan (18,000 yrs B.P.) glacial drainage regime of the marine ice sheet in the Ross Sea region (Anderson et al., 1984b). These data support the paleodrainage model of Denton and Hughes (1981), which calls for ice sheets grounded at the continental shelf edge at this time.

Glacial-marine sediments contain a significant quantity of material deposited from floating ice, either ice shelves, ice tongues or icebergs. This ice-rafted debris is associated with mixtures of pelagic and terrigenous sediments. Variations in the concentration of these different components reflect the relative influence of glacial, biological and oceanographic processes (Chriss and Frakes, 1972; Barrett, 1975; Anderson et al., 1980). Fig. 7.2 shows a surface sediment distribution map for the Ross Sea.

The actual fate of sediment transported to the coast by glaciers is still problematic. What we do know is that the concentration of ice-rafted debris in surface sediments of the continental shelf is highly variable and decreases markedly seaward of the shelf break (Anderson et al., 1979, 1984a). There is a consensus amongst glaciologists that the basal layer of ice shelves (and tongues) is melted before reaching the calving line where icebergs are produced (Robin, 1979; Thomas, 1979a; Drewry and Cooper, 1981; Drewry, 1986). This conclusion is based mainly on theoretical considerations, but is supported by physical oceanographic observations which indicate net melting at the base of the Ross Ice Shelf (Jacobs et al., 1979) and by the absence of a basal debris zone in a hole drilled through the Ross Ice Shelf (Drewry and Cooper, 1981). Furthermore, surface sediments collected near the calving line of the Ross Ice Shelf contain only minor quantities of ice-rafted debris (Dunbar et al., 1985).

Most basal glacial debris probably melts out near the grounding line of ice shelves and glacier tongues (Drewry and Cooper, 1981; Drewey, 1986). Relict sediments formed by melting of the basal debris layer are believed to occur throughout the Ross Sea region (Anderson et al., 1984b) and modern sediments deposited in this manner have been sampled from beneath the Mackay Glacier Tongue in the southwestern corner of the Ross Sea (Macpherson, 1986, 1987). They are similar to basal tills in that they are unsorted to very poorly sorted, generally massive, and display textural and mineralogical homogeneity downcore. They differ from basal tills only in that they are not overcompacted and they frequently contain marine fossils.

Modern glacial marine sediments of the Antarctic continental shelf consist of two distinct groups. The first group includes fine-grained sediments composed of a mixture of terrigenous silt and clay and pelagic material (mostly diatom frustules) and associated ice-rafted debris. These sediments have been termed "compound glacial marine sediment" by Anderson et al. (1980) because they represent a combination of sedimentation by marine currents, pelagic sedimentation, and ice rafting in relatively low energy settings (Chriss and Frakes, 1972). Near the coast, aeolian material may comprise a significant component of surface sediments (Barrett et al., 1983). The proportion of ice-rafted debris in these sediments varies appreciably but is most concentrated in nearshore regions bound by outlet glaciers and ice streams, such as in the westernmost Ross Sea, off the Pennell Coast, and off the Marie Byrd Land Coast (Anderson et al., 1984a). Dirty icebergs and glacial ice show that debris containing layers of ice tongues is not always melted out before their calving zone is reached (J.R. Keys, pers. comm.). During a dozen expeditions to the Antarctic region, I have observed many sediment-laden icebergs on the continental shelf but most were within a few tens of kilometres of the continent, and only rarely were they in the open ocean.

A second group of glacial marine sediments is composed of poorly-sorted mixtures of sand and gravel with various amounts of calcareous, bioclastic sand and gravel (mainly foraminiferal tests and fragments of bryozoans, barnacles, molluscs, corals and echinoderms). These sediments reflect ice-rafting in areas where marine currents are sufficiently strong to remove fine-grained material, either as it settles through the water column or via bottom erosion and resuspension (Chriss and Frakes, 1972; Anderson et al., 1980, 1984a). They are therefore termed by Anderson et al. (1980) "residual glacial marine sediment". Residual glacial marine sediments occur on the outer continental shelf (Fig. 7.2), where impinging deep-sea currents are influential sedimentary agents (Anderson and Smith, 1989) and on relatively shallow (< 300 m) banks and inner shelf regions where wind-driven currents influence sedimentation (Anderson et al., 1984a). Residual glacial marine sediments are typically associated with relatively well-sorted sands, which are the products of bottom current transport. These sediments indicate that relatively strong marine currents are active to depths of up to 300 m (Anderson and Smith, 1989).

Perhaps one of the most intriguing aspects of modern surface sediments of the Antarctic continental shelf is that ice-rafted debris is typically a minor component of these sediments, certainly relative to ancient deposits of the shelf. In fact, siliceous muds and oozes consisting of 10 to 40% biogenic silica, mainly diatom frustules, and less than 10% ice-rafted debris are widespread on the shelf and are the dominant sediment type in shelf basins (Fig. 7.2). Accumulation rates for these siliceous sediments are as high as 2.5 mm/yr in the western Ross Sea, and biogenic silica accumulation in this area is comparable to that of low-latitude upwelling environments (Ledford-Hoffman et al., 1986). In general, the biogenic silica content of surface sediments increases from east to west across the Ross Sea shelf and in an onshore direction (Truesdale and Kellogg, 1979; Dunbar et al., 1985). Siliceous muds and oozes occur as far south as McMurdo Sound (Fig. 7.2). This distribution pattern is attributed to greater productivity in the western Ross Sea, probably due to less persistent sea ice cover there (Truesdale and Kellogg, 1979; Anderson et al., 1984b), and to redistribution of fine-grained sediments by marine currents (Dunbar et al., 1985). Siliceous sediments are also concentrated in glacial troughs off the Pennell Coast (Fig. 7.2). Their occurrence there results from marine currents sweeping fine-grained sediments from the shallower portions of the shelf and into these small basins (Anderson et al., 1984a).

On the inner shelf of the eastern Ross Sea and in the Sulzberger Bay area, fine-

192

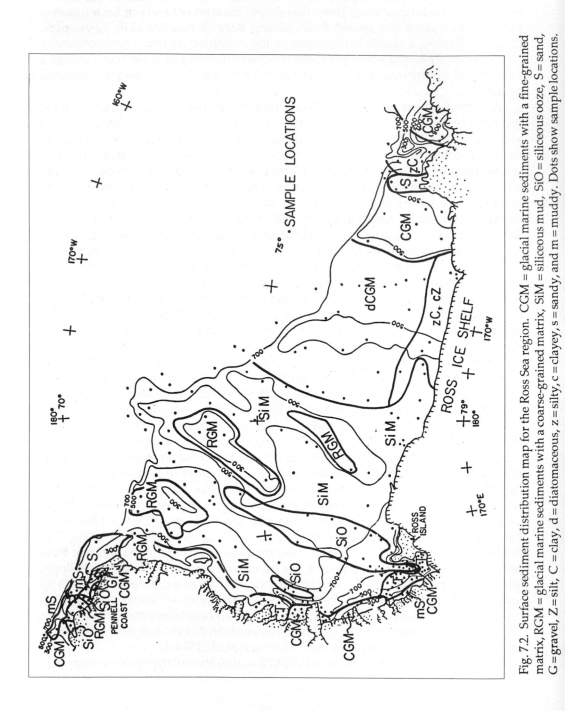

Fig. 7.2. Surface sediment distribution map for the Ross Sea region. CGM = glacial marine sediments with a fine-grained matrix, RGM = glacial marine sediments with a coarse-grained matrix, SiM = siliceous mud, SiO = siliceous ooze, S = sand, G = gravel, Z = silt, C = clay, d = diatomaceous, z = silty, c = clayey, s = sandy, and m = muddy. Dots show sample locations.

grained sediments (clayey silts) with very little biogenic and ice-rafted material (< 10% of each) are accumulating (Fig. 7.2). These fine-grained sediments are attributed to redistribution of suspended material by marine currents in the absence of significant biogenic sediment input (Dunbar et al., 1985). Nittrouer et al. (1984) argued that the volume of terrigenous sediment accumulating on the Ross Sea floor today is comparable to that of continental shelves which have major fluvial dispersal systems.

In summary, the surface sediment distribution pattern in the Ross Sea indicates that only in nearshore areas adjoining outlet glaciers and ice streams is ice-rafting an important contributor to marine sediments. Ice-rafted debris is a minor component of sediments collected adjacent to the calving wall of the Ross Ice Shelf. Fine-grained sediments consist of both terrigenous material and siliceous biogenic material. These fine-grained sediments are swept from the outer shelf into inner shelf basins where they accumulate rapidly. Shallow banks are covered by coarse-grained residual sediments comprised largely of bioclastic (carbonate) material. These sediments indicate relatively strong marine currents at depths above approximately 300 m.

Surficial sediment dispersal patterns for the remainder of the Antarctic margin of the Pacific are poorly known. The only other detailed work has been conducted in the area of Bransfield Strait at the northern tip of the Antarctic Peninsula (Anderson et al., 1984a) and in Marguerite Bay between longitudes 66°W and 70°W on the Antarctic Peninsula (Kennedy, 1987). In these areas, glacial marine sediments occur on the shallow portions of the continental shelf, and diatomaceous muds and oozes occur in shelf basins and in bays and fjords of the peninsula (Griffiths and Anderson, 1989). Bioclastic sediments, similar to those which blanket the shallower portions of the Ross Sea floor, have not been cored. Recent work in the fjords and bays of the Antarctic Peninsula region has led to the observation that meltwater is a significant factor in the delivery of sediments to the sea only in the South Shetland Islands (Anderson et al., 1987).

Continental Slope Sedimentation

Sedimentation on the Antarctic continental slope has been described in detail by Anderson et al. (1979). Unfortunately, only a few sediment cores have been collected on the Antarctic slope in the Pacific and most of these were collected in the Ross Sea. It is therefore not possible to describe sediment distribution patterns on the slope. However, sediment types, and therefore processes, can be described for the Ross Sea continental slope.

The Ross Sea continental slope is divided into two distinct physiographic portions with Iselin Bank the dividing line (Fig. 7.1). East of Iselin Bank, the slope is relatively gentle (average gradient of 2°) and unbroken by submarine canyons. West of Iselin bank, the slope is steeper with the upper slope averaging 5° and the lower sloper 1.5°, and is dissected by several submarine canyons (Fig. 7.3a).

Surface sediment samples from the upper continental slope of the western Ross Sea (to depths of approximately 1,000 m) consist of sandy, gravelly mud and bioclastic sands and gravels. Bottom photographs from the upper slope also show

194

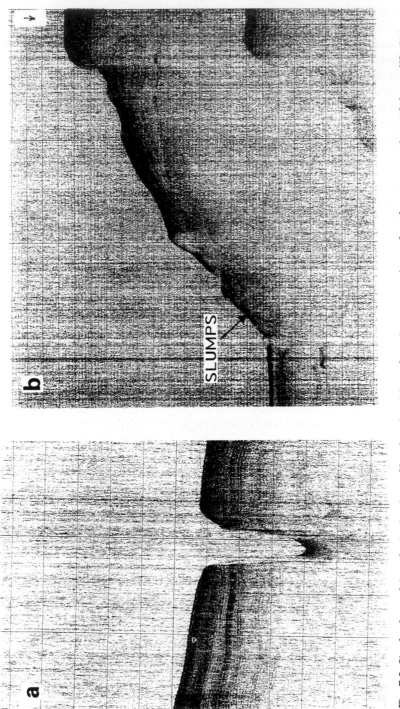

Fig. 7.3. Single-channel (sparker) seismic profiles showing (a) a submarine canyon situated on the upper continental slope off Iselin Bank, and (b) large slumps on the continental slope, again off Iselin Bank

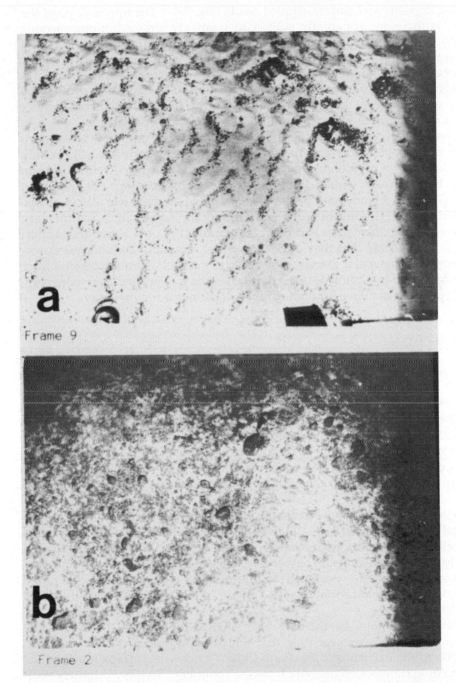

Fig. 7.4. Bottom photographs from the western Ross Sea continental slope showing (a) rippled sands (*Eltanin* camera station 2 in 1,720 m of water), and (b) gravelly lag deposits (*Eltanin* camera station 7, in 2,040 m of water).

surface lag deposits and current-rippled sands (Fig. 7.4). The upper slope of the Ross Sea is therefore apparently subject to relatively strong bottom currents (Dunbar et al., 1985; Anderson and Smith, 1989). Piston cores from the region have penetrated thin (< 1 m) graded sands. Both detrital and bioclastic carbonate sands occur, and are apparently derived from nearby Iselin Bank. Turbidity currents are therefore important agents on this part of the Ross Sea continental slope. Seismic lines from the slope show huge slumps (Fig. 7.3b), which is another important mechanism of sediment transport on the steep, upper slope.

Only two piston cores have been collected on the upper portion of the eastern Ross Sea continental slope, and these penetrated poorly-sorted sandy, pebbly muds which show no evidence of current winnowing. Marine currents therefore appear to be effective in winnowing sediments on the upper slope but not on the lower slope in this region. Four piston cores collected on the lower, eastern slope penetrated unsorted sediments (diamictons) and laminated silts. Sedimentary properties of these diamictons and displaced foraminifera led Kurtz and Anderson (1979) to conclude that they are debris flows, probably transported downslope during the last major glacial advance on to the shelf. Laminated silts were possibly deposited by sediment-laden bottom currents. They indicate more sluggish bottom currents than exist on the upper slope in this region today.

ABYSSAL SEDIMENTS

Distribution Patterns

The distribution pattern of abyssal sediments on the Antarctic Sector of the Pacific Ocean floor has been mapped and described by several workers (Goodell, 1968, 1973; Lisitzin, 1962, 1970; Nayudu, 1971; Piper et al., 1985). The sediment distribution maps generated by these authors were used in conjunction with the results of my own examination of surface sediments to compile the surface sediment map shown in Fig. 7.5. The following discussion is based largely on this map.

Terrigenous silts and clays occupy a broad belt extending from the Antarctic continenal slope to well out on to the abyssal floor. These hemipelagic sediments are typically poorly-sorted, polymodal, and include both laminated and massive, frequently bioturbated units. They consist mainly of detrital quartz, and clay minerals are mainly well-crystallized chlorite and illite (Goodell, 1973). Ice-rafted debris, volcanic ash, and ferromanganese micronodules are minor constituents of these sediments.

A belt of terrigenous sediments is also situated offshore of the Peru–Chile margin, but is much narrower than that which occurs off Antarctica. This is largely due to the existence of the Peru–Chile Trench which traps much of the sediment being transported offshore from the continent. To the west, these sediments grade into carbonate ooze. The distribution of these sediment types is regulated by the Carbonate Compensation Depth (C.C.D.), with calcareous ooze occurring above approximately 4,500 m and pelagic clay below this depth. As off

South America, terrigenous sands and silts are virtually confined to the continental shelf and slope of New Zealand. Except for a belt of pelagic clay situated along the northeastern margin of New Zealand, these terrigenous sediments grade offshore into pelagic carbonates.

North of the terrigenous silt and clay belt that surrounds Antarctica, there is a broad belt of siliceous ooze, which consists primarily of diatom frustules. The southern limit of the siliceous ooze belt corresponds approximately with the surface water 0°C isotherm and the northern limit with the Antarctic Convergence (Fig. 7.5; Goodell, 1973). North of the convergence, a relatively narrow belt of mixed diatom-calcareous ooze (foraminiferal ooze) occurs. North of the mixed ooze belt, foraminiferal ooze blankets the abyssal floor to a depth of approximately 4,500 m (the C.C.D.) (Goodell, 1973; Piper et al., 1985). Brown pelagic clays are accumulating in those portions of the Southeastern Pacific Basin and Southwestern Pacific Basin that are situated below the C.C.D. Unlike the terrigenous sediments that occur in belts off Antarctica and South America, these pelagic clays consist almost exclusively of clay minerals, zeolites and detrital grains (Skornyakova and Petelin, 1967; Nayudu, 1971). Montmorillonite is the dominant clay mineral. The dominant zeolite in these sediments is phillipsite, which may comprise upwards of 50% of the sediment by volume, and pyroxene, plagioclase, and opaques are the dominant mineral grains (Nayudu, 1971). These pelagic clays may also contain abundant fish bones (Nayudu, 1971). Hemipelagic clay and calcareous clay also occur in a broad belt west of the South American continent, within the deeper part of the Southeastern Pacific Basin.

Abyssal Sedimentary Processes

A number of factors contributes to the distribution of surface sediments on the deep seafloor of the South Pacific Ocean. Among these are the offshore flux of fine-grained terrigenous sediment from the continents (by ocean currents and turbidity currents), surface productivity of biogenic material, dissolution of biogenic sediments at depth, reworking by marine currents, and, to a much lesser degree, ice-rafting and authigenic mineral formation (Lisitzin, 1962, 1970; Nayudu, 1971; Goodell, 1973).

The Antarctic continent is producing an abundance of terrigenous silt and clay, substantially more than the other continents of the South Pacific. The mineralogies of surface sediments on the seafloor in the area of the Antarctic Peninsula show that the peninsula is a major source of terrigenous sediment for the southeastern Pacific Ocean (Edwards, 1968). The subpolar glacial maritime setting of that region is conducive to glacial erosion and transport of sediment, the occurrence of meltwater being a leading contributor to this supply. South of approximately 65°S, a polar glacial regime exists, and the delivery of sediment to the sea by surface meltwater streams is virtually nonexistent.

It is also noteworthy that the belt of terrigenous sediments surrounding the continent is much broader around West Antarctica than East Antarctica (Goodell, 1973). This is explained, in part, by the fact that the vast ice shelves which drain into the West Antarctic margin have a larger glacial drainage basin, and therefore

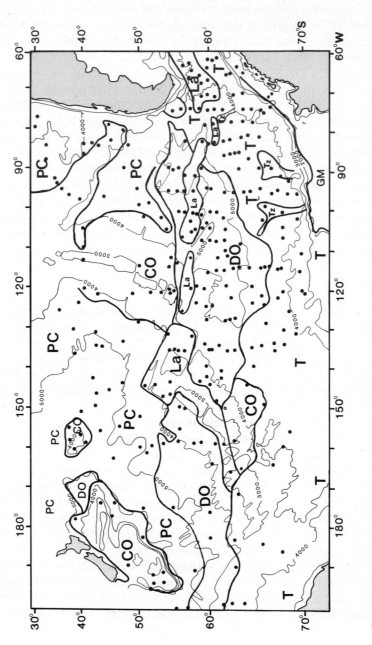

Fig. 7.5. Surface sediment distribution map for the South Pacific Ocean. Dots show sample locations. T = terrigenous silts and clays, Tz = sandy turbidites, DO = diatomaceous ooze and mud, CO = calcareous ooze and mud, PC = pelagic clay, La = gravelly or sandy lag deposits. Bathymetry in metres.

a larger sediment source area, than do glaciers draining into any given portion of the East Antarctic margin. The exception to this is the Amery Ice Shelf and adjacent continental margin. Furthermore, the glacial setting of West Antarctica (wet-based marine ice sheets) is more conducive to sediment erosion and transport than the dry-based terrestrial glacial regime of East Antarctica (Drewry, 1986). The seaward extent of the terrigenous sediment belt around Antarctica is also a function of the efficiency with which these sediments are being transported offshore by marine processes, a subject about which we know relatively little. It is, however, clear that turbidity currents have played a significant role in delivering terrigenous sediments to those portions of the South Pacific seafloor situated near Antarctica, and this mechanism is probably active today (Wright et al., 1985).

The continental slopes and rises of the Amundsen and Bellinghausen Seas are quite extensive and are dissected by numerous submarine canyons (Dangeard et al., 1977). These canyons extend well out on to the abyssal floor and are major conduits through which terrigenous sediments are supplied to the deep (Dangeard et al., 1977). The role of turbidity currents in delivering terrigenous sediments to the deep seafloor is expressed in the form of deep-sea fans that occur on the Bellingshausen continental rise and abyssal plain (Wright et al., 1984). Two large submarine fans, the Charcot and Palmer Fans, have been mapped (Tucholke and Houtz, 1976; Dangeard et al., 1977). These fans systems are apparently inactive today, as turbidites are mainly confined to canyons (Wright et al., 1984). Disorganized gravels and graded gravels and sands cored within these channels consist of glacially-striated grains and include a variety of mineral and rock types. Recent petrographic work by Baegi (1985) has shown that the mineralogical compositions of these deposits vary from canyon-to-canyon, and these data indicate direct input of glacial debris to canyon heads by glaciers during a previous glacial maximum when ice was grounded at or near the shelf break. Piston cores collected from interchannel areas contain finely laminated, very fine sands, silts and clays, interpreted as overbank deposits.

In general, hemipelagic sediments become finer in an offshore direction, away from the Antarctic continent. This simply reflects increasing distance from the source of these sediments. The ice-rafted component of these sediments decreases sharply away from the Antarctic continent (Anderson et al., 1979), and ice-rafted debris is virtually lacking in bottom sediments north of the Antarctic Convergence (Goodell, 1973). This is due to the accelerated decay rate of icebergs as they are subjected to the relatively warm (> 0°C) and rougher surface waters situated just offshore of the continental shelf, and to the tendency of icebergs to drift parallel to the continent once they encounter the circumpolar currents situated seaward of the shelf break.

The siliceous ooze belt shown in Fig. 7.5 results from high surface productivity. It also marks the northern limit of terrigenous sediment transport by turbidity currents. This boundary between siliceous ooze and hemipelagic sediments also corresponds roughly to a major divergence in abyssal circulation. South of this boundary, abyssal currents flow in a westward direction along the Antarctic continental margin while, to the north of this boundary, abyssal flow is more eastward (Heezen and Hollister, 1971). Terrigenous sediments that are transported northward from the Antarctic continental margin may be entrained by westward flowing currents, thus restricting their distribution to the north. North of this boundary, siliceous sediments are transported to the east during their final descent to the seafloor.

The northern boundary of the diatomaceous ooze belt marks the northern limit of bottom waters that are undersaturated with respect to calcium carbonate and where calcareous biogenic sediments mask siliceous sediments (Lisitzin, 1970). In the central South Pacific, this boundary corresponds approximately to the position of the mid-ocean ridge, which impedes northward flow of corrosive Antarctic Bottom Water (Heezen and Hollister, 1971).

Nayudu (1971) and Zemmels (1978) carried out detailed geochemical analyses of South Pacific abyssal sediments. Nayudu found that pelagic clays there are enriched in minerals and elements of volcanic origin. He also concluded that the distribution of diatomaceous and terrigenous sediments is influenced by abyssal circulation and that dilution of terrigenous sediment by biogenic phases is the main factor regulating their concentration on the seafloor. Several studies have indicated the possible occurrence of metalliferous sediments of hydrothermal origin at the crest of the Pacific–Antarctic Ridge (Zemmels, 1978; Glasby et al., 1980; Stoffers et al., 1985).

The dispersal of fine-grained sediments once they reach abyssal depths can, in part, be inferred from bottom photographs. A large collection of bottom photographs exists, particularly for the Southeastern Pacific Basin, as a result of early *Eltanin* and *Conrad* cruises. These were studied by Goodell (1968) and Heezen and Hollister (1971) for visible evidence of bottom currents, and their combined results are shown in Fig. 7.6. These results show that the Southeastern Pacific Basin may be subdivided into three east-west oriented belts. Photographs taken on the abyssal floor nearest the Antarctic continental margin display evidence for weak bottom currents (Fig. 7.7). This area corresponds approximately to the belt of fine-grained terrigenous sediments situated north of the margin (Fig. 7.5).

North of the low energy depositional belt, bottom photographs display evidence of strong to moderate bottom currents in the form of deflected sessile organisms, scour around pebbles and nodules, current lineation, and ripples. A few photographs taken in the vicinity of oceanic fracture zones and the mid-ocean ridge show exposed basement rocks. This zone of bottom scour also corresponds to an extensive field of manganese nodules (Fig. 7.6). Bottom samples from this region also show rippled foraminiferal sands and gravelly lag deposits. Surface sediment samples from the area reveal that both sediment types contain ferro-manganese micronodules and manganese-coated sand and gravel of ice-rafted origin. Megaripples and ripples in predominantly sand-sized sediments and scour around features on the seafloor imply current velocities of several tens of centimetres per second (Goodell, 1973). Elsewhere, below the C.C.D. , this scour zone is characterized by siliceous oozes containing ferromanganese micronodules and manganese-coated ice-rafted grains. Magnetostratigraphic analysis of piston cores from the South Pacific has shown that Brunhes age sediments are thinner, and locally absent, in this sector of the abyssal floor (Goodell and Watkins, 1968).

The South Pacific Scour Zone (Fig. 7.7) is associated with eastwardly transport

201

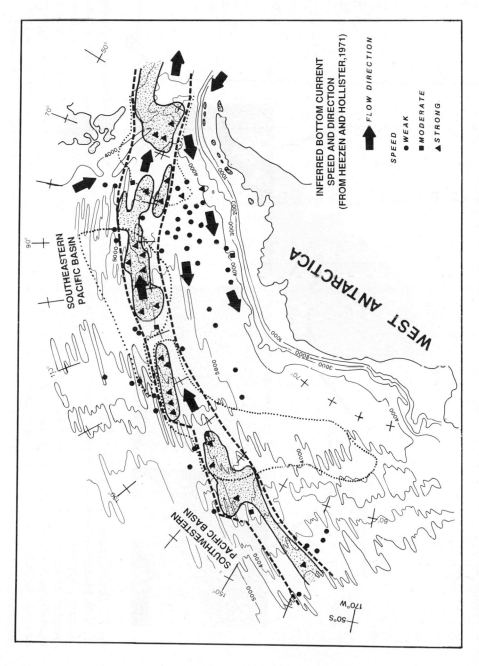

Fig. 7.6. Map showing the distribution of scour zones, manganese nodule distributions, and inferred bottom current information in the South Pacific Ocean. Areas in which lag deposits and rippled sands occur is shown with a stippled pattern. The dotted lines show the outer limits of seafloor that is covered by manganese nodules (Piper et al., 1986). The dashed lines show the limits of the South Pacific Scour Zone (from Heezen and Hollister, 1971). Also shown are inferred bottom current directions and speed (from Heezen and Hollister, 1971).

202

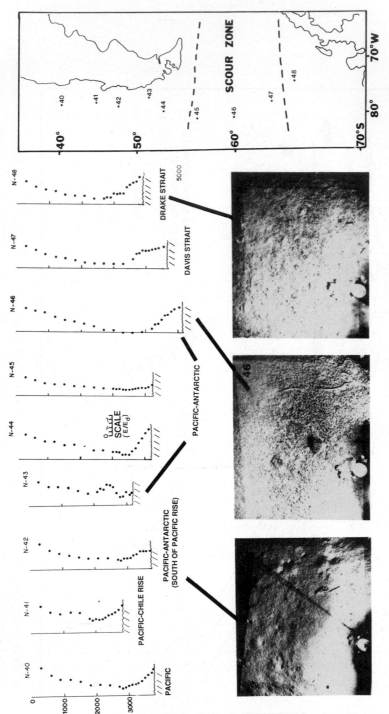

Fig. 7.7. Bottom photographs and nephelometer profiles from a transect across the southeastern Pacific Ocean (data from Sullivan et al., 1973). Muddy bottom with tracks and trails occurs north of the South Pacific Scour Zone, and manganese nodules occur within the scour zone. The muddy seafloor near Antarctica is covered by ice-rafted stones. A bottom nepheloid layer extends throughout the area, except in the northern part of the scour zone. Nephelometer data are recorded with a photometering/transmission densitometer. Optical density is converted to log-exposure using a calibration curve constructed from sensitometer patches. The log exposures for two scattered-light strips are averaged and the log exposure for one of the direct strips is subtracted from the average to obtain E/E_D. See Sullivan et al. (1973) for additional discussion of methods used to obtain and quantify nephelometer measurements.

of bottom water through gaps in the Pacific–Antarctic Ridge, along the deepest part of the abyssal plain, and through the Drake Passage (Heezen and Hollister, 1971). North of this scour zone is a belt where bottom photographs reflect weak bottom current energy (Fig. 7.7), and where fine-grained siliceous oozes and pelagic muds blanket the seafloor (Fig. 7.5).

Nephelometer profiles collected along a N–S transect across the eastern edge of the Southeastern Pacific Basin crosses the South Pacific Scour Zone (Fig. 7.7). Bottom nepheloid layers are associated with the two low energy zones, whereas there is no bottom nepheloid layer associated with the northern portion of the scour zone. The nepheloid layer situated nearest the Antarctic continent is associated with westwardly directed bottom currents (Fig. 7.6), and probably consists of fine-grained terrigenous sediments derived from the continent. In the central region, the bottom nepheloid layer is less extensive (Fig. 7.7). This area is associated with eastward flowing bottom currents (Fig. 7.6). The northern sector has a near bottom nepheloid layer that is probably comprised of sediment derived from the South American continent and is associated with bottom currents which flow to the south (Fig. 7.6).

During R.V. *Conrad* Cruise 15, a series of nephelometer profiles and bottom photographs was gathered along a transect across the northern portion of the South Pacific Ocean (Fig. 7.8). These data, together with the surface sediment map for the region, can be used to illustrate some of the important sedimentological provinces and processes in an east–west transect across the basin. The seafloor in the northeastern part of the region (between 150° and 140°W) is floored by manganese nodules (Fig. 7.8), and there is no bottom nepheloid layer in this area. The transect crosses an area of basalt outcrop at 138°W, which separates the manganese nodule fields to the west from a relatively featureless seafloor (Fig. 7.8) which has a near bottom nepheloid layer (Fig. 7.8). Sediments in this area consist of pelagic clays (Fig. 7.5). Between approximately 130° and 90°W, the seafloor is covered with tracks and trails (Fig. 7.8) and the bottom sediments consist of calcareous clay and ooze (Fig. 7.5). Rock outcrops occur where the transect crosses the mid-ocean ridge (Fig. 7.8). There is no near bottom nepheloid layer in this central province (Fig. 7.8). A bottom nepheloid layer occurs within about 500 m of the bottom in the eastern portion of the East Pacific Basin, and coincides approximately with the boundary between calcareous clays and calcareous ooze (Fig. 7.5). This nepheloid layer probably consists of terrigenous sediments derived from the South American continent.

More recently, Schmitz et al. (1986) have determined sediment accumulation rates in the Southwestern Pacific Basin and demonstrated the importance of erosion and sediment focusing by Antarctic Bottom Water (A.A.B.W.) there.

Ferromanganese Deposits

The distribution and abundance of manganese nodules on the floor of the Antarctic Sector of the Pacific have been mapped by a number of investigators (Goodell, 1968, 1973; Goodell et al., 1971; Glasby, 1976a; Piper at al., 1985). Geochemical studies of nodules from this region have been reported by Goodell et al. (1971), Glasby (1976b) and Meylan and Goodell (1976).

204

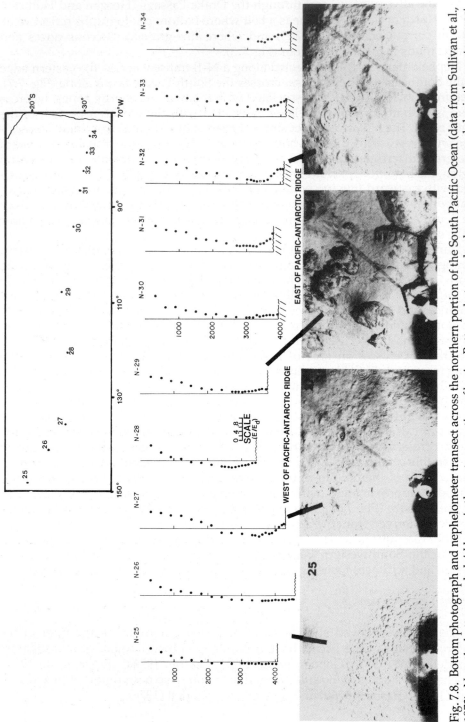

Fig. 7.8. Bottom photograph and nephelometer transect across the northern portion of the South Pacific Ocean (data from Sullivan et al., 1973). Note the bottom nepheloid layer in the eastern portion of basin. Bottom photographs show manganese nodules in the westernmost part of the area. Relatively featureless bottom occurs over most of the western South Pacific seafloor and is separated from seafloor with abundant tracks and trails by the mid-ocean ridge, where basalt outcrops occur. See Fig. 7.7 for discussion of methods used to obtain nephelometer measurements.

According to Glasby (1976a), high concentrations of nodules (> 75% coverage of the seafloor) occur in five main areas : the Southwestern Pacific Basin, the Tasman manganese pavement, the Bellingshausen Basin (centred on 60°S, 100°W), the central region of the Drake Passage, and the crest of the Pacific–Antarctic Ridge (as manganese-encrusted boulders). High surface densities of nodules on the seafloor are due to a combination of low sedimentation rates and high bottom current velocities. Goodell et al. (1971) argued that the elements comprising the concretions are derived mainly from volcanic sources and transported to the site of deposition by bottom currents, coprecipitating en route. Glasby (1976a), on the other hand, concluded that the high abundance of nodules in the two basins on the flanks of the Pacific–Antarctic Ridge is, in part, due to the high availability of potential nucleating agents derived from the erosion and palagonitization of the volcanic rocks extruded at the ridge crest. The difference in composition between nodules from the Southwestern Pacific Basin enriched in Mn, Ni, Mo, Cu, and Co and those from the Bellingshausen Basin was thought to reflect either differences in sediment type in the two regions (red clay and diatomaceous ooze, respectively), or the characteristics of the nodule nuclei (Glasby, 1976a; Meylan and Goodell, 1976).

Glasby (1976b) concluded that the most extensive manganese deposits in the South Pacific are probably located in the circumpolar siliceous ooze province. Nonetheless, these deposits were considered to have no real economic value because of their relatively low Ni + Cu + Co contents, their dilution by glacial erratics, their great distance from land and the unfavourable weather conditions in the region (cf. Zumberge, 1979, 1983).

SUMMARY

Its polar glacial setting, sea ice cover, and great depth combine to make the Antarctic continental shelf a unique sedimentary environment. A myriad of glacial settings occurs along the Pacific Sector of the Antarctic continental margin, which extends from the Antarctic Peninsula to the Ross Sea. These range from vast ice shelves, the largest being the Ross Ice Shelf, to mountainous coasts where valley glaciers flow into the sea. The Ross Sea continental shelf is the most thoroughly studied portion of the margin.

At present, outlet glaciers play the greatest role in delivering sediment to the continental shelf. Many sediment-laden icebergs have been observed in the region, but most are relatively small. Large ice shelves deposit the bulk of their debris near their grounding lines. Large tabular icebergs calved from the ice shelves are therefore mostly barren of sediment. The concentration of ice-rafted debris in surface sediments decreases sharply seaward of the continental shelf, which implies that most debris-laden icebergs melt before reaching the South Pacific Ocean. Even on the continental shelf, ice-rafted debris comprises a relatively small proportion of surface sediments. Sediments of the inner shelf consist mainly of terrigenous silt, with variable concentrations of siliceous biogenic material (mostly diatom frustules). The only areas where marine currents are winnowing fine-grained sediments to produce coarse-grained deposits is on shallow banks and at the shelf edge and upper slope. Sediment gravity flow processes are active sedimentary agents on the continental slope and on those portions of the continental shelf where glacial erosion has resulted in steep gradients. Piston cores have penetrated through these surface sediments into relict deposits that are mainly of glacial origin. These include glacial marine sediments as well as till.

An extensive belt of fine-grained terrigenous sediment surrounds the Antarctic continent. The northern limits of this belt corresponds approximately with a divergence in the direction of bottom current flow directions. Turbidity currents also play an active role in the dispersal of terrigenous sediments on the abyssal floor. An extensive siliceous ooze belt is situated north of the terrigenous sediment belt and coresponds approximately to the Antarctic Convergence. North of this belt, calcareous sediments blanket those portions of the abyssal floor that are shallower than 4,500 m, which is taken as the level of the Carbonate Compensation Depth. Below this, pelagic clays are accumulating. This overall sediment distribution pattern is disrupted by strong bottom currents, which winnow fine-grained sediments as they settle to the seafloor and actually scour the seafloor in some areas. Bottom photographs show lag deposits and current ripples within scour zones. These scour zones are also marked by extensive zones of manganese deposits.

CHAPTER 8

PLANKTON

S.Z. EL-SAYED

INTRODUCTION

In general, early studies of plankton of the Southern Ocean, and of the Pacific Sector of the Southern Ocean in particular, are closely linked to the history of exploration of the Antarctic continent and its surrounding seas. J.D. Hooker, the famed botanist and surgeon of the *Erebus* and *Terror* Expeditions (1839–43), collected the first plankton samples in Antarctic waters. Hooker sent samples collected between Cape Horn and the Ross Sea to the German diatomist, C.G. Ehrenberg, who published the first paper on Antarctic diatoms in 1844. At about the same time, Dumont d'Urville published an interesting account of the Antarctic waters in his "Voyage au Pole Sud et dans l'Oceanie", noting the rich plant and animal life. During the following three-quarters of a century, extensive collection of Antarctic phytoplankton was conducted by members of such celebrated expeditions as the *Challenger* (1873–76), *Belgica* (1897–99), *Valdivia* (1898–99), *Gauss* (1901–08), *Scotia* (1902–04), *Pourquoi Pas?* (1908–10) and *Meteor* (1925). The *Discovery II* investigations (1925–39, 1950–61) substantially increased our knowledge of the distribution and abundance of the phytoplankton and zooplankton populations, especially krill, in the Atlantic, Indian and Pacific Sectors of the Southern Ocean.

In the Pacific Sector of the Southern Ocean, systematic studies of the plankton commenced in the mid-1950s and early 1960s with the cruises of the Russian ships *Ob, Slava* and *Vitiaz*, the United States Navy ship, *Eltanin*, as well as with the numerous Japanese Antarctic Research Expeditions (JARE). As a result of these investigations, a large body of valuable data was obtained on the geographic and temporal distributions of phytoplankton and zooplankton populations, especially for the high latitudes of the South Pacific. El-Sayed (1970a), Knox (1970) and Bary (1970) provided comprehensive reviews of the knowledge about plankton of the South Pacific accumulated up until the late 1960s. Moreover, in a paper on the abundance, composition and distribution of phytoplankton in the Pacific Antarctic, Hasle (1969) gave an excellent overview of the history of phytoplankton investigations of the Southern Ocean up to that time.

Study of the structure and function of the Antarctic marine ecosystem began in the southwestern Pacific Sector of the Antarctic with *Eltanin* Cruise 38 (March to May 1969). This cruise (together with *Eltanin* Cruises 46 and 51 in the Indian and Pacific Sectors, respectively) constitutes a landmark in the history of ecosystem-oriented study of the seas surrounding Antarctica (El-Sayed, 1973; McWhinnie, 1973). *Eltanin* Cruise 51 completed an integrated study of the biology, chemistry and physical oceanography of the Ross Sea which served as a prelude to the Ross Ice Shelf Project (RISP) investigations in the late 1970s. Research efforts in the early 1980s, under the auspices of the program, Biological Investigations of Marine Antarctic Systems and Stocks (BIOMASS) has enhanced our knowledge of the plankton populations in the Pacific Sector of the Southern Ocean, although not to the same extent as the Atlantic and Indian Sectors. The publications by Heywood and Whitaker (1984) and Everson (1984b) provide recent comprehensive overviews of the Southern Ocean phytoplankton and zooplankton, respectively.

Knowledge about the plankton and, for that matter, about other biological components of the Pacific Sector of the Antarctic lags behind that of the better-studied waters of the Atlantic Sector. In addition, while the broad distributional features of Antarctic plankton are now known, many ecological questions remain unanswered. Fortunately, due to the circumpolar nature of the Southern Ocean, knowledge gained in one sector can be applied to other sectors, provided that due allowances are made for characteristic hydrographic and environmental conditions (Hart, 1942). The reader should keep these allowances in mind, as information provided in this chapter is not strictly limited to the Pacific Sector of the Antarctic.

PHYSICAL AND CHEMICAL CHARACTERISTICS

The discussion of plankton in this chapter will be prefaced by a brief examination of the unique physical and chemical characteristics of the Antarctic seas, since these have a strong bearing on the biology, distribution, and abundance of the planktonic organisms. A more detailed account of the hydrology of the Pacific Sector of the Southern Ocean is given by Whitworth and Patterson (this volume).

Unique features of the waters surrounding Antarctica include : (a) the presence of pack-ice around the Antarctic continent and its seasonal waxing and waning; (b) variability of the light regime, which, south of the Antarctic Circle, alternates between continuous darkness in the winter and continuous daylight during the summer; (c) extensive cloud cover; (d) the circumpolarity of Antarctic waters, and (e) high concentrations of inorganic nutrients. It is in response to the physico-chemical environments that the Antarctic planktonic organisms have developed their characteristic features.

The Southern Ocean is a region of relatively simple hydrographic conditions. These conditions have been discussed in detail by Sverdrup (1933) and Deacon (1933, 1963, 1964, 1984) and are only briefly summarized here. The waters between 40°S and the Antarctic continent can be divided into several well-defined circumpolar zones (Nowlin, 1985). Of the several fronts, the Polar Front appears most stationary (Fig. 8.1), and it forms one of the major boundary zones of the World Ocean. The principal physical property by which its location can be mapped is the steep temperature gradient at the sea surface. At the northern limit of the Polar Front, Antarctic Surface Water sinks beneath the less dense, south-flowing sub-Antarctic Water to form the Antarctic Intermediate Water which flows northward (Fig. 8.2). The Antarctic Bottom Water is formed close to the Antarctic continent. Immediately above this Bottom Water, there is an exception-

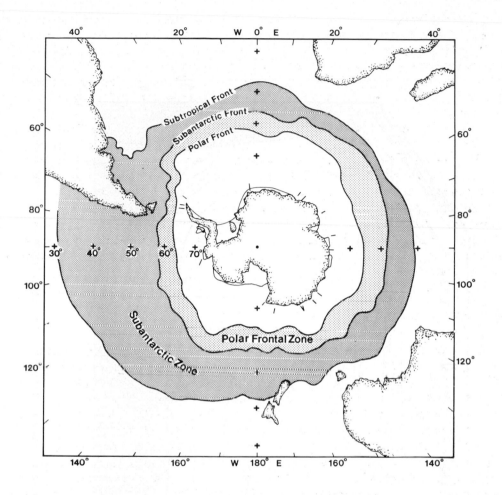

Fig. 8.1.   Surface regimes of the Southern Ocean.   Position of the Subtropical Front separating the subtropics from the Subantarctic Zone is after Deacon (1982). Locations of the Subantarctic Front and Polar Front bounding the polar frontal zone are modified from a figure by Clifford (1983). The antarctic zone is south of the Polar Front. Summer ice extent is shown near Antarctica as are locations where a water mass transition near the continental slope has been observed (Clifford, 1983) (after Nowlin, 1985, and Nowlin and Klinck, 1986).

ally thick relatively warm water mass, the Circumpolar Deep Water, character-ized by high salinity and high concentrations of nutrients.

The distributions of the three inorganic nutrient salts best studied in the Southern Ocean (i.e., phosphate, nitrate and silicate) show marked geographic variations. The effect of the Antarctic Converge on the distribution of these nutrient salts is quite significant. In general, the nutrient distributions show higher concentrations south of the convergence than north of it. However, it is interesting to note that even their lowest levels of concentrations are higher, in

210

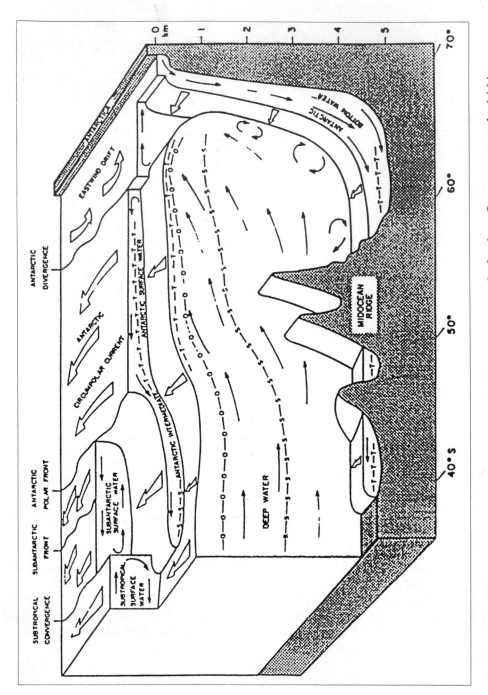

Fig. 8.2. Schematic representation of water masses and their movements in the Southern Ocean sector south of Africa (after Lutjeharms et al., 1985).

general, than the winter maximum of temperate regions. At a deeper level, between the northward-moving Antarctic Intermediate Water and the southward-moving Deep Water, phosphate and nitrate appear to be regenerated, possibly because of the large mortality of sinking phytoplankton as indicated by the abundant deposits of diatom ooze below this region. The decomposition enriches the south-going deep water and, in the Antarctic zone, the highest phosphate and nitrate concentrations are found in the Circumpolar Deep Water. Silicates are most abundant in the Antarctic Bottom Water, possibly because of regeneration from the dissolution of the diatom frustules near the bottom.

According to Foster (1984), there does not seem to be a clear correlation between the surface distribution of nutrients and upwelling, although the Circumpolar Deep Water is probably the source of the nutrients in the surface waters south of the convergence.

PHYTOPLANKTON

The numerous phytoplankton investigations carried out in Antarctic waters during the past few decades have dealt primarily with the taxonomy and distribution of the organisms. The publications of Kozlova (1964) and Hasle (1969) dealing with the systematic composition and distribution of the phytoplankton (diatoms in particular) in the Pacific Sector of the Southern Ocean are of special interest. Very little attention has been given to the study of the life history, physiology, metabolism, and population dynamics of these algal communities.

COMPOSITION

Diatoms

The phytoplankton assemblage of the Pacific Sector of the Southern Ocean (and in the Southern Ocean generally) is dominated by diatoms, with smaller numbers of dinoflagellates and silicoflagellates. In a detailed study of the water samples of the Pacific Sector of the Southern Ocean from the Norwegian *Brategg* Expedition (1947–48), Hasle (1969) listed about 100 diatom, 70 dinoflagellate, 5 coccolithophorid, and 5 silicoflagellate species. Diatoms of the genera *Chaetoceros*, *Coscinodiscus*, *Nitzschia*, *Rhizosolenia* and *Thalassiosira* generally dominate the Antarctic phytoplankton (Fig. 8.3). Each of these genera is represented by 10–15 species. Hasle (1969) listed *Chaetoceros neglectus*, *Nitzschia* "barkleyi", and *Coccolithus huxleyi* (a coccolithophorid) as the dominant species in the flora of the Subantarctic Zone; *Chaetoceros dichaeta*, *C. neglectus*, *Nitzschia* "nana", and *N.* "closterioides" as dominants in the northern Antarctic Zone; and *Nitzschia curta*, *N. cylindrus* and *N. subcurvata* as dominants in the southern part of the Antarctic Zone.

Endemism is fairly high among Antarctic diatoms; however, their general distribution pattern is circumpolar. Very few species are thought to be bipolar in

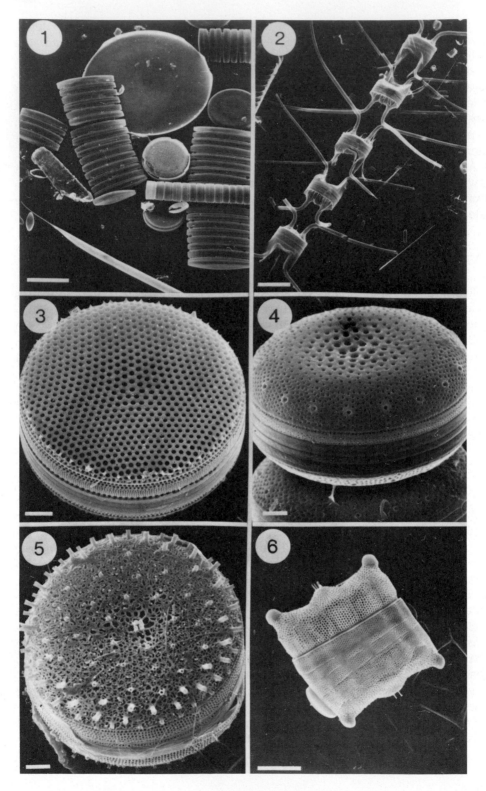

distribution (with truly disjunct biogeographical populations), but examples do exist. Bipolar species include *Thalassiosira antarctica, Porosira glacialis,* and *Nitzschia cylindrus* (Hasle, 1976).

Dinoflagellates

Because Antarctic dinoflagellates (Fig. 8.4) are rather small and are often encased in weak and easily deformed plates, they have been only poorly studied. Although the number of dinoflagellates appears to be significantly smaller than the number of diatoms, the dinoflagellate biomass in the Antarctic has probably been underestimated. Dinoflagellate-dominated phytoplankton assemblages have been reported; therefore, at least in isolated cases, their contribution to the biomass is significant (Balech, 1970).

Only a few thecate genera (those encased in cellulose plates), chiefly *Protoperidinium* and *Dinophysis,* are represented in the Antarctic dinoflagellates. Of these, *Protoperidinium* is by far the most abundant, both in number of species and in number of individuals.

Naked, or thin-walled, dinoflagellates are probably not as rare in Antarctic waters as they seem. The assumption that they are rare is due, in part, to preservation and fixation procedures which render them unrecognizable. However, eight naked species of *Gymnodinium,* four of *Gyrodinium,* and two of *Amphidinium,* as well as the species *Pyrocystis pseudonoctiluca* have been identified in the Antarctic (Balech, 1975).

As far as we know, Arctic and Antarctic waters have only a very few cosmopolitan species in common. Three bipolar species are known : *Protoperidinium antarcticum, P. saltans,* and *P. thulescence.* The latter has also been reported in sub-Antarctic waters. Endemism is high among Antarctic dinoflagellates; no less than 35 species, many belonging to the genus *Protoperidinium,* being limited to the Antarctic region. However, cells are occasionally found in sub-Antarctic waters, probably transported by the isolated "rings" or meanders of Antarctic waters in the region of the Polar Front (El-Sayed and Hofmann, 1986). In no other oceanic region do the dinoflagellates attain such a high degree of endemism (80–85%) (Balech, 1970).

Fig. 8.3. Antarctic diatoms. (Photos from : F.C. Stephens, C. Park, and Dr G. Fryxell)

3–1 *Rhizosolenia hebetata, Actinocyclus* sp., *Thalassiosira* sp., *Nitzschia kerguelensis, Nitzschia* sp., Scale marker = 50 µm.
3–2 *Chaetoceros dichaeta,* Scale marker = 25 µm.
3–3 *Thalassiosira symmetrica,* Scale marker = 5 µm.
3–4 *Thalassiosira gracilis,* Scale marker = 2 µm.
3–5 *Thalassiosira gravida,* Scale marker = 2 µm.
3–6 *Biddulphia* sp., Scale marker = 50 µm.

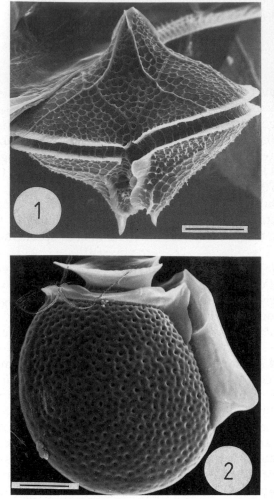

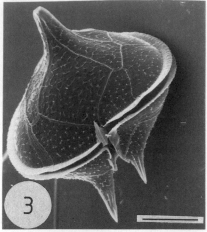

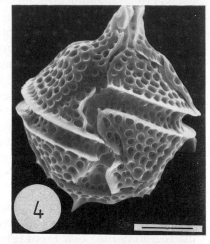

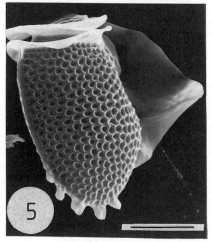

Fig. 8.4 Dinoflagellates.

(Photos from : Dr C. McKenzie)

4–1 *Protoperidinium crassipes,*
Scale marker = 20 μm.
4–2 *Dinophysis antarctica,* Scale marker = 10 μm.
4–3 *Protoperidinium antarcticum,*
Scale marker = 30 μm.
4–4 *Gonyaulax digitale,* Scale marker = 10 μm.
4–5 *Dinophysis tuberculata,* Scale marker = 20 μm.

Phaeocystis pouchetii

Phaeocystis pouchetii belongs to the order Prymnesiales and is one of the few non-diatom algae which is exceedingly plentiful in southern Antarctic waters. *Phaeocystis* occurs in either a unicellular motile form or a colonial palmelloid stage which can be large enough to be visible to the naked eye. This alga is very widely distributed in warm and temperate waters as well as in Antarctic and Arctic seas. Its gelatinous blooms are sometimes known as "Dutchman's baccy juice", and the jelly-like colonies are so thick that they clog plankton nets.

Extensive blooms of *Phaeocystis* have been reported in the Ross Sea (El-Sayed et al., 1983) where high cell concentrations extended from the surface to depths of 100–150 m. Distinct disoloration of the water (greenish-grey to greenish-brown) accompanied this bloom, resulting in considerable submarine light attenuation.

Silicoflagellates

Silicoflagellates are unicellular chrysophycean algae. Occasionally, cells may be linked together to form simple, small colonies. The silicoflagellates have an internal skeleton of conspicuous hollow siliceous tubes, forming a spectacular symmetrical structure containing many chloroplasts. Only one species of silico-flagellate, *Dictyocha (Distephanes) speculum* (Fig. 8.5), is generally abundant in Antarctic waters; it sometimes outnumbers any species of diatom (Balech, 1970). *Dictyocha speculum* is larger than many diatoms and should not be overlooked as a contributor to phytoplankton biomass and primary production in Antarctic waters.

Monads, Flagellates, and Coccolithophorids

Hasle (1969) listed monads, flagellates, and coccolithophorids as regular components of the phytoplankton within the Pacific Sector of the Southern Ocean. The coccolithophorids are generally restricted to the Subantarctic Zone.

STANDING CROP AND PRIMARY PRODUCTION

Chlorophyll a

The extensive phytoplankton studies carried out in the Pacific Sector of the Southern Ocean on board the U.S.N.S. *Eltanin* (see Fig. 8.6 for positions of stations occupied) clearly indicate that the phytoplankton standing crop is generally poor (Table 8.1). The average chlorophyll *a* (here used as an index of phytoplankton biomass) concentration in the surface waters during *Eltanin* Cruises 19–28 (less 22) was only 0.26 mg/m^3. More recently, Fukuchi (1980) reported surface chlorophyll *a* concentrations in the Pacific Sector of the Southern Ocean ranging generally from 0.12 to 0.29 mg/m^3, with a maximum value of 0.66 mg/m^3. Integrated chlorophyll *a* values for the euphotic zone (i.e., values integrated through a

216

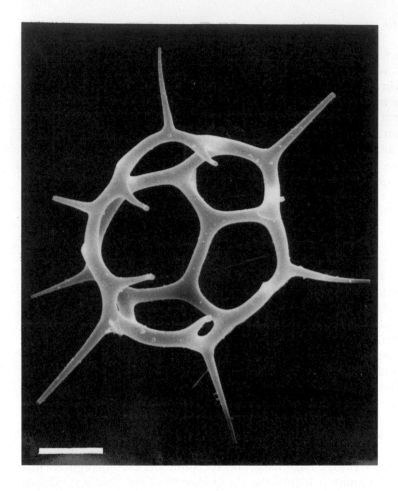

Fig. 8.5. Antarctic marine silicoflagellate *Distephanes speculum*, Scale marker = 5μm.
(Photo from : C. Park).

column of water extending from sea surface to the depth to which 1% of surface
light intensity penetrates; in the Pacific Sector this depth averages 80 m with a
range of 50–150 m) average 12.62 mg/m² in the Pacific Antarctic (El-Sayed, 1968).

Within the water column, chlorophyll *a* exhibits maximum concentrations at
depths corresponding to 25–50% of surface light intensity (Fig. 8.7). Below these
maxima, there is a gradual decrease in phytoplankton biomass to the bottom of
the euphotic zone, below which the biomass is usually much reduced (El-Sayed,
1970a; El-Sayed and Turner, 1977; Holm-Hansen et al., 1977). However, substantial amounts of chlorophyll *a* are sometimes found below the euphotic zone, as for
example, at several stations during *Eltanin* Cruise 51 in the Ross Sea (Fig. 8.8).

The average surface chlorophyll *a* concentration for the Pacific Antarctic (0.26
mg/m³) is 3–4 times lower than for the Atlantic Antarctic (0.89 mg/m³). However,

TABLE 8.1

Observations made of the standing crop of phytoplankton during *Eltanin* Cruises 19–28 (less Cruise 22) in the South Pacific and in the Pacific Sector of the Southern Ocean (from El-Sayed, 1968).

	Min.	Max.	Mean	Standard deviation	Number of observations
*Chl *a* (mg/m³)	0.01	5.80	0.26	0.34	723
**Chl *a* (mg/m²)	0.23	41.32	12.62	6.32	217
*^{14}C (mgC/m³/hr)	0.03	22.50	1.22	1.69	656
**^{14}C (mgC/m²/hr)	3.54	194.73	32.01	23.93	213

* Surface values
** Integrated values for the euphotic zone

integrated values for the Atlantic Sector are not markedly higher than those for the Pacific (15.94 mg/m² and 12.62 mg/m², respectively; El-Sayed, 1968). Caution should be exercised in interpreting these results, however. While a great many of the stations occupied in the Atlantic Sector were located in relatively productive coastal regions, most of the stations occupied in the Pacific Antarctic were in oceanic regions noted for their lower productivity (El Sayed, 1970a).

Primary Production

The rate at which photosynthetic organisms synthesize organic matter from inorganic substances (primary productivity) is generally measured in oceanic waters by the ^{14}C uptake method (Steemann Nielsen, 1952). Primary productivity in the Pacific Sector generally correlates very well with the distribution of the standing crop of phytoplankton. As with chlorophyll *a* concentration, primary productivity shows wide point-to-point variation. However, rates of photo-synthesis are generally low (< 5.0 mgC/m³/hr), with an average integrated value for the euphotic zone of only 0.134 gC/m²/day (El-Sayed and Turner, 1977; Holm-Hansen et al., 1977). This production value is similar to that reported for other open waters of the world's oceans (Steemann Nielsen, 1954).

In general, maximum photosynthetic activity (like chlorophyll *a*) occurs at depths corresponding to between 25% and 50% of surface light intensity. Carbon uptake often extends well below the depth of 1% surface illumination. At some stations in the Ross Sea, primary production below the euphotic zone was slightly in excess of 25% of the total production in the water column (El-Sayed et al., 1983). However, in other parts of the Pacific Sector, the percentage could be much lower (< 10%).

As in the case of the phytoplankton standing crop, the primary productivity of surface water samples in the Atlantic Sector was about four times the Pacific value (5.25 mgC/m³/hr compared to 1.22 mgC/m³/hr, respectively). In terms of inte-

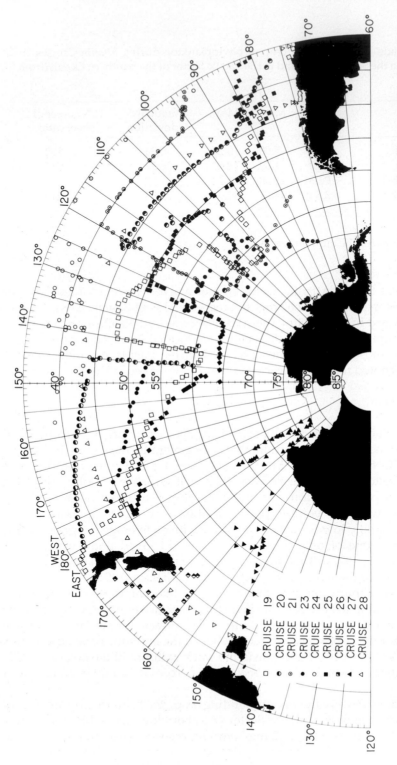

Fig. 8.6. Stations occupied by U.S.N.S. *Eltanin* in the Pacific Sector of Antarctic during Cruises 19–28, less Cruise 27 (after El-Sayed, 1970b).

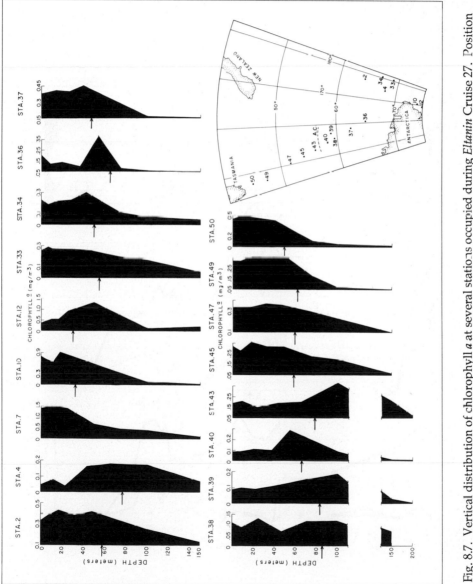

Fig. 8.7. Vertical distribution of chlorophyll *a* at several stations occupied during *Eltanin* Cruise 27. Position of arrows indicates depth of euphotic zone (after El-Sayed, 1970a).

220

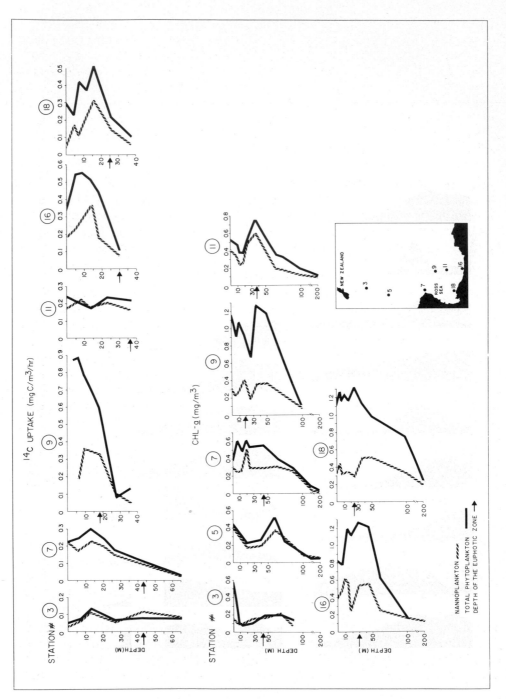

Fig. 8.8. Vertical distributions of total and nanoplankton (< 10 μm) primary production and chlorophyll *a* at stations occupied during *Eltanin* Cruise 51 (after El-Sayed and Turner, 1977).

grated values, however, the Atlantic stations were not substantially more productive than the Pacific stations (50.70 and 32.01 mgC/m^2/hr, respectively; El-Sayed, 1968).

Although the Southern Ocean has always been described in terms which reflect its proverbial richness, the results of the primary productivity measurements made in recent years have clearly demonstrated that the high productivity of Antarctic waters is real only with regard to the inshore waters, and not with respect to the oceanic regions. According to Holm-Hansen et al. (1977), the average primary productivity of the Southern Ocean is 0.134 gC/m^2/day which is about the same as that of the oligotrophic Gulf of Mexico (El-Sayed and Turner, 1977). This together with the recognition that the productive season in the Antarctic seas is about 120 days per year, forces us to qualify earlier emphasis on the high productivity of the Southern Ocean.

Latitudinal and Longitudinal Variations

Due to the vast expanses of the Antarctic and sub-Antarctic waters in the Pacific Sector of the Southern Ocean, it is instructive to study the latitudinal and longitudinal variations in the phytoplankton standing crop and primary productivity in these regions. When data from *Eltanin* Cruises 19–28 (less 22) are averaged over 5° of latitude and plotted (Fig. 8.9), it is apparent that values of chlorophyll *a* and ^{14}C uptake in surface water samples between 40° and 60°S show little variation with latitude. However, substantial increases in these parameters are noted south of 70°S. Averaging over 10° of longitude (Fig. 8.10) shows that the western section of the Pacific Sector of the Southern Ocean between 140°E and 170°W (excluding 150°–160°E) has conspicuously higher values of chlorophyll *a* and ^{14}C uptake than the central and eastern sections. This richness can be attributed, in part, to the proximity of the observation sites to New Zealand, Australia, and Tasmania, and the so-called "landmass effect" proposed by Doty and Oguri (1956).

The region to the west of the Antarctic Peninsula is also noted for its rich phytoplankton populations; surface chlorophyll *a* concentrations as high as 18 mg/m^3 were recorded by the author from the Gerlache Strait (El-Sayed, 1967). Even higher values (25 mg/m^3) are reported by Burkholder and Mandelli (1965) from the same Strait.

Seasonal Variations

The seasonal variations of pigment and primary productivity values collected in the Pacific Sector during nine cruises of the *Eltanin* are shown in Fig. 8.11. Standing crop and photosynthetic activity of the primary producers were substantially higher during the austral spring and summer cruises than during the autumn and winter cruises. Hart (1942) observed similar seasonal variations in the phytoplankton population and related these variations to seasonal changes in the physico-chemical environment. Such seasonal variations in abundance are most pronounced for the diatoms, which reach their maximum density in mid-

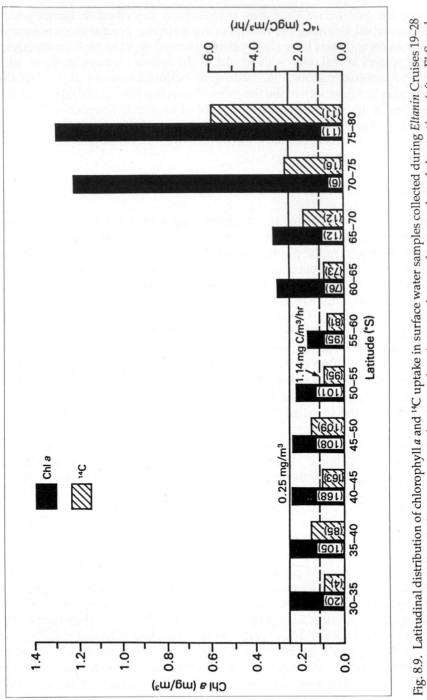

Fig. 8.9. Latitudinal distribution of chlorophyll *a* and ¹⁴C uptake in surface water samples collected during *Eltanin* Cruises 19–28 (less Cruise 22). Dashed lines indicate average values; numbers in parentheses refer to number of observations (after El-Sayed, 1968).

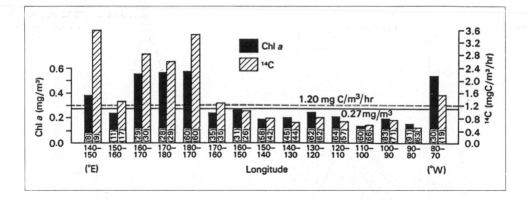

Fig. 8.10. Longitudinal distribution of chlorophyll *a* and ^{14}C uptake in surface water samples collected during *Eltanin* Cruises 19–28 (less Cruise 22). Dashed lines indicate average values; numbers in parentheses refer to number of observations (after El-Sayed, 1968).

January in what Hart referred to as the Intermediate Zone (i.e. c. 55°50'–60°00'S) or at the end of January and in the first half of February further south (Hasle, 1969). The dinoflagellates, in general, parallel the diatoms in their seasonal variations.

FACTORS GOVERNING PRIMARY PRODUCTION

The factors governing variability in primary production in Antarctic waters have been discussed by Holm-Hansen et al. (1977) and Fogg (1977), and more recently by El-Sayed (1984, 1987) and Sakshaug and Holm-Hansen (1986). A brief account of the factors influencing primary production of the Southern Ocean is given below.

Light

It is well known that variations in incoming solar radiation between summer and winter in the Antarctic are extreme. Mean monthly values of radiant energy plotted against ^{14}C uptake and chlorophyll *a* concentration (Fig. 8.12) show clearly that the rise and fall of phytoplankton biomass and primary production in Antarctic waters are in direct response to the amount of incident radiation.

In their study of the effect of radiant energy on the photosynthetic activity of the phytoplankton in the Ross Sea, Holm-Hansen et al. (1977) found that, on days when light intensity was high, photosynthetic rates were low in surface waters, and maximal at depths corresponding to between 25% and 50% of incident radiation. On the other hand, when incident light was low during the *in situ* incubation period, photosynthetic rates remained fairly constant in the upper waters of the euphotic zone, or they were highest at the surface (Fig. 8.13). These results are

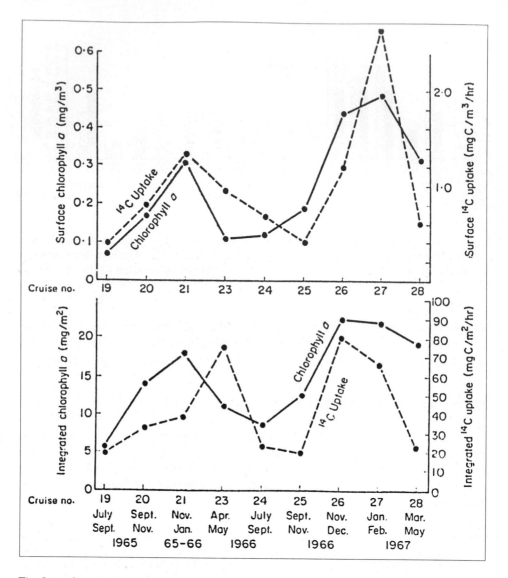

Fig. 8.11. Seasonal variations in surface and integrated chlorophyll *a* and ¹⁴C carbon uptake in the Pacific Sector of the Southern Ocean (from El-Sayed, 1970a).

most probably due to photo-inhibition, whereby high light intensity causes a decrease in photosynthetic rates. The threshold of photo-inhibition for Antarctic phytoplankton was calculated to be in the range of 40–50 cal/cm²/half-light day.

Light penetration in Antarctic waters is determined not only by the intensity and angle of incidence of light, surface reflectance, and absorption by suspended particles, but also by the presence of thick fast-ice and pack-ice, which appreciably reduces the amount of submarine illumination.

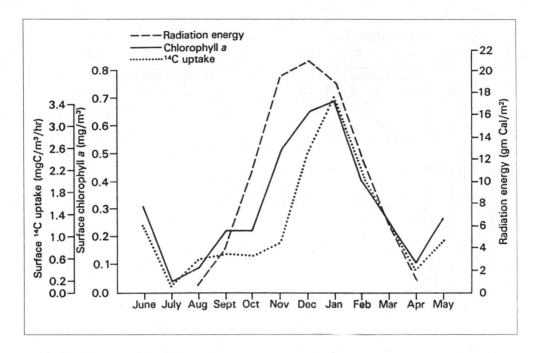

Fig. 8.12. Monthly variation of radiation energy (with average cloudiness) at "Maudheim" station (71°03'S, 10°56'W) compared with monthly changes in surface chlorophyll *a* and ¹⁴C uptake in Antarctic waters (after El-Sayed, 1971b).

Temperature

Temperature is commonly listed as one of the factors, if not the main factor (Saijo and Kawashima, 1964), influencing the rate of primary production in Antarctic waters. Antarctic phytoplankton appear to be obligate psychrophiles (cold-loving) since they grow well at low temperatures, but show a sharp drop in photosynthetic rate at temperatures above 10°C. Neori and Holm-Hansen (1982) concluded that temperature limits primary production rates at times when light intensity is saturating the photo-chemical apparatus of the cell. Since the phytoplankton are saturated by a light intensity approximately 10–15% of that generally incident upon the sea surface, it is apparent that temperature can be a rate-controlling factor in the upper 10–20 m of the water column.

Nutrients

The numerous observations on nutrients (phosphate, nitrate and silicate) in Antarctic waters clearly show that these nutrients appear to be in excess of phytoplankton requirements. There are no data available to suggest that phytoplankton

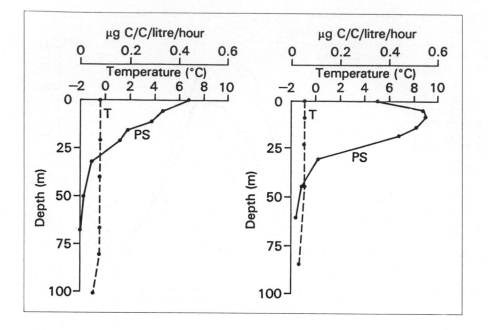

Fig. 8.13. Vertical distribution of photosynthesis (PS) measured in µg/litre/hr and temperature at Station 14 (left) and Station 16 (right) of *Eltanin* Cruise 51 (January/February 1972) in the Ross Sea (after Holm-Hansen et al., 1977).

growth in the Antarctic is limited by nutrient deficiency (Hayes et al., 1984). Even at the peak of phytoplankton growth, the concentration of nutrients remains well above limiting values. For instance, during the heavy bloom of *Phaeocystis pouchetii* in the Ross Sea (El-Sayed et al., 1983), the nitrate concentration was still high, with euphotic zone values averaging 17 µg at./l. It is therefore unlikely that nutrients are sufficiently low at any one time to become limiting factors to the growth of the phytoplankton. However, according to Walsh (1971) and Allanson et al. (1981), patterns of silicate distribution indicate that SiO_3 may be the most limiting of the major nutrients for the growth of Antarctic diatoms, thus corroborating a similar conclusion arrived at earlier by Hart (1942). With regard to the trace elements, Jacques (1983) carried out enrichment experiments using Zn, Mo, Co, Mn, and Fe, and showed that they are not limiting factors. It is, however, possible that organic factors, e.g., vitamin B_{12} and thiamin (see Carlucci and Cuhel, 1977), may alter the species composition of the phytoplankton without changing the overall rate of primary production. It is also possible that the availability of trace micronutrients may be altered by pack-ice and iceberg melt-water, thus affecting the productivity or species composition of the waters in the vicinity of pack-ice and icebergs.

Water Column Stability

Several investigators have drawn attention to the importance of the stability of the water column in controlling production (Braarud and Klem, 1931; Gran, 1932; Sverdrup, 1953; Pingree, 1978). Of the several processes which have been suggested to be important in initiating and sustaining near-ice blooms, the most significant is the vertical stability induced by melt-water. According to this suggestion, first proposed by Marshall (1957) for Arctic waters, the low salinity of melt-water contributes to the stability of the near-ice water column, thus helping to retain the phytoplankton near the surface and promoting a bloom. Corroborative evidence that this mechanism is important in the initiation of ice-edge blooms in the Antarctic is furnished by Jacobs and Amos (1967), El-Sayed (1971a) and Smith and Nelson (1985). Stability of the upper water layers may therefore play an important role in the development of Antarctic phytoplankton blooms. Sakshaug and Holm-Hansen (1986) report that for all "bloom stations", where chlorophyll a was > 2 mg/m^3, the pycnocline (zone where water density changes markedly with depth) was between 20 m and 40 m deep. They speculate that 50 m is the maximum pycnocline depth for a bloom to develop. The presence of an homogeneous (i.e., isothermal) water column reaching to a depth of 50–100 m during most of the year therefore hinders the development of blooms and contributes to the low primary production of Antarctic waters.

Grazing

In the Southern Ocean, euphausiids (principally *Euphausia superba*, "krill"), which may constitute half of the Antarctic zooplankton biomass (Holdgate, 1970), are the dominant herbivores. Several investigators have observed that areas of high krill concentration are usually noted for their low standing crop of phytoplankton. In 1981, during the First International BIOMASS Experiment (FIBEX), Polish investigators found that, in the central parts of the Bransfield Strait, areas of dense krill concentration exhibited low chlorophyll a values at the surface (< 0.5 mg/m^3) and in the water column (< 50 mg/m^2) (Rakusa-Suszczewski, 1982). Chilean scientists also reported similar findings during FIBEX. For example, in the region to the south of the South Shetland Islands, Uribe (1982) measured low values of chlorophyll a (< 0.5 mg/m^3) in the central part of the Bransfield Strait where high krill concentrations in the 10–200 m layer were found. According to Uribe (1982), the poverty of the phytoplankton was not due to nutrient limitation (phosphate : 1.4 µg at./l; nitrate : 17.9 µg at./l) but was most likely due to intensive krill feeding. In addition, data from the R.V. *Melville* cruise (also during FIBEX) demonstrated, on a temporal basis, the inverse relationship often noted between phytoplankton biomass and zooplankton (mainly krill) abundance (Holm-Hansen and Huntley, 1984).

SIGNIFICANCE OF NANOPLANKTON AND PICOPLANKTON

In contrast to phytoplankton larger than 35 μm in size (net phytoplankton), which in the past have received considerable attention and form the basis of the classic food chain, the contribution of nanoplankton (< 20 μm) to the standing crop and primary production has been overlooked until recently (Pomeroy, 1974). Fay (1973) was the first to show that nanoplankton contribute about 70% of phytoplankton biomass and primary production of the Ross Sea. El-Sayed and Taguchi (1981) reported on the abundance and significance of the nanoplankton in the Weddell Sea. South of Australia, Yamaguchi and Shibata (1982) have shown that cells < 10 μm in size constitute about 50% of the total phytoplankton biomass in Antarctic waters. The abundance of this size group was relatively constant in all water masses, whereas the size fraction > 10 μm showed large variations.

In recent years, there has been increased awareness of the existence of a subpopulation of still smaller organisms, collectively known as picoplankton (< 2 μm). In the tropical Pacific and Atlantic Oceans, it has been estimated that picoplankton makes a substantial contribution to the turnover rate of phytoplankton biomass (Li et al., 1983; Platt et al., 1983). Kosaki et al. (1985), in a survey of phytoplankton size distribution in waters south of Australia, found that the nanoplankton (3–20 μm) were predominant in Antarctic waters.

Recent investigations have demonstrated that, in agreement with findings from lower and temperate latitudes, a significant portion of the photoautotrophs in the Antarctic Ocean is in the picoplankton (< 1 μm) size range (Weber and El-Sayed, 1987).

Taken together, the results of the nanoplankton and picoplankton investigations underscore the importance of the smallest organisms in the biomass spectrum. According to Platt et al. (1983) "... we have to modify the way in which we perceive the structure and function of the pelagic ecosystem in the oligotrophic waters." Although the Antarctic is not oligotrophic in terms of its nutrient concentrations, this conclusion may be applicable to the Southern Ocean with its generally low phytoplankton biomass.

ICE ALGAE

Hooker (1847) was among the first to report on the association of marine flora with sea ice and the discoloring effect of algal growth on icebergs and pack-ice. He observed, " ... they occurred in such countless myriads, as to stain the Berg and the pack-ice a pale ocherous colour." These brown stains are caused by a community of organisms, principally diatoms, living either in the ice or in the brine pockets of the ice. This group of microflora includes over 50 species of mainly neritic diatoms, some chrysophytes, dinoflagellates and green flagellates. Of these, diatoms are ubiquitous and generally dominant. The ice diatom community is composed of both attached species such as *Pleurosigma, Nitzschia, Amphiprora,* and *Fragilaria,* and nonattached species such as *Odontella, Coscinodiscus,* and *Asteromphalus.* This community is quite distinct from the planktonic community.

Dinoflagellates are generally rare, although occasionally they may achieve dominance. *Phaeocystis*, on the other hand, may be present in some areas in enormous numbers at certain times of the year.

Because of the large area that experiences seasonal ice advance and retreat in the Southern Ocean (ice covers on average an area as large as 18.5×10^6 km^2 in winter but only about 3.6×10^6 km^2 at the end of the austral summer), the influence of the ice-edge on the Antarctic marine ecosystem is expected to be pronounced. One potentially significant impact of the ice-edge is its influence on phytoplankton distribution. Marginal ice zones have been shown to support large blooms of phytoplankton. A dense bloom of *Nitzschia curta* was encountered near the receding ice-edge off the coast of Victoria Land, Antarctica (Smith and Nelson, 1985). A possible explanation of ice-edge blooms is that the low-density meltwater creates a vertically stable water column.

With the ice microflora serving as a bloom innoculum, phytoplankton accumulation within the euphotic zone is thus promoted. Kozlova (1964) contended that ice conditions determine the quantitative development of diatoms to a greater degree than does the time of year.

Recent studies of the ice-edge zone in the Weddell Sea indicate that, next to the diatoms and *Phaeocystis*, the protistan choanoflagellates (collared heterotrophic flagellates bearing an extracellular lorica) are the third most abundant group in the water column and are, at times, locally dominant (Buck and Garrison, 1983). These authors provided the first quantitative estimates of the composition of nanoplankton and microplankton in the ice-edge region of the Weddell Sea. The choanoflagellates constitute a conspicuous component of Antarctic nanoplankton, comprising 10–40% of the total number of living nanoplankton (Marchant, 1985). The great abundance of the choanoflagellates and other heterotrophic forms in the ice-edge zone suggests that a tightly coupled food web composed of bacterial, detrital and nano-algal production exists. These microheterotrophs are sometimes as abundant as diatoms and may be an important food source for pelagic consumers such as euphausiids (von Brockel, 1981; Kils, 1982).

PLANKTON UNDER THE ROSS ICE SHELF

Until recently, the existence of life in the relatively deep cul-de-sacs beneath the large Antarctic ice shelves was primarily a topic of speculation. Because the thickness of the Ross Ice Shelf (400–500 m) precludes photosynthesis in the underlying water column, it was originally suggested that a sub-ice biota might be absent altogether or that a highly specialized, novel assemblage might exist in which chemosynthesis (formation of organic compounds from inorganic substances using energy derived from oxidation reactions) rather than photosynthesis takes place. Efforts by the scientific community to put this speculation to test resulted in the successful undertaking of the Ross Ice Shelf Project (RISP). One of the objectives of the RISP was to examine interactions between the biota of the Ross Sea and that underneath the Ross Ice Shelf, if found. In 1977 and 1978, a hole was successfully drilled at a site about 430 km from the open Ross Sea

(82°22.5'S, 168°37.5'W) through 420 m of ice which was underlain by a 237 m water column (Clough and Hansen, 1979). At all depths studied, investigators found that the water had sparse populations of micro- and macro-organisms, components of which might comprise a food web. Sampled organisms included bacteria, algae, microzooplankton, and large zooplankton.

Samples from three depths in the water column (20, 110 and 200 m) were concentrated on 35 μm mesh Nitex and were examined for microplankton. Pennate diatoms accounted for about 80% of the microplankton at 20 m. Forms of several genera, including *Amphiprora, Fragilariopsis, Navicula, Nitzschia, Pinnularia* and *Pleurosigma*, were observed. No pennate diatoms were seen at 200 m. Centric diatoms were represented by a few empty frustules of *Coscinodiscus* and *Triancria* found at 20 and 110 m.

The only dinoflagellates recognized were species of *Peridinium (Protoperidinium)*, principally *P. depressum* and *P. antarcticum*. A few naked dinoflagellates (10–20 μm in length) and a few specimens of the silicoflagellate *Distephanes speculum*, including several which retained their protoplast, were observed (Azam et al., 1979).

Metazoan forms observed included naupliar and postnaupliar copepods. In addition to the copepods, two specimens, probably of polychaete larva, were found in the sample from 20 m (Azam et al., 1979).

Based on the available data, RISP investigators could not determine whether these microbial organisms represent an indigenous population or if they represent the remnants of populations advected from the Ross Sea. For this reason, no conclusions can be drawn as to whether the organisms found constitute a functioning *in situ* food web. However, based on ^{14}C fixation experiments carried out in the water beneath the Ross Ice Shelf, it is concluded that the food web is ultimately dependent on water advected from the Ross Sea (Horrigan, 1981).

ZOOPLANKTON

As with the phytoplankton, the extensive *Discovery II* investigations have contributed a wealth of knowledge about the composition, distribution, and life histories of the most dominant zooplankton species. The *Discovery II* investigations, together with the more recent investigations carried out on board the *Eltanin* and other research vessels, have added substantially to our knowledge of the zooplankton in the Pacific Sector of the Southern Ocean. However, there is still a tremendous amount of work that must be done before our level of understanding concerning the zooplankton of the region resembles the more detailed knowledge of the plankton off the coast of California, for example, or even of the Scotia Sea/Bransfield Strait region. The recent investigations carried out off Campbell Island and in the Ross Sea are contributing to a better understanding of the systematics and ecology of the zooplankton in the southwestern Pacific Ocean (Bradford and Wells, 1983).

Although there are many species of Antarctic zooplankton which vary considerably in size, density, distribution and behaviour, discussion in this section will be limited to those components of the Antarctic zooplankton which constitute the bulk of the biomass. A separate section will be devoted to krill since they comprise the most important group, biologically and economically, in the Antarctic marine ecosystem.

COMPOSITION

The copepods constitute the bulk of the Antarctic mesoplankton (middle-sized zooplankton), accounting for an average of about 70% of its total biomass (Fig. 8.14) The three most prevalent species are *Calanoides acutus, Calanus propinquus,* and *Rhincalanus gigas.* Hopkins (1971) contended that the principal contributors to zooplankton biomass in samples taken in the Pacific Sector of the Southern Ocean are the copepods, chaetognaths and euphausiids, in that order. He found that the copepods constitute 67.7 and 59.6% of the zooplankton standing crop in the Antarctic and sub-Antarctic regions, respectively. Russian investigators found similar percentages (72.8 and 61.5%) for the Antarctic and sub-Antarctic copepods in the Indian Sector (Voronina, 1966). The paucity of euphausiids in Hopkins' plankton samples can be attributed to the fact that his collections were made further north in the West Wind Drift, in areas not frequented by the krill. Russian investigators found similarly low numbers of krill because they used a type of net (Juday net) which is poorly suited to capturing adult krill.

The chaetognaths (arrow worms) are an important ecological group because of their abundance among the zooplankton, second only to copepods, and because of their role as carnivorous predators. In both abundance of individuals and frequency of occurrence, *Eukrohnia hamata* is the most common of the 18 species of chaetognaths which are found in both the Antarctic and sub-Antarctic regions.

DISTRIBUTION

Several species of zooplankton appear to be present literally everywhere in the Southern Ocean. The chaetognaths *Sagitta gazellae* and *Eukrohnia hamata* were found in almost all the samples examined by David (1965). The copepods *Calanoides acutus, Calanus propinquus,* and *Rhincalanus gigas* (Baker, 1954) as well as the euphausiid *Thysanoessa* also have a wide distribution.

Most, if not all, Antarctic zooplankton species are circumpolar in distribution, but frequently show centres of concentrations at different depths or in different latitudes. Voronina (1966, 1968) reported that zooplankton may concentrate in the oceanic areas of convergence and divergence; furthermore, she found the total zooplankton biomass at the Polar Front to be 3 to 3.5 times greater than in adjacent areas.

Hydrographic conditions play an important role in the distribution of Southern Ocean zooplankton. As mentioned above, the sinking of Antarctic Surface Water at the Polar Front contributed to the Antarctic Intermediate Water which flows northward at around 800–1,000 m. Planktonic organisms retained in this

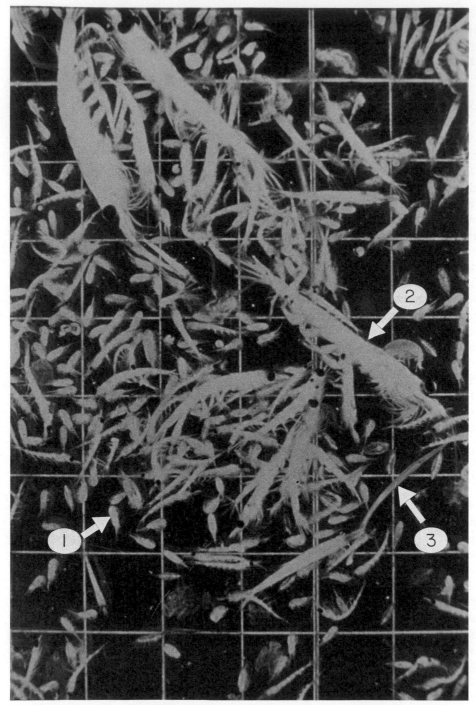

Fig. 8.14. Antarctic zooplankton showing its three main components : copepods (1), euphausiids (2) and chaetognaths (arrow worms) (3) (Photo : Dr J. Dearborn).

water thus extend their distribution range northward, but at a deeper level. Examples of species so entrained include *Rhincalanus gigas, Calanoides acutus, Sagitta maxima, S. marri,* and *Eukrohnia hamata.* It is not known, however, how far to the north these organisms may be distributed.

The Subtropical Convergence and the Polar Front are effective barriers to the distribution of some organisms. It is well known, however, that several species "cross" these barriers. John (1936) indicated that the distributions of some euphausiid species in the Pacific Sector are limited by either the Polar Front (e.g., *Euphausia frigida*) or Subtropical Convergence (*E. longirostris*). Mackintosh (1946) observed that the other euphausiids cross one or another of the convergences (e.g., *E. triacantha*) or occur apparently without relation to known oceanographic features (e.g., *E. crystallorophias* and *E. similis*).

STANDING CROP

Despite the extensive zooplankton investigations carried out in the Southern Ocean, it is difficult to arrive at reasonable estimates of the zooplankton standing crop in Antarctic waters because of problems related to sampling techniques, patchy distribution, and seasonal vertical migration. It is usually assumed, however, that the biomass of zooplankton, in general, is the same as that of krill.

The total biomass of zooplankton in the upper 1,000 m in the Pacific Sector averages 3.50, 2.55, and 2.76 g dry weight/m² in the areas of the Antarctic, sub-Antarctic, and Polar Front, respectively (Hopkins, 1971). In comparison, Atlantic Sector values of zooplankton/micronekton abundance averaged 5.9 g dry weight/m² in the upper 1,000 m (Hopkins, 1966).

SEASONAL VARIATIONS

Several investigators have shown that there is a seasonal change in the vertical distribution of several species (e.g., *Sagitta gazellae, Euphausia superba,* and *Calanoides acutus*) in Antarctic waters; specimens occur in the upper levels in summer and descend to deep water in winter. Hopkins (1971) noted that over half of the zooplankton biomass of the upper 1,000 m of sampled waters occurred in the top 250 m in late spring, summer, and early autumn months (November through April); while during the remainder of the year (May through October), most of the biomass was below 250 m. It is suggested that vertically migrating species, even though they move northward (and eastward) during the summer, are retained within the Antarctic circumpolar system when they descend to the deep water and are returned southward during winter, either as adults, or at an earlier stage in life development. Breeding habits appear to be associated with this seasonal migration so that species at various stages of the life cycle may inhabit different environments (water masses).

The seasonal changes of the zooplankton biomass in surface waters are characterized by two peaks. The first peak seems to result from the formation of pre-spawning concentrations of organisms following the spring migration upward in the water column. This change merely represents vertical re-distribution of plankton rather than an actual increase in abundance, as can be seen from the fact that the biomass in the upper 1,000 m layer as a whole remains practically unchanged. The second peak (summer) reflects development of the new generation until the annual peak is reached. Later, the downward migration of older organisms marks a more or less sharp decline in the biomass within surface waters to a level which persists throughout the long austral winter. The summer peak of zooplankton first appears in northern latitudes and then develops further to the south. Zooplankton spawning is attuned to the marked seasonality of the primary production so that larvae are able to obtain abundant food prior to winter. During the summer in the northern region of the Southern Ocean, the zooplankton biomass peaks two months later than that of the phytoplankton. In the southern region, on the other hand, one month elapses between the peaks of phyto- and zooplankton (Hart, 1942).

KRILL

The Organism

As a result of the extensive collections made during the *Discovery II* investigations in the 1920s and 1930s, almost all that is known about krill comes from the classic studies of the late J.W.S. Marr during that expedition (Marr, 1962). Of the 11 species of Antarctic krill, interest centres around *Euphausia superba, E. crystallorophias, Thysanoessa macrura*, and *E. valentini*. These euphausiids are located as follows : *E. valentini* is found north of the Polar Front; *E. crystallorophias* inhabits the pack-ice zone; and *E. frigida* and *E. superba* are found in open waters south of the Polar Front. Although *E. superba* (Fig. 8.15) is often considered to be synonymous with krill and, indeed, is the dominant species, a number of other euphausiids which are particularly important at the ice-edge should be included under the term.

Due to the circumpolar distribution of the Antarctic krill and the apparent similarity of the biology, breeding, and swarming of krill from the Atlantic, Pacific and Indian Sectors, the following discussion of krill for circum-Antarctic waters is pertinent to the Pacific Sector krill population.

DISTRIBUTION

The circumpolar distribution of krill seems to be lopsided; there are large populations in the Atlantic Sector of the Antarctic, and thinner bands around the rest of the continent (Fig. 8.16). Whether these areas of high krill concentration represent separate stocks is not at present known. However, this is an issue of crucial importance to the way the krill resource is to be managed (Laws, 1985b).

Krill have a strongly aggregated distribution. The average krill patch size

Fig. 8.15. Krill (*Euphausia superba*) (Photo : Dr U. Kils).

appears to measure < 100–150 m horizontally and 40–50 m in depth. In February 1981, U.S. scientists on board the R.V. *Melville* north of Elephant Island, encountered a "super swarm" which occupied a surface area of 450 km² and had an estimated biomass of more than two million tonnes (Macaulay et al., 1984).

It is well established that krill migrate vertically, but only on rare occasions has a recognizable pattern been discernible (Marr, 1962; Mohr, 1976; Fisher and Mohr, 1978; Kubota, 1981; Hampton, 1985). One can generalize that by day krill tend to be deep, while after dark they tend to congregate near the surface.

The relationship between the distribution of krill and their physical/chemical environment is one of the vexing problems facing krill ecologists. The southern circumpolar seas are often considered to be relatively uniform in thermal regimes and radiant energy; they are, however, seasonally variable. The physical oceanographic characteristics of the Southern Ocean have well known vertical and horizontal variabilities, but these and other environmental parameters have not been fully correlated with krill distribution. Interseasonal and interannual variations in krill populations also add to the list of unknowns. For instance, krill investigators reported a substantial decrease in the krill populations in 1983/84 austral summer (Heywood et al., 1985), coincident with an increase in the surface sea temperature. Some investigators speak of the possible influence of El Niño Southern Oscillation events.

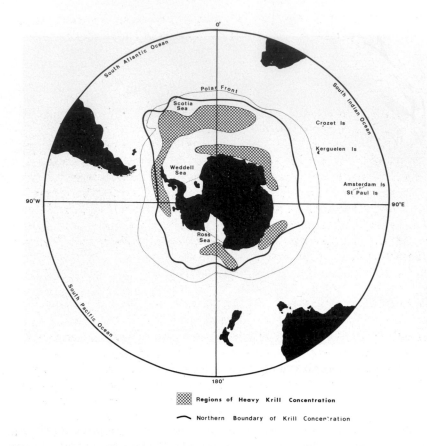

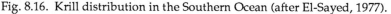

Fig. 8.16. Krill distribution in the Southern Ocean (after El-Sayed, 1977).

BREEDING AND SPAWNING OF KRILL

Breeding takes place in at least four areas : the Bellingshausen Sea, the Bransfield Strait, Davis Strait, and in the vicinity of South Georgia Island. We do not know whether there is a main breeding area in the Pacific Sector or how many breeding stocks there are. A female krill produces from as few as 500 eggs to as many as 8,000 eggs (average of 2,500) per brood with a brood interval of 6.5 days. The spawning season lasts two months, yielding an annual egg production of 22,000 eggs per season per female (Ross and Quetin, 1983). Early larval stages readily become acclimatized to high pressure conditions of up to 200 atm., while adult krill, including gravid females, are sensitive to pressure and can acclimatize only to 20 atm. Spawning cannot therefore occur at depths greater than 200 m. Krill egg development is also influenced by temperature but not by salinity or hydrostatic pressure.

While our knowledge of krill spawning and hatching in the shelf areas has increased in recent years, virtually nothing is known about the fate of eggs spawned over oceanic depths. We do not know, for instance, how deep these eggs will sink or at what depth the very early larval development takes place.

LONGEVITY

The longevity of krill is still a matter of controversy; however, there are indications that krill may live for more than four years. The traditional and often misleading method of determining krill age has been to examine the length frequency distribution of catches, regarding peaks in the histrogram as year-classes. Since krill moult and shrink in body size as an overwintering strategy, successive year-classes of mature krill can overlap, obscuring the length-age relationship. This method is being replaced by an innovative approach using lipofuscin, also called age pigment, which accumulates in the organism over time (Ettershank, 1984). The lipofuscin molecule is easily identified, since it is very large and characteristically fluorescent.

FOOD AND FEEDING

Until recently, krill have been considered to be exclusively herbivorous and, therefore, primary consumers in the ecosystem. Winter feeding and growth have been considered to be negligible since phytoplankton productivity decreases due to the extensive ice cover in the seas adjacent to the Antarctic. However, during 12 months of laboratory experiments with krill, carnivorous, detritivorous, and cannibalistic feeding were demonstrated (McWhinnie and Denys, 1978). Kott-meier and Sullivan (pers. comm.) have observed larval and juvenile krill feeding on the sea-ice microkrill community. This new knowledge of the occurrence of such feeding habits will require revision of established annual growth rate and, ultimately, longevity estimates of krill.

Experiments using a high-speed macro-photo-registration technique (Kils, 1983) suggest that krill are not limited to one feeding method, but employ a variety of highly efficient mechanisms. Depending on several factors such as food density, food quality, size of krill and, probably, activity level of the animal, different methods are employed by the animal to get the energy it needs.

KRILL STOCKS

Many computations have been made of production and standing stock of krill, and most estimates of annual harvestable yield range from 100 to 150 million tonnes. These figures have been derived using a variety of approaches including the consumption of past and present stocks of whales (based on their length of residence in Antarctic waters, volume of stomach contents, and energy require-ments); the consumption by other vertebrate predators; the catch rates of krill in plankton nets; and the proportion of primary production that is converted to krill.

However, there are no accurate data on the magnitude of either the standing stock or annual production of *E. superba*. It is popularly believed that krill stocks increased after whale stocks decreased. While there is indirect evidence that this occurred (e.g., increase in the population of winged birds, penguins and seals that feed on krill), direct evidence is lacking. Present techniques of estimating krill biomass directly from net hauls or by acoustic methods are subject to considerable variance because of the structure and highly irregular distribution of the swarms and the proportion of krill living outside the swarms. Such estimates may also be biased because of other factors; for example, large krill escape from most nets, and scientists lack information on the acoustic properties of krill, either individually or in swarms, which limits the accuracy of estimates based on use of an echosounder.

KRILL EXPLOITATION

Concern over the need for proper management and conservation of Antarctic krill (and other living resources as well) has been voiced by members of the scientific community and by international organizations. The former's concern stems from the lack of adequate information on a host of questions concerning krill growth rates, rate of advance to maturity, longevity, fecundity and spawning events, and the temporal and spatial differences within the populations through-out their circumpolar range. Effective management and conservation depend on the availability of this kind of information.

In response to a request from the Antarctic Treaty Organization regarding the Antarctic marine living resources, the Scientific Committee on Antarctic Research (SCAR) established the Group of Specialists on Southern Ocean Ecosystems and their Living Resources to expand the scientific understanding of the Antarctic marine ecosystem. The group developed a plan for the "Biological Investigations of Antarctic Marine Systems and Stocks" (BIOMASS). The principal objective of the BIOMASS Programme is, "to gain a deeper understanding of the structure and dynamic functioning of the Antarctic marine ecosystem as a basis for the future management of potential living resources" (El-Sayed, 1977). Implementation of the programme began with the planning and execution of a coordinated, multi-national, multidisciplinary research effort. This effort was planned to develop a better understanding of (a) krill's fundamental biology, (b) the dependence of higher trophic levels on krill stocks, and (c) the interrelations between krill swarming and the hydrographic features of Antarctic waters. The austral sum-mer of 1980/81 was chosen for the First International BIOMASS Experiment (FIBEX) in which 13 ships from 11 nations participated in the largest biological oceanographic expedition ever mounted in the Southern Ocean. The Second International BIOMASS Experiment (SIBEX-I and SIBEX-II) was carried out in the 1983/84 and 1984/85 austral summers. The primary objective of SIBEX was to obtain a better understanding of the dynamics of the krill-dominated part of the Antarctic marine ecosystem, particularly the relationship between the advance and retreat of sea-ice and krill distribution and abundance. From these studies, sufficient information should become available before intensive krill exploitation begins.

In response to a recommendation of the Antarctic Treaty, a Special Antarctic Treaty Consultative meeting was also held in 1978 to begin negotiating a convention on the conservation of Antarctic marine living resources. The Convention on the Conservation of Antarctic Marine Living Resources was ratified in April 1982 and will provide comprehensive research into krill ecology and a monitored quota system based on gradually expanding knowledge about krill. The convention is intended to ensure that the Antarctic marine ecosystem is not affected adversely by the harvesting of Antarctic krill or other marine living resources. To this end, the convention has set up a commission to pose questions and facilitate research, adopt conservation measures, and generally work toward implementing the conservation principles so strongly advocated by the scientific community.

SUMMARY AND CONCLUSIONS

Despite the great strides made in recent years in the study of the Antarctic marine ecosystem, in part stimulated by the prospect of harvesting its marine living resources, our knowledge of the plankton in the Pacific Sector of the Southern Ocean is far from satisfactory and lags behind that of the better studied Atlantic Sector. Research carried out under the BIOMASS programme has, to some extent, ameliorated this deficiency.

Phytoplankton biomass in the Pacific Sector varies spatially and temporally as a function of a variety of physical, chemical and biological factors; notable among these are light, temperature, water column stability and grazing. Phytoplankton investigations carried out to date underscore four important points : (1) that the phytoplankton biomass and primary production rates vary by at least one to two orders of magnitude; (2) that the seasonal variabilities of phytoplankton biomass and productivity are overshadowed by geographical variations in these parameters; (3) that, like the Atlantic and Indian Sectors, Pacific Sector waters, in general, display their richness mainly in coastal regions; and (4) that Pacific Sector waters do not show an outstandingly high rate of primary production.

The copepods constitute the bulk of the Antarctic mesoplankton (accounting for an average of about 70% of its total biomass) with the chaetognaths as distant second. Most, if not all, Antarctic zooplankton species are circumpolar in distribution; however, they frequently show centres of concentrations at different depths or in different latitudes. Hydrographic conditions play an important role in the distribution of Southern Ocean zooplankton. For instance, the Subtropical Convergence and the Polar Front act as effective barriers to the distribution of some organisms. As to the zooplankton standing crop, it is difficult to arrive at reasonable estimates of their biomass because of problems related to sampling techniques, patchy distribution, and seasonal vertical migration.

Krill investigations carried out in recent years have contributed substantially to our knowledge of the biology, distribution, longevity, food and feeding behavior of this organism. However, much remains to be learned, as even the estimates of krill biomass are still a matter of controversy.

240

As a result of the recent investigations carried out on phytoplankton/zoo-plankton/krill interrelationships, we may find it necessary to modify our concept of the structure and function of the Antarctic marine ecosystem. In light of these investigations we are being forced to re-examine the classical description of a simple food chain from diatoms→ krill→ whales. Recent studies on Antarctic bacterioplankton, dissolved organic matter, nanoplankton, picoplankton, sea ice-algae and krill food sources suggest the presence of hitherto overlooked path-ways through which a major part of the avilable energy may be flowing. A new paradigm of the Antarctic ocean's food web is now emerging (Fig. 8.17). This paradigm may contain yet other strands, so that the classic pathway may con-stitute only a part of the energy flow within the Antarctic marine ecosystem.

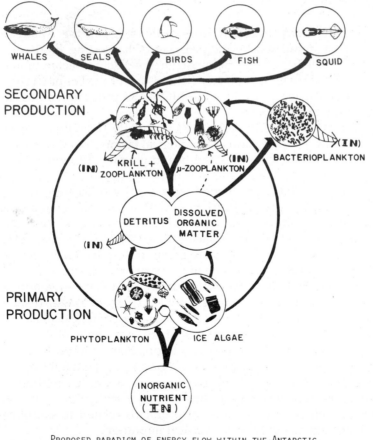

PROPOSED PARADIGM OF ENERGY FLOW WITHIN THE ANTARCTIC
MARINE ECOSYSTEM (FROM EL-SAYED, 1984).

Fig. 8.17. Paradigm of energy flow within the Antarctic marine ecosystem (after El-Sayed, 1984).

CHAPTER 9

MARINE MAMMALS

A.N. Baker

Twenty-seven species of whales and dolphins, and 14 species of seals live in or adjacent to the Antarctic Sector of the Pacific Ocean. Some are permanent residents, other migrate in and out of the region, and a few are itinerants from northern waters. This chapter reviews the occurrence, past exploitation and present status of these southern marine mammal species.

Until the late 18th century, marine mammals in the Southern Ocean lived unmolested in large numbers in a productive, yet relatively simple, ecosystem with an abundance of food, birds, and other marine organisms (Fig. 9.1).

The basis for the Antarctic ecosystem is a combination of the nutrient-rich waters circulating around the continent, and the consequent rich phytoplankton growth in the long hours of daylight during summer (El-Sayed, this volume). The plankton growth supports a high concentration of the staple food item of the region, the small shrimp-like crustacean called *krill*. There are many high-level

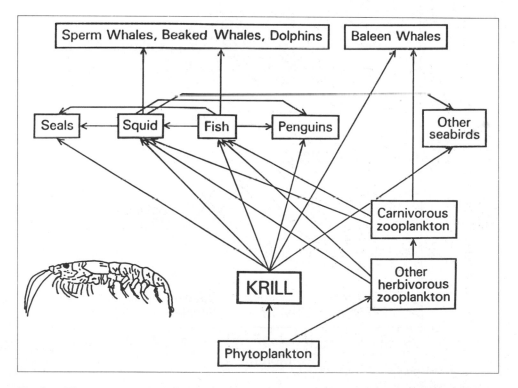

Fig. 9.1. The crustacean krill forms the central link in the Antarctic food web (after Barnes, 1982).

242

consumers in Antarctic waters, including all the marine mammals, which are ultimately dependent on krill and other low-level species (Fig. 9.2).

Explorers who first traversed the Southern Ocean in the late 18th century reported in their journals large numbers of seals and whales in those waters, and it was only a few years later that commercial exploitation began on the openly accessible species. It was inevitable that in time the resource would be over-exploited, given its open-access (Bonner, 1982).

HISTORY OF EXPLOITATION

Sealers from Britain and America were first on the scene, being attracted to the islands of the Scotia Sea, South Georgia and South Shetlands in particular. The elephant seal and Antarctic fur seal were the prime targets from about 1778 onwards, because of their valuable oil and fur respectively.

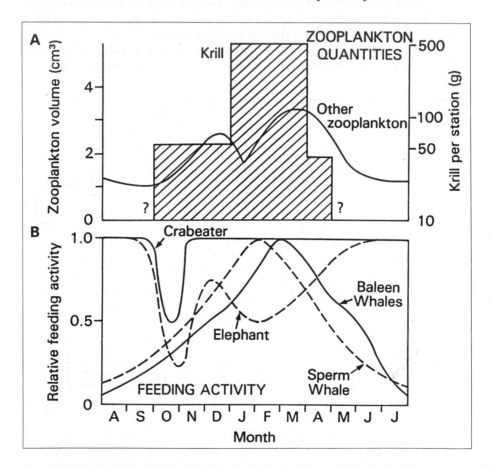

Fig. 9.2. Relative abundance of krill and plankton (A), and relative feeding activity of the main Antarctic consumers (B), on a seasonal basis (after Laws, 1977).

The ensuing slaughter was so effective that by 1823 elephant seals were almost extinct in the Scotia Sea, and sealers began moving into the Pacific, especially the islands to the south of New Zealand and Australia (McNab, 1907; Hindell and Burton, 1988a). Hunting of seals continued in these areas until after the Second World War, with some population extinctions. Surveys of fur seals and sea lions over the past 20 years have shown, however, that at least on the islands of the southwestern Pacific, the numbers are generally recovering (Croxall and Gentry, 1984; papers in Ridgway and Harrison, 1981a, b).

Whaling ships worked the Chilean and New Zealand coasts from 1785 and 1791 respectively and many shore-based whaling stations began in the latter country in the 1820s (McNab, 1913; Morton, 1982). The deep-sea whalers from Europe and America hunted mostly right whales and sperm whales to the south and east of New Zealand, while "bay whalers" took only the highly vulnerable right whale close to the coast (Fig. 9.3), (papers in Tillman and Donovan, 1983, and Forster, 1985).

Despite the fact that both coastal and deep-sea whaling in the sub-tropical and temperate waters of the South Pacific declined after the 1840s, it was a further 50 years before whaling activities reached into the Southern Ocean south of 50°S, towards the Antarctic continent. Antarctic coastal waters were still poorly explored at that time, and indeed the first landing on the continent was not made until 1895.

Although Cook, Weddell, Ross and other explorers had reported concentrations of whales close to Antarctica, nothing was known about them, not even what kinds were present there. Eventually, expeditions to the western parts of Antarctica by Dallman in the German whaling ship *Gronland* in 1873–74, and the Norwegian whaler *C.A. Larsen* in 1892, established that the abundant whales (several hundred would sometimes surround their boats) were not the sought-after right whales, but the then commercially less-attractive rorquals — blue, fin, and humpback whales. It was not until after the turn of the century that the value of the oil from the "great whales" was fully appreciated (Tønnessen and Johnsen, 1982).

The first reconnaissance of the Ross Sea area of Antarctica since Sir James Clark Ross's 1842 visit in *Erebus* and *Terror* was by the Norwegian whaling ship *Antarctic* in 1894–95, looking for right whales. The only ones seen were at Campbell Island on the voyage south from New Zealand, but the expedition achieved distinction by placing the first people (Bull and Borchgrevink) on the Antarctic continent at Cape Adare, Victoria Land.

Around the turn of the century, knowledge of the zoology of the Southern Ocean, particularly its whales and krill, increased markedly as a result of a number of scientific expeditions from Belgium, Germany and Britain (Deacon, 1984). The study of Antarctic natural history was further enhanced by investigations carried out in conjunction with the Heroic Age of Antarctic land exploration prior to the First World War.

Modern commercial-scale whaling began in Antarctic waters in 1904 and, like the sealing industry over one hundred years before, it centred on the islands of the South Atlantic.

Intense competition amongst whalers in the North Atlantic, and low world

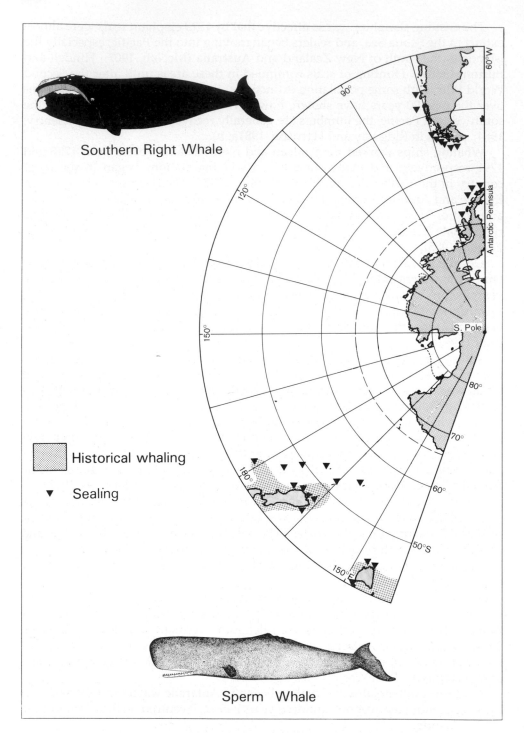

Fig. 9.3. Historical (pre–1900) whaling and sealing grounds in the South Pacific.

prices for a significant amount of the whale oil from the region (50% of the oil was second-grade and thus unusable for soap manufacture), forced whalers to transfer their operations to the southern grounds. Here, the whales were so abundant that whalers could afford to render down only the best portions of blubber, thus increasing the percentage of top quality oil for use in the soap, tanning and textile industries, and for lubrication and lighting.

South Georgia was the base for Antarctic whaling in the first years of this century. The industry evolved fast, and technological changes soon increased the catching and processing efficiency to levels previously undreamt-of. C.A. Larsen, who had set up the original operation on South Georgia, introduced factory ships which were capable of processing whales at sea, independent of the shore station. This was in fact the same system that operated in the early whaling years, with sailing boats, tri-pots on deck, and oil storage below. But the technology was better – explosive harpoons, fast steam driven whale chasers, and increased oil storage capacity on the factory ships.

The advent of mobile whale-processing factories meant that, as the numbers of whales in the South Atlantic declined, the chasers and factory ships began following the whales to the other parts of the Southern Ocean, including the Antarctic Sector of the Pacific. The abundance of whales in this sector supported a major whaling industry for 60 years, which successively over-exploited the various species there (Mackintosh, 1965; Clark and Lamberson, 1982).

The highly efficient factory ships, with their slipways for hauling whales out of the water, rotary steam cookers for rendering blubber to oil, and large capacity built-in oil tanks, were initially modified tramp steamers or passenger ships. Later, in the 1930s, purpose-built whale processing ships of up to 21,500 gross tonnes were constructed for the Southern Ocean whaling industry.

In 1923–24, the modern whaling pioneer Larsen was again to the fore by being the first whaler to use a factory ship in the Ross Sea. The *Sir James Clark Ross*, a 14,000 tonne ship, searched for blue and humpback whales along the coast of Victoria Land, but the expedition was not a success because the ship did not have a slipway, and flensing whales in the freezing conditions alongside the ship amongst ice-floes, proved impossible. The following year Larsen died on the Ross Sea grounds, but his ship encountered better conditions and found numerous whales, resulting in the first large-scale catching of whales in Antarctic waters (Tønnesen and Johnsen, 1982).

During the first three seasons south of New Zealand, Larsen's company operated 1 ship and 5 chasers, but in 1926–27 another more efficient ship, the *C.A. Larsen*, named after the founder, went south from the company's base at Stewart Island, New Zealand. Many whales were caught in the Ross Sea, along the Victoria Land coast, and around the Balleny Islands (Fig. 9.4.). This region was at that time a dependency of New Zealand, and all whaling was carried out under licences controlled by the New Zealand government. The licences were intended to ensure that the whale carcasses were not discarded, but were utilized to the fullest extent for oil production.

Larsen's company was joined in the Ross Sea in 1926 by an unlicenced whaling ship, the *N.T. Nielsen Alonso*, which, it was suspected at the time, was wasteful in

Fig. 9.4. Blue whales alongside a Norwegian chaser in the Ross Sea; protected for many years, these whales are recovering slowly (Photo : National Museum of N.Z.).

its processing methods. This practice stimulated the need for licences. Catch figures for the first six seasons in the Ross Sea are as follows (from Tønnesen and Johnsen, 1982) :

Season	No. of Whales	Barrels of Oil (1 barrel = 182 litres)
1923–24	221	17,299
1924–25	427	31,850
1925–26	531	30,630
1926–27	1,117	100,838
1927–28	2,012	171,311
1928–29	1,742	160,010

The most dramatic expansion in Southern Ocean whaling took place over only three seasons between 1927 and 1931, when the effort and catches quadrupled (Tønnesen and Johnsen, 1982). In 1930–31, there were 6 shore stations, 41 factory ships and 238 chasers involved in Antarctic whaling. 40,201 whales which produced 3,608,348 barrels of oil were caught in that season alone. Despite a lull in the depression years caused by over-production, low prices and reluctant forward-buying of oil, catches continued to increase throughout that decade. Figure 9.5 shows the areas of the Antarctic Sector of the Pacific that modern whalers concentrated on.

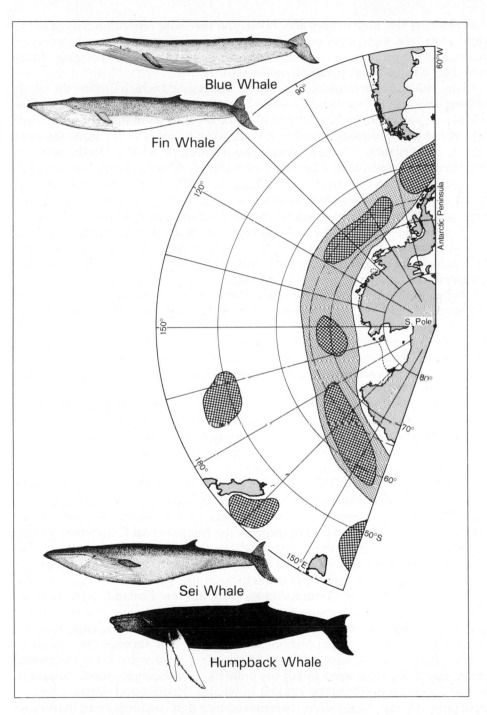

Fig. 9.5. Areas of modern (post–1900) whaling (light hatching). Darker hatching corresponds to concentrated catch zones (after Gaskin, 1977).

In the Ross Sea, blue whales abounded, and therefore represented most of the catch. However, there were soon signs of over-catching – younger whales being caught, and the proportion of different species in the catch were changing. More fin and sei whales were appearing on the records.

In the 1930s, an international agreement was reached which limited the whale catching season in the Southern Ocean to 3 months. It also afforded female whales and calves protection, and prescribed humane (as they were thought to be then) methods of killing whales. Although there were many cries for some stronger form of conservation of whale stocks, the number of whales caught was not controlled until much later when the International Whaling Commission (IWC) was formed in 1946 (McHugh, 1974; Gulland, 1988). Annual catch quotas also served to prevent over-production of whale oil and corresponding market instability. Even during the war years, 46,656 whales were caught in southern waters. Many of the old factory ships were damaged or destroyed during the 1940s as they were pressed into service to support the war effort. The post-war years saw big development of new ships, and the entry into Southern Ocean whaling of the new modern whaling nations Russia and Japan.

Catches in the Antarctic Sector of the Pacific averaged 6,151 whales a season between 1946 and 1964, reaching a peak of 12,979 in 1956–57. Britain, Norway and the Netherlands found the poor catches of the early 1960s uneconomic, and by 1964–65 had given up sending whaling fleets to the Southern Ocean, leaving the grounds for Japan and Russia. It has been estimated that almost 1.4 million whales were removed from Antarctic waters between 1904 and 1978 (Tønnesen and Johnsen, 1982).

The graphs in Fig. 9.6 show the numbers of different kinds of whales that were caught annually in the Antarctic Sector of the Pacific between 1946 and 1986 (data courtesy Dr. R. Gambell, International Whaling Commission). The graphs demonstrate the successive concentration of catching on humpback, blue, fin, sei and minke whales as each species was depleted.

From 1979, the small minke whale was the only species allowed to be caught in Antarctic waters under the International Whaling Commission's regulations, and since 1986 there has been a total moratorium on commercial whaling in the Antarctic. There is, however, provision in the International Convention for the Regulation of Whaling for the taking of whales for scientific purpose. Japan has continued to catch minke whales (241 in 1989) in the interests of scientific research.

There is now considerable opposition to "scientific whaling" amongst the IWC nations, and, at the 1988 Commission meeting in New Zealand, 10 nations co-sponsored resolutions opposing the issuing of special whaling permits. It has been argued that it is necessary to catch whales to provide the basic data for monitoring the status of populations and the age and reproductive status of individuals. However, new methods of sampling whales are being developed which may reduce the need to kill the animals. For example, the technique of genetic "fingerprinting" can be applied to whales (Hoelzel and Amos, 1988). A small plug of body tissue painlessly removed by a dart can identify an individual, patterns of paternity and, in some cases, maternity, and be used to assess the amount of genetic variation with populations of whales. There are also new benign study techniques involving photo-identification of whales, and analysis of their vocalizations, which, for some species, can provide data on migrations, population sizes and life histories.

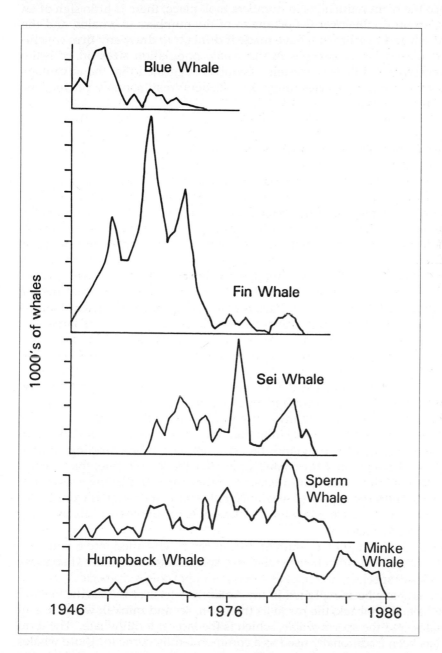

Fig. 9.6. Numbers of whales caught in the Antarctic Sector of the Pacific Ocean, south of 40°S, between 1946 and 1986 (from IWC data).

Gambell (1987) has reviewed the effects of exploitation on the whale stocks of Antarctica and has pointed out that, although there is some strong evidence that both pregnancy rates and age at sexual maturity have changed in the big baleen whales since the main reductions in numbers took place, there is little sign of an increase. Current doubts over the estimates of the numbers of whales, and the rates of growth and recruitment, have made it difficult to draw any firm conclusions about the impact of changes in the whale population sizes on both the whales themselves and their ecosystem. Gambell suggested that the advantage now taken by competing species (other krill-feeders) may actually prevent the recovery of whale stocks.

OCCURRENCE AND STATUS OF MARINE MAMMALS

WHALES

The Southern Hemisphere fossil record shows that whales have inhabited the region for over 40 million years from the Late Eocene to the present (Fordyce, 1985). The earliest cetaceans (archeocetes) were toothed whales, but opinions differ as to whether they gave rise to the modern toothed whales (odontocetes) and baleen whales (mysticetes) which appeared in the Oligocene (Barnes, 1984). Baleen whales are those that feed by straining krill or small fishes from the sea water through a filtering system of baleen plates — an energy-efficient method that has proved very successful, as demonstrated by the baleen whales' large size. Baleen whales probably evolved from the odontocete whales, which are active predators possessing teeth used for grasping larger prey such as fishes and squids.

Fordyce (1977) has postulated that the mid-Oligocene seas over eastern New Zealand and the Campbell Plateau region could have provided a focal point for the evolution of the filter-feeding mysticete whales. Productivity changes in the Southern Ocean associated with the initiation of the Circum-Antarctic Current in the mid-Oligocene possibly triggered the evolution of the new feeding adaptation. As Australia separated from Antarctica after the late Eocene, the Circum-Antarctic Current brought cool, nutrient-rich waters into the shallow seas east of New Zealand. The large supply of nutrients in this temperate region would have resulted in a huge increase in plankton biomass, able to support rapidly evolving and radiating organisms.

Cetaceans now living in the Southern Ocean can be classified into 6 families : right whales (2 species), other baleen whales (5 species), sperm whales (1 species), beaked whales (9 species), dolphins (8 species) and porpoises (2 species).

Whales that have been exploited in the Antarctic Sector of the Pacific include the right whale, humpback, the rorquals (blue, fin, sei and minke), which are all baleen whales, and the sperm whale, which is the largest tooth whale. The term "rorqual" has been traditionally used as a common family name for those whales belonging to the genus *Balaenoptera*. The general natural history of the great whales is well covered by Ellis (1981) and Evans (1987), and the distributional ecology by Gulland (1974) and Gaskin (1976).

Existing in the Southern Ocean are a further 20 species of smaller cetaceans that have never been seriously considered as commercial propositions by whalers. They include the pygmy right whale, the beaked whales and the dolphins and porpoises. Descriptions and illustrations of the whales, dolphins and porpoises of the Antarctic Sector of the Pacific can be found in Leatherwood and Reeves (1983), all regions; Sielfeld (1980), South American region; and Daniel and Baker (1986), New Zealand region.

Baleen Whales and the Sperm Whale

Southern right whales occur throughout the Antarctic Sector of the Pacific, usually north of 55°S. Although now one of the world's rarest whales, a few can still be seen regularly south of New Zealand at Campbell Island and the Auckland Islands, and on the southern and eastern Australian, New Zealand, and Chilean coasts. They are slow swimmers, and often frequent shallow coastal waters. Right whales have been recorded in schools of 11–12, but mostly occur singly or with a calf.

The prime target for early shore-based whaling in New Zealand, Australia and Chile, the right whale was easy prey because of its coastal habit and slow swimming speed. Some 193,000 southern right whales are thought to have been caught in the southwestern Pacific between 1804 and 1817 (Harmer, 1931). Records show that, between 1827 and 1848, 23,060 right whales were taken from the waters of eastern and southern Australia and New Zealand by both "bay whalers" and the pelagic fleets (Dawbin, 1987). American whalers took 6,262 right whales from Chilean waters between 30°S and 50°S, during the years 1785–1913 (Aguayo, 1974). The whale's value in those early days lay in high-quality oil and baleen (used then for corset stays, umbrella ribs, etc.) and the natural flotation of the carcasses, which made retrieval by small boats relatively easy.

By 1848, right whale stocks in the southwestern Pacific had been heavily depleted, and the species accounted for only a small proportion of the whale catch thereafter, until it was fully protected in 1931. In Chile, right whales continued to be caught up until 1966, but the total number caught between 1920 and 1966 was only 119 whales. The size of the current southern right whale population is thought to be small, and estimates range from 1,030 to 4,300 individuals (Cummings, 1985).

Humpback whales were prominent in the early South Pacific whale catches despite their widespread general distribution because they tend to concentrate on winter and summer grounds, making them easy targets. In the South Pacific, there are several largely isolated stocks of humpbacks, which spend the summer in Antarctic waters and migrate north past the coasts of Australia, New Zealand and Chile to winter in subtropical waters (see summary in Gaskin, 1968, 1972). Like the right whale, humpbacks are not fast swimmers, and could be taken on their migratory routes by shore-based whalers. In the 1930s, humpbacks were heavily depleted in Antarctic waters by the pelagic whaling fleets. Although shore stations in Australia and New Zealand continued to catch them through the

1950s (Fig. 9.7), the stocks had declined to a few hundred individuals by the early 1960s making whaling uneconomic (Mackintosh, 1965). In 1939, the humpback was protected in Antarctic waters, but this was only temporary, as catching resumed in 1949. Final protection in southern waters came in 1963 through the International Whaling Commission.

Around 9,300 humpbacks are estimated to remain worldwide, including about 1,000 in the South Pacific (Winn and Reichley, 1985). The latter number may be a minimum, however, for a recent photo-identification survey of humpbacks in the Antarctic Peninsula area (Stone and Hamner, 1988) showed that these whales were more numerous there than have been previously estimated. There is a need to extend such surveys to other parts of the Antarctic to clarify the distribution and abundance of humpback whales.

Humpbacks travel alone or in small groups and may congregate in groups of up to 15 when feeding on krill.

Rorquals — blue whales, fin whales, sei whales and minkes — were the main-stay of pelagic whaling in the Antarctic Sector of the Pacific (Mackintosh, 1965). *Blue whales* are found in all oceans and, in the South Pacific, usually spend the summer south of 40°S. It is believed that the population of blue whales in Antarctic seas was reduced from some 150,000 whales in the 1930s, to between 5,000

Fig. 9.7. A humpback whale being flensed at the former shore whaling station at Whangamumu, New Zealand (Photo : National Museum of New Zealand).

and 10,000 by the late 1950s (Chapman, 1974). They are still extremely rare in the Southern Hemisphere despite complete protection since 1966. Gulland (1981) estimated the total blue whale population in the Southern Ocean to be about 10,000, and increasing at the rate of 4–5% each year.

The largest of living animals, blue whales of the Southern Ocean, were recorded at 30 m length in the early days of whaling but, as catching increased, their maximum lengths decreased. Blue whales do not form schools; they are usually found alone or in pairs. A detailed summary of the blue whale's natural history is given by Yochem and Leatherwood (1985).

Fin whales also occur world-wide, and were probably the most abundant whales in Antarctic waters when whaling began there. Like the blue and sei whales, the fin feeds mostly on krill in southern waters. It is more gregarious than the blue whale, and is sometimes seen in groups of about 100, but usually travels in pods of less than 10. In the South Pacific, fin whales migrate annually from the Antarctic feeding grounds north to temperate and subtropical seas for breeding in the winter. It is thought that separated breeding stocks of fin whales exist broadly on each side of the South Pacific and that they overlap to some degree in the Antarctic feeding grounds (Gambell, 1985a).

Although the fin whale was hunted only occasionally in Antarctic seas from the early 1900s, it became the most sought-after commercial species once the blue whale had been virtually eliminated from Antarctic waters, and was heavily depleted during the years 1946–65. Off the coast of Chile, the fin whale was caught consistently between 1920 and 1968, accounting for 4,503 whales (Aguayo, 1974). There is still argument over assessments of the numbers of fin whales presently living, and their population trends, but it has been estimated that 125,000 may still exist in the Southern Hemisphere (Gambell, 1987).

Sei whales are found in all major oceans and, in the Southern Hemisphere, they occur mostly south of 40°S in the summer, but do not live as close to polar waters as the other rorquals. They possibly migrate north to about 30°S in winter (Aguayo, 1974, gives some evidence of a northward movement to at least 39°S in Chilean waters), but their true wintering grounds are at present unknown (Gambell, 1985b). Sei whales usually travel alone or in pairs but sometimes form larger feeding aggregations. These whales were also hunted in the Antarctic from the earliest days of mechanized whaling, but became the most important target for whalers much later in the 1960s as fin whale numbers were declining rapidly. They were fully protected in 1977. The Southern Hemisphere stocks of sei whales have been calculated at 191,000 before whaling began, and about 37,000 at present (Gambell, 1985b).

Minke whales are the smallest baleen whales to have been commercially exploited, reaching only 10 m in length and 0.98 tonnes weight. Although a few minkes were caught in the Antarctic earlier this century, the main exploitation began in the 1960s — 22,427 were taken between 1963 and 1978 (Stewart and Leatherwood, 1985). Since then, catches have fluctuated between about 800 and 2,000 whales each season. Following the International Whaling Commission's 1986 moratorium, several hundred have been caught for research purposes. The present Antarctic population is estimated by the IWC to be between 440,000 and

690,000 whales. It has been suggested that more should be caught to reduce competition with other whales and so allow recovery of the blue, fin and hump-backs (Oshumi, 1979).

Minkes are gregarious (Fig. 9.8) and may form groups of several hundred. There are two distinct forms of minke whale in the Southern Hemisphere, one being a dwarf, reaching only about 7 m in length, and possibly having a more northerly distribution than its larger relative (Arnold et al., 1987).

Sperm whales are found in all oceans and have a somewhat clumped distribution. Best (1974) used catch statistics for sperm whales to demonstrate that certain regions had the high densities of whales. South of 40°S in the Pacific, there are probably several segregated stocks, which he termed the "New Zealand and East Australian Stock" (140°–160°W), the "Central South Pacific Stock" (160°–100°W), and the "Western South American Stock (100°–60°W). In the South Pacific, female sperm whales are not found south of 45°–50°S, whereas the males occur south to between 60°S and 70°S. They do not approach the polar pack ice, and are generally regarded as an oceanic species. They were hunted in the Southern Ocean in the last century (Harmer, 1931), but the main exploitation by modern whalers began after World War II, peaked in 1973–74 (3,765 whales), and ceased in 1979. Sperm whales may be found alone or in large groups of 50 or more, sometimes sexually segregated. Gambell (1987) estimated the total Southern Hemisphere population to be 750,000.

Fig. 9.8. Minke whales in Antarctic waters: this species is the subject of "scientific whaling" (Photo : P. Ensor).

Small cetaceans

The remaining species of cetaceans found in the Antarctic Sector of the Pacific are regarded as the "small cetaceans" and are not commerical species, although a few have been taken by modern whalers from time to time for research purposes. With the exception of the pygmy right whale, which is a krill filter-feeder, the small cetaceans are primarily squid and fish eaters. They are mostly known from occasional sea sightings and strandings and some, for example the beaked whales, are extremely rare. Brownell (1974) gave a good summary of Antarctic small cetaceans. Goodall and Galeazzi (1985) have reviewed the distribution and food habits of small cetaceans from both Antarctic and Subantarctic waters, and Goodall and Cameron (1980) the exploitation of small cetaceans off southern South America.

The only baleen whale not to have received the attention of whalers is the *pygmy right whale*, a relative of the large right whale. The pygmy right whale lives only in the Southern Hemisphere between about 31°S and 52°S, and reaches about 6.5 m in length. It is rare in the South Pacific, where it has only been recorded from the New Zealand region and Tasmania (Baker, 1985).

Arnoux's beaked whale, the largest of the southern beaked whales, has a circumpolar distribution from about 34°S to the Antarctic ice edge. In the South Pacific, it is known from New Zealand and Antarctic waters, where it has been observed well south of the Antarctic Convergence (Miyazaki and Kato, 1988), but is not common. This whale can be gregarious, occurring in groups of 6–10, and occasionally up to about 80 (K. Balcomb, pers. comm.), but is also solitary.

The *southern bottlenose whale* has a similar distribution to that of Arnoux's whale, is similar in general appearance, and is probably more common in Antarctic waters (Miyazaki and Kato, 1988). Some specimens have been caught by whalers in the Antarctic Sector of the Pacific (Goodall and Galeazzi, 1985).

Shepherd's beaked whale is known from only 18 specimens south of 35°S (Ross et al., in press), mostly from New Zealand. The southernmost record is from Tierra del Fuego at 55°S (Goodall and Galeazzi, 1985), and it has not been reported from Antarctic waters.

Cuvier's beaked whale is widely distributed in most oceans, and has been recorded many times from the South Pacific through sea sightings and strandings. It has been reported from Subantarctic South American waters at 60°S by R.N.P. Goodall (pers. comm.), and south of New Zealand at 52°S by Baker (1977).

Five species of beaked whales of the genus *Mesoplodon* have been recorded from south of 45°S in the Pacific, but none close to the Antarctic continent. They range in length from 4 to 6 m, are rarely sighted, and are notoriously difficult to identify at sea.

The biggest *Mesoplodon* species is the *strap-toothed whale*, which seems to be a truly Southern Hemisphere whale, being found off all the southern temperate continents, and in the Subantarctic it has been recorded from Tierra del Fuego (Sielfeld, 1980) and Heard Island (Guiler et al., 1987). The male of this species, which reaches just over 6 m in length, is the most easily recognized beaked whale because of its pair of long, strap-like teeth.

The *dense-beaked whale,* normally an inhabitant of tropical oceans, is included in this summary of southern Pacific cetaceans because of records of specimens from Tasmania and Macquarie Island (Guiler, 1966; Ross et al., in press). Notable for its raised lower jaws and, in the male, a pair of massive teeth, the dense-beaked whale must be regarded as an occasional straggler into southern waters.

Gray's beaked whale is the most commonly reported species of the remaining three small species of *Mesoplodon* beaked whale known from the Southern Ocean (Gray's, Hector's and Andrew's). About 60 specimens have been recorded, all north of 55°S, mostly from strandings, although there are some sea sightings east of New Zealand (Ross et al., in press). Gray's beaked whale is unusual amongst the species of *Mesoplodon* for its sometime habit of travelling in small (< 25) schools. *Hector's beaked whale* is known from less than 20 specimens from mainly temperate waters of both Pacific hemispheres, but a stranded specimen has been recovered from southern Chile at about 55°S (Sielfeld, 1979; Mead and Baker, 1987). *Andrew's whale,* known mainly from the Australasian region, is even rarer but skeletal remains have been found on the Subantarctic islands to the south of New Zealand (Baker, 1983; Goodall and Galeazzi, 1985).

Eight species of dolphins and two true porpoises complete the list of Southern Ocean cetaceans. Only the killer whale, hourglass dolphin, and the southern right whale dolphin are known to travel south of the Antarctic Convergence. The *killer whale* is commonly seen amongst the pack ice in summer, but the dolphins are oceanic, the *hourglass dolphin* (Fig. 9.9) approaching the pack ice south of 60°S, but not actually entering the ice, and the *right whale dolphin* being found further north, beyond 60°S (Miyazaki and Kato, 1988). The remaining dolphins (pilot, dusky, Peale's, Hector's and Chilean) are cool temperature species and are mostly associated with coastal waters of the South Pacific. In the Subantarctic, the pilot whale and dusky dolphin are known from the Auckland Islands and Campbell Islands respectively (Baker, 1977), and pilot whales have been recorded close to Antarctica at 64°24'S (Miyazaki and Kato, 1988). The *Chilean* and *Peale's dolphins* are known from the southern coast of Chile, and are common around Chiloé Island. Peale's dolphin is frequently seen along the Pacific coast south to Cape Horn (J. Oporto, pers. comm.). *Hector's dolphin,* a close relative of the Chilean dolphin, is known only from the inshore waters of southern New Zealand, where it is relatively common to 48°S in certain localities, but the total population may be less than 4,000 (Dawson and Slooten, 1988).

Of the two porpoises known from the Southern Ocean, the *spectacled porpoise* is truly Subantarctic, having been recorded from the Auckland Islands (Baker, 1977). Macquarie Island (Fordyce et al., 1984), Heard Island (Guiler et al., 1987), Tierra del Fuego, and the southwestern Atlantic islands (Goodall, 1978). *Burmeister's porpoise* is included here because of its rare occurrence in the Cape Horn area of South America; otherwise its Pacific distribution is northward along the coast of Chile, particuarly north of Chiloé Island (43°S). A report of this porpoise at Heard Island in the Antarctic (Guiler et al., 1987) is, however, a mis-identification of the spectacled porpoise.

Fig. 9.9. An hourglass dolphin south of the Antarctic Convergence (Photo : P. Ensor).

SEALS

Fourteen species of seals are found in or adjacent to the Antarctic Sector of the Pacific. Breeding colonies occur on the coasts of southern New Zealand, southern Chile, the Subantartic islands, and on the ice itself. It was the Subantarctic and temperate seal colonies that attracted the 18th century sealers, and so started the massive depletion of marine mammal stocks in the Southern Ocean. Many Subantarctic islands were discovered by sealing expeditions.

Between the late 1700s and 1830, many seals were taken from the islands to the south of New Zealand, as well as from the Antarctic Peninsula, with the result that by 1830 the fur seal (hunted for its soft fur) and the elephant seal (oil) were so rare that the industry ceased (Chapman, 1893). By 1870, fur seals had recovered enough to allow a sealing industry to begin again in the Subantarctic islands, but this was short-lived, and by 1894 a total ban on catching was in force in that region (Csordas and Ingham, 1965).

In 1971–72, the U.S.S.R. took 1,000 crabeater seals from Antarctica as an experiment, but did not develop an industry on that species.

The biology of Antarctic seals has been summarized by Laws (1981, 1984), papers in Ridgway and Harrison (1981), and King (1983), and the interactions between man and seals by Bonner (1982). Daniel and Baker (1986) provided an identification guide to seals of the New Zealand region, which includes species found in the Ross Sea. Laws (1981) referred to the Antarctic seals as those that breed on land, and those that breed on the ice. The fur seals, sea lions, and elephant seal fall into the land-breeding category, and the leopard, Ross, crab-eater, and Weddell seals into the ice-breeding group.

Fur Seals

The Southern Hemisphere fur seals all belong to the same genus, *Arctocephalus*. The *Antarctic* and *Subantarctic fur seals*, primarily southern Atlantic and Indian Ocean species, come within the geographical scope of this account as breeding colonies only at Macquarie Island (Shaughnessy and Fletcher, 1987) and as stragglers to the Chilean coast (Guerra and Torres, 1987) and (the Subantarctic fur seal only) to southwestern New Zealand (Csordas, 1962) and the Antipodes Islands (Taylor, 1979).

Four other species of fur seals are found mainly in the South Pacific region : the Australian, New Zealand, Juan Fernandez, and South American fur seals. The Australian fur seal is found on the southeastern Australian coast, including the islands of Bass Strait and Tasmania north of 45°S (Warneke and Shaughnessy, 1985). The *New Zealand fur seal* also occurs on the coast of southern Australia, and at Macquarie Island, but its main populations are in the New Zealand region including the Subantarctic islands south to Campbell Island (Mattlin, 1987). The *Juan Fernandez fur seal* occurs only at that group of islands and the San Felix Group slightly further north off the coast of Chile whereas, on the mainland, the South American fur seal ranges from near Cape Horn along the coast of Chile to southern Peru (Guerra and Torres, 1987; Majluf, 1987).

	Total population size	Trend
Antarctic fur seal	1,100,000	rapid increase
Subantarctic fur seal	300,000	rapid increase
New Zealand fur seal	50,000	increasing
Australian fur seal	25,000	stable
South American fur seal	500,000	increasing
Juan Fernandez fur seal	6,000	increasing

The above figures show the total population sizes and trends for Southern Hemisphere fur seals (from Croxall and Gentry, 1987, and King, 1988). The rapid increase in populations of the Antarctic fur seal since 1956 (when monitoring began) has been attributed to decreased competition for food (krill) with the now depleted baleen whales (Bonner, 1982).

Sea Lions

Three species of sea lions are found in the South Pacific : Hooker's sea lion, the

Australian sea lion, and the South American sea lion. *Hooker's sea lion* has breeding colonies on the islands to the south of New Zealand, primarily Auckland Islands and Campbell Island (Fig. 9.10). Some breeding also occurs on the Snares Islands, and occasional stragglers, mostly young males, reach Macquarie Island and the New Zealand mainland (King, 1983). Hooker's sea lion was exploited commercially in the early 1800s, and had almost vanished by 1830. The population has built up slowly since then, and is now estimated to be over 6,000 animals. It is currently under some threat as a by-catch in the squid trawl fishery near the Auckland Islands (Cawthorn et al., 1985).

The *Australian sea lion* has a restricted distribution amongst the offshore islands of southern and western Australia east to about 140°W, so is just on the edge of the region covered in this volume. The total population is thought to be between 3,000 and 5,000 seals.

The *South American sea lion* has a wide distribution along both coasts of southern South America, reaching northern Peru in the west. It is common throughout the Chilean archipelagoes from Tierra del Fuego to Chiloé Island (pers. observ.), and breeding colonies are known as far north as Islas Lobos de Tierra at 6°30'S. The Peruvian population was thought to be about 20,000 and increasing in 1968 (Grimwood, 1969). The South American sea lion was exploited once the eastern Pacific was opened to ships by the discovery of the Straits of Magellan in the sixteenth century. Sea lions are protected in both Peru and Chile, but some are still killed by fishermen who farm salmon and suffer predation on

Fig. 9.10. Female Hooker's sea lions at the Auckland Islands : a species threatened by commercial fishing (Photo : National Museum of N.Z.).

the salmon by sea lions, or who use the seal flesh for bait in the king-crab fishery of southern Chile (pers. observ.).

Elephant Seal

The southern elephant seal's main breeding populations occur on the circumpolar Subantarctic islands, which, in the Antarctic Sector of the Pacific, are Macquarie Island, Campbell Island, and the Auckland Islands. The largest population is on Macquarie Island which is estimated at 136,000 animals (McCann, 1985). Southern elephant seals were extensively hunted in the early 1800s, and the populations were severely reduced in most places. Sealing had ceased in the Antarctic Sector of the Pacific by early this century, and it was thought that the elephant seals had regained their former population level by 1950 (Carrick et al., 1962). However, recent studies at Macquarie Island by Hindell and Burton (1988b) indicated a 40–50% decrease there over the past 36 years. The reasons for this decline are not known, but some of the potential underlying causes suggested are natural fluctuations in population size generated by such intrinsic factors as density dependent pup mortality, increased predation, depletion of resources and environmental changes. Elephant seals regularly reach the coasts of New Zealand and Tasmania (Fig. 9.11) and, although one has been recorded from Peru, none has yet been found in Chilean waters (King, 1983). The biology of southern elephant seals is reviewed by Ling and Bryden (1981).

Fig. 9.11. A male elephant seal, a regular visitor to New Zealand shores, but whose numbers are decreasing in the Southern Ocean (Photo : National Museum of N.Z.).

The Ice-breeding Seals

The *leopard seal* is found in the circumpolar pack ice in summer and north through the Subantarctic islands occasionally to the coasts of New Zealand, southern Australia, and Tierra del Fuego in winter. It is a solitary animal, but the total population could be quite large (about 220,000) (Gilbert and Erickson, 1977). Because of its solitary habit, the leopard seal has not been subject to exploitation. The *Ross seal* also lives in the ice, apparently preferring consolidated, heavy ice rather than open pack ice in the Ross Sea (Hofman, 1975). It does not often move north from Antarctica during the winter, there being only a few records from Australia and New Zealand. In Antarctic seas, the Ross seal is commonest in the Ross Sea and King Haakon VII Sea. Like the leopard seal, it seems to be largely solitary. Population estimates by Hofman et al. (1973) were in the order of 100,000–650,000 animals but Ray (1981) believed that there are still insufficient sightings of the Ross seal to make any reasonable estimates of its numbers.

The *crabeater seal* lives on the drifting pack ice surrounding Antarctica (Kooyman, 1981a). It is regarded as the most abundant seal in the world, with population estimates ranging up to 75 million animals (Erickson et al., 1971). However, more recent and accurate estimates by Gilbert and Erickson (1977) put the numbers at about 15 million. It is especially abundant in the waters west of the Antarctic Peninsula and in the southern part of the Ross Sea. A few stragglers have reached the coasts of New Zealand and Australia. The crabeater actually feeds on krill rather than crabs, having teeth specialized for straining small crustaceans from the water. It is thought that, like the Antarctic fur seal, stocks of crabeaters have increased substantially this century as a result of the greater availability of krill following the demise of Antarctic whales (Laws, 1977). This seal has not been significantly exploited. The mummified seals known from the inland Dry Valleys of Victoria Land, Antarctica, are mostly crabeaters.

The *Weddell seal* is unusual because it spends its entire life more or less literally in Antarctic waters, feeding under the pack ice, and breeding there. In the spring and summer, they can be seen lying languorously about on the ice surface. Like the other ice-breeders, the Weddell seal is sometimes seen at the Subantarctic islands and, more rarely, in New Zealand and southern Australia. Stirling (1971) and Kooyman (1981b) reviewed the knowledge of this species of well-studied seal, and Tedman (1985) listed important references to more recent work. Total population estimates vary from 250,000 to 750,000 animals, with about 50,000 in the western part of the Ross Sea (Laws, 1971; De Master, 1979). Weddell seals were hunted briefly in 1821, but otherwise they have not attracted commercial attention.

THE FUTURE

With the cessation of commercial whaling and sealing in the Antarctic Sector of the Pacific, one is tempted to say there cannot now be any serious threat to the survival of the animals in that isolated region. Indeed, we have seen that for some marine mammals the signs are encouraging — the populations are increasing rapidly (fur seals) or slowly (blue whales), and there are substantial numbers of other species still present (sperm whales, crabeater and Weddell seals).

There are, however, some disquieting facts as yet not fully understood or explained — the well documented decrease in elephant seal numbers at Macquarie Island and elsewhere in the Southern Ocean (Pascal, 1985), and the still very small numbers of southern right whales and humpbacks, whale species that have had the longest protection from exploitation.

It now seems obvious that the removal of huge numbers of whales and seals from the Southern Ocean over the past 200 years must have affected the Antarctic ecosystem : the competitive balance is such that a change in the abundance of any one species in the food web can have consequent changes in the abundance of other species. Laws (1977, 1981) referred to the possible increased availability of krill and other low-level consumers, such as fish and squid, and warned of the consequences to the Antarctic ecosystem of high levels of uncontrolled harvesting of those species. Already there have been significant depletions of Antarctic and Subantarctic fish stocks, indicating poor management of that resource (see Beddington, 1987).

One concern is that extensive harvesting of krill, for example, could reduce the food resources available to the depleted baleen whale populations, and thus restrict their recovery. Krill is potentially the largest resource in the Southern Ocean, and can be marketed whole, processed into proteins and vitamins used in cheese manufacture, or used for fish meal to feed farm animals.

New threats to the Southern Ocean ecosystem include pollution (oil, plastics, abandoned fishing gear, etc.) and environmental changes such as global warming due to the "greenhouse effect", with consequent changes in ocean current patterns.

The conservation of marine mammals in the Antarctic Sector of the Pacific has been commented on by many writers over the past century. It must be emphasized that successful conservation still depends on the dynamics of the Antarctic ecosytem, of which we are still largely ignorant, being constantly addressed through international scientific effort, and a satisfactory international management regime being developed within the Convention of Antarctic Living Marine Resources, which can be enforced under the Antarctic Treaty. The machinery for co-operative research is in place and operating (BIOMASS — "Biological Investigations of Marine Antarctic Systems and Stocks" — is a 10-year non-governmental programme co-sponsored by the FAO and the International Association of Biological Oceanographers), and the IWC conducts research on whales within that framework. There must be continuing international logistic and financial support for such programmes to ensure their long-term survival. The welfare of marine mammals in the Antarctic ecosystem may well depend on them.

CHAPTER 10

SEABIRDS

P.C. HARPER, E.B. SPURR, and R.H. TAYLOR

INTRODUCTION

Limiting factors influencing the distibution of seabirds in the Antarctic Sector of the Pacific include the paucity of islands where birds can breed and the lack of a reliable food supply in the region. This lack of food arises because there are few continental margins not covered by pack ice where deep nutrient-rich water can upwell to provide a consistent source for zooplankton on which oceanic birds prey.

The main body of the southern Pacific is in fact a vast relentless ocean where incessant gales generated by deep low-pressure cells chase each other from west to east. These storm systems provide a benefit for seabirds in creating an important migration corridor which extends from the New Zealand Province, where subantarctic bird species are abundant, to the Scotia Sea, where there is abundant summer food for both the migrant and indigenous avian predators.

The object of this chapter is to review briefly the available information on the birds of the polar Pacific and to highlight some of the problems associated with studying birds in this little-known region.

ORIGINS

Although the Antarctic Sector of the Pacific appears little more than a windswept ocean with places of ornithological interest restricted to its periphery, it was not always so. The region was probably the cradle from which the early penguin/petrel stock began its evolutionary growth and diversification in the late Cretaceous and early Tertiary. That the penguins (Sphenisciformes) and the petrels (Procellariiformes) originated in the Late Cretaceous seems clear since none of the region's Tertiary penguin faunas show primitive features (e.g., *Palaeeudyptes marplesi* and *Pachydyptes ponderosus* from late Eocene at Kakanui, New Zealand (Simpson, 1975) and others from Australia, Patagonia and Seymour Island off the Antarctic Peninsula).

Harper (1978) proposed that the environmental trigger which helped initiate the mid-Tertiary radiation of the penguin and petrel faunas in the Pacific Sector was the major global cooling which began at the Eocene/Oligocene boundary (c. 38 m.yrs B.P.). Continuing crustal movements led to substantial climatic and oceanographic changes, the most pivotal of which was the northward displacement of the Australian continent and the development of the circumpolar Antarctic current during the late Oligocene 30–25 m.yrs B.P. (Kennett et al., 1975b). Changes in sea levels and land area in the New Zealand region throughout the Tertiary and Recent (Fleming, 1979) created a range of marine habitats into which the oceanic birds diversified with considerable success. Recolonization of Antarctica by penguins, petrels, and skuas occurred only very recently, c. 6,500 years ago in McMurdo Sound, and a little earlier than this further north (Young, 1981).

According to Kennett et al. (1975b), the Polar Front became a prominent feature in the Pacific as long ago as the Miocene, so that its influence on the ecology and evolution of southern avifaunas has been important for some 15 million years. Penguins reached their maximum diversity during the Miocene and the sub-sequent extinctions, especially of the larger species as suggested by Simpson (1975) may have resulted from increasing competition from the rapidly-evolving marine mammals.

TAXONOMY

Post-Pleistocene differentiation is less marked in the penguins than in the petrels. Of 13 penguin species resident in this region, only the Macaroni (Royal) Penguin (*Eudyptes chrysolophus*) has a well defined subspecies, *schlegeli,* which breeds at Macquarie Island. In contrast, subspeciation in the endemic South Pacific forms of the albatrosses (Diomedeidae) has been strong. Some full species are clearly masquerading as subspecies in the present taxonomy. Needing revision are: the Southern and Northern Royal Albatrosses (*Diomedea epomophora*); the New Zealand forms of the Wandering Albatross (*D. exulans*); the two Black-browed Mollymawks (*D. m. melanophris* and *D. m. impavida*), the two colour morphs of the Buller's Mollymawk (*D. bulleri*); and the three distinctive 'cauta' mollymawks, (*D. c. cauta, c. salvini,* and *c. eremita*). On the basis of morphology, behaviour, distribution and genetics, there is a good case for separating the mollymawks from the greater albatrosses at the genus level (i.e., retention of the name *Thalassarche*).

The smaller petrels of the region are mostly circumpolar in their distributions, although there are some geographical and behavioural differences because of the urge to return to their place of birth. Two sibling species of the Giant Petrel (*Macronectes giganteus* and *M. halli*) at Macquarie Island are reproductively isolated by a difference of some six weeks in their breeding schedules (Bourne and Warham, 1966). Unsuccessful interbreeding has been observed there by Johnstone (1977). Successful hybridization occurs at South Georgia, a fact attributed by Hunter (1983) to abundant local food supplies. This highlights the taxonomic difficulties that can arise with widely distributed species and demonstrates that birds of the same species living in different regions of the circumpolar ocean can adopt differing behaviours as a result of food abundance. Another behavioural difference occurs with the Snow Petrel (*Pagodroma nivea*) which is common in ice-free waters of the Scotia Sea (J.P. Croxall, pers. comm.); yet in the Pacific, the Snow Petrel rarely ventures far from the ice edge. Paucity of the region's food north of the ice edge may be a reason, but other factors might include flight distances to nest sites. The sea ice in this region from open water to Marie Byrd

Land on the Antarctic coast can be as much as 500-1,000 km — even in summer.

The increasing number of specimens of oceanic birds from their breeding localities in recent years has the potential to aid taxonomy greatly, and this information could be combined with modern biochemical techniques to unravel the complexities in several groups, such as the *urinatrix* subspecies of the Common Diving Petrel (Family Pelecanoididae). Much further work remains to be done.

BREEDING DISTRIBUTION

Watson et al. (1971) recognized five zoogeographical provinces in the Antarctic and Subantarctic regions. Of these, three are relevant to the Antarctic Sector of the Pacific : the Antarctic Continental Province which encompasses all the area south of the maximum pack ice limit, the New Zealand Province, and the Magellanic District of the Atlantic Province which includes the Chilean coast of South America. The composition of species within these provinces is shown in Table 10.1. Table 10.2 illustrates the breeding distribution of birds within the Antarctic Sector of the Pacific.

The Antarctic Continental Province

The Ross, Amundsen and Bellingshausen Seas adjacent to the Antarctic continent comprise the region's truly polar element. New Zealand and American ornithologists have studied the bird life from a number of research stations in the Ross Sea region (Young, 1981) such as those at Capes Adare, Bird, Crozier, Hallett and Royds (Fig. 10.1). Brief observations at the Ballenys and Scott, Possession, Franklin, Beaufort Islands and Terra Nova Bay have been made from ships travelling to and from the region.

Three species of penguins, Emperor (*Aptenodytes forsteri*), Adélie (*Pygoscelis adeliae*), and Chinstrap (*Pygoscelis antarctica*), six species of petrel, Cape Pigeon (*Daption capense*), Antarctic Fulmar (*Fulmarus glacialoides*), Antarctic Petrel (*Thalassoica antarctica*), Snow Petrel (*Pagodroma nivea*), Antarctic Prion (*Pachyptila desolata*), Wilson's Storm Petrel (*Oceanites oceanicus*) and two species of skuas (Antarctic Skua *Catharacta maccormicki* and Southern Skua *C. lonnbergi*) breed on the continental coast and its adjacent islands (Table 10. 2).

Although the Antarctic Continental Province has only 11 breeding bird species, most of these have large populations. The avian population of the Ross Sea region alone was estimated by Ainley (1986) to be some 10 million birds, with an average density of 16 birds per km^2 and a biomass of 44 kg per km^2 (in December–early January). The avifauna is dominated in numbers by the Antarctic Petrel (55%), and in biomass by the Emperor Penguin (43%) and the Adélie Penguin (39%). The Ross Sea contains approximately one third of the world's population of Emperor and Adélie penguins (Wilson, 1983; Ainley et al., 1984; Harper et al., 1984).

The birdlife of the Marie Byrd Land coast and the coasts south of the Amund-

TABLE 10.1

The composition of bird species within the zoogeographical zones of the Antarctic Sector of the Pacific.

CIRCUMPOLAR IN BOTH ANTARCTIC AND SUBANTARCTIC REGIONS

Southern Giant Petrel	Antarctic Prion	Blue-eyed Shag	Kelp Gull
Cape Pigeon	Wilson's Storm Petrel	Southern Skua	Antarctic Tern

CIRCUMPOLAR IN SUBANTARCTIC REGION

Northern Giant Petrel	Little Shearwater
White-chinned Petrel	Black-bellied Storm Petrel
Grey Petrel	Grey-backed Storm Petrel
White-headed Petrel	Common Diving Petrel
Soft-plumaged Petrel	South Georgian Diving Petrel
Blue Petrel	Subantarctic Diving Petrel
Fairy Prion	King Shag

CIRCUMPOLAR IN ANTARCTIC REGION

Adélie Penguin
Chinstrap Penguin
Antarctic Fulmar
Snow Petrel
Wilson's Storm Petrel
Antarctic Skua

CIRCUMPOLAR IN SUBANTARCTIC REGION

King Penguin
Gentoo Penguin
Rockhopper Penguin
Macaroni Penguin
Wandering Albatross
Black-browed Mollymawk
Grey-headed Mollymawk
Light-mantled Sooty Albatross

CONFINED TO CONTINENTAL PROVINCE

Emperor Penguin
Antarctic Petrel
Snow Petrel

CONFINED TO NEW ZEALAND PROVINCE

Royal Penguin	Shy Mollymawk	White-faced Storm Petrel
Yellow-eyed Penguin	Salvins Mollymawk	Southern Diving Petrel
Snares Crested Penguin	Chatham Is Mollymawk	Bounty Is Shag
Erect-crested Penguin	Snares Cape Pigeon	Campbell Is Shag
Chatham Is Blue Penguin	Fulmar Prion	Pitt Is Shag
Northern Royal Albatross	Mottled Petrel	Red-billed Gull
Southern Royal Albatross	Chatham Is Taiko	White-fronted Tern
NZ Black-browed Mollymawk	Chatham Is Petrel	
Southern Bullers Mollymawk	Black-winged Petrel	
Northern Bullers Mollymawk		

CONFINED TO ATLANTIC PROVINCE (MAGELLANIC DISTRICT)

Chilian Skua
Magellanic Diving Petrel
South American Tern

SHARED WITH MAGELLANIC DISTRICT

Sooty Shearwater

sen and Bellingshausen Seas has been little studied, largely because of the vast and impenetrable pack ice that dominates this region. Adélie Penguins, Snow Petrels and Antarctic Skuas are known to breed in Marie Byrd Land (information reviewed in Harper et al., 1984). Recently, Broady et al. (1989) reported 10,000 nests of Antarctic Petrels on Edward VII Peninsula. Peter I Island, the only oceanic island in the southeastern part of the region, is reported to have a few breeding Adélie and Chinstrap Penguins, Antarctic Fulmars, Cape Pigeons, Snow Petrels and Wilson's Storm Petrels (Holgersen, 1951; Fevolden, 1987). Antarctic Skuas may also breed there.

The distribution of Adélie Penguin breeding sites illustrates the uneven distribution of birds along the Antarctic coast of the Pacific. Adélie Penguins nest on stony areas free of ice and snow. They also nest adjacent to seas where winter fast ice regularly breaks out in spring, so that food is close by in mid-December to feed the newly hatched chicks. Of more than 1 million pairs of Adélie Penguins breeding in 45 colonies along approximately 10,000 km of coastline, over 90% nest in 26 colonies along one 1,500 km stretch — the western fringe of the Ross Sea from Ross Island to Cape Adare (Fig. 10.2). In this area, where inshore sea ice breaks up earlier than elsewhere there are several very extensive Adélie Penguin colonies including the largest known — Cape Adare with over 240,000 breeding pairs. Along the remaining 8,500 km of the Antarctic coast — encompassing the Bellingshausen and Amundsen Seas, Marie Byrd Land, Pennell Coast and Oates Land — where solid shelf ice commonly occurs until late in summer, only 19 scattered colonies are known, and only two of these are thought to contain more than 5,000 pairs each (Table 10.3). This coast has, however, been poorly surveyed.

Fig. 10.1. Nesting Adélie Penguins at Cape Royds, Antarctica.

TABLE 10.2

Breeding distribution of Antarctic and Subantarctic seabirds within the Pacific Sector.

SPECIES	ANTARCTIC PROVINCE		NEW ZEALAND PROVINCE							ATLANTIC PROVINCE	NOTES
	Balleny Is.	Antarctica	Macquarie Is.	Campbell Is.	Auckland Is.	Antipodes Is.	Bounty Is.	The Snares	Chatham Is.	Chile	
PENGUINS											
Emperor Penguin		x									
King Penguin			x*								* See Table 10.3.
Yellow-eyed Penguin				x	x			x			
Adélie Penguin	x	x*									
Gentoo Penguin			x								
Chinstrap Penguin	x										
Blue Penguin								x	x		
Royal Penguin			x*								* *Eudyptes c. schlegeli*: sub-species of Macaroni Penguin
Rockhopper Penguin			x	x	x	x				x	
Snares Crested Penguin								x			
Erect-crested Penguin				x	x	x	x				
Magellanic Penguin										x	

	Balleny Is.	Antarctica	Macquarie Is.	Campbell Is.	Auckland Is.	Antipodes Is.	Bounty Is.	The Snares	Chatham Is.	Chile	Notes
ALBATROSSES, MOLLYMAWKS and PETRELS											
Wandering Albatross				x*	x	x	x				*Diomedea e. chionoptera: Snowy Albatross
Royal Albatross				x	x					x*	*Diomedea e. sandfordi: Northern Royal Albatross
Black-browed Mollymawk			x	x*		x					*Diomedea m. impavida: New Zealand subspecies
Grey-headed Mollymawk			x	x						x	
Buller's Mollymawk					x			x	x*		*Diomedea b. platei: Northern Buller's Mollym'k
White-capped Mollymawk				x	x		x*	x*	x**		Three species exist in New Zealand (see text) *Salvins, **Chatham Is
Light-mantled Sooty Albatross			x	x	x	x					
Antarctic Petrel	x	x									
Antarctic Fulmar	x	x									
Southern Giant Petrel			x								
Northern Giant Petrel			x	x	x	x	x	x			
Cape Pigeon	x	x		x	x*	x*	x*	x*			*Endemic subspecies: Daption c. australe
Snow Petrel	x	x									
White-headed Petrel			x	x	x	x		x			
Mottled Petrel											

	Balleny Is.	Antarctica	Macquarie Is.	Campbell Is.	Auckland Is.	Antipodes Is.	Bounty Is.	The Snares	Chatham Is.	Chile	
Soft-plumaged Petrel						x					
Blue Petrel			x							x	
Antarctic Prion		x*	x		x						*Known only from Scott Is. (Harper et al., 1984)
Thin-billed Prion			x*							x	*Offshore islets only
Fairy Prion			x		x	x		x	x		Bollons Is ?
Fulmar Prion					x	x?	x	x	x		
Grey Petrel			*	x	x	x					*Formerly on Macquarie Is.
White-chinned Petrel				x	x	x					
Sooty Shearwater			x	x	x	x		x	x	x	
Little Shearwater					x	x			x	x	
Wilson's Storm Petrel	x	x				x				x	
Grey-backed Storm Petrel				x?	x	x			x		
White-faced Storm Petrel					x						
Black-bellied Storm Petrel				x	x	x					
Common Diving Petrel			x*	x*	x*	x*		x	x	x	*Subantarctic subspecies: Pelecanoides u. exsul
Magellanic Diving Petrel										x	
South Georgia Diving Petrel*											*Codfish Is (Stewart Is)
SKUAS											
Antarctic Skua	x?	x									
Southern Skua	x?		x	x	x	x	x?	x	x		
Chilean Skua										x	

TABLE 10.3

Breeding populations of Adélie Penguins in the Pacific Sector.

Region	Location	No. of breeding pairs (approx.)
Bellingshausen Sea	Charcot Island	50
	Peter I Island	20
Marie Byrd Land	Mt Siple	? small
	Maher Island	? small
	Mathewson Point	30,000
	Worley Point	10,000
	Cruzen Island	100
Ross Island	Cape Royds	4,000
	Cape Bird South	15,800
	Cape Bird Middle	3,200
	Cape Bird North	40,100
	Cape Crozier West	151,500
	Cape Crozier East	28,400
Ross Sea Islands	Beaufort Island	53,700
	Franklin Island West	55,300
	Franklin Island East	1,200
Terra Nova / Wood Bays	Inexpressible Island	28,000
	Terra Nova Bay	11,600
	Edmonson Point	2,400
Coulman Island	Cape Anne	500
	Coulman Island South	22,600
	Coulman Island Middle	5,500
	Coulman Island North	1,900
Daniel Peninsula	Cape Jones	200
	Mandible Cirque	19,500
	Cape Phillips	4,400
Hallett Peninsula	Cape Wheatstone	2,300
	Cape Cotter	49,500
	Cape Hallett	57,600
Possession Islands	Foyn Island	41,900
	Possession Island	157,600
Adare Peninsula	Downshire Cliffs	22,600
	Cape Adare	240,000
Pennell Coast	Duke-of-York Island	4,600
	Sentry Rock	80
	Unger Island	150
	Nella Island	200
Oates Land	Aviation Is. "Conical Island"	150
	Aviation Is. "Dome Island"	150
	Aviation Is. "South West Island"	700
Balleny Islands	Sabrina Island	4,400
	Chinstrap Island	2,400
	South West Promontory	300
	Cape Davis	550
	Cape Cornish	500
Totals	45 colonies	> 1,076,000

Three species of petrels that breed near to or north of the Subtropical Convergence regularly forage close to the Antarctic pack ice in summer : they are the Sooty Shearwater (*Puffinus griseus*), Short-tailed Shearwater (*Puffinus tenuirostris*) and Mottled Petrel (*Pterodroma inexpectata*.) These are joined by many subantarctic species of procellariids which migrate south to forage chiefly on the summer swarms of Antarctic krill (e.g., Harper, 1973, 1987; Croxall, 1984).

Since the review of Young (1981), the main advances in knowledge about seabirds in the Antarctic Sector of the Pacific have been concerning their status and conservation (Harper et al., 1984; Schlatter, 1984) and their marine ecology in summer (Ainley et al., 1984). However, there is still virtually nothing known about the winter life of these birds.

Aerial reconnaissance and photography have been used in the Ross Sea region since 1981 to determine the breeding locations of Adélie Penguins and to count the numbers of nests occupied during the early incubation period (Taylor and Wilson, 1982; Wilson and Taylor, 1984). Despite years of exploration in the region, new colonies continue to be found (Wilson and Thomas, 1988).

Since 1985, radio transmitters have been attached to penguins at Cape Bird on Ross Island to track them at sea. During the incubation stage, most penguins went northwards beyond the range of the tracking equipment (100 km) for most of their time at sea (Ward et al., 1985; Davis et al., 1988). During the chick-feeding stage, most penguins stayed in McMurdo Sound within 5 km of the colony, but a few disappeared around the north end of Ross Island more than 10 km away (Sadleir, 1987). This project is the beginning of new developments which may extend to tracking the critical winter movements of penguins. It may also provide useful data in the event of an increase in shipping or air traffic for tourism, fishing, oil or mineral exploration, with consequent increased risk of serious oil pollution.

The New Zealand Province

The New Zealand plateau is the only large continental platform adjacent to the Antarctic Sector of the Pacific, and consists of a substantial area of relatively shallow seas (depth less than 2,000 m) which allows a complex mixing of waters about its margins. The New Zealand plateau contains six subantarctic island groups. These islands, together with the three main islands of New Zealand, support a seabird diversity unmatched anywhere else on Earth. Accounts of these islands and their avifauna are given in Clark and Dingwall (1985) and Fraser (1986). About 60 seabird species breed in the New Zealand Province, but only about half of these breed south of the Subtropical Convergence (Table 10.2). The remainder are subtropical and/or transequatorial species and lie outside the scope of this chapter. Apart from the Taiko (*Pterodroma magentae*), a subtropical species on the Chatham Islands, perhaps the most interesting finding in recent years was the discovery of the South Georgia Diving Petrel (*Pelecanoides georgicus*) nesting in consolidated sand dunes at Codfish Island, off Stewart Island, by Imber and Nilsson (1980). The presence of warm subtropical waters in Foveaux Strait makes the find of this subantarctic species all the more remarkable.

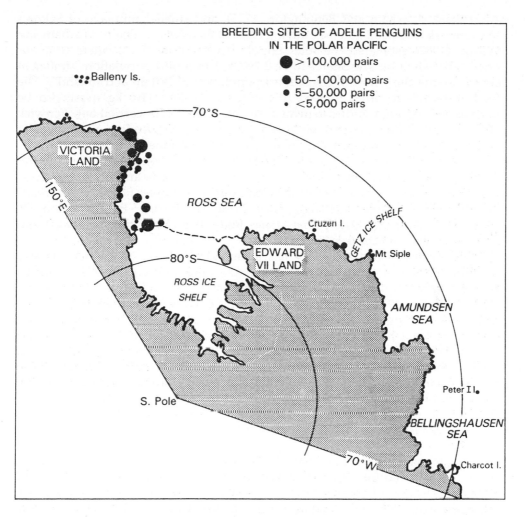

Fig. 10.2. The location of Adélie Penguin colonies within the Antarctic Sector of the Pacific.

The Snares

This small (3.3 km²) group of two low-lying and mainly forest-covered islands, and several small islets and rocks, has no introduced mammals and remains virtually in a natural state. At 48°02'S, 166°33'E, The Snares lie just north of the Subtropical Convergence. The seabirds which breed there represent a mingling of subtropical and subantarctic elements.

Twenty-one species of seabirds breed on The Snares. The endemic Snares Crested Penguin (*Eudyptes robustus*) has a population of 30,000–50,000 birds in 133 scattered colonies (Warham, 1974). Two species of albatross breed at the islands, about 700 pairs of Buller's Mollymawk on Northeast and Broughton Islands and

Alert Stack (Warham and Bennington, 1983), and smaller numbers of Salvin's Mollymawk (*D. salvini*) on the outlying islets of the Western Chain. Warham and Wilson (1982) estimated the total population of Sooty Shearwaters (*Puffinus griseus*) breeding on The Snares to be 2,750,000, or a bird population "similar in size to that of the whole of the seabird population of Britain and Ireland". The food resources required to feed this biomass of 4.4×10^6 kg must also be impressive, although studies to investigate this remain to be carried out. Fenwick (1978) reported four species of birds and six species of fish feeding on euphausiid and amphipod swarms near The Snares during the summer of 1976/77.

Another common species on The Snares is the Southern Diving Petrel (*Pelecanoides urinatrix chathamensis*). Other breeding birds are the Snares Cape Pigeons (*Daption capense australe*), Mottled Petrel (*Pterodroma inexpectata*), Broad-billed Prion (*Pachyptilla vittata*), Fairy Prion (*P. turtur*), Fulmar Prion (*P. crassirostris*), Antarctic Tern (*Sterna vittata*), Red-billed Gull (*Larus scopulinus*), and Southern Skua (*Catharacta lonnbergi*).

The University of Canterbury has a biological station on the islands and scientific parties have visited there regularly since 1961. Research on Snares Islands seabirds has included studies on the Snares Crested Penguin (Stonehouse, 1971; Warham, 1974), Buller's Mollymawk (Richdale and Warham, 1973; Warham and Bennington, 1983; Warham and Fitzsimons, 1987), Mottled Petrel (Warham et al., 1977), Sooty Shearwater (Warham et al., 1982; Warham and Wilson, 1982), Snares Cape Pigeon (Sagar 1979, 1986), Antarctic Tern (Sagar, 1978). There are also several general accounts of the island's birdlife (Warham, 1967a; Warham and Keeley, 1969; Fleming and Baker, 1973; Horning and Horning, 1974; Sagar, 1977a, b; Miskelly, 1984).

The Auckland Islands

The uninhabited Auckland Islands (50°40'S, 166°10'E) extend for 52 km from north to south and for 35 km from east to west, and have a land area of about 620 km². The group consists of two large, partly forested islands with peaks over 600 m, four smaller islands, and numerous small islets and stacks. Although there are pigs, goats, cats and mice on the main island — and cattle, rabbits and mice on a few others — the group as a whole still supports a rich and plentiful birdlife.

These islands are a known breeding station for 25 species of seabird — including 3 penguins and 16 albatrosses and petrels. The colonial nesting Rockhopper Penguin (*Eudyptes c. chrysocome*) is the most numerous penguin with 5–10,000 pairs breeding (Bell, 1975). There are also considerable numbers of the solitary nesting Yellow-eyed Penguin (*Megadyptes antipodes*) on Adams, Enderby and Rose Islands where there are no introduced predators. The Erect-crested Penguin (*E. sclateri*) also breeds in small numbers on the Auckland group. There are over 13,500 pairs of Wandering Albatross (*Diomedea exulans*) and 64,000 pairs of White-capped Mollymawk (*D. cauta steadi*) — the former mainly on predator-free Adams Islands and the latter mainly on Disappointment Island (Robertson, 1975). Smaller numbers of Southern Royal Albatross (*D. epomorphora*), Light-mantled Sooty Albatross (*Phoebetria palpebrata*), and Northern Giant Petrel (*Macronectes halli*) also nest on various islands in the group.

Crevice or burrow nesting petrels are the Snares Cape Pigeon, White-headed Petrel (*Pterodroma lessoni*), Antarctic Prion (*Pachyptila desolata*), Subantarctic Fulmar Prion (*P. crassirostris eatoni*), White-chinned Petrel (*Procellaria aequin-octialis*), Sooty Shearwater, Subantarctic Little Shearwater (*P. assimilis elegans*), Grey-backed Storm Petrel (*Garrodia nereis*), White-faced Storm Petrel (*Pelago-droma marina maoriana*), Black-bellied Storm Petrel (*Fregetta tropica*), Subantarctic Diving Petrel (*Pelecanoides urinatrix exsul*), and South Georgia Diving Petrel.

The Southern Skua, Southern Black-backed Gull (*Larus dominicanus*), Red-billed Gull, Antarctic Tern and White-fronted Tern (*Sterna striata*) also breed at the islands. There is one marine cormorant, the endemic Auckland Island Shag (*Leucocarbo campbelli colensoi*) which nests in small scattered colonies on cliff tops and ledges, and fishes inshore waters.

The lack of permanent bases or regular expeditions has affected the type of research carried out on the Auckland Islands. Seabird studies have been confined to surveys, banding (movement) studies, and the incidental collection of data on breeding and other aspects (Falla, 1965; Bell, 1975; Robertson, 1975; van Tets, 1975; Falla et al., 1979; Anonymous, 1985c; Penniket et al., 1986). Greater oppor-tunities for in-depth research on Auckland Island seabirds may occur in the near future. Much more detailed ecological information is needed on the different seabird species using the islands. Such information is essential to help formulate sound management policies, not only for these important Nature Reserves but also for the surrounding seas from which the birds derive their food.

The Campbell Islands

The Campbell Islands, situated at 52°33'S, 169°E, are the most southerly of the islands on the New Zealand Plateau. They comprise Campbell Island (113 km²), which reaches 567 m a.s.l. and a number of small islets and stacks. The vegetation is mainly tussock grassland, shrubland and herbfield. The plant cover and wildlife of the main island are much modified by past farming ventures and the presence of feral sheep, cats and Norway rats. Only the small offshore islets remain in a natural state.

Three penguin species breed on the islands. The most common species is the Rockhopper Penguin which previously bred in millions (Bailey and Sorensen, 1962) but more recently their numbers have declined drastically (Moors, 1986). Reasons for this are uncertain but are probably connected with food supplies at sea. Small numbers of Erect-crested Penguins also breed amongst the Rock-hoppers. Campbell Island has the southernmost population of the Yellow-eyed Penguin, with several hundred pairs nesting behind beaches and sheltered sloping shores on many parts of the island.

The island is the main nesting locality of the Southern Royal Albatross. The breeding population has been increasing since the 1930s and now numbers about 10,000 pairs (Taylor et al., 1970; Dilks and Wilson, 1979). The Light-mantled Sooty Albatross nests on the coastal cliffs and offshore stacks, and a few Wandering Albatrosses also breed on the main island (Fig. 10.3). Campbell is also the main breeding station of the New Zealand Black-browed Mollymawk (*D. m. impavida*), and of the Grey-headed Mollymawk (*D. chysostoma*) in the South Pacific, but the numbers of both these species appear to have declined recently, perhaps from the same factors affecting Rockhopper Penguins. Northern Giant Petrels nest in small colonies on several parts of Campbell Island and on offshore islets. The numbers of these scavengers have also declined in recent years, a trend that is probably linked to the large decline in the island's penguin and elephant seal populations.

The burrowing petrel populations of the Campbell Islands have been severely reduced by predation from cats and rats over the past 100 years. Medium-sized petrels still breeding in small numbers on the main island include the Snares Cape Pigeon, Grey Petrel, White-chinned Petrel, and Sooty Shearwater (Bailey and Sorensen, 1962). However, it is only on the small outlying islets that there are any numbers of White-chinned Petrels, Sooty Shearwaters, Grey-backed Storm Petrels, Black-bellied Storm Petrels, and Subantarctic Diving Petrels (Robertson, 1980; Foggo and Meurk, 1981). There is a breeding population of about 2,000 pairs of the endemic Campbell Island Shag (*Leucocarbo campbelli campbelli*) that nest on the cliff ledges on the main island and on several offshore islets (van Tets, 1980). Southern Skuas, Southern Black-backed Gulls, Red-billed Gulls and Antarctic Terns are the other seabird species breeding at the Campbell Islands.

Campbell Island was the site of continuous coast-watching expeditions during World War II and has had a manned meteorological station since 1946. Conse-

Fig. 10.3. A breeding pair of Wandering Albatrosses (paler plumaged male on nest) from Campbell Island.

quently, more biological investigations have been carried out there than at most other New Zealand subantarctic islands. Unfortunately, with the exception of J.H. Sorensen in the 1940s, no professional ornithologist was attached to these expeditions for more than a few summer months until 1984. Published research on Campbell Island seabirds includes studies on the Rockhopper Penguin (Moors, 1985), Southern Royal Albatross (Sorensen, 1950a; Westerskov, 1959, 1963; Taylor et al., 1970; Dilks and Wilson, 1979), Light-mantled Sooty Albatross (Sorensen, 1950b), Campbell Island Shag (van Tets, 1980), as well as many more general surveys and reviews (Westerskov, 1960; Bailey and Sorensen, 1962; Falla, 1965; Kinsky, 1969; Robertson, 1980).

The Antipodes Islands

This group is situated at 49°42'S, 178°47'E and consists of Antipodes Island (20.2 km²), six small offshore islets and several stacks. The main island consists of an elevated plateau with hills reaching about 400 m a.s.l. Small, sparse patches of low shrubs form the only woody vegetation, and the plant cover is predominantly tussock grassland and fern. There has been little human impact on the islands, and mice — which are confined to the main island — are the only introduced mammals.

Twenty species of seabirds, including 2 penguins and 15 petrels, breed at the islands. Erect-crested Penguins and Rockhopper Penguins occur in over 80 mixed colonies on all suitable parts of the coastline, and on Bollons, Archway and Windward Islands (Fig. 10.4).

Fig. 10.4. Part of a very large breeding colony of Erect-crested Penguins on the west coast of Antipodes Island.

About 1,500–1,800 pairs of Wandering Albatross breed on the main island (Warham and Bell, 1979) and 150 pairs of Black-browed Mollymawk (*D. melanophrys melanophrys*) on Bollons Island (Robertson, 1985a). Numerous Light-mantled Sooty Albatrosses nest on steep coastal slopes and cliff ledges, and c. 320 pairs of Northern Giant Petrels nest in small scattered colonies. Of the burrow-nesting petrels, the White-headed Petrel is the most abundant, and the White-chinned Petrel and the winter-breeding Grey Petrel are also common. The Subantarctic Little Shearwater nests on the offshore islets in vast numbers. Imber (1983) considered that the Antipodes group has the largest population of this species in the South Pacific — in excess of 100,000 pairs. Other petrels breeding in smaller numbers are the Subantarctic Diving Petrel, Grey-backed Storm Petrel, Black-bellied Storm Petrel, Snares Cape Pigeon (c. 300 pairs), Subantarctic Fairy Prion, Soft-plumaged Petrel (*Pterodroma mollis*), and Sooty Shearwater. Other breeding seabirds are the Southern Skua and the Antarctic Tern. Rather surprisingly there are no shags, but the surrounding waters are much deeper than around the other New Zealand subantarctic islands and it is probable that no suitable niche exists for them.

There have been several major expeditions to the islands since 1950. Resulting publications on seabirds include a general account of the birdlife (Warham and Bell, 1979) as well as the results of studies on the Southern Skua (Moors, 1980), the lesser petrels (Imber, 1979, 1983), and the Antarctic Tern (Sadleir et al., 1986).

The Bounty Islands

The Bounty Islands (1.3 km²) are a group of more than 20 small granite islands and rocks situated at 47°45'S, 179°03'E. The islands are all less than 75 m a.s.l. and the only land plants are lichens and green algae.

Seven species of seabirds breed on the Bounty Islands. According to Robertson and van Tets (1982), there are about 115,000 pairs of Erect-crested Penguins, 76,000 pairs of Salvin's Mollymawks, many thousands of Fulmar Prions, small numbers of Snares Cape Pigeon and Antarctic Terns and fewer than 600 pairs of the endemic Bounty Island Shag (*Leucocarbo campbelli ranfurlyi*). Three predatory or scavenging species — Northern Giant Petrels, Southern Black-backed Gulls and Southern Skuas — are found in some numbers at the Bounty Islands during the summer but do not breed there. Their nearest breeding sites are at the Antipodes Islands, 250 km away.

Few ornithologists have made more than a fleeting visit to the Bounty Islands, and only one scientific party has camped ashore. Consequently, most accounts of the birdlife are in general terms (Oliver, 1955; Darby, 1970; Falla et al., 1979; Robertson and van Tets, 1982; Anonymous, 1985c).

The Chatham Islands

The Chatham Island archipelago (963 km²) is situated at 44°00'S, 176°30'W, 800 km east of New Zealand's South Island. It consists of two large islands (Chatham and Pitt) and about 10 smaller islands as well as many stacks and rocks.

As a result of centuries of human occupation, the vegetation and birdlife of the larger islands have been seriously depleted. Feral farm stock, pigs, cats, rats and mice occur on Chatham Island, and all these pests except for rats are also on Pitt Island. Fortunately, all other islands and islets are now uninhabited and free of introduced mammals, and provide safe refuge for most of the surviving seabird species. Several of the smaller islands and large parts of Pitt Island are now Nature Reserves. The islands lie within the Subtropical Convergence. The seabird fauna of the islands is therefore made up of species of warmer waters, species of cooler waters, and local endemics — most of which feed in the productive waters along the convergence zone.

One species of penguin and 16 petrels breed at the islands. The predominantly warm-water species include the Blue Penguin (*Eudyptula minor*), Northern Royal Albatross (*Diomedea sanfordi*), Northern Buller's Mollymawk (*D. bulleri platei*), and the Black-winged Petrel (*Pterodroma nigripennis*). Local endemic petrels are the Chatham Island Mollymawk (*D. eremita*) with a total population of about 4,000 pairs breeding on the Pyramid (Robertson, 1985b), the recently re-discovered and extremely rare Chatham Island Taiko (*Pterodroma magentae*) with a total population of perhaps only 40 birds (Crockett, 1985), and the Chatham Island Petrel (*P. axillaris*) which is also rare and breeds only on South East Island (Imber, 1985). Petrels breeding at the Chathams which also breed further south in the subantarctic are the Northern Giant Petrel, Snares Cape Pigeon, Broad-billed Prion, Fairy Prion, Fulmar Prion, Sooty Shearwater, Subantarctic Little Shearwater, Grey-backed Storm Petrel, White-faced Storm Petrel, and the Southern Diving Petrel (*Pelecanoides urinatrix chathamensis*).

There are two endemic shags, the Chatham Island Shag (*Leucocarbo c. carunculatus*) and the Pitt Island Shag (*Stictocarbo punctatus featherstoni*). Other breeding seabirds are the Southern Skua, Southern Black-backed Gull, Red-billed Gull and White-fronted Tern.

Although much fieldwork has been carried out on Chatham Island seabirds by both privately funded and government expeditions over the last 20 years, few results have been published in detail. Notable exceptions are Dawson's (1973) work on Albatross and mollymawk colonies, and Young's (1978) study of the Southern Skua. Other papers and short notes published on Chatham Island seabirds since Fleming's (1939) standard work deal with survey results (Bell, 1954), Northern Royal Albatross and Northern Buller's Mollymawk (Robertson, 1974), Northern Giant Petrel (Hemmings and Bailey, 1985), Chatham Island Taiko (Crocket, 1979), Black-winged Petrel (Merton, 1984), various small petrels (Imber, 1978), subfossil petrel bones (Bourne, 1964, 1967; Scarlett, 1976), and the Chatham Island Shag (Morris, 1977). Much original information on the different species has also been published in field guides and books on New Zealand birds (e.g., Oliver, 1955; Falla et al., 1979; Anonymous, 1985c).

Macquarie Island

The most southerly of the islands in the New Zealand Province is Macquarie Island, situated at 54°37'S, 158°54'E. The island lies on the Macquarie Ridge which is separated from the New Zealand Plateau by the Emerald Basin. It has four species of penguins, including one endemic subspecies of the Macaroni Penguin (*Eudyptes chrysolophus schlegeli*), 13 species of procellariids, an endemic sub-species of shag, the circumpolar Southern Skua, the Black-backed Gull and the Antarctic Tern. The lack of endemicity in Macquarie Island seabirds reflects the dominant circumpolar elements in its avifauna.

Since the island's discovery in 1810, Macquarie has suffered severely from the impact of human exploitation by early sealers, and the associated introduction of predators and vermin such as mice, rats, cats, dogs, rabbits, and the Stewart Island Weka (*Gallirallus australis scotti*). These imports have devastated the island's marine avifauna to the extent that the Grey Petrel (*Procellaria cinerea*) has been exterminated as a breeding species, and the population of most of the remaining species have been greatly reduced (Falla, 1947; Jones, 1980; Brothers, 1984).

Studies on Macquarie birds have included those of the Royal Penguin (Shaughnessy, 1970, 1975), Rockhopper Penguin (Warham, 1963), the feeding ecology of the Giant Petrels (Johnstone, 1977) and White-headed Petrel (Warham, 1967b). The status and conservation of the Macquarie Island birds has recently been reviewed by Rounsevell and Brothers (1984).

The Atlantic Province – Magellanic District

The Magellanic District of the Atlantic Province embraces the southern fjords and archipelagoes of Chile where Murphy's (1936) pioneering treatise on South American seabirds remains the definitive work (see also Johnson, 1965). As recently as 1984, Roberto Schlatter of Valdivia University, Chile, remarked, "few ornithologists have conducted searches for and surveys of breeding colonies, and more work in this vast and inaccessible area is urgently needed." Jehl (1973) has discussed the distribution of marine birds in Chilean waters in winter, and, more recently, the Totorore expedition made valuable seabird observations in the southern Chilean fjords in 1983, including the discovery of Thin-billed Prions (*Pachyptila belcheri*) breeding on Ilsa Noir and a new colony of 200,000 Sooty Shearwaters breeding on Ilsa Guafo (Clark et al., 1984a, b).

The dominant influence in this region is the Peru Current which carries sub-antarctic waters northwards along the west coast of South America to just south of the equator. This cool-water system enables 18 species of chiefly subantarctic seabirds to nest in Chile (Murphy, 1936; Schlatter, 1984). The breeding list includes four species of penguin, including one endemic (*Sphenicus magellanicus*) to the Fuegian coasts, nine species of petrels (one endemic), five species of cormorants (one endemic), the Chilean Skua, and four species of gulls and terns (two endemic). Boswell and MacIver (1975) reviewed the breeding biology and ecology of Magellanic Penguins, which are numbered "in millions, possibly tens of millions".

DISTRIBUTION AT SEA

The distribution of birds at sea is a complex issue made more difficult by our limited understanding of what controls it. Distributional studies are, at the very least, reliant upon comprehensive oceanographic data being available and understandable to the ornithologist at sea. Sadly, this is often not the case. As Brown (1980) has noted, an appreciation by ornithologists that the ocean is not merely a wet provider of food but is in fact a myriad of patches and pathways affected by water temperature, salinity, colour, currents, depth, wind and weather has been a long time in coming. The modern-day field observer needs to have a thorough background in marine biology as well as knowing something of the physiology, metabolic rates, and ecological relationships of the birds under study. For many, it is a daunting prospect.

Attempts to integrate bird distributions with a few of the above parameters has begun (e.g., Szijj, 1967; Pockington, 1979; Brown, 1980; Ainley et al., 1984; Abrams, 1985) but these studies reveal just how elusive meaningful results are. Preliminary findings (Manikowski, 1971; Brown et al., 1975) suggest that any correlation between oceanographic and meteorological factors and seabird distribution is probably subtle and complex, involving permutations of the above, together with biotic factors such as food availability, the nature of seabird communities, and the age structure of birds at sea. Intuitively, one would expect seabirds to seek out large and conspicuous physical features, such as frontal systems or ice edges, first and to then seek prey associated with such boundaries. Designing experiments to test these speculations will prove interesting.

The Polar Front

The Polar Front has long been cited as being an important boundary zone both to plankton and to birds (e.g., Murphy, 1936). According to Mackintosh (1960, fig. 75), for example, the distribution of *Euphausia triacantha* straddles the Polar Front and he further stated that "the Antarctic Convergence is not necessarily a sharp boundary to the total range of many species, but there are many contrasts in the planktonic fauna to the north and south of it."

Recent research has shown the Polar Front to be a complex zone, with up to three "fronts" separating different water masses. These can migrate laterally to form wavelike disturbances that frequently close on themselves, forming current rings and eddies which may have lifetimes from days to years (Foster, 1984). The effect of the Polar Front on ocean birds depends on whether it forms sharp discontinuities of temperature and salinity. In some places outside the Antarctic Sector of the Pacific, such as the Scotia Sea in the South Atlantic, the Polar Front forms over shallow submarine ridges where deflected currents and eddies can disrupt, displace and mix the water. There, the Polar Front can be hard to detect at the sea's surface. Whether oceanic birds are capable of discerning the Polar Front under these conditions is unknown, but certainly many species of subantarctic birds cross the Polar Front in the Scotia Sea area with seeming impunity (e.g., Harper, 1973). Kock and Reinsch (1978) and Ainley et al. (1984) considered the

Polar Front to be greatly overrated as a faunal barrier to birds in the Scotia Sea.

In the Antarctic Sector of the Pacific, the Polar Front forms over deep waters (3,000–6,000 m) and can thus form sharply. In calm weather, dense sea-mists frequently occur above it. In rough weather, when considerable mixing of surface waters takes place, its effect on birds is an enigma. To give an example, during a voyage from Auckland, New Zealand, to Valparaiso, Chile, in 1965, the Antarctic research ship U.S.N.S. *Eltanin* while heading due south along longitude 144°32'W encountered heavy sea-mists and a clear Polar Front on 28 September 1965 between 55°21'S and 55°41'S in the western Pacific. Between these two positions, the sea surface temperature dropped from 3.7°C to 0.7°C. This occurrence of the Polar Front was very sharp and it abruptly halted the southern movement of seven subantarctic species (Wandering Albatross, Black-browed Mollymawk, Grey-headed Mollymawk, Light-mantled Sooty Albatross, Thin-billed Prion, Grey Petrel, White-headed Petrel). It similarly affected the northward movement of Blue Petrel, Antarctic Petrel, Antarctic Fulmar, and interestingly, the Kerguelen Petrel (*Pterodroma brevirostris*) (Fig. 10.5). Proceeding north again in a stormy ocean in the eastern Pacific between longitudes 104°W and 120°W the ship did not detect the Polar Front at the surface on 18 October 1965 (56°38'S, 105°W) but six of the above seven subantarctic species all reappeared on this date.

When the *Eltanin* returned to the area in relatively calm weather on 25 November, 55 days later, the Polar Front had moved some 460 km south to 60°S (at 120°W longitude) and the subantarctic species had all followed it south. They vanished as soon as the *Eltanin* passed south over the Polar Front and reappeared immediately after the ship returned northwards en route to Punta Arenas in the Magellan Straits. The two most reliable subantarctic water indicator species in the polar Pacific proved to be the Grey Petrel (*Procellaria cinerea*) and the White-headed Petrel (*Pterodroma lessoni*). They were better at indicating the Polar Front than most of the instruments onboard ship.

Clearly, one of the greatest gaps in our understanding of seabird ecology is the effect of faunistic barriers such as the Polar Front on bird distributions, particularly since the behaviour of the birds in the Pacific appears to be quite different from that of birds frequenting the South Atlantic. Here, numerous species, including the Grey Petrel, apparently cross the Polar Front freely (Eakin et al., 1986). Why they should do so may be related to the availability of krill in the region, but more information is needed.

The Ice Edge

Adjacent to the Antarctic coastline and its land-fast ice is a belt of shifting pack ice which extends well northwards in winter and spring to cover more than half of the ocean between the continent and the Polar Front. During late spring and early summer, the ice melts and retreats south, and in doing so uncovers a substantial area of sea to sunlight, which results in rapid primary production by phytoplankton and a resulting large jump in zooplankton numbers. Mackintosh (1970) reported krill hundreds of kilometres south of the spring position of the ice edge, and noted that it "cannot have travelled there with the open water, for there is no

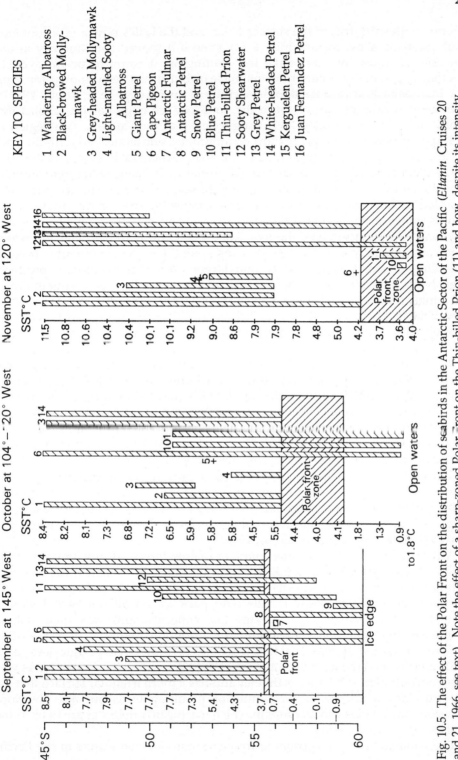

KEY TO SPECIES

1 Wandering Albatross
2 Black-browed Molly-
    mawk
3 Grey-headed Mollymawk
4 Light-mantled Sooty
    Albatross
5 Giant Petrel
6 Cape Pigeon
7 Antarctic Fulmar
8 Antarctic Petrel
9 Snow Petrel
10 Blue Petrel
11 Thin-billed Prion
12 Sooty Shearwater
13 Grey Petrel
14 White-headed Petrel
15 Kerguelen Petrel
16 Juan Fernandez Petrel

Fig. 10.5. The effect of the Polar Front on the distribution of seabirds in the Antarctic Sector of the Pacific (*Eltanin* Cruises 20 and 21, 1966, see text). Note the effect of a sharp-zoned Polar Front on the Thin-billed Prion (11) and how, despite its intensity, the Polar Front can effectively halt species such as the Wandering Albatross.

general southward drift of the surface layer, and the krill's power of locomotion would scarcely allow for one mile a day even if it moved continuously in one direction. It must live under the ice, waiting, as it were, to be uncovered." Whether this actually occurs remains unclear, but it has been known for some time that seabirds are attracted to the vicinity of the ice edge (e.g., Routh, 1949).

In their review of the influence the Antarctic ice edge has on seabird distribution, Fraser and Ainley (1986) suggested that the ice edge is a region of overlap between two distinct seabird communities, one associated with the pack ice (Emperor and Adélie Penguins, and Snow and Antarctic Petrels) and the other with waters generally free of ice, but still under its influence (Antarctic Fulmar, Cape Pigeon, Wilson's Storm Petrel, and Mottled Petrel). The ice edge was regarded as important to both bird communities because of the intense algal blooms which occur in the Antarctic spring in the numerous open leads and polynyas. As the ice melts, the associated algal communities seed the water, which are gradually exposed to increasing sunlight as the ice retreats. It is the coalescing of small algal blooms into larger ones that eventually produces extensive oceanic blooms so characteristic of the Antarctic. According to Fraser and Ainley (1986), recent information suggests that seabirds congregate not at the edge of the ice but rather 7–10 km further north, reflecting the time lag between ice disintegration and the surge in productivity of the water previously covered by ice.

In addition, not merely the presence of ice but also its age and general condition are possibly important in the distribution of polar seabirds. Pack ice surveys by Zink (1981) and Ainley et al. (1984) have shown birds are directly associated with intrusions of extremely thick, densely concentrated, multi-year ice. "Seabird numbers peaked over these intrusions, which were laced with floes showing both extraordinary algal and bacterial communities and advanced stages of decomposition. These were also the only sites within the pack where euphausiids, decapod crustaceans, and other prey regularly occurred. Again, heavy ice cover, infrequent foraging behaviour, and abrupt discontinuities in seabird abundance that corresponded with the boundaries of these intrusions all suggested that the birds were responding to physical features of the ice, not to prey availability" (Fraser and Ainley, 1986).

Antarctic birds live in an environment of low temperatures, unpredictable winds, and ice-strewn seas. Zink (1981), in his study of oceanic birds during a high-latitude voyage from Ross Island to Anvers Island between 16 January and 7 February 1976, sighted Snow Petrels over pack ice on all but two days and suggested an ice cover of 3–5 oktas (ice concentration) was their habitat preference. In recognition of their limited distribution, Shuntov (1974) classified the Snow and Antarctic Petrels as neritic-ice species rather than pelagic ones. Zink (1981) emphasized the need for future studies to determine the type of ice as well as its concentration. Older ice is thinner and has a more irregular surface that not only provides wind shelter for resting or moulting birds but also develops numerous small holes and crannies in which marine invertebrates are to be found (Watson, 1975; Zink, 1981).

The Antarctic Fulmar appears to frequent more ice-free waters in the Pacific

(Zink, 1981; Ainley et al., 1984; P.C. Harper, pers. observ.), although this may not be so in the Australian Polar region (Johnston and Kerry, 1974) or the Scotia Sea (Murphy, 1936; J.P. Croxall, pers. comm.). Dissimilarities in bird behaviour between resident populations of the three major polar basins surrounding Antarctica emphasize the need for careful behavioural studies and the recognition that, despite being contiguous, populations of birds can remain separate entities rather than forming a homogeneous whole within the Antarctic domain.

The Status of Birds at Sea

The distances that breeding birds can forage away from their eggs and chicks depends on food availability, incubation duties, chick feeding, and the more subtle limitations such as competition, predators, and the oscillations of convergences where birds tend to congregate. Antarctic species have the added problem of flying considerable distances over pack ice to reach open water.

During summer, the breeding season for most oceanic birds, the great influx of birds to the waters surrounding their breeding islands tends to obscure distributional patterns of other birds in the region, while at the same time exposing the migration patterns and movements of sexually immature and non-breeding birds which range far to sea. Whereas breeding birds are restricted in how far away they can forage from nest-sites, non-breeding birds have no such limitations. Because young Procellariiformes delay breeding for several years, pre-breeders make up a substantial percentage of at-sea populations.

But what exactly are these non-breeding birds doing at sea for perhaps a third of their total life-span? The answer lies initially in determining the status of birds seen at sea. This is not an easy task because an at-sea observer rarely has any way of determining the status of an observed bird unless specific age-groups can be conspicuously marked. Are, for example, the Mottled Petrels (*Pterodroma inexpectata*) which forage along the Antarctic ice edge in summer non-breeding birds; or are they, as Warham et al. (1977) suggested, breeding adult birds which can make the 4,000 km round trip during the week-long stints between incubation or chick feeding duties? Are squid and crustaceans in such short supply in the New Zealand region that breeding Mottled Petrels must fly such distances? We doubt it.

The age structure of New Zealand storm-driven birds such as Antarctic Fulmars, prions and the Kerguelen Petrel clearly shows that fledglings have a much greater range than adults (Harper, 1980; Veitch, 1980; Imber, 1984). If it could be shown that the majority of zoneless procellariids are only five or six years old, and that the adult birds tend to remain within their adopted life zones, then we would be much closer to understanding the real nature of marine bird distributions.

The so-called "tendency to wander" by juvenile birds appears to have been largely misunderstood for many years. Baker (1978, 1980, 1982), in his challenging discussions on bird migrations, argued that post-fledglings do not "disperse" but use "exploratory migration" instead; the need to search for new feeding areas and possible places to breed which do not necessarily match those of adult birds.

Baker believes that a bird's process of familiarization with its environment consists of three parts : "(1) *exploratory migration* (i.e., the act of moving along unfamiliar routes to unfamiliar destinations but always with the intention of eventually returning to a familiar site); (2) *habitat assessment* (i.e., judging the suitability of a route or place, identifying what resources it can offer, and ranking it against other places already discovered); and (3) *navigation* (i.e., negotiating the way back to a familiar site)." Baker's hypotheses on bird migration are, at the very least, intriguing, and worthy of testing. His hypotheses could be usefully tested using colour-banded fledgling Giant Petrels, a programme initiated by Dr S. Hunter (British Antarctic Survey) as part of the International Survey of Antarctic Seabirds (ISAS). Giant Petrels are large, abundant, and easily identified birds, an excellent species with which to begin seeking some answers.

Pacific Migrations

In describing the pelagic distribution of marine birds in the eastern Bering Sea, Hunt et al. (1981) remarked : "The general pattern of bird distribution in the area is one of highly mobile units, frequently single birds, scattered over the ocean, coalescing into small or large assemblages for short periods, and then dispersing. This produces a permutating web of high and low densities over the surface waters of the eastern Bering Sea." This description typifies the birds of the Antarctic Sector of the Pacific, for without island refuges, birds can use this vast habitat only as a place to feed and as a migration corridor.

Many southern Procellariiformes engage in west–east migrations. Examples include Wandering and Royal Albatrosses, which move from their New Zealand breeding grounds to the region around the Horn and Patagonia (e.g., Robertson and Kinsky, 1972); whether these birds have a circumpolar distribution remains unproved. Subtropical Buller's Mollymawks probably travel well to the north of the Polar Front to winter in waters adjacent to the Chilean coast (Murphy, 1936). Warham (1982) reported a bird banded as a chick on The Snares being recovered on a fisherman's long-line 7,460 km away at 12°25'S, 105°06'W, some 2,000 km southwest of the Galapagos Islands. Fledgling Giant Petrels (*Macronectes* sp.) were encountered by the *Eltanin* from 21 March 1966 in position 58°06'S, 103°55'W all the way west to near the Chatham Islands (44°00'S, 176°30'W) on 25 April 1966, a distance encompassing most of the polar Pacific (P.C. Harper, pers. observ.). These birds were migrating from the New Zealand region eastwards. Diving Petrels are extremely difficult to see at sea at the best of times, but observations made in the polar Pacific between New Zealand and Chile during 1965–66 clearly indicate that some birds are migrating eastwards in the 52°–57° latitudes (Watson et al., 1971; P.C. Harper, pers. observ.). Their identity remains unknown.

BIRD DENSITIES AT SEA

Attempts to understand the relationship between oceanic birds and their prey at sea have been hastened by the need for information on human krill harvesting

(Knox, 1984) and possible oil and mineral exploitation in the Ross Sea and other basins adjacent to Antarctica. One facet of this endeavour is to obtain an index of seabird biomass.

With hindsight, it was inevitable that field observers might adopt their own approach to counting birds at sea. This made comparative analyses extremely difficult, if not impossible, to achieve with any degree of reliability. Tasker et al. (1984) have been singularly helpful to future studies by reviewing the various methods used to count seabirds from ships and proposing a standardized approach.

Problems in assessing bird numbers at sea result from several factors. Some species are attracted to ships, others avoid them. Rafts of birds resting or feeding from the surface can be invisible in a moderate swell to observers even close-by. The greatest problem, however, is surely the patchy nature of bird distributions at sea. In early March and April, one can search for days in the southeastern Pacific Ocean without seeing a single bird (P.C. Harper, pers. observ.).

Birds are highly mobile, with energy requirements related to their flying efficiency and body size. Abrams (1985) estimated that to sustain continual flight, albatrosses require between 85 g and 160 g of squid daily. Hence, with a meal of 650 g (Prince, 1980) a relatively small albatross could forage for six days, and a Wandering Albatross for 3–4 days before losing body mass. Prions, on the other hand, use 67 g of food per day for flight alone, which is over 50% of their daily energy expenditure. At 12 g per meal, they require 5–6 meals per day, or a meal every 4–5 hours, just for flight.

Such information suggests that smaller species of procellariids need to be skilled at finding plankton swarms, especially at night when the vertical migrations of krill bring these organisms to the sea surface. It follows that a ship might fortuitously steam through most of the plankton swarms with their attendant birds, or miss them entirely. Either way, the resultant data will give an erroneous picture of the biomass of birds in any particular area. Certainly, convergence zones and places of regular upwelling such as continental margin waters may seasonally generate reliable plankton stocks which may in turn routinely attract birds. However, it is our belief that, because the Antarctic Sector of the Pacific is a deep, remote ocean where there are few foci on which productive upwelling waters can develop with any predictability, any such foci are probably ephemeral and are not the consistent food resources that birds require. In consequence, Pacific birds must range widely over their ocean in search of food and this may explain why large flocks of birds, so common in the Scotia Sea, are comparatively rare in the Pacific.

FORAGING BEHAVIOUR AND FOOD

What seabirds eat and how they obtain their food has, until recently, been one of the least studied aspects of Antarctic bird ecology (Ashmole, 1971; Ainley, 1977; Croxall and Prince, 1980; Croxall, 1984; Harper et al., 1985; Schramm, 1986; Harper, 1987).

Croxall (1984) reviewed the feeding methods of seabirds and gave examples of feeding techniques based upon the terminology of Ashmole (1971) and the morphology of bill structure. Although some species scavenge food from ships and fishing vessels, most Procellariiformes appear to catch their prey at night by taking advantage of the vertical migration to the surface of zooplankton and their attendant predators such as squid and fish. During a two and a half year research period aboard U.S.N.S. *Eltanin*, one of the authors (P.C.H.) made 4,926 observations on 20 species of petrels feeding at sea. Most of these observations were made at night during oceanographic stations, when the ship's moveable signalling lights and other techniques could be effectively used to study the feeding behaviour of seabirds. Eleven feeding methods were distinguished, the most common of which were surface seizing (49.1%, used by 14 species); dipping (25.2%, 9 species), and surface plunging (c. 6%, 6 species). Seven species foraged entirely at night, and five fed by day only. Live food seen to be caught at the surface was chiefly crustaceans and squid (for further details, see Harper, 1987).

Nearly all studies on what oceanic birds eat have analyzed food samples brought by adults to feed their chicks by regurgitation (Croxall, 1984). Recent techniques of water offloading to obtain seabird stomach contents (Wilson, 1984) have lessened the need to kill birds, which therefore can be resampled as necessary (e.g., penguins (van Heezik, 1988) and Cape Pigeons (Green, 1987)).

There may be biases in data collected by both regurgitation and water offloading techniques, however. In his study of three species of gadfly petrels breeding at the Prince Edward Islands, Schramm (1986) showed that the percentage of the total weight of stomach contents regurgitated by chicks was 69% (range 0–100%) for *Pterodroma macroptera*, 29% (33–73%) for *P. brevirostris*, and 7% (0–89%) for *P. mollis*. He stated that "it was therefore necessary to kill chicks to obtain representative samples of stomach contents."

On the basis of such studies, some authors (e.g., Abrams, 1985) have classified seabirds as planktivores, squid-eaters, piscivores, or "mixed". Such classifications are open to error for the following reasons.

1. There is a lack of sufficient seasonal data to determine whether birds take the same types of food prey throughout the year. Intuitively, one would expect this notion to be extremely unlikely, and that winter prey ought to be quite different from summer prey. For example, breeding birds, because of their restricted foraging zones, may be less choosy in their food preferences than they are at other times. A counter argument to this might assert that because more prey species are available to birds in summer they merely take advantage of this abundance of available food. Which, if either, of these hypotheses is correct is not known.

As an example, the Broad-billed Prion (*Pachyptila vittata*) takes copepods and other crustaceans during summer, but catches small squid at other times, especially during winter when crustaceans are much less plentiful. The bill of *P. vittata* is remarkably structured to sieve small plankton such as copepods from the water (Murphy, 1936) yet is also efficient at grasping and holding squid approximately 50 mm in length (Harper, 1987). Using Abram's terminology, *P. vittata* could be regarded as a planktivore in summer, and a squid-eater in winter.

In another important corollary to the above, Hunter (1983) showed that differences in diet are greater between sexes than between species in the sexually dimorphic Giant Petrels (*Macronectes giganteus* and *M. halli*) at South Georgia where males take more carrion and females more crustaceans. If this occurs in other sexually dimorphic procellariids, then the true nature of interspecific and intersexual competition, and niche partioning among such oceanic birds may prove more challenging to researchers than is currently realized.

2. In analyzing regurgitated food samples and gizzard contents, there is a strong bias towards hard-bodied prey. Some soft-bodied food can pass through the gut of prions and shearwaters quickly, such that the glandular stomach is empty about five hours after food intake (P.C. Harper, pers. observ.).

3. Adult birds may collect different foods for their chicks than for their own energy needs (e.g., Bradstreet and Brown, 1985). This can be tested experimentally by analyzing the foods of non-breeding birds and comparing them with those of breeding birds.

4. *Pterodroma* petrels are often cited as squid-eaters (e.g., Imber, 1973; Abrams, 1985; Schramm, 1986) which, of course, they are, but some species are also extremely adept at catching crustaceans from the sea surface (Harper, 1987). Which of these prey species is the more important component in the diet of these birds? And does the important prey change throughout the year? Data are lacking.

5. Griffiths (1983) suggested that Snow and Antarctic Petrels are restricted to areas of sea ice because of their non-specialized, flapping flight which, although more expensive energetically than the gliding flight of most pelagic procellariids (Pennycuick, 1972) allows them to exploit the generally unpredictable wind gradients associated with polar sea ice and around icebergs (Fig. 10.6). A lack of diet specialization enables Snow and Antarctic Petrels to feed opportunistically on crustaceans, fish and squid. Is this lack of diet specialization a summer feature, or is it prevalent throughout the year in these species?

Precisely what the correlations are between bird abundance at sea, their energy requirements, and their "principal food types" will remain open to speculation until much more information on foraging behaviour and the seasonal nature of foods taken by birds is available.

Whether the Antarctic Sector of the Pacific will be the place for such oceanic bird studies appears unlikely. Future prospects for ornithological research in the Antarctic Sector of the Pacific look certain to be largely landbased, with radio telemetry used to follow some birds during their foraging to sea. Improvements in miniaturization and placement of transmitters on birds, which can supply data to satellites passing overhead, may provide the vital key to discovering where birds go during the Antarctic winter. The formidable costs of putting scientific research ships into remote areas appears, at least for the present, to mean the end of prolonged scientific journeys such as those of the U.S.N.S. *Eltanin* in the 1960s. Ornithological observations from an increasing number of tourist ships frequenting southern seas (e.g., Rogers, 1980) will continue to provide a useful, if tenuous, link to our understanding of the distribution of marine birds at sea.

Fig. 10.6. Snow Petrel in the Ross Sea.

CHAPTER 11

ENVIRONMENTAL AND POLLUTION ASPECTS

M.R. Gregory

INTRODUCTION

For centuries, the world's oceans were viewed as a vast sink into which one could cast waste of any kind. In the past couple of decades, however, there has been a growing awareness that the oceans do not possess an infinite capacity to absorb the wastes of modern industrial society. Whilst there is some general consensus that the 'health' of northern hemisphere seas, and particularly inshore waters adjacent to heavily populated and industrialized regions, has been progressively deteriorating, there has been little comment on the state of the Southern Ocean. Lying, as it does, remote from industrial pollution sources, with little shipping traffic and minimal population pressure, there is a widely held belief that these waters remain largely in a pristine state. Furthermore, geographic isolation, together with the vastness and storminess of this very dynamic ocean, ensure that globally-identified significant marine pollutants, such as hydrocarbons, polychlorinated hydrocarbons, sewage, heavy metals and radioactive waste, are so dispersed and diluted that any environmental impact is inconsequential (e.g., Waldichuk, 1977). Nevertheless, some concern is gathering over the increasing evidence of both local and regional contamination of these southern waters and adjacent shores.

Sources of marine pollution are accidental, incidental and deliberate, and may be either on- or off-shore. Global distribution of pelagic tar balls and persistent synthetic debris suggests spread from frequently traversed tanker routes (e.g., Levy et al., 1981) and other well-travelled shipping lanes (e.g., Horsman, 1982) as well as both local and distant-water fishing activities (e.g., Merrell, 1980, 1984; Mattlin and Cawthorn, 1986). Ocean dump sites (Dahlberg and Day, 1985) are of comparable importance to land-derived, often river-borne, industrial effluent, commercial and domestic waste and casual recreational litter (e.g., Dixon and Dixon, 1981; Laist, 1987). In their review of marine by pollution around New Zealand, Ridgway and Glasby (1984) noted that coastal waters were by many criteria uncontaminated, particularly if compared to the North Atlantic. The only area of concern which they identified was sewage disposal in semi-enclosed waters near metropolitan centres.

The pioneering studies of Russell (1885, 1897) on driftwood and icebergs have long established the dominating role in Southern Ocean circulation of the west-wind driven, easterly flowing Circumpolar Current (cf. Patterson and Whitworth, this volume). This current is evident both from oceanographic data and also from reports of pumice from the 1962 South Sandwich Islands eruption which reached southern New Zealand some four years later (Coombs and Landis, 1966). In addition, there are numerous reports of exotic driftwood and seeds stranding on

Subantarctic and maritime Antarctic Island shores (e.g., Barber et al., 1959; Smith, 1985). Whilst this circumpolar broadcasting is noteworthy, floating debris also tends to concentrate along oceanic fronts (Heaton et al., 1980; Bourne and Clark, 1984; Gregory et al., 1984b) and cast up on windward shores (Gregory, 1987).

METHODS/OBSERVATIONS

This review deals primarily with observations made and data acquired over the austral summers of 1981/82, 1982/83, early 1985 and 1985/86 during the course of an ongoing research programme on marine pollution between New Zealand and Antarctica. Some preliminary results, together with the descriptive details and tabulation of raw data lists, are to be found in the reports of Gregory et al. (1984a) and Gregory (1987). Accessible shores around New Zealand's Subantarctic islands and along the Victoria Land and Ross Island coasts of the Ross Dependency have been surveyed extensively on foot for stranded seaborne litter, whilst the quantities afloat have been established using a neuston net (Fig. 11.1).

PLASTICS AND THE SUBANTARCTIC ISLANDS

A great diversity of discarded plastic and other manufactured objects wash up on the shores of the Subantarctic Islands (Figs 11.2 and 11.3). Plastic crates, con-

Fig. 11.1 Aluminum-framed, otter-style neuston net used in surface trawling for pelagic plastics and tar balls; suspended over ship's side (a) and streaming away from ship's side (b). The mouth of the frame is 0.4 m x 0.4 m.

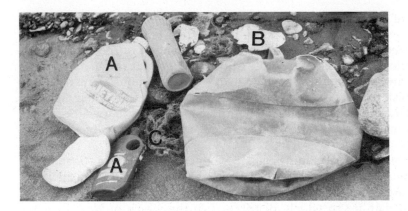

Fig. 11.2. Plastic items washed up on the sandy beach of North West Bay, Campbell Island. The large crushed container is of French origin, and the two smaller items (A) are of U.K. manufacture. Note the pieces of broken high density plastic fishing float (B) and cordage (C).

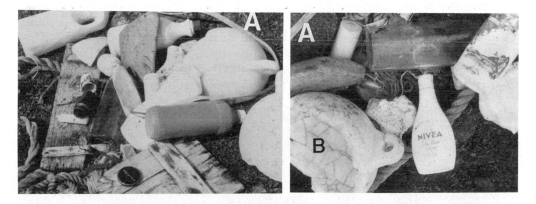

Fig. 11.3 Assembled representative items recovered in the vicinity of Derry Castle Reef, Enderby Island. Note the polypropylene strapping (A), cordage, parts of wooden packing crates, and also incipient crazing evident on the inside of a broken high density plastic fishing float (B).

tainers and bottles in varying shapes, colours and sizes, with a multitude of uses from the cosmetic and medical to detergents and agricultural chemicals abound. Their various caps and tops are also abundant. Polypropylene strapping in all lengths up to several metres, and generally blue but sometimes yellow, together with varying-sized chunks of foamed (polystyrene) plastic are widespread. Polythene sheeting and bags of all sizes are quite common. Several bulky (c. 5 kg) masses of colourless plastic wrapping sheet were also recorded.

Small pieces of string and twine, together with frayed rope and cordage, frequently green or orange, were ever present. Knotted, tangled and lengthy (> 10 m) pieces of heavy rope and hawsers, as well as general purpose cargo and fishing net of various dimensions are quite common (Figs 11.3 and 11.4). Several kinds of plastic and aluminium fishing floats are a conspicuous element of the litter. Other persistent items include glass bottles, light bulbs, disposable cigarette lighters, cloth and clothing and footware, but these together with metallic objects such as drums, cans, tins and aerosol containers are seldom as visually obvious as the plastic debris.

The quantity of smaller degrading plastic fragments observed is surprisingly small, when the numbers of larger more or less unbroken as well as crushed and partly broken plastic containers are considered. Small virgin plastic granules (or nibs) of the kind that are so widely distributed in the wrack of New Zealand beaches (Gregory, 1978) have not been found on these Subantarctic island shores.

Paper and cardboard containers or boxes, together with cellophane and other wrapping materials of the kinds which are common in the domestic litter of mainland New Zealand shores (e.g., Hayward, 1984; Ridgway and Glasby, 1984) are a very minor component of that stranding on these remote, seldom visited, islands.

Pieces of lumber, dunnage, sawn and dressed timber, and parts of packing crates and boxes, together with obvious ship wreckage such as spars and fittings, are particularly plentiful near Derry Castle Reef, Enderby Island, and minor quantities were found elsewhere. Natural driftwood is not uncommon. Most pieces are small and gnarled and, like the worked wood, bleached white from long exposure to the elements and much abraded and worn. Rounded pumice clasts, up to and exceeding 300 mm across, are almost invariably present.

Fig. 11.4. Large piece of (green) netting stranded on Enderby Island.

DISTRIBUTION AND SOURCES

The amounts of seaborne plastic and other persistent synthetic litter being cast up on the larger Subantarctic islands are greatest on windward (western) shores such as North West Bay, Campbell Island, and Derry Castle Reef, Enderby Island, and least on leeward (eastern) shores (cf. Gregory, 1987). This same pattern is also evident around the semi-enclosed waters of Port Ross, Auckland Islands. Few littering items appear on the protected south facing sandy beach of Enderby Island. Across the harbour some 5 km to the southeast, litter concentrates on the narrow west-facing bouldery beach of Ewing Island, but it is not evident on its open-ocean eastern side. At the southern end of the Auckland Islands, plastic, wood and rubber items and other flotsam and jetsam are swept through Victoria Passage or blasted over Fairchilds Garden, Adams Island. It spreads eastwards in diminishing quantities along the shores of Carnley Harbour (Gregory, 1987).

The cliff-girt coasts of the smaller island groups (The Snares, Antipodes and Bounty Islands) provide little chance for litter accumulation and fewer for inspection. Where examined, only minor quantities, mostly chunks of foamed plastic and plastic strapping together with pieces of wood, cord and the rare fishing float, were identified (Gregory, 1987). Floating debris of all kinds tends to be entrapped in surge pools and guts around all these islands. On the barren Bounty Islands, some items have been driven by wind, far above the wave-swept zone.

Today, apart from the permanent occupants of the meteorological station at the head of Perseverance Harbour, Campbell Island, the only human presence on these islands, which are otherwise nature reserves with restricted entry by permit, are occasional scientific parties who stay from several days to a month or more and sporadic day trippers from passing tourist vessels.

It follows that the plastics and other persistent litter on these shores are unlikely to have a local land-based origin or reflect casual visitors. Indeed, until quite recently, the meterorological station's residents dumped their domestic garbage directly into the waters of Perseverance Harbour and yet, apart from a couple of confectionary wrappers, no modern litter is to be seen on nearby shores — presumably the strong westerly winds carried this material out to sea (Gregory, 1987).

The character, composition and country of origin for the plastic and other persistent synthetic litter (Table 11.1), on these remote shores, suggest that it is introduced from commercial fishing activity around the region, with particular emphasis to be placed on the lucrative squid fishery centred close offshore around these islands. Several reports have drawn attention to the noticeable increase in materials of these kinds over the past decade or more, and which have accompanied expansion of the fishing industry in coastal and distant waters of New Zealand's Exclusive Economic Zone (e.g., Hayward, 1984; Ridgway and Glasby, 1984; Cawthorn, 1985; Mattlin and Cawthorn, 1986). There is conclusive evidence that some contamination of shores around Port Ross comes from domestic trash and broken fishing gear indiscriminately thrown overboard from vessels seeking haven from the stormy seas outside this harbour (Gregory, 1987; M.W. Cawthorn, pers. comm.).

TABLE 11.1

Summary of numbers of those plastic items on New Zealand's Subantarctic island shores whose country of origin could be determined (for details see Gregory, 1987).

Locality Source	Campbell Island	Carnley Harbour	Enderby and Ewing Islands	The Snares	Total
Asia	1	2	8		11
United Kingdom	3		2		5
New Zealand			4		4
Australia			3		3
Spain		1	1		2
Bulgaria			1		1
France	1				1
Norway			1		1
U.S.S.R.			1		1
Argentina				1	1

It is now recognized that enormous quantities of plastic and other persistent debris are afloat today across the global ocean (Laist, 1987; Pruter, 1987). It has been suggested by Horsman (1982) that there is a daily contribution of at least 600,000 plastic containers from merchant ships alone to the estimated 6.4×10^6 tonne yr^{-1} that is dumped overboard worldwide (NAS, 1975). As a typical example, Merrell (1980) indicated that 1,635 tonne yr^{-1} of fishing gear was being lost in waters off Alaska and that, on the island of Amchitka, this litter together with discarded garbage increased in quantity rapidly during 1972–82 (from 122 to 345 kg km^{-1} of beach) but this decreased by 1982 to 255 kg km^{-1} (Merrell, 1984).

Whilst it is clear that quantities of discarded fishing gear and other litter stranded on New Zealand's Subantarctic islands are not yet of the magnitude apparent on Northern Hemisphere shores adjacent to heavily fished areas, that is no reason for complacency. With expanding distant water fisheries all around the Southern Ocean, quantities of discarded fishing gear and other litter can only increase. Already significant amounts of this litter are being reported from amongst the wood and pumice strewn wrack of the South Shetland Island (Torres and Gajardo, 1985), the Falklands and South Georgia (Croxall et al., 1984), as well as Heard and Macquarie Islands (H.R. Burton, pers. comm.). Plastic objects, and other artefacts of local and distant origin, are also not uncommon on the shores of Prince Edward and Marion Islands as well as those of Gough, Tristan da Cunha and Inaccessible Islands in the African Sector of the Southern Ocean (Ryan, 1987a). Further evidence of this wide dispersal in the circumpolar current is the discovery of an Argentinian fishing float at The Snares Islands (C.M. Miskelly, pers. comm.), a large French plastic chemical container, possibly from Kerguelen, stranding on the sandy beach of North West Harbour, Campbell Island, and South African drift cards reaching Macquarie Island and New Zealand (Gregory, 1987).

From the numerous reports of Southern Ocean seabirds ingesting the small virgin plastic granules, as well as other plastics (Table 11.2), it is evident that these pollutants have wide circumpolar distribution, although not with the density found in the Northern Hemisphere (cf. Day et al., 1985). Seasonal migrants may bring some plastic granules with them from the North before feeding commences (e.g., Skira, 1986) but this is not likely to be a source of great importance (cf. Harper and Fowler, 1987).

From the data in Gregory et al. (1984b) and Gregory (1987), it is estimated that virgin plastic granules are dispersed with densities of 15–20 km^{-2} across the remote higher latitude (45°–60°S) waters south of New Zealand. This figure is substantially less than that of 1,500–3,600 km^{-2} recorded by Morris (1980) for the Cape Basin of the South Atlantic lying west of southern Africa, and a region also under the influence of the strong circum-Antarctic west wind drift, although at a lower latitude (c. 35°S). At > 10,000 km^{-2} (Hauraki Gulf) and > 40,000 km^{-2} (Cook Strait), pellet densities for inshore New Zealand waters are considerably greater, whilst across the South Pacific Ocean north of New Zealand a figure of c. 1,000 km^{-2} is appropriate (unpubl. data).

Although the data base is inadequate, available evidence suggests there is a strong latitudinal gradient in the areal density distribution of virgin plastic granules in passing southwards from the southern Pacific and Atlantic (and ? Indian) Oceans (> 1,000 km^{-2}) to the Southern Ocean (< 20 km^{-2}). It is inferred (Gregory et al., 1984b) that the southward spread of plastic and other persistent synthetic pelagic debris is effectively arrested at the Polar Front, along which it tends to accumulate with other flotsam (Fig. 11.5). Drifting garbage is known to accumulate at the Humbolt Front off Valparaiso, Chile (Bourne and Clarke, 1984) and has been noted along windrows in the Hauraki Gulf, New Zealand (pers. observ.).

Ross Sea Beaches

Very minor amounts of seaborne man-made debris reach these shores and it is all demonstrably of local origin (Gregory et al., 1984b). The only material to be at all persistent is dressed lumber (Fig. 11.6), much of which appears to come from disintegrating cargo pallets. Exotic logs like those reaching Macquarie, South Sandwich and Campbell Islands (Barber et al., 1969; Smith, 1985; Gregory, 1987) are never seen. Netting, floats and other evidence of distant pelagic fishing activity have not been encountered (Gregory et al., 1984b). Apart from relics of the "Heroic" era spread about at Cape Evans, the most unsightly localities are dump sites at McMurdo Sound and Hallett Stations. Debris-laden, ice-bonded rafts calve from the former and join islands of inorganic waste dumped for disposal on annual sea ice. Sunken debris locally litters the seafloor and has had some detrimental impact on the benthic biota of McMurdo Sound (Dayton and Robilliard, 1971). The rubbish dump of abandoned Hallett Station lies exposed at the foreshore and is today being eroded by ice push and wave action. Released debris

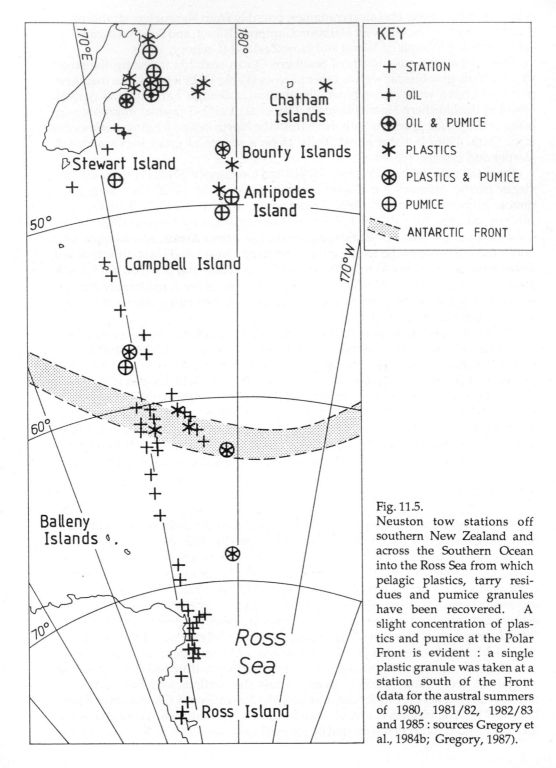

KEY

+ STATION

+ OIL

⊕ OIL & PUMICE

✳ PLASTICS

⊛ PLASTICS & PUMICE

⊕ PUMICE

ANTARCTIC FRONT

Fig. 11.5.
Neuston tow stations off
southern New Zealand and
across the Southern Ocean
into the Ross Sea from which
pelagic plastics, tarry residues and pumice granules
have been recovered. A
slight concentration of plastics and pumice at the Polar
Front is evident : a single
plastic granule was taken at a
station south of the Front
(data for the austral summers
of 1980, 1981/82, 1982/83
and 1985 : sources Gregory et
al., 1984b; Gregory, 1987).

Fig. 11.6. Lumber thrown up on the beach at Foyn Island in the Possession Group, northern Ross Sea. Size and shape of some pieces suggest that they come from disintegrating discarded cargo pallets with a source at the abandoned Hallet Station over 50 km to the south.

spreads northwards along the coast (Gregory et al., 1984b). A further source of litter pollution exists in domestic garbage and trash dumped haphazardly overboard in the traditional seafarer manner (Fig. 11.7), since vessels operating in this region seldom have onboard incineration or other disposal facilities.

Gregory et al. (1984b) suggested that pollutants from these sources spread northwards along the coast (see Fig. 11.11) driven by the strong clockwise gyral circulation of the western Ross Sea, which effectively isolates this pelagic litter system from any exchange with material trapped at the Polar Front to the north.

Fig. 11.7. Ships's garbage afloat on a tranquil Ross Sea.

An encrusting biota, of the kind common in middle and low latitudes (Winstone, 1982; Gregory, 1983), has not so far been observed on metal, wood, plastic and other items of the litter stranding around the Ross Sea (Gregory et al., 1984b).

Gregory et al. (1984b) expressed the opinion that, while the minor quantities of pollutants stranding on these high latitude shores are aesthetically distasteful, they are not of any great environmental consequence at present. On the other hand, and although not a marine pollution matter in the strict sense, it should be noted that Johnston (1971) has recorded the death of skuas (*Catharacta maccormicki*) at Cape Hallett through crop rupture following ingestion of corn cobs.

ENVIRONMENTAL IMPLICATIONS

There can be little question that the presence of plastic debris and other persistent synthetic litter on remote and wilderness beaches, let alone shores close to metropolitan centres, is aesthetically offensive. While larger items are a particular eyesore to most observers, the environmental hazards and problems they and less conspicuous smaller fragments present are not so clearly manifest.

Entanglements

There are numerous reports of marine mammals, reptiles, birds and fish becoming entangled in marine litter, particularly abandoned netting, strapping loops and recently the plastic carrying yokes for six-packs. Marine mammals appear particularly susceptible because of their well known curiosity in, and attraction to, floating rubbish of all kinds. The problem has been widely publicized for the lucrative fishing grounds of the North Pacific and Alaska where the annual mortality of northern fur seals has been estimated to exceed 50,000 (Coleman and Wehl, 1984; Wallace, 1985). Ultimate death comes from starvation, mutilation, laceration and infection, drowning or increased vulnerability to predation (e.g., Fowler, 1987; Laist, 1987). There are also reports of rope and plastic neck collars on Cape fur seals (*Arctocephalus pusillus*) from Southern Africa (Shaughnessy, 1980) and Antarctic fur seals (*Arctocephalus gazella*) from South Georgia (Bonner and McCann, 1982).

There is increasing evidence that the same problems are developing in the waters around New Zealand and its Subantarctic islands. Since an initial observation in 1975, there have been increasingly frequent reports of New Zealand fur seals (*Arctocephalus forsteri*) and the Hooker's sea lion (*Phocarctos hookeri*) which is endemic from Cook Strait to Campbell Island and the Auckland Islands, being snared in netting (Fig. 11.8) or collared by plastic loops (see Cawthorn, 1985, 1987). Both species are acknowledged to be endangered. Some indication of the magnitude of the threat is evident in Dawson and Slooten's (1987) claim that accidental gillnet entanglement annually kills 10–15% of Hector's dolphins (*Cephalorhynchus hectori*) in the Banks Peninsula area; they have estimated that the entire population of this endemic species is only 3–4,000 individuals. There are few records of cetacean entanglement around New Zealand waters, probably because large set nets and traps are not a feature of the local inshore fishery. Cawthron (1985) has reported on two recent instances which at the time received reasonably wide publicity. In 1979, a distressed killer whale (*Orcinus orca*) fouled by ropes and floats was observed in the eastern Bay of Plenty. In February 1984, a juvenile male southern right whale (*Eubalaena australis*), which died shortly after stranding north of Banks Peninsula, was found to have a lengthy piece of polypropylene rope and attached small polystyrene buoy, wrapped around its tail stock. Cawthorn (1985) noted that the rope had cut 200 mm into the leading edges of both flukes.

Fig. 11.8. Hooker's sea lion (*Phocarctos hookeri*) entangled in netting on deck of trawler near the Auckland Islands (Photo : M. Donoghue, World Wildlife Fund).

For the Subantarctic islands, as well as mainland New Zealand, Cawthron (1985) identified hard, embossed polypropylene strapping loops and crimped bands as constituting a particular hazard to seals and sea lions. He made a general appeal for them to be cut or severed before being discarded rather than being simply slipped off any package. Subsequent observations suggest that this plea is being heeded for very few uncut straps were seen in a 1985 survey of the southern regions (Gregory, 1987).

Seabirds of the New Zealand region are also at risk as recent illustrations in Cawthorn (1987) would attest. He recorded the death of a black-backed gull

(*Larus dominicanus*) following capture in a plastic six-pack carrying yoke, and also the drowning of 14 spotted shags in an Otago Harbour set net. Incidental snaring of both birds and fish by ghost-fishing abandoned or derelict drift nets is a further issue that needs to be addressed (cf. Mattlin and Cawthorn, 1986).

The magnitude of the entanglement mortality problem for the Subantarctic islands is impossible to assess. It has been estimated that up to 130 sea lions die through drowning in trawl nets each year (Donoghue, 1987). However, no animals which had been mutilated through entrapment, snared or collared were sighted during an extensive survey in 1985 (Gregory, 1987), although several bird carcasses entrapped in monofilament fishing line were noted on the Bounty Islands.

Encrustations

Plastics and other synthetic litter afloat on the global ocean afford an important and expanding ecologic niche for a pseudoplanktonic biota (Winston, 1982). Many taxa, including foraminiferids, hydroids, bryozoans, calcareous annelid tubes, barnacles and coralline algae, as well as diatoms and bacteria are known to encrust or attach to floating plastic (see Gregory, 1983). In surveys of Southern Ocean waters and shores between New Zealand and the Ross Sea, the only encrusters so far identified have been goose barnacles and *"Spirorbis"* on larger plastic objects (Gregory, 1987). No biota have been identified on any of those few virgin plastic granules collected south of New Zealand.

Patches of lichen, identified as *Canderlariella* sp. and *Lecanora dispersa* Agg. by C. Meurk (pers. comm.) encrust several large pieces of abraded dense plastic from broken fishing floats, which had been cast-up high and dry beyond the reach of waves on the northeast shore of Enderby Island (Auckland Islands). These are taxa characteristic of rocky, Subantarctic island, coastal environments.

Ingestion

Ingestion of plastic pollutants has been recorded in at least 50 species of marine birds worldwide (Day et al., 1985). Although there are several records from Australasian waters and elsewhere around the Southern Ocean (Table 11.2), where there is evidence for prions ingesting plastics from the early 1960s (Harper and Fowler, 1987), quantity and frequency for the region do not yet seem to have reached the Northern Hemisphere levels reported in the comprehensive review of Day et al. (1985). Plastic objects have been identified in the gizzards and proventriculi of birds examined but never in the intestinal tract or faeces (Day et al., 1985) which is surprising because some prions can void intact fish vertebrae with no apparent difficulty (Harper and Fowler, 1987). In a review of seabird conservation in the New Zealand region, Robertson and Bell (1984) concluded that the ingestion of rubbish, plastics and plastic pellets was not a significant problem.

The small mostly colourless, virgin or raw polyethylene granules which are so abundant on New Zealand beaches (Gregory, 1978) and widely dispersed across the Southern Ocean (Gregory et al., 1984b; Gregory, 1987) are the most commonly

TABLE 11.2

Seabirds of the New Zealand region of the Southern Ocean known to ingest plastic particles (sources : Jehl et al., 1980; Reed, 1981; Bourne and Imber, 1982; Furness, 1983, 1985; Randall et al., 1983; Day et al., 1985; Brown et al., 1986; Skira, 1986; Harper and Fowler, 1987; Ryan, 1987b, c; Ryan and Jackson, 1987).

Common Name	Formal Scientific Name
Blue Penguin (?)	*Eudyptula minor*
Rockhopper Penguin	*Eudyptes chrysocome*
Adélie Penguin (?)	*Pygoscelis adeliae*
Wandering Albatross	*Diomedea exulans*
Southern Royal Albatross	*Diomedea epomophora*
Salvin's Mollymawk	*Diomedea cauta salvini*
Black-browed Mollymawk	*Diomedea melanophris*
Grey-headed Mollymawk	*Diomedea chrysostoma*
Yellow-nosed Mollymawk	*Diomedea chlororhynchus*
Sooty Albatross	*Phoebetria fusca*
Northern Giant Petrel	*Macronectes halli*
Southern Giant Petrel	*Macronectes giganteus*
Cape Pigeon	*Daption capense*
Kerguelen Petrel	*Pterodroma brevirostris*
Soft-plumaged Petrel	*Pterodroma mollis*
Atlantic Petrel	*Pterodroma incerta*
Blue Petrel	*Halobaena caerulea*
Broad-billed Prion	*Pachyptila vittata*
Antarctic Prion	*Pachyptila desolata*
Salvin's Prion	*Pachyptila salvini*
Thin-billed Prion	*Pachyptila belcheri*
Fairy Prion	*Pachyptila turtur*
Great Shearwater	*Puffinus gravis*
Sooty Shearwater	*Puffinus griseus*
Little Shearwater	*Puffinus assimilis*
Grey-backed Storm Petrel	*Garrodia nereis*
White-faced Storm Petrel	*Pelagodroma marina*
White-bellied Storm Petrel	*Fregetta grallaria*
Gannet (?)	*Sula serrator*
Southern Skua	*Catharacta antarctica*
Black-backed Gull	*Larus dominicanus*

ingested form of plastic pollutants in this region. Following the wreck of several hundred sea birds on beaches of the west coast of the North Island, New Zealand, in September 1981, Reed (1981) noted that all 27 Blue Petrels dissected contained plastic pellets. In contrast, only one of 26 Kerguelen Petrels contained a plastic pellet (Reed, 1981). Similarly, in Victoria, Australia, Brown et al. (1986) found plastic pellets in 60% of beach-washed Blue Petrels but only in one Kerguelen Petrel. Furthermore, Harper and Fowler (1987) have shown that between 1958 and 1977 over 15% of storm-killed prions recovered from beaches near Wellington contained plastic pellets, with incidence being greatest in local residents (Broad-billed Prion, Fairy Prion) and least in Indian Ocean migrants (Thin-billed Prion).

Larger fragments of plastic and items such as bottle tops and small fishing floats are also ingested (Day et al., 1985). Gregory (1987) reported a Salvin's Mollymawk chick on Proclamation Island (Bounty Islands) regurgitating a small handline type, orange fishing float at the foot of an observer, and various plastic objects (Fig. 11.9) are scattered around Southern Royal Albatross nesting sites on Campbell Island. It has also been noted that pieces of cordage and strips of blue coloured plastic, derived from packing straps, were incorporated into nesting mounds of Salvin's Mollymawk on both the Bounty and Snares Islands (Gregory, 1987). Regurgitations are not necessary evidence for extensive contamination of local waters, for albatrosses from Auckland Island are known to feed off Sydney, Australia (C.J.R. Robertson, pers. comm.). Although Day et al. (1985) commented that the phenomenon is not known in penguins, several pieces of shredded plastic and a small ball of thread partly buried amongst pebbles of Adélie Penguin nesting sites at Cape Adare, North Victoria Land, Antarctica, suggest that this species may also in rare instances ingest plastics. Careful inspection of several other large Adélie Penguin colonies around the Ross Sea revealed no further examples.

Whilst some species of seabird apparently ingest plastic randomly, the feeding strategies of many suggest selective preference for certain types of plastic (Day et al., 1985; Harper and Fowler, 1987). Plastic objects of all consumable sizes are probably mistaken for normally-sought prey. The encrusting biota is seldom present in other than minor amounts, suggesting it is not an important food objective. Prince (1980) has commented that red coloured toothpaste-tube tops and melamine laminate, regurgitated by Grey-headed Albatross chicks on Bird Island, South Georgia, could easily have been mistaken for reddish crustacean prey. Similarly many of the plastic items observed in Southern Royal Albatross regurgitations from Campbell Island sites are red or pinkish (Fig. 11.9). It has also been suggested that small colourless virgin plastic pellets could be taken on board as an unwitting substitute for the pumice granules that many seabirds use as cropstones. Granule- and larger-sized pieces of pumice are broadcast across surface waters of the Southern Ocean (Gregory et al., 1984b; Gregory, 1987) and frequently ingested by seabirds of the region.

Effects

Intuitively, many would argue that ingestion of plastics should be harmful to life, if not a significant cause of death. The direct effects, it has been suggested (e.g., Bourne and Imber, 1982; Day et al., 1985), could include intestinal blockage leading to starvation, or local ulceration of delicate internal tissue following damage by sharp and irregularly jagged objects. The "quality" of life and repro-ductive performance could also be detrimentally affected. On the other hand, it must also be acknowledged that plastic granules could behave as crop stones im-proving digestive efficiency through grinding action (Day, 1980).

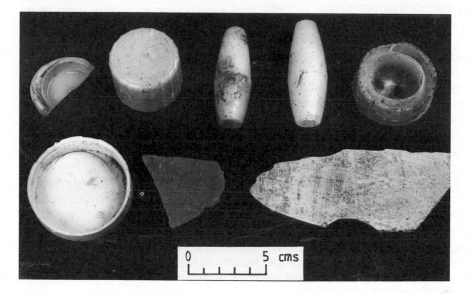

Fig. 11.9. Regurgitated plastic artefacts from a Southern Royal Albatross nesting site on Campbell Island; all but two of the items are pink or reddish in colour (Collected by C.J.R. Robertson).

The frequency with which seabirds swallow, and regurgitate, naturally occurring, hard and resistant objects such as pebbles, bones, nuts and squid beaks with little apparent ill-effect (Kenyon and Kridler, 1969; Rothstein, 1973; Hays and Cormons, 1974) suggests that plastic items are similarly unlikely to be of any great biological consequence (Gregory, 1978, 1983; Bourne and Imber, 1982; Day et al., 1985). Whilst the presence of ingested plastics is, without question, of concern to all environmentalists, recent studies suggest that it seldom impairs digestive efficiency (Harper and Fowler, 1987; Ryan and Jackson, 1987) and the direct risk to adult birds is considered minimal (Fry et al., 1987). Larger plastic objects may well cause death of seabirds through intestinal blockage (e.g., Dickerman and Goelet, 1987), but, with pellets and granules, it is difficult to decide whether they are a cause or effect of starvation (Bourne and Imber, 1982; Harper and Fowler, 1987).

Although ingestion of discarded plastic items by larger marine animals appears to be less of a problem than entanglement (Laist, 1987), intestinal blockage leads to some deaths (cf. Wehle and Coleman, 1983). Cawthorn (1985) has cited two New Zealand examples. Leatherback turtles, although uncommon, are not rare visitors to these waters. Necroscopy of a specimen that died shortly after beaching near Whakatane, Bay of Plenty, in the summer of 1979–80 revealed an oesophagus packed by polythene bread bags. It is assumed these were mistaken for its normal prey of salps and medusoids, for marine turtles are known to have an appetite for synthetic drift items (Wehle and Coleman, 1983; Balazs, 1985). Similarly, a juvenile minke whale (*Balaenoptera acutorostrata*), stranded at

Palliser Bay east of Wellington in 1976, had a polythene bag stuck deep in its oesophagus.

Degradation and Persistence

Those very properties which mankind finds so highly desirable in plastics, lightness, strength, manufacturing adaptability and flexibility, together with relative inertness and resistance to degradational processes, are also the reasons why today they are a marine pollutant of global proportions. At the present time, it is difficult to estimate disappearance rates for plastics and other synthetic debris from the marine milieu (Gerrodette, 1985).

Gregory (1978, 1983) cited evidence to suggest that, despite their unquestioned durability, raw plastic granules both afloat and left stranded and exposed on sandy shores at low to middle latitudes may have a life expectancy of five years or less. Ingested pellets have an expected half life of at least one year (Ryan and Jackson, 1987). Progressive embrittlement through oxidative ageing may lead to initial fragmentation of fabricated high density polyethylene objects, like plastic bottles and containers, within three years of disposal at sea (Dixon and Dixon, 1981). On the other hand, antioxidants or other additives may ensure survival of 50 or more years for some monofilament netting and polypropylene cordage (Gregory, 1978; Wehle and Coleman, 1983). At higher latitudes where insolation is much less and temperatures lower, degradation rates will be reduced (Merrell, 1980; Gregory, 1987). If they survive physical battering, some objects may persist almost indefinitely.

Many plastic items cast up on the Subantarctic island shores are much abraded or exhibit other signs of physical battering and mechanical battering (Figs 11.2 and 11.3). Although impossible to quantify at present, evidence for disintegration through oxidative ageing appears to be of less significance than for comparable materials found on mainland New Zealand shores to the north. Similarly, most pellets taken from these southern waters have a fresh, non-crazed surface.

Gill net floats and sandals stranded on Amchitka island, Alaska, are often gnawed by rats (Merrell, 1980). There is no evidence of this taking place on Campbell and Enderby Islands. Lichen encrustations could also lead to the deterioration of some plastics in a manner analogous to their pedogenic weathering action on rocks (Jones et al., 1980).

Longevity of plastics and continued input of fresh material outpaces ultimate loss of visibility and/or adsorption into the environment through processes such as :
1. physical and mechanical disintegration;
2. degradation and deterioration in response to embrittlement following photo-oxidation, reaction with seawater, microbial and other biological activity;
3. burial after stranding at the shore;
4. sinking as buoyancy is lost either by fouling of marine growth or becoming water-logged.

As a consequence, unlike pelagic tar balls where numbers have reached an equilibrium state (Butler, 1975a), seaborne plastics are likely to continue increasing in quantity for the foreseeable future (Gregory, 1978).

PETROLEUM PRODUCTS

It has been variously estimated that >10[6] tonnes of petroleum hydrocarbons are yearly released into the marine milieu (NAS, 1975). Public sensitivity to the visual effects of oil slicks and tar balls (Butler, 1975a) ensures that this pollution problem attracts wide attention. The global distribution of pelagic oil and tar balls closely follows established tanker shipping routes (Levy et al., 1981). Anecdotal evidence, and what few data there are (e.g., Benzhitsky and Polikarpov, 1977; Mileykovskiy, 1979; Levy et al., 1981; Maslov and Nesterova, 1981; Ventajas and Comes, 1982), indicate that, by comparison with the North Atlantic and other heavily traversed waters, or near major industrial and population centres, those encircling Antarctica remain virtually pristine. Nevertheless, Maslov and Nesterov (1981, fig. 1), in a small scale and much simplified map, defined an isolated patch of Subantarctic water to the south of New Zealand and Tasmania where surface oil film occurs in 5% of observations (number of stations is not stated).

With increased tanker and other shipping traffic around southern Africa over the past two decades, there have been several major accidental oil spills and numerous minor incidents, and today relatively high levels of chronic oil pollution exist around the region (cf. Watling, 1980). Oil slicks and tar balls are not uncommon in surface waters around and south of Cape of Good Hope, but they disperse rapidly in these stormy seas (Eagle et al., 1979). As the "residence time" is unlikely to exceed one year (Butler, 1976b) and may be as little as 58 days (Levy and Walton, 1976), it is highly improbable pollutants from this source would ever reach waters to the south of New Zealand, for the drift transit time is a year or so (Gregory, 1987).

In August 1974, following the grounding of the VLCC *Metula*, over 400,000 barrels of light Arabian Crude were released into the Straits of Magellan. There was no clean-up response, and approximately 250 km of shoreline were contaminated. The environmental impact was considerable and included destruction of a tern (*Sterna hirundinaceae*) breeding colony which had not re-established 5 years after the event (Guzman and Campodonico, 1980). On the other hand, kelp (*Macrocystis pyrifera*) beds were little affected. Extensive ashphaltic pavements persist to this day, with some samples showing little evidence of weathering (Gundlach et al., 1982; Owens et al., 1987).

Similarly, there is evidence from South Georgia's abandoned shore whaling station that the impact of massive local hydrocarbon spills persists for many years, although the marine environment ultimately recovers (Platt, 1979).

New Zealand Waters

Stranded pelagic tar balls and degrading oily residues are rare to absent on New Zealand shores (Gregory, 1977; Oostdam, 1984) as they are elsewhere across the South Pacific Ocean (Lee, in Butler et al., 1973; Bourne, 1976; Oostdam, 1984). Even near production, storage and refinery facilities at New Plymouth and Whangarei, as well as other major ports, they are rarely encountered, and those that are have a short life expectancy on either beaches or rocky shores (pers. observ.). Whilst minor oil spills occur from time to time, clean-up response is quick, environmental impacts appear minimal, and the visual evidence seldom persists (Fig. 11.10).

Fig. 11.10. A rare sight : tar balls stranded on a sandy beach near Whangarei, northern New Zealand.

Rare oily residues and tar flecks have been recorded from Cook Strait, off Banks Peninsula as well as east of the southern South Island of New Zealand and across Chatham Rise. None has yet been recognized at over forty stations southwards across Subantarctic waters and the Polar Front to the Ross Sea (Fig. 11.5; Gregory et al., 1984b; Gregory, 1987). No tar balls or tarry encrustations have been observed on Ross Sea shores or those of New Zealand's Sub-antarctic islands despite the high level of fishing activity around the latter region (Gregory et al., 1984b; Gregory, 1987).

Oiling of Penguins and other Seabirds

Being completely aquatic, penguins are far more vulnerable to oil pollution than flighted seabirds (Clark, 1984). Around southern Africa, the Jackass Penguin (*Spheniscus demersus*) has been subjected to quite severe oil pollution with fatalities numerous and frequent (e.g., Randall et al., 1980), although an extensive bird-cleaning programme has been initiated (Kerley and Erasmus, 1987). Deaths amongst the sympatric Cape Gannet (*Sula capensis*) are less common. The Magellanic Penguin (*Sphensicus magellanicus*) of Argentinian shelf waters is under similar threat (Jehl, 1975; Perkins, 1983) but the problem here appears much less than around southern Africa.

Other major penguin populations lie south of, or remote from, major shipping routes, and are unlikely to be subjected to other than occasional oil pollution. However, there are a disturbing number of oiling reports from higher southern latitudes, which fortunately to date have involved only a few individuals. Although Croxall et al. (1984) has noted that oil pollution is not a problem for seabirds around the Antarctic Peninsula, isolated instances of fouling of Adélie Penguins (*Pygoscelis adeliae*) in the vicinity of Palmer Station are known (Parker, 1971). From South Georgia, Jehl et al. (1979) have reported freshly oiled Gentoo Penguins (*Pygoscelis papua*), while Copestake et al. (1983) recorded the oil staining of a single King Penguin (*Aptenodytes patagonica*). At Marion Island, several hundred oiled Rockhopper Penguins (*Eudyptes crestatus*) have been seen (Kerley and Erasmus, 1987). Minor oil pollution has occurred at Biae du Marin, Île de la Possession, Crozet Islands, and also at Grande Terre, Kerguelen Islands, where in 1980 a Russian tanker ran aground spilling 600 tonnes of petroleum (Jouventin et al., 1984). In none of these instances does the writer know of any report of seabird fatalities.

Sightings of oiled seabirds are not infrequent around New Zealand. Fortunately, the numbers involved are generally low. An environmentally more serious incident was the spillage of over 20,000 litres of fuel oil in Lyttelton Harbour in July 1965, which spread over a distance of almost 50 km and resulted in the loss of many seabirds (Norris, 1965). The worst affected were Spotted Shags (*Stictocarbo punctatus*) and White-flippered Penguins (*Euptytula albosignata*). Giant Petrels (*Macronectes giganteus*), Red-billed Gulls (*Larus novaehollandiae scopulinus*) and Black-backed Gulls (*Larus dominicanus*) were also affected.

During the 1972 Snares Islands Expedition, D.S. Horning (pers. comm.) observed the landing of a Snares Crested Penguin (*Eudyptes robustus*) with oil staining on its chest. There have been no further reports to this author's knowledge. During the 1985 Subantarctic Islands Expedition, no sightings were made of oil-fouled penguins or any other seabird for that matter (Gregory, 1987).

In January 1979, at least 20 oil-fouled Adelie Penguins (*Pygoscelis adeliae*) were seen at Cape Bird, Ross Island, Antarctica (Wilson, 1980). The source of this contamination was never established. It most probably came from either bilge pumping or a small spill from a passing vessel. However, there is also the possibility of a natural seep, although none has yet been reported from Antarctica (cf. Wilson et al., 1974).

EXPLORATION AND EXPLOITATION

Subantarctic New Zealand

There is considerable offshore petroleum potential for areas to the south and southeast of New Zealand (Katz, 1974; Cook and Davey, this volume). Exploratory drilling in the Great South Basin east and southeast of Stewart Island and Solander Basin immediately to the west has proved promising but exploitable hydrocabon accumulations await discovery (Sanford, 1980). Management plans prepared for The Snares, Campbell and Auckland Islands (Department of Lands and Survey, 1983, 1984, 1987) acknowledge the environmental problems that an offshore oil spill could create for these protected Nature Reserves.

Gregory (1985) has noted that Campbell, Auckland and The Snares Islands lie to the west and south of Great South Basin hydrocarbon prospects. Spills at these sources would degrade and disperse rapidly bcause of stormy seas. The persistent, strong westerly wind and wave climate should also ensure that oil slicks are carried rapidly away from these islands. Solander Trough prospects lie to windward of The Snares, but they would be a small target, and again distance and stormy seas should ensure that spills there have minimal shoreline impact. Similarly, the Bounty and Antipodes Islands, although lying downwind from possible spill sites, are small and so distant that little impact can be envisaged.

The towering cliffed and rocky coasts of these islands are high energy exposed shores which, in the event of an oil spill, can be considerd "low risk" for they would self cleanse rapidly of any impacting oil (Gregory, 1985). Wave reflection would probably keep most oil offshore. Oil fouling of the few sandy beaches is unlikely to persist for more than a few months. With the prevailing strong westerly winds, it is most improbable that oil slicks would ever reach the areally-restricted, tidal flats and salt marshes at the heads of east-facing fjards of Campbell and Auckland Islands. These are sensitive "at risk" environments, which, if experience following the *Metula* spill in the Straits of Magellan is any guide (cf. Gundlach et al., 1982), could take decades to re-establish.

Long term, chronic low-level releases of hydrocarbons from offshore production platforms, would probably have little environmental significance because of dilution, dispersal and rapid degradation. Of more immediate concern would be massive, acute, spills following catastrophic platform failure, rupture of seabed pipelines, tanker groundings or accidents involving onshore (storage) facilities. These could have immediate detrimental effects upon fisheries, sea birds and sea mammals.

One can conclude that for the present the probability of an oil spill in the vicinity of New Zealand's Subantarctic islands is extremely remote, and that clean-up intervention would only be warranted in most exceptional circumstances. There were no reported oil or other pollution incidents during exploratory drilling around this region.

Large icebergs occasionally stray from their usual southern tracks, reaching waters as far north as Chatham Rise (Brodie and Dawson, 1971; Burrows, 1976). It is not idle comment to suggest that they could be an unexpected and unpredictable threat to large, fixed, offshore production platforms, in these middle latitudes.

Ross Sea Prospects

Authorities and observers from many countries have speculated for a number of years on the hydrocarbon prospects for parts of the over-deepened continental margin encircling Antarctica (cf. Cook and Davey, this volume). Of the ten offshore basins that St. John (1986) considered to be viable hydrocarbon targets, those of the Ross Sea region rank highly (e.g., Holdgate and Tinker, 1979; Lock, 1983). Modelling studies suggest that, of the three Ross Sea basins (Fig. 11.11), the Eastern and Victoria Land basins have good exploration potential, while the Central Trough is barely marginal (Cook and Davey, 1984). Discovery of ashphaltic residues at a depth of c. 633 m near the base of CIROS–1 (Barrett, 1987) will further tantalize hydrocarbon prospectors.

Any commercial hydrocarbon development in the Ross Sea, as elsewhere around Antarctica, would of necessity be at a large scale. It is difficult to establish minimum or optimum sizes for such operations, but a productive field will need to be of giant (500 x 10^6 barrels) to supergiant (500 x 10^9 barrels) proportions, and with a daily yield capability of at least 3–400,000 barrels (see Holdgate and Tinker, 1979; Ivanhoe, 1980; Gregory, 1982; Garrett, 1985; St. John, 1986).

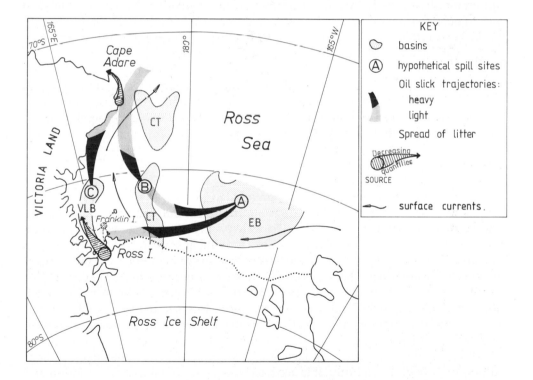

Fig. 11.11. Predicted oil-slick trajectories for hypothetical spills sited on the Eastern (A), Central (B) and Victoria Land Basins (C) of the Ross Sea. During the short, open-water summer season, most rocky shores and beaches, many of which are important penguin rookeries, of Ross Island and adjacent Victoria Land coast could be under threat, by a spill comparable in magnitude to IXTOC 1. The strong gyral circulation also spreads locally-derived litter northwards along the coast as shown (Based on Gregory, 1982, fig. 3; Gregory et al., 1984a, fig. 6; Cook and Davey, 1984, fig. 1).

Antarctica, it is widely acknowledged, is the most severe, physically and technologically demanding and environmentally hazardous place on earth, in which to conduct hydrocarbon exploration and exploitation. Nevertheless, seismic surveying and the consequential exploratory drilling for identified targets in the Ross Sea could take place today using currently available technology (Anonymous, 1977; Hodgate and Tinker, 1979; Zumberge, 1979, 1982; Burroughs, 1986). Successful exploitation will require costly evolution and adaptation of technology developed for Arctic conditions (e.g., Roots, 1983), although conceptual feasibility has been demonstrated (Splettstoesser, 1979; Sanderson, 1983; St. John, 1986). There is an evolving consensus, however, that, because of economic constraints alone, hydrocarbon exploitation is unlikely in the foreseeable future (cf. Holdgate, 1984; Garrett, 1985).

Because of the great water depths of the Ross Sea (e.g., 200–900 m over prospective parts of the Victoria Land Basin) and the short open water season of 3 months or less (Keys, 1984), it has been suggested that the only sensible long-term option for oil production would be a subsea well completion (Sanderson, 1983). It would need to function without surface maintenance for at least nine months or it could be serviced by submarine — a technology awaiting development. Any subsea completion and pipeline(s) would need to be buried some 5–10 m for protection against iceberg scour. Sanderson (1983) considered that the most likely "export" method would be by seafloor storage and large icebreaking tankers (VLCC) capable of coping with ice conditions year round. Another option could be large submarines (McLaren, 1984). Alternatively, oil could be pipelined to a shore storage facility to await onward delivery.

Environmental and Pollution Aspects

Crude and processed oils vary greatly in their physical and chemical properties, although in both the lighter and more soluble aromatic fractions are highly toxic to marine life. Even in cold waters, spreading of oil as ever-thinning films on the sea surface is rapid, with slicks moving at some 60% of water current rate and 3% of wind speed. The fate and behaviour of oil spilled in cold (Arctic) ice-infested waters have been reviewed by several authors (e.g., Weller, 1980b; Nelson-Smith, 1982; Hume et al., 1983; Weeks and Weller, 1984; Mackay, 1985; Bobra and Fingas, 1986) and amongst the more important processes identified are : evaporative ageing and weathering, mechanical and physical dispersal, dissolution and emulsification, sea-ice and shoreline inter-actions and microbial activities together with seasonal factors and amount of oil that has been spilled. Although difficult to quantify, it is accepted that rates of natural degradation and decomposition are substantially slower in polar environments than they are in temperate ones. Conclusions from the extensive and important Canadian contributions to the study of oil spills in northern high latitudes (e.g., Sergy and Blackall, 1987) are not entirely relevant to the Ross Sea (Holdgate and Tinker, 1979; Keys, 1984). As examples, the Ross Sea pack-ice is lighter and there is less, thick multiyear ice than that which is experienced in the Arctic (Mitchell, 1983), water depths at likely offshore hydrocarbon prospects are too deep for the bottom-founded structures typical of the Beaufort Sea and icebergs are more numerous and larger.

Many authors have addressed the possible environmental consequences and issues likely to arise from the exploration for and exploitation of hydrocarbon resources lying beneath Antarctica's continental shelf (e.g., Elliot, 1977; Dugger, 1978; Holdgate and Tinker, 1979; Zumberge, 1979, 1982; Brewster, 1982; Gregory, 1982; Gregory and Kirk, 1983; Holdgate, 1983, 1984; Sanderson, 1983; Keys, 1984; Joyner, 1985). The environmental factors and problems identified, which are many, have been summarized by Holdgate and Tinker (1979) and repeated elsewhere (e.g., Holdgate, 1983, 1984). They are presented in Table 11.3, and only some aspects of particular relevance to the Ross Sea are developed in the following discussion. In a review of Southern Ocean pollution, some readers may consider these remarks unnecessary and little better than informed speculation. Others may be more concilliatory viewing them as anticipatory, having a forecasting role, and a necessary part of establishing the planning criteria should hydrocarbon exploration and exploitation ever eventuate around the region.

Shore Line Impact

Gregory (1982) suggested that much of the coast around the Ross Sea could be at risk following a large tanker accident, pipeline rupture, or well head blowout comparable in magnitude to the IXTOC 1 incident in Campeche Bay, Gulf of Mexico (cf. Fig. 11.11). This was the largest spill in history releasing > 4,000,000 tonnes of oil into the sea between June 3, 1979 and March 23, 1980, with impact reaching Texas beaches over 800 km from the spill site. Ross Sea impact potential would be greatest during relative ice-free periods of the brief summer season (December–March) and environmental response determined by hydrocarbon type and weather conditions at the time, as well as shore-line character and processes. Shores of the region are dominated by high ice cliffs (Gregory et al., 1984a; Kirk and Gregory, in press). Seasonally variable landfast sea ice may comprise more than 90% of the effective shore (Fig. 11.12). Ice-free or bare rocky shores comprise little more than a quarter of the coast (Fig. 11.13). The coastal categories of high ice cliffs, high rocky cliffs, low partially ice-covered rocky shores and beaches together with fast ice, identified in the mapping programme of Gregory et al. (1984a) do not fit into a hierarchy of oil spill persistence or physical sensitivity indices of the kinds favoured for mid-latitude coastal landforms (e.g., Gundlach and Hayes, 1978; Michel et al, 1978; Gregory, 1981).

Furthermore, the Arctic experience with retention indices (Nummedal, 1980) and the breakdown of major shore type into several subdivisions (e.g., McLaren, 1980; Owens et al., 1981; Sempels, 1982; Welch, 1984) is inappropriate because coastal landforms of protected low energy environments, such as marshes, lagoons, broad intertidal mud and sand flats, vegetated and non-vegetated low banks and bluffs or cliffs in weakly consolidated materials, have no expression around the Ross Sea.

From observations reported widely in the literature, it has been concluded that high ice cliffs and other permanent and seasonal ice shores around the Ross Sea

TABLE 11.3

Environmental factors affecting hydrocarbon exploration and exploitation in the Ross Sea (from Holdgate and Tinker, 1979; *additions from Zumberge, 1982).

Factors that Influence Site Selection
   Geological indications of oil potential
   Bathymetry and structure of the sea bed
   Iceberg and pack ice condition and distribution
   Currents (surface and deep)
   Climate – weather
   Special biological features of site (and alternatives)
   Cost of operation

Technological Factors that Influence Impacts
   Use of seismic explosives
   Drilling procedures and processes
   Nature of rigs or platforms
   Nature of well head completion structure (e.g., on or below seabed)
   Nature of oil storage system (e.g., seabed or shore-based tank farm)
   Nature of transport system (ship, submarine, pipeline)
   Nature of pollution control system (including training and management)
   Nature of emergency procedures (including training)
   *Short season and limitation on drilling of relief well(s)
   *Lack of timely and accurate ice-climate and weather forecasting

Environmental Factors Affecting Impact
   Types and concentration of pollutants released (e.g., oil, condensate, gas,
      drilling mud, sewage, domestic garbage)
   Rates of physical and biological degradation of hydrocarbons and other pollutants
   Rates and direction of dispersion and dilution of hydrocarbons and other pollutants
   Relative locations of accidental, incidental and deliberate releases and living targets
      (e.g., benthos, sea-ice microbial community, phytoplankton, krill and zooplankton,
      fish, seals, whales, seabirds, etc.)
   Sensitivity of living targets to hydrocarbons and other pollutants and to substances
      used in clean-up operations

would rapidly self-cleanse of any impacting oil through vigorous wave action and the abrasive effects of drifting ice (Gregory et al., 1984a). Similarly, there would be no significant retention of oil on rocky shores, whether low, glacially muted bluffs or high precipitous cliffs (Fig. 11.14), for these also would self-cleanse. In addition, landfast sea ice and a protective ice foot would further shield these shores from drifting oil.

Beaches, which are mostly composed of coarse granule sands and pebble-to-boulder-sized material constitute less than 5% of the entire coast of the western Ross Sea (Figs 11.12 and 11.13), and most are occupied by Adélie Penguin rook-

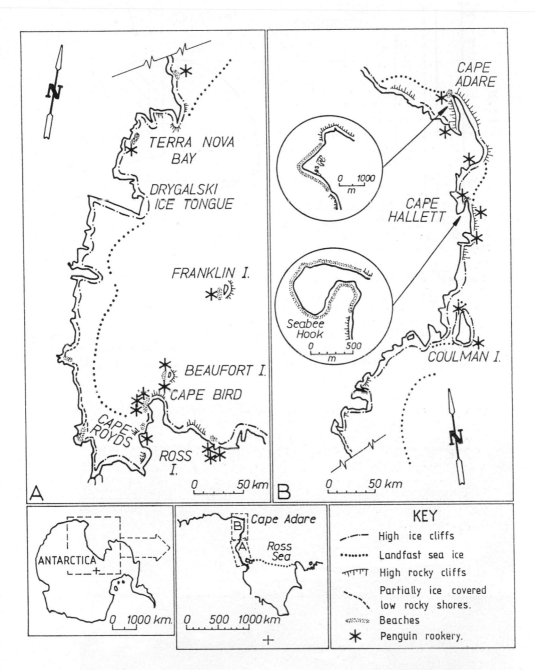

Fig. 11.12. Simplified map of coastal types for Victoria Land and Ross Island. Note the very limited distribution of beach and low rocky shore categories – environments likely to bear the brunt of any on-shore facility development.

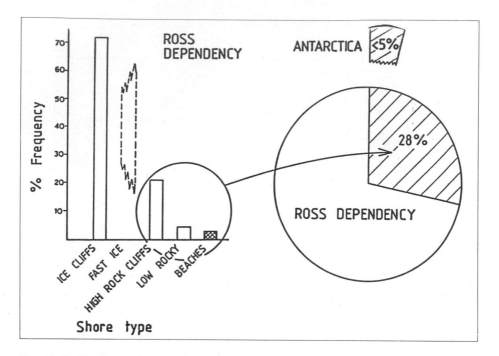

Fig. 11.13. Frequency bar graph illustrating proportions of each coastal type for the region shown in Fig. 11.12. Seasonal, ice-free shores are far more common in this region than they are for most of the continent with the exception of the Antarctic Peninsula region.

Fig. 11.14. Precipitous cliffs, like these in Cenozoic volcanic breccias south of Cape Adare, North Victoria Land, would self cleanse rapidly even when not protected by ice.

eries (Fig. 11.15). Once the protective ice-foot disintegrates and disappears from these beaches in summer, they would be wide open to oil spill contamination. In the porous, coarse gravels of the intertidal zone and wave-swept active beach face, stranded oil could rapidly penetrate, possibly to the depth of the impervious ice or permafrost core. It could also be buried by rapid changes in beach morphology induced by wave action or ice-push. The irregularly hummocky relief and large hollows left by melting blocks of stranded ice would also provide sumps for the oil. Preliminary estimates suggest vast quantites of oil could be retained in these beaches (Table 11.4) to be released slowly by sediment redistribution and erosion over subsequent decades. Repeated fouling long after the spill occurred is likely. Recent observations following an experimental oil spill on a sheltered beach at Cape Hatt, Baffin Island in the Canadian Arctic (cf. Owens et al., 1987; Owens and Robson, 1987) suggest that, on seasonally exposed Ross Sea beaches, oil will be removed more rapidly and in more substantial quantities than this writer has previously envisaged (e.g., Gregory and Kirk, 1983).

Storm wave action would probably throw oil high on to and across seawardsmost ridges of cuspate forelands (Fig. 11.15) leading to ashphaltic pavement formation and progressive immobilization of gravelly sediment. This could well enhance the erosion evident at the southern ends of most Ross Sea beaches as well as reduce pebble availability for penguins' nest building activities (Kirk and Gregory, in press).

Fig. 11.15. Cuspate foreland with raised beach ridges on Possession Island, off North Victoria Land Coast, and with its modern gravelly beach almost continuously protected by an ice foot. There are an estimated 100–150,000 breeding pairs of Adélie Penguins at this locality (Harper et al., 1984).

TABLE 11.4

Potential retention capacity of Ross Sea beaches for spilled oil based on the assumption of complete filling of all void spaces above the permanently ice-cemented zone, from behind and above the modern reach ridge to immediately below the wave-swept active beach face, and in the absence of a protecting ice foot.

Locality	Quantity	
Cape Adare	$> 2.5 \times 10^6$ barrels	(350,000 tonnes)
Possession Island	$< 1 \times 10^6$ barrels	(130,000 tonnes)
Cape Hallett	$> 1.3 \times 10^6$ barrels	(170,000 tonnes)
Franklin Island	$> 2.0 \times 10^6$ barrels	(275,000 tonnes)
Beaufort Island	$> 1.5 \times 10^6$ barrels	(215,000 tonnes)
Cape Bird	$\gg 6.0 \times 10^6$ barrels	(863,000 tonnes)

Penguins are particularly vulnerable to oil fouling (Kerley and Erasmus, 1987) and it seems likely that in the event of a major spill impacting the site of a rookery (e.g., Fig. 11.15), mortality would be greatest during the period the beach was protected by an ice-foot. At that time, the birds coming on shore would be herded through narrow leads and passages where congealing oil would concentrate. This risk to individuals would be lessened if the beach were open to the sea.

Oil-ice Interaction

The behaviour of oil released in a frozen sea or under ice is schematically illustrated in Fig. 11.16. Ice will tend to limit the rapid spread of the oil. Biodegradation and mechanical dispersal of oil trapped in leads between flows, pumped on to the ice surface, or held in oil-slush-ice mixtures is likely to be slow. Wind, wave, tidal action or broad oceanic circulation could spread this contamination far from its place of origin (e.g., Fig. 11.11). Oil, seasonally entrained and encapsulated in ice, would migrate to the surface ponding in summer melt pools (Martin, 1979; Wadhams, 1981) to be released back into the sea. It has been argued that release of large quantities of oil on to the Antarctic pack ice surface could significantly lower its albedo and consequentially trigger a rise in sea level (cf. Mitchell, 1982). However, dilution effects over the vastness of the Southern Ocean, and seasonal variations in the extent of sea ice cover suggest that oil-induced melting in this manner should not significantly effect either local or global climate.

Polynyas

A polynya centred on Terra Nova Bay and induced by strong westerly katabatic winds is a persistent wintertime feature of the western Ross Sea (Kurtz and

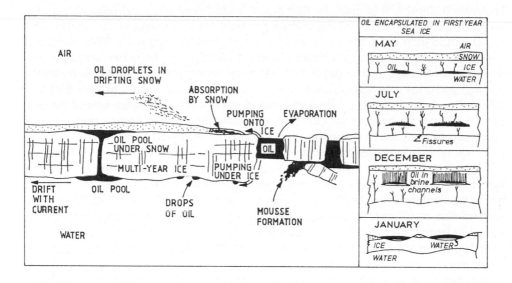

Fig. 11.16. Schematic illustration of interactions between sea ice and water (after Wadhams, 1981; Bobra and Fingas, 1986). Oil can be trapped in pools beneath pack ice or amongst leads between flows. It can be pumped under or on to the ice surface to be covered and/or absorbed by drifting snow. Oil is lost to the atmosphere through evaporation, and dispersed in sea water through droplet formation, solution and emulsification (mousse formation). Encapsulated oil migrates upwards during winter through brine channels in first year sea ice to pond at the surface in the following summer (inset, right).

Bromwich, 1983). The open water area averages 1,000 km² over most years and reaches a maximum of 5,000 km². Other polynyas in this region are reported from McMurdo Sound and off the Ross Ice Shelf (cf. Knapp, 1972).

The extent to which the Ross Sea polynyas are winter refuges for seals, penguins and other animals has not been established. However, Arctic studies suggest they are likely to be regions of high productivity and considerable ecological importance, where an oil spill or blowout could be environmentally devastating (Stirling et al., 1981). Oil from a spill in Terra Nova Bay would probably be held offshore by strong westerly winds and seldom directly threaten the penguin colony of Inexpressible Island. On the other hand, oil would be dispersed to the eastern margin of the polynya where it would be driven against the pack ice margin, and also into leads through the ice, and where it could imperil marine mammals and birds.

Subsea Blowout

Water depths over postulated exploitable hydrocarbon prospects around the Ross Sea, and in particular over the Victoria Land Basin (cf. Cook and Davey, 1984, this volume) are generally greater than 350 m and may exceed 1,000 m.

From such depths, it is unlikely that a constricted conical or cylindrical, rapidly ascending column of oil and expanding gas bubbles as illustrated by Lewis (1979, fig. 2) would ever reach the surface to form a gas boil in open water (Westergaard, 1980), or interact with an ice cover (Lewis, 1970, fig. 3). In water within a few degrees of freezing and at depths of 300 m or more, formation of gas hydrates having densities and appearance similar to ice is likely (Topham and Bishnoi, 1980). Slowly ascending oil droplets and decomposing hydrates would be dispersed widely by even weak currents, reaching the surface over a much wider area than in the case of a shallow-water blowout, and perhaps spreading many unpredictable kilometres downdrift from the release point (cf. Lewis, 1979, fig. 4).

Iceberg scour and furrow marks have yet to be reported from the floor of the Ross Sea. Occasional icebergs in this region may have drafts greater than 400 m, but in general most are unlikely to greatly exceed 300 m (Keys, 1984). Elsewhere around the continent, side-scan sonar surveys have reported modern iceberg scouring from water depths of at least 300 m in the Weddell Sea (Lien, 1981) and over 500 m off Wilkes Land to the west of the Ross Sea, although the age of the latter remain uncertain (Eittreim et al., 1984). It is likely that scour features in water depths of 400–600 m or more are relict (Lien, 1981; Orheim and Elverhoi, 1981). Thus, the potentially most favourable sites for subsea well head completions, and pipelines over most of their length along possible routes to shore facilities, will be at depths more or less safely beyond iceberg scour limits. Only near the coast, where water depths shoal abruptly would pipelines be at risk to ice scour and need to be buried for protection. Here also, pipeline landfalls and onshore facilities face the threat of ice-piling and ride-up (e.g., Kovacs and Sodhi, 1981).

Hydrocarbon Spills and the Marine Biota

The marine biota of the Southern Ocean and Ross Sea are described elsewhere in this volume. Extrapolation from Arctic studies (cf. Dunbar, 1985), predicting the possible effects that a major oil/condensate/gas spill would have on the local and regional biota, needs to be approached with caution (Knox, 1982). The central and key role that krill plays in Southern Ocean and Ross Sea ecosystems is often emphasized (e.g., Knox, 1984). Crustacea are widely recognized as being particularly sensitive to oil fouling and large spills could jeopardize krill concentrations of the Ross Sea. The short, simple food webs of lower species diversity that characterize high latitudes are often considered vulnerable to man-induced perturbations, but to term these ecosystems "fragile" may be a misconception (e.g., Weller, 1980; Dunbar, 1985). Adaptation to seasonal extremes of light, temperature and other environmental parameters indicates a resilience that popular opinion seldom acknowledges. Regionally separated and isolated dense populations (e.g., penguin rookeries, krill swarms) scattered but widely distributed, suggest that local extirpations through pollution could be repaired by immigration from adjacent areas (e.g., Dunbar, 1985). It must also be noted that the impact of even the most massive imaginable spills would be mitigated by the dilution properties of the very vastness of the Southern Ocean (Zumberge, 1979).

The importance of the unique and specialized sea-ice microbial community has been reviewed by Bradford (1978). Like ice-margin phytoplankton blooms (e.g., Smith and Nelson, 1985), it is a highly significant part of the productive Ross Sea ecosystem (Palmisano and Sullivan, 1983; El-Sayed, this volume). Zooplankton biomass is lower inshore than it is offshore (see Foster, 1987). The vulnerability of the sea-ice microbial community to oil contamination is substantially greater than that of either zoo- or phytoplankton, where effects would probably be both local and transient (Keys, 1984). It has been emphasized that hydrocarbon-degrading and -utilizing bacteria are absent from Antarctic waters (Keys, 1984). However, Platt's (1979) observations near Grytviken, South Georgia, and Konlechner's (1985) study at Cape Bird, Ross Island, attest to the presence of hydrocarbon-degrading micro-organisms. Decomposition rates at these high latitudes would be much lower than at mid to low latitudes.

The deeper-water benthos of possible well sites is unlikely to be imperilled through seafloor dumping or accidental release of oil contaminated drill cuttings and drilling muds, although some local environmental deterioration may be evident (cf. Macdonald, 1982).

The shallow benthos below the abrasion limit of sea ice (0–c. 30 m) is abundant and diverse. Sensitivity of this community to hydrocarbon pollution has been demonstrated by Robilliard and Busdosh (1981). They described a depleted biota, including a bed of dead clam shells, over a small area of petroliferous-smelling sediment, alongside the wharf in Winter Quarters Bay, McMurdo Sound, at a depth of 25 m.

There is popular perception that larger marine mammals (whales, sea elephants, sea lions, seals) of the region would be at risk in a large oil spill. This scenario may be correct for Mysticeti (baleen whales) where vulnerability is likely to be through a contaminated food vector, rather than in direct oiling. On the other hand, there is evidence that Odontoceti (toothed whales) and Phocidae (seals) can detect and hence avoid oil slicks (e.g. Smith et al., 1983), although it must be noted that many years ago Lillie (1954) reported oil-fouled seals in Antarctic waters. These animals would be more susceptible to oiling when sea-ice cover was extensive and congealing oil was imprisoned in the leads through which they were forced to surface. The relative defenselessness of penguins to oil-fouling has been briefly discussed elsewhere in this review. Harper (1983) and Harper et al. (1984) have commented on the prospect of a large spill in the Ross Sea decimating neighbourhood penguin populations and detrimentally affecting other local seabird species.

Pesticides and Other Persistent Compounds

Polychlorinated biphenyls (PCBs) and several other persistent synthetic organic compounds (DDT, DDE and TDE) are stable contaminants that have global distribution and are an acknowledged environmental hazard. Such residues are widespread around Antarctica (Risebrough et al., 1976) and have been detected in Adélie Penguins and Crabeater Seals from Cape Crozier, Ross Island (Sladen et al., 1966). Wildlife from mainland New Zealand and offshore Subantarctic islands are also known to be contaminated (Bennington et al., 1975;

Solly and Shanks, 1976), as they are from elsewhere in the region (e.g., Kerguelen Islands — Abarnou et al., 1986). PCBs and pesticide residues have been detected in the atmosphere and surface waters across the Southern Ocean between Australia and Antarctica, with higher concentrations noted in the vicinity of the Balleny Islands and off the Sabrina Coast (Tanabe et al., 1983).

In general, contamination levels determined in both wildlife (Bennington et al., 1975) and oceanic waters (Tanabe et al., 1983) become progressively less with increasing distance from local Australian and New Zealand sources. These levels are substantially lower than those reported from lower latitudes and the Northern Hemisphere. Other than some slight evidence from Syowa Station (Hidaka et al., 1984), Antarctic scientific bases do not appear to be significant point sources of chlorinated hydrocarbon contamination (Riseborough, 1977). The dominant pathway for the transfer of PCB and DDT residues to these remote southern regions is through atmospheric circulation, ocean currents and seasonal migrants from the north (Risebrough et al., 1976; Risebrough, 1977; Tanabe et al., 1983). However, a recently available report (Manheim, 1988) reveals that waters off McMurdo base are grossly contaminated with PCBs. A local source through indiscriminate waste disposal is indicated with reported PCB levels (18–340 ppb) significantly greater than those of polluted United States estuaries. Although established by conservative measurement techniques, these results need to be verified.

Base Installations

Other than inland stations, permanent and seasonal or temporary bases are preferentially situated on snow- and ice-free reasonably level areas close to the sea. Such places are almost invariably occupied by bird colonies and/or plant communities (e.g., Capes Adare, Hallett, Bird, Royds and Evans), and displacement of the original colonists as well as some other environmental interference is inevitable (e.g., Johnston, 1971). Around all bases, there is an accumulation of both organic and inorganic waste (e.g., Cameron, 1972; Cameron et al., 1977; Lipps, 1978). Environmental contamination and pollution is an acknowledged consequence. Today, for Antarctic sites, both casual and controlled landfill dumping is as unacceptable as is the still common practice of indiscriminate annual disposal of obsolete and worn-out equipment, discarded packaging and other waste by piling it on the sea ice. With the seasonal ice breakout, it disappears — out of sight out of mind seems an accepted credo. On the other hand, it is perhaps ironic to note that otherwise aesthetically distasteful rubbish scattered around "Heroic" era huts is to many considered of historic importance, and deserving of protection. Is there a contradiction here — what are we going to leave to future generations of industrial age archaeologists? Of the pelagic whaling which took place around the Ross Sea in the 1920s, there remains no visible testimony.

Most observers find sewage disposal at Antarctic bases a vexatious issue. Release of human wastes, whether untreated, "blended" and macerated, or treated, is viewed with much distaste. Of more immediate concern should be toxic chemical wastes. Manheim (1988) has noted unacceptable heavy metal concentrations in waters off McMurdo base. At outfalls, marine ecosystems will be stressed and biologically impoverished aureoles may develop. Tyler (1972), in discussing sewage treatment at McMurdo Sound, suggested that it is simply a change to something more aesthetically acceptable to delicate human senses. It is perhaps a simplistic overstatement to note that the excreta of some 1,500 Weddell Seals are absorbed into the McMurdo Sound marine ecosystem. At the turn of the century, they were more numerous (Testa and Siniff, 1987). Is there any reason to believe that base populations (reaching summer maxima of c. 1,000) will cause any great environmental perturbation other than that localized at outfalls. Microbial breakdown processes are surely the same for all mammalian wastes. Recent observations by Venkatesan et al. (1986) indicate coprostanols in McMurdo Sound sediment cores are not necessarily evidence of human sewage contamination, but a biomarker for marine mammals.

With the exeption of dead clams in Winter Quarters Bay described previously, it has yet to be established if pollution from the McMurdo Sound bases has harmed the local biota. The observed decline in local Weddell Seal populations may have an independent cause.

CONCLUDING COMMENTARY

It is apparent that remoteness and isolation have not insulated the New Zealand Sector of the Southern Ocean and adjacent shores from mankind's contaminants. On the other hand, it is an emotional overstatement to suggest the region is now becoming "befouled" (see Joyner, 1985, p. 169). Certainly, the shores of New Zealand's Subantarctic islands no longer have quite the unsullied and pristine character savoured by Guthrie-Smith (1936) but they can in no way be considered significantly polluted. Similarly, whilst waters of the region may carry the imprint of man's activities, it is slight and remains of little environmental significance.

Man's activities are also locally evident around the Ross Sea and across oceanic waters to the north. The evidence reviewed suggests that the impact of polluting plastics, hydrocarbons, persistent synthetic compounds, and other non-biodegradable material is not yet of great environmental consequence. Nevertheless, their progressive encroachment is aesthetically distasteful, creating environmental problems that for the present appear minor, but which need to be monitored and carefully addressed rather than casually dismissed. It is important that Antarctica's primordial and pristine state be retained, insofar as it is possible, for the continent provides the baseline standards so vital for global environmental monitoring and surveillance, and against which future changes can be moderated (see Weller et al., 1987).

For the foreseeable future, the most serious pollution hazards are likely to arise from increasing distant water fishing activities and offshore petroleum developments, although tourism should not be ignored. If these are not to have major environmental consequences, there is need for sound, internationally accepted, management procedures, and an ever-vigilant, scientifically informed and aware community. It is my belief that in the event of a major hydrocarbon spill, current clean-up procedures and technology could not cope with the Ross Sea environment.

NOTE ADDED IN PRESS

Since preparing this review, there has been a significant diesel oil spill in waters adjacent to the Antarctic Peninsula. In late January 1989, the Argentinian vessel *Bahia Paraiso* sank after grounding on shoals off southwestern Anvers Island, a short distance from Palmer Station (U.S.A.). Soon after, in February, the Peruvian vessel *Humbolt* was refloated after running aground off King George Island some 400 km to the north.

The *Bahia Paraiso* was carrying almost one million litres of diesel as well as other petroleum products. Although measures to contain the spilling oil were prompt, a slick spread some distance from the wrecked vessel. It is the considered opinion of several commentators that this spill has threatened the viability of some biological research projects at Palmer Station. Preliminary reports mentioned considerable krill mortality in the vicinity, and later observations noted detrimental impact on Skuas, Chinstrap and Adélie Penguins, and Blue-eyed Shags. There was oil-fouling and deaths amongst the penguins and evidence of internal haemorrhaging in Blue-eyed Shags. There was also evidence that the season's offspring of 54 local pairs of breeding Skuas had been lost.

The *Bahia Paraiso* spill was a "minor" incident, luckily involving diesel, which although highly toxic, evaporated quickly and did not form mousse.

An event of more momentous significance was the March 1989 spill of over 35 million litres of crude oil from the tanker *Exxon Valdez* in Prince William Sound, Alaska. This is the first large spill to occur in a relatively enclosed body of cold water. The area is one of ecological richness and diversity and there is wide agreement that this is an environmental disaster of catastrophic proportions. Clean-up operations have been hampered by the physical environment, climate and logistics, and an economically important fishery has been threatened. The wildlife of the area has sustained damage, the magnitude of which is difficult to assess — particularly at risk are sea lions, otters, migratory birds and carrion feeders such as Bald Eagles and bears. While wave action may clean exposed sites of oil, sheltered spots may remain contaminated for years.

From the *Bahia Paraiso* and *Exxon Valdez* incidents, one minor and the other catastrophic, we will learn much. There are both warnings and lessons that must be heeded by all who contemplate and/or authorize expansion of shipping traffic or fisheries activity, as well as hydrocarbon exploration and exploitation in Antarctic waters. This environment is an unforgiving one and complacency is an attribute of all mankind. The *Exxon Valdez* incident suggests that we should take no risks with Antarctica.

REFERENCES

Aagaard, K., Roach, A.T. and Schumacher, J.D., 1985. On the wind-driven variability of the flow through Bering Strait. J. Geophys. Res., 90: 7213–7221.

Abarnou, A., Robineau, D. and Michel, P., 1986. Contamination par les organo-chlorés des dauphins de Commerson des îles Kerguelen. Oceanol. Acta, 9: 19–29.

Abrams, R.W., 1985. Energy and food requirements of pelagic aerial seabirds in different regions of the African Sector of the Southern Ocean. In: W.R. Siegfried, P.R. Condy, and R.M. Laws (Editors), Antarctic Nutrient Cycles and Food Webs. Springer-Verlag, Berlin, pp. 467–472.

Ackley, S.F., 1981: A review of sea ice weather relationships in the Southern Hemisphere. In: I. Allison (Editor), Sea Level, Ice and Climatic Change. International Association of Hydrological Sciences, Publ. No. 131, pp. 127–159.

Adams, R.D. and Christoffel, D.A., 1962. Total magnetic field surveys between New Zealand and the Ross Sea. J. Geophys. Res., 67: 805–813.

Aguayo, A., 1974. Baleen whales off Chile. In: W.E. Scheville (Editor), The Whale Problem A Status Report. Havard University Press, Cambridge, Mass., pp. 209–217.

Ainley, D.G., 1977. Feeding methods in seabirds: a comparison of polar and tropical nesting communities in the eastern Pacific Ocean. In: G.A. Llano (Editor), Adaptations within Antarctic Ecosystems. Smithsonian Institution, Washington, D.C., pp. 669–685.

Ainley, D.G., 1986. Biomass of birds and mammals in the Ross Sea. In: W.R. Siegfried, P.R. Condy, and R.M. Laws (Editors), Antarctic Nutrient Cycles and Food Webs. Springer-Verlag, Berlin, pp. 498–515.

Ainley, D.G., Fraser, W.R., Sullivan, C.W., Torres, J.J., Hopkins, T.L. and Smith, W.D., 1986. Antarctic mesopelagic micronekton: evidence from seabirds that pack ice affects community structure. Science, 232: 847–849.

Ainley, D.G. and Jacobs, S.S., 1981. Sea bird affinities for ocean and ice boundaries in the Antarctic. Deep-Sea Res., 28: 1173–1185.

Ainley, D.G., O'Connor, E.F. and Boekleheide, R.J., 1984. The marine ecology of birds in the Ross Sea, Antarctica. Ornith. Monogr. No. 32. Amer. Ornith. Union, Washington, D.C., 97 pp.

Aliyeva, Ye. R. and Kucheruk, Ye. V., 1985. Geodynamic reconstructions and the prediction of oil and gas potential of poorly known regions : the case of Antarctica. Int. Geol. Rev., 27: 1383–1395.

Allanson, B.R., Hart, R.C. and Lutjeharms, J.R.E., 1981. Observations on the nutrients, chlorophyll and primary productivity of the Southern Ocean south of Africa. S. Afr. J. Antarctic Res., 10/11: 3–14.

Allen, K.R., 1980. Conservation and Management of Whales. Butterworths, London, 107 pp.

Allis, R.G., Barrett, P.J. and Christoffel, D.A., 1975. A paleomagnetic stratigraphy for Oligocene and early Miocene marine glacial sediments at site 270, Ross Sea, Antarctica. In: Initial Reports of the Deep Sea Drilling Project, Vol. 28. U.S. Govt Printing Office, Washington D.C., pp. 879–884.

Anderson, J.B., 1987. Natural constraints on exploring Antarctica's continental margin, existing geophysical and geological data bases, and proposed drilling program. AAPG Convention (Abstr.).

Anderson, J.B., Brake, C., Domack, E.W., Myers, N. and Singer, J., 1984a. Sedimentary dynamics on the Antarctic continental shelf. In: R.L. Oliver, P.R. James, and J.B. Jago (Editors), Antarctic Earth Science. Australian Academy of Science, Canberra, pp. 387–389.

Anderson, J.B., Brake, C., Domack, E., Myers, N. and Wright, R., 1983. Development of a polar glacial-marine sedimentation model from Antarctic Quaternary deposits and glaciological information. In: B.F. Molnia (Editor), Glacial-Marine Sedimentation. Plenum Press, N.Y., pp. 223–264.

Anderson, J.B., Brake, C.F. and Myers, N.C., 1984b. Sedimentation on the Ross Sea continental shelf, Antarctica. Mar. Geol., 57: 295–333.

Anderson, J.B., Griffith, T., Smith, M. and Singer, J., 1987. Sedimentation in Antarctic fiords and bays. INQUA 87 Programme with Abstracts, Ottawa, Canada, pp. 121 (Abstr.).

Anderson, J.B., Kurtz, D.D., Domack, E.W. and Balshaw, K.M., 1980. Glacial and glacial marine sediments of the Antarctic continental shelf. J. Geol., 88: 399–414.

Anderson, J.B., Kurtz, D.D. and Weaver, F.M., 1979. Sedimentation on the Antarctic continental slope. In: L.J. Doyle and O.H. Pilkey (Editors), Geology of Continental Slopes. Society of Economic Paleontologists and Mineralogists Spec. Publ. 27, pp. 61–73.

Anderson, J.B. and Smith, M.J., 1989. Formation of modern sand-rich facies by marine currents on the Antarctic continental shelf. In: R. Morton and D. Nummedahl (Editors), Shelf Sedimentation, Shelf Sequences and Related Hydrocarbon Accumulation. Society of Economic Paleontologists and Mineralogists Spec. Publ., pp. 41–52.

Anderton, P.W., Holloway, N.H., Engstrom, J.C., Ahmad, , pp. 41–52.H.M. and Chong, B., 1982. Evaluation of geology and hydrocarbon potential of the Great South and Campbell basins. N.Z. Geol. Surv. open-file, Petroleum Report, No. 828, 7 vols.

Angel, M.V., 1987. Criteria for protected areas and other conservation measures in the Antarctic region. Environment Internat., 13 : 105–114.

Angino, E.E. and Lepley, L.K., 1966. Ross Sea. In: R.W. Fairbridge (Editor), The Encyclopedia of Oceanography. Reinhold Publishing Co., N.Y., pp. 751–753.

Anonymous, 1957. Oceanographic Atlas of the Polar Seas, Part I, Antarctic. U.S. Navy Hydrographic Office, Washington D.C. (H.O. Pub. No. 705), 70 pp.

Anonymous, 1966a. Atlas of Antarctica, vol. 1. Moscow, 225 pp. [translation of text in Soviet Geography Review and Translation 1967, 8(5–6): 261–507].

Anonymous, 1966b. Coulman Island. Department of Lands and Survey, New Zealand, N.Z. Map Series 166: Sheet SS58–60, 6.

Anonymous, 1977. Northern skills may go south to Antarctica within a decade. Offshore Engineer, Supplement, December 1977: 36–37.

Anonymous, 1979. Shipping losses caused by ice 1890–1977. Polar Rec., 19: 343–362.

Anonymous, 1982. Japanese oil survey in Ross Sea. Antarctic, 9(11): 398.

Anonymous, 1983a. Research Emphases from the U.S. Antarctic Program. National Academy Press, Washington, D.C., 52 pp.

Anonymous, 1983b. Soviet ships circumnavigate Antarctica. Antarctic, 10(9): 113.

Anonymous, 1984. Environmental data inventory for the Antarctic area. U.S. Dept. of Commerce NESDIS Environmental Inventory, No. 1, 53 pp.

Anonymous, 1985a. Glaciers, Ice Sheets, and Sea Level : Effect of a CO_2-induced Climatic Change. Report of a Workshop held in Seattle, Washington September 13–15, 1984, 348 pp.

Anonymous, 1985b. Oil and gas technologies for the Arctic and deepwater. U.S. Congress Office of Technology Assessment, OTA–0–270 : 227 pp. (plus summary volume).

Anonymous, 1985c. Readers Digest Complete Book of New Zealand Birds. Readers Digest, Reed Methuen, Sydney, 319 pp.

Anonymous, 1986a. U.S. Research in Antarctica in 2000 A.D. and Beyond A Preliminary Assessment. National Academy Press, Washington, D.C., 35 pp.

Anonymous, 1986b. World Ocean Circulation Experiment. U.S. W.O.C.E. Planning Report

No.3: 229 pp.

Anonymous, 1986c. Marine Resources of the Polar Regions: Scientific and Technological Priorities. Marine Resources Project (PRFST), University of Manchester.

Anonymous, 1987a. The Role of the National Science Foundation in Polar Regions A Report to the National Science Board. National Science Foundation, Washington, D.C., 57 pp.

Anonymous, 1987b. Antarctic ice is smaller. EOS Trans. Am. Geophys. Un., 68(48): 1625.

Anonymous, 1988. More countries making seismic surveys. Antarctic (N.Z. Antarctic Soc.), 11(7/12): 292–294.

Anonymous, 1989. Italy and Japan continue seismic surveys. Antarctic (N.Z. Antarctic Soc.), 11(9 & 10): 374–375.

Apostolescu, V. and Wanneson, J., 1982. Y a-t-il du pétrole dans L'Antarctique? La Recherche, 13: 1340–1343.

Arnold, P., Marsh, H., and Heinsohn, G., 1987. The occurrence of two forms of minke whale in east Australia waters with a description of external characteristics and skeleton of the diminutive or dwarf form. Scient. Rep. Whales Res. Inst., 38: 1–46.

Ashcroft, W.A., 1972. Crustal structure of the South Shetland Islands and Bransfield Strait. Scientific Report No. 66, British Antarctic Survey, London, 43 pp.

Ashmole, N.P., 1971. Sea bird ecology and the marine environment. In: D.A. Farner and J.R. King (Editors), Avian Ecology, Vol.1. Academic Press, London, pp. 223–286.

Auburn, F.M., 1982. Antarctic Law and Politics. C. Hurst & Company, London, 361 pp.

Azam, F., Beers, J.R., Campbell, L., Carlucci, A.F., Holm-Hansen, O. and Reid, F.M.H. 1979. Occurrence and metabolic activity of organisms under the Ross Ice Shelf, Antarctica, at Station J9. Science, 203: 451–453.

Bacgi, M., 1985. Turbidite deposition on the Bellingshausen abyssal plain: sedi-mentologic implications. Unpubl. M.A. thesis, Rice University, Houston, Texas, 109 pp.

Bailey, A.M. and Sorensen, J.H., 1962. Subantarctic Campbell Island. Proc. Denver Mus. Nat. Hist., Vol. 10, 305 pp.

Bainbridge, A.E., 1981. GEOSECS Atlantic Expedition, Volume 2, Sections and Profiles. National Science Foundation, Washington, D.C., 198 pp.

Baker, A.deC., 1954. The circumpolar continuity of Antarctic plankton species. Discovery Reps, 27: 201–218.

Baker, A.N., 1977. Spectacled porpoise, Phocoena dioptrica, new to the subantarctic Pacific ocean. N.Z. Jl Mar. Freshwater Res., 11: 401–406.

Baker, A.N., 1983. Whales and Dolphins of New Zealand and Australia, Victoria University Press, Wellington, 133 pp.

Baker, A.N., 1985. Pygmy Right Whale Caperea marginata (Gray, 1946). In: S.H. Ridgway and R. Harrison (Editors), Handbook of Marine Mammals 3: The Sirenians and Baleen Whales. Academic Press, London, pp. 345–354.

Baker, R.R., 1978. The Evolutionary Ecology of Animal Migration. Hodder and Stoughton, London, 1000 pp.

Baker, R.R., 1980. The significance of the Lesser Black-backed gull, Larus fascus, to models of bird migration. Bird Study, 27: 41–50.

Baker, R.R., 1982. Migration Paths Through Time and Space. Hodder and Stoughton, London, 248 pp.

Balazs, G.H., 1985. Impact of ocean debris on marine turtles: entanglement and ingestion. In: R.S. Shomura and H.O. Yoshida (Editors), Proceedings of the Workshop on the Fate and Impact of Marine Debris, 26–29 November 1984, Honolulu, Hawaii. U.S. Dept. Commer. NOAA Tech. Memo. NMFS, NOAA-TM-NMFS-SWFC-54: pp. 387–429.

Balech, E., 1970. The distribution and endemism of some Antarctic microplankters. In:

M.W. Holdgate (Editor), Antarctic Ecology, Vol. I. Academic Press, London, pp. 143–147.

Balech, E., 1975. La distribution de algunos microplanctores en el Atlantico sudoeste. Tirada aparte del Boletin del Servico de Hidrografia Naval, 12(2/3): 15–24.

Barber, H.N., Badswell, H.E. and Ingle, H.D., 1959. Transport of driftwood from South America to Tasmania and Macquarie Island. Nature, 184: 203–204.

Bardach, J.E., 1986. Fish far away: Comments on Antarctic Fisheries. Ocean Yb., 6: 38–54.

Barker, P.F., 1982. The Cenozoic subduction history of the Pacific margin of the Antarctic Peninsula: ridge crest-trench interactions. J. Geol. Soc. Lond., 139: 787–801.

Barkov, N.I., 1985. Ice shelves of Antarctica. (English translation of 1971 publication in Russian). Amerind Publishing Co., New Dehli, 262 pp.

Barnes, J.N., 1982. Let's Save Antarctica! Greenhouse Publications, Richmond, Australia, 96 pp.

Barnes, J.N., 1982. The emerging Convention on the Conservation of Antarctic Marine Living Resources : An attempt to meet the new realities of resource exploitation in the Southern Ocean. In: J.I. Charney (Editor), New Nationalism and the Use of Common Space. Allenheld, Osmun Publishers, Totowa, New Jersey, pp. 239–286.

Barnes, L.G., 1984. Search for the first whale. Retracing the ancestry of cetaceans. Oceans, 17: 20–23.

Barnes, P.W. and Lien, R., 1988. Icebergs rework shelf sediments to 500 m off Antarctica. Geology, 16: 1130–1133.

Barnola, J.M., Raynaud, D., Korotkevich, Y.S. and Lorius, C., 1987. Vostok ice core provides 160,000-year record of atmospheric CO_2. Nature, 329: 408–414.

Barrett, P.J., 1975. Textural characteristics of Cenozoic preglacial and glacial sediments at Site 270, Ross Sea, Antarctica. In: Initial Reports of the Deep Sea Drilling Project, Vol. 28. U.S. Govt Printing Office, Washington, D.C., pp. 757–767.

Barrett, P.J., 1981. History of the Ross Sea region during the deposition of the Beacon Supergroup 400–180 million years ago. J. Roy. Soc. N.Z., 11: 447–458.

Barrett, P.J. (Editor), 1986. Antarctic Cenozoic history from the MSSTS–1 drillhole, McMurdo Sound. N.Z. Dep. Scient. Ind. Res. Bull., 237: 174 pp.

Barrett, P.J., 1987. Oligocene sequence cored at CIROS–1, western McMurdo Sound. N.Z. Antarctic Rec., 7(3): 1–7.

Barrett, P.J. (Editor), 1989. Antarctic Cenozoic history from CIROS–1 Drillhole, McMurdo Sound. N.Z. Dep. Scient. Ind. Res. Bull., 245: in press.

Barrett, P.J. and McKelvey, B.C., 1986. Stratigraphy. In: P.J. Barrett (Editor), Antarctic Cenozoic history from MSSTS–1 drillhole, McMurdo Sound. N.Z. Dep. Scient. Ind. Res. Bull., 237: 9–52.

Barrett, P.J., Pyne, A.R. and Ward, B.L., 1983. Modern sedimentation in McMurdo Sound, Antarctica. In: R.L. Oliver, P.R. James and J.B. Jago (Editors), Antarctic Earth Science. Australian Academy of Science, Canberra, pp. 550–554.

Barrett, P.J. and Scientific Staff, 1985. Plio-Pleistocene glacial sequence cored at CIROS 2, Ferrar Fjord, western McMurdo Sound. N.Z. Antarctic Rec., 6(2): 8–19.

Barron, J., Larsen, B. and Baldauf, J.G., 1988. Early glaciation of Antarctica. Nature, London, 333: 303–304.

Bary, B.McK., 1970. Biogeography and ecology of plankton in the South Pacific. In: W.S. Wooster (Editor), Scientific Exploration of the South Pacific. National Academy of Sciences, Washington, D.C., pp. 211–225.

Baumgartner, A. and Reichel, E., 1975. The World Water Balance Mean Annual Global, Continental and Maritime Precipitation, Evaporation and Run-off. Elsevier, Amsterdam, 179 pp.

Beck, P.J., 1983. British Antarctic policy in the early 20th Century. Polar Rec., 21(134): 475–483.

Beddington, J.R., 1987. The scientific requirements for the conservation of exploited living marine resources in the Antarctic. Environment Internat., 13: 115–118.

Beggs, J.M., 1978. Geology of the metamorphic basement and late Cretaceous to Oligocene sedimentary sequence of Campbell Island, Southwest Pacific Ocean. J. Roy. Soc. N.Z., 8: 161–177.

Behrendt, J.C., 1983a. Geophysical and geological studies relevant to assessment of the petroleum resources of Antarctica. In: R.L. Oliver, P.R. James, and J.B. Jago (Editors), Antarctic Earth Science. Australian Academy of Science, Canberra, pp. 423–428.

Behrendt, J.C. (Editor), 1983b. Petroleum and mineral resources of Antarctica. U.S. Geol. Surv. Circ., 909: 75 pp.

Behrendt, J.C., In press. Scientific studies relevant to the question of Antarctica's petroleum resource potential. In : R.J. Tingey (Editor), Geology of Antarctica. Oxford University Press, Oxford.

Bek-Bulat, G.Z. and Zalishchak, B.L., 1985. A find of phosphorite on a seamount in the Eltanin Fracture Zone (Pacific Ocean). Oceanol., 24(6): 763–765.

Bell, A., 1988. Chlorine blamed for growing 'ozone hole'. Ecos, 56: 3–6.

Bell, B.D., 1975. Report on the birds of the Auckland Islands Expedition 1972–73. In: J.C. Yaldwyn (Editor), Preliminary Results of the Auckland Islands Expedition 1972–1973. Dept. of Lands and Survey, Wellington, pp. 136–142.

Bell, L.C., 1954. Notes on the birds of the Chatham Islands. Notornis, 6: 65–68.

Benninghoff, W.S. and Bonner, W.N., 1985. Man's impact on the Antarctic environment : A procedure for evaluating impacts from scientific and logistic activities. Scientific Committee on Antarctic Research, Cambridge, 56 pp.

Bennington, S.L., Connors, P.G., Connors, C.W. and Risebrough, R.W., 1975. Patterns of chlorinated hydrocarbon contamination in New Zealand Subantarctic and coastal marine birds. Environ. Pollut. Ser. A, 8: 135–147.

Bentley, C.R., 1984. The Ross Ice Shelf Geophysical and Glaciological Survey (RIGGS): Introduction and summary of measurements performed. Antarctic Res. Ser., 42: 1–20.

Bentley, C.R., 1985. Glaciological evidence: the Ross Sea sector. In: Glaciers, Ice Sheets, and Sea Level: Effect of a CO_2-induced Climatic Change. Report of a Workshop held in Seattle, Washington September 13–15, 1984, pp. 178–196.

Bentley, C.R., 1987. Antarctic ice streams: a review. J. Geophys. Res., 92: 8843–8858.

Bentley, C.R., Clough, J.W., Jezek, K.C. and Shabtaie, S., 1979. Ice thickness patterns and the dynamics of the Ross Ice Shelf, Antarctica. J. Gaciol., 24: 287–294.

Bentley, C.R. and Jezek, K.C., 1981: RISS, RISP and RIGGS : Post-IGY glaciological investigations of the Ross Ice Shelf in the U.S. programme. J. Roy. Soc. N.Z., 11: 366–372.

Bentley, C.R., Shabtaie, S., Blankenship, D.D., Rooney, S.T., Schultz, D.G., Anandakrishnan, S. and Alley, R.B., 1987. Remote sensing of the Ross ice streams and adjacent Ross Ice Shelf, Antarctica. Annals Glaciol., 9: 20–29.

Benzhitsky, A.G. and Polikarpov, G.G., 1977. Distribution of oil aggregates with neuston periphyton in the surface layer of the Atlantic, Southern and Indian Oceans. Biologiya Morya (Vladivostok), 2: 88–91 (in Russian).

Bergsager, E., 1983. Basic conditions for the exploration and exploitation of mineral resources in Antarctica: options and precedents. In: F.O. Vicuña (Editor), Antarctic Resource Policy Scientific, Legal and Political Issues. Cambridge University Press, Cambridge, pp. 167–183.

Best, P.B., 1974. The biology of the sperm whale as it relates to stock management. In: W.E. Schevill (Editor), The Whale Problem A Status Report. Havard University Press,

330

Cambridge, Mass., pp. 247–293.

Black, P.M., 1980. A reconnaissance survey of the petrology of New Zealand coals. N.Z. Energy Research and Development Committee Rep., 51: 49 pp.

Blackman, D.K., von Herzen, R.P. and Lawver, L.A., 1984. Heatflow and tectonics in the Ross Sea. EOS Trans. Am. Geophys. Un., 65: 1120 (Abstr.).

Bobra, A.M. and Fingas, M.F., 1986. The behaviour and fate of Arctic oil spills. Water Sci. Technol., 18: 13–23.

Bolin, B., Döös, B.R., Jäger, J. and Warrick, R.A. (Editors), 1986. SCOPE 29 The Greenhouse Effect, Climate Change and Ecosystems. John Wiley & Sons, Chichester, 541 pp.

Bonner, W.N., 1982. Seals and Man A Study of Interactions. University of Washing-ton Press, Seattle, 170 pp.

Bonner, W.N., 1984. Conservation and the Antarctic. In: R.M. Laws (Editor), Antarctic Ecology, Vol. 2. Academic Press, London, pp. 821–850.

Bonner, W.N. and Angel, M.V., 1987. Conservation and the Antarctic environment : The working group reports of the joint IUCN/SCAR symposium on the scientific require-ments for Antarctic conservation. Environment Internat., 13 : 137–144.

Bonner, W.N. and Laws, R.M., 1964. Seals and sealing. In: R. Priestley, R.J. Adie and G. deQ. Robin (Editors), Antarctic Research. Butterworths, London, pp. 163–190.

Bonner, W.N. and McCann, T.S., 1982. Neck collars on fur seals, Arctocephalus gazella, at South Georgia. Br. Antarct. Surv. Bull., No. 57: 73–77.

Borchgrevink, C.E., 1900. The "Southern Cross" expedition to the Antarctic, 1899–1900. Geogr. J., 16: 381–414.

Boswell, J. and MacIver, D., 1975. The Magellanic Penguin Sphenisens magellanicus. In: B. Stonehouse (Editor), The Biology of Penguins. Macmillan, London, pp. 271–308.

Bourne, W.R.P., 1964. The relationship between the Magenta Petrel and the Chatham Island Taiko. Notornis, 11: 139–144.

Bourne, W.R.P., 1967. Subfossil petrel bones from the Chatham Islands. Ibis, 109: 1–7.

Bourne, W.R.P., 1976. Seabirds and pollution. In: R. Johnston (Editor), Marine Pollution. Academic Press, London, pp. 403–502.

Bourne, W.R.P. and Clark, G.C., 1984. The occurrence of birds and garbage at the Humbolt Front off Valparaiso, Chile. Mar. Pollut. Bull., 15: 343–344.

Bourne, W.R.P. and Imber, M.J., 1982. Plastic pellets collected by a prion on Gough Island, central South Atlantic Ocean. Mar. Pollut. Bull., 13: 20–21.

Bourne, W.R.P. and Warham, J., 1966. Geographical variation in giant petrels of the genus Macronectes. Ardea, 54: 45–67.

Boyer, D.L. and Guala, J.R., 1972. Model of the Antarctic Circumpolar Current in the vicinity of the Macquarie Ridge. Antarctic Res. Ser., 19: 79–93.

Braarud, T. and Klem, A., 1931. Hydrographical and chemical investigations in the coastal waters off More and in the Romsdalfjord. Hvalraadets Skrifter, 1: 1–88.

Bradford, J.M., 1978. Sea ice organisms and their importance to the Antarctic ecosystem. N.Z. Antarctic Rec., 1(2): 43–50.

Bradford, J.M. and Wells, J.B.J., 1983. New calanoid and harpacticoid copepods from beneath the Ross Ice Shelf, Antarctica. Polar Biol., 2: 1–15.

Bradstreet, M.S.W. and Brown, R.G.B., 1985. Feeding ecology of the Atlantic Alcidae. In: D.N. Nettleship and T.R. Birkhead (Editors), The Atlantic Alcidae. Academic Press, London, pp. 263–318.

Brewster, B., 1982. Antarctica: Wilderness at risk. A.H. & A.W. Reed, Wellington, 125 pp.

Brigham, L.W., 1988. The Soviet Antarctic program. Oceanus, 31(2): 87–92.

Broady, P.A., Adams, C.J., Cleary, P.J., and Weaver, S.D., 1989. Ornithological observations at Edward VII Peninsula, Antarctica, in 1987–88. Notornis, 36: 53–61.

Brodie, J.W., 1965. Oceanography. In: T. Hatherton (Editor), Antarctica. A.H. & A.W. Reed, Wellington, pp. 101–127.

Brodie, J.W. and Dawson, E.W., 1971. Antarctic icebergs near New Zealand. N.Z. Jl Mar. Freshwater Res., 5: 80–85.

Broecker, W.S., Spencer, D.W. and Craig, H., 1982. GEOSECS Pacific Expedition volume 3 Hydrographic data 1973–1974. National Science Foundation, Washington, D.C., 137 pp.

Bromwich, D.H. and Kurtz, D.D., 1982. Experiences of Scott's northern party: evidence for a relationship between winter katabatic winds and the Terra Nova Bay polynya. Polar Rec., 131: 137–146.

Brooks, J. and Fleet, A.J. (Editors), 1987. Marine petroleum source rocks. Geol. Soc. Lond. Spec. Publ., 26: 444 pp.

Brothers, N.P., 1984. The weka on Macquarie Island. Notornis, 31: 145–154.

Brown, G.G. and Lackyer, C.H., 1984. Whales. In: R.M. Laws (Editor), Antarctic Ecology, Vol. 2. Academic Press, London, pp. 717–781.

Brown, R.G.B., 1980. Seabirds as marine animals. In: J. Burger, B.L. Olla, and H.E. Winn (Editors), Behaviour of Marine Animals. Marine Birds, Vol. 14. Plenum Press, London, pp. 1–39.

Brown, R.G.B., Barker, S.P., Gaskin, D.E. and Sandeman, M.R., 1981. The foods of great and sooty shearwaters *Puffinus gravis* and *P. griseus* in eastern Canadian waters. Ibis, 123: 19–30.

Brown, R.G.B., Cooke, F., Kinnear, P.K., and Mills, E.L. 1975. Summer seabird distribution in Drake Passage, the Chilean fiords and off southern South America. Ibis, 117: 339–356.

Brown, R.S., Norman, F.I. and Eades, D.W., 1986. Notes on Blue and Kerguelen Petrels found beach-washed in Victoria, 1984. Emu, 86: 228–238.

Brownell, R.L., 1974. Small odontocetes of the Antarctic. In: V.C. Bushnell (Editor), Antarctic Map Folio Ser., Folio 18, pp. 13–19.

Bruhn, R.L. and Dalziel, I.W.D., 1977. Destruction of the early Cretaceous marginal basin in the Andes of Tierra del Fuego. In: M. Talwani and W.C. Pitman (Editors), Island Arcs Deep Sea Trenches and Back-Arc Basins. Am. Geophys. Un., Maurice Ewing Ser., 1: 393–405.

Bryden, H.L., 1983. The Southern Ocean. In: A.R. Robinson (Editor), Eddies in Marine Science. Springer-Verlag, N.Y., pp. 265–277.

Bryden, H.L. and Heath, R.A., 1985. Energetic eddies at the northern edge of the Antarctic Circumpolar Current in the Southwest Pacific. Prog. Oceanogr., 14: 65–87.

Buck, K.R. and Garrison, D.L., 1983. Protists from the ice-edge region of the Weddell Sea. Deep-Sea Res., 30: 1261–1277.

Budd, W.F., 1981. The role of Antarctica in southern hemisphere weather and climate. In: N.W. Young (Editor), Antarctica : Weather and Climate. Melbourne University Press, Australia, 20 pp.

Budd, W.F., 1982. The role of Antarctica in southern hemisphere weather and climate. Aust. Met. Mag., 30: 265–272.

Budd, W.F., 1986a. The Antarctic Treaty as a scientific mechanism (Post-IGY) – Contribution of Antarctic scientific research. In: Antarctic Treaty System An Assessment Proceedings of a Workshop held at Beardmore South Field Camp, Antarctica January 7–13, 1985. National Academy Press, Washington, D.C., pp. 103–151.

Budd, W.F., 1986b: The Southern Hemisphere circulation of atmosphere, ocean and sea ice. Proceedings of the Second International Conference on Southern Hemisphere Meteorology, December 1–5, 1986, Wellington, New Zealand, American Meteorological Society, Boston, Mass., pp. 101–106.

Budd, W.F., Jacka, T.H. and Morgon, V.I., 1980. Antarctic iceberg melt rates derived from size distributions and movement rates. Annals Glaciol., 1: 103–112.

Budd, W.F. and Smith, I.N., 1985. The state of balance of the Antarctic ice sheet an updated assessment 1984. In: Glaciers, Ice Sheets, and Sea Level: Effect of a CO_2-induced Climatic Change. Report of a Workshop held in Seattle, Washington September 13–15, 1984, pp. 172–177.

Bullivant, J.S., 1967. New Zealand Oceanographic Institute Ross Sea investigations, 1968–60: General account and station list. Mem. N.Z. Oceanogr. Inst., 32: 9–29.

Burckle, L.H., Robinson, D. and Cooke, D., 1982. Reappraisal of sea-ice distribution in Atlantic and Pacific sectors of the Southern Ocean at 18,000 yr BP. Nature, 299: 435–437.

Burkholder, P.R. and Mandelli, E.F., 1965. Carbon assimilation of marine phytoplankton in Antarctica. Proc. Natn Acad. Sci., 544: 437–444.

Burling, R.W., 1960. New Zealand Oceanographic Institute investigations in the Southern Ocean. N.Z. Sci. Revs, 18: 22–26.

Burling, R.W., 1961. Hydrology of circumpolar waters south of New Zealand. Mem. N.Z. Oceanogr. Inst., 10: 66 pp. + 1 chart.

Burns, B.J., James, A.T., Emmett, J.K., 1984. The use of gas isotopes in determining the source of some Gippsland basin oils. APEA J., 24: 217–221.

Burroughs, R.H., 1986. Seafloor area within reach of petroleum technology. Ocean Management, 10: 125–135.

Burrows, C.J., 1976. Icebergs in the Southern Ocean. N.Z. Geographer, 32: 127–138.

Butler, J.N., 1975a. Pelagic tar. Scient. Am., 232: 90–97.

Butler, J.N., 1975b. Evaporative weathering of petroleum residues: the age of pelagic tar. Mar. Chem., 3: 9–21.

Butler, J.N., Morris, B.F. and Sass, J., 1973. Pelagic tar from Bermuda and the Sargasso sea. Bermuda Biological Station for Research Spec. Publ., No. 10: 346 pp.

Callahan, J.E., 1971. Velocity structure and flux of the Antarctic Circumpolar Current south of Australia. J. Geophys. Res., 76: 5859–5864.

Callahan, J.E., 1972. The structure and circulation of deep water in the Antarctic. Deep-Sea Res., 19: 563–575.

Cameron, P.J., 1981. The petroleum potential of Antarctica and its continental margin. APEA J. 21: 99–111.

Cameron, R.E., 1972. Pollution and conservation of the Antarctic terrestrial ecosystem. In; B.C. Parker (Editor), Conservation Problems in Antarctica. Allen Press, Lawrence, Kansas, pp. 267–307.

Cameron, R.E., Honour, R.C. and Morelli, F.A., 1977. Environmental impact studies of Antarctic sites. In: G.A. Llano (Editor), Adaptations within Antarctic Ecosystems. Smithsonian Institution, Washington, pp. 1157–1176.

Cande, S.G., Herron, E.M. and Hall, B.R., 1982. The early Cenozoic tectonic history of the southeast Pacific. Earth Planet. Sci. Letts, 57: 63–74.

Cande, S.G. and Mutter, J.C., 1982. A revised identification of the oldest seafloor spreading anomalies between Australia and Antarctica. Earth Planet. Sci. Letts, 58: 151–160.

Carleton, A.M., 1979. A synoptic climatology of satellite-observed extratropical cyclone activity for the southern hemisphere winter. Arch. Met. Geophys. Bioklim., Ser. B, 27: 265–279.

Carleton, A.M., 1981a. Monthly variability of satellite-derived cyclonic activity for the southern hemisphere winter. J. Climatol., 1: 21–38.

Carleton, A.M., 1981b. Ice-ocean-atmosphere interactions at high southern latitudes in winter from satellite observation. Aust. Met. Mag., 29: 183–195.

Carlucci, A.F. and Cuhel, R.L., 1977. Vitamins in the south polar seas: distribution and significance of dissolved and particulate vitamin B_{12}, thiamine and biotin in the south Indian Ocean. In: G.A. Llano (Editor), Adaptations Within Antarctic Ecosystems. Proceedings of Third SCAR Symposium on Antarctic Biology, Smithsonian Institution, Washington, D.C., pp. 115–128.

Carmack, E.C., 1977. Water characteristics of the Southern Ocean south of the Polar Front. In: M. Angel (Editor), A Voyage of Discovery George Deacon 70th Anniversary Volume, Supplement to Deep-Sea Res., Pegamon, Oxford, pp. 15–41.

Carmack, E.C. and Killworth, P.D., 1978. Formation and interleaving of abyssal water masses off Wilkes Land, Antarctica. Deep-Sea Res., 25: 357–369.

Carrick, R., Csordas, S.E., Ingham, S.E. and Keith, K., 1962. Studies on the southern elephant seal *Mirounga leonina* (L.) III, the annual cycle in relation to age and sex. CSIRO Wildl. Res., 7: 119–160.

Carter, L. and Mitchell, J.S., 1987. Late Quaternary sediment pathways through the deep ocean, east of New Zealand. Paleoceanography, 2: 409–422.

Carter, L., Mitchell, J.S. and Day, N.J., 1981. Suspended sediment beneath permanent and seasonal ice, Ross Ice Shelf, Antarctica. N.Z. Jl Geol. Geophys., 24: 249–262.

Carter, R.M. and Norris, R.J., 1976. Cainozoic history of southern New Zealand : an accord between geological observations and plate-tectonic predictions. Earth Planet. Sci. Letts, 31: 85–94.

Cassie, V., 1963. Distribution of surface phytoplankton between New Zealand and Antarctica December 1957. Trans-Antarctic Expedition 1955–1958 Sci. Reps, No. 7: 11 pp.

Cavalieri, D.J. and Parkinson, C.L., 1981. Large-scale variations in observed Antarctic sea ice extent and associated atmospheric circulation. Mon. Wea. Rev., 109: 2323–2336.

Cawthorn, M.W., 1985. Entanglement in, and ingestion of, plastic litter by marine mammals, sharks, and turtles in New Zealand waters. In: R.S. Shomura and H.O. Yoshida (Editors), Proceedings of the Workshop on the Fate and Impact of Marine Debris, 26–29 November 1984, Honolulu, Hawaii. U.S. Dept. Commer, NOAA Tech. Memo NMFS, NOAA-TM-NMFS-SWFC-54: pp. 336–343.

Cawthorn, M., 1987. Rubbishing the ocean. Forest and Bird, 18: 217–219.

Cawthorn, M.W., Crawley, M.C., Mattlin, R.H. and Wilson, G.J., 1985. Research on Pinnipeds in New Zealand. Wildlife Research Liaison Group Research Review, Wellington, 7: 29 pp.

Chapman, D.G., 1974. Status of Antarctic rorqual stocks. In: W.E. Schevill (Editor), The Whale Problem A Status Report. Harvard University Press, Cambridge, Mass., pp. 218–238.

Chapman, F.R., 1893. Notes on the depletion of the fur seal in the Southern Oceans. Canad. Rec. Sci., Oct., 1893: 446–549.

Cheney, R.E., Marsh, J.G. and Beckely, B.D., 1983. Global mesoscale variability from collinear tracks of SEASAT altimeter data. J. Geophys. Res., 88: 4343–4354.

Chittleborough G., 1984. Nature, extent and management of Antarctic living resources. In: S. Harris (Editor), Australia's Antarctic Policy Options. ANU Centre for Resource and Environmental Studies Monograph, 11: 135–161.

Chriss, T. and Frakes, L.A., 1972. Glacial marine sedimentation in the Ross Sea. In: R.J. Adie (Editor), Antarctic Geology and Geophysics. Universitetsforlaget, Oslo, pp. 747–762.

Christoffel, D.A. and Falconer, R.K.H., 1972. Marine magnetic measurements in the southwest Pacific Ocean and the identifications of new tectonic features. Antarctic Res. Ser., 19: 197–209.

Clapperton, C.M. and Sugden, D.E., 1982. Glacier fluctuations in George VI Sound area,

334

West Antarctica. Annals Glaciol., 3: 345 (Abstr.).

Clark, A.H., 1884–87. The Antarctic fur-seal and sea-elephant industry. In: G.B. Goode, The Fisheries and Fishery Industries of the United States, Vol. 2 (18). U.S. Govt. Printing Office, Washington, D.C., pp. 400–467.

Clark, C.W. and Lamberson, R., 1982. An economic history and analysis of pelagic whaling. Mar. Policy, 5: 103–120.

Clark, G.S., Goodwin, R.D. and von Meyer, A.P., 1984a. Extension of the known range of some seabirds on the coast of southern Chile. Notornis, 31: 320–324.

Clark, G.S., von Meyer, A.P., Nelson, J.W. and Watt, J.N., 1984b. Notes on sooty shearwaters and other avifauna of the Chilean offshore island of Guafo. Notornis, 31: 225–231.

Clark, M.R. and Dingwall, P.R., 1985. Conservation of islands in the Southern Ocean: A review of the protected areas of Insulantarctica. IUCN, Cambridge University Press, Cambridge, 188 pp. + Appendix.

Clark, R.B., 1984. Impact of oil pollution on seabirds. Environ. Pollut. Ser. A, 33: 1–22.

Clarke, A., 1985. Food webs and interactions: an overview of the Antarctic ecosystems. In: W.N. Bonner and D.W.H. Walton (Editors), Key Environments Antarctica. Pergamon Press, Oxford, pp. 329–350.

Clausen, H.B., Dansgaard, W., Nielsen, J.O. and Clough, J.W., 1979. Surface accumulation on the Ross Ice Shelf. Antarctic Jl U.S. 14(5): 68–72.

Clifford, M.A. 1983. A descriptive study of the zonation of the Antarctic Circum-polar Current and its relation to wind stress and ice cover. Unpubl. M.S. Thesis, Texas A&M University, 93 pp.

Clough, J.W. and Hansen, B.L., 1979. The Ross Ice Shelf Project. Science, 203: 433–434.

Coachman, L.K. and Aagaard, K., 1981. Reevaluation of water transports in the vicinity of Bering Strait. In: D.W. Hood and J.A. Calder (Editors), The Eastern Bering Sea Shelf Oceanography and Resources, Vol. I. National Oceanic and Atmospheric Administration, Washington, D.C., 1: pp. 95–110.

Cochrane, J.D., 1958. The frequency distribution of water characteristics in the Pacific Ocean. Deep-Sea Res., 5: 111–127.

Coleman, F.C. and Wehle, D.H.S., 1984. Plastic pollution: a worldwide oceanic problem. Parks, 9: 9–12.

Coleman-Cooke, J., 1963. Discovery II in the Antarctic. Odhams, Watford, 255 pp.

Collen, J.D. and Froggatt, P.C., 1986, Depth of burial and hydrocarbon source rock potential. In: P.J. Barrett (Editor), Antarctic Cenozoic history from MSSTS–1 drillhole, McMurdo Sound. N.Z. Dep. Scient. Ind. Res. Bull., 237: 9–52.

Collins, I.F. and McCrae, I.R., 1985. Creep buckling of ice shelves and the formation of pressure rollers, J. Glaciol., 31: 242–252.

Colman, J.A.R., 1976. Gippsland Basin on-shore. In: R.B. Leslie, H.J. Evans and C.L. Knight (Editors), Economic Geology of Australia and Papua New Guinea 3. Petroleum. Australasian Institute of Mining and Metallurgy, Parkville, Victoria, pp. 34–40.

Colton, M.T. and Chase, R.R.P., 1983. Interactions of the Antarctic Circumpolar Current with bottom topography: An investigation using satellite altimetry. J. Geophys. Res., 88: 1825–1843.

Comiso, J.C. and Zwally, H.J., 1984. Concentration gradients and growth/decay characteristics of the seasonal sea ice cover. J. Geophys. Res., 89: 8081–8103.

Cook, R.A., 1981. Geology and bibliography of the Campbell Plateau, New Zealand. N.Z. Geol. Surv. Rep., 97: 48 pp.

Cook, R.A., 1985. Trends in New Zealand hydrocarbon exploration and discovery 1950–1985. N.Z. Geol. Surv. Rep., G96: 21 pp.

Cook, R.A., 1988. Interpretation of the geochemistry of oils of Taranaki and West Coast region, western New Zealand. Energy Exploration and Exploitation, 6: 201–212.

Cook, R.A. and Davey, F.J., 1984. The hydrocarbon exploration of the basins of the Ross Sea, Antarctica, from modelling of the geophyical data. J. Petroleum Geol., 7: 213–226.

Cook, R.A. and Woolhouse, A.D., 1989. Hydrocarbon residue. In: P.J. Barrett (Editor), Antarctic Cenozoic History from CIROS–1 Drillhole, McMurdo Sound. N.Z. Dep. Scient. Ind. Res. Bull., 245: in press.

Coombs, D.S. and Landis, C.A., 1966. Pumice from the South Sandwich eruption of March 1962 reaches New Zealand. Nature, 209: 289–290.

Cooper, A.K. and Davey, F.J., 1985. Episodic rifting of Phanerozoic rocks in the Victoria Land Basin, western Ross Sea, Antarctica. Science, 229: 1085–1087.

Cooper, A.K. and Davey, F.J. (Editors), 1987. The Antarctic Continental Margin : Geology and Geophysics of the Western Ross Sea. Circum-Pacific Council for Energy and Mineral Resources, Earth Science Series, Vol. 5B, 253 pp.

Cooper, A.K., Davey, F.J. and Behrendt, J.C., 1987. Seismic stratigraphy and structure of the Victoria Land Basin, Western Ross Sea, Antarctica. In: A.K. Cooper and F.J. Davey (Editors), The Antarctic Continental Margin: Geology and Geophysics of the western Ross Sea. Circum-Pacific Council for Energy and Mineral Resources, Earth Science Series, Vol. 5B, pp. 27–76.

Cooper, A.K., Davey, F.J. and Hinz, K., 1988. Antarctica – 1 Ross Sea – geology, hydrocarbon potential; Antarctica – 2 Liquid hydrocarbons probable under Ross Sea. Oil & Gas J., 86(45, 46): 54–58, 118–128.

Cooper, A.K., Davey, F.J. and Hinz, K., in press. Crustal extension and origin of sedimentary basins beneath the Ross Sea and Ross Ice Shelf, Antarctica. In: M.R.A. Thompson, J.A. Crame and J.W. Thomson (Editors), Geological Evolution of Antarctica. Cambridge University Press, Cambridge.

Copestake, P.G., Croxall, J.P. and Prince, P.A., 1983. Food digestion and energy consumption experiments on a king penguin Aptendoytes patagonicus. Br. Antarct. Surv. Bull., No. 58: 83–87.

Cortes, R.R., 1985. Perspectivas de desarrollo de recursos de hidrocarburos en la Antártica. Revista Minerales, 40: 21–25.

Crabtree, R.D. and Doake, C.S.M., 1982. Pine Island Glacier and its drainage basin: results from radio echo-sounding. Annals Glaciol., 3: 65–70.

Craddock, C., 1978. Antarctica and Gondwanaland. In: M.A. McWhinnie (Editor), Polar Research to the Present, and the Future. Westview Press, Colorado, pp. 62–96.

Craddock, C., 1982. Antarctica and Gondwanaland Review paper. In: C. Craddock (Editor), Antarctic Geoscience. University of Wisconsin Press, Madison, pp. 3–13.

Craddock, C. and Hollister, C.D., 1976. Geological evolution of the Southeast Pacific Basin. In: Initial Reports of the Deep Sea Drilling Project, Vol. 35. U.S. Govt Printing Office, Washington, D.C., pp. 723–743.

Craig, H., 1970. Abyssal carbon 13 in the South Pacific. J. Geophys. Res., 75: 691–695.

Craig, H., Broecker, W.S. and Spencer, D., 1981. GEOSECS Pacific Expedition, Vol. 4, Sections and Profiles. National Science Foundation, Washington, D.C., 251 pp.

Craig, H., Weiss, R.F. and Clarke, W.B., 1967. Dissolved gases in the equatorial and South Pacific Ocean. J. Geophys. Res., 72: 6165–6181.

Crockett, D.E., 1979. Rediscovery of the Chatham Island taiko solved century-old mystery. Forest and Bird, 13(4): 8, 9, 11–13.

Crockett, D.E., 1985. Chatham Island Taiko Pterodroma magentae. In: Readers Digest Complete Book of New Zealand Birds. Readers Digest, Reed Methuen, Sydney, pp. 78.

Crockett, R.N. and Clarkson, P.D., 1987. The exploitation of Antarctic minerals. Environment Internat., 13: 121–132.

336

Croxall, J.P., 1984. Seabirds. In: R.M. Laws (Editor), Antarctic Ecology, Vol. 2. Academic Press, London, pp. 533–619.

Croxall, J.P. and Gentry, R.L. (Editors), 1987. Status, Biology, and Ecology of Fur Seals. Proceeding of an International Symposium and Workshop, Cambridge, England, 23–27 April 1984. NOAA Tech. Rep., NMFS 51: 212 pp.

Croxall, J.P. and Prince, P.A., 1980. Food, feeding ecology and ecological segregation of seabirds at South Georgia. Biol. J. Linn. Soc., 14: 103–131.

Croxall, J.P., Prince, P.A., Hunter, I., McInnes, S.J. and Copestake, P.G., 1984. The seabirds of the Antarctic Peninsula, Islands of the Scotia Sea, and Antarctica Continent between 80°W and 20°W: their status and conservation. In: J.P. Croxall, P.G.H. Evans and R.W. Schreiber (Editors), Status and Conservation of the World's Seabirds. International Council for Bird Preservation Tech. Publ., No. 2: 637–666.

Croxall, J.P., Ricketts, C., and Prince, P.A., 1984. Impact of seabirds on marine resources, especially krill, of South Georgia waters. In: G.C. Whittow and H. Rahn (Editors), Seabird Energetics. Plenum Press, N.Y., pp. 285–317.

Csordas, S.E., 1962. The Kerguelen fur seal on Macquarie Island. Victorian Nat., 79: 226–229.

Csordas, S.E. and Ingham, S.E., 1965. The New Zealand fur seal Arctocephalus forsteri (Lesson) at Macquarie Island 1949–64. CSIRO Wildl. Res., 10: 83–99.

Cullen, D.J., 1967. Island arc development in the Southwest Pacific. Tectonophysics, 4: 163–172.

Cummings, W.C., 1985. Right Whales Eubalaena glacialis (Muller, 1776) and Eubalaena australis (Desmoulins, 1822). In: S.H. Ridgway and R. Harrison (Editors), Handbook of Marine Mammals 3: The Sirenians and Baleen Whales. Academic Press, London, pp. 275–304.

Curlin, J.W., Johnson, P., Westermeyer, W. and Stevens, C., 1986. Arctic offshore petroleum technologies. Oceanus, 29(1): 73–77.

Dahlberg, M.L. and Day, R.H., 1985. Observations of man-made objects on the surface of the North Pacific Ocean. In: R.S. Shomura and H.O. Yoshida (Editors), Proceedings of the Worksholp on the Fate and Impact of Marine Debris, 26–29 November 1984, Honolulu, Hawaii. U.S. Dept. Commer. NOAA Tech. Memo. NMFS, NOAA-TM-NMFS-SWFC-54: pp. 198–212.

Dalziel, I.W.D., 1981. Back-arc extension in the southern Andes: a review and critical appraisal. Philos. Trans. R. Soc. London, Ser. A, 300: 319–335.

Dalziel, I.W.D., 1982. The early (pre Middle Jurassic) history of the Scotia arc region: a review and progress report. In: C. Craddock (Editor), Antarctic Geoscience, University of Wisconsin Press, Madison, pp. 111–126.

Dalziel, I.W.D., 1983. The evolution of the Scotia Arc: a review. In: R.L. Oliver, P.R. James and J.B. Jago (Editors), Antarctic Earth Science, Australian Academy of Science, Canberra, pp. 283–288.

Dalziel, I.W.D. and Elliot, D.H., 1973. The Scotia arc and Antarctic margin. In: A.E.M. Nairn and G.F. Stehli (Editors), The Ocean Basins and Margins Vol. 1, The South Atlantic. Plenum Press, N.Y., pp. 171–246.

Dangeard, L., Vanney, J.R. and Johnson, G.L., 1977. Affleurements, courants et faciès dan la zone Antarctique du Pacifique Oriental (Mers de Bellingshausen et d'Amundsen). Ann. Inst. océanogr., Paris, 53: 105–124.

Daniel, M. and Baker, A., 1986. Collins Guide to the Mammals of New Zealand. Collins, Auckland, 228 pp.

Darby, M., 1970. Natural history of the Bounty Islands. Animals, 13: 171–177.

Dater, H.M., 1975. History of Antarctic exploration and scientific investigation. Antarctic

Map Folio Ser., Folio 19, 6 pp. + 15 plates.

Davey, F.J., 1981. Geophysical studies in the Ross Sea region. J. Roy. Soc. N.Z., 11: 465–479.

Davey, F.J., 1985. The Antarctic margin and its possible hydrocarbon potential. Tectonophysics, 114: 443–470.

Davey, F.J., Bennett, D.J. and Houtz, R.E., 1982. Sedimentary basins of the Ross Sea, Antarctica. N.Z. Jl Geol. Geophys., 25: 245–255.

Davey, F.J. and Christoffel, D.A., 1984. The correlation of the MSSTS–1 drillhole results with seismic reflection data from McMurdo Sound, Antarctica. N.Z. Jl Geol. Geophys., 27: 405–412.

Davey, F.J. and Cooper, A.K., 1987. Gravity studies of the Victoria Land Basin and Iselin Bank. In: A.K. Cooper and F. J. Davey (Editors), The Antarctic Continental Margin: Geology and Geophysics of the Western Ross Sea. Circum Pacific Council for Energy and Mineral Resources, Earth Science Series, Vol. 5B, pp. 119–137.

Davey, F.J., Hinz, K. and Schroeder, H., 1983. Sedimentary basins of the Ross Sea, Antarctica. In: R.L. Oliver, P.R. James and J.B. Jago (Editors), Antarctic Earth Science, Australian Academy of Science, Camberra, pp. 533–438.

Davey, F.J. and Houtz, R.E., 1977. The Campbell Plateau and its relationship with the Ross Sea, Antarctica. Mar. Geol., 25: 61–72.

David, P.M., 1965. The chaetognatha of the Southern Ocean. In: J. van Mieghem and P. van Oye (Editors), Biogeography and Ecology in Antarctica. Junk, The Hague, pp. 296–325.

Davis, L.S., Ward, G.D. and Sadleir, R.M.F.S., 1988. Foraging by Adélie penguins during the incubation period. Notornis, 35: 15–23.

Dawbin, W.H., 1952. Whales and whaling in the Southern Ocean. In: F.A. Simpson (Editor), The Antarctic Today. A.H. & A.W. Reed, Wellington, pp. 151–194.

Dawbin, W.H., 1987. Right whales caught in the waters around south eastern Australia and New Zealand during the 19th and 20th centuries. Rep. Int. Whal. Commn Spec. Issue 10: 261–267.

Dawson, E.W., 1973. Albatross populations at the Chatham Islands. Notornis, 20: 210–230.

Dawson, S. and Slooten, E., 1987. The down under dolphin. Forest and Bird, 18(4): 32–34.

Dawson, S. and Slooten, E., 1988.. Hector's dolphin, Cephalorhynchus hectori: Distribution and Abundance. In: R.L. Brownell and G.P. Donovan (Editors), The Biology of the Genus Cephalorhynchus. Rep. Int. Whal. Commn Spec. Issue 9: 315–324.

Day, R.H., 1980. The occurrence and characteristics of plastic pollution in Alaska's marine birds. Unpubl. M.S. thesis, University of Alaska, Fairbanks, Alaska, 111 pp.

Day, R.H., Wehle, D.H.S. and Coleman, F.C., 1985. Ingestion of plastic pollutants by marine birds. In: R.S. Shomura and H.O. Yoshida (Editors), Proceedings of the Workshop on the Fate and Impact of Marine Debris, 26–29 November 1984, Honolulu, Hawaii. U.S. Dept. Commer. NOAA Tech. Memo. NMFS, NOAA-TM-NMFS-SWFC-54: pp. 344–386.

Dayton, P.K. and Robilliard, G.A., 1971. Implications of pollution to the McMurdo Sound benthos. Antarct. Jl U.S. 6: 53–56.

de Wit, M.J., 1985. Minerals and Mining in Antarctica Science and Technology, Economics and Politics. Clarendon Press, Oxford, 127 pp.

Deacon, G.E.R., 1933. A general account of the hydrology of the South Atlantic Ocean. Discovery Reps, 7: 171–238.

Deacon, G.E.R., 1937. The hydrology of the Southern Ocean. Discovery Reps, 15: 1–124.

Deacon, G.E.R., 1963. The Southern Ocean. In: M.N. Hill (Editor), The Sea, Vol. 2. Interscience Publishers, N.Y., pp. 281–296.

Deacon, G.E.R., 1964. Antarctic oceanography: The physical environment. In: R. Carrick,

338

M. Holdgate and J. Prévost (Editors), Biologie Antarctique. Hermann, Paris, pp. 81–86.

Deacon, G.E.R., 1975a. Southern Ocean exploration. Oceanus, 18(4): 2–7.

Deacon, G.E.R., 1975b. The oceanographical observations on Scott's last expedition. Polar Rec., 17(109): 391–396.

Deacon, G.E.R., 1977a. The Southern Ocean: History of exploration. In: G.A. Llano (Editor), Adaptations within Antarctic Ecosystems. Proceedings of the Third SCAR Symposium on Antarctic Biology. Smithsonian Institution, Washington, D.S., pp. xv–xxxvii.

Deacon, G.E.R., 1977b. Comments on a counterclockwise circulation in the Pacific sub-antarctic sector of the Southern Ocean suggested by McGinnis. Deep-Sea Res., 24: 927–930.

Deacon, G.E.R., 1982. Physical and biological zonation in the Southern Ocean. Deep-Sea Res., 29: 1–15.

Deacon, G., 1984. The Antarctic Circumpolar Ocean. Cambridge University Press, Cambridge, 180 pp.

Deacon, M., 1971. Scientists and the Sea 1650–1900 A Study of Marine Science. Academic Press, London, 445 pp.

Dean, W.E., Claypool, G.E. and Thiede, J., 1984. Accumulation of organic matter in Cretaceous oxygen-deficient depositional environments in the Central Pacific Ocean. Org. Geochem., 7: 39–51.

Debenham, F., 1948. The problem of the Great Ross Barrier. Geogr. J., 112: 196–218.

Decker, E.R., 1978. Geothermal models of the Ross Island–Dry Valleys Region. Dry Valley Drilling Project Bull., No. 8: 11.

Demaison, G., 1984. The generative basin concept. In: G. Demaison and R.J. Murris, Petroleum Geochemistry and Basin Evaluation. AAPG Memoir, 35: 1–14.

De Master, D.P., 1979. Weddell Seal. In: Mammals of the Seas 2, FAO Fish. Ser., 5, pp. 130–134.

Denton, G.H. and Hughes, T.J., 1981. The Last Great Ice Sheets. Wiley, N.Y., 484 pp.

Department of Lands and Survey, 1983. Management plan for the Campbell Islands Nature Reserve. Department of Lands and Survey, Wellington, 77 pp.

Department of Lands and Survey, 1984. Management plan for the Snares Islands Nature Reserve. Department of Lands and Survey, Wellington, 58 pp.

Department of Lands and Survey, 1987. Management plan for the Auckland Islands Nature Reserve. Department of Lands and Survey, Wellington, 78 pp.

De Rycke, R.J., 1973. Sea ice motions off Antarctica in the vicinity of the eastern Ross Sea as observed by satellite. J. Geophys. Res., 78: 8873–8879.

Dickerman, R.W. and Goelet, R.G., 1987. Northern gannet starvation after swallowing styrofoam. Mar. Pollut. Bull., 18: 293.

Dietz, R.S., 1952. Some Pacific and Antarctic sea-floor features discovered during the U.S. Navy Antarctic Expedition, 1946–1947. Proc. 7th Pacif. Sci. Congr., 3: 335–344.

Dilks, P.J. and Wilson, P.R., 1979. Feral sheep and cattle and Royal Albatrosses on Campbell Island: population trends and habitat changes. N.Z. Jl Zool., 6: 127–139.

Dixon, T.R. and Dixon, T.J., 1981. Marine litter surveillance. Mar. Pollut. Bull., 12: 289–295.

Dixon, T.H. and Parke, M.E., 1983. Bathymetry estimates in the southern oceans from Seasat altimetry. Nature, 304: 406–411.

Doake, C.S.M., 1982. State of balance of the ice sheet in the Antarctic Peninsula. Annls Glaciol., 3: 77–82.

Doake, C.S.M., 1985. Antarctic mass balance: glaciological evidence from Antarctic Peninsula and Weddell Sea sector. In: Glaciers, Ice Sheets, and Sea Level: Effect of a CO_2-induced Climatic Change. Report of a workshop held in Seattle, Washington, September 13–15, 1984, pp. 197–209.

Donoghue, M., 1987. Marine debris: plastic not so fantastic. Catch, 14(6): 15–18.

Dott, R.H., 1976. Contrasts in tectonic history along the eastern Pacific rim. Am. Geophys. Un. Geophys. Monogr., No. 19: 299–308.

Doty, M. and Oguri, M., 1956. The island mass effect. Cons. Perm. Int. Explor. Mer, 22: 33–37.

Drewry, D.J., 1979. Late Wisconsin reconstruction for the Ross Sea region, Antarctica. J. Glaciol., 24: 231–244.

Drewry, D.J. (Editor), 1983. Antarctica: glaciological and geophysical folio. Scott Polar Research Institute, University of Cambridge, Cambridge.

Drewry, D.J., 1986. Glacial Geologic Processes. Edward Arnold, Baltimore, Md, 276 pp.

Drewry, D.J. and Cooper, A.P.R., 1981. Processes and models of Antarctic glaciomarine sedimentation. Annals Glaciol., 2: 117–122.

Drewry, D.J., Jordon, S.R. and Jankowski, E., 1982. Measured properties of the Antarctic Ice Sheet: surface configuration, ice thickness, volume and bedrock characteristics. Annals Glaciol., 3: 83–91.

Driscoll, M.L. and Parsons, B., 1988. Cooling of the oceanic lithosphere – evidence from geoid anomalies across the Udintsev and Eltanin Fracture Zones. Earth Planet. Sci. Letts, 88: 289–307.

Dugger, J.A., 1978. Exploiting Antarctic mineral resources – technology, economics and the environment. Univ. Miami Law Rev., 33: 315–339.

Dunbar, M.J., 1985. The Arctic marine ecosystem. In: F.R. Engelhardt (Editor), Petroleum Effects in the Arctic Environment. Elsevier Applied Science Publishers, London, pp. 1 35.

Dunbar, R.B., Anderson, J.B., Domack, E.W. and Jacobs, S.S., 1985. Oceanographic influences on sedimentation along the Antarctic continental shelf. Antarctic Res. Ser., 43: 291–312.

Dunbar, R.B., Leventer, A.R. and Stockton, W.L., 1989. Biogenic sedimentation in McMurdo Sound, Antarctica. Mar. Geol., 85: 155–179.

Du Toit, A.L., 1937. Our Wandering Continents An Hypothesis of Continental Drifting. Oliver and Boyd, Edinburgh, 366 pp.

Eagle, G.A., Green, A. and Williams, J., 1979. Tar ball concentrations in the ocean around the Cape of Good Hope before and after a major oil spill. Mar. Pollut. Bull., 10: 321–325.

Eakin, R.R., Dearborn, J.H. and Townend, W.C., 1986. Observations of marine birds in the South Atlantic Ocean in the late austral autumn. Antarctic Res. Ser., 44: 69–86.

Earland, A., 1935. Foraminifera Part III. The Falklands sector of the Antarctic (excluding South Georgia). Discovery Reps, 10: 3–208.

Editorial Committee, 1952. Recent expeditions and institutional activities. In: F.A. Simpson (Editor), The Antarctic Today. A.H. & A.W. Reed, Wellington, pp. 313–324.

Edmond, J.M., Jacobs, S.S., Gordon, A.L., Mantyla, A.W. and Weiss, R.F., 1979. Water column anomalies in dissolved silica over opaline pelagic sediments and the origin of the deep silica maximum. J. Geophys. Res., 84: 7809–7826.

Edwards, D.M. and Heap, J.A., 1981. Convention on the Conservation of Antarctic Marine Living Resources : A commentary. Polar Rec., 20(127): 353–362.

Edwards, D.S., 1968. The detrital mineralogy of surface sediments of the ocean floor in the area of the Antarctic Peninsula, Antarctica. Contr. Sediment. Res. Lab. Fla State Univ., 25: 68 pp.

Ehrenberg, C.G., 1844. Einige vorlaufige Resultate der Untersuchungen der von der Sudpolreise des Capitain Ross, so wie von den Herren Schayer und Darwin zugekommenen Materialien. Mber. Preuss. Akad. Wiss.: 182–207.

Eittreim, S.L., Cooper, A.K., and Scientific Staff, 1984. Marine geological and geophysical investigations of the Antarctic continental margin, 1984. U.S. Geol. Surv. Circ., 935: 12 pp.

Ekman, V.W., 1905. On the influence of the earth's rotation on ocean currents. Ark. Math., Astron. Fysik., 2: 1–53.

Elliot, D.H., 1977. A Framework for Assessing Environmental Impacts of Possible Antarctic Mineral Development. Institute of Polar Studies, Ohio State University, Columbus, Ohio (2 Parts).

Elliot, D.H., 1988. Antarctica : Is there any oil and natural gas? Oceanus, 31(2): 32–38.

Ellis, R., 1981. The Book of Whales. Robert Hale, London, 202 pp.

El-Sayed, S.Z., 1967. On the productivity of the southwest Atlantic Ocean and the waters west of the Antarctic Peninsula. Antarctic Res. Ser., 11: 15–47.

El-Sayed, S.Z., 1968. Primary productivity of the Antarctic and Subantarctic. In: V.C. Bushnell (Editor) and S.Z. El-Sayed (Co-editor), Primary productivity and benthic marine algae of the Antarctic and Subantarctic. Antarctic Map Folio Ser., Folio 10, pp. 1–6.

El-Sayed, S.Z., 1970a. On the productivity of the Southern Ocean (Atlantic and Pacific sectors). In: M.W. Holdgate (Editor), Antarctic Ecology, Vol. 1. Academic Press, London, pp. 119–135.

El-Sayed, S.Z, 1970b. Phytoplankton productivity of the South Pacific and the Pacific Sector of the Antarctic. In: W.S. Wooster (Editor), Scientific Exploration of the South Pacific. National Academy of Sciences, Washington, D.C., pp. 194–210.

El-Sayed, S.Z., 1971a. Observations on the phytoplankton bloom in the Weddell Sea. Antarctic Res. Ser., 17: 301–312.

El-Sayed, S.Z., 1971b. Dynamics of trophic relations in the Southern Ocean. In: L.O. Quam (Editor), Research in the Antarctic. American Association for the Advancement of Science, Washington, D.C., pp. 73–92.

El-Sayed, S.Z., 1973. Biological oceanography. Antarctic Jl U.S., 8(3): 93–100.

El-Sayed, S.Z. (Editor), 1977. Biological Investigations of Marine Antarctic Systems and Stocks (BIOMASS), Vol. 1. Research Proposals prepared by SCAR/SCOR Group of Specialists on Living Resources of the Southern Ocean, 79 pp.

El-Sayed, S.Z., 1978. Primary productivity and estimates of potential yields of the Southern Ocean. In: M.A. McWhinnie (Editor), Polar Research to the Present, and the Future. Westview Press, Colorado, pp. 141–160.

El-Sayed, S.Z., 1984. Productivity of Antarctic waters – A Reappraisal. In: O. Holm-Hansen, L. Bolis and R. Gils (Editors), Marine Phytoplankton and Productivity. Springer-Verlag, Berlin, pp. 19–34.

El-Sayed, S.Z., 1987. Biological productivity of the Antarctic waters : present paradoxes and emerging paradigms. In: S.Z. El-Sayed and A.P. Tomo (Editors), Regional Symposium on Recent Advances in Antarctic Aquatic Biology, with special reference to the Antarctic Peninsula, San Carlos de Bariloche, Argentina, 6–10 June, 1983, pp. 1–21.

El-Sayed, S.Z., Bigg, D.C. and Holm-Hansen, O., 1983. Primary productivity, standing crop of phytoplankton and ammonium chemistry of the Ross Sea. Deep-Sea Res., 30: 871–886.

El-Sayed, S.Z. and Hofmann, E.E., 1986. Drake Passage and Western Scotia Sea (Antarctica). In: W.A. Hovis (Editor), Nimbus-7 CZCS Coastal Zone Color Scanner Imagery for Selected Coastal Regions, pp. 97–99.

El-Sayed, S.Z. and Taguchi, S., 1981. Primary production and standing crop along the ice edge in the Weddell Sea. Deep-Sea Res., 28: 1017–1032.

El-Sayed, S.Z. and Turner, J.T., 1977. Productivity of the Antarctic and tropical/subtropic regions: A comparative study. In: M.J. Dunbar (Editor), Polar Oceans. Arctic Institute of North America, Calgary, pp. 463–503.

Emery, W.J., 1977. Antarctic Polar Frontal Zone from Australia to the Drake Passage. J. Phys. Oceanogr., 7: 811–822.

Erickson, A.W. and Hofman, R.J., 1974. Antarctic Seals. In: V.C. Bushnell (Editor), Antarctic Map Folio Ser., Folio 18, pp. 4–13.

Erickson, A.W., Siniff, D.B., Cline, D.R., and Hofman, R.J., 1971. Distributional ecology of Antarctic seals. In: G. Deacon (Editor), Symposium of Antarctic Ice and Water Masses. Proceedings. Scientific Committee on Antarctic Research, Cambridge, pp. 55–76.

Ettershank, G., 1984. A new approach to the assessment of longevity in the Antarctic krill *Euphausia superba*. J. Crustacean Biol., 4 (Spec. No. 1): 295–305.

Evans, P.G.H., 1987. The Natural History of Whales and Dolphins. Christopher Helm, London, 343 pp.

Everson, I., 1977. The living resources of the Southern Ocean. FAO Southern Ocean Fisheries Survey Programme, GLO/80/77/1: 156 pp.

Everson, I., 1984a. Fish biology. In: R.M. Laws (Editor), Antarctic Ecology, Vol. 2. Academic Press, London, pp. 491–532.

Everson, I., 1984b. Marine zooplankton. In: R.M. Laws (Editor), Antarctic Ecology, Vol. 2. Academic Press, London, pp. 463–490.

Ewing, M. and Heezen, B.C., 1956. Some problems of Antarctic submarine geology. Am. Geophys. Un. Geophys. Monogr., No. 1: 75–81.

Falla, R.A., 1937. Birds. B.A.N.Z. Antarct. Res. Exped. Reps, Ser. B, Vol. II, 288 pp.

Falla, R.A., 1962. Exploitation of seals, whales and penguins in New Zealand. Proc. N.Z. Ecol. Soc., 9: 34–38.

Falla, R.A., 1965. Birds and mammals of the subantarctic islands. Proc. N.Z. Ecol. Soc., 12: 63–68.

Falla, R.A., Sibson, R.B. and Turbott, E.G., 1979. The New Guide to the Birds of New Zealand. Collins, Auckland, 247 pp.

Falla, R.A., Taylor, R.H. and Black, C., 1979. Survey of Dundas Island, Auckland Islands, with particular reference to Hooker's sea lion (*Phocarctos hookeri*). N.Z. Jl Zool., 6: 347–355.

Falvey, D.A., 1974. The development of continental margins in plate tectonic theory. APEA J., 14: 95–106.

FAO, 1985. FAO species identification sheets for fishery purposes Southern Ocean CCAMLR Convention Area Fishing Areas 48, 58 and 88. Food and Agriculture Organisation of the United Nations, Rome, 2 vols.

Farman, J.C. and Gardiner, B.G., 1987. Ozone depletion over Antarctica. Nature, 329: 574.

Fay, R.R., 1973. Significance of nanoplankton in primary production of the Ross Sea, Antarctica during the 1972 austral summer. Unpubl. Ph.D. thesis, Texas A&M University, 184 pp.

Fenwick, G.D., 1978. Plankton swarms and their predators at the Snares Islands. N.Z. Jl Mar. Freshwater Res., 12: 223–224.

Fevolden, S.E., 1987. Norwegian expedition to Peter I. Island. BIOMASS Newsletter 9(1): 14.

Fischer, A.G., 1982. Long-term climatic oscillations recorded in stratigraphy. In: Climate in Earth History. National Academy Press, Washington, D.C., pp. 97–104.

Fisher, W. and Mohr, H., 1978. Verhaltensbeobachtungen an krill (*Euphausia superba* Dana). Arch. FischWiss., 29 (Beih. 1): 71–79.

Fleming, C.A., 1939. Birds of the Chatham Islands. Emu, 38: 380–412, 492–509.

Fleming, C.A., 1952. The seas between. In: F.A. Simpson (Editor), The Antarctic Today. A.H. & A.W. Reed, Wellington, pp. 102–126.

Fleming, C.A., 1979. The Geological History of New Zealand and its Life. Auckland

University Press, Auckland. 141 pp.

Fleming, C.A. and Baker, A.N., 1973. The Snares Western Chain. Notornis, 20: 37–45.

Fogg, G.E., 1977. Aquatic primary production in the Antarctic. Philos. Trans. R. Soc. London, Ser. B., 279: 27–38.

Foggo, M.N. and Meurk, C.D., 1981. Notes on a visit to Jacquemart Island in the Campbell Island Group. N.Z. Jl Zool., 4: 29–32.

Forbes, L.M., 1966. New Zealand and United States expedition to the Ross Sea, the Balleny Islands and Macquarie Ridge, 1965. Polar Rec., 13(82): 52–54.

Fordyce, R.E., 1977. The development of the Circum-Antarctic Current and the evolution of the Mysticeti (Mammalia : Cetacea). Palaeogeogr. Palaeoclimatol. Palaeoecol., 21: 265–271.

Fordyce, R.E., 1985. The history of southern whales. In: J.K. Ling and M.M. Bryden (Editors), Studies of Sea Mammals in South Latitudes. South Australia Museum, Adelaide, pp. 79–104.

Fordyce, R.E., Mattlin, R.H. and Dixon, J.M., 1984. Second record of spectacled porpoise from the subantarctic southwest Pacific. Scient. Rep. Whal. Res. Inst., 35: 159–164.

Forster, H., 1985. The South Sea Whaler An Annotated Bibliography. The Kendall Whaling Museum, Saron and Edward J. Lefkowicz, Fairhaven, U.S.A., 157 pp.

Forsythe, R., 1982. The Late Palaeozoic to Early Mesozoic evolution of southern South America: a plate tectonic interpretation. J. Geol. Soc. Lond., 139: 671–682.

Foster, B.A., 1987. Composition and abundance of zooplankton under the spring sea-ice of McMurdo Sound, Antarctica. Polar Biol., 8: 41–48.

Foster, T.D., 1984. The marine environment. In: R.M. Laws (Editor), Antarctic Ecology, Vol. 2. Academic Press, London, pp. 345–371.

Fowler, C.W., 1987. Marine debris and northern fur seals: a case study. Mar. Pollut. Bull., 18: 326–335.

Frakes, L.A., 1983. Problems in Antarctic marine geology: A review. In: R.L. Oliver, P.R. James and J.B. Jago (Editors), Antarctic Earth Science. Australian Academy of Science, Canberra, pp. 375–378.

Fraser, C., 1986. Beyond the Roaring Forties New Zealand's Subantarctic Islands. Government Printing Office, Wellington, 214 pp.

Fraser, W.A. and Ainley, D.G., 1986. Ice edges and seabird occurrence in Antarctica. Bioscience, 36: 258–263.

Fredrickson, L.H., 1971. Environmental awareness at Hallett Station. Antarct. Jl U.S., 6: 57.

French, G.A. (Editor), 1974. Antarctic Pilot, comprising the coasts of Antarctica and all islands southward of the usual route of vessels 4th ed. U.K. Hydrographic Dept., Tauton, Somerset, 336 pp.

Fry, D.M., Fefer, S.I. and Sileo, L., 1987. Ingestion of plastic debris by Lysan Albatrosses and Wedge-tailed Shearwaters in the Hawaiian Islands. Mar. Pollut. Bull., 16: 339–343.

Fu, L.-L. and Chelton, D.B., 1984. Temporal variability of the Antarctic Circumpolar Current observed by satellite altimetry. Science, 226: 343–346.

Fukuchi, M., 1980. Phytoplankton chlorophyll stocks in the Antarctic Ocean. J. Oceanogr. Soc. Japan, 36: 73–84.

Furness, B.L., 1983. Plastic particles in three procellariiform seabirds from the Benguela Current, South Africa. Mar. Pollut. Bull., 14: 307–308.

Furness, R.W., 1985. Ingestion of plastic particles by seabirds at Gough Island, South Atlantic Ocean. Environ. Pollut., Ser. A, 38: 261–272.

Gambell, R., 1985a. Fin Whale *Balaenoptera physalis* (Linnaeus, 1758). In: S.H. Ridgway and R. Harrison (Editors), Handbook of Marine Mammals 3: The Sirenians and Baleen Whales. Academic Press, London, pp. 171–192.

Gambell, R., 1985b. Sei Whale *Balaenoptera borealis* Lesson, 1828. In: S.H. Ridgway and R. Harrison (Editors), Handbook of Marine Mammals 3: The Sirenians and Baleen Whales. Academic Press, London, pp. 155–170.

Gambell, R., 1987. Whales in the antarctic ecosystem. Environment Internat., 13: 47–54.

Garner, D.M., 1958. The Antartcic Convergence south of New Zealand. N.Z. Jl Geol. Geophys., 1: 577–594.

Garrett, J.F., 1980. Availability of the FGGE drifting buoy system data set. Deep-Sea Res., 27: 1083–1086.

Garrett, J.N., 1984. The economics of Antarctic oil. In: L.M. Alexander and L.C. Hanson (Editors), Antarctic Politics and Marine Resources : Critical Choices for the 1980s. Center for Ocean Management Studies, Kingston, Rhode Island, pp. 185–190.

Gaskin, D.E., 1968. The New Zealand Cetacea. Fish. Res. Bull. (N.Z.), 1: 1–92.

Gaskin, D.E., 1972. Whales, dolphins and seals. Heinemann Educational Books, Auckland, 200 pp.

Gaskin, D.E., 1976. The evolution, zoogeography and ecology of Cetacea. Oceanogr. Mar. Biol. Ann. Rev., 14: 257–346.

Gaskin, D.E., 1983. The Ecology of Whales and Dolphins. Heinemann, London, 480 pp.

Gerrodette, G., 1985. Toward a population dynamics of marine debris. In: R.S. Shomura and H.O. Yoshida (Editors), Proceedings of the Workshop on the Fate and Impact of Marine Debris, 26–29 November 1984, Honolulu, Hawaii. U.S. Dept. Commer. NOAA Tech. Mem. NMFS, NOAA-TM-NMFS-SWFC--54: pp. 508–518.

Gilbert, J.R. and Erickson, A.W., 1977. Distribution and abundance of seals in the pack ice of the Pacific sector of the Southern Ocean. In: G.A. Llano (Editor), Adaptations within Antarctic Ecosystems. Smithsonian Institution, Washington, D.C., pp. 703–748.

Gill, A.E., 1973. Circulation and bottom water production in the Weddell Sea. Deep-Sea Res., 20: 111–140.

Gilmour, A.E., 1979. Sea temperatures from McMurdo Sound and White Island, Antarctica. N.Z. Jl Mar. Freshwater Res., 13: 141–142.

Giovinetto, M.B. and Bentley, C.R., 1985. Surface balance of ice drainage systems of Antarctica. Antarctic Jl U.S., 20(4): 6–13.

Gjelsvik, T., 1983. The mineral resources of Antarctica: Progress in their identification. In: F.O. Vicuña (Editor), Antarctic Resources Policy Scientific, Legal and Politcal Issues. Cambridge University Press, Cambridge, pp. 61–76.

Glasby, G.P., 1976a. Surface densities of manganese nodules in the southern sector of the South Pacific. N.Z. Jl Geol. Geophys., 19: 771–790.

Glasby, G.P., 1976b. Manganese nodules in the South Pacific: a review. N.Z. Jl Geol. Geophys., 19: 707–736.

Glasby, G.P., 1983. The Southwestern Pacific and Samoan Basins. N.Z. Geographer, 39: 3–11.

Glasby, G.P., Barrett, P.J., McDougall, J.C. and McKnight, D.G., 1976. Localised variations in sedimentation characteristics in the Ross Sea and McMurdo Sound regions, Antarctica. N.Z. Jl Geol. Geophys. 18: 605–621.

Glasby, G.P., Meylan, M.A., Margolis, S.V. and Bäcker, H., 1980. Manganese deposits of the Southwestern Pacific Basin. In: I.M. Varentsov and Gy. Grasselly (Editors), Geology and Geochemistry of Manganese, Vol. 3. Hungarian Academy of Science, Budapest, pp. 137–183.

Gleadow, A.J.W. and Fitzgerald, P., 1987. Uplift history and structure of the Transantarctic Mountains: New evidence from fission track dating on basement apatites in the Dry Valley area, southern Victoria Land. Earth Planet. Sci. Lett, 82: 1–14.

Goodall, R.N.P., 1978. Report on the small cetaceans stranded on the coasts of Tierra del

Fuego. Scient. Rep. Whales Res. Inst., 30: 197–230.

Goodall, R.N.P. and Cameron, I.S., 1980. Exploitation of small cetaceans off southern South America. Rep. Int. Whal. Commn, 30: 445–450.

Goodall, R.N.P. and Galeazzi, A.R., 1985. A review of the food habits of the small cetaceans of the Antarctic and sub-Antarctic. In: W.R. Siegfried, P.R. Condy and R.M. Laws (Editors), Antactic Nutrient Cycles and Food Webs. Springer-Verlag, Berlin, pp. 566–572.

Goodell, H.G., 1968. The marine geology of the Southern Ocean, USNS Eltanin Cruises 16–27. Contr. sediment. Res. Lab. Fla State Univ., 25: 245 pp.

Goodell, H.G., 1973. The sediments. Antarctic Map Ser., Folio 17, pp. 1–9.

Goodell, H.G., Meylan, M.A. and Grant, B., 1971. Ferromanganese deposits of the South Pacific Ocean, Drake Passage, and Scotia Sea. Antarctic Res. Ser., 15: 27–92.

Goodell, H.G. and Watkins, N.D., 1968. The paleomagnetic stratigraphy of the Southern Ocean: 20° West to 160° East longitude. Deep-Sea Res., 15: 89–112.

Gordon, A.L., 1966. Potential temperature, oxygen and circulation of bottom water in the Southern Ocean. Deep-Sea Res., 13: 1125–1138.

Gordon, A.L., 1967a. Geostrophic transport through the Drake Passage. Science, 156: 1732–1734.

Gordon, A.L., 1967b. Structure of Antarctic waters between 20°W and 170°W. Antarctic Map Folio Ser., 6: 1–10, pls 1–14.

Gordon, A.L., 1971. Antarctic Polar Front Zone. Antarctic Res. Ser., 15: 205–221.

Gordon, A.L., 1972a. On the interaction of the Antarctic Circumpolar Current and the Macquarie Ridge. Antarctic Res. Ser., 19: 71–78.

Gordon, A.L., 1972b. Spreading of Antarctic Bottom Waters II. In: A.L. Gordon (Editor), Studies in Physical Oceanography A tribute of George Wüst on his 80th birthday. Gordon and Breach, London, 2: pp 1–17.

Gordon, A.L., 1973. Physical oceanography. Antarctic Jl U.S., 8: 61–69.

Gordon, A.L., 1975. An Antarctic oceanographic section along 170°E. Deep-Sea Res., 22: 357–377.

Gordon, A.L., 1977. International Southern Ocean Studies. In: M.J. Dunbar (Editor), Polar Oceans. Arctic Institute of North America, Calgary, pp. 219–225.

Gordon, A.L., 1978. Deep Antarctic convection west of Maud Rise. J. Phys. Oceanogr., 8: 600–612.

Gordon, A.L., 1981. Seasonality of Southern Ocean sea ice. J. Geophys. Res., 86: 4193–4197.

Gordon, A.L., 1986. Interocean exchange of thermocline water. J. Geophys. Res., 91: 5037–5046.

Gordon, A.L., 1987. Is there a global scale ocean circulation? EOS Trans. Am. geophys. Un. 67: 109–110.

Gordon, A.L. and Bye, J.A.T., 1972. Surface dynamic topography of Antarctic waters. J. Geophys. Res., 77: 5993–5999.

Gordon, A.L., Georgi, D.T. and Taylor, H.W., 1977a. Antarctic Polar Front Zone in the western Scotia Sea – summer 1975. J. Phys. Oceanogr., 7: 309–328.

Gordon, A.L. and Goldberg, R.D., 1970. Circumpolar characteristics of Antarctic waters. Antarctic Map Folio Ser., Folio 13, pp. 1–5 + plates 1–18.

Gordon, A.L. and Molinelli, E.J., 1982. Thermohaline and chemical distributions and the atlas data set. In: Southern Ocean Atlas, Columbia University Press, N.Y., pp 3–11 + 233 plates.

Gordon, A.L., Molinelli, E. and Baker, T., 1978. Large-scale relative dynamic topography of the Southern Ocean. J. Geophys. Res., 83: 3023–3032.

Gordon, A.L., Molinelli, E.J. and Baker, T.N., 1982. Southern Ocean Atlas. Columbia

University Press, N.Y., 34 pp. + 233 plates.

Gordon, A.L., Taylor, H.W. and Georgi, D.T., 1977b. Antarctic oceanographic zonation. In: M.J. Dunbar (Editor), Polar Oceans. Arctic Institute of North America, Calgary, pp. 45–76.

Gordon, A.L. and Tchernia, P., 1972. Waters of the continental margin off Adelie Coast, Antarctica. Antarctic Res. Ser., 19: 59–69.

Gow, A.J., 1965. The Ice Sheet. In: T. Hatherton (Editor), Antarctica. A.H. & A.W. Reed, Wellington, pp. 221–258.

Gow, A.J., Ackley, S.F., Weeks, W.F. and Govoni, J.W., 1982. Physical and structural characteristics of Antarctic sea ice. Annals Glaciol., 3: 113–117.

Gran, H.H., 1932. Phytoplankton. Methods and problems. J. Cons. Perm. Int. Explor. Mer, 7: 344–358.

Grant, A.C., 1985. Structural evolution of the head of the Solander Trough based on analysis of seismic basement. N.Z. Jl Geol. Geophys., 28: 5–22.

Greely, A.W., 1929. The Polar Regions in the Twentieth Century Their Discovery and Industrial Evolution. George G. Harrap, London, 223 pp.

Green, K., 1986. Food of the Cape Pigeon (*Daption capense*) from Princess Elizabeth Land, East Antarctica. Notornis, 33: 151–154.

Green Hammond, K.A., 1981. Modelling of Antarctic ecosystems. In: Biological Investigations of Marine Antarctic Systems and Stocks (BIOMASS), Vol. II. SCAR/SCOR. Scott Polar Research Institute, Cambridge, pp. 23–29.

Gregory, M.R., 1977. Plastic pellets on New Zealand beaches. Mar. Pollut. Bull., 8: 82–84.

Gregory, M.R., 1978. Accumulation and distribution of virgin plastic granules on New Zealand beaches. N.Z. Jl Mar. Freshwater Res., 12: 399–414.

Gregory, M.R., 1981. Oil and the coast. In: P. Tortell (Editor), New Zealand Atlas of Coastal Resources. New Zealand Government Printer, Wellington. 28 pp.

Gregory, M.R., 1982. Ross Sea hydrocarbon prospects and the IXTOC 1 oil blowout, Campeche Bay, Gulf of Mexico: comparisons and lessons. N.Z. Antarctic Rec., 4(2): 40–45.

Gregory, M.R., 1983. Virgin plastic granules on some beaches of eastern Canada and Bermuda. Mar. Environmental Res., 10: 73–92.

Gregory, M.R., 1985. The Subantarctic Islands and oil-spill persistence (or physical sensitivity) index mapping. (Unpubl. report to Department of Lands and Survey, Wellington, New Zealand), 23 pp.

Gregory, M.R., 1987. Plastics and other seaborne litter on the shores of New Zealand's Subantarctic Islands. N.Z. Antarctic Rec., 7(3): 32–47.

Gregory, M.R. and Kirk, R.M., 1983. Possible environmental consequences of and planning for oil spills in the Ross Sea: application of an oil spill sensitivity index. N.Z. Antarctic Rec., 5(2): 22.

Gregory, M.R., Kirk, R.M. and Mabin, M.C.G., 1984a. Shore types of Victoria Land, Ross Dependency, Antarctica. N.Z. Antarctic Rec., 5(3): 23–40.

Gregory, M.R., Kirk, R.M. and Mabin, M.C.G., 1984b. Pelagic tar, oil, plastics and other litter in surface waters of the New Zealand sector of the Southern Ocean, and on Ross Dependency shores. N.Z. Antarctic Rec., 6(1): 12–28.

Gretener, P.E., 1981. Geothermics: using temperature in hydrocarbon exploration. AAPG Education Course Note Series No. 17, American Association of Petroleum Geologists, Tulsa, 170 pp.

Griffiths, A.M., 1983. Factors affecting the distribution of the Snow Petrel (*Pagodroma nivea*) and the Antarctic Petrel (*Thalassoica antarctica*). Ardea, 71: 145–150.

Griffiths, T.W. and Anderson, J.B., 1989. Climatic control of sedimentation in bays and fjords of the northern Antarctic Peninsula. Mar. Geol., 85: 181–204.

Grimwood, I.R., 1969. Notes on the distribution and status of some Peruvian mammala. Am. Committee for Internat. Wildl. Protection and N.Y. Zool. Soc. Spec. Publ., 21: 86.

Grindley, G.W. and Davey, F.J., 1982. The reconstruction of New Zealand, Australia, and Antarctica. In: C. Craddock (Editor), Antarctic Geoscience. The University of Wisconsin Press, Madison, pp. 15–29.

Gudmandsen, P.E., 1983. Application of microwave remote sensing to studies of sea ice. Philos. Trans. R. Soc. London, Ser. A, 309: 433–445.

Guerra, C., and Torres, D., 1987. Presences of the South American fur seal *Arctocephalus australis* in northern Chile. In: J.P. Croxall and R.L. Gentry (Editors), Status, Biology, and Ecology of Fur Seals. Proceedings of an International Symposium and Workshop, Cambridge, England, 23–27 April 1984. NOAA Tech. Rep. NMFS 51, pp. 169–173.

Guiler, E.R., 1966. A stranding of *Mesoplodon densirostris* in Tasmania. J. Mamm., 47(2): 327.

Guiler, E.R., Burton, H.R. and Gales, N.J., 1987. On three odontocete skulls from Heard Island. Scient. Rep. Whales Res. Inst., 38: 117–124.

Guillaume, G., 1983. Oil as a special resource : problems and experiences. In: F.O. Vicuña (Editor), Antarctic Resources Policy Scientific, Legal and Political Issues. Cambridge University Press, Cambridge, pp. 185–190.

Gulland, J., 1981. A note on the abundance of the Antarctic blue whales. In: Mammals of the Sea., III. FAO Fish. Ser. 5, pp. 219–228.

Gulland, J.A., 1974. Distribution and abundance of whales in relation to basic productivity. In: W.E. Schevill (Editor), The Whale Problem A Status Report, Harvard University Press, Cambridge, Mass., pp. 27–52.

Gulland, J.A., 1986. The Antarctic Treaty System as a resource management mechanism – living resources. In: Antarctic Treaty System An Assessment Proceedings of a Workshop held at Beardmore South Field Camp, Antarctica January 7–13, 1985. National Academy Press, Washington, D.C., pp. 221–234.

Gulland, J.A., 1988. The end of whaling? New Scientist, 1636: 42–47.

Gundlach, E.R., Domeracki, D.D. and Thebeau, L.C., 1982. Persistence of *Metula* oil in the Strait of Magellan six and one-half years after the incident. Oil Petrochem. Pollut., 1: 37–48.

Gundlach, E.R. and Hayes, M.O., 1978. Vulnerability of coastal environments to oil spill impacts. Mar. Technol. Soc. J., 12: 18–27.

Guterch, A., Grad, M., Janik, T., Perchuc, E. and Pajchel, J., 1985. Seismic studies of the crustal structure in west Antarctica 1979–80 – Preliminary results. Tectonophysics, 114: 411–429.

Guthrie-Smith, H., 1936. Sorrows and joys of a New Zealand naturalist. A.H. and A.W. Reed, Dunedin, 252 pp.

Guymer, L.B., 1978. Operational application of satellite imagery to synoptic analysis in the southern hemisphere. Tech. Rep. 29, Bureau of Met., Australia, 88 pp.

Guymer, L.B. and Le Marshall, J.F., 1980. Impact of FGGE buoy data on southern hemisphere analysis. Aust. Met. Mag., 28: 19–42.

Guzman, L. and Campodonico, I., 1981. Studies after the Metula oil spill in the Straits of Magellan. In: Petroleum and the marine environment. Petromar 80 Eurocean. Graham and Trotman Ltd, London, pp 363–376.

Halbouty, M.T., Meyerhoff, A.A., King, R.E., Dott, R.H., Klemme, H.D. and Shabad, T., 1970. World's giant oil and gas fields, geologic factors affecting their formation and basin classification. In: M.T. Halbouty (Editor), Geology of Giant Petroleum Fields. APPG Memoir, 14: pp. 502–55.

Hallam, A., 1984. Continental humid and arid zones during the Jurassic and Cretaceous. Palaeogeogr. Palaeoclimatol. Palaeoecol., 47: 195–223.

Hamley, T.C. and Budd, W.F., 1986. Antarctic iceberg distribution and dissolution. J. Glaciol., 32: 235–241.

Hampton, I., 1985. Abundance, distribution and behaviour of *Euphausia superba* in the Southern Ocean between 15° and 30°E during FIBEX. In: W.R. Siegfried, P.R. Condy and R.M. Laws (Editors), Antarctic Nutrient Cycles and Food Webs. Springer-Verlag, Berlin, pp. 294–303.

Han, Y.-J. and Lee, S.-W., 1981. A new analysis of monthly mean wind stress over the global ocean. Climate Research Institute, Oregon State Univ., Corvallis, Oregon, 26: 151 pp.

Handschumacher, D.W., 1976. Post-Eocene plate tectonics of the eastern Pacific. Am. Geophys. Un. Geophys. Monogr., No. 19: 177–202.

Hanson, M.B. and Erickson, A.W., 1985. Sightings of toothed whales along the Antarctic coast and in the South Atlantic Ocean. Antarctic Jl U.S., 20(2): 16–19

Hantke, H., 1986. The use of icebergs for water supply. Natural Resources and Development, 23: 35–44.

Hanzawa, M. and Tsuchida, T., 1954. A report on the oceanographical observations in the Antarctic Ocean carried out on board the Japanese whaling fleet during the years 1946 to 1952. J. Oceanogr. Soc. Japan, 10(3): 99–111.

Hardy, A., 1967. Great Waters. Collins, London, 542 pp.

Harmer, S.F., 1931. Southern whaling. Proc. Linn. Soc., Sess. 142: 84–163.

Harper, P.C., 1973. The field identification and supplementary notes on the Soft-plumaged Petrel (*Pterodroma mollis* Gould, 1844). Notornis, 20: 193–201.

Harper, P.C., 1976. Breeding biology of the Fairy Prion (*Pachyptila turtur*) at the Poor Knights Islands, New Zealand. N.Z. Jl Zool., 3: 351–371.

Harper, P.C., 1978. The plasma proteins of some albatrosses and petrels as an index of relationship in the Procellariiformes. N.Z. Jl Zool., 5: 509–549.

Harper, P.C., 1979. Colour vision in the Procellariiformes. Mauri Ora, 7: 151–155.

Harper, P.C., 1980. The field identification and distribution of the prions (genus *Pachyptila*). Notornis, 27: 235–286.

Harper, P.C., 1983. Future of birds of Antarctica could be in jeopardy. Forest and Bird, 14(7): 8–14.

Harper, P.C., 1987. Feeding behaviour and other notes on 20 species of Procellariiformes at sea. Notornis, 34: 169–192.

Harper, P.C., Croxall, J.P. and Cooper, J., 1985. A guide to foraging methods used by marine birds in Antarctic and Subantarctic seas. BIOMASS Handbook, No. 24: 22 pp.

Harper, P.C. and Fowler, J.A., 1987. Plastic pellets in New Zealand storm-killed prions (*Pachyptila* spp.) 1958–1977. Notornis, 34: 65–70.

Harper, P.C. and Kinsky, F.C., 1978. Southern Albatrosses and Petrels: an identification guide. Victoria University Press, Wellington, 116 pp.

Harper, P.C., Knox, G.A., Spurr, E.B., Taylor, R.H., Wilson, G.J. and Young, E.C., 1984. The status and conservation of birds in the Ross Sea sector of Antarctica. In: J.P. Croxall, P.G.H. Evans and R.W. Schreiber (Editors), Status and Conservation of the World's Seabirds. International Council for Bird Preservation Tech. Publ., No. 2: 593–608.

Harper, P.C., Watson, G.E. and Angle, P.A., 1972. New records of the Kerguelen Petrel (*Pterodroma brevirostris*) in the South Atlantic and Pacific Oceans. Notornis, 19: 56–60.

Hart, T.J., 1942. Phytoplankton periodicity in the Antarctic surface waters. Discovery Reps, 21: 261–356.

Harwood, D.M., 1986. Diatoms. In: P.J. Barrett (Editor), Antarctic Cenozoic history from the MSSTS–1 drillhole, McMurdo Sound. N.Z. Dep. Scient. Ind. Res. Bull., 237: 69–107.

Harwood, D.M., Sherer, R.P. and Webb, P.N., 1989. Multiple Miocene marine productivity events in West Antarctica as recorded in upper Miocene sediments beneath the Ross Ice Shelf (Site J–9). Mar. Micropaleontol.

Hasle, G.R., 1969. An analysis of the phytoplankton of the Pacific Southern Ocean : Abundance, composition and distribution during the Brategg Expedition, 1947–48. Hvalraadets Skrifter, 52: 1–168.

Hasle, G.R., 1976. The biogeography of some marine planktonic diatoms. Deep-Sea Res., 23: 319–328.

Hatherton, T., 1986. Antarctica prior to the Antarctic Treaty – a historical perspective. In: Antarctic Treaty Symposium An Assessment Proceedings of a Workshop held at Beardmore South Field Camp, Antarctica, January 7–13, 1985. National Academy Press, Washington, D.C., pp. 15–32.

Hatherton, T. (Editor), in press. Antarctica : The Ross Sea Region. DSIR Publishing, Wellington, New Zealand

Hatherton, T., Dawson, E.W. and Kinsky, F.C., 1965. Balleny Islands reconnaissance expedition, 1964. N.Z. Jl Geol. Geophys., 8: 164–179.

Hay, W.W., 1981. Sedimentological and geochemical trends resulting from the breakup of Pangea. Oceanologica Acta, N° SP: 135–147.

Hay, W.W., 1984. The breakup of Pangea : Climate, erosional and sedimentological effects. Proc. 27th Internat. Geol. Congress, 6: 15–38.

Hay, W.W., Barron, E.J., Sloan, J.L. and Southam, J.R., 1981. Continental drift and the global pattern of sedimentation. Geol. Rdsch., 70: 302–315.

Hayes, D.E. and Davey, F.J., 1975. A geophysical study of the Ross Sea, Antarctica. In: Initial Reports of the Deep Sea Drilling Project, Vol. 28. U.S. Govt Printing Office, Washington, D.C., pp. 887–907.

Hayes, D.E. et al., 1975a. Sites 270, 271, 272. Initial Reports of the Deep Sea Drilling Project, Vol. 28. U.S. Govt Printing Office, Washington, D.C., pp. 211–334.

Hayes, D.E. et al., 1975b. Site 273. Initial Reports of the Deep Sea Drilling Project, Vol. 28. U.S. Govt Printing Office, Washington, D.C., pp. 335–343.

Hayes, D.E. and Pitman, W.C., 1972. Review of marine geophysical observations in the Southern Ocean. In: R.J. Adie (Editor), Antarctic Geology and Geophysics. Universitetsforlaget, Oslo, pp. 725–732.

Hayes, D.E. and Ringis, J., 1973. Seafloor spreading in the Tasman Sea. Nature, 243: 454–458.

Hayes, P.K., Whitaker, T.M. and Fogg, G.E., 1984. The distribution and nutrient status of phytoplankton in the Southern Ocean between 2 and 70°W. Polar Biol., 3: 153–165.

Hays, H. and Cormons, G., 1974. Plastic particles found in tern pellets on coastal beaches and at factory sites. Mar. Pollut. Bull., 5: 44–46.

Hayward, B.W., 1984. Rubbish trends – beach litter surveys at Kawerua, 1972–1984. Tane, 30: 209–217.

Heath, R.A., 1981. Oceanic fronts around southern New Zealand. Deep-Sea Res., 28: 547–560.

Heaton, M.G., Wilke, R.J. and Bowman, M.J., 1980. Formation of tar balls in a simulated oceanic front. Texas J. Sci., 32: 265–268.

Heezen, B.C. and Hollister, C.D., 1971. The Face of the Deep. Oxford University Press, N.Y., 657 pp.

Heine, A.J., 1967. The McMurdo Ice Shelf, Antarctica: A preliminary report. N.Z. Jl Geol. Geophys., 10: 474–478.

Heirtzler, J.R. (Editor), 1985. Relief of the surface of the earth Computer generated color-coded shaded relief. World Data Center for Marine Geology and Geophysics Report MGG–2 Sheet 2, National Geophysical Data Center, National Oceanic and Atmospheric Administration. Chart

Heirtzler, J.R., Dickson, G.O., Herron, E.M. Pitman, W.C. and Le Pichon, X., 1968. Marine magnetic anomalies, geomagnetic field reversals, and motions of the ocean floor and continents. J. Geophys. Res., 73: 2119–2136.

Hemmings, A.D. and Bailey, E.C., 1985. Pursuit diving by Northern Giant Petrels at the Chatham Island. Notornis, 32: 330–331.

Hempel, G., 1985. Antarctic marine food webs. In: W.R. Siegfried, P.R. Condy and R.M. Laws (Editors), Antarctic Nutrient Cycles and Food Webs. Springer-Verlag, Berlin, pp. 266–270.

Hempel, G., 1986. Changing of the guard – New Meteor enters service. German Research, 1/86: 22–24.

Hempel, G., 1987. BIOMASS. Environment Internat., 13 : 27–31.

Hempel, G., 1988. Antarctic marine research in winter: the Winter Weddell Sea Project 1986. Polar Rec., 24(148): 43–48.

Herdman, H.F.P., 1952. The voyage of Discovery II, 1950–51. Geogr. J., 118: 429–442.

Herdman, H.F.P., 1959. Some notes on sea-ice observed by Captain James Cook, R.N., during his circumnavigation of Antarctica, 1772–75. J. Glaciol., 3(26): 534–541.

Herman, G.F. and Johnson, W.J., 1980. Arctic and Antarctic climatology of a GLAS general circulation model. Mon. Wea. Rev., 108: 1974–1991.

Héroux, Y., Chagnon, A. and Bertrand, R., 1979. Compilation and correlation of major thermal maturation indicators. AAPG Bull., 63: 2128–2144.

Herron, E.M., 1971. Crustal plates and seafloor spreading in the southeastern Pacific. Antarctic Res. Ser., 15: 229–237.

Herron, E.M., 1972. Seafloor spreading and the Cenozoic history of the East Central Pacific. Bull. Geol. Soc. Am., 83: 1671–1692.

Herron, E.M. and Hayes, D.E., 1969. A geophysical study of the Chile Ridge. Earth Planet. Sci. Lett, 6: 77–83.

Herron, E.M. and Tucholke, B.E., 1976. Seafloor magnetic pattens and basement structure in the southeastern Pacific. In: Initial Reports of the Deep Sea Drilling Project, Vol. 35. U.S. Govt Printing Office, Washington, D.C., pp. 236–278.

Heywood, R.B., Everson, I. and Priddle, J., 1985. The absence of krill from the South Georgia zone, winter 1983. Deep-Sea Res., 32: 369–379.

Heywood, R.B., and Whitaker, T.M., 1984. The Antarctic marine flora. In: R.M. Laws (Editor), Antarctic Ecology, Vol. 2. Academic Press, London, pp. 373–421.

Hidaka, H., Tanabe, S., Kawano, M. and Tatsukawa, R., 1984. Fate of DDT's, PCB's and Chlordane compounds in the Antarctic marine ecosystem. Mem. Nat. Inst. Polar Research Spec. Issue, No. 32: 151–161.

Hill, H.W., 1980. The mechanics of fronts and depressions in the atmosphere. N.Z. Meteorological Service Misc. Publ. No. 165, 14 pp.

Hindell, M.A. and Burton, H.R., 1988a. The history of the elephant seal industry at Macquarie Island and an estimate of the pre-saling numbers. Pap. Proc. R. Soc. Tasmania 122: 159–176.

Hindell, M.A. and Burton, H.R., 1988b. Past and present status of the southern elephant seal (Mirounga leonina Linn.) at Macquarie Island. J. Zool., 213: 365–380.

Hinz, K. and Block, M., 1983. Results of geophysical investigations in the Weddell Sea and in the Ross Sea, Antarctica. Proc. Eleventh World Petroleum Congress, London, PD 2, (1): 1–13.

Hinz, K. and Kristoffersen, Y., 1987. Antarctica Recent advances in the understanding of the continental shelf. Geol. Jb., E37: 3–54.

Hoelzel, A.R. and Amos, W., 1988. DNA fingerprinting in "scientific whaling". Nature, 333: 305.

Hofman, R., Erickson, A. and Siniff, D., 1973. The Ross seal (*Ommatophoca rossi*). In: Seals, IUCN Supp. Pap., 39, pp. 129–139.

Hofmann, E.E., 1985. The large-scale horizontal structure of the Antarctic Circumpolar Current from FGGE drifters. J. Geophys. Res., 90: 7087–7097.

Hofmann, E.E. and Whitworth, T., 1985. A synoptic description of the flow at Drake Passage from year-long measurements. J. Geophys. Res., 90: 7177–7188.

Holdgate, M.W., 1970. Plankton and its pelagic consumers. In: M.W. Holdgate (Editor), Antarctic Ecology, Vol. 1. Academic Press, London, pp. 117.

Holdgate, M.W., 1983. Environmental factors in the development of Antarctica. In: F.O. Vicuña (Editor), Antarctic Resources Policy Scientific, Legal and Political Issues. Cambridge University Press, Cambridge, pp. 77–101.

Holdgate, M.W., 1984. The use and abuse of polar environmental resources. Polar Rec., 22: 25–48.

Holdgate, M.W., 1987. Regulated development and conservation of Antarctic resources. In: G.D. Triggs (Editor), The Antarctic Treaty Regime Law, Environment and Resources. Cambridge University Press, Cambridge, pp. 128–142.

Holdgate, M.W. and Tinker, J., 1979. Oil and other minerals in the Antarctic. SCAR, Cambridge, 51 pp.

Holdsworth, G., 1978. Some mechanisms for the calving of icebergs. In: A.A. Husseiny (Editor), Iceberg Utilization. Proceedings of the First International Conference. Pergamon Press, N.Y., pp. 160–175.

Holdsworth, G., 1982. Dynamics of Erebus Glacier Tongue. Annals Glaciol., 3: 131–137.

Holdsworth, G., 1985. Some effects of ocean currents and wave motion on the dynamics of floating glacier tongues. Antarctic Res. Ser., 43: 253–271.

Holgersen, H., 1951. On the birds of Peter I Island. Proc. 10th Int. Ornithol. Congr.: 614–616.

Hollister, C.D., Nowell, A.R.M. and Jumers, P.A., 1984. The dynamic abyss. Scient. Am., 250(3): 42–53.

Holm-Hansen, O. and Chapman, A.S., 1983. Antarctic circumnavigation cruise, 1983. Antarctic Jl U.S., 18(5): 162–163.

Holm-Hansen, O. and Huntley, M., 1984. Feeding requirements of krill in relation to food sources. J. Crustacean Biol., 4 (Spec. No. 1): 156–173.

Holm-Hansen, O., El-Sayed, S.Z., Franceschini, G.A. and Cuhel, R.L., 1977. Primary production and the factors controlling phytoplankton growth in the Southern Ocean. In: G.A. Llano (Editor), Adaptations within Antarctic Ecosystems. Proceedings of the Third SCAR Synposium on Antarctic Biology. Smithsonian Institution, Washington, D.C., pp. 11–50.

Holtedahl, O. (Editor), 1935. Scientific results of the Norwegian Antarctic Expeditions 1927–1928 et sqq., instituted and financed by Consul Lars Christiansen, vol. 1. Det Norske Videnskaps-Akademi, Oslo, 14 chapters.

Hood, A., Gutjahr, C.C.M. and Heacock, R.L., 1975. Organic metamorphism and the generation of petroleum. AAPG Bull., 59: 986–996.

Hooker, J.D., 1847. Diatomaceae. In: The Botany of the Antarctic Voyage of H.M. Discovery ships Erebus and Terror in the years 1839–1843. Reeve Brothers, London, pp. 503–519.

Hopkins, T.L., 1966. A volumetric analysis of the catch of the Isaac-Kidd midwater trawl and two types of plankton nets in the Antarctic. Australian Jl Mar. Freshwater Res., 17: 147–154.

Hopkins, T.L., 1971. Zooplankton standing crop in the Pacific sector of the Antarctic. Antarctic Res. Ser., 17: 347–382.

Horning, D.S. and Horning, C.J., 1974. Bird records of the 1971–73 Snares Islands, New Zealand, Expedition. Notornis, 21: 13–24.

Horrigan, S.G., 1981. Primary production under the Ross Ice Shelf, Antarctica. Limnol. Oceanogr. 26: 378–382.

Horsman, P.V., 1982. The amount of garbage pollution from merchant ships. Mar. Pollut. Bull., 13: 167–169.

Hough, J.L., 1956. Sediment distribution in the Southern Oceans around Antarctica. J. Sedim. Petrol., 26: 301–306.

Houtman, Th.J., 1967. Water masses and fronts in the Southern Ocean south of New Zealand. N.Z. Oceanogr. Inst. Mem., 36: 40 pp + 1 chart.

Houtz, R., 1974. Continental Margin of Antarctica: Pacific–Indian sectors. In: C.A. Burk and C.L. Drake (Editors), The Geology of Continental Margins. Springer-Verlag, Berlin, pp. 655–658.

Houtz, R.E. and Davey, F.J., 1973. Seismic profiler and sonobuoy measurements in the Ross Sea, Antarctica. J. Geophys. Res., 78: 3448–3458.

Houtz, R.E. and Meijer, R., 1970. Structure of the Ross Sea shelf from profiler data. J. Geophys. Res., 75: 6592–6597.

Hughes, T., 1973. Is the West Antarctic Ice Sheet disintegrating? J. Geophys. Res., 78: 7884–7910.

Hughes, T., 1975. The West Antarctic Ice Sheet: instability, disintegration, and initiation of ice ages. Revs Geophys. Space Phys., 13: 502–526.

Hughes, T., 1983. On the disintegration of ice shelves: the role of fracture. J. Glaciol., 29: 98–117.

Hult, J.L. and Ostrander, N.C., 1973. Applicability of ERTS for surveying Antarctic iceberg resources. NASA/NSF, Report 1354: 50 pp.

Hume, H.R., Buist, I., Betts, D. and Goodman, R., 1983. Arctic marine oil spill research. Cold Regions Sci. Technol., 7: 313–341.

Hunt, G.L., Gould, P.J., Forsell, D.J. and Peterson, H., 1981. Pelagic distribution of marine birds in the Eastern Bering Sea. In: The Eastern Bering Sea Shelf: Oceanography and Resources, Vol. 2. Office of Maritime Pollution Assessment, NOAA, University of Washington Press, Seattle, Washington, pp. 689–718.

Hunter, S., 1983. The food and feeding ecology of the giant petrels Macronectes halli and M. giganteus at South Georgia. J. Zool., 200: 521–538.

Huntford, R., 1979. Scott and Amundsen. Hodder and Stoughton, London, 665 pp.

Ibach, L.E.J., 1982. Relationship between sedimentation rate and total organic carbon content in ancient marine sediments. Am. Assoc. Petrol. Geol. Bull., 66: 170–188.

Imber, M.J., 1973. The food of grey-faced petrels (Pterodroma macroptera gouldi (Hutton)), with special reference to diurnal vertical migration of their prey. J. Anim. Ecol., 42: 645–662.

Imber, M.J., 1978. Recent petrel research. Wildlife – A review, 9: 9–15.

Imber, M.J., 1979. Petrels of the Antipodes Islands. Wildlife – A review, 10: 11–15.

Imber, M.J., 1983. The lesser Petrels of Antipodes Islands, with notes from Price Edward and Gough Island. Notornis, 30: 283–298.

Imber, M.J., 1984. The age of Kerguelen Petrels found in New Zealand. Notornis, 31: 89–91.

Imber, M.J., 1985. Chatham Island Petrel Pterodroma axillaris. In: Readers Digest Complete Book of New Zealand Birds. Readers Digest, Reed Methuen, Sydney, 319 pp.

Imber, M.J. and Nilsson, R.J., 1980: South Georgian Diving Petrels (Pelecanoides georgicus)

352

breeding on Codfish Island. Notornis, 27: 325–330.

Ingram, C.W.N. and Wheatley, P.O., 1961. New Zealand Shipwrecks 1795–1960. A.H. & A.W. Reed, Wellington, 408 pp.

Ivanhoe, L.F., 1980. Antarctica – operating conditions and petroleum prospects. Oil & Gas J., 78(52): 212, 214, 217, 219, 220.

Ivanov, V.L., 1985. The geological prerequisites for petroleum prediction in Antarctica. Int. Geol. Rev., 27: 757–769.

Jacka, T.H., 1983. A computer data base for Antarctic sea ice extent. ANARE Res. Notes, 13: 54 pp.

Jacka, T.H., Allison, I., Thwaites, R. and Wilson, J.C., 1987. Characteristics of the seasonal sea ice of East Antarctica and comparisons with satellite observations. Annals Glaciol., 9: 85–91.

Jacobs, S.S. (Editor), 1985. Oceanology of the Antarctic Continental Shelf. Antarctic Res. Ser., 43: 312 pp.

Jacobs, S.S. and Amos, A., 1967. Physical and chemical oceanographic observations in the Southern Ocean. Tech. Rep. 1–CU-1-67. Lamont-Doherty Geological Observatory.

Jacobs, S.S., Amos, A.F. and Bruchhausen, P.M., 1970. Ross Sea oceanography and Antarctic bottom water formation. Deep-Sea Res., 17: 935–962.

Jacobs, S.S., Fairbanks, R.G. and Horibe, Y., 1985. Origin and evolution of water masses near the Antarctic continental margin: evidence from $H_2^{18}O/H_2^{16}O$ ratios in seawater. Antarctic Res. Ser., 43: 59–85.

Jacobs, S.S. and Georgi, D.T., 1977. Observations on the southwest Indian/Antarctic Ocean. In: M. Angel (Editor), A Voyage of Discovery George Deacon 70th Anniversary Volume, Supplement to Deep-Sea Res., Pergamon, Oxford, pp. 43–84.

Jacobs, S.S., Gordon A.L. and Ardai, J.L., 1979. Circulation and melting beneath the Ross Ice Shelf. Science, 203: 439–443.

Jacobs, S.S., Huppert, H.E., Holdsworth, G. and Drewry, D.J., 1981. Thermohaline steps induced by melting of the Erebus Glacier Tongue. J. Geophys. Res., 86: 6547–6555.

Jacobs, S.S., MacAyeal, D.R. and Ardai, J.L., 1986. The recent advances of the Ross Ice Shelf, Antarctica. J. Glaciol., 32: 464–474.

Jacques, G., 1983. Some eco-physiological aspects of the Antarctic phytoplankton. Polar Biol., 2: 27–34.

Jehl, J.R., 1973. The distribution of marine birds in Chilean waters in winter. Auk, 90: 114–135.

Jehl, J.R., 1975. Mortality of Magellanic penguins in Argentina. Auk, 92: 596–598.

Jehl, J.R., Todd, F.S., Rumboll, M.A.E. and Schwartz, D., 1979. Pelagic birds in the South Atlantic Ocean and at South Georgia in the austral autumn. Le Gerfaut, 69: 13–27.

Jenne, R.L, Crutcher, H.L., van Loon, H. and Taljaard, J.J., 1971. Climate of the upper air: southern hemisphere, Vol. III, Vector mean geostrophic winds; isogon and isotach analyses, National Center for Atmospheric Research, Boulder, Colorado, NCAR–TN/STR–58.

Jezek, K.C. and Bentley, C.R., 1984. A reconsideration of the mass balance of a portion of the Ross Ice Shelf. J. Glaciol., 30: 381–384.

John, D., 1936. The southern species of the genus *Euphausia*. Discovery Reps, 14: 193–324.

Johnson, A.W., 1965. The birds of Chile and adjacent regions of Argentina, Bolivia and Peru. Vol. 1. Platt Establecimentos Graficos, Buenos Aires.

Johnson, G.L., Vanney, J.R. and Hayes, D., 1982. The Antarctic continental shelf. In: C. Craddock (Editor), Antarctic Geoscience. University of Wisconsin Press, Madison, pp. 995–1002.

Johnston, B.R., 1971. Skua numbers and conservation problems at Cape Hallett, Antarctica.

Nature, 231: 468.

Johnstone, G.W., 1977. comparative feeding ecology of the giant petrels *Macronectes giganteus* (Gmelin) and *M. halli* (Mathews). In: G.A. Llano (Editor), Adaptations within Antarctic Ecosystems. Smithsonian Institution, Washington, D.C., pp. 647–668.

Johnstone, G.W. and Kerry, K.R., 1974. Ornithological observations in the Australian sector of the Southern Ocean. Proc. 16th Int. Ornithol. Congr.: 725–738.

Jones, D., Wilson, M.J. and Tait, J.M. 1980. Weathering of a basalt by *Pertusaria corallina*. The Lichenologist, 12: 277–289.

Jones, E., 1980. A survey of burrow-nesting petrels at Macquarie Island based upon remains left by predators. Notornis, 27: 11–20.

Jouventin, P., Stahl, J.C., Weimerskirch, H. and Mougin, J.L., 1984. The seabirds of the French Subantarctic Islands and Adelie Land, their status and conservation. In: J.P. Croxall, P.G.H. Evans and R.W. Schreiber (Editors), Status and Conservation of the World's Seabirds. International Council for Bird Preservation Tech. Publ., No. 2: 609–625.

Joyce, T.M. and Patterson, S.L., 1977. Cyclonic ring formation at the Polar Front in the Drake Passage. Nature, 265: 131–133.

Joyce, T.M., Patterson, S.L. and Millard, R.C., 1981. Anatomy of a cyclonic ring in the Drake Passage. Deep-Sea Res., 28: 1265–1287.

Joyner, C.C., 1985. Southern Ocean and marine pollution: problems and prospects. Case Western Reserve Jl Internat. Law, 17: 165–194.

Kaczynski, V.M., 1984. Economic aspects of Antarctic fisheries. In: L.M. Alexander and L.C. Hanson (Editors), Antarctic Politics and Marine Resources : critical Choices for the 1980s. Center for Ocean Management Studies, Kingston, Rhode Island, pp. 141–158.

Karl, H.A., 1989. High-resolution seismic-reflection interpretations of some sediment deposits, Antarctic continental margin : Focus on the western Ross Sea. Mar. Geol., 85: 205–223.

Katz, H.R., 1968. Potential oil formations in New Zealand and their stratigraphic position as related to basin evolution. N.Z. Jl Geol. Geophys., 11: 1077–1133.

Katz, H.R., 1974. Offshore petroleum potential in New Zealand. APEA Jl, 14: 3–13.

Katz, H.R., 1982. West Antarctica and New Zealand: A geologic test of the model of continental split. In: C. Craddock (Editor), Antarctic Geoscience. The University of Wisconsin Press, Madison, pp. 31–41.

Katz, H.R. and Herzer, R.H., 1986. Oil and gas developments in New Zealand and Southwest Pacific islands in 1985. AAPG Bull., 70: 1625–1631.

Kaylor, J.D. and Learson, R.J., 1983. Krill and its utilization : A review. NOAA Tech. Rep., NMFS SSRF–769: 10 pp.

Keffer, T., 1985. The ventilation of the world's oceans: maps of the potential vorticity field. J. Phys. Oceanogr., 15: 509–523.

Kellogg, D.E. and Kellogg, T.B., 1986. Biotic provinces in modern Amundsen Sea sediments : Implications for glacial history. Antarctic Jl U.S., 21(5): 154–156.

Kellogg, T.B. and Kellogg, D.E., 1988. Antarctic cryogenic sediments : biotic and inorganic facies of ice shelf marine-based ice sheet environments. Palaeogeogr. Palaeoclimatol. Palaeoecol., 67: 51–74.

Kellogg, T.B., Truesdale, R.S. and Osterman, L.E., 1979. Late Quaternary extent of the West Antarctic Ice Sheet: new evidence from Ross Sea cores. Geology, 7: 249–253.

Kennedy, D., 1987. Modern sedimentary dynamics and Quaternary glacial history of Marguerite Bay, Antarctic Peninsula. Unpubl. M.A. thesis, Rice University, Houston, Texas, 203 pp.

Kennett, J.P., 1977. Cenozoic evolution of Antarctic glaciation, the Circum-Antarctic

354

Ocean, and their impact on global paleoceanography. J. Geophys. Res., 82: 3843–3860.

Kennett, J.P., 1980. Paleoceanographic and biogeographic evolution of the Southern Ocean during the Cenozoic, and Cenozoic microfossil datums. Palaeogeogr. Palaeoclimatol. Palaeoecol., 31: 123–152.

Kennett, J.P., 1983. Paleo-oceanography : Global ocean evolution. Revs Geophys. Space Phys., 21: 1258–1274.

Kennett, J.P., Burns, R.E., Andrews, J.E., Churkin, M., Davies, T.A., Dumitrica, P., Edwards, A.R., Galehouse, J.S., Packham, G.H. and van der Lingen, G.J., 1972. Australian–Antarctic continental drift palaeocirculation changes and Oligocene deep-sea erosion. Nature Phys. Sci., 239: 51–55.

Kennett, J.P. and von der Borch, C.C., 1986. Southwest Pacific Cenozoic paleoceanography. In: Initial Reports of the Deep Sea Drilling Project, vol. 90. U.S. Govt Printing Office, Washington, D.C., pp. 1493–1517.

Kennett, J.P. et al., 1975a. Site 281. Initial Reports of the Deep Sea Drilling Project, Vol. 29. U.S. Govt Printing Office, Washington, D.C., pp. 271–315.

Kennett, J.P. et al., 1975b. Cenozoic paleoceanography in the Southwest Pacific Ocean, Antarctic glaciation, and the development of the Circum-Antarctic Current. In: Initial Reports of the Deep Sea Drilling Project, Vol. 29. U.S. Govt Printing Office, Washington, D.C., pp. 1155–1169.

Kenyon, K.W. and Kridler, E., 1969. Laysan albatrosses swallow indigestable matter. Auk, 86: 339–343.

Kerley, G.I.H. and Erasmus, T., 1987. The management of oiled penguins. Proc. 1987 Oil Spill Conference, Baltimore, U.S.A., pp. 465–468.

Keys, J.R., 1983. Iceberg quantities, shapes and sizes in western Ross and D'Urville Seas. Antarctic Jl U.S., 18(5): 125–127.

Keys, J.R., 1984. Antarctic Marine Environments and Offshore Oil. Commission for the Environment, Wellington, 168 pp. + 4 Appendices.

Keys, J.R., 1985. Icebergs off South Victoria Land, Antarctica. N.Z. Antarctic Rec., 6(2): 1–7.

Keys, J.R., 1988. B–9 moves more slowly than expected. Antarctic (N.Z. Antarctic Soc.), 11(7): 280–281.

Keys, J.R., 1989. Iceberg B–9: update. Antarctic (N.Z. Antarctic Soc.), 11(9 & 10): 364–365.

Keys, J.R. and Fowler, A.D.W., 1989. Sources and movement of icebergs in south-west Ross Sea, Antarctica. Annals Glaciol., 12: 85–88.

Keys, J.R. and Williams, K.L., 1984. Rates and mechanisms of iceberg ablation in the D'Urville Sea, Southern Ocean. J. Glaciol., 30: 218–222.

Kils, U., 1982. Swimming behaviour, swimming performance and energy balance of Antarctic krill, Euphausia superba. BIOMASS Scientific Ser., 3: 1–121.

Kils, U., 1983. Swimming and feeding of Antarctic krill, Euphausia superba – some outstanding energetics and dynamics – some unique morphological details. Ber. Polarforsch., 4: 130–135.

Killworth, P.D., 1983. Deep convection in the world ocean. Revs Geophys. Space Phys., 21: 1–26.

Kimura, K., 1982. Geological and geophysical survey in the Bellingshausen basin, off Antarctica. Japanese Antarctic Rec., 75: 12–24.

King, J.E., 1983. Seals of the World. British Museum (Natural History) and Oxford University Press, London and Oxford, 240 pp.

King, J.E., 1988. Australasian Pinniipeds. In: M.L. Augee (Editor), Marine Mammals of Australasia Field Biology and Captive Management. Spec. Publ. R. Soc. N.S.W., pp, 3–8.

King, P.R. and Robinson, P.H., 1988. An overview of Taranaki region geology New Zealand. Energy Exploration and Exploitation, 6: 213–232.

Kinsky, F.C., 1969. New and rare birds on Campbell Island. Notornis, 16: 225–236.

Kirk, R.M. and Gregory, M.R. In press. The coastline of the Ross Sea. In: T. Hatherton (Editor), Antarctica – The Ross Sea Region. DSIR Publishing, Wellington, New Zealand

Kirwan, L.P., 1959. A History of Polar Exploration. Penguin, London, 408 pp.

Knapp, W.W., 1972. Satellite observations of large polynyas in polar waters. In: T. Karlsson (Editor), Sea Ice. National Research Council, Reykjavik, pp. 201–212.

Knox, G.A. 1970. Biological oceanography of the South Pacific. In: W.S. Wooster (Editor), Scientific Exploration of the South Pacific. National Academy of Sciences, Washington, D.C., pp. 155–182.

Knox, G.A., 1982. The Southern Ocean: an ecosystem under threat. N.Z. Internat. Rev., 7(3): 15–18.

Knox, G.A., 1983. The living resources of the Southern Ocean : A scientific review. In: F.O. Vicuña (Editor), Antarctic Resources Policy Scientific, Legal and Political Issues. Cambridge University Press, Cambridge, pp. 21–60.

Knox, G.A., 1984. The key role of krill in the ecosystem of the Southern Ocean with special reference to the Convention on the Conservation of Antarctic Marine Living Resources. Ocean Management, 9: 113–156.

Knox, G.A., 1986. Recent New Zealand marine research in the Ross Sea sector of Antarctica. Mem. Natl Inst. Polar Res., Spec. Issue, 40: 345–363.

Knox, G.A. 1987. The littoral ecology of the subantarctic region: with special reference to the New Zealand subantarctic regions. In: Colloque sur l'Écologie Marine des Îles Subantarctiques et Antarctiques (Paris 25 juin 1985). Comité national français des recherches antarctiques Nᵘ 57: 47–79.

Knox, G.J., 1982. Taranaki Basin, structural style and tectonic settings. N.Z. Jl Geol. Geophys., 25: 125–140.

Kock, K.-H., 1985. Marine habitats – Antarctic fish. In: W.N. Bonner and D.W.H. Walton (Editors), Key Environments Antarctica. Pergamon Press, Oxford, pp. 173–192.

Kock, K.-H., 1987. Marine consumers : fish and squid. Environment Internat., 13 : 37–45.

Kock, K.-H. and Reinch, H.H., 1978. Ornithological observations during the "German Antarctic Expedition 1975/76". Beit. Vogelkd., 24: 305–328.

Konlechner, J.C., 1985. An investigation of the fate and effects of a paraffin based crude oil in an Antarctic terrestrial ecosystem. N.Z. Antarctic Rec., 6(3): 40–46.

Kooyman, G.L., 1981a. Crabeater Seal Lobodon carcinophagus (Hombron & Jacquinot, 1842). In: S.H. Ridgway and R. Harrison (Editors), Handbook of Marine Mammals 2: Seals. Academic Press, London, pp. 221–235.

Kooyman, G.L., 1981b. Weddell Seal Leptonychotes weddelli Lesson, 1826. In: S.H. Ridgway and R. Harrison (Editors), Handbook of Marine Mammals 2: Seals. Academic Press, London, pp. 275–296.

Korsch, R.J. and Wellman, H.W., 1988. The geological evolution of New Zealand and the New Zealand region. In: A.E.M. Nairn, F.G. Stehli and S. Uyeda (Editors), The Ocean Basins and Margins, Vol. 7B The Pacific Ocean. Plenum Press, N.Y., pp. 411–482.

Kort, V.G., 1962. The Antarctic Ocean. Scient. Am., 207(3): 113–128

Kosaki, S., Takahashi, M., Yamaguchi, Y. and Aruga, Y., 1985. Size characteristics of chlorophyll particles in the Southern Ocean. Trans. Tokyo Univ. Fisheries, 6: 85–97.

Kothe, J., Tessensohn, F., Thonhauser, W. and Wendebourg, R., 1981. The expedition and its logistics. Geol. Jb., 41B: 3–30.

Kovacs, A. and Sodhi, D.S., 1981. Ice pile-up and ride-up on Arctic and Subarctic beaches. Coastal Engineering, 5: 247–273.

Kozlova, O.G., 1964. Diatoms of the Indian and Pacific Sectors of the Antarctic. Academy

356

of Sciences of the U.S.S.R. Institute of Oceanology, Moscow, 191 pp. (translated from Russian).

Kristensen, M., 1983. Iceberg calving and deterioration in Antarctica. Progr. Phys. Geogr., 7: 313–328.

Kubota, K., 1981. Relation between solar light intensity and vertical distribution of krill swams. Antarctic Rec., 73: 88–96.

Kudrass, H.-R. and von Rad, U., 1984. Underwater television and photography observations, side-scan sonar and acoustic reflectivity measurements of phosphorite-rich areas on the Chatham Rise (New Zealand). Geol. Jb., 65: 69–89.

Kukla, G. and Gavin, J., 1981. Summer ice and carbon dioxide. Science, 214: 497–503.

Kurtz, D.D. and Anderson, J.B., 1979. Recognition and sedimentologic description of recent debris flow deposits from the Ross and Weddell Seas, Antarctica. J. Sediment. Petrol., 49: 1159–1170.

Kurtz, D.D. and Bromwich, D.H., 1983. Satellite obsreved behavior of the Terra Nova Bay polynya. J. Geophys. Res., 88: 9717–9722.

Kurtz, D.D. and Bromwich, D.H., 1985. A recurring, atmospherically forced polynya in Terra Nova Bay. Antarctic Res. Ser., 43: 177–201.

Laist, D.W., 1987. Overview of the biological effects of lost and discarded plastic debris in the marine environment. Mar. Pollut. Bull., 18: 319–326.

Larminie, F.G., 1987. Mineral resources : commercial prospects for Antarctic minerals. In: G.D. Triggs (Editor), The Antarctic Treaty Regime Law, Environment and Resources. Cambridge University Press, Cambridge, pp. 176–181.

Larson, R.L., Cande, S.C., Bodine, J.H. and Watts, A.B., 1979. The origin of the Eltanin Fracture Zone. EOS Trans. Am. Geophys. Un., 60: 967 (Abstr.).

Larson, R.L. and Chase, C.G., 1972. Late Mesozoic evolution of the western Pacific Ocean. Bull. Geol. Soc. Am., 83: 3627–3644.

Larson, R.L. and Pitman, W., 1972. World-wide correlation of Mesozoic magnetic anomalies, and its implications. Bull. Geol. Soc. Am., 83: 3645–3662.

Laws, R.M., 1973. The current status of seals in the southern hemisphere. In: Seals, ICUN Suppl. Pap., 39: 144–161.

Laws, R.M., 1977. Seals and whales of the Southern Ocean. Philos. Trans. R. Soc. London, Ser. B, 279: 81–96.

Laws, R.M., 1981. Biology of Antarctic seals. Sci. Prog. Oxf., 67: 377–397.

Laws, R.M., 1983. Antarctica : a convergence of life. New Scient., 99(1373): 508–516.

Laws, R.M., 1984. Seals. In: R.M. Laws (Editor), Antarctic Ecology, Vol. 2. Academic Press, London, pp. 621–715.

Laws, R.M., 1985a. International stewardship of the Antarctic: Problems, successes and future options. Mar. Pollut. Bull., 16(2): 49–55.

Laws, R.M., 1985b. The ecology of the Southern Ocean. Am. Scient., 73: 26–40.

Laws, R.M., 1987. Scientific opportunities in the Antarctic. In: G.D. Triggs (Editor), The Antarctic Treaty Regime Law, Environment and Resources. Cambridge University Press, Cambridge, pp. 28–48.

Leatherwood, S. and Reeves, R.R., 1983. The Sierra Club Handbook of Whales and Dolphins, Sierra Club Books, San Francisco, 302 pp.

Ledford-Hoffman, P.A., DeMaster, D.J. and Nittrouer, C.A., 1986. Biogenic silica accumulation in the Ross Sea and the importance of Antarctic continental shelf deposits in the marine silica budget. Geochim. Cosmochim. Acta, 50: 2099–2110.

Legeckis, R., 1977. Oceanic Polar Front in the Drake Passage - satellite observations during 1976. Deep-Sea Res., 24: 701–704.

Lejenas, H., 1984. Characteristics of southern hemisphere blocking as determined from a time series of observational data. Q. J. R. Meteorol. Soc., 110: 967–979.

LeMasurier, W.E. and Rex, D.C., 1982. Volcanic record of Cenozoic glacial history in Marie Byrd Land and western Ellsworth Land : revised chronology and evaluation of tectonic factors. In: C. Craddock (Editor), Antarctic Geoscience. University of Wisconsin Press, Madison, pp. 725–734.

Le Marshall, J.F., Kelly, G.A.M. and Karoly, D.J., 1985. An atmospheric climatology of the southern hemisphere based on ten years of daily numerical analyses (1972–1982): I. Overview. Aust. Met. Mag., 33: 65–85.

Leventer, A. and Dunbar, R.B., 1988. Recent diatom record of McMurdo Sound, Antarctica : Implications for history of sea ice extent. Paleontology, 3: 259–274.

Levy, E.M., Ehrhandt, M., Kohnke, D., Sobtchenko, E., Suzuoki, T. and Tokuhiro, A., 1981. Global Oil Pollution. Intergovernmental Oceanographic Commission, UNESCO, Paris, 35 pp.

Levy, E.M. and Walton, A., 1976. High seas oil pollution: particulate petroleum residues in the North Atlantic. J. Fish. Res. Bd Canada, 33: 2781–2791.

Lewis, D., 1975. Ice Bird. William Collins Sons and Co. Ltd, London, 224 pp.

Lewis, E.L., 1979. Some possible effects of Arctic industrial developments on the marine environment. Proceedings POAC '79, Vol. 1; Fifth International Conference on Port and Ocean Engineering under Arctic Conditions, Trondheim, pp. 369–392.

Lewis, E.L., 1987. Fifty years of progress in understanding sea ice. J. Glaciol., Spec. Issue: 48–51.

Lewis, E.L. and Perkins, R.G., 1985. The winter oceanography of McMurdo Sound, Antarctica. Antarctic Res. Ser., 43: 145–165.

Lewis, E.L. and Weeks, W.F., 1970. Sea ice: some polar contrasts. In: G. Deacon (Editor), Symposium on Antarctic Ice and Water Masses. Scientific Committee on Antarctic Research, Cambridge, pp. 23–34.

Li, W.K.W., Subba Rao, D.V., Harrison, W.G., Smith, J.C., Cullen, J., Irwin, B. and Platt, T., 1983. Autotrophic picoplankton in the tropical ocean. Science, 219: 292–295.

Lien, R., 1981. Sea bed features in the Blaaenga area, Weddell Sea, Antarctica. Proceedings POAC '81, Vol. II. Sixth International Conference, Quebec, pp. 706–716.

Lillie, H., 1954. Comments in discussion. Proceedings International Conference on Oil Pollution of the Sea, London (1953), pp. 31–33.

Lindley, D., 1987. Ozone hole deeper than ever. Nature, 329: 473.

Lindstrom, D. and Tyler, D., 1984. Preliminary results of Pine Island and Thwaites Glacier study. Antarctic Jl U.S., 19(5): 53–55.

Ling, J.K. and Bryden, M.M., 1981. Southern Elephant Seal *Mirounga leonina* Linnaeus, 1758. In: S.H. Ridgway and R. Harrison (Editors), Handbook of Marine Mammals 2: Seals. Academic Press, London, pp. 297–327.

Ling, J.K. and Bryden, M.M. (Editors), 1985. Studies of Sea Mammals in South Latitudes. South Australian Museum, Adelaide, 132 pp.

Lipps, J.H., 1978. Man's impact along the Antarctic Peninsula. In: B.C. Parker (Editor), Environmental Impact in Antarctica. Virginia Polytechnic Institute, Blacksburg, Virginia, pp. 333–371.

Lisitzin, A.P., 1962. Bottom sediments of the Antarctic. Am. Geophys. Un. Geophys. Monograph, No. 7: 81–88.

Lisitzin, A.P., 1970. Sedimentation and geochemical considerations. In: W.S. Wooster (Editor), Scientific Exploration of the South Pacific. National Academy of Sciences, Washington, D.C., pp. 89–132.

Lock, R.G., 1983. Continental margin petroleum potential in the Ross Sea region. N.Z. Antarctic Rec., 5(1): 6–15.

Lonsdale, P. and Smith, S.M., 1980. "Lower insular rise hills" shaped by a bottom boundary current in the mid-Pacific. Mar. Geol., 34: M19–M25.

Loutit, T.S., Kennett, J.P. and Savin, S.M., 1983. Miocene equatorial and southwest Pacific paleoceanography from stable isotope evidence. Mar. Micropaleontol., 8: 215–233.

Lovering, J.F. and Prescott, J.R.V., 1979. Last of Lands Antarctica. Melbourne University Press, Melbourne, 212 pp.

Lucchitta, B.K. and Ferguson, H.M., 1986. Antarctica: measuring glacier velocity from satellite images. Science, 234: 1105–1108.

Lutjeharms, J.R.E. and Baker, D.J., 1980. A statistical analysis of the meso-scale dynamics of the Southern Ocean. Deep-Sea Res., 27: 145–149.

Lutjeharms, J.R.E., Walters, N.M. and Allanson, R.B. 1985. Oceanic frontal systems and biological enhancement. In: W.R. Siegfried, P.R. Condy and R.M. Laws (Editors), Antarctic Nutrient Cycles and Food Webs. Springer-Verlag, Berlin, pp. 11–21.

Lyman, J., 1958. The U.S. Navy International Geophysical Year Antarctic Program in oceanography. Int. Hydrograph. Rev., 35(2): 111–126.

Macaulay, M.C., English, T.S. and Mathisen, O.A., 1984. Acoustic characterization of swarms of Antarctic krill (*Euphausia superba*) from Elephant Island and Bransfield Strait. J. Crustacean Biol., 4 (Spec. No. 1): 16–44.

MacAyeal, D.R., 1984. Thermohaline circulation below the Ross Ice Shelf: a consequence of tidally induced vertical mixing and basal melting. J. Geophys. Res., 89: 597–606.

MacAyeal, D.R. and Thomas, R.H., 1986. The effects of basal melting on the present flow of the Ross Ice Shelf, Antarctica. J. Glaciol., 32: 72–86.

McCann, T.S., 1985. Size, status and demography of southern elephant seal (*Mirounga leonina*) population. In: J.K. Ling and M.M. Bryden (Editors), Studies of Sea Mammals in South Latitudes. South Australian Museum, Adelaide, pp. 1–17.

McCartney, M.S., 1976. The interaction of zonal currents with topography with applications to the Southern Ocean. Deep-Sea Res., 23: 413–427.

McCartney, M.S., 1977. Subantarctic Mode Water. In: M. Angel (Editor), A Voyage of Discovery: George Deacon 70th Anniversary Volume, Supplement to Deep-Sea Res., Pergamon, Oxford, 24: 103–119.

McCartney, M.S., 1982. The subtropical recirculation of mode waters. J. Mar. Res., 40 (Suppl.): 427–464.

Macdonald, R.W., 1982. An examination of metal inputs to the southern Beaufort Sea by disposal of waste barite in drilling fluid. Ocean Management, 8: 29–49.

McDougall, I., 1977. Potassium-argon dating of glauconite from a grensand drilled at Site 270 in the Ross Sea, DSDP leg 28. In: Initial Reports of the Deep Sea Drilling Project, Vol. 36. U.S. Govt Printing Office, Washington, D.C., pp. 1071–1072.

McGinnis, L.D., Bowen, R.H., Ericson, J.M., Allred, B.J. and Kreamer, J.L., 1985. East-west Antarctic boundary in McMurdo Sound. Tectonophysics, 114: 341–356.

McHugh, J.L., 1974. The role and history of the International Whaling Comission. In: W.E. Schevill (Editor), The Whale Problem A Status Report. Harvard University Press, Cambridge, Mass., pp. 305–355.

McIntyre, N.F., 1985. The dynamics of ice sheet outlets. J. Glaciol., 31: 99–107.

McIver, R.D., 1975. Hydrocarbon gases in canned core samples from Leg 28 sites 271, 272, and 273, Ross Sea. In: Initial Reports of the Deep Sea Drilling Project, Vol. 28. U.S. Govt. Printing Office, Washington, D.C., pp. 815–817.

Mackay, D., 1985. The physical and chemical fate of spilled oil. In: F.R. Englehardt (Editor), Petroleum Effects in the Arctic Environment. Elsevier Applied science Publishers, London, pp. 37–61.

Mackintosh, N.A., 1946. The Antarctic Convergence and the distribution of surface temperatures in Antarctic waters. Discovery Reps, 23: 177–212.

Mackintosh, N.A., 1960. The pattern of distribution of the Antarctic fauna. Proc. Roy. Soc. Lond., 152B: 624–631.

Mackintosh, N.A., 1964. A survey of Antarctic biology up to 1945. In: R. Carrick, M. Holdgate, and J. Prévost (Editors), Biologique Antarctique. Hermann Press, Paris, pp. 29–38.

Mackintosh, N.A., 1965. The Stocks of Whales. Fishing News Books, London, 232 pp.

Mackintosh, N.A. 1970. Whales and krill in the Twentieth Century. In: M.W. Holdgate (Editor), Antarctic Ecology, Vol. 1. Academic Press, London, pp. 195–212.

McLaren, A.S., 1984. Transporting Arctic petroleum: a role for commercial submarines. Polar Rec., 21(133): 369–381.

McLaren, P., 1980. The coastal morphology and sedimentology of Labrador: a study of shoreline sensitivity to a potential oil spill. Geol. Surv. Canada, Pap. 79–28, 41 pp.

McNab, R., 1907. Murihuku and the Southern Islands. Fasc. ed. Wilson and Horton, Auckland, 377 pp.

McNab, R., 1913. The Old Whaling Days. Whitcombe and Tombs, Christchurch, 408 pp.

Macpherson, A.J., 1986. Glaciological, oceanographic and sedimentological data from Mackay Glacier and Granite Harbour, Antarctica. Victoria University of Wellington Antarctic Data Series., No. 12: 81 pp.

Macpherson, A.J., 1987. The Mackay Glacier/Granite Harbour system (Ross Dependency, Antarctica) – A study in nearshore glacial marine sedimentation. Unpubl. Ph.D. thesis (Victoria University of Wellington, N.Z.). 85 pp. + 2 Appendices.

McWhinnie, M.A., 1973. Physiology and biochemistry: USNS Eltanin, 1962–1972. Antarctic Jl U.S., 1(5): 210.

McWhinnie, M.A. and Denys, C.J., 1978. Biological studies of Antarctic krill, austral summer, 1977–1978. Antarctic Jl U.S., 13: 133–135.

Majluf, P., 1987. South American fur seal *Arctocephalus australis* in Peru. In: J.P. Croxall and R.L. Gentry (Editors), Status, Biology, and Ecology of Fur Seals. Proceedings of an International Symposium and Workshop, Cambridge, England, 23–27 April 1984. NOAA Tech. Rep. NMFS 51, pp. 33–35.

Maksimov, L.V., 1964. Oceanographic Research of Soviet Antarctic Expeditions, Vol. 1. Elsevier, Amsterdam, 404 pp.

Manabe, S., Hahn, D.G. and Holloway, J.L., 1978. Climate simulations with GFDL spectral models of the atmosphere: effect of spectral truncation. In: Report of the JOC study conference on climate models: performance, intercomparison and sensitivity studies. GARP Publication Ser. No. 22, W.M.O., Geneva, pp. 41–94.

Manheim, B.S., 1988. On thin ice. The failure of the National Science Foundation to protect Antarctica. Environmental Defence Fund, Washington, D.C., 112 pp.

Manikowski, S., 1971. The influence of meteorological factors on the behaviour of seabirds. Acta Zool., 13: 581–668.

Mantyla, A.W. and Reid, J.L., 1983. Abyssal characteristics of the world ocean waters. Deep-Sea Res., 30: 805–833.

Marchant, H.J., 1985. Choanoflagellates in the Antarctic marine food chain. In: W.R. Siegfried, P.R. Condy and R.M. Laws (Editors), Antarctic Nutrient Cycles and Food Webs. Springer-Verlag, Berlin, pp. 271–276.

Markham, C., 1986. Antarctic Obsession – The British National Antarctic Expedition 1901–4. Bluntisham Books and the Erskine Press, Harleston, Norfolk, 179 pp.

Markov, K.K., Bardin, V.I., Lebedev, V.L., Orlove, A.I. and Suyetova, I.A., 1970. The Geography of Antarctica. Israel program for scientific translations, Jerusalem, 370 pp.

Marr, J.W.S., 1962. The natural history of and geography of the Antarctic krill (*Euphausia superba* Dana). Discovery Reps, 32: 33–464.

Marshall, P.T., 1957. Primary production in the Arctic. J. Cons. Perm. Int. Explor. Mer, 23: 173–177.

Martin, S., 1979. A field study of brine drainage of oil entrainment in first-year sea ice. J. Glaciol., 22: 473–502.

Maslov, V.Yu. and Nesterova, M.N., 1981. The fluorescence method and an instrument for monitoring the pollution of the sea surface. Oceanology, 21: 801–803.

Mattlin, R.H., 1987. New Zealand fur seal *Arctocephalus forsteri*, within the New Zeland region. In: J.P. Croxall and R.L. Gentry (Editors), Status, Biology, and Ecology of Fur Seals. Proceedings of an International Symposium and Workshop, Cambridge, England, 23–27 April 1984. NOAA Tech. Rep. NMFS 51, pp. 49–51.

Mattlin, R.H. and Cawthorn, M.W., 1986. Marine debris – an international problem. N.Z. Environment, No. 51: 3–6.

Maury, M.F., 1968. The Physical Geography of the Sea and its Meteorology. Harvard University Press, Cambridge, 432 pp. (original volume published in 1855).

Mawson, D., 1915. The Home of the Blizzard. William Heinemann, London, 2 vols.

May, J., 1988. The Greenpeace Book of Antarctica A New View of the Seventh Continent. Darling Kindersley, London, 192 pp.

Mead, J.G. and Baker, A.N., 1987. Notes on the rare beaked whale *Mesoplodon hectori* (Gray). J. Roy. Soc. N.Z., 17: 303–312.

Mead, K.L., 1978. Bibliography of N.Z.A.R.P. publications 1956–1976. Antarctic Division, D.S.I.R., 185 pp.

Mechoso, C.R., 1981. Topographic influences on the general circulation of the Southern Hemisphere: a numerical experiment. Mon. Wea. Rev., 109: 2131–2139.

Mercer, J.H., 1978. West Antarctic ice sheet and CO_2 greenhouse effect: a threat of disaster. Nature, 271: 321–325.

Mercer, J.H., 1983. Cenozoic glaciation in the southern hemisphere. Ann. Rev. Earth Planet. Sci., 11: 99–132.

Mero, J.L., 1965. The Mineral Resources of the Sea. Elsevier, Amsterdam, 312 pp.

Merrell, T.R., 1980. Accumulation of plastic litter on beaches of Amchitka Island. Mar. Environmental Res., 3: 171–184.

Merrell, T.R., 1984. A decade of change in nets and plastic litter from fisheries off Alaska. Mar. Pollut. Bull., 15: 378–384.

Merton, D., 1984. Confirmation of breeding by Black-winged Petrel on South East Island, Chatham Islands. Notornis, 31: 265–266.

Metcalfe, A., Sporli, K.B. and Craddock, C., 1978. Plutonic rocks from the Ruppert Coast, West Antarctica. Antarctic Jl U.S., 13(4): 5–7.

Meylan, M.A. and Goodell, H.G., 1976. Chemical composition of manganese nodules from the Pacific–Antarctic Ocean, Drake Passage and Scotia Sea: relation to ferromanganese oxide mineralogy and nucleus type. CCOP/SOPAC Tech. Bull., 2: 99–117.

Michel, J., Hayes, M.O. and Brown, P.J., 1978. Application of an oil spill vulnerability index to the shoreline of Lower Cook Inlet, Alaska. Environmental Geol., 2: 107–117.

Mickleburgh, E., 1987. Beyond the Frozen Sea Visions of Antarctica. The Bodley Head, London, 256 pp.

Mildenhall, D.C., 1980. New Zealand late Cretaceous and Cenozoic plant biogeography: a contribution. Palaeogeogr. Palaeoclimatol. Palaeoecol., 31: 197–233.

Mileykovskiy, S.A., 1979. Extent of the oil pollution of the world ocean (literature review). Oceanology, 19: 547–551.

Mill, H.R., 1905. The Seige of the South Pole. Alston Rivers, London, 449 pp.

Miller, B.M., Thomsen, H.L., Dolton, G.L., Coury, A.B., Hendricks, T.A., Lennartz, F.E.,

Powers, R.B., Sable, E.G. and Varnes, K.L., 1975. Geological estimates of undiscovered recoverable oil and gas resources in the United States. U.S. Geol. Surv. Circ., 725: 78 pp.

Miskelly, C.K., 1984. Birds of the Western Chain, Snares Islands, 1983–1984. Notornis, 31: 209–224.

Mitchell, B., 1982. The Southern Ocean in the 1980s. In: E.M. Borgese and N. Ginsburg (Editors), Ocean Yearbook 3. University of Chicago Press, Chicago, pp. 349–385.

Mitchell, B., 1983. Frozen Stakes : The Future of Antarctic Minerals. International Institute for Environment and Development, London, 135 pp.

Mitchell, B. and Sandbrook, R., 1980. The Management of the Southern Ocean. International Institute for Environment and Development, London, 162 pp.

Mitchell, B. and Tinker, J., 1980. Antarctica and its Resources. An Earthscan Publication, International Institute for Environment and Development, London, 98 pp.

Miyazaki, N. and Kato, H., 1988. Sighting records of small cetaceans in the southern hemisphere. Bull. Natn Sci. Mus. Tokyo, Ser. A., 14(1): 47–65.

Mognard, N.M., Campbell, W.J., Cheney, R.E. and Marsh, J.B., 1983. Southern Ocean mean monthly waves and surface winds for winter 1978 by Seasat radar altimeter. J. Geophys. Res., 88: 1736–1744.

Mohr, H., 1976. Tageszeitlich bedingte Rhythmik im Verhalten von halbwüchsigem Krill (*Euphausia superba*). Inf. Fischwirt. 4/5, 132–134. Bundesforschungsdnst. Fisch, Hamburg.

Molinelli, E., 1978. Isohaline thermoclines in the southeast Pacific Ocean. J. Phys. Oceanogr., 8: 1139–1145.

Molnar, P., Atwater, T., Mammerickx, J. and Smith, S.M., 1975. Magnetic anomalies, bathymetry and tectonic evolution of the South Pacific since the Late Cretaceous. Geophys. J. Roy. Astr. Soc., 40: 383–420.

Molors, P.J., 1980. Southern Great Skuas on Antipodes Island, New Zealand: observations on foods, breding and growth of chicks. Notornis, 27: 133–146.

Montgomery, R.B., 1958. Water characteristics of Atlantic Ocean and of world ocean. Deep-Sea Res., 5: 134–148.

Moors, P.J., 1986. Decline in numbers of Rockhopper Penguins at Campbell Island. Polar Rec., 23: 69–73.

Morris, R.B., 1977. Juvenile Chatham Island shag observed offering nest material to a breeding adult. Notornis, 24: 141.

Morris, R.J., 1980. Plastic debris in the surface waters of the South Atlantic. Mar. Pollut. Bull., 11: 164–166.

Morton, H.A., 1983. The Whale's Wake. John McIndoe, Dunedin, 396 pp.

Mosby, H., 1956. The Norwegian Antarctic expedition in the «Brategg» 1947–1948. Scient. Results of the «Brategg» Expedition, 1957–48, No.1: 3–9.

Mosby, H., 1968. Bottom water formation. SCAR/SCOR/IAPO/IUBS Symposium on Antarctic oceanography, Santiago, Chile, Sept. 13–16, 1966. Scott Polar Res. Inst., Sci. Comm. on Antarctic Res., pp. 47–57.

Mullan, A.B., 1985. Zonal asymmetry in the Southern Hemisphere 500 hPa height field: Long-term means and monthly variability. In: Proceedings of the First WMO Workshop on the Diagnosis and Prediction of Monthly and Seasonal Atmospheric Variations over the Globe. 29 Jul–2 Aug 1985 (College Park, USA). World Meteorological Organisation, Tech. Doc. No. 87, pp. 404–410.

Mullan, A.B., Hill, H.W. and Dini, P.W., 1986. The relationship of Southern Hemisphere planetary waves to typical weather regimes of the southern Indian and Pacific Oceans. In: Proceedings of Second International Conference on Southern Hemisphere Meteorology, 1–5 December 1986, Wellington, New Zealand. American Meteorological

Society, Boston, pp. 180–183.

Murphy, R.C., 1936. Oceanic Birds of South America. American Museum of Natural History, N.Y., 2 vols.

Murray, G., 1901. The Antarctic Manual for the use of the expedition of 1901. Royal Geographical Society, London, 566 pp.

Murray, J., 1886. The exploration of the Antarctic regions. Scot. Geogr. Mag., 2: 527–548.

Murray, J. 1894. The renewal of Antarctic exploration. Geogr. J., 3: 1–42.

Nagata, T., 1983. The implementation of the Convention on the Conservation of Antarctic Marine Living Resources : needs and problems. In: F.O. Vicuña (Editor), Antarctic Resources Policy Scientific, Legal and Political Issues. Cambridge University Press, Cambridge, pp. 119–137.

National Academy of Science, 1975. Assessing potential ocean pollutants. A report of the Study Panel on Assessing Potential Ocean Pollutants to the Ocean Affairs Board, Commission on Natural Resources, National Research Council, Washington, D.C.

Nayudu, Y.R., 1971. Lithology and chemistry of surface sediments in subAntarctic regions of the Pacific Ocean. Antarctic Res. Ser., 15: 247–282.

Neal, C.S., 1979. The dynamics of the Ross Ice Shelf revealed by radio echo-sounding. J. Glaciol., 24: 295–308.

Neal, V.T. and Newlin, W.D., 1979. International Southern Ocean studies of circumpolar dynamics. Polar Rec., 19(122): 461–470.

Neaverson, E., 1934. The sea-floor deposits 1. General characteristics and distribution. Discovery Reps, 9: 295–350.

Nelson, D.M. and Gordon, L.I., 1982. Production and pelagic dissolution of biogenic silica in the Southern Ocean. Geochim. Cosmochim. Acta, 46: 491–501.

Nelson, D.M. and Smith, W.O., 1986. Phytoplankton bloom dynamics of the western Ross Sea ice edge – II. Mesoscale cycling of nitrogen and silicon. Deep-Sea Res., 33: 1389–1412.

Nelson-Smith, A., 1982. Biological consequences of oil-spills in Arctic waters. In: L. Rey (Editor), The Arctic Ocean: The hydrographic environment and the fate of pollutants. MacMillan, London, pp. 275–293.

Neori, A. and Holm-Hansen, O., 1982. Effect of temperature on rate of photosynthesis in Antarctic phytoplankton. Polar Biol., 1: 33–38.

Neshyba, S., 1980. On the size distribution of Antarctic icebergs. Cold Regions Science and Technology, 1: 241–248.

Neshyba, S. and Fonseca, T.R., 1980. Evidence for counterflow to the West Wind Drift off South America. J. Geophys. Res., 85: 4888–4892.

Nittrouer, C.A., Ledford-Hoffman, P.A., DeMaster, D.J. and Dadey, K.A., 1984. Accumulation of Modern sediment in the Ross Sea, Antarctica. EOS Trans. Am. Geophys. Un., 65: 916 (Abstr.).

NOAA, 1974. Catalog of meteorological satellite data – ESSA 9 television cloud photography, January 1 – March 31, 1972. Key to meteorological records documentation No. 5.333, U.S. Dept. of Commerce.

Norris, B.N., 1965. Caring for white flippered penguins. Notornis, 12: 185–186.

Norris, R.J. and Carter, R.M., 1980. Offshore sedimentary basins at the southern end of the Alpine Fault, New Zealand. Spec. Publ. Int. Assoc. Sedimentol., 4: 237–265.

Northey, D.J., Brown, C., Christoffel, D.A., Wong, H.K. and Barrett, P.J., 1975. A continuous seismic profiling survey in McMurdo Sound, Antarctica – 1975. Dry Valley Drilling Project Bull., No. 5: 167–179.

Nowlin, W.D., 1985. General circulation of the Southern Ocean : Status and recommendations for research. A Report by SCOR Working Group, September, 1985. 70 pp.

Nowlin, W.D. and Clifford, M., 1982. The kinematic and thermohaline zonation of the Antarctic Circumpolar Current at Drake Passage. J. Mar. Res., 40 (Suppl): 481–507.

Nowlin, W.D. and Klinck, J.M., 1986. The physics of the Antarctic Circumpolar Current. Revs Geophys., 24: 469–491.

Nowlin, W.D., Pillsbury, R.D. and Bottero, J., 1981. Observations of kinetic energy levels in the Antarctic Circumpolar Current at Drake Passage. Deep-Sea Res., 28: 1–17.

Nowlin, W.D., Whitworth, T., and Pillsbury, R.D., 1977. Structure and transport of the Antarctic Circumpolar Current at Drake Passage from short-term measurements. J. Phys. Oceanogr., 7: 788–802.

Nowlin, W.D. and Zenk, W., 1988. Westward bottom currents along the margin of the South Shetland Island Arc. Deep-Sea Res., 35: 269–301.

Nummedal, D., 1980. Persistence of spilled oil along the Beaufort Sea coast. Final Report to National Oceanic and Atmospheric Administration, Outer Continental Shelf Environmental Assessment Program. Contract 03–5022–82, 48 pp.

Oerlemans, J. and van der Veen, C.J., 1984. Ice Sheets and Climate. D. Reidel Publ. Co., Dordrecht, 217 pp.

Oliver, R.L., James, P.R. and Jago, J.B. (Editors), 1983. Antarctic Earth Science. Australian Academy of Science, Canberra, 597 pp.

Oliver, W.R.B., 1955. New Zealand Birds. A.H. & A.W. Reed, Wellington. 661 pp.

Oostdam, B.L., 1984. Tar pollution of beaches in the Indian Ocean, the South China Sea and the South Pacific Ocean. Mar. Pollut. Bull., 15: 267–270.

Orheim, O., 1980. Physical characteristics and life expectancy of tabular Antarctic icebergs. Annals Glaciol., 1: 11–18.

Orheim, O., 1985. Iceberg discharge and the mass balance of Antarctica. In: Glaciers, Ice Sheets and Sea Level: Effect of a CO_2-induced Climatic Change. Report of a Workshop held in Seattle, Washington September 13–15, 1984, pp. 210–215.

Orheim, O. and Elverhoi, A., 1981. Model for submarine glacial deposition. Annals Glaciol., 2: 123–128.

Oshumi, S., 1979. Population assessment of the Antarctic minke whale. Rep. Int. Whal. Commn, 29: 407–420.

Ostapoff, F., 1961. A contribution to the problem of the Drake Passage circulation. Deep-Sea Res., 8: 111–120.

Owen, R., 1941. The Antarctic Ocean. Whittlesey House, N.Y., 254 pp.

Owens, E.H., Harper, J.R., Robson, W. and Boehm, P.D., 1987. Fate and persistence of crude oil stranded on a sheltered beach. Arctic, 40 (Suppl. 1): 109–123.

Owens, E.H. and Robson, W., 1987. Experimental design and the retention of oil on Arctic test beaches. Arctic, 40 (Suppl. 1): 230–243.

Owens, E.H., Robson, W. and Humphrey, B., 1987. Obsrevations from a site visit to the "Metula" spill 12 years after the incident. Spill Technology Newsletter, 12: 83–96.

Owens, E.H., Taylor, R.B., Miles, M. and Forbes, D.L., 1981. Coastal geology mapping: an example from the Sverdrup Lowland, District of Franklin. Current Research, Part B, Geological Survey of Canada, Paper 81–1B, 39–48.

Palmisano, A.C. and Sullivan, C.W., 1983. Sea ice microbial communities (SIMCO) 1. Distribution, abundance, and primary production of ice microalgae in McMurdo Sound, Antarctica in 1980. Polar Biol., 2: 171–177.

Parish, T.R., 1982. Surface airflow over East Antarctica. Mon. Wea. Rev., 110: 84–90.

Parker, B.C., 1971. The case for conservation in Antarctica. Antarctic Jl U.S., 6: 50–53.

Parkinson, C.L. and Bindschadler, R.A., 1984. Response of Antarctic sea ice to uniform atmospheric temperature increases. In: J.E. Hansen and T. Takahashi (Editors), Climate Processes and Climate Sensitivity. American Geophysical Union, Washington,

D.C., pp. 254–264.

Parsons, A., 1987. Antarctica : The Next Decade. Cambridge University Press, Cambridge, 164 pp.

Pascal, M., 1985. Numerical changes in the population of elephant seals (*Mirounga leonina* L.) in the Kergulen Archipelago during the past 30 years. In: J.R. Beddington, R.H. Beverton and D.M. Lavigne (Editors), Marine Mammals and Fisheries. Allen and Unwin, London, pp. 170–186.

Patterson, S.L., 1985. Surface circulation and kinetic energy distributions in the southern hemisphere oceans from FGGE drifting buoys. J. Phys., Oceanogr., 15: 865–884.

Patterson, S.L. and Sievers, H.A., 1979/80. Mesoscale thermal structure of the polar front zone in Drake Passage during the austral summer of 1976. Serie Cientifica Inst. Antart. Chileno, 25/26:: 49–112.

Penniket, A., Garrick, A. and Breese, E. (Editors), 1986. Preliminary reports of Expeditions to the Auckland Islands Nature Reserve 1973–84. Dept. of Lands and Survey, Welling ton. 231 pp.

Pennycuick, C.J., 1972. Animal Flight. Edward Arnold, London, 68 pp.

Pennycuick, C.J., Croxall, J.P. and Prince, P.A., 1984. Scaling of foraging radius and growth rate in petrels and albatrosses (Procellariiformes). Ornis Scandinavica, 15: 145–154.

Perkins, J.S., 1983. Oiled Magellanic penguins in Golfo San Jose, Argentina. Mar. Pollut. Bull, 14: 383–387.

Peterson, R.G., 1985. Drifter trajectories through a current meter array at Drake Passage. J. Geophys. Res., 90: 4883–4893.

Peterson, R.G., Nowlin, W.D. and Whitworth, T., 1982. Generation and evolution of a cyclonic ring at Drake Passage in early 1979. J. Phys. Oceangor., 12: 712–719.

Phillips Petroleum New Zealand Ltd, 1976. Phillips Geochemical Reports – source rock potential. Wells and field samples. N.Z. Geol. Surv., open-file Petroleum Rep., No. 737, 147 pp.

Pilaar, W.F.H. and Whakefield, L.L., 1984. Hydrocarbon generation in the Taranaki Basin, New Zealand. In: G. Demaison and R.J. Murris (Editors), Petroleum Geochemistry and Basin Evaluation. APPG Memoir, 35: 405–423.

Pillsbury, R.D. and Bottero, J.S., 1984. Observations of current rings in the Antarctic Zone at Drake Passage. J. Mar. Res., 42: 853–874.

Pillsbury, R.D. and Jacobs, S.S., 1985. Preliminary observations from long-term current meter moorings near the Ross Ice Shelf, Antarctica. Antarctic Res. Ser., 43: 87–107.

Pingree, R.D., 1978. Cyclonic eddies and cross frontal mixing. J. Mar. Biol. Assoc. U.K., 58: 955–963.

Piola, A.R. and Georgi, D.T., 1982. Circumpolar properties of Antarctic Intermediate Water and Subantarctic Mode Water. Deep-Sea Res., 29: 687–711.

Piper, D.Z., Swint, T.R., Sullivan, L.G. and McCoy, F.W., 1985. Manganese nodules, seafloor sediment, and sedimentation rates of the Circum–Pacific region. Circum-Pacific Council for Energy and Mineral Resources, AAPG, Tulsa, Oklahoma (Chart).

Pitman, W.C., Herron, E.M. and Heirtzler, J.R., 1968. Magnetic anomalies in the Pacific and seafloor spreading. J. Geophys. Res., 73: 2069–2085.

Platt, H.M., 1979. Exploitation and pollution in Antarctica: a case history. Progr. Underwater Sci., 5: 188–200.

Platt, T., Subba Rao, D.V. and Irwin, B., 1983. Photosynthesis of picoplankton in the oligotrophic ocean. Nature, 300: 700–704.

Ploshay, J.J., White, R.K, and Miyakoda, K., 1983. FGGE level III–B daily global analyses. NOAA Data Report ERL GFDL–1, Geophysical Fluid Dynamics Laboratory, Princeton, New Jersey, 4 parts.

Pockington, R., 1979. An oceanographic interpretation of seabird distributions in the Indian Ocean. Mar. Biol., 51: 9–21.

Polar Group, 1980. Polar atmosphere-ice-ocean processes: A review of polar problems in climate research. Revs. Geophys. Space Phys., 18: 525–543.

Pomeroy, L.R., 1974. The ocean's food web, a changing paradigm. Bioscience, 24: 499–504.

Pontecorvo, G., 1982. The economics of the resources of Antarctica. In: J.I. Charney (Editor), The New Nationalism and the Use of Common Spaces. Allenheld, Osmun Publishers, Totowa, New Jersey, pp. 155–166.

Potter, N., 1969. Natural resource potentials of the Antarctic. American Geographical Society Occ. Publ. No. 4: 97 pp.

Powell, D.L., 1983. Scientific and economic considerations relating to the conservation of marine living resources in Antarctica. In: F.O. Vicuña (Editor), Antarctic Resources Policy Scientific, Legal and Political Issues. Cambridge University Press, Cambridge, pp. 111–118.

Prebble, M.M., 1968. Ice breakout, McMurdo Sound, Antarctica. N.Z. Jl Geol Geophys., 11: 908–921.

Priestley, R., 1956. Twentieth Century man against Antarctica. Advancement of Science, 13: 3–16.

Prince, P.A., 1980. The food and feeding ecology of grey-headed albatross Diomedea chrysostoma and black-browed albatross D. melanophris. Ibis., 122: 476–488.

Prince, P.A. and Francis, M.D., 1984. Activity budgets of foraging gray-headed albatrosses. Condor, 86: 297–300.

Pritchard, D.W. and LaFond, E.C., 1952. Some recent temperature sections across the Antarctic Convergence. Proc. 7th Pacif. Sci. Congr., 3: 209–297.

Pruter, A.T., 1987. Sources, quantities and distribution of persistent plastics in the marine environment. Mar. Pollut. Bull., 18. 305–310.

Pyne, A. and Waghorn, D.B. (Editors), 1980. Victoria University of Wellington Antarctic Expedition 24 and MSSTS, Immediate Report. Victoria University of Wellington, 56 pp. + 16 plates.

Pyne, A.R., Ward, B.L., Macpherson, A.J. and Barrett, P.J. , 1985. McMurdo Sound bathymetry, 1:250,000. N.Z. Oceanogr. Inst. Chart, Misc. Ser. 62.

Pyne, S.J., 1986. The Ice A Journey to Antarctica. University of Iowa Press, Iowa City, 428 pp.

Quartermain, L.B., 1967. South to the Pole The Early History of the Ross Sea Sector, Antarctica. Oxford University Press, Wellington, 481 pp.

Quilty, P.G., 1984. Mineral resources of the Australian Antarctic Territory. In: S. Harris (Editor), Australia's Antarctic Policy Options. ANU Centre for Resources and Environmental Studies Monograph, 11: 165–203 (also published in ANARE Research Notes, 27: 165–203, 1985).

Quilty, P.G., 1987. Identification and evolution of Antarctic sedimentary basins. Trans. Fourth Circum-Pacific Energy and Mineral Resources Conf.: 317–333.

Rabinowitz, P.D. and LaBreque, J.L., 1979. The Mesozoic South Atlantic Ocean and evolution of its continental margins. J. Geophys. Res., 84: 5976–6002.

Rakusa-Sauszczewski, S., 1982. Feeding of Euphausia superba Dana under natural conditions. Pol. Polar Res., 3: 289–297.

Randall, B.M., Randall, R.M. and Roussow, G.J., 1983. Plastic particle pollution in great shearwaters (Puffinus gravis) from Gough Island. South African Jl Antarctic Res., 13: 49–50.

Randall, R.M., Randall, B.M. and Bevan, J., 1980. Oil pollution and penguins – is cleaning justified? Mar. Pollut. Bull., 11: 234–237.

Ray, G.C., 1981. Ross Seal *Ommatophoca rossi* Gray, 1844. In: S.H. Ridgway and R. Harrison (Editors), Handbook of Marine Mammals 2: Seals. Academic Press, London, pp. 237–260.

Reed, S., 1981. Wreck of Kerguelen and blue petrels. Notornis, 28: 239–240.

Reid, J.L., 1965. Intermediate waters of the Pacific Ocean. The Johns Hopkins Oceanographic Studies, 2: 85 pp.

Reid, J.L., 1973. Transpacific hydrographic sections at Lats. 43°S and 28°S: the SCORPIO Expedition–III. Upper water and a note on southward flow at mid-depth. Deep-Sea Res., 20: 39–49.

Reid, J.L., 1986. On the total geostrophic circulation of the South Pacific Ocean: flow patterns, tracers and transports. Progr. Oceanogr., 16: 1–61.

Reid, J.L. and Arthur, R.S., 1975. Interpretation of maps of geopotential anomaly for the deep Pacific Ocean. J. Mar. Res., 33 (Suppl.): 37–52.

Reid, J.L. and Lynn, R.J., 1971. On the influence of the Norwegian–Greenland and Weddell seas upon the bottom waters of the Indian and Pacific oceans. Deep-Sea Res., 18: 1063–1088.

Reid, J.L. and Nowlin, W.D., 1971. Transport of water through the Drake Passage. Deep-Sea Res., 18: 51–64.

Reid, J.L., Nowlin, W.D. and Patzert, W.C., 1977. On the characteristics and circulation of the southwestern Atlantic Ocean. J. Phys. Oceanogr., 7: 62–91.

Richardson, J. and Gray, J.E. (Editors), 1844–75. The zoology of the voyage of H.M.S. Erebus & Terror, under the command of Captain Sir James Clark Ross, R.N., F.R.S., during the years 1829 to 1843. E.W. Janson, London, 2 vols.

Richdale, L.E. and Warham, J., 1973. Survival, pair bond retention and nest-site tenacity in Buller's Mollymawk. Ibis, 115: 257–263.

Ridgway, N.M. and Glasby, G.P., 1984. Sources of marine pollution around New Zealand. N.Z. Oceanogr. Inst. Oceanogr. Summary, No. 23, 21 pp.

Ridgway, S.H. and Harrison, R. (Editors), 1981a. Handbook of Marine Mammals 1: The Walrus, Sea Lions, Fur Seals and Sea Otters. Academic Press, London, 235 pp.

Ridgway, S.H. and Harrison, R. (Editors), 1981b. Handbook of Marine Mammals 2: Seals. Academic Press, London, 359 pp.

Ridgway, S.H. and Harrison, R. (Editors), 1985. Handbook of Marine Mammals 3: The Sirenians and Baleen Whales. Academic Press, London, 362 pp.

Risebrough, R.W., 1977. Transfer of Organochlorine pollutants to Antarctica. In: G.A. Llano (Editor), Adaptations within Antarctic Ecosystems. Proceedings of the Third SCAR Symposium on Antarctic Biology, pp. 1203–1210.

Risebrough, R.W., Walker, W., Schmidt, T.T., De Lappe, B.W. and Connors, C.W., 1976. Transfer of chlorinated biphenyls to Antarctica. Nature, 264: 738–739.

Risk, G.F. and Hochstein, M.P., 1974. Heatflow at Arrival Heights, Ross Island, Antarctica. N.Z. Jl Geol. Geophys., 17: 629–644.

Roberts, B., 1958. Chronological list of Antarctic expeditions. Polar Rec., 9(60): 191–239.

Robertson, C.J.R., 1974. Albatrosses of the Chatham Islands. Wildlife – A review, 5: 20–22.

Robertson, C.J.R., 1975. Report on the distribution, status and breeding biology of the Royal Albatross, Wandering Albatross and White-capped Mollymawk on the Auckland Islands. In: J.C. Yaldwyn (Editor), Preliminary Results of the Auckland Islands Expedition 1972–1973. Dept. of Lands and Survey, Wellington, pp. 143–151.

Robertson, C.J.R., 1980. Birds on Campbell Islands. Preliminary reports of the Campbell Island Expedition 1975–76. N.Z. Dept. of Lands and Survey, pp. 106–116.

Robertson, C.J.R., 1985a. Black-browed Mollymawk *Diomedes melanophrys.* In: Readers Digest Complete Book of New Zealand Birds. Readers Digest, Reed Methuen, Sydney, pp. 61.

Robertson, C.J.R., 1985b. Shy Mollymawk *Diomedea cauta*. In: Readers Digest Complete Book of New Zealand Birds. Readers Digest, Reed Methuen, Sydney, pp. 65.

Robertson, C.J.R. and Bell, B.D., 1984. Seabird status and conservation in the New Zealand region. In: J.P. Croxall, P.G.H. Evans and R.W. Schreiber (Editors), Status and Conservation of the World's Seabirds. International Council for Bird Preservation Tech. Publ., No. 2: 573–586.

Robertson, C.J.R. and Kinsky, F.C., 1972. The dispersal movements of the Royal Albatross (*Diomedea epomophora*). Notornis, 19: 289–301.

Robertson, C.J.R. and van Tets, G.F., 1982. Status of the birds at the Bounty Islands. Notornis, 29: 311–336.

Robilliard, G.A. and Busdosh, M., 1981. Need for real world assessment of the environmental effects of oil spills in ice-infested marine environments. Proceedings POAC '81, Vol. II. Sixth International Conference, Quebec, pp. 937–944.

Robin, G. de Q., 1979. Formation, flow, and disintegration of ice shelves. J. Glaciol., 24: 259–271.

Robin, G. de Q., 1986. Changing the sea level. In: B. Bolin, B.R. Döös, J. Jäger and R.A. Warrick (Editors), SCOPE 29 The Greenhouse Effect, Climate Change, and Ecosystems. John Wiley & Sons, Chichester, pp. 323–359.

Robin, G. de Q., 1988. The Antarctic ice sheet; its history and response to sea level and climatic changes over the past 100 million years. Palaeogeogr. Palaeoclimatol. Palaeoecol., 67: 31–50.

Robin, G. de Q., Drewry, D.J. and Squire, V.A., 1983. Satellite observations of polar ice fields. Philos. Trans. R. Soc. London, Ser. A, 309: 447–461.

Robin, G. de Q. and Swithinbank, C., 1987. Fifty years of progress in understanding ice sheets. J. Glaciol., Spec. Issue, pp. 33–47.

Robinson, P.H. and King, P.R., 1988. Hydrocarbon reservoir potential of the Taranaki Basin, western New Zealand. Energy Exploration and Exploitation, 6: 248–262.

Rodman, M.R. and Gordon, A.L., 1982. Southern Ocean bottom water of the Australian–New Zealand sector. J. Geophys. Res., 87: 5771–5778.

Rogers, A.E.F., 1980. Seabirds observed between Sydney and Buenos Aires. Notornis, 27: 69–78.

Roland, N.W., 1986. Prospecting in Antarctica?: Geological economic and political aspects. In: Prospecting in areas of glaciated terrain 1986. The Institution of Mining and Metallurgy, London, pp. 175–186.

Romanov, A.A., 1984. Ice of the Southern Ocean (in navigable conditions). Gidrometeoizdat, Leningrad, 150 pp. (In Russian).

Roos, S.E., 1937. Some geographical results of the second Byrd Antarctic expedition, 1933–1935 I The submarine topography of the Ross Sea and adjacent waters. Geogr. Rev., 17: 574–583.

Roots, E.F., 1983. Resource development in polar regions: comments on technology. In: F.O. Vicuña (Editor), Antarctic Resource Policy Scientific, Legal and Political Issues. Cambridge University Press, Cambridge, pp. 297–315.

Ross, D.A., Uchupi, E., Summerhayes, C.P., Koelsch, D.E. and El Shazly, E.M., 1978. Sedimentation and structure of the Nile Cone and Levant Platform area. In: D.J. Stanley and G. Kelling (Editors), Sedimentation in Submarine Canyons, Fans, and Trenches. Dowden, Hutchinson and Ross, Stroudsburg, Pa, pp. 261–275.

Ross, D.I., 1967. Magnetic and bathymetric measurements across the Pacific–Antarctic Ridge south of New Zealand. N.Z. Jl Geol. Geophys., 10: 1452–1465.

Ross, G.J.B., Baker, A.N., Goodall, R.N.P., Lichter, A.A. and Meade, J.G., in press. The distribution of beaked whales in the Southern Hemisphere. Rep. Int. Whal. Commn

Spec. Issue

Ross, M.J., 1982. Ross in the Antarctic. Caedmon, Whitby, 276 pp.

Ross, R.M. and Quetin, L.B., 1983. Spawning frequency and fecundity of the Antarctic krill, *Euphausia superba*. Mar. Biol., 77: 201–205.

Rothstein, S.I., 1973. Plastic particle pollution on the surface of the Atlantic Ocean: evidence from a seabird. The Condor, 75: 344–345.

Rounsevell, D.E. and Brothers, N.P., 1984. The status and conservation of seabirds at Macquarie Island. In: J.P. Croxall, P.G.H. Evans, and R.W. Schreiber (Editors), Status and Conservation of the World's Seabirds. International Council for Bird Preservation Tech. Publ., 2: 587–592.

Routh, M., 1949. Ornithological observations in Antarctic seas. Ibis, 91: 577–606.

Rubin, M.J., 1982a. James Cook's scientific programme in the Southern Ocean, 1772–75. Polar Rec., 21(130): 33–49.

Rubin, M.J., 1982b. Thaddeus Bellingshausen's scientific programme in the Southern Ocean, 1818–21. Polar Rec., 21(132): 215–229.

Runnells, D.D., 1970. Continental drift and economic minerals in Antarctica. Earth Planet. Sci. Letts, 8: 400–402.

Russell, H.C., 1885. Icebergs in the Southern Ocean. J. Roy. Soc. N.S.W., 29: 286–315.

Russell, H.C., 1897. Current papers, No. 2. J. Roy. Soc. N.S.W., 30: 202–210.

Ryan, P.G., 1987a. The origin and fate of artefacts stranded on islands in the African sector of the Southern Ocean. Environ. Conserv., 14: 341–346.

Ryan, P.G., 1987b. The incidence and characteristics of plastic particles ingested by seabirds. Mar. Environmental Res., 23: 175–206.

Ryan, P.G., 1987c. The effects of ingested plastic on seabirds: correlations between plastic load and body condition. Environ. Pollut., 46: 119–125.

Ryan, P.G. and Jackson, S., 1987. The lifespan of ingested plastic particles in seabirds and their effect on digestive efficiency. Mar. Pollut. Bull., 18: 217–219.

Sadleir, R.M., 1987. Movements at sea of Adelie penguins during the chick-feeding stage. N.Z. Antarctic Rec., 7(3): 57 (Abstr.).

Sadleir, R.M.F.S., Taylor, R.H. and Taylor, G.A., 1986. Breeding of Antarctic Terns (*Sterna vittata bethunei*). Notornis, 33: 264–265.

Sagar, P.M., 1977a. Birds of the Western Chain, Snares Islands, New Zealand. Notornis, 24: 178–183.

Sagar, P.M., 1977b. Birds of the 1976–77 Snares Islands Expedition. Notornis, 24: 205–209.

Sagar, P.M., 1978. Breeding of Antarctic Terns at the Snares Islands, New Zealand. Notornis, 25: 59–70.

Sagar, P.M., 1979. Breeding of the Cape Pigeon at the Snares Islands. Notornis, 26: 23–36.

Sagar, P.M., 1986. The sexual dimorphism of Snares Cape Pigeons (*Daption Capense australe*). Notornis, 33: 259–263.

Sage, B., 1985. Conservation and exploitation. In: W.N. Bonner and D.W.H. Walton (Editors), Key Environments Antarctica. Pergamon Press, Oxford, pp. 351–369.

Sahrhage, D. (Editor), 1988. Antarctic Ocean and Resources Variability. Springer-Verlag, Berlin, 304 pp.

Saijo, Y. and Kawashima, T., 1964. Primary production in the Antarctic Ocean. J. Oceanogr. Soc, Japan, 19: 190–196.

St. John, W., 1986. Antarctica – Geology and hydrocarbon potential. In: M.T. Halbouty (Editor), Future Petroleum Provinces of the World. AAPG Memoir, 40: 55–100.

Sakshaug, E. and Holm-Hansen, O., 1984. Factors governing pelagic production in Polar Oceans. In: O. Holm-Hansen, L. Bolis and R. Gils (Editors), Marine Phytoplankton and Productivity. Springer-Verlag, Berlin, pp. 1–18.

Sakshaug, E. and Holm-Hansen, O., 1986. Photoadaptation in Antarctic phytoplanton : variations in growth rate, chemical composition and P versus I curves. J. Plankton Res., 8: 459–473.

Sanderson, T.J.O., 1983. Offshore oil development in Polar regions. N.Z. Antarctic Rec., 5(1): 30–44.

Sanford, R.M., 1980. Exploration results off S. New Zealand. Oil & Gas J., 78(5): 83–85, 88–90.

Sarnthein, M., Winn, K. and Duplessy, J.-C., 1988. Global variations of surface ocean productivity in low and mid latitudes : Influence in CO_2 reservoirs of the deep ocean and atmosphere during the last 21,000 years. Paleoceanography, 3: 361–399.

Sarukhanyan, E'.I., 1985. Structure and variability of the Antarctic Circumpolar Current. Division of Ocean Sciences, National Science Foundation, Washington, D.C., 108 pp. (translated from Russian).

Sato, S., Askura, N., Saki, T., Oikawa, N. and Kaneda, Y., 1984. Preliminary results of geological and geophysical surveys in the Ross Sea and in the Dumont D'Urville Sea, off Antarctica. Mem. Nat. Inst. Polar Res. (Tokyo) Special Issue No. 33: 66–92.

Savage, M.L. and Ciesielski, P.F., 1983. A revised history of glacial sedimentation in the Ross Sea region. In: R.L. Oliver, P.R. James and J.B. Jago (Editors), Antarctic Earth Science. Australian Academy of Science, Canberra, pp. 555–559.

Savatyugin, L.M., 1970. Obizmeneniye konfiguratsii fronta shel'fovykh lednikov Bellings-gauzena, Tueytsa i Lazareva. Soviet Antarct Exped. Inform. Bull., 79: 56–58.

Savchenko, V.G., Emery, W.J. and Vladiminov, O.A., 1978. A cyclonic eddy in the Antarctic Circumpolar Current south of Australia: results of Soviet–American observations aboard the R/V PROFESSOR ZUBOV. J. Phys. Oceanogr., 8: 825–837.

Savours, A., 1983. John Biscoe, master mariner 1794–1843. Polar Rec., 21(134): 485–491.

Scarlett, R.J., 1976. Further records of the Grey Petrel on Chatham Island. Notornis, 23: 178.

SC CAMLR V, 1986. Report of the Fifth Meeting of the Scientific Committee (Hobart, Australia, 8–15 September 1986). Scientific Committee for the Conservation of Antarctic Marine Living Resources, Hobart, Australia, 271 pp.

Schlanger, S.O., 1986. High frequency sea-level fluctuations in Cretaceous time: An emerging geophysical problem. In: K.J. Hsü (Editor), Mesozoic and Cenozoic Oceans. Am. Geophys. Un. Geodynamics Ser., 15: pp. 61–74.

Schlatter, R.P., 1984. The status and conservation of seabirds in Chile. In: J.P. Croxall, P.G.H. Evans, and R.W. Schreiber, (Editors), Status and Conservation of the World's Seabirds. International Council for Bird Preservation Tech. Publ., 2: 261–269.

Schlemmer, F.C., 1978. Structure and spreading of Antarctic Bottom Water in oceanic basins adjacent to Antarctica. Unpubl. Ph.D. dissertation, Texas A&M University, College Station, Texas. 127 pp.

Schmitz, W., Mangini, A., Stoffers, P., Glasby, G.P. and Plüger, W.L., 1986. Sediment accumulation rates in the Southwestern Pacific Basin and Aitutaki Passage. Mar. Geol., 73: 181–190.

Schramm, M., 1986. The diet of chicks of greatwinged, Kerguelen and softplumaged Petrels at the Prince Edward Islands. Ostrich, 57: 9–15.

Schwerdtfeger, P., 1979. On icebergs and their uses. Cold Regions Sci. Technol., 1: 59–79.

Schwerdtfeger, W., 1970. The climate of the Antarctic. In: S. Orvig (Editor), Climates of the Polar Regions, Vol. 14, World Survey of Climatology. Elsevier, Amsterdam, pp. 253–355.

Schwerdtfeger, W. and Kachelhoffer, St., 1973. The frequency of cyclonic vortices over the southern ocean in relation to the extension of the pack ice belt. Antarctic Jl U.S., 8: 234.

370

Sciremammano, F., 1979. Observations of Antarctic Polar Front motions in a deep water expression. J. Phys. Oceanogr., 9: 223–226.

SCOR Working Group 74, 1985. General circulation of the Southern Ocean: Status and recommendations for research. World Climate Programme Report, 109: 50 pp. + 2 Appendices (published by World Meteorological Organization).

Scotese, C.R., 1987. Development of the circum-Pacific Panthalassic Ocean during the early Palaeozoic. In: J.W.H. Monger and J. Francheteau (Editors), Circum Pacific Orogenic Belts and Evolution of the Pacific Ocean Basin, Geodynamic Series, Vol. 18. American Geophysical Union, Washington, D.C., pp. 49–58.

Scott, R.F., 1913. Scott's Last Expedition. MacMillan, London, 2 vols.

Sempels, J.-M., 1982. Coastlines of the eastern Arctic. Arctic, 35: 170–179.

Sergy, G.A. and Blackall, P.J., 1987. Design and conclusions of the Baffin Island oil spill project. Arctic, 40 (Suppl. 1): 1–9.

Shabtaie, S. and Bentley, C.R., 1982. Tabular icebergs: implications from geophysical studies of ice shelves. J. Glaciol., 28: 413–430.

Shackleton, E., 1909. The Heart of Antarctica. William Heinemann, London, 368 pp.

Shapley, D., 1985. The Seventh Continent Antarctica in a Resource Age. Resources for the Future, Inc., Washington, D.C., 315 pp.

Shaughnessy, P.D., 1970. The genetics of plumage phase dimorphism of the Southern Giant Petrel Macronectes giganteus. Heredity, 25: 501–506.

Shaughnessy, P.D., 1975. Variation in facial colour of the Royal Penguin. Emu, 75: 147–152.

Shaughnessy, P.D., 1980. Entanglement of Cape fur seals with man-made objects. Mar. Pollut. Bull., 11: 332–336.

Shaughnessy, P.D. and Fletcher, L., 1987. Fur seals, Arctocephalus spp. at Macquarie Island. In: J.P. Croxall and R.L. Gentry (Editors), Status, Biology, and Ecology of Fur Seals. Proceedings of an International Symposium and Workshop, Cambridge, England, 23–27 April 1984. NOAA Tech. Rep. NMFS 51, pp. 177–188.

Shibaoka, M., Saxby, J.D. and Taylor, G.H., 1978. Hydrocarbon generation in Gippsland Basin, Australia – Comparison with Cooper Basin, Australia. APPG Bull., 62: 1151–1158.

Shuntov, V.P., 1974. Seabirds and the biological structure of the ocean. U.S. Dept. of Commerce (Washington, D.C.), Nat. Tech. Inf. Ser. TT–74–55032, 566 pp. (English translation).

Siegfried, W.R., Condy, P.R. and Laws, R.M. (Editors), 1985. Antarctic Nutrient Cycles and Food Webs. Springer-Verlag, Berlin, 700 pp.

Sielfeld, W., 1979. Consideraciones acerca de tres especes de Mesoplodon Gervais (Cetacean : Ziphiidae) presentes en las aguas Chileans. Annls. Inst. Patagonia, Punta Arenas, Chile, 10: 179–187.

Sielfeld, W., 1983. Mamiferos marinos de Chile. Ediciones de Universidad de Chile, Santiago, 199 pp.

Sielfeld, W., Venegas, C., Atalah, A. and Torres, J., 1978. Prospecion de Otaridos en las costas de Magallanes, Annls Inst. Patagonia, Punta Arenas, Chile, 9: 157–169.

Sievers, H.A. and Emergy, W.J., 1978. Variability of the Antarctic Polar Frontal Zone in the Drake Passage – Summer 1976–1977. J. Geophys. Res., 83: 3010–3022.

Sievers, H.A. and Nowlin, W.D., 1984. The stratification and water masses in Drake Passage. J. Geophys. Res., 89: 10489–10514.

Silva, N. and Neshyba, S., 1979/80. Masas de agua y circulación geostrófica frente a la costa de Chile Austral. Serie Científica Inst. Antárt. Chileno, 25/26: 5–32.

Simmonds, I. and Lin, Y.-B., 1983. Topographic and thermal forcing in a general circulation model of the Southern Hemisphere – January case. University of Melbourne Meteorology Dept. Publ. No. 24, 88 pp.

Simpson, G.G., 1975. Fossil Penguins. In: B. Stonehouse (Editor), The Biology of Penguins. Macmillan, N.Y., pp. 19–41.

Sissons, B.A., 1980. Downhole temperatures. In: A. Pyne and D.B. Waghorn (Editors), Victoria University of Wellington Antarctic Expedition 24 and MSSTS, Immediate Report. Victoria University of Wellington, pp. 14 (Abstr.).

Skira, I.J., 1986. Food of the short-tailed shearwater, *Puffinus tenuirostris*, in Tasmania. Aust. Wildlife Res., 13: 481–488.

Skornyakova, N.S. and Petelin, V.P., 1967. Sediments in the central part of the South Pacific. Oceanology, 7: 779–793.

Sladen, W.J.L., Menzie, C.M. and Reichel, W.L., 1966. DDT residues in Adelie penguins and a crabeater seal from Antarctica. Nature, 210: 670–671.

Smith, G.C., 1982. A review of the Tertiary–Cretaceous tectonic history of the Gippsland Basin and its control on coal measure sedimentation. Aust. Coal Geol., 4: 1–28.

Smith, R.I. Lewis, 1985. Nothofagus and other trees stranded on islands in the Atlantic sector of the Southern Ocean. Br. Antarct. Surv. Bull., No. 66: 47–55.

Smith, T.G., Geraci, J.R. and Aubin, D.J., St., 1983. Reaction of bottlenose dolphins, *Tursiops truncatus*, to a controlled oil spill. Canadian J. Fisheries Aquatic Sci., 40: 1522–1525.

Smith, W.O., 1987. Phytoplankton dynamics in marginal ice zones. Oceanogr. Mar. Biol. Ann. Rev., 25: 11–38.

Smith, W.O. and Nelson, D.M., 1985. Phytoplankton bloom produced by a receding ice edge in the Ross Sea : Spatial coherence with the density field. Science, 227: 163–166.

Solly, S.R.B. and Shanks, V., 1976. Organochlorine residues in New Zealand birds, and mammals. 2. Polychlorinated biphenyls. N.Z. Jl Sci., 19: 53–55.

Sorensen, J.H., 1950a. The Royal Albatross. N.Z. Dept. Sci. Indus. Res. Cape Expedition Ser. Bull. ,No. 2: 39 pp.

Sorensen, J.H., 1950b. The Light-mantled Sooty Albatross at Campbell Island. N.Z. Dept. Sci. Ind. Res. Cape Expedition Series Bull., No. 8: 30 pp.

Splettstoesser, J.F., 1979. Underground technology for offshore hydrocarbon development in Antarctica. Proceedings POAC '79, Vol. 3; Fifth International Conference on Port and Ocean Engineering under Arctic Conditions, Trondheim, pp. 233–245.

Sporli, K.B. and Craddock, C., 1981. Geology of Ruppert Coast, Marie Byrd Land, Antarctica. In: M.M. Cresswell and P. Vella (Editors), Gondwana Five. A.A. Balkema, Rotherdam, pp. 243–250.

Steemann Nielsen, E., 1952. The use of radio-active carbon (C^{14}) for measuring organic production in the sea. J. Cons. Perm. Int. Explor. Mer, 18: 117–140.

Steemann Nielsen, E. 1954. On organic production in the oceans. J. Cons. Perm. Int. Explor. Mer, 19: 309–328.

Stetson, H.C. and Upson, J.E., 1937. Bottom deposits of the Ross Sea. J. Sedim. Petrol., 7: 55–66.

Stewart, B.S. and Leatherwood, S., 1985. Minke Whale *Balaenoptera acutorostrata* Lacé-pède, 1804. In: S.H. Ridgway and R. Harrison (Editors), Handbook of Marine Marine Mammals 3: The Sirenians and Baleen Whales. Academic Press, London, pp. 91–136.

Stirling, I., 1971. Population dynamics of the Weddell sea (*Leptonychotes weddelli*) in McMurdo Sound, Antarctica, 1966–1968. Antarctic Pinnipedia. Antarctic Res. Ser., 18: 141–161.

Stirling, I., Cleator, H. and Smith, T.G., 1981. Marine mammals. In: I. Stirling and H. Cleator (Editors), Polynyas in the Canadian Arctic. Canadian Wildlife Service Occ. Pap., No. 45: 45–58.

Stock, J. and Molnar, P., 1987. Revised history of early Tertiary plate motion in the south-west Pacific. Nature, 325: 495–499.

Stoffers, P., Schmitz, W., Glasby, G.P., Plüger, W.L. and Walter, P., 1985. Mineralogy and geochemistry of sediments in the Southwestern Pacific Basin: Tahiti–East Pacific Rise–New Zealand. N.Z. Jl Geol. Geophys., 28: 513–530.

Stommel, H., 1957. A survey of ocean current theory. Deep-Sea Res., 4: 149–184.

Stommel, H., 1984. Lost Islands The Story of Islands that have Vanished from Nautical Charts. University of British Columbia Press, Vancouver, 146 pp.

Stone, G.S. and Hamner, W.M. 1988: Humpback whales Megaptera novaeangliae and south ern right whales Eubalaena australis in the Gerlache Strait, Antartica. Polar Rec., 234(148): 15–20.

Stonehouse, B., 1971. The Snares Islands penguin Euidyptes robustus. Ibis, 113: 1–7.

Stonehouse, B., 1972. Animals of the Antarctic The Ecology of the Far South. Holt, Rinehart & Winston, N.Y., 171 pp.

Streten, N.A., 1980. Some synoptic indices of the southern hemisphere mean sea level circulation 1972–1977. Mon. Wea. Rev., 108: 18–36.

Streten, N.A. and Pike, D.J., 1980. Characteristics of the broadscale Antarctic sea ice extent and the associated atmospheric circulation 1972–1977. Arch. Met. Geophys. Bioklim., Ser. A, 29: 279–299.

Streten, N.A. and Troup, A.J., 1973. A synoptic climatology of satellite observed cloud vortices over the Southern Hemisphere. Q. J. R. Meteorol. Soc., 99: 56–72.

Streten, N.A. and Zillman, J.W., 1984. Climate of the South Pacific Ocean. In: H. van Loon (Editor), Climates of the Oceans, Vol. 15, World Survey of Climatology. Elsevier, Amsterdam, pp. 263–429.

Stuiver, M., Denton, G.H., Hughes, T.J. and Fastook, J.L., 1981. History of the marine ice sheet in West Antarctica during the last glaciation: A working hypothesis. In: G.H. Denton and T.J. Hughes (Editors), The Last Great Ice Sheets. Wiley– Interscience, N.Y., pp. 319–436.

Sturman, A.P. and Anderson, M.P., 1986. On the sea ice regime of the Ross Sea, Antarctica. J. Glaciol., 32: 60–64.

Suess, E., 1909. The Face of the Earth, Vol. 4. Clarendon Press, Oxford, 673 pp.

Suess, E. and Ungerer, C.A., 1981. Element and phase composition of particulate matter from the circumpolar current between New Zealand and Antarctica. Oceanol. Acta, 4: 151–160.

Sugden, D., 1982. Arctic and Antarctic, a Modern Geographical Synthesis. B. Blackwell, Oxford, 472 pp.

Suggate, R.P., 1963. The Alpine Fault. Trans. Roy. Soc. N.Z., Geology, 2: 105–129.

Sullivan, L., Thorndike, E., Ewing, M. and Eittreim, S., 1973. Nephelometer measurements, Hach turbidity measurements and bottom photographs from Conrad Cruise 15. Lamont-Doherty Geol. Obs. Tech. Rept., 8–CU–8–73: 259 pp.

Summerhayes, C.P., 1967. Note on Macquarie Ridge and the Tonga–Kermadec complex Are they parts of the mid-ocean ridge system? N.Z. Jl Sci., 10: 808–812.

Summerhayes, C.P., 1969. Marine geology of the New Zealand subantarctic sea floor. Mem. N.Z. Oceanogr. Inst., 50: 92 pp.

Sutton, J., 1977. Antarctica, a key to the understanding of the evolution of Gondwanaland. Philos. Trans. R. Soc. London, Ser. B, 279: 197–205.

Sverdrup, H.U., 1933. On vertical circulation in the ocean due to the action of the wind with application to conditions within the Antarctic Circumpolar Current. Discovery Reps, 7: 141–169.

Sverdrup, H.U., 1953. On conditions for the vernal blooming of phytoplankton. J. Cons.

Perm. Int. Explor. Mer, 18: 287–295.

Sverdrup, H.U., Johnson, M.W. and Fleming, R.H., 1942. The Oceans, their Physics, Chemistry and General Biology. Prentice-Hall, Englewood Cliffs, N.J., 1087 pp.

Swithinbank, C., 1970. Ice movement in the McMurdo Sound area of Antarctica. Proc. Internat. Symp. Antarctic Glacial Explor.: 472–487.

Swithinbank, C. and Zumberge, J.H., 1965. The Ice Shelves. In: T. Hatherton (Editor), Antarctica. A.H. & A.W. Reed, Wellington, pp. 99–220.

Swithinbank, C., McClain, P. and Little, P., 1977. Drift tracks of Antarctic icebergs. Polar Rec., 18: 495–501.

Szijj, L.J., 1967. Notes on the winter distributions of birds in the western Antarctic and adjacent Pacific waters. Auk, 84: 366–378.

Taljaard, J.J., 1968. Climatic frontal zones of the Southern Hemisphere. Notos, 17: 23–34.

Taljaard, J.J., 1972. Synoptic meteorology of the Southern Hemisphere. In: C.W. Newton (Editor), Meteorology of the Southern Hemisphere. American Meteorological Society Monograph, Vol. 13, No. 35, pp. 139–213.

Taljaard, J.J., van Loon, H., Crutcher, H.L. and Jenne, R.L., 1969. Climate of the upper air: southern hemisphere, Vol. I, Temperatures, dew points, and heights at selected pressure levels, NAVAIR 50–IC–55, U.S. Naval Weather Serv., Washington, D.C.

Tanabe, S., Hidaka, H. and Tatsukawa, R., 1983. PCBS and chlorinated hydrocarbon pesticides in Antarctic atmosphere and hydrosphere. Chemosphere, 12: 277–288.

Tasker, M.L., Hope-Jones, P., Dixon, T. and Blake, B.F., 1984. Counting seabirds at sea from ships: a review of methods employed and a suggestion for a standardized approach. Auk, 101: 567–577.

Taylor, R.H., 1979. Fur seals at Antipodes Islands, 1969. In: J.H. Sorensen (Editor), New Zealand fur seals with special reference to the 1946 open season. N.Z. Mar. Dept. Fish Tech. Rep., 42: 79–80.

Taylor, H.W., Gordon, A.L. and Molinelli, E., 1978. Climatic characteristics of the Antarctic Polar Front Zone. J. Geophys. Res., 83: 4572–4578.

Taylor, R.H., Bell, B.D. and Wilson, P.R., 1970. Royal Albatrosses, feral sheep and cattle on Campbell Island. N.Z. Jl Sci., 13: 78–88.

Taylor, R.H. and Wilson, P., 1982. Counting Antarctic penguins from the air. Antarctic, 9: 366–368.

Tchernia, P., 1977. Etude de la derive Antarctique est-ouest au moyen d'icebergs suivis par le satellite EOLE. In: M.J. Dunbar (Editor), Polar Oceans. Arctic Institute of North America, Calgary, Alberta, pp. 107–120.

Tchernia, P., 1980. Descriptive Regional Oceanography. Pergamon Press, Oxford, 253 pp.

Tchernia, P. and Jeannin, P.F., 1983. Quelques aspects de la circulation océanique Antarctique révélé's par l'observation de la derive d'icebergs (1972–1983). Centre National d'Etudes Spatiales, Expeditions Polaires Francaises, Museum National d'Histoire Naturelle, Paris, 93 pp. + 18 plates.

Tedman, R.A., 1985. The Weddell seal Leptonychotes weddelli at McMurdo Sound, Antarctica: milk production in relation to pup growth. In: J.K. Ling and M.M Bryden (Editors), Studies of Sea Mammals in South Latitudes. South Australian Museum, Adeliade, pp. 41–52.

Teichert, C., 1952. A brief history of the Gondwanaland concept and of the inter-national Gondwana Commission. XIXe Congress Géologique International, Alger, Symposium sur les Séries de Gondwana, pp. 7–12.

Tessensohn, F., 1984. Das Ross-Meer-Gebiet im Schnittpunkt geotektonischer Fragen-Stand der geowissenschaftlichen Antarktisforschung der BGR. Geol. Jb., A75: 261–263.

Tessensohn, F., 1986. Antarctic mineral resources: Tell us where the riches are ... In: R.

Wolfrum (Editor), Antarctic Challenge II Conflicting Interests, Cooperation Environmental Protection, Economic Development. Duncker & Humblot, Berlin, pp. 19–35.

Testa, J.W. and Siniff, D.B., 1987. Population dynamics of Weddell Seals (*Leptonychotes weddelli*) in McMurdo Sound, Antarctica. Ecol. Monogr., 57: 149–165.

Thomas, B.M., 1982. Land-plant source rocks for oil and their significance in Australian basins. APEA J., 22: 164–178.

Thomas, C.W., 1959. Lithology and zoology of an Antarctic Ocean bottom core. Deep-Sea Res., 6: 5–15.

Thomas, C.W., 1960. Late Pleistocene and Recent limits of the Ross Ice Shelf. J. Geophys. Res., 65: 1789–1792.

Thomas, R.H., 1979a. The dynamics of marine ice sheets. J. Glaciol., 24: 167–177.

Thomas, R.H., 1979b. Ice shelves: a review. J. Glaciol., 24: 273–286.

Thomas, R.H. and MacAyeal, D.R., 1982. Derived characteristics of the Ross Ice Shelf, Antarctica. J. Glaciol., 20: 397–412.

Thompson, R.O.R.Y., 1971. Structure of the Antarctic Circumpolar Current. J. Geophys. Res., 76: 8694.

Thomson, M.R.A., 1982. Mesozoic paleogeography of West Antarctica. In: C. Craddock (Editor), Antarctic Geoscience. The University of Wisconsin Press, Madison, pp. 331–337.

Thomson, M. and Swithinbank, C., 1985. The prospects for Antarctic minerals. New Scientist, No. 1467: 31–35.

Threlfall, W.F., Brown, B.R. and Griffith, B.R., 1976. Gippsland Basin, off-shore. In: R.B. Leslie, H.J. Evans and C.L. Knight (Editors), Economic Geology of Australia and Papua New Guinea 3. Petroleum. Australasian Institute of Mining and Metallurgy, Parkville, Victoria, pp. 41–67.

Tillman, M.F. and Donovan, G.P. (Editors), 1983. Historical Whaling Records, Rep. Int. Whal. Commn Spec. Issue, 5, 269 pp.

Tissot, B.P. and Welte, D.H., 1978. Petroleum Formation and Occurrence. Springer Verlag, Berlin, 538 pp.

Toggwiller, J.R. and Sarmiento, J.L., 1985. Glacial to interglacial changes in atmospheric carbon dioxide: The critical role of ocean surface water in high latitudes. In: E.T. Sundquist and W.S. Broeker (Editors), The Carbon Cycle and Atmospheric CO_2 : Natural Variations Archean to Present. Am. Geophys. Un. Monogr., 32: 163–184.

Tønnessen, J.N. and Johnsen, A.O., 1982. The History of Modern Whaling. C. Hurst, London, 798 pp.

Topham, D.R. and Bishnoi, P.R., 1980. Deep water blowouts. Spill Technology Newsletter, 5: 88–94.

Torres, N.D. and Gajardo, M., 1985. Informacion preliminar sabre desechos plasticos hallados en Cabo Shirreff, isla Livingston Shetland del Sur. Boletin anartico Chileno, 5: 12–13.

Trenberth, K.E., 1980. Planetary waves at 500 mb in the Southern Hemisphere. Mon. Wea. Rev., 108: 1378–1389.

Trenberth, K.E., 1981. Observed Southern Hemisphere eddy statistics at 500 mb: Frequency and spatial dependence. J. Atmos. Sci., 38: 2585–2605.

Trenberth, K.E. and Mo, K.C., 1985. Blocking in the Southern Hemisphere. Mon. Wea. Rev., 113: 3–21.

Treshnikov, A.F., 1964. Surface water circulation in the Antarctic Ocean. Information Bulletin of the Soviet Antarctic Expedition, 5: 81–83 (English translation).

Truesdale, R.S. and Kellogg, T.B., 1979. Ross Sea diatoms: Modern assemblage distributions and their relationship to ecologic, oceanographic, and sedimentary conditions.

Mar. Micropaleontol., 4: 13–31.

Tucholke, B.E. and Houtz, R.E., 1976. Sedimentary framework of the Bellingshausen Basin from seismic profiler data. In: Initial Repts Deep Sea Drilling Project, Vol. 35. U.S. Govt Printing Office, Washington, D.C., pp. 197–227.

Turbott, E.G., 1952. Seals of the Southern Ocean. In: F.A. Simpson (Editor), The Antarctic Today. A.H. & A.W. Reed, Wellington, pp. 195–215.

Turcotte, D.L., 1980. Models for the evolution of sedimentary basins. In: A.W. Bally, P.L. Bender, T.R. McGetchin and R.I. Walcott (Editors), Dynamics of Plate Interiors. Geodynamics Series 1. American Geophysical Union, Washington, D.C., pp. 21–26.

Tyler, P.E., 1972. Sanitation and waste disposal in Antarctica. In: B.C. Parker (Editor), Conservation Problems in Antarctica. Allen Press, Lawrence, Kansas, pp. 241–246.

Uribe, F., 1982. Influence of the phytoplankton and primary production of the Antarctic waters in relationship with the distribution and behavior of krill. Instituto Antarctico Chileno, Scient. Ser., 28: 147–163.

U.S. Navy, 1965. Marine Climatic Atlas of the World Volume VII Antarctic. NAVWEPS 50–1C–50. U.S. Govt Printing Office, Washington, D.C., 361 pp.

U.S. Navy, 1979. Marine Climatic Atlas of the World Volume V South Pacific Ocean. NAVAIR 50–1C–532. U.S. Govt Printing Office, Washington, D.C., 350 pp.

U.S. Navy, 1985. Sea Ice Climatic Atlas: Volume I Antarctic. Naval Oceanography Command, Department of the Navy, NAVAIR 50–1C–540, 132 pp.

U.S. Navy Task Force 43, 1969. Report of Operation Deep Freeze 69, 1968–69: 52 pp.

USSR, 1985. Results of research into distribution and status by stocks of target species in the convention area - Atlantic, Indian and Pacific Ocean sectors of the Antarctic. Selected Papers Presented to the Scientific Committee of CCAMLR 1982–1984 Part 1: 227–327.

van Heezik, Y., 1988. Diet of Adelie penguins during the incubation period at Cape Bird, Ross Island, Antarctica. Notornis, 35: 23–26.

van Loon, H., 1967. The half-yearly oscillations in middle and high southern latitudes and the coreless winter. J. Atmos. Sci., 24: 472–486.

Vanney, J.R., Falconer, R.K.H. and Johnson, G.L., 1981. Geomorphology of the Ross Sea and adjacent oceanic provinces. Mar. Geol., 41: 73–102.

Vanney, J.R. and Johnson, G.L., 1976. The Bellingshausen–Amundsen Basin (South-east Pacific): Major seafloor units and problems. Mar. Geol., 22: 71–101.

van Tets, G.F., 1975. Observations on the Auckland Island shag, 1972–73. In: J.C. Yaldwyn (Editor), Preliminary Results of the Auckland Islands Expedition 1972–1973. Dept. of Lands and Survey, Wellington, pp. 152–153.

van Tets, G.F., 1980. The Campbell Island Shag. Preliminary reports of the Campbell Island Expedition 1975–76. N.Z. Dept. of Lands and Survey, Wellington, pp. 117–119.

Varne, R. and Rubenach, M.J., 1972. Geology of Macquarie Island and its relationship to oceanic crust. Antarctic Res. Ser., 19: 251–266.

Varne, R., Gee, R.D. and Quilty, P.G.J., 1969. Macquarie Island and the cause of oceanic linear magnetic anomalies. Science, 166: 230–233.

Vaz-Ferreira, R., 1981. South American Sea Lion Otaria flavescens (Shaw, 1800). In: S.H. Ridgway and R. Harrison (Editors), Handbook of Marine Mammals 1: The Walrus, Sea Lions, Fur Seals and Sea Otters. Academic Press, London, pp. 39–65.

Veitch, C.R., 1980. Seabirds found dead on New Zealand beaches in 1978. Notornis, 27: 115–124.

Venkatesan, M.I., Ruth, E. and Kaplan, I.R., 1986. Coprostanols in Antarctic marine sediments: A biomarker for marine mammals and not human pollution. Mar. Pollut. Bull., 17: 554–557.

Ventajas, L.M. and Comes, R., 1982. Determinación de hidrocarburos de petroleo en aquas del Oceano Austral: Pasaje de Drake, Mar del Scotia, Mar de Weddell y Mar de Bellingshausen. Contribuciones Cientificas del Instituto Antarctico Argentino, 5: 13–27.

Vincent, W.F., 1988. Microbial Ecosystems of Antarctica. Cambridge University Press, Cambridge, 304 pp.

von Brockel, K., 1981. The importance of nanoplankton within the pelagic Antarctic ecosystem. Kieler Meeresforch. Sonderh., 5: 61–67.

Voronina, N.M. 1966. Distribution of the zooplankton biomass in the Southern Ocean. Oceanology, 6: 836–846.

Voronina, N.M. 1968. The distribution of zooplankton in the Southern Ocean and its dependence on the circulation of water. Sarsia, 34: 277–284. Wade, F.A. and Wilbanks, J.R., 1972. Geology of Marie Byrd and Ellsworth lands. In: R.J. Adie (Editor), Antarctic Geology and Geophysics. Universitetsforlaget, Oslo, pp. 207–214.

Wadhams, P., 1981. Oil and ice in the Beaufort Sea – the physical effects of a hypothetical blowout. In: Petroleum and the Marine Environment. Petromar 80 Eurocean. Graham and Trotman Ltd, London, pp. 299–318.

Wadhams, P., Kristensen, M. and Orheim, O., 1983. The response of Antarctic icebergs to ocean waves. J. Geophys. Res., 88: 6053–6065.

Waldichuk, M., 1977. Global marine pollution: an overview. Intergovernmental Oceanographic Commission Technical Ser., 18, 96 pp.

Walker, G.E. and Ling, J.K., 1981a. New Zealand Sea Lion *Phocarctos hookeri* (Gray, 1844). In: S.H. Ridgway and R. Harrison (Editors), Handbook of Marine Mammals 1: The Walrus, Sea Lions, Fur Seals and Sea Otters. Academic Press, London, pp. 25–38.

Walker, G.E. and Ling, J.K., 1981b. Australian Sea Lion *Neophoca cinerea* (Peron, 1816). In: S.H. Ridgway and R. Harrison (Editors), Handbook of Marine Mammals 1: The Walrus, Sea Lions, Fur Seals and Sea Otters. Academic Press, London, pp. 99–118.

Wallace, N., 1985. Debris entanglement in the marine environment: a review. In: R.S. Shomura and H.O. Yoshida (Editors), Proceedings on the Fate and Impact of Marine Debris, 26–29 November, 1984, Honolulu, Hawaii. U.S. Dept. Commer., NOAA Tech. Memo. NMFS, NOAA-TN-NMFS-SWFC-54: 259–277.

Walsh, J.J., 1971. Relative importance of habitat variables in predicting the distribution of phytoplankton at the ecotone of the Antarctic upwelling ecosystem. Ecol. Monogr., 41: 291–308.

Walton, D., 1988. Antarctic metalliferous minerals assessment – no "bonanza". NERC News, No. 4: 8–9.

Walton, D.W.H. (Editor), 1987. Antarctic Science. Cambridge University Press, Cambridge, 280 pp.

Walton D.W.H. and Bonner, W.N., 1985. History and exploration in Antarctic biology. In: W.N. Bonner and D.W.H. Walton (Editors), Key Environments Antarctica. Pergamon Press, Oxford, pp. 1–20.

Ward, B.L., Barrett, P.J. and Vella, P., 1987. Distribution and ecology of benthic foraminifera from McMurdo Sound, Antarctica. Palaeogeogr. Palaeoclimatol. Palaeoecol., 58: 138–153.

Ward, G.D., Davis, L.S. and Sadlier, R.M.F.S., 1986. Foraging movements of Adelie penguins at Cape Bird. N.Z. Antarctic Rec., 7(2): 14–18.

Warham, J., 1963. The Rockhopper Penguin *Eudyptes chrysocome*, at Macquarie Island. Auk, 80: 229–256.

Warham, J., 1967a. Snares island birds. Notornis, 14: 122–139.

Warham, J., 1967b. The white-headed petrel *Pterodroma lessoni* at Macquarie Island. Emu,

67: 1–22.

Warham, J., 1974. The breeding biology and behaviour of the Snares Crested Penguin. J. Roy. Soc. N.Z., 4: 63–108.

Warham, J., 1982. A distant recovery of a Buller's Mollymawk. Notornis, 29: 213–214.

Warham, J. and Bell, B.D., 1979. The birds of Antipodes Islands, New Zealand. Notornis, 26: 121–169.

Warham, J. and Bennington, S.L., 1983. A census of Bullers Albatross *Diomedea bulleri* at the Snares Islands, New Zealand. Emu, 83: 112–114.

Warham, J. and Fitzsimons, C.N., 1987. The vocalisation of Bullers Mollymawk, *Diomedea bulleri*, (Aves : Diomedeidae), with some comparative data on other albatrosses. N.Z. Jl Zool., 14: 65–79.

Warham, J. and Keeley, B.R., 1969. New and rare birds at Snares Island during 1968–69. Notornis, 16: 221–224.

Warham, J., Keeley, B.R. and Wilson, G.J., 1977. Breeding of the Mottled Petrel. Auck, 94: 1–17.

Warham, J. and Wilson, G.J., 1982. The size of the Sooty Shearwater population at the Snares Islands, New Zealand. Notornis, 29: 23–30.

Warham, J., Wilson, G.J. and Keeley, B.R., 1982. The annual cycle of the Sooty Shearwater at The Snares Islands, New Zealand. Notornis, 29: 269–292.

Warneke, R.M. and Shaughnessy, P.D., 1985. *Arctocephalus pusillus*, the South African and Australian fur seal: taxonomy, evolution, biogeography, and life history. In: J.K. Ling and M.M. Bryden (Editors), Studies of Sea Mammals in South Latitudes. South Australian Museum, Adelaide, pp. 53–77.

Warren, B.A. 1971. Antarctic deep water contribution to the world ocean. In: L.O. Quam (Editor), Research in the Antarctic. American Association for the Advancement of Science, Washington, D.C., pp. 631–643.

Warren, B.A., 1973. Transpacific hydrographic sections at Lats. 43°S and 28°S: the SCOR-PIO Expedition–II. Deep Water. Deep-Sea Res., 20: 9–38.

Warren, B.A., 1976. Structure of deep western boundary currents. Deep-Sea Res., 23: 129–142.

Warren, B.A. 1981. Deep circulation of the world ocean. In: B.A. Warren and C. Wunsch (Editors), Evolution of Physical Oceanography. The MIT Press, Cambridge, Mass., pp. 6–41.

Washington, W.M. and Meehl, G.A., 1984. Seasonal cycle experiment on the climate sensitivity due to a doubling of CO_2 with an atmospheric general circulation model coupled to a simple mixed-layer ocean model. J. Geophys. Res., 89: 9475–9503.

Watling, R.J., 1980. Don't touch: tanker traffic around the Cape of Good Hope. Oceans, 13: 62–64.

Watson, G.E., 1975. Birds of the Antarctic and Sub-Antarctic. American Geophysical Union, Washington, D.C., 350 pp.

Watson, G.E., Angle, J.P., Harper, P.C., Bridge, M.A., Schlatter, R.P., Tickell, W.L.N., Boyd, J.C. and Boyd, M.M., 1971. Birds of the Antarctic and Subantarctic. Antarctic Map Ser., Folio 14, 18 pp. + 15 plates.

Watt, J.P.C., 1989. Stewart Island's Kaipipi shipyard and the Ross Sea whalers. Jim Watt, Havelock North, New Zealand.

Webb, P.N., 1983. A review of Late Cretaceous–Cenozoic stratigraphy, tectonics, palaeontology and climate in the Ross Sector. In: R.L. Oliver, P.R. James and J.B. Jago (Editors), Antarctic Earth Science. Australian Academy of Science, Camberra, pp. 545 (Abstr.).

Webb, P.N., Harwood, D.M., McKelvey, B.C., Mercer, J.H. and Stott, L.D., 1984. Cenozoic marine sedimentation and ice-volume variation on the East Antarctic craton. Geology,

12: 287–291.

Weber, L.H. and El-Sayed, S.Z., 1987. Contributions of the net, nano, and picoplankton to the phytoplankton standing crop and primary productivity in the Southern Ocean. J. Plankton Res., 9: 973–994.

Weeks, W.F. and Campbell, W.J., 1973. Icebergs as a freshwater source: an appraisal. J. Glaciol., 12: 207–233.

Weeks, W.F. and Mellor, M., 1978. Some elements of iceberg technology. In: A.A. Husseiny (Editor), Iceberg Utilization. Proceedings of the First International Conference, Pergamon Press, New York, pp. 45–98.

Weeks, W.F. and Weller, G., 1984. Offshore oil in the Alaskan Arctic. Science, 225: 371–378.

Weertman, J., 1974. Stability of the junction of an ice sheet and an ice shelf. J. Glaciol., 13: 3–11.

Wegener, A., 1924. The origin of the continents and oceans. Methven and Co., London, 212 pp.

Wehle, D.H.S. and Coleman, F.C., 1983. Plastics at sea. Natural History, 92(2): 20–26.

Weissel, J.K. and Hayes, D.E., 1972. Magnetic anomalies in the southeast Indian Ocean. Antarctic Res. Ser., 19: 165–196.

Weissel, J.K. and Hayes, D.E., 1977. Evolution of the Tasman Sea reappraised. Earth Planet. Sci. Letts, 36: 77–84.

Weissel, J.K., Hayes, D.E. and Herron, E.M., 1977. Plate tectonic synthesis: displacements between Australian, New Zealand and Antarctica since the Late Cretaceous. Mar. Geol., 25: 231–277.

Welch, D.M., 1984. Arctic marine shore classification for regional planning and environmental assessment. Water Sci. and Technol., 16: 569–579.

Weller, G., 1980a. Spatial and temporal variations in the south polar surface energy balance. Mon. Wea. Rev., 108: 2006–2014.

Weller, G., 1980b. Oil pollution in ice-covered Arctic waters. In: R.A. Geyer (Editor), Marine Environmental Pollution, 1 Hydrocarbons. Elsevier, Amsterdam, pp. 353–369.

Weller, G., 1982. Polar problems in climate research: some comparisons between the Arctic and Antarctic. Aust. Met. Mag., 30: 163–168.

Weller, G., 1986. Meteorology. Antarctic Jl U.S., 21(2): 7–12.

Weller, G., Bentley, C.R., Elliot, D.H., Lanzerotti, L.J. and Webber, P.J., 1987. Laboratory Antarctica : Research contributions to global problems. Science, 238: 1361–1368.

Wenk, T. and Siegenthaler, U., 1985. The high-latitude ocean as a control of atmospheric CO_2. In: E.T. Sundquist and W.S. Broecker (Editors), The Carbon Cycle and Atmospheric CO_2 : Natural Variations Archean to Present. Am. Geophys. Un. Monogr., 32: 185–194.

Westergaard, R.H., 1980. Underwater blowout. Environment Internat., 3: 177–184.

Westerskov, K., 1959. The nesting habitat of the Royal Albatross on Campbell Island. Proc. N.Z. Ecol. Soc., 6: 16–20.

Westerskov, K., 1960. Birds of Campbell Islands. N.Z. Dept. of Internal Affairs, Wildlife Service Publ. 61: 83 pp.

Westerskov, K., 1963. Ecological factors affecting distribution of a nesting Royal Albatross populations. Proc. 13th Int. Ornith. Congr.: 795–811.

Whillans, I.M., 1976. Radio-echo layers and the recent stability of the West Antarctic Ice Sheet. Nature, 264: 152–155.

Whitworth, T., 1980. Zonation and geostrophic flow of the Antarctic Circumpolar Current at Drake Passage. Deep-Sea Res., 27: 497–507.

Whitworth, T., 1988. The Antarctic Circumpolar Current. Oceanus, 31(2): 53–58.

Whitworth, T. and Nowlin, W.D., 1987. Water masses and currents of the Southern Ocean at the Greenwich meridian. J. Geophys. Res., 92: 6462–6476.

Whitworth, T., Nowlin, W.D. and Worley, S.J., 1982. The net transport of the Antarctic Circumpolar Current through Drake Passage. J. Phys. Oceanogr., 12: 960–971.

Whitworth, T., and Peterson, R.G., 1985. Volume transport of the Antarctic Circumpolar Current from bottom pressure measurements. J. Phys. Oceanogr., 15: 810–816.

Williams, F.L., 1963. Matthew Fontaine Maury Scientist of the Sea. Rutgers University Press, New Brunswick, 720 pp.

Wilson, A.T., 1964. Origin of ice ages: an ice shelf theory for Pleistocene glaciation. Nature, 313: 535–540.

Wilson, D.D., McGinnis, L.D., Burdelik, W.J. and Fasnacht, T.L., 1981. McMurdo Sound upper crustal geophysics. Antarctic Jl U.S., 16(5): 31–33.

Wilson, D.L., Smith, W.O. and Nelson, D.M., 1986. Phytoplankton bloom dynamics of the western Ross Sea ice edge – I. Primary productivity and species-specific production. Deep-Sea Res., 33: 1375–1387.

Wilson, G.J., 1980. Oiled penguins in Antarctica. N.Z. Antarctic Rec., 2(2): 3.

Wilson, G.J. (Editor), 1983. Distribution and abundance of Antarctic and Subantarctic penguins: a synthesis of current knowledge. BIOMASS Scient. Ser., 4: 46 pp.

Wilson, G.J. and Taylor, R.H., 1984. Distribution and abundance of penguins in the Ross Sea sector of Antarctica. N.Z. Antarctic Rec., 5(1): 1–7.

Wilson, P. and Thomas, B., 1988. Penguin photographic survey from first R.N.Z.A.F. C–130 dedicated science flight. N.Z. Antarctic Rec., 8(2): 11–13.

Wilson, R.D., Monaghan, P.H., Osanik, A., Price, L.C. and Rogers, M.A., 1974. Natural marine oil seepage. Science, 184: 857–865.

Wilson, R.P., 1984. An improved stomach pump for penguins and other seabirds. J. Field Orn., 55: 109 112.

Winn, H.E. and Riechley, N.E., 1985. Humpback Whale *Megaptera novaeangliae* (Browoski, 1781). In: S.H. Ridgway and R. Harrison (Editors), Handbook of Marine Mammals 3: The Sirenians and Baleen Whales. Academic Press, London, pp. 242 273.

Winstone, J.E., 1982. Drift plastic – an expanding niche for a marine invertebrate? Mar. Pollut. Bull., 13: 348–351.

Wong, H.K. and Christoffel, D.A., 1981. A reconnaissance seismic survey of McMurdo Sound and Terra Nova Bay, Ross Sea. Antarctic Res. Ser., 33: 37–62.

Wordie, J.M., 1921. The Ross Sea drift of the Aurora in 1915–16. Geogr. J., 58: 219–225.

Wordie, J.M. and Kempe, S., 1933. Observations on certain Antarctic icebergs. Geogr. J., 81: 426–434.

Worthington, B., 1986. Soviet krill-chaser in Lyttelton. Catch, 13(4–5): 7.

Worthington, L.V., 1981. The water masses of the world ocean: some results of a fine-scale census. In: B. Warren and C. Wunsch (Editors), Evolution of Physical Oceanography, MIT Press, Cambridge, Mass., pp. 42–59.

Wright, C.S. and Priestley, R.E., 1922. Glaciology. British (Terra Nova) Antarctic Expedition 1910–1913. Harrison & Sons Ltd, London, 581 pp.

Wright, N.A. and Williams, P.L. (Editors), 1974. Mineral resources of Antarctica. U.S. Geol. Surv. Circ., 705: 29 pp.

Wright, R., Anderson, J.B. and Fisco, P.P., 1984. Distribution and association of sediment gravity flow deposits and glacial/glacial-marine sediments around the continental margin of Antarctica. In: B. Molnia (Editor), Glacial–Marine Sedimentation. Plenum Press, N.Y., pp. 265–300.

Yamaguchi, Y. and Shibata, Y., 1982. Standing stock and distribution of phytoplankton chlorophyll in the Southern Ocean south of Australia. Trans. Tokyo Univ. Fisheries, 5: 111–128.

380

Yeskin, L.I., 1982. Iceberg drift in the Antarctic Circumpolar Current. Polar Geog. Geophys., 6: 239–242.

Yochem, P.K. and Leatherwood, S., 1985. Blue Whale *Balaneoptera musculus* (Linnaeus, 1758). In: S.H. Ridgway and R. Harrison (Editors), Handbook of Marine Mammals 3: The Sirenians and Baleen Whales. Academic Press, London, pp. 193–240.

Young, E.C., 1978. Behavioural ecology of *Ionnbergi* skuas in relation to environment on the Chatham Island, New Zealand. N.Z. Jl Zool., 5: 4–6.

Young, E.C., 1981. The ornithology of the Ross Sea. J. Roy. Soc. N.Z., 11: 287–315.

Zeller, E.J., Saunders, D.F. and Angino, E.E., 1974. A proposal for the establishment of a permanent high-level radioactive waste depository in Antarctica. In: Proceedings of the OECD–IAEA Symposium on Management of Radioactive Wastes from Fuel Processing, Paris, 1973, pp. 431–446.

Zemmels, I., 1978. A study of the sediment composition and sedimentary geochemical processes in the vicinity of the Pacific–Antarctic Ridge. Unpubl. Ph.D. thesis, Fla State Univ, Tallahassee, 334 pp.

Zernova, V.V., 1970. Phytoplankton of the Southern Ocean. In: M.W. Holdgate (Editor), Antarctic Ecology, Vol. 1. Academic Press, London, pp. 136–142.

Zhivago, A.V., 1962. Outlines of Southern Ocean geomorphology. Am. Geophys. Un. Geophys. Monograph, No. 7: 74–80.

Zink, R.M., 1981. Observations of seabirds during a cruise from Ross Island to Anvers Island, Antarctica. Wilson Bull., 93: 1–20.

Zorn, S.A., 1984. Antarctic minerals A common heritage approach. Resources Policy, 10(1): 2–18.

Zotikov, I.A., Zagorodnov, V.S. and Raikovsky, Ju.V., 1980. Core drilling through the Ross Ice Shelf (Antarctica) confirmed basal freezing. Science, 207: 1463–1465.

Zumberge, J.H., 1979. Mineral resources and politics in Antarctica. Am. Scient., 67(1): 68–77.

Zumberge, J.H. (Editor), 1979. Possible environmental effects of mineral exploitation in Antarctica. EAMREA Report. Scientific Committee on Antarctic Research, 59 pp.

Zumberge, J.H., 1982. Potential mineral resource availability and possible environment problems in Antarctica. In: J.I. Charney (Editor), New Nationalism and the Use of Common Spaces. Allenheld, Osmund and Company, Totowa, New Jersey, pp. 115–154

Zwally, H.J., Comiso, J.C. and Gordon, A.L., 1985. Antarctic offshore leads and polynyas and oceanographic effects. Antarctic Res. Ser., 43: 203–226.

Zwally, H.J., Comiso, J.C., Parkinson, C.L., Campbell, W.J., Carsey, F.D. and Gloersen, P., 1983a. Antarctic Sea Ice 1973–76: Satellite Passive-Microwave Observations. National Aeronautics and Space Administration, Washington, D.C., NASA SP–459, 206 pp.

Zwally, H.J., Parkinson, C.L., Carsey, F.D., Gloersen, P., Campbell, W.J. and Ramseier, R.O., 1979. Seasonal variations of total Antarctic sea ice area, 1973–75. Antarctic Jl U.S., 14(5): 102–103.

Zwally, H.J., Parkinson, C.L. and Comiso, J.C., 1983b. Variability of Antarctic sea ice and changes in carbon dioxide. Science, 220: 1005–1012.

386

390